# American Soldiers

# American Soldiers

## Ground Combat in the World Wars, Korea, and Vietnam

Peter S. Kindsvatter

Foreword by Russell F. Weigley

University Press of Kansas

© 2003 by the University Press of Kansas
All rights reserved

Published by the University Press of Kansas (Lawrence, Kansas 66049), which was organized by the Kansas Board of Regents and is operated and funded by Emporia State University, Fort Hays State University, Kansas State University, Pittsburg State University, the
University of Kansas, and Wichita State University

Library of Congress Cataloging-in-Publication Data

Kindsvatter, Peter S.
    American soldiers : ground combat in the World Wars, Korea, and
Vietnam / Peter S. Kindsvatter ; foreword by Russell F. Weigley.
        p. cm. — (Modern war studies)
Includes bibliographical references (p. ) and index.

    ISBN-0-7006-1229-7 (alk. paper)
    1. Combat—History—20th century. 2. United States. Army.
Infantry—History—20th century. 3. United States. Marine
Corps—History—20th century. I. Title. II. Series.
    UA28 .K55 2003
    355'.00973'0904—dc21
                7365                    2002012957

British Library Cataloguing in Publication Data is available.

Printed in the United States of America

10 9 8 7 6 5 4 3 2 1

# Contents

# Foreword

John Keegan introduced his classic study of the experience of combat, *The Face of Battle*, with the lament that no military historian had hitherto succeeded in conveying that experience realistically.* Just what it felt like to place yourself in the way of numerous deadly missiles, blade strokes and bayonet thrusts, and clubbing weapons of various kinds and to persist in moving forward into the storm had, he believed, eluded previous historians. Keegan set out to offer a corrective, and he did so impressively, keeping sight of the simple, central point, amid a good deal of complex exposition, that the dominant emotion and experience in battle is to be scared.

Notwithstanding the classic stature of Keegan's book, there is an element of the self-serving in his introductory remarks about how writers before him had failed to get matters right regarding combat. Disappointed by that apparent attitude, I myself initially put *The Face of Battle* aside. It required insistent friends to persuade me to pick it up again, conquer my distaste for what proved to be a small part of it, and discover that on the whole it is a great book. Putting aside, however, the self-satisfaction of Keegan's contrasting his own work with other historians' accounts of the nature of combat, his position is not without merit. It is exceedingly difficult to capture in writing the chaos of events and emotions that occur in combat. All descriptions of the climactic events of war dilute them.

A great virtue of the present volume by Peter Kindsvatter is that, by reading and passing on to us his findings in an extraordinary number of American soldiers' narratives of combat during the four major conscript-army wars of the

*John Keegan, *The Face of Battle* (New York: Viking Press, 1976), pp. 15–54, 72–78.

twentieth century, he has identified a surprisingly large number of writers who have in some measure overcome this difficulty and who actually tell us what it is to be in battle. He presents generous samplings of such writings within his own interpretive analysis to create a major addition to that slim body of literature that does convey a sense of the reality of battle. Kindsvatter's book is based firmly on the firsthand accounts of combat written by twentieth-century American soldiers and marines of the World Wars, Korea, and Vietnam. Its author acts as a sensitive, skillful mediator between the writers and us.

One of the merits of John Keegan's *The Face of Battle* is that Keegan provides so much insight into the social history of the British soldiers with whom he is concerned because he knows that without understanding whence the soldiers came the reader will not be able to comprehend properly how they behaved in combat. Similarly, Peter Kindsvatter leads up to the combat experience with detailed examinations of his writers' accounts of the entire process of living in the armed forces, from induction through basic and advanced training. Through the soldiers' writings he sympathetically explores their ambivalent relationships with their families and friends back home to whom they knew they could not adequately communicate what they experienced, and their less ambivalent, more often hostile attitudes toward the rear echelons of men who wore military uniforms but did not share the trials at the cutting edge.

Yet it is experiencing combat and how men could enter and endure it with which Kindsvatter is principally concerned. Similar issues of why men were able to enter the hell of combat and why they stuck to it have been addressed recently for the American Civil War by James M. McPherson in *For Cause and Comrades*.* As his title implies, McPherson found that the writings of Civil War soldiers indicate that they fought first for ideological reasons—for their cause and country—and secondarily for their comrades—for motives having to do with the bonding of friends and with unit solidarity. Kindsvatter finds the same scale of motivational values among his twentieth-century soldiers, which will cause some of us to rethink accustomed beliefs. We have had a tendency, drawn from impressionistic and insufficient evidence, to believe that the more worldly wise soldiers of the century just ended were more likely than the romantic rustics of the Victorian era to fight simply and cynically just to get an unpleasant job over with. Kindsvatter shows that combat motivation remained rooted in the same kind of

---

*James M. McPherson, *For Cause and Comrades: Why Men Fought in the Civil War* (New York, Oxford: Oxford University Press, 1997). McPherson deals with similar themes, although with more emphasis on why men enlisted in the first place and somewhat less on why they continued fighting, in *What They Fought For, 1861–1865* (Baton Rouge: Louisiana State University Press, 1994).

ideological, patriotic, and comradeship values in twentieth-century American mass armies as in our first mass army, even if less sentimentally expressed.

Kindsvatter has used more self-consciously literary sources than McPherson; where the latter relied mainly on unpublished letters and diaries, Kindsvatter has drawn from published fiction, memoirs, and histories by combat veterans. Fiction and nonfiction have been of nearly equal value for his purposes, but if there is an edge, fictionalized memories of combat seem to come a bit closer to presenting a cogent version of the experience of battle. Perhaps feeling obliged to adhere to what can be confirmed as the literal truth interferes with capturing a fuller truth, even in memoirs, let alone in the work of historians, thus reaffirming the degree of accuracy within John Keegan's complaint about military historians who preceded him.

We can hope that by introducing these literary sources—that approach about as closely as words are able toward conveying what it is like to be part of war—Kindsvatter will bring us all to a better appreciation of that uniquely intense experience. We can hope, too, that Kindsvatter will succeed in sending his readers to examine the best of his sources for themselves. Perhaps a better comprehension of the realities of war will help us stay away from warlike policies, but I do not intend this Foreword to convey any such simpleminded antiwar message, nor is that by any means the purpose of Kindsvatter's book. Through the book, however, we learn that those soldiers who approached combat informed by the best literary descriptions of it, though they could not fully be prepared for what they were entering—nothing could accomplish that—were at least more ready than those who came only with romantic images from the movies. If we are to continue to engage in combat, as we will, even that slight advantage for those new to it might make them better soldiers. More than that, it surely must be of some value for policymakers and for those who vote for policymakers to possess a modicum of understanding of what war is. Peter Kindsvatter gives us more than that modicum.

*—Russell F. Weigley*

# Acknowledgments

This book, substantial as it is, started out as an even longer dissertation that required considerable refining. The dissertation and resulting book would not have been possible without the help of my devoted and talented wife, Marty. She not only typed the dissertation and the revised manuscript that followed but also applied her editing skills and common sense to make them better. She did these tasks while working full time to support us.

That this dissertation had publication potential in the first place owes much to my committee at Temple University. I was yet another student fortunate enough to have his work receive the thoughtful criticism and close attention of Dr. Russell F. Weigley, who supported and encouraged me during the entire Ph.D. process, right through the job-hunting stage. Dr. Richard H. Immerman, a skillful editor, went beyond the call of duty to carefully read and thoughtfully edit my dissertation. Dr. David Alan Rosenberg added his considerable breadth of knowledge to the process. My outside reader, historian and retired U.S. Army colonel Dr. Henry G. Gole, shared my interest in the study of the soldier in combat, provided thoughtful insights, and shared his personal experiences as a combatant in two wars.

I must also thank Dr. Dennis E. Showalter, who not only read the manuscript I sent to the University Press of Kansas, twice (the long and longer versions), but also provided constructive criticism and comments while remaining steadfastly supportive. Finally, I want to thank Dr. Jack Atwater, the director of the U.S. Army Ordnance Museum, and his staff, Ed Heasley, Alan Killinger, Tim Tidwell, Judy Garrett, and Elmer Wymer. They have assisted me in my official duties as the Ordnance Corps historian in myriad ways and have also provided moral support while I finished this project.

What it is that makes a man go out into dangerous places
and get himself shot at with increasing consistency until finally he dies,
is an interesting subject for speculation.
And an interesting study.

—James Jones, *WWII: A Chronicle of Soldiering*

# Introduction

What, indeed, motivated novelist James Jones and his fellow GIs in World War II, or American soldiers in World War I or the Korean and Vietnam Wars, to go out into dangerous places? And once there—in the combat zone—what enabled them to persevere until all too often they did die, or were wounded or emotionally broken? These questions generate more than just interesting speculation. The answers are critically important. Men facing battle or charged with leading troops need to understand the nature of these "dangerous places" to be better prepared to deal with them. Civilian leaders who order American soldiers into harm's way need to appreciate the potentially devastating effect that combat can have on those soldiers. The American people must realize how vital their unequivocal support is to soldiers trying to endure war's hardships and dangers. Too often in the twentieth century novice soldiers, leaders, and citizens alike did not comprehend these basic realities.

Gaining an appreciation for the nature of combat involves an examination of why the citizen joined, or at least consented to serve in, the U.S. Army or Marine Corps; the role of training in converting the recruit into a soldier; the physical and emotional hardships and dangers of combat; how soldiers coped, or failed to cope, with the combat environment; what motivated them to carry the fight to the enemy; and the soldiers' relationships with the home front.

Speculation on James Jones's "interesting subject" thus encompasses a wide range of topics. The scope of this book, therefore, is necessarily broad but remains manageable because of several constraints. The discussion is limited to the experiences of American soldiers and marines. This experience certainly invites comparison with soldiers in other armies, but such a comparison would be a book in itself. The focus is on ground combat at the individual and small-unit level. Central to this approach is the American infantryman and, to a lesser extent, other combatants such as tank crewmen, artillerymen, and engineers. The perspectives of noncombatants who were close to the fighting, such as war correspondents, medical personnel, and chaplains, are also included. This book is neither a combat history nor a tactical treatise but an examination of what the combat environment was like and how soldiers reacted to it.

The American soldier is examined through the course of four wars—the world wars, and the Korean and Vietnam Wars. The soldiers' experiences in these wars certainly varied in important ways, but these wars, despite their differences, also encompass a distinct period of American military history. They are the wars of the draft era, fought primarily, though by no means exclusively, by the conscripted citizen-soldier. They are also modern wars, largely fought conventionally, and of sufficient duration and violence to have a serious impact on the physical and emotional well being of those who fought them. These characteristics distinguish them from the wars that preceded or followed.

Where best to learn about the soldier's experience in the wars of the draft era? From what the veterans themselves have to say. This book draws upon memoirs, novels, and oral histories. A few of these works were written by war correspondents, but most reflect the experiences of enlisted men and junior officers. Works by marines and soldiers have been consulted, and the term "soldiers" in this study includes marines, unless otherwise specified. Each war, and in the case of World War II the Pacific theater and Mediterranean/European theater, is represented by twenty-one to thirty works.

A wide range of secondary sources in military psychiatry, military sociology, literary criticism, and history supplements the direct testimony of the veterans. This secondary literature is invaluable for several reasons. The psychiatrists, psychologists, and sociologists provide useful insights, often based directly on their work with soldiers or veterans, concerning the causes of stress in combat, how men try to cope with that stress, and what motivates them to "stick it out." The sociological studies and surveys also provide statistical support, at least from World War II on, for many claims made by the soldiers in their memoirs and novels. The literary critics, many of whom are also veterans, provide recommendations as to which memoirs and novels are most significant. More important, some critics go beyond matters of style and structure to assess the themes, or messages, contained in these works. The historical studies either provide a narrative combat history told from the soldier's perspective or specifically address soldier behavior.

As for the primary sources, the vast majority are soldiers' memoirs or first-hand accounts written by war correspondents. Some of these books are based on thoughts and experiences recorded shortly after the fact, as in the case of memoirs based on diaries and letters and the accounts written by the correspondents. Historian William L. Langer explains that such contemporary accounts can be refreshingly straightforward and unaffected, as was his combination memoir and unit history, written immediately after the Armistice in November 1918: "As I reread this simple narrative after a lifetime spent in the teaching and writing of history, I found its immediacy rather appealing. It has nothing of the sophisticated rationalization that invariably creeps into reminiscences recorded long after the event."[1]

Soldiers' diaries and letters may possess this virtue of immediacy, but men in combat did not have much time to record their thoughts and experiences in detail, and they often had little pocket space for more than a small notebook. Not surprisingly, most memoirs were written after war's end, sometimes many years after, and the authors relied on recollections. Even memoirs based on diaries and letters were often fleshed out with added-on commentary. Critics argue the pros and cons of these after-the-fact recollections. The most obvious problem, as historian Ronald Schaffer points out, is the potential for distortion: "Postwar reconstructions of what happened were subject to distortions of memory and reflected not simply immediate wartime experiences but later thoughts and occurrences as well."[2]

Another concern, voiced by James Jones, is that memories fade with time, especially memories of war's unpleasantries: "Thus we old men can in all good conscience sit over our beers at the American Legion on Friday nights and recall with affection moments of terror thirty years before. Thus we are able to tell the youngsters that it wasn't all really so bad."[3]

Jones's conventional wisdom aside, however, the reality is that long-term memory of traumatic, unusual, or dramatic events remains vivid and constant. One memoir in this book is unique in doubling as a research device to measure memory. Alice M. Hoffman, an oral historian, interviewed her husband, Howard, an experimental psychologist who had been a mortarman in World War II, about his wartime experiences. A series of interviews, conducted in 1978 and 1982, were checked against unit histories, photographs, and corroborating testimony from other unit veterans. The Hoffmans discovered that Howard's memories about "unique happenings" or the "first occurrence of an event" were remarkably clear and accurate: "The forty-year-old memories that Howard retains are extraordinarily resistant to change. They appear to have been protected from decay by rehearsal and reinforced by salience so that they have become fixed in the mind."[4]

Put in less clinical terms by Paul Boesch, a veteran of the bitter fighting in the Huertgen Forest in World War II, memories about details may fade, but traumatic events remain indelibly etched in the mind: "It is difficult to recall the sequence in which events occurred. Each episode appears to claim precedence over the others. But though it is hard to recall exactly when a thing happened, it is impossible to erase the events themselves, for the sheer, stark, exhausting terror burned them inextricably in our memory."[5]

Given this book's focus on the soldier's experience in combat, it is exactly these sharply recalled events, not the details of date, time, and place, that are important. Nevertheless, the nagging suspicion remains, as literature professor and onetime combat pilot Samuel Hynes explains, that veterans' memoirs contain "failures of observation . . . , the confined vision of witnesses, the infidelities of memories after the events, the inevitable distortions of language."[6] Thus the only sort of truth that can be gained from after-the-fact accounts is collective.

Hynes takes this approach in his own excellent study, *The Soldiers' Tale,* the plural "soldiers" indicative of his use of multiple experiences to reconstruct memory. This book proceeds in a similar vein, citing numerous examples in the text and notes to support a point.

This book also draws upon war novels in the search for collective truth. The use of fictional works in a historical study is bound to raise eyebrows, but these novels were included for two reasons. First, although some of them are obscure, others are well known, such as the works of Ernest Hemingway, John Dos Passos, Norman Mailer, and James Jones. In any discussion of the influence of war literature on successive generations, a topic addressed in the conclusion, these popular fictional works cannot be left out. Second, and more important, these fictional works speak directly and eloquently to the soldier's condition in war. Every author whose fictional work is included is a veteran or seasoned war correspondent, and many of these works are semiautobiographical. In short, they are realistic, or "mimetic" to use a term common to literary criticism, meaning they accurately imitate or represent human behavior. These novels, to paraphrase the literature professor Stanley Cooperman, dramatize rather than invent historical reality.[7] Historian and veteran Henry G. Gole believes that this literature is as important to seeking the truth about man's condition in wartime as is historical analysis:

> The historian's attempt at detachment stands in sharp contrast to the artist's passionate personal involvement and raises the question of truth and who comes closer to it—the historian or artist. We are well advised to rely upon both the artist and the historian, one for "essential truth" produced by the creative imagination so the reader has a sense of being there, and one for analysis of known facts available. It should be clear that both artist and historian demand from us a leap of faith as the former invents the plausible, while the latter ultimately uses analysis to take us from what is known to what is probably true.[8]

Nevertheless, though novels are valuable for their portrayal of soldiers' responses to war, they should be used with caution concerning matters outside the human experience. For example, war-novel plots tend to be tactically illogical, often involving the physical isolation of a small unit to an unrealistic degree. This technique allows the author to keep his cast of characters within reasonable bounds and free from outside interference. As historian Roger A. Beaumont points out, these plots are not only unrealistic but also leave out many aspects of the military picture: "The fiction writer . . . is faced, as is the historian, with shaping meaning. It is not surprising that the dullness of mass bureaucracy is ignored in favor of colorful if improbable microcosms. . . . Fictional accounts most often fall flat treating the complexities of command, logistics, and organization, and show a vague sense of the administrative realities of military life."[9]

While the microcosms established by the novelist may sometimes be improbable, within that microcosm, the reactions of the characters to the stress and hardships of combat usually ring true. But there can be a problem here as well, not in the portrayal of specific incidents, but in cumulative effect. Some novelists have heavily weighted their presentation of events in the direction of brutality, negativity, and immorality to support an antiwar theme. Thus it is possible to have a novel, like Norman Mailer's *The Naked and the Dead,* that provides powerful and plausible examples of soldier behavior in combat, yet the overall effect is sharply, and unrealistically, skewed to the negative. Literature professor and Vietnam veteran Tobey C. Herzog notes that Mailer's novel is "devoid of heroes": "Values—personal and religious—crumble; positive actions result in failure; integrity, concern for others, noble struggles for survival, and heroic actions are absent; and rare moments of personal insight are quickly dismissed."[10]

Mailer's novel is every bit as negative in overall theme as Herzog's assessment indicates, yet *The Naked and the Dead* has provided valuable excerpts, and eloquent ones at that, for this book. The problem of imbalance in any one novel can be avoided by using multiple examples from different sources to illustrate a point and by not relying solely on fiction—in sum, the collective memory approach.

A final issue raised by historians concerning memoirs and novels involves representativeness. Soldier-authors tend to be better educated and from a higher social standing than the average soldier and hence are potentially "unrepresentative." Though this observation has validity, some of the memoirists in this study are not atypical, in that their education and social backgrounds are modest. Their accounts are not polished, and often someone has assisted in editing their memoirs or diaries. In other cases, authors may have gone on to successful careers in business, journalism, or academia, but they were relatively young and unsophisticated, and hence fairly typical, soldiers when they recorded their experiences. Thus, the memoirs are probably not as unrepresentative as some critics suggest. In any case, twelve oral histories have been included to help ensure representativeness. Veterans who were neither sufficiently educated nor motivated to write down their war experiences were often at least willing to talk about them to oral historians.

The more important, though generally overlooked, issue concerning representativeness is not that these soldier-authors are somehow different from the average soldier but that they represent only the successful soldier. Deserters, soldiers who inflicted wounds on themselves to escape combat, or men who broke down in their first firefight did not write memoirs. Some of the soldier-authors cited in this book were unenthusiastic draftees or only average performers, or they suffered bouts of combat fatigue, but on the whole they acquitted themselves satisfactorily. The secondary sources, especially the sociological and psychiatric studies, are thus essential for providing insight into desertion, self-inflicted wounds, and psychological breakdown.

Ultimately, although the use of memoirs, novels, and oral histories raises legitimate questions about representativeness, accuracy of memory, and objectivity of perspective, the fact remains that this written and oral testimony is the primary available source for learning about the combat experience. Hynes, after raising typical concerns about distortions in memory that could compromise after-the-fact recollections of battle, concedes that these accounts are essential: "What other route do we have to understanding the human experience of war—how it felt, what it was like—than the witness of the men who were there?"[11] Whatever their shortcomings, these eyewitness testimonies, including those re-created in fictional form, reveal a great deal about what prompted men "to go out into dangerous places" and what enabled them to carry on in the face of danger and grievous hardships. This book synthesizes and assesses what those testimonies have to say.

Beyond the issue of the general relevance of memoirs, novels, and oral histories is the question of which specific works to consult from the hundreds available. Certainly the number of sources used in this book is not sufficient to satisfy any scientific criteria for a statistically significant sample. There was some method to the selection process, however. Each war received roughly equal representation. A balance between army and marine memoirs was also sought, one not easily struck in the Pacific theater in World War II because most of the memoirs are by marines, despite the large number of soldiers who also fought there. Availability was thus a factor, as it was in the case of World War I and the Korean War, for which far fewer published primary sources exist than for World War II and Vietnam. Sources are more than adequate, but less selectivity was involved in choosing works. The same is true for accounts by African-American soldiers and, in the days of the segregated army, their white leaders, although again the number of available sources is sufficient.

For those wars where primary sources are plentiful, I chose memoirs and novels deemed significant by literary critics and historians. Noted professor of literature and World War II combat veteran Paul Fussell, for example, praises the memoirs of World War II marine Eugene B. Sledge and Vietnam War marine William D. Ehrhart, and rightly so; hence, these works are included, as is Fussell's own memoir. Moreover, chance entered in as a factor. For example, I stumbled upon Paul Boesch's obscure but superb World War II memoir at a used bookstore—a memoir long overdue for reprinting.

While reading and assessing these memoirs, novels, and oral histories, a revelatory process occurred that, in retrospect, should have been obvious. Combat is a human experience, and because individuals react to it in typically human ways, the student of soldier behavior first notices the remarkable similarities in soldiers' attitudes and motivations. Historian Peter Karsten, in preparing a book of documents and narrative excerpts on the effects of war on American life, "was struck by the degree to which the experiences and attitudes of eighteenth-, nineteenth-, and twentieth-century American soldiers were more alike than they were different."[12] Literature professors such as Herzog, who study soldiers' memoirs and novels, are also struck by the consistencies in human reactions to war: "In spite of obvious differences involving the nature, conduct, and perceptions of the

Vietnam War and other modern wars, the best stories from these conflicts suggest a fundamental universality among wars: emotions, combat experiences, battlefield rituals, and changes soldiers undergo."[13]

The more that one compares soldiers' experiences, however, the more obvious it becomes, as the historian Richard H. Kohn points out, that individual reactions to war are as complex and diverse as humans themselves: "The problem, in both scholarship and popular thinking, is our propensity to search for typicality, to think in terms of stereotypes, and to aim for universal generalizations that fit across all of American history. The truth of the matter is that the 'American soldier' never existed; the most pernicious myth of all is that there has ever been a prototypical American in uniform."[14]

Thus, each soldier experiences his own war, as the psychiatrists Herbert Hendin and Ann Pollinger Haas discovered in talking with Vietnam veterans: "The unique personal and social characteristics that each individual brought to combat played a role in shaping his combat experiences, in influencing his perceptions of traumatic combat events, and in determining the specific meanings that such events had, and continue to have, for him."[15]

What complicates the study of the soldier's experience in war is that both Karsten and Herzog on the one hand, and Kohn, Hendin, and Haas on the other, are correct. Generalizations can be made about soldiers' attitudes and behavior, but they must allow for any number of individual differences. For example, the closest thing to a truism about soldiers in combat is that they are afraid, and what they fear most is death or mutilation; but even this truism must admit to exceptions, such as the psychotic soldier who knows no fear, or the rare individual who never loses his belief in his own invulnerability and hence does not fear death. This book, therefore, draws conclusions about soldier behavior and motivations while allowing for numerous exceptions and variances.

And what conclusions can be made concerning American soldier behavior in the wars of the draft era? Chapter 1 examines why men volunteered to serve or honored their draft notices. The common perception is that doughboys marched off to World War I enthusiastically, that the GIs of World War II and the Korean War donned their uniforms reluctantly albeit with a certain grim determination, and that the young men of the Vietnam War era, if they answered the call to serve at all, did so only with thinly veiled resentment. These perceptions are not without validity, but they also oversimplify. The reality is that myriad factors, positive and negative, motivated young men to rally to the flag in each of the wars of the draft era.

New recruits then went through basic training or, for marines, boot camp. They were literally and figuratively stripped of their civilian identities and rebuilt into soldiers. This "soldierization process," as the U.S. Army calls it, produced a physically fit soldier skilled in basic tasks and confident in his new profession. This process did not produce, its critics notwithstanding, some sort of automaton or amoral killer. Nor did all recruits react the same to the soldierization process. The degree to which they rallied to the flag either enthusiastically or reluctantly influenced the degree to which they responded positively or negatively to their training.

Following training, these newly minted soldiers found themselves en route to the war zone. To appreciate the soldier's behavior in combat, it is first necessary to understand the environment in which he fought and struggled to survive. Chapter 2 examines the harsh physical and emotional environment of war. The green soldier had learned in training that he needed to be physically fit, but he was unpleasantly surprised to learn just how hard, dirty, and exhausting soldiering could be. When not on the move, and often carrying a staggering load, the soldier prepared defensive positions and maintained vigilance. He did not get enough sleep, often did not get enough to eat or drink, went without a bath or clean clothes for weeks at a time, and suffered the effects of climatic extremes.

While this harsh physical environment was wearing the soldier down, he was simultaneously forced to cope with enormous emotional stresses. Danger and the fear of death were ever present. During air or artillery attack, when the soldier could not retaliate, the feeling of helplessness could be overpowering. Soldiers were dismayed to discover that they were expendable cogs in a huge war machine. Chance more than martial prowess determined a soldier's fate, and he was alarmed at the prospect that not only might he be killed by the enemy, but he could also die in a senseless accident, perhaps at the hands of his own comrades.

Over time, the soldier found himself immersed deeper and deeper in this malevolent environment. Chapter 3 describes the immersion process. The soldier first entered combat either as an individual replacement or as part of a green unit, and his experiences varied accordingly. Relief, even elation, replaced anxiety after surviving first combat. The soldier had proven himself. He began functioning effectively, gaining experience and confidence in his martial skills. Sooner or later, however, perhaps following a wound or the death of a comrade, the soldier's confidence was shattered—it *could* happen to him. He was not invulnerable. He became increasingly aware of the many dangers around him, and his fears grew accordingly. At the same time, the harsh physical environment wore him down physically. The soldier became shaky. Eventually he could not take it any more—psychological breakdown or even suicidal fatalism ensued.

Immersion in the environment of war was thus an inevitably debilitating process, yet some soldiers endured it for an amazingly long time without losing their sanity or their humanity. Chapter 4 examines the various ways a soldier coped. Perhaps most important was removing him from the malevolent environment as often as the situation permitted. Breaks in the action, be it a rotation into reserve or the granting of leave for rest and relaxation (R and R), afforded the soldier a chance to recover physically and emotionally. He also learned to resist a military environment that he often perceived of as uncaring, unnecessarily hierarchical, and inefficient by rebelling in various ways, from going over the hill to enjoy a drink at an off-limits establishment to carrying out midnight requisitions for needed or desirable supplies.

When soldiers could not physically escape the environment through minor rebellions or a break in the action, they resorted to various mind games that provided mental escape. Soldiers were notorious daydreamers, dwelling on prewar good times and swapping stories about plans for their postwar futures. At the same time, they learned not to dwell on present circumstances, such as yesterday's costly firefight or tomorrow's sure-to-be-grueling road march. Soldiers learned to live in the moment and focus on the mundane tasks at hand. Some soldiers found comfort in religious faith; others did not. Some put their faith in good luck charms. Humor, often black, provided relief from stress. Ultimately, soldiers clung to the hope of a departure from the combat zone by way of a non-life-threatening "million dollar wound" or, in the cases of the Korean and Vietnam Wars, by reaching the end of their tour of duty.

One coping mechanism was so complex and so important that it warrants special consideration. Chapter 5 addresses the role of comradeship, not just as a means of coping but as an essential element in motivating the soldier to fight. The varying bonds of friendship that formed within the soldier's squad and platoon, his "primary group" to use a sociological term, cannot be viewed in isolation. The group's relationship to its parent unit (company and higher) and, most significantly, its members' attitudes toward their country and its war aims must also be considered. Morale and effectiveness declined sharply if the soldier's belief in cause and country began to fade, as it did during the latter stages of the Korean and Vietnam Wars.

Despite the various means of coping with the environment of war, some soldiers just could not bear the strain. They broke down. Chapter 6 examines how, during the wars of the draft era, psychological breakdown became recognized as a serious casualty producer, and means of treatment were devised. Many soldiers were treated successfully and returned to duty. Some never fully recovered. Psychiatrists and sociologists have debated why men "cracked up," as the soldiers call it. Individual personality traits and characteristics affected a soldier's susceptibility—indeed, some broke down in their first fight or even before reaching the front. The harsh physical environment and the exhausting nature of combat also contributed to psychological breakdown. The determining factor for most men, however, was the constant fear of death or mutilation and the enormous stress that it produced, although other fears often added to the strain.

Some soldiers who couldn't take it any more, many of whom were on the verge of cracking up, opted out of combat through self-inflicted wounds or desertion. Their comrades might be expected to take a dim view of such "cowards" who abandoned the group, and often they did, but surprisingly the group sometimes accepted the fact that many of these men had reached the end of their rope after making a sincere effort to do their part.

At the other extreme from the shaky soldier who couldn't take it anymore was the soldier-adventurer, who seemed to thrive on war. Chapter 7 describes these soldier-adventurers, whose impact on the battlefield far outweighed their numbers. They were neither avid killers nor psychotics, but they did not mind killing as part of their job and excelled at soldierly skills, for which they were recognized and admired. This recognition was a powerful motivator for the soldier-adventurer, but as the term "adventurer" implies, these soldiers were also thrilled by the excitement. Combat was a fascinating if lethal game. Besting the enemy was a challenge.

Certainly only a minority of soldiers thrived on war, but even the average GI discovered that war was not without some redeeming qualities. Even veterans who denounced the brutality and senselessness of war often noted, with some nostalgia, that the friendships formed were intense and unforgettable. Soldiers also took pride in a job well done. Defeating the enemy was cause for satisfaction. A firefight could be deadly but also an exhilarating experience against which humdrum peacetime activities paled in comparison. On occasion soldiers were tourists, enjoying sights unlike anything in their hometowns. And the spectacle of war itself could be breathtaking. Awestruck soldiers were fascinated by aerial dogfights, off-shore naval battles, artillery barrages, and the sight of massed men and machinery.

That the soldier could take considerable satisfaction in defeating his enemy indicates the extent to which he had accepted his new profession of trained killer. A few students of soldier behavior have claimed, however, that American troops were so fear-ridden or guilty over the prospect of taking human life that they literally failed to pull the trigger. Chapter 8 debunks this theory. There were as many attitudes toward killing as there were individual personalities, and certainly some soldiers were reluctant to kill, but in the kill-or-be-killed catalyst of the battlefield, few hesitated to pull triggers. Some enjoyed it. The degree to which the enemy was dehumanized by propaganda and racial hatred enhanced the soldier's willingness to kill, as did the extent to which he perceived that his enemy committed atrocities or refused to fight "fair." Hence the Asian foe, more than the German foe, was considered an enemy to whom quarter was not to be granted.

The extent to which soldiers stayed within the acceptable bounds of conduct in warfare, albeit bounds that varied by war, enemy, and situation, was influenced in no small part by the small-unit leader. Chapter 9 reviews the leadership traits and skills essential for junior officers and noncommissioned officers: possessing tactical and technical competence, ensuring that soldiers are cared for, and sharing in the hardships and dangers. Morale and cohesion in units without such leaders suffered accordingly.

The good junior officer shared the hardships and dangers with his men, and together they resented, and complained about, those soldiers and civilians who did not have to suffer with them. Chapter 10 explores the combat soldier's attitude toward the rear echelon that provided his logistics and supporting arms. The front-line soldier believed, sometimes not without reason, that the rear echelons lived in safety and comfort, kept the best supplies for themselves, or even profited at his expense through black-market operations. The soldier likewise resented homefront slackers who made a comfortable living in war-related business and industry or who even, in the case of the Vietnam War, denigrated the fighting soldier while they obtained educational, medical, or occupational draft deferments.

At the same time that the soldier resented the home front, however, he also sought its support and acceptance. The home front represented, in the tangible form of friends, neighbors, and family, the country that had sent him off to war. The memory of loved ones, reinforced by letters from home, helped the soldier cope. He also scanned the hometown newspapers he received for any mention of himself or his unit. He wanted recognition for his efforts and, more important, appreciation for his sacrifices. When that recognition was not forthcoming, the results could be devastating to morale.

One group in particular sought their country's recognition and acceptance — African-American soldiers. Chapter 11 addresses the black soldier in the wars of the draft era, a period that witnessed a shift from a segregated to an integrated army and Marine Corps. The inherent flaws in the segregated "Jim Crow" army ensured not only relative obscurity for black troops but also inequalities and inefficiencies that forced black units to operate with distinct disadvantages. Integration during the Korean War ensured that blacks and whites would fight side by side in Vietnam, and African-American performance under fire shattered forever the myth that blacks did not make good soldiers. Black grunts also garnered an overdue measure of recognition for African-American contributions in war. Integration did not erase all vestiges of real and perceived discrimination within the military, however.

Despite overwhelming evidence of war's brutality and how devastating to mind and body sustained combat can be, the phenomenon remains that in all the wars of the draft era, a substantial number of men, especially early on in each of those conflicts, volunteered or accepted their draft notices with enthusiasm. Their positive, even cavalier, approach to wartime service can be explained only by the circumstance that their notions about what combat would be like were wrongheaded. The Conclusion briefly examines how each generation's roseate notions of combat were propagated by the memorialization process and the popular media. Conversely, some young men went to war with a more realistic idea of what it would be like, and while the truism remains that no green soldier fully understands what he is in for, those young soldiers fared better than their comrades whose heads were full of romanticized images of glorious combat. Perhaps this book, and certainly the memoirs and novels cited, can provide new generations with a more realistic appraisal of what war is all about.

# 1

# Rallying to the Flag

Before 1917, America relied primarily on volunteer soldiers in wartime. Upon signing the Selective Draft Act on May 18, 1917, however, President Woodrow Wilson ushered in the draft era.[1] The draft, or Selective Service System as it was officially designated, would be the tool for conscripting American manpower in four wars, ending only in 1973 with the adoption of an all-volunteer force. The draft was introduced because, unlike volunteerism, it allowed for the efficient, centralized management of manpower. Men with jobs critical to the war effort, in fields such as agriculture and industry, were exempted from military service, but the rest were subject to call-up based on various categories of age, marital status, and health. What should not be forgotten, however, is that multiple avenues remained for entering military service, despite the draft. For example, though draftees constituted 72 percent of the army by the end of World War I in November 1918, voluntary enlistments outpaced draft inductions throughout 1917. These volunteers were urgently needed to bring regular army and federally activated National Guard units up to strength while the draft apparatus was still being established.[2] These volunteers were the first into combat in France.

While the specifics varied, this pattern was repeated in each of the wars of the draft era. Regular army or marine units, consisting solely or mostly of volunteers, often saw action first, usually followed by federalized National Guard units containing a large proportion of volunteers. Units formed primarily from draftees followed, at least during the world wars, and in all the wars individual replacements were most often draftees. These various paths to service accommodated a wide range of motivational levels, from enthusiastic volunteer to resentful draftee.

## COMMON PERCEPTIONS: ENTHUSIASTIC DOUGHBOYS, RESIGNED GIs, AND RESENTFUL GRUNTS

Historians have drawn generalized conclusions about how willingly Americans served in time of war. The perception is that young men rallied to the colors in 1917 with an enthusiasm that reflected contemporary, middle-class, Victorian mores. "The nineteenth and early twentieth centuries," notes the historian Michael C. C. Adams, "created a cultural milieu in which war could be seen as an intrinsically valuable human endeavor."[3] War would cleanse and strengthen American society, which had become soft and decadent. Duty to country and wartime self-sacrifice would curb the sordid materialism of a rapidly expanding industrial society. Indeed, nothing less than a moral renaissance would occur, both in America and, thanks to American influence and intervention, in Europe as well.[4]

War was also considered an exciting, chivalrous pursuit that would provide young men "a liberating release from the stultifying conventions of civilized society," according to historian David M. Kennedy.[5] The Great War would allow an escape from boring, petit-bourgeois work and female-dominated home life while also providing an opportunity for a young adventurer to prove his courage and manhood.[6] Many young men volunteered in 1917, or served even earlier with Allied forces, in search of excitement.

The notion that war was an adventurous and intrinsically valuable endeavor was not unique to America. European society displayed a similar attitude when war broke out in 1914.[7] The war literature that Americans read from 1914 to 1917, much of it originating in Europe, reinforced the idea that war was chivalrous and uplifting. This literature, overwhelmingly pro-Allied, nurtured the growing belief that America must act to save the culture and democratic heritage of England and France from the evils of Prussianism.[8]

Perhaps even more influential than the literature was the stance taken by America's opinion leaders in championing the Allied cause and condemning Teutonic barbarity. These "custodians of culture," as the historian Henry F. May calls them, included leading men of letters, college presidents, conservative politicians, and editors.[9] Kennedy notes the impact of these opinion leaders, coupled with the pro-Allied, romantic literature: "An affirmative and inspiring attitude toward war, preached by guardians of tradition like [Oliver Wendell] Holmes and [Theodore] Roosevelt, nurtured by popular war writers like [Alan] Seeger and [Arthur Guy] Empey, filled men's imaginations in 1917."[10] The result was enthusiasm for the war and the Allied cause, especially among young idealists from the Ivy League colleges and exclusive prep schools.[11]

The custodians of culture and the purveyors of popular war literature proved to be wrong, however. The Great War did not cleanse and uplift society, American or European, nor did it prove to be chivalrous. Americans were thoroughly disabused of any notion of war as a positive force. Thus, when the United States was pushed into war in December 1941, the "naive idealism" and "noisy confidence" of the World War I doughboy were no longer in evidence, according to historian Lee Kennett.[12] Americans donned their uniforms with "a certain grim determination," writes literature professor William E. Matsen, "far removed from the innocent idealism displayed in 1917 by the Great War's doughboys."[13] Romanticized, prowar literature would be notably absent during World War II.[14] Marine private Robert Leckie's farewell to his mother before heading off to the Pacific encapsulates America's attitude toward World War II: "It was not a heart-rending leave-taking, nor was it brave, resolute—any of those words that fail to describe the thing. It was like so much else in this war that was to produce unbounded heroism, yet not a single stirring song: it was resigned."[15]

While the resigned GI rejected his doughboy predecessor's lofty goal of making the world safe for democracy, he nevertheless believed that America's involvement in World War II was necessary and just. When the specter of a North Korean takeover of South Korea by military force loomed large in 1950, a resid-ual faith in the nation and its leadership left over from World War II came into play. Americans equated Communism with the recently defunct Nazi regime and uncritically assumed that the cause of defending South Korea was just. Robert Lekachman, a World War II veteran, commented on this residual fervor: "I think everybody still felt good about the war in '47, '48, '49. One wonders: could Tru-man have unilaterally committed American troops to Korea unless there had been the lingering romance of the Second World War? I rather doubt it."[16]

Once the Communist Chinese intervened in the Korean War, however, vic-tory in the World War II sense of totally defeating the enemy became an impos-sibility. As the war dragged on, disillusionment grew, and American draftees were increasingly reluctant to fight in an unwinnable war. A few historians and journalists warned that a new type of army, a professional, Cold War "legion," would be needed if America was to fight any more such wars. War correspondent Marguerite Higgins advised as early as 1951 that the "Third World War is on. It began in Korea." Therefore, in the future, "American leadership is going to have to impress on every potential GI that there are strong odds that he's going to fight some dirty battles to keep the vanilla-ice-cream kind of world he has been brought up in."[17]

Historian and Korean War veteran Theodore R. Fehrenbach argued the case for a new type of army even more vehemently in 1963, pointing out that "Korea was the kind of war that since the dawn of history was fought by professionals, by legions." America must take to heart a critical lesson from the Korean War: "In Korea, Americans had to fight, not a popular, righteous war, but to send men to die on a bloody checkerboard, with hard heads and without exalted motiva-tions, in the hope of preserving the kind of world order Americans desired."[18]

Yet, except for the establishment and expansion of the Special Forces, with their famous green berets, no special legion emerged. Thus when President Lyn-don B. Johnson committed major American ground forces to what proved to be the quagmire of Vietnam and failed to call the reserves to active duty, as had occurred in previous wars, manpower requirements could be met only by greatly increased draft calls. The Vietnam-era draftee was not merely resigned, as were his counterparts in World War II and Korea, but downright resentful. The perceived inequities of the Vietnam-era draft were a major source of this resentment. As Lawrence M. Baskir and William A. Strauss, both of whom served on the Presidential Clemency Board established by Gerald R. Ford, observe: "The draft . . . worked as an instrument of Darwinian social policy. The 'fittest'—those with background, wit, or money—managed to escape. Through an elaborate structure of deferments, exemptions, legal technicalities, and noncombatant military alternatives, the draft rewarded those who manipulated the system."[19] As the war dragged on and the foxholes were increasingly filled by draftees, the Vietnam War grunt's level of resentment over having to fight while others avoided serving only increased.

## THE REALITIES OF RALLYING TO THE FLAG

This overview of motivations, or lack thereof, for serving in the wars of the draft era certainly contains much truth. It is also simplistic and therefore misleading. In reality, a mix of enthusiasm, resignation, and resentment can be found among those serving in each of the wars in question. David M. Kennedy's concept of "coercive volunteerism" provides a useful starting point for a more sophisticated examination of wartime motivations. Kennedy rejects the common perception of Victorian, middle-class American men enthusiastic for war in 1917. He concedes that many were eager to join up, but this reservoir of enthusiasts was far from bottomless. Thus, the governing bureaucracy and its elite supporters, while ostensibly championing volunteerism, increasingly resorted to social pressure and stricter regulations to keep the ranks filled. Indeed, if World War I had continued, Kennedy believes that coercive measures would have been even more necessary: "Had the crisis continued to deepen, and the government been forced to sift the population ever more finely for men to send to France, it was altogether likely that ballyhoo would have increasingly given way to bayonets."[20] With variations, this process occurred in all the wars of the draft era. When the supply of prewar regulars and enthusiastic volunteers gave out, the country coerced growing numbers of reluctant, even resentful, draftees into serving.

The first to rally to the wartime colors were the volunteers, and despite the workings of the Selective Service System, various channels remained available for them to enter service. During World War I many volunteers did indeed conform to the generalization about idealistic crusaders. They were Francophiles or Anglophiles who feared that Europe would be crushed under the Prussian boot heel.[21] None were more idealistic than the thousands of Americans who volunteered to serve in the Allied armies or in American volunteer ambulance and truck units, even before the United States entered the war. Amos N. Wilder was one such volunteer, joining more illustrious compatriots such as John Dos Passos and Ernest Hemingway in serving as an ambulance driver. As did many of his colleagues, he transferred to the American forces following the U.S. entry into the war, serving as a corporal in an AEF artillery battalion. Wilder saw himself and his fellow volunteers as ideological bellwethers: "Thus when it came to motivation of whatever elements and ranks in the armed forces, one should recognize the leavening influence of those with a more grounded perception of the issues at stake and a more enlightened dedication."[22]

More than a few Americans volunteered to serve because they believed the stories, actively fed by Allied propaganda, of German atrocities and worried that America might share the Allies' fate. Private Alphonso Bulz quit high school in Texas to enlist, fearing the war was going so badly for the Allies that they might lose and that the Kaiser's next target might be America. Then there were "all those awful things the Germans were doing to the Belgians—cutting the fingers off the men so they couldn't pull the trigger on a gun and raping all those nuns and all that."[23] Corporal Horatio Rogers joined his local National Guard outfit in Massachusetts out of similar concerns: "The papers were full of German atrocities and Allied unsuccess. Each 'great drive' the Allies made seemed to accomplish nothing. Then Russia was overthrown, and I had visions of a Prussianized world."[24]

The accepted wisdom is that such idealistic concerns did not figure so prominently in later conflicts, given the disillusionment with war as a force for good generated by the Great War, but belief in the cause continued to motivate some volunteers. GIs in World War II considered Nazism more evil than its Prussian predecessor and were proud, as Lieutenants Harold P. Leinbaugh and John D. Campbell put it in their memoir about a World War II rifle company, to be "part of the mighty endeavor, the Great Crusade to free Europe."[25] Or put more prosaically by marine private Robert Stiles, "There was no question who wore the white hats—we did."[26]

Korean War soldiers equated Communism with Nazism and believed America was justified, even obligated, to save South Korea. Historian Henry Berry noted the prevalence of this attitude among the Korean War veterans he interviewed. One of his interviewees commented, "The Communists seemed just as bad as the Nazis to us. I think my age group had been bred on the patriotic fervor of World War II. You either went into the service or you were a bad guy."[27]

Ideological motivations are rarely discussed as a factor in why the Vietnam-era soldier served, but many who enlisted believed in the cause—a far cry from the perception that most grunts were resentful draftees. A significant minority of soldiers, at least early in the war, believed in stopping the spread of Communism, defending the fledgling Republic of South Vietnam, and heeding their charismatic president John F. Kennedy's call to serve one's country.[28]

Marine corporal and Vietnam veteran William D. Ehrhart believes that "those who went to Vietnam—well into the 1960's and contrary to popular perception—were largely young volunteers, eager and idealistic."[29] Marine sergeant Ron

Kovic was one such volunteer. He and others joined so "that we could serve our country like the young president [Kennedy] had asked us to do."[30] Both Ehrhart and Kovic, like others, eventually became disillusioned with the war, but their beliefs provided a strong incentive for initially volunteering.

While some men volunteered out of a genuine belief in the cause, even more joined up looking for excitement, or at least for a change of pace from their boring civilian lives. Many World War I volunteers conformed to the generalization about middle-class, Victorian-era men seeking adventure in the chivalrous, masculine arena of combat. Corporal William L. Langer spoke for the men in his unit, the all-volunteer First Gas Regiment: "I can hardly remember a single instance of serious discussion of American policy or of larger war issues. We men, most of us young, were simply fascinated by the prospect of adventure and heroism. Most of us, I think, had the feeling that life, if we survived, would run in the familiar, routine channel. Here was our one great chance for excitement and risk. We could not afford to pass it up."[31]

Even some of the self-proclaimed idealists like Amos N. Wilder admitted that, beyond their "crusading spirit," they were animated by "a sense of high adventure." The "main idea," he added, "was to be where the action was, and with this was mixed the romance of adventure."[32] Will Judy, a clerk in the Thirty-third Division, noted a similar combination of eagerness and idealism in his called-up National Guard outfit: "The spirit of great adventure is upon us and we compare ourselves not too modestly with the crusaders of other centuries."[33]

Of course, these eager crusaders soon discovered that modern warfare was not so much adventurous as deadly and impersonal; hence the perception that American GIs went to war reluctantly in World War II and even less enthusiastically in the Korean and Vietnam Wars. In reality, however, thousands of volunteers went off to those later wars with as much eagerness and naïveté as did their doughboy predecessors. Most of these adventure seekers were young, without family responsibilities, and a war promised more excitement than going to school or getting a job.

Novelist James Jones, a World War II veteran, believes that the lure of adventure drew many to the colors: "There is always that exciting feeling about the beginning of a war. . . . All restraints are off, everyday life and its dull routines, its responsibilities, are scratched and a new set of rules take over."[34] Audie Murphy, who received a battlefield commission in World War II and survived the war as America's most decorated soldier, was a classic case of a young man attracted to war as an alternative to life's "dull routines." One of nine children born into a family of poor sharecroppers, Murphy dreamed about the glories of combat as his "one escape from a grimly realistic world." On reaching his eighteenth birthday, he wasted no time in joining up, finally being accepted into the infantry after being rejected by the marines and the paratroops because of his small size and weight.[35]

John L. Munschauer came from a background quite different from Murphy's. The college-educated son of a comfortably middle-class family, he had by 1944 received a commission in the army's Medical Service Corps and was safely ensconced as a training company commander in Colorado. Yet he decided to transfer to the infantry and was soon in combat in the Philippines, because sitting the war out in Colorado meant "missing out on the greatest event of the century, and deep down that was the strongest pull. I did not want to miss the show."[36]

A sense that they had, indeed, "missed the show" in World War II, usually because they were too young, motivated some men to jump at the chance for action when the Korean War erupted in 1950. John A. Sullivan was too young to serve during World War II, but the war had "left a strong impression" on him: "Our young men were fighting the twin evils of German and Japanese dictatorship, and the entire nation seemed mobilized to support them."[37] In 1950, Sullivan was old enough to seek the adventure he had missed out on a few years earlier: "Boyhood dreams from military school and the Second World War flooded back. Could I now lead troops in combat? Could I ever earn the right to wear the Combat Infantry Badge?"[38]

By the time that President Lyndon Johnson decided to commit substantial ground forces to Vietnam in 1965, a new generation of young men, weaned on romanticized accounts of World War II provided by authors, historians, and especially filmmakers, was ready for its share of wartime adventure, or at least escape from a humdrum civilian existence.[39] Ron Kovic, who saw in the Vietnam War a chance to meet President Kennedy's challenge of service to America, also sought to escape a dead-end civilian life: "I didn't want to be like my Dad, coming home from the A&P every night. . . . I didn't want to be like that, working in that stinking A&P, six days a week, twelve hours a day. I wanted to be somebody."[40] Lieutenant Alfred S. Bradford and his fellow Army Reserve Officers' Training Corps comrades volunteered with visions of future glory: "Even before we (ROTC officers) had gone to war, we imagined ourselves back, telling our own stories to an awe-stricken audience. After all, Vietnam was our generation's great adventure and we had volunteered for it; we wanted to go to war."[41]

Thus, each new generation sought its "great adventure," and for the American youth of the twentieth century, that adventure was as often as not a war. Yet each generation also produced, along with its would-be heroes and crusaders, a large contingent of men content to forgo adventure for the security and prosperity of peacetime, no matter how boring. Historian Peter Karsten notes that in an ideal democratic society, "young men, conscious of the freedoms and rights they possess . . . , will freely consent to military service with a sense of political obligation."[42] While some Americans served out of just such a sense of obligation, Karsten adds that many more men "acquiesced," at best, to serve, leaving their peacetime lives, families, and jobs to heed the call to arms only with great reluctance.[43]

Certainly not every doughboy conformed to the generalization of the eager volunteer in search of adventure, out to rid the world of Prussianism. Wilder noticed that the draftee replacements arriving to fill up his artillery battalion shared neither his ideals nor his enthusiasm: "The drafted soldiers here in camp as replacements—who have had only a dull experience on top of their first home-sickness—really exhibit blueness over the failure of [President Woodrow Wilson's] peace proposition. They really hope not to go to the front."[44] Many reluctant doughboys undoubtedly shared the sentiments of Tennessee mountain man Sergeant Alvin C. York, who, unlike the Anglophile and Francophile Ivy Leaguers and custodians of culture, "had no time nohow to bother much about a lot of foreigners quarrelling and killing each other over there in Europe."[45] Then there is the case of Jack Herschowitz, pulled from his thriving dried-food business in New York City by his induction notice. He ended up a rifleman in the AEF, but he was not happy about it for the most sensible reason: "I didn't feel like going—who wants to get killed?"[46]

The workings of Kennedy's coercive volunteerism explain in part why so many Americans were willing, if not exactly eager, to go to war. An important aspect of coercive volunteerism was social and peer pressure, which could be coercive indeed, as when vigilantes tracked down draft dodgers during World War I. More typically, however, it involved young men who could not face the scorn, disappointment, or rejection from schoolmates, girlfriends, relatives, and community leaders that their draft evading would generate. Conversely, volunteering or at least stoically accepting one's draft notice brought congratulations and sympathetic support.

Ronald Schaffer discusses the various reasons why men served during World War I, noting that they were often "influenced by their connections to others in their hometowns or neighborhoods or schools or colleges or families."[47] Marine private Carl Andrew Brannen was so influenced. He believed his family had to "do their bit in uniform," so he "joined the exodus from Texas A&M College, as cadets went into different branches of service."[48]

The fear of public condemnation coerced a reluctant Charles F. Minder into serving in the AEF, and into not seeking a possible draft deferment as the sole supporter of his mother: "I wish now that I had claimed exemption when they asked me; like a fool I said, 'No,' just because I was too much a coward to be a Conscientious Objector. I was afraid of what others would think of me."[49]

Peer and social pressure remained a central aspect of coercive volunteerism during World War II. Leon C. Standifer provides an excellent assessment of the multiple pressures working on a young man in a small, conservative, rural community. In Clinton, Mississippi, one did not dodge the draft: "Clinton would not tolerate a man who took a war-essential job just for draft deferment." The high school football team members set the standard, wanting "to become marines or fighter pilots." Then there were the girls, whose opinions mattered a great deal to an eighteen-year-old boy: "Girls were fascinated with the whole war. They seemed to want us all to become fighter pilots, marines, or at the very least paratroopers." This was enough for Standifer: "Personally, I was eager to be in uniform. I wanted to come home on leave, have everyone brag about me, and be able to date any girl in town."[50]

James Jones sees this peer pressure as a critical feature differentiating World War II from the wars that followed: "The only real difference, the main difference, between World War II and later wars was the greater overall social commitment and, therefore, the greater social stigma attached to refusing to go."[51] Jones is no doubt correct in a relative sense, but young men in those later wars continued to serve in part because they feared the condemnation that would ensue if they refused to do so. At least until the later stages of the Korean and Vietnam conflicts, when public opinion had turned against those wars, young men who dodged the draft or deserted from the service could not expect the blessings or the support of their communities.[52]

Vietnam veterans confirm that fear of censure by friends and community was often an important factor in convincing them to comply with their greetings from Uncle Sam. Tim O'Brien was one such draftee who ultimately decided, because of social pressure, to fight in a war he believed was wrong: "Here we are. Mama has been kissed goodbye, we've grabbed our rifles, we're ready for war. All this not because of conviction, not for ideology; rather it's from fear of society's censure."[53] Or, to put the problem into sharper perspective, as one of Christian Appy's interviewees did: "Suppose I had found a way out. How could I face my friends who were drafted or joining up? And how would I feel walking around town, seeing their parents, and knowing that they were over in Nam getting shot at while I'm home partying? I'd feel like a chickenshit."[54]

Another aspect of coercive volunteerism that persuaded the reluctant to serve was the threat of punishment. Draft evading or desertion could mean jail or exile, in addition to social censure. Often, as in the case of Korean War private Rudolph W. Stephens, a mix of social pressure and fear of punishment convinced a wavering draftee to serve: "Inside I wanted to run away, assume a strange name, and get lost in this big country of ours, but there was no way I could do such a thing when other boys were leaving to do the part they were called to do. Besides, the military would be looking for me for a long time to come, and I wasn't raised to be a coward. I also didn't want to take the chance of going to Fort Leavenworth, Kansas, to spend time behind bars."[55]

In all the wars of the draft era, some men failed to register for the draft or evaded induction when called up, despite the potential punishments. Draft evasion, for example, reached serious proportions during the later stages of the Vietnam War. Baskir and Strauss describe how the legal system became swamped, to the point of virtual breakdown, by the thousands of potential legal cases generated by this draft evasion. But no matter how dysfunctional the system became, enough draft evaders were convicted in often highly publicized cases that "the choice was made clear for nineteen- and twenty-year-olds who might have had second thoughts about obeying their draft boards: Report for induction, or you'll go to prison."[56]

Many young men thus shared Charles Strong's rationale for heeding the call during the Vietnam War: "I chose not to evade the draft but to conform to it. I figured it was better to spend two years in the service than five years in prison. And I figured that for nineteen years I had enjoyed a whole lot of fruits of this society. I knew that you don't get anything free in this world."[57]

Once of age and registered for the draft, and if no deferment or exemption was forthcoming, then the potential draftee knew that it was just a matter of time before he received his induction notice. At that point, many men elected to volunteer for duty in the hope of being accepted by a service or for a military specialty that would be the least dangerous. The U.S. Army Research Branch conducted thousands of surveys and studies of American soldiers during World War II, the results of which were consolidated after the war in a four-volume report, commonly referred to as the Stouffer Study (after Samuel A. Stouffer, director of the Research Branch's professional staff and one of the editors of the report). The Research Branch discovered that except for the adventure seekers, draftees sought safe jobs, and only a small fraction of those who had managed, by whatever means, to land a safe job (defined as "noninfantry") had any desire to leave it to join the infantry.[58]

In a similar vein, a survey of Vietnam veterans showed that as many as two-thirds of those who had volunteered were "draft-motivated." That is, they volunteered in the face of probable induction in the hope of joining a service (the navy or air force) or acquiring a military specialty that would keep them out of Vietnam, or at least out of ground combat.[59] Enlistment meant three or four years' service instead of the usual two for draftees, but most men considered this a reasonable price to pay. John Ketwig was one of those draft-motivated enlistees. After passing his preinduction physical examination, he saw the handwriting on the wall. He considered running away but did not want to dishonor his family and feared that he would never be able to return home. The waiting list to join the reserves or National Guard was too long—he would probably be called up first. The air force and navy were not accepting any more recruits at that time. Finally, he enlisted to become a mechanic.[60] This choice, as it turned out, did not keep him out of Vietnam, but it did keep him out of the infantry.

Similar stories can be found from earlier wars. Howard S. Hoffman, facing imminent induction on reaching his eighteenth birthday during World War II, attempted unsuccessfully to enlist in the navy's flight training program (not necessarily a safe occupation, but better than a foxhole).[61] Robert G. Thobaben, like thousands of other young men during World War II, opted for the Army Specialized Training Program (ASTP) because it allowed him to stay in college, obtain a commission upon graduation, and then serve in some specialized (as in noncombat) field.[62] To the dismay of most ASTP participants, the program was later canceled and many of them found themselves in the infantry, which desperately needed fresh replacements.

In another case, James Brady faced the unwanted prospect of peacetime induction for a two-year tour of duty in the years following World War II. He thought he would beat the system by joining the Marine Corps's Platoon Leaders' Class (PLC). It exempted him from the draft and presented him with a Marine Reserve commission upon his graduation from college—which occurred about a week before the Korean War broke out. Brady was soon on his way.[63]

Coercive volunteerism, with its social pressures backed by the threat of legal consequences, was not the only influence pushing draft-age men toward military service. Many felt a genuine obligation to serve, as their fathers and grandfathers had done. They believed that they owed their country something for educating, raising, and sustaining them. Kennedy acknowledges that this sense of obligation was an important corollary to the coercive aspects of volunteerism: "Few words were so widely bruited in American society in the World War I era as 'service,' and it is a matter of some importance that the term was incorporated into the official title of the draft agency. . . . Everywhere Americans agreed that a commitment to 'service' was an attribute of the national soul that the war had quickened."[64] Bob Hoffman, whose father had fought in the Spanish-American War and his grandfathers in the Civil War, was one of those who believed "that it was a man's duty to fight and die for his country," and he immediately enlisted in April 1917 "in an endeavor to live up to the tradition of our family."[65]

A sense of obligation to family, community, and country was an important motivator in later wars as well. Sergeant Floyd Jones, a World War II artilleryman, had no illusions about war being an adventure, but he went without question when called: "I served because it was my job and I don't dodge jobs I feel I must do whether I like them or not."[66] Many a man attributed his sense of duty, as World War II paratrooper George William Sefton did, to being "eminently pre-conditioned to volunteer for military service based on his upbringing."[67] These men had relatives who had fought in previous wars (Sefton held his father, a company commander in World War I, in high esteem), and they had a strong sense of community (Sefton was raised in a small, church-going, midwestern town). William Manchester is another case in point. His father, a marine corporal in World War I, had been seriously wounded in the Meuse-Argonne fighting. Manchester grew up in a close, religious New England family of old stock. His ancestors on his mother's side had fought for the Lost Cause in the Civil War. Thus, "in the spring of 1942, guided by the compass that had been built into me, I hitchhiked to Springfield and presented myself to the Marine Corps recruiting station."[68]

Such feelings were not dead with the advent of Vietnam, despite Jones's earlier comment that soldiers in the wars since World War II lacked "social commitment." One Vietnam veteran told oral historian Mark Baker that his family's tradition of service was a key factor in his complying with his induction notice: "One way or another in every generation when there was a war, some male in the family on my father's side went to it. I had never had it drilled into me, but there was a lot of attention paid to the past, a lot of not-so-subtle 'This is what a man does with his life' stuff when I was growing up."[69]

John Foote, a draftee who went to Vietnam even though he could have obtained a medical deferment for allergies, was another man driven by a sense of duty. His father had served in World War II and his ancestors in the Civil War. Moreover, Foote said, "Both of my parents, though not particularly warlike, were strong believers in the duty to serve and the honor that was associated with honorable service."[70] Sergeant Bill Morgan, the protagonist in Jack Fuller's novel *Fragments,* was the quintessential reluctant warrior driven to accept his draft notice, despite misgivings about the Vietnam War, because he could not do otherwise: "When you come from where I did, when you'd been raised on certain tales, when you'd learned to respect your father and his friends, not because of what they did in the wars but rather because of what they suffered, then you simply had no alternative when your number came up. You were swept along despite the arguments [against the war]. And it wasn't the great historic ebbs and flows or even the coercive power of the state that did it. You were moved forward by your own ineradicable past."[71]

Most of the soldiers discussed thus far, whether reluctant draftees or eager volunteers, came from the ranks of the citizenry. In discussing the American soldier in the wars of the draft era, historians understandably focus on these citizen-soldiers since they constituted a majority. But a fair number of regular army soldiers and salty leathernecks from the peacetime forces also went to war, and their motives for joining the service often differed from those of the citizen-soldier.

Having joined in time of peace, these soldiers, though patriotic enough, clearly were not motivated by wartime ideology or any immediate desire to experience combat. Some hoped to see something of the world or to do interesting things while in the military, but many were simply in search of a decent job. The service offered security and a chance for advancement.

Schaffer explains that many of those entering the regular army prior to World War I were impelled to enlist because of "lack of opportunity or disappointment in civilian life" or just sought a warm place to sleep.[72] Several of Henry Berry's interviewees joined the National Guard units being called up and deployed to the United States–Mexican border in 1916 because they were bored with civilian life, and going to the "Wild West" sounded exciting.[73] Many of these men were still in uniform when America went to war in 1917.

Prior to World War II, hard times during the depression made military service an acceptable option for some men, despite the poor pay and the low esteem in which the army was held by the general populace. Sergeant Henry Giles was one such enlistee: "I was sick and tired of the scrabbling and the shame of the commodity lines and no jobs. . . . Nobody knows what the army meant to me — security and pride and something fine and good . . . putting on that uniform not only meant that for the first time in my life I had clothes I wasn't ashamed of, but for the first time in my life I was *somebody*."[74]

For Rod Rodriguez, the son of a poor Cuban immigrant, joining the just-federalized Florida National Guard in 1940 was a good idea, despite the lowly private's pay of thirty-one dollars a month: "In truth, compared to the poverty I had known in Tampa, the army seemed like a good deal. All my material needs were provided."[75] By 1948 a slump had hit the American steel industry, and John Babyak could not find a job after graduating from high school in Youngstown, Ohio: "So, rather than hang around, I decided to join the [Marine] Corps." Winter 1950–1951 found Babyak in Korea, "up to my rear end in snow with God knows how many Chinamen trying to kill me," when to his chagrin he received a letter from home telling him that "there are plenty of jobs available back in Youngstown."[76]

With the integration of the armed forces in the 1950s, the army provided a steady job and upward mobility for blacks as well as whites. A 1954 Gallup Poll showed that 92 percent of black veterans—twice as many as white veterans—felt that they were better off for their army service and had found it rewarding.[77] Increasingly, blacks made the military a career. By 1965, black reenlistment rates in the armed forces were more than twice those of whites.[78] Blacks enlisted for many of the same reasons as whites, citing personal factors, patriotic duty, or draft-motivated enlistment, but blacks mentioned self-advancement almost twice as often as white enlistees did as a reason for joining the military.[79]

Significantly, even when enlistment in the army during the Vietnam era usually entailed a tour of duty in Southeast Asia, young men from the minorities continued to enlist, seeking socioeconomic benefits.[80] Captain Joseph B. Anderson Jr., a platoon leader and company commander in Vietnam, observed that "for many black men, the service, even during a war, was the best of a number of alternatives to staying home and working in the fields or bumming around the streets of Chicago or New York."[81] Albert French, a black marine corporal, certainly felt that way. While he and a hometown buddy from Pittsburgh, Pennsylvania, were on their way to Vietnam, French told his friend that the Marine Corps was not so bad: "You get used to it—it's better than the streets. Half the dudes in jail already, ain't a job nowhere, mills ain't doing shit."[82]

Moreover, a measure of self-esteem came with donning the uniform. Sergeant Emilio P. Milett, a poor Puerto Rican immigrant, had shined shoes in Harlem, but "then he had found the Army, where a life to be proud of lay within a man's aspirations: even a Puerto Rican's."[83] A career in the army, or even just a tour of duty, meant for many minority soldiers what it did for Arthur E. Woodley Jr.: "I felt I could escape from my environment and get ahead in life."[84]

Some young men joined the peacetime army to learn a skill useful in the civilian world or, during the period of the GI bill, to earn educational benefits. Many of these men joined up never expecting, or wanting, to experience combat. War came as a rude, unwelcome surprise. The army itself often made matters worse by championing the material benefits of service while downplaying, in its recruiting program, the fact that soldiers exist to fight. Historian Roy E. Appleman notes that this was the case in the peacetime army before the Korean War: "The great majority of the enlisted men were young and not really interested in being soldiers. The recruiting posters that had induced most of these men to enter the Army mentioned all conceivable advantages . . . , but never suggested that the principal business of an army is to fight."[85]

A similar situation existed in army and marine reserve units prior to the Korean War. Many men had joined the reserves for the drill pay and the camaraderie. No one had anticipated a war. Thus occurred the ironic phenomenon of soldiers and marines bemoaning the fact that they had not bargained on fighting. The Seventh Marine Regiment, hastily cobbled together for the Inchon landing, contained many unhappy, called-up reservists: "Some had just begun their first civilian jobs; others were college boys. A few were on summer vacation from high school. All of them had been called abruptly from their homes, and none had signed on for reserve duty with expectations of a shooting war."[86]

Despite the lesson of Korea—that war could come at any time—men continued to join the peacetime army with thoughts of combat far from their minds. Robert Mason, who loved to fly and held a civilian pilot's license, joined the army's helicopter flight program in 1964, earning his wings and becoming a warrant officer. He had not factored a war into his plans, but he soon found himself en route to Vietnam with the First Cavalry Division: "It was a revelation . . . that came too late. I was going. I owed the army three years of service for teaching me to fly helicopters. And there you had it."[87]

While some men joined the service as a temporary expedient, hoping to learn a skill, earn educational benefits, or simply tide themselves over until something better turned up "on the outside," others found that they liked soldiering and made the service a career. Cynical commentators have charged that professional soldiers welcome war because it provides for advancement, and wartime often did lead to expansion of the military and promotions. Most professional soldiers, however, did not wish for a war to boost their careers. Indeed, because of their training, they had a better appreciation of war's hardships and dangers than most naive citizen-soldiers. Career soldiers were nevertheless drawn to the fighting once war broke out for the elementary reason that it was what they were trained to do. Historian Richard Holmes, in his study on soldier behavior, is one of the few to appreciate this basic fact: "Regular [army] soldiers . . . share an intense professional curiosity as to how well their weapons, tactics and training will work in a real war. War is—and I mean this in no derogatory sense—the opportunity for them to apply what they have studied."[88]

Thus, when a war broke out, most professional soldiers wanted to be in on it. Bill Mauldin, visiting the front in Korea as a correspondent for *Collier's* magazine, encountered a rare species—a soldier voluntarily serving a second tour. As the soldier, an engineer, explained, "I'm a career man and this is my business, so it seemed like this is where I ought to be."[89] Corporal Ehrhart's equally laconic sergeant in Vietnam, a career marine, likewise chose combat duty over a safe job in the rear: "I'd rather be out here where I can keep you boys out of trouble."[90]

Career officer Joseph R. Owen, upon hearing of the outbreak of war in Korea, saw a chance to prove himself: "The news about Korea had inflamed my hope for an opportunity to lead troops in combat, to put myself to the test. I was a twenty-four-year-old second lieutenant, a professional marine officer, intensively trained for combat leadership but as yet untried in battle."[91] Marine captain Richard D. Camp, about to take command of a rifle company in Vietnam, shared Owen's sentiments: "This is it! . . . This is what I had been working up to for all those years. . . . Now, at last, I was really part of it. It was *my* turn."[92]

Some initially reluctant wartime draftees came to adopt a similar attitude. After months of individual and unit training, many citizen-soldiers were as ready as their regular army counterparts, whom they now closely resembled, to try out their new skills. Sergeant Hoffman, to his own surprise, found that he and his comrades were eager to get into action in World War I: "I couldn't understand how men could desire to go out and fight and die. But it is something that grows on you. You train and expect so long that finally you become anxious to get into it, to get it over with."[93]

After two years of training, the citizen-soldiers of K Company, 333d Infantry, Eighty-fourth Infantry Division, felt much the same way on the eve of their first battle in World War II: "After journeying this far and working so long and hard to become soldiers, we would have felt cheated to miss out on the fighting."[94] Lieutenant Sullivan felt an urge to try out his newly acquired skills during the Korean War: "The education process is over, and I am about to put into practice the accumulated knowledge of two years of training. It actually felt good to be a member of the team that my government had fielded to stem the Marxist hordes."[95]

In sum, the generalization of enthusiastic doughboys in World War I, resigned GIs in World War II and Korea, and resentful grunts in Vietnam, though not entirely inaccurate, is too simplistic to encompass the myriad attitudes displayed by those who rallied to the flag. In each war of the draft era, belief in the cause, a quest for adventure, a desire for socioeconomic betterment, military professionalism, social pressure, the threat of legal action, and a sense of obligation affected each individual differently, producing soldiers whose motivations varied from enthusiastically positive to glumly resigned.

Even this list does not exhaust the factors that motivated men to serve. A few soldiers joined seeking revenge, making for a very personal war. One of Audie Murphy's comrades in World War II was a recently immigrated Pole named Novak, to whom all Germans were "sonsabeeches" for overrunning his beloved homeland in 1939. Novak hated Germans "personally and passionately."[96] George Ahlhausen, one of the men in Lester Atwell's squad, volunteered for service in World War II after his kid brother was killed in the Pacific. Ahlhausen, who as guardian had signed the papers allowing his seventeen-year-old brother to join the marines, decided he could not remain idle: "I start thinking *I* should do something, you know, like to make up to him for. . . . Well, I wanted to get into it."[97]

Matthew Brennan tells the story of his platoon sergeant, Sergeant Terry, who had been seriously wounded earlier in Vietnam and discharged. When his brother was killed in Vietnam, Terry rejoined the army. Because of his disabilities he could serve only in a noncombat specialty, but by becoming a helicopter mechanic, he landed a tour of duty in Vietnam, after which he finagled his way into an aero-rifle platoon in the First Cavalry Division. Earlier, Terry "swore a vendetta with the Communists," and now he could carry it out.[98]

Some men served because they believed that the war would be the defining event of their generation, and they did not want to miss it. Walter Rosenblum, a combat photographer in World War II, believed he was "doing something worth-while" in capturing on film the demise of fascism: "You felt you were an actor in a tremendous drama that was unfolding. It was the most important moment of my life."[99] Michael Lee Lanning felt an obligation to serve his country during the Vietnam War, but he also did not want to "miss the chance to experience the major significant event of my generation."[100] John Foote felt the same way: "I began to see Vietnam as the preeminent historical experience of my lifetime, certainly of my youth."[101]

Other men served for less inspired reasons. Their choice was the army or the penitentiary. As Baskir and Strauss write, "Many judges agreed with [Lewis B.] Hershey [director of the Selective Service System] that military service was a good way to rehabilitate social misfits and petty criminals. They sometimes gave convicted offenders a choice between joining the military or going to jail."[102] The enforced discipline and responsibilities of military service did turn some wayward rowdies around. In most cases, however, hoodlums and misfits did not make good soldiers. Men who could not conform to society's norms and laws were even less successful at complying with military standards of discipline and behavior.[103]

At the opposite extreme from the criminal who chose the army over jail was the young volunteer who believed that combat was a proving ground, or rite of passage, from which he would emerge a man. For eighteen-year-old Robert G. Thobaben, even the simple act of registering for the draft in 1942 seemed a step toward manhood: "Suddenly I felt older, more mature. I was a boy who had become a man, courtesy of a small paper [draft] card."[104] If a young man had a reputation as a coward or weakling, he was often especially eager to go to war to prove his detractors wrong. Robert Rasmus, a World War II rifleman and self-admitted "mama's boy," looked forward to going overseas: "I was going to gain my manhood then. I would forever be liberated from the sense of inferiority that I wasn't rugged. I would prove that I had the guts and the manhood to stand up to these things."[105]

Some seekers of manhood, to their horror, found themselves doing "women's work" while in uniform. Corporal Charles S. Crawford manned a tele-phone switchboard in Quantico, Virginia, at the height of the Korean War: "Imagine how I felt when people asked me what I did in the Marine Corps."[106] Crawford soon managed a transfer to Korea as an individual replacement, where he took up the more manly pursuit of forward observer.

The macho, war-as-rite-of-passage theme is also evident in Vietnam War memoirs. Marine lieutenant Caputo "needed to prove something — my courage, my toughness, my manhood, call it what you like." Caputo's battalion went to Vietnam as a unit, hence his platoon experienced first combat together. Caputo saw this combat, at least in retrospect, as a passage to manhood: "Having received that primary sacrament of war, baptism of fire, their boyhoods were behind them. Neither they nor I thought of it in those terms at the time. . . . We were simply aware, in a way we could not express, that something significant had happened to us."[107] One of Baker's interviewees felt much as Caputo did: "I wanted to go to war. It was a test that I wanted to pass. It was a manhood test, no question about it."[108]

For some, as was the case for Corporal Ehrhart's fellow marine in Vietnam, the Japanese immigrant Kenokura Amagasu, duty in the military was a shortcut to American citizenship.[109] Thousands of immigrants became citizens by serving in the military. Many immigrants, even those already holding citizenship, joined the military and fought because they wanted to show their loyalty and gratitude to their new American homeland. Russian immigrant Morry Morrison, for example, joined up in World War I even though, since he was not yet a citizen, he was exempt from the draft. He wanted to fight for his adopted country, and other immigrants he met in uniform felt the same: "Germans, Irish, Polish—no matter what country the man I talked to had come from, it was always the same. 'Sure, I went. Why not? It was as much my country as anyone else's, wasn't it?'"[110]

Yet for whatever reason, or more often multiple reasons, that a man decided to rally to the flag, he soon found himself, as a new recruit, in an alien and distinctly unpleasant world—the army or marine training camp.

## TRAINING IN THE DRAFT ERA: THE SOLDIERIZATION PROCESS

The training a recruit received before his baptism of fire varied significantly in duration and quality. During the massive mobilizations of World War I and II, the army and marines scrambled to expand their minuscule peacetime training apparatus. Equipment, facilities, and instructors were initially in short supply. Most soldiers trained as part of the unit they would go to war with, but in both wars camps were also established to train individual replacements.

The recognition, based on the experiences of the two world wars, that soldiers could be more efficiently trained at centralized camps by experienced cadre led to the system common to the Korean and Vietnam Wars of first training individual recruits in basic soldier skills (marching, military courtesy, physical conditioning, rifle marksmanship, and so on) followed by advanced training in a designated special skill such as infantryman, artilleryman, or truck driver. Only then was a trainee assigned to a unit, often one already in combat, but possibly one still preparing to be sent overseas.

Despite these somewhat different approaches, the twin goals of the training, or soldierization process, were understandably consistent: to teach recruits basic tactical, physical, and weapons skills while simultaneously instilling the discipline and behavioral norms necessary to succeed in combat.[111] This soldierization process, as sociologists Arthur J. Vidich and Maurice R. Stein explain, entailed the transformation of the "civilian-minded recruit" into a "reliable soldier who will respond according to expectation. The institutional techniques for accomplishing this involve a process of self-dissolution and reconstruction."[112] Or, to put it in less clinical terms, as one of the Vietnam War veterans interviewed by Christian G. Appy did, "they tore you down. They tore everything civilian out of your existence . . . and then they re-built you and made you over."[113]

"Tear down" and "build up" imply an extreme, even violent, process. Most of the soldier-authors who comment on their training experience did indeed find it physically demanding and emotionally traumatic. The degree of harassment and stress varied, largely depending on the personality of the recruit's all-important and seemingly omnipotent cadre noncommissioned officer (NCO), or drill instructor/drill sergeant, as he was commonly called during much of this period. Whatever the variations in individual experiences, most recruits considered their initial training an important preliminary to combat, and most emerged from it just as they were supposed to—feeling like soldiers and proud of it.

Though a proud soldier may have been the end product, the process of getting there was painful, especially during the tearing-down phase, which lasted the first several weeks of a recruit's army basic training or marine boot camp. Canadian broadcaster Gwynne Dyer, in researching his television series on war for the Canadian Broadcasting Company, visited the Marine Corps boot camp at Parris Island, where he learned that the first step in the "conversion process" of turning civilians into marines "is the destruction of an individual's former beliefs and confidence, and his reduction to a position of helplessness and need."[114] This conversion process was intentionally stressful.[115] James R. Ebert, in studying army basic training in the Vietnam era, found that "harassment and regimentation gradually increased over the first four weeks of training" as part of a calculated effort "to expose the men to tolerable levels of stress," because stress was something they would surely have to deal with in combat.[116]

The separation from all things civilian began immediately and often dramatically when the new recruits arrived at the induction center (or "reception station," as it was called in the Vietnam era). The reception process lasted several days, during which the trainees turned in their civilian clothes for uniforms, received haircuts (meaning shaved heads), learned to maintain their bunks and footlockers, and began learning the rudiments of military drill and courtesy.[117]

Many recruits vividly remember exactly when this process began—the moment the drill instructor stepped aboard their bus after it arrived at the reception station. The process of transporting enlistees to their induction centers or reception stations varied but generally involved a train trip followed by a final bus or truck ride to the center, there to be met by a drill sergeant. Robert Leckie and his fellow marine recruits received a typically ominous greeting from their drill sergeant when they arrived at Parris Island during World War II: "Boys—Ah want to tell yawl something. Give youah hearts to Jesus, boys—cause youah ass belongs to me!"[118]

William D. Ehrhart has similar memories of his arrival at Parris Island in 1966. The drill instructor who met his bus, whom Ehrhart nicknamed "the Voice of God," quickly set the ground rules: "You will do everything you're told instantly, and you will do nothing else. I'll kill the first cocksucker that fucks it up. You scuzzy shitbirds are *mine,* ladies! And I do not like you. Now, MOVE!"[119] The "Voice of God" revealed, in these few sentences, all the characteristics of verbal abuse that the trainees would learn to endure during the tear-down process: abrasively loud commands, shockingly vulgar language, demeaning references to their lack of masculinity, and no positive encouragement whatsoever—indeed, just the opposite ("I do not like you").

At the end of their first day in the army or Marine Corps, more than a few recruits wondered, as World War II enlistee Howard S. Hoffman did while lying on his bunk at the induction center, just what they had let themselves in for: "I didn't cry or break into tears or anything, but I felt very, very much threatened; I felt that I was now in the grip of forces that I couldn't do anything about; that what was happening to me was largely a matter of chance; that I was at the very bottom of the totem pole."[120] If anything, Ehrhart was even more distraught as he lay on his bunk at the end of his first day: "With all my heart and soul, I did not want to be here. I couldn't understand how any of this had happened. I lay there for what seemed like hours in a kind of trance, staring at the ceiling, my mind in neutral and somebody flooring the accelerator."[121]

Adding to the new recruit's anxiety was his total separation from his previous, comforting civilian life, except for mail and in recent times limited telephone contact. To make matters worse, many young recruits were away from home for the first time. After only a few days at the induction station, World War II draftee John L. Munschauer noticed that "some of the biggest, toughest-looking bruisers were already showing signs of homesickness. Many of these men had never been out of the state, some hardly out of their neighborhood, and more than one had never slept in a house other than their own." At the same time that the recruit was separated from his previous life and "torn down," he was also "leveled off." The recruits discovered that their previous civilian status and accomplishments meant nothing. All were treated the same—badly, as far as they were concerned. Munschauer learned about the leveling process on his first day at the induction station: "Rich or poor, . . . all of us were rabble."[122]

If anything, civilian accomplishments, such as being a "college boy," could bring scorn and extra harassment. Prate Stack and his brother, both former Yale students, made the tactical error of arriving at Parris Island during World War II in a private Pullman railroad car arranged for by their father. The drill sergeant was not impressed: "I've already got what is undoubtedly the dumbest bunch of college bastards who will ever come to Parris Island," he snarled, "and now I have a couple of big-time clowns like you two. You college guys are a swift pain in the ass."[123]

During the reception process, the recruit was relieved of his previous identity. First to go were any physical signs of his civilian past. Leckie and his fellow marine recruits, after turning in their civilian clothes for fatigues and receiving their buzz haircuts, felt "stripped of all vestiges of personality."[124] The Vietnam-era recruit felt as humiliated as his World War II predecessors, as evidenced by a comment by Bill Morgan, the protagonist in Fuller's novel *Fragments:* "We were stripped down to the essentials, heads shaven, uniforms all the same, no past and damned little in the way of a future."[125]

After the reception process, the recruits were formed into platoons of about forty men for the duration of their training.[126] As part of his platoon, the recruit continued the process begun at the reception station of learning to make his bunk, keep his footlocker, and maintain his uniform and equipment to the demanding standards of the drill sergeant. Every waking moment of a long training day was regulated. Uniformity was demanded. The recruits learned to march, talk, and look the same. Recruit Leckie soon realized that it was a "process of surrender" of individual personality and freedom in order to meet group standards of appearance and behavior: "At every turn, at every hour, it seemed, a habit or preference had to be given up, an adjustment had to be made."[127] Many recruits, like Hoffman, found this loss of individuality alarming and demeaning: "You quickly lost your identity in the sense that you became a number very quickly or an item. I was very depressed by the whole situation."[128]

The drill sergeant often resorted to group punishments for individual infractions, thereby reinforcing the idea that the recruit was part of a group first and an individual a distant second. Leon Uris provides an example in *Battle Cry* of one of the most common causes of group punishment—a recruit dropped his rifle (an even more heinous crime than referring to one's rifle as a gun). The entire platoon paid for this accident by having to balance their rifles on the tops of their fingers with arms extended straight out to the front, palms down.[129]

Recruits resented being punished as a group for an individual's mistake, but because they could not change the system, they began to zero in instead on the "screw-ups" who were causing the punishments.[130] They might try to help a well-meaning but slow-learning comrade avoid mistakes, but as one World War II study points out, "deviants" who brought on group punishment by angering the drill sergeant were another matter: "When a whole platoon or an entire company is penalized because of a recalcitrant few, the collective wrath turns upon these few."[131] As Ebert explains in his discussion of Vietnam-era basic training, such deviants "were ostracized and verbally humiliated or bullied into conducting themselves properly," and in a few extreme cases, "group frustrations toward a recalcitrant 'screw-up' resulted in acts of violence, such as 'blanket parties' in which the target of the group's wrath was beaten."[132] In this way the group learned to police itself, and this self-enforcement was exactly what the drill sergeants were out to achieve.

In addition to resorting to group punishments, the drill sergeants went out of their way to harass the trainees verbally and physically. To avoid such harassment, trainees tried to keep a low profile. They learned, according to one World War II study, "to avert attention from themselves by avoiding any erratic behavior."[133] (Many trainees, incidentally, sought to keep a low profile for the remainder of their time in service, perhaps best summed up by the army adage, "never volunteer.") In 1951, army basic trainee Rudolph W. Stephens struggled to keep a low profile: "You did your job and tried to keep everything in order so the noncoms would stay off your back; these people did everything they could to break you down."[134] This advice remained sound for trainees in the Vietnam era as well, as Ebert learned from one marine veteran: "Marine Corps boots learned early that if they did what was asked and did so quickly, they could make it through training without drawing attention to themselves. Anonymity was the key to avoiding punishment."[135]

While trainees, at least some of the time, succeeded in avoiding the attention and hence ire of the drill sergeant, they could not avoid the close physical proximity of the rest of the men in their training platoon. Trainees lived in communal-style barracks. The loss of privacy was yet one more shock the recruit had to adjust to during the tearing-down phase.[136] Leckie found the total lack of privacy to be the worst part of the "process of surrender" of his individuality in boot camp: "Everything was done in the open. Rising, waking, writing letters, receiving mail, making beds, washing, shaving, combing one's hair, emptying one's bowels—all was done in public and shaped to the style and stricture of the sergeant."[137] This lack of privacy would prove to be a hallmark of military service, and the recruits would find they had even less, if that were possible, when living in the combat zone.

During the tearing-down phase, the recruit, for the life of him, could not see what any of this unpleasantness had to do with preparing him for combat. Learning to shine shoes, march, salute, pull kitchen duty, and make a bunk in a military fashion did not strike him as useful skills. After several weeks of such training, the recruits hit a nadir. They were demeaned, frustrated, and angry. They had worked hard but received little in the way of positive reinforcement, and they certainly did not feel like soldiers—slaves perhaps.[138] David Parks's attitude only a week into army basic training in 1965 indicates just how fed up the trainees could become: "These drill instructors drive you nuts. They go around hollering the same thing every day. . . . Hour after hour they're bugging us, how to salute, how to present ourselves to an officer, how to say 'sir,' how to obey orders—how to become robots. . . . Drill—drill—drill. March—march—march. I've had it."[139]

Yet just when trainees' frustrations hit a high point and their morale a low point, things began to change, albeit almost imperceptibly at first. The tear-down phase ended and the buildup began. Appy summarizes the shift: "Having been broken down to nothing—their identities stripped, their compliance won, and their aggression heightened—recruits were gradually rebuilt into soldiers."[140]

The skills the recruits began to learn took on a decidedly more military flavor and hence were more interesting and important in their eyes. Lee Kennett, in his study of the World War II GI, observes: "What the soldiers liked best were those activities that fitted their preconceptions of what a soldier should be doing, and to be precise, they liked those things that had the violence and flavor of combat."[141]

The first activity that most trainees recall as being "useful" and interesting was rifle qualification. They had been issued rifles, taught to march with them, disassemble and assemble them, clean them, and memorize their performance characteristics, all of which was tedious and boring—that is, until they went to the rifle range. Leckie remembers the rifle range as a distinct turning point: "If you are undone in Parris Island, taken apart in those first few weeks, it is at the rifle range that they start to put you together again."[142] No matter how naive, the trainee understood that marksmanship was a skill that he was very possibly going to need in the near future. David Parks, for example, paid special attention to the night-firing training: "The word is that they do a lot of night fighting in Vietnam. So it was an important class."[143]

The trainees began learning other decidedly martial skills also, such as throwing a hand grenade, using a bayonet, and moving in basic tactical formations. Even the hated forced marches, often to the firing ranges and back, made sense— soldiers had to be in top physical condition. World War II surgeon Klaus H. Heubner, after marching all night with his infantry battalion in Italy, conceded the value of his training marches: "I guess these are the sort of forced marches we trained for in the States. One needs stamina to keep up."[144] The training marches not only built stamina but also confidence and a sense of accomplishment. Paul Fussell, no eager soldier by his own admission, nevertheless felt "pleasure and pride" on completing the final forced march during basic training, adding that "happiness . . . can be consistent . . . with deprivation and pain, exhaustion and tears—as long as self-respect is intact, and even, as here, augmented."[145]

Not only did the soldier find the training more relevant and interesting during the buildup phase, but he also began receiving some recognition, earning a marksmanship badge and perhaps a certificate for good performance on the obstacle course or in bayonet drill.[146] Fussell, beginning to feel fit and tan as a result of his training, "attained the grade of Expert Rifleman and won thereby a carton of Chesterfields [cigarettes]. Scared of loud noises as a child, I grew to love them. I enjoyed the bang of the rifle in my ear, as well as the kick against my shoulder."[147] Parks earned the marksmanship rating of Sharpshooter: "It felt good. A lot of guys didn't even come close." He was also proud of winning his training company's bayonet contest.[148]

Even the drill sergeants seemed less like ogres during the buildup phase. The trainees came to realize, at least in retrospect, that their drill sergeant was deliberately starting to bolster their confidence and group pride.[149] Howard Matthias, going through marine officer candidate training at Parris Island in summer 1951, noticed that "the process worked": "Loyalty and pride started to show itself quickly. We were proud to belong to the finest squad, the best platoon and the greatest battalion in the Marine Corps. We could out drill, outmarch, and outfight any other outfit."[150] World War II marine veteran Roger Tuttrup shared Matthias's belief in the process. The drill sergeants "really put you in your place. That's a polite way of sayin' it. They humiliate ya, they make ya do things that you don't think are physically possible. At the same time, they're makin' you feel you're something. That you're part of something. . . . It was the high point of my life."[151]

During the buildup phase, the trainee did not feel as humiliated and demeaned as he had during the tear down, not only because the drill sergeants began mixing in some praise with the chewing outs but also because he was getting over his "environmental shock."[152] He was becoming habituated to army life, learning to blow off steam through the time-honored ritual of griping. Trainees learned to complain about virtually every aspect of basic training—the food, the drill sergeants, the inspections, the harassment, and the lack of freedom and free time. They did not expect anyone in authority to listen, but they could at least voice their displeasure.[153]

Griping was also a form of social interaction, allowing trainees to commiserate over their fate, making use of their newly acquired military foul mouths in the process.[154] Many recruits were shocked at first, as Leckie was, by the stream of four-letter expletives flowing from the mouths of their drill sergeants, but "we would become inured to it, in time, have it even on our own lips."[155] Many recruits were soon equaling, in color and profusion, the language of their veteran sergeants, as Kennett notes: "The younger and more impressionable probably took to obscene expressions the way they took to wearing their overseas caps at a jaunty angle—it fitted their image of a soldier."[156] Swearing was thus one more way, during the buildup phase, that the trainee continued his conversion from civilian, in whose society such language was not acceptable, to soldier, for whom swearing was a virtual art form.

As the trainees' anxiety lessened, the platoon comics began to get up the nerve to challenge the drill sergeants in small ways, or at least to mimic them behind their backs. Much like griping, the humorous antics of the platoon cutups provided a relief valve for frustrations. John Faris, who paid close attention to the role of the drill sergeants in his study of basic training, noticed that they not only began sprinkling some praise and recognition amid the criticism but also began to allow, within limits, some trainee–drill sergeant banter.[157]

Uris provides a classic example of a platoon comic, L. Q. Jones, in *Battle Cry*. During boot camp, Jones mimicked the southern accent and colorful language of the platoon's drill instructor, Corporal Whitlock. Unfortunately for Jones and his audience, Whitlock entered the barracks and witnessed Jones's performance. For punishment, Whitlock had the culprits march about camp with buckets on their heads, chanting "I'm a craphead," much to the amusement of all, trainee and cadre alike.[158] The punishment imposed by Corporal Whitlock, though no doubt embarrassing to the marchers, was deliberately mild and provided some comic relief for the entire camp. The value of such antics was not lost on Robert G. Thobaben, going through army basic training in 1943. He praised the comic skills of his platoon's cutup, "Strap": "He could duplicate the voice and actions of anyone. His sense of humor was finely honed, and his quick wit and droll burlesque brightened many a bivouac and march."[159]

The trainees also mastered the art of "goldbricking," to use the term common in World War II, as a way to beat the system. Work details could be dodged, or at least the effort expended on them kept to a bare minimum. The trainee would not goldbrick if by so doing he brought punishment on the group. At other times he was too closely supervised to get away with it. But he goldbricked when he could, and Irving L. Janis believes he did so as an overt, if minor, act of rebellion: "In making the independent decision to goldbrick rather than to carry out his assignment adequately, the recruit asserts his willfulness. He creates for himself the illusion that he is achieving a victory over the superior who required him to perform the menial job."[160] Goldbricking, "slacking," or "ghosting," like griping, was a time-honored soldier skill that the recruit would practice, within certain bounds, throughout his military career.

Another factor contributing to the trainee's improving morale and confidence during the buildup phase was the support he received from his friends. After several weeks of living together, most trainees formed friendships with one or more of their bunkmates. Buddies encouraged and helped each other.[161] George William Sefton, after describing the diverse characters in his platoon, went on to praise his "closest buddy," an older man named Donald Townsend, who took "a big-brother interest" in Sefton's welfare.[162]

These personal friendships shifted somewhat as buddies had a falling out or became sick or injured and had to recycle with a different platoon not as far along in the training program, but overall they grew stronger with shared hardships and experiences. The platoon started to bond together, and thanks also to the group recognition and praise that the drill sergeant occasionally provided, the trainees began to consider themselves a unit, and a good one at that. This phenomenon occurred in Thobaben's World War II training platoon. After more than three months of training together, the platoon had become "a genuine unit. We were bound by a hundred common experiences. We had become friends."[163]

During the buildup phase, the trainee began to think of himself not as a lowly recruit but as a budding soldier. Not only did he find marksmanship to be the first interesting subject encountered in his training, but he also noticed that the army considered it a distinctly "soldierly," as opposed to "trainee," skill.[164] The trainee also began to realize that his job was to kill. The drill sergeants reinforced this theme by unabashedly emphasizing that where the recruit was heading, kill-or-be-killed was the order of the day. Morgan, in the novel *Fragments,* came to just such a realization in basic training: "The longer training went on, the more you had to confront just what it was they were training you for. You could grumble about the wet, endless days on the rifle range, but when the target popped up, it had the silhouette of a man. You could bitch about the way they made you crawl up and down the piny dunes, but you had to admit that it made sense to keep your profile low. You did not even try to kid yourself about what you might be facing. You sought it out. You grilled the drill sergeants about their experiences in the jungles across the pond."[165]

Stanley Goff and his fellow army trainees adopted a "war mentality" similar to Morgan's: "We got to feel that these people [the instructors] knew what they were doing. . . . Once we were into the war mentality, . . . psychologically our training got to us. Even though you didn't want to succumb to it, we couldn't help it. . . . We were brainwashed. . . . We were ready to go to Vietnam. Nobody was crying about it."[166] Certainly not all soldiers were as "ready" to go to Vietnam as Goff claims, but his basic point about the conversion to a war mentality is valid. Most trainees came to think of themselves as soldiers. This awareness was in itself an important step in the process of converting civilians to soldiers.

By the end of the training process, a transformation had occurred. The angry, fed-up, demoralized trainee had become a physically fit, skilled, confident, even cocky soldier.[167] By the end of boot camp during World War II, Eugene B. Sledge and his fellow trainees "were hard physically, had developed endurance, and had learned our lessons. Perhaps more importantly, we were tough mentally."[168] Rudolph W. Stephens, after completing army basic training in 1951, was confident and fit: "Somehow I managed to endure this sixteen weeks and that put me in the best physical condition I have ever been in in my life. I felt I could handle any situation that might come my way."[169] William Ehrhart, who had lain in his bunk the first night of boot camp in a state of shock, graduated eight weeks later with a promotion and a chestful of pride: "I burst into a broad grin, barely able to contain the pride struggling to get out of me in a mighty shout. In a few moments, I would be meritoriously promoted to Private First Class W. D. Ehrhart, United States Marine."[170]

The graduating trainees had even developed a grudging admiration for their drill sergeants, although there were a few notable exceptions.[171] Indeed, as Dyer had discovered in observing marine boot camp, the drill instructors had become "not just role models and authority figures, but the focus of the recruits' developing loyalty to the organization."[172] Robert Leckie came to understand that the drill sergeants had been tough for a reason: "On the whole, the sergeants were not cruel. They were not sadists. They believed in making it tough on us, but they believed this for the purpose of making us turn out tough."[173] Stan Goff and his fellow army trainees came to the same conclusion two wars later concerning their drill sergeant: "We found that he was damned serious and very concerned about the men. We could read it in him. Even though he was very, very mean, we could tell he was sincere. He felt that it was his responsibility whether we made it through the Nam or not."[174]

In sum, drill sergeants, who worked long, hard hours to implement the training program, were for the most part neither deliberately cruel nor callous. The training had to be tough and stressful to prepare the trainees for the physical and emotional trauma of combat, as observers of the process, including Dyer, came to appreciate: "The men . . . who teach the recruits how to kill and how to die are not cynical in their manipulation of the minds of impressionable teenagers; they believe every word they say. And if you accept the necessity of armed force in the world as it is . . . [then they] are absolutely right."[175]

## PERSONAL VALUES VERSUS CONDITIONED BEHAVIOR

Once the erstwhile civilian was torn down and rebuilt into a fit, confident, and aggressive soldier, he proceeded to more advanced training, either as part of a tactical unit or as an individual. Those trainees with combat specialties learned to use machine guns, mortars, antitank weapons, tanks, armored personnel carriers, or artillery. Thus the desired product, from the first day at the reception station through completion of advanced training, was a trained killer. Not surprisingly, some observers found this process abhorrent. The pacific, civilizing values had been stripped from the trainee, and a soldier conditioned to kill emerged in his stead. The philosopher and World War II veteran Jesse Glenn Gray saw this emergent soldier as a different breed from his previous civilian self: "Man as warrior is only partly a man, yet, fatefully enough, this aspect of him is capable of transforming the whole. When given free play, it is able to subordinate other aspects of the personality, repress civilian habits of mind, and make the soldier as fighter a different kind of creature from the former worker, farmer, or clerk." Gray went so far as to establish a new species for the combat soldier—Homo furens.[176]

Psychiatrist Robert Jay Lifton was even more alarmed over this conversion process and specifically charged the training system, at least in the Vietnam era, with responsibility for turning mild-mannered civilians into "socialized warriors": "To reach the desired psychological state, the socialized warrior has always required some kind of initiation process. . . . In that rite (now called *basic training*), his civil identity, with its built-in restraints, is eradicated, or at least undermined and set aside in favor of the warrior identity and its central focus on killing. Only through such a prescribed process can the warrior become psychically numbed toward killing and dying, shielded from complexity, and totalized in his commitment to the warrior role."[177]

Certainly the soldierization process generated "uncivilian" norms of behavior, but some experts question the extent to which a recruit could be programmed by a few months of military training to modify or reject personal values instilled by years of parental, educational, and social influences. Sociologists Morris Janowitz and Roger W. Little are two such skeptics, who point out that recruits are not cultural tabula rasa, nor does the military train in a social vacuum: "It is a fundamental error to assume that the military establishment is some sort of self-contained organism which digests and assimilates foreign bodies."[178] The beliefs and attitudes the recruit brings with him from civilian society must therefore be taken into account when examining the effect of the soldierization process.

Furthermore, as Lee Kennett points out in his study of the World War II GI, the average American citizen-soldier was never fully purged of those civilian beliefs and attitudes. Military training introduced new skills and norms of behavior, but it did not destroy those values a recruit brought with him into the service. The GI was thus "suspended between two ways of life and held in that state of suspension as long as he wore a uniform. Physically he left civilian life, yet mentally he never joined the Army; he was in the service but not of it."[179]

A citizen-soldier "suspended" between two worlds is a far cry from a "socialized warrior," devoid of civilized values. Further complicating the debate is the lack of consensus over exactly what values a recruit brought with him in the first place. Perhaps, as Dyer suggests, violence is not so much programmed into recruits as it is a carryover from civilian society: "There is aggression in all of us. . . . Armies don't have to create it, and they can't even increase it."[180] The philosopher Sam Keen also sees a connection between military and civilian violence: "Sadism in war is hard to explain only if we assume that there is a discontinuity between soldiers who enjoy inflicting pain and normal men and women. The assumption that there is a vast difference between the moral fiber of the man who enjoys killing in battle and you and me is the illusion on which the notion of normality is built."[181]

The level of violence in civilian society certainly lends credence to Dyer's and Keen's arguments, but if the average recruit entered service with a natural or socialized propensity for aggression, then how does one explain those soldiers who fought, and killed, only reluctantly, gaining no enjoyment from doing what they considered a necessary but distasteful job?

The reality is that recruits did bring deeply ingrained beliefs and attitudes with them into the service but that each individual's beliefs were unique.[182] Too often the experts assumed a degree of cultural homogeneity that simply did not exist.[183] Just as individual motives for rallying to the flag varied significantly, so too did the recruit's reaction to the soldierization process, depending on his attitude and past experiences. "The orientation which the civilian society gives to recruits," note Janowitz and Little, "will either assist or retard their assimilation of military roles."[184] Thus the enthusiastic volunteer tended to emerge from training as an enthusiastic soldier and the reluctant draftee a reluctant soldier. A study of Vietnam-era trainees found, for example, that their reaction to basic training was positive or negative in about the same ratio as their attitude toward the military upon entering service.[185]

The World War II trainee Kurt Gabel conducted his own one-man sociological study of those around him at the reception station. He noted a wide range of reactions to army life based on the inductees' attitudes and backgrounds. There was the young, homesick type; the older, married type who worried and missed the comforts of home; the well-to-do fraternity type, disdainful of his ignorant companions and spartan surroundings; and the Oakie type, who was content with army life because he was used to austerity and hard work.[186] Gabel failed to mention his own type—the eager volunteer who enthusiastically took to the training (he became a paratrooper).

Although Gabel is guilty of stereotyping, his point about the diversity of attitudes among trainees is valid. Based on those attitudes, recruits' reactions to basic training varied, as Fuller's trainee Bill Morgan observed: "You saw some men crumble, some men grow. You saw who was selfish, who was scared. . . . Some guys became isolated in adversity; they were afraid of having to carry any more than their own weight. But others bonded together against it, and the worse it got the closer they became."[187]

Some recruits found the training process so stressful and the values of military life so alien that they broke down or even committed suicide. An interdisciplinary group of scholars commissioned after World War II to study American military manpower policy during the war examined, among other things, why some recruits failed to complete their initial training and had to be discharged from the army. They found that some trainees broke down because they could not stand the separation from home or had received disturbing news from home about sickness, financial problems, or infidelity. Others did not suffer a mental breakdown, but they lacked any sense of social responsibility or obligation, refusing "to make much of an effort once they had been inducted," resulting in their discharge as unfit for service.[188]

Psychiatrists discovered further reasons why recruits broke down during World War II. Robert A. Clark learned that some trainees could not adapt to the aggressive behavior that basic training demanded of them because they suffered from inferiority complexes, excessive dependence on others, and various other emotional instabilities.[189] Psychiatrists Meyer H. Maskin and Leon L. Altman cataloged a variety of reasons why some trainees could not cope: unwillingness to submit to authority, fear of assuming responsibility, depression over leaving home and loved ones, inability to make friends or work as part of a group, and resentment over the loss of personal identity.[190]

To the average recruit, untutored in psychological terminology, compatriots who broke down were labeled "mama's boys" because they exhibited homesickness, physical weakness, or a milquetoast demeanor.[191] John L. Munschauer recalls a mama's boy who broke down on his second day in the army. The young man had lived at home with his mother all his life, ate only food "fixed the way he liked it," and had built his social life around this woman, "who was a widow and pretty well managed her son."[192] Such insecure, sheltered young men often fared poorly in the alien, stressful world of the barracks room.

At the other extreme were those recruits, most often volunteers, who entered service with positive attitudes toward soldiering. For them, training was a challenge, not a stress. A phrase commonly shouted by recruits during training was

"WETSU"—"We Eat This Shit Up." According to Marlowe's study of army recruits in the 1950s, 10 to 15 percent of the trainees actually meant it: "There are those . . . who experience an absolute minimum of anxiety or dislocation on entering the service and perform and function with ease from the very first day."[193] Not surprisingly, these eager recruits were the ones who most often volunteered for even more challenging training and service with elite units such as the Special Forces, Rangers, or airborne.[194]

Some recruits, although they completed the training process, were not so much proud and confident, like their fellow trainees, as they were disappointed and unhappy over their training experience. They hated the inconveniences and the loss of freedom and individuality that being a soldier entailed. Disgruntled World War II trainee Carl M. Becker went so far as to claim that the army's effort to build "obedience to command, subordination of individualism, loyalty to the group, and bonding to one another" had failed completely in the case of his training platoon: "Such desiderata were a will-o'-the-wisp. Our ordinary routines fostered instead an ethos of every man for himself and the devil take the hindmost."[195]

David Parks, whose basic-training experience was not entirely negative, had nothing good to say about the advanced infantry training (AIT) that followed: "Finally finished A.I.T. Eight sickening, boring weeks of pure crap."[196] John Ketwig was equally negative about his advanced training as a mechanic in 1967 at Aberdeen Proving Ground, Maryland. He had "expected the humiliation and harassment to end after basic, but it had followed us to Aberdeen." He had hoped that his army training would parallel his experience playing high school sports, where his coaches had instilled team discipline, but "this was not teamwork. The lifers [training cadre] had stripped us of all dignity and self-respect and seemed to delight in rubbing our noses in our impotence."[197]

Like Ketwig, each recruit brought his own set of personal values, expectations, and motivations with him into the army. Some found army training to be all that they expected and more. Others were as disappointed as Ketwig. A few were so traumatized that they broke down before completing basic. The training process did succeed in "conditioning" most trainees to believe that they were well-trained, fit, and confident soldiers or marines; but as the wide variation in individual reactions to the soldierization process indicates, the trainee was neither purged of all his previous beliefs and attitudes nor turned into some sort of automated killer.

Whatever their attitude on completing training, many of these freshly minted soldiers soon faced the prospect of combat. Their newly acquired skills, stamina, and military discipline would be sorely tested in the environment of war.

# 2

# The Environment of War

The newly trained soldier, reasonably confident in his fitness and skills, soon found himself en route to war. No matter how well prepared, however, he discovered that combat was more physically demanding and emotionally traumatic than he had expected. Indeed, the environment of war proved to be such a "radical discontinuity" from peacetime existence, to use Eric J. Leed's term, that it "posed the most severe psychic contradictions."[1] The soldier was shocked to discover just how cruel, dangerous, and unforgiving this new world was: "In no other circumstances than the battlefield does man confront the knowledge that he is present in that place for the purpose of suffering death at the hands of fellow man, and that he must kill if he is not to be killed himself. The battlefield, in short, is a place almost without mercy and utterly without pity, where the emotions which humanity cultivates and admires elsewhere— gentleness, compassion, tolerance, amity—have neither room to operate nor place to exist."[2]

Up to a point, the soldier understood from his training that his job was to kill the enemy and that he would in turn be in danger, but few soldiers apprehended the harshness of the environment in which this life-or-death struggle would be played out. The physical and emotional aspects of that environment must be appreciated to understand just how radical the discontinuity was for those soldiers in the combat zone.

## THE PHYSICAL ENVIRONMENT OF WAR

One of the first shocking discoveries was that soldiering is hard, menial, dirty work. The work often began as soon as the soldiers disembarked in the war zone. Lieutenant Joseph R. Owen was mortar platoon leader in a marine rifle company that went ashore in the follow-up wave during the Inchon landing in the Korean War. Instead of plunging into the fray, however, the company was put to work in the heat of the Korean summer as stevedores: "Our troops, stripped to their skivvies, sweated, labored, and bitched."[3]

Most combat troops, including Owen's company, certainly found themselves in action soon enough. But to their dismay, they discovered that the hard work did not end even in combat. Indeed, despite their physical conditioning and the resilience of youth, soldiers found that combat could wear them down to a degree that they had never imagined. Lieutenant Michael Lee Lanning arrived in Vietnam with the eagerness typical of a young man off to his first war, but "after less than two weeks in-country, much, if not all, of the glamour had faded. It was simply hard, tiring, dangerous, and usually boring work."[4] Lieutenant Philip Caputo, arriving in Vietnam with his marine battalion in 1965, was even more eager than Lanning. Yet after a few weeks of defending an air base day and night, in the oppressive heat and humidity, filling sandbags, stringing barbed wire, and building bunkers, Caputo could only conclude that "this was not war, it was forced labor."[5]

Sustaining and protecting themselves took up much of the soldiers' time and energy. As Caputo's mission of guarding an air base illustrates, establishing a defensive position involved many chores. After the leaders selected positions for the men to occupy, soldiers dug one- or two-man foxholes to protect themselves from direct and indirect fire. Digging in often came at the end of an exhausting day of marching, and perhaps fighting, and leaders sometimes had to ride the tired troops to get them to dig.

Digging in at night was a common occurrence for the doughboy in summer and fall 1918, when the fighting was far more fluid than the stereotypical image of static trench warfare would suggest. Marine private Elton E. Mackin describes the miseries of digging in at night in the rain, using bayonets because entrenching tools were in short supply: "Dark figures crouched on knees, their shoulders hunched, helmets hanging low across their eyes while a driving rain beats ceaselessly across their backs and drains in little rivulets from the exposed napes of their necks, to run down inside their collars in icy streams that cut against the sweaty warmth of their bodies. . . . To see them, hear them growl as they tear away at the earth like burrowing animals reminds you of mad beasts."[6]

Perhaps the only condition worse than darkness and rain for digging in was a winter freeze. Lieutenant George William Sefton and his platoon of paratroopers discovered just how difficult digging into a frozen hillside in the Vosges Mountains of France in February 1945 could be: "That seemed like the longest night of my life. We would hit the frozen soil with a full swing of an engineer's pick, to be rewarded with an icy chip the size of a silver dollar. . . . Within four hours, the blisters on our hands were broken and bleeding."[7]

Even when a unit remained in a defensive position for some time, the work did not stop. Positions had to be improved, which involved filling sandbags, building overhead cover using logs and dirt to protect against artillery airbursts, and putting in barbed wire and mines. Most of the material needed for this improvement, plus food, water, and ammunition, had to be brought forward, often by carrying parties when rugged terrain or the danger of enemy fire precluded the use of supply vehicles.

Even refilling canteens could be a far from routine task. When the front lines remained stationary for any length of time, the enemy frequently discovered and targeted the local water holes and springs. The army corporal Ben Judd explains that even though a water hole was only 300 yards from his bunker in Korea, "the Chinese, if they chose, could drop a mortar round directly into it. . . . Many men were injured going to supply their units with water."[8]

Hauling water or supplies of any sort up the steep Korean mountains was a challenge, as Lieutenant Owen notes: "Keeping the forward weapons supplied with ammunition was a dangerous job that required exposure to enemy view. Under lethal small arms and mortar fire the bearers lugged heavy boxes of rifle, BAR [Browning Automatic Rifle], and machine gun ammunition, as well as crates of grenades, up steep, uneven grades. It was hard labor."[9] Carrying ammunition forward was equally arduous during the fighting on Okinawa in World War II, as marine private Eugene B. Sledge remembered: "We spent a great deal of time in combat carrying this heavy ammunition on our shoulders to places where it was needed—spots often totally inaccessible to all types of vehicles—and breaking it out of the packages and crates. On Okinawa this was often done under enemy fire, in driving rain, and through knee-deep mud for hours on end. Such activity drove the infantryman, weary from the mental and physical stress of combat, almost to the brink of physical collapse."[10]

The carrying-party traffic was not all one way. The wounded had to be carried to the rear. This task could be especially demanding because time was of the essence if a man's life was to be saved. Most units had stretcher bearers assigned as part of their medical detachment, but there were never enough of them, and the infantrymen often had to carry their own buddies to safety, using makeshift stretchers. War correspondent John Hersey accompanied a stretcher party on Guadalcanal during World War II. He describes negotiating stretchers up and down slippery gullies, over fallen trees, and across dangerously swift jungle streams.[11] Not all of the wounded made it to the aid station alive, and the stretcher bearers were not much better off themselves: "It was hard to tell the difference between the wounded men and the bearers."[12]

Establishing and improving defensive positions was hard work for the infantry, but life for the artilleryman was perhaps even more arduous, if less dangerous. Artillery units made frequent displacements during the Allied offensives of summer and fall 1918. Each new position had to be consolidated, and artilleryman Charles MacArthur quickly learned that "consolidate means dig. Dig means work."[13] An artillery battery was a likely candidate for counterbattery fire or aerial attack, so the crews had to dig firing pits for the guns, bunkers to protect the projectiles and powder charges, and foxholes for themselves.

Consolidation also meant downloading heavy projectiles from caissons or supply wagons, laying telephone lines, cleaning the guns, putting up camouflage, and caring for the battery's horses—the last by all accounts the bane of the artilleryman's existence. Horses had to be watered, fed, curried, and their tackle and harness cleaned and repaired. For MacArthur and his battery mates, the order to turn in their horses was a cause for celebration exceeding the Armistice: "For the first time since we had enlisted, the war was over. The Armistice had been a joke so long as we had to go on massaging and feeding two hundred lousy horses every day."[14]

The horse's replacement by the truck and artillery tractor eased the artilleryman's burden in later wars, but establishing a firing position continued to be demanding work. Lieutenant Frederick Downs, an infantryman, captured the essence of the artilleryman's exhausting world in his description of a cannoneer pushing at the mired wheel of his howitzer in the heat and mud of a Vietnam firebase: "His body taut, with his shoulder to the wheel and his feet hard in the mud, eyes closed, head lying in the mud on the wheel, a cigarette dangling out of the corner of his mouth, and his arms dangling down into the mud—that is how I will always remember the artillery man in Vietnam."[15]

In addition to performing these burdensome tasks, soldiers had to remain on guard for the enemy. Some of the men had to be alert at all times, manning crew-served weapons, observation posts, and listening posts. Others pulled radio or telephone watch. Marine corporal William D. Ehrhart, for example, after performing his normal duties as an intelligence specialist in his battalion command post in Vietnam, found himself on the perimeter at night guarding against a possible Viet Cong attack. His comment that "sleep was always at a premium" is classic understatement.[16]

The enemy was well aware that sleep was a precious commodity and did what he could to deprive the American soldier of his sacktime, as the GI called it. Air attacks were especially nerve-racking, and thus the Germans and Japanese during World War II (and to a lesser extent the Chinese during the Korean War) sent bombers, which the GIs dubbed "Washing Machine Charlie" or "Bed Check Charlie," on night harassment raids over American lines.[17] The few bombs scattered about did minimal damage, but as Robert Leckie pointed out, "the drone of Charlie's circling progress kept everyone awake and uneasy. . . . Charlie did not kill many people, but, like MacBeth, he murdered sleep."[18]

Even when Bed Check Charlie was gone and things seemed peaceful, the soldier could not let his guard down, especially if the enemy was adept at infiltration and surprise attack. Knowing that the enemy might appear at any moment made night watch stressful. The soldier on guard, often alone in his foxhole or bunker, began to let his imagination get the best of him. The dim outlines of bushes or rocks took on human form. Stationary objects seemed to be moving. At times an animal would stir the bushes.[19] Sometimes the sound of the wind or a pounding rain made detecting an approaching enemy almost impossible. Even a veteran soldier who could keep his imagination in check felt drained after a few hours of maintaining such alertness.

The need for constant vigilance coupled with the many "housekeeping" chores involved in maintaining a frontline position meant that soldiers were deprived of sleep. Soldiers in combat averaged less than six hours' sleep a day, often considerably less.[20] Sleep deprivation, exposure to the elements, hard work, and stress eventually lowered morale, impaired a soldier's judgment, and reduced his physical stamina.[21]

Corporal Amos N. Wilder became aware, during the Soissons counteroffensive in World War I, of the impact that fatigue was having on his artillery battalion: "Strange when one is tired, it not only affects one's physical force, but one's powers of addition, memory, the presence and bearing of the person, his greeting and authority, but most strangely, one's conscience, one's ethical standard is blurred and one becomes curiously lax."[22] Conditions were no better three wars later. The marine company that Lieutenant Caputo served in had "run nearly two hundred patrols in the month I had been with it, and then there had been all those nights on the line. The men were in a permanent state of exhaustion. They were in a shaft, plunging daily from one level of fatigue to the next."[23]

An overly fatigued soldier might even begin to hallucinate. Captain Charles R. Cawthon, suffering "from fatigue long-sustained" after several months of fighting in the European theater in World War II, thought he saw an approaching German patrol one night—not remarkable in itself, except that the patrol was outfitted in World War I uniforms and equipment. Cawthon, not sure to this day if the entire patrol or just their garb was a hallucination, let the ghostly apparition proceed out of his sight.[24]

When not defending a position, the soldier was on the move, either shifting to a new location or off in search of the enemy. Sometimes this move involved trains or trucks, modes of transport that did not provide as much respite for the weary soldier as might be assumed. Virtually every doughboy rode on the French trains, usually in boxcars called "forty and eights," referring to their posted capacity of forty men or eight horses. A trip in "those devil's gift to transportation," as one doughboy called them, ranged from mildly unpleasant to abjectly miserable.[25] There were no seats in the drafty, unheated, wooden cars. On a good ride, the floor was covered with fresh straw. On a bad ride, the car had not been cleaned out after the previous equine passengers had detrained. In either case, the soldiers were packed in so tightly that they barely had room to sit on the floor. Stretching out to sleep was impossible.[26]

World War II accounts, interestingly, reveal that the French forty and eights, sans improvements, were as common as they had been in 1918 and just as miserable to ride in.[27] Lieutenant George Wilson summed up the World War II GI's opinion of the "infamous" boxcars in his comment about their capacity: "Forty men or eight horses—and I wouldn't treat a horse that way."[28]

The doughboys rode in trucks almost as often as they did in trains. Truck units, usually French, conveyed them from one sector to another or forward from a railhead. This *camion* ride, to use the French term, was as uncomfortable and tiring as a trip in the forty and eights. The roads were marginal and usually damaged by heavy military traffic. Solid-rubber tires and rudimentary suspension systems further ensured a bone-jarring ride. The trucks' open tops, or at best canvas covers, and the wooden seats added to the discomfort, especially on a long ride in the cold and rain. A warm, dry day was better, but that meant clouds of choking dust.

Marine lieutenant John W. Thomason Jr. renders the troops' assessment of truck convoying while en route to the Soissons counteroffensive in World War I: "'Lord forgive me, I uster kick about them noble [forty and eight] box cars. . . . They say it was taxicabs an' motortrucks that won the first battle of the Marne— yeh! If they rushed them Frogs up packed like this, you know they felt like fightin' when they got out!'"[29]

Truck transport was even more common in later wars. Balloon tires and better suspension systems improved the ride—but only just. Private Lester Atwell recounts a grueling, nonstop, sixteen-hour truck ride in the dead of winter in France in World War II. The trucks were heavily overloaded with troops. Wind blew through the gaps in the canvas cover. The men could not move about to restore circulation. An empty five-gallon can was passed around to urinate into. Men with dysentery had to hang their backsides over the tailgate while buddies held their arms to prevent them from falling out.[30]

On top of the physical discomfort, a truck convoy could generate considerable anxiety. Most units did not possess sufficient trucks to move their infantry about routinely. A truck ride, therefore, indicated that something out of the ordinary was up. Lieutenant Paul Boesch recalls a relatively pleasant truck convoy on a mild fall day in France in 1944, but "instead of enjoying the ride, we were justifiably suspicious. We could detect a tough assignment ahead."[31] His suspicions were soon confirmed when his infantry company was committed to an attack.

Despite increasing mechanization during the wars of the draft era, the soldier's move often involved a foot march. During late summer and fall 1918, the doughboys marched in chilling rain and sticky mud, usually at night to avoid enemy observation. Lieutenant Joseph D. Lawrence describes such a march. The men in his infantry company could not see in the pitch-black, rainy night and frequently slipped off the road into the muddy, water-filled ditches. During halts they shivered in the cold. The mud clung to their boots with every step. Cigarettes or lights of any sort were forbidden. Daybreak brought only a breakfast of cold coffee and bread.[32]

The artillery batteries found the going even more difficult. Despite their designation as horse drawn, the cannoneers almost always marched beside their guns. In fall 1918, horse losses to enemy fire and exhaustion were so severe that there were barely enough sickly nags to pull the guns. Cannon and caissons frequently mired in the mud or slipped off the road into the ditches, and the crews strained and pushed to keep the battery moving. Limbers and tackle broke and had to be repaired.[33]

The post–World War I mechanization of the artillery greatly eased the burdens of the march, if not the amount of work awaiting the cannoneers when they got to their next position. For the infantry, however, the exhausting foot march remained a staple. The World War II correspondent Ernie Pyle captured the essence of the infantry foot march near the end of the fighting in Tunisia: "The men were walking. They were fifty feet apart for dispersal. Their walk was slow, for they were dead weary, as a person could tell even when looking at them from behind. Every line and sag of their bodies spoke their inhuman exhaustion. On their shoulders and backs they carried heavy steel tripods, machine-gun barrels, leaden boxes of ammunition. Their feet seemed to sink into the ground from the overload they were bearing."[34]

The grunt in Vietnam was also no stranger to hard marching. Lieutenant Downs discovered early on how grueling the daily routine of searching for the enemy could be: "My first days on combat patrol introduced me to . . . ten-foot-deep punji pits; wait-a-minute vines that collected around the feet and legs until their combined strength stopped you and you had to say 'wait-a-minute' while you untangled or cut yourself loose; the hot sun beating down on us as we marched with seventy-pound packs, the sweat pouring off us; bugs so thick around our faces that we sometimes inhaled them; and the physical agony of forcing tired muscles to keep on going."[35]

Downs's catalog of miseries is if anything incomplete. Grunts also had to wade across rice paddies fertilized with human feces or cross areas covered with tall elephant grass sharp enough to cut the skin. Sometimes soldiers had to hack their way through jungle undergrowth with machetes. They had to stop periodically to remove blood-sucking leeches. Sweat and constant chafing caused painful "crotch rot." And most important, the grunts could not let these nuisances or their growing exhaustion throw them off guard, because the enemy or his booby traps could strike at any time.[36]

Further, the infantry soldier, as evidenced by Downs's almost casual mention of a seventy-pound pack, was more often than not weighed down with an onerous load. The historian Samuel L. A. Marshall is one of the few observers of the soldier's condition to note, and criticize, the army's tendency, even if well-meant, grossly to overload the infantry soldier in an effort to ensure that he had everything needed to fight and survive.[37] Soldiers regularly carried seventy pounds or more. Radio operators, machine-gun crews, and mortarmen carried an even heavier load.[38]

And although the army could tell the soldier what he was supposed to carry, what he actually kept once in the combat zone was another matter. The infantryman quickly learned to lighten his load by discarding nonessentials. Doughboy Joseph Lawrence and his Thirtieth Division conducted a forced march into Belgium shortly after arriving in France in 1918. The troops, out of shape after a long sea voyage and sweltering in the July heat, sneaked away from their bivouac sites that evening to hide or bury what they did not want to carry the next day, when the march was to continue. The officers noticed that the local inhabitants were suddenly in possession of all manner of doughboy equipment. They then "made an investigation and found that practically all the men had thrown away everything but their guns, the clothes they wore, and their overcoats—which they used to sleep under."[39]

During Operation OVERLORD, the World War II invasion of France, the paratroopers who jumped into Normandy the evening before D-Day were almost as overloaded as the troops who assaulted the beaches the next morning. Like Lawrence and his fellow doughboys, however, they did not remain so for long. Lieutenant Sefton, jumping in with the 101st Airborne Division, was separated from his unit but soon caught up with it by following "the trail of discarded equipment, primarily gas masks" (except during World War I, when gas attack was common, the mask was the first thing to go).[40]

Leaders learned, as they gained combat experience, to allow the soldier to lighten his load, if not during a march behind the lines then at least when going into combat. Even a relatively light combat load, however, still tipped the scales at thirty to forty pounds, given the weight of a weapon, ammunition, grenades, helmet, canteen, entrenching tool, clothing, first aid packet, and some emergency rations.[41]

Knowing what to keep and what to discard or leave behind in the supply truck came only with experience, and Marshall has pointed out that it came at a price: "Many will say, I know, looking back to their own experience in battle, that troops learned automatically to discard the things that they did not need, and that therefore there is no problem. That may be true. But they only gained this kind of wisdom by hard experience, and it is invariably in the *first* battle that the greatest damage is done."[42]

Aggravating the problem was the fact that the inexperienced soldier facing his first battle often voluntarily overloaded himself. Marine lieutenant Tony Balsa describes the green soldier's tendency to load up on ammunition in the Pacific in World War II: "Just the thought of running out of ammunition made you feel uneasy: you'd have an empty rifle. Actually, a problem for some of the new guys was carrying too much. Too many clips, or grenades. You had to balance the needs of fighting with getting overloaded."[43] Then there was the case of "Peewee" Budny in Leon C. Standifer's rifle platoon in France in World War II, who prior to his first battle "looked like a Mexican bandit," with bandoliers of rifle ammunition draped across his chest and a grenade stuffed in every pocket. His comrades persuaded him to put most of the extra ammunition back.[44] The green soldier in the Vietnam War acted much the same. When the marines in Richard E. Ogden's rifle platoon, on the day prior to landing at Danang (an amphibious landing that they had been falsely told might be opposed by the Viet

Cong), drew their ammunition, he noticed that "many tried to get more than the regular allotment of ammunition and grenades."[45]

Thus the soldier, through his own volition or the directives of his superiors, marched with a staggering amount of weight. On reaching his destination, he found little respite, given the work required to establish a defensive position and remain vigilant for the enemy. Surely the exhausted soldier at least got a chance to rest when his unit was in reserve or undergoing training? As a general rule, he did, but he also found himself doing construction work, stevedoring, graves registration, and battlefield salvage when the support troops normally assigned those duties were in short supply. These chores were not only strenuous but also demoralizing—such work did not befit warriors.

The African-American soldiers of the 369th Infantry Regiment, on arriving in France in January 1918, expected to be rushed to the front. Instead they drained swamps, built railroads, and constructed warehouses as part of the effort to build up the AEF logistics base at the port of St. Nazaire. Major Arthur W. Little, who later commanded a battalion in the 369th, noticed a sharp drop in morale: "This pick and shovel work was most destructive of the morale of men who had enlisted to fight."[46]

Even near the front lines, doughboys found themselves detailed to non-combatant duties. Lieutenant Lawrence and his infantry platoon were told that they had to clean up the very battlefield they had just fought on: "Of all jobs that a soldier hates, that of policing—picking up trash—takes first place, and on October 21 [1918], while still in the valley, our pride was much hurt by being ordered to police the battlefield over which we had fought the first day of our heavy fighting."[47]

During World War II in the Pacific, especially early in the war, combat troops performed noncombatant jobs because sufficient support troops were unavailable. Leckie and his fellow marines on Guadalcanal were exhausted from working by day at Henderson Airfield, the island's critical link to the outside, and defending against the Japanese by night: "We hated working parties. We were weak from hunger. We manned the lines at night. By day, they formed us into working parties and took us to the airfield."[48] One of the most common, and hated, jobs that combat soldiers in the Pacific theater performed was unloading supply ships, usually in brutal heat and humidity. Private Arliss Franklin's attitude was typical: "That kind of work is not why I'd joined the Corps."[49]

GIs in the Korean War were not exempt from hard labor, either. During the static warfare common to the last years of the fighting, units rotated from the front line were put to work digging trenches and bunkers for a second or third line of defense. The American soldier has never been known for his enthusiasm for shovel work, and the Korean War GI was no exception. Lieutenant Matthias and his marine rifle platoon discovered that being in reserve "was not . . . any vacation," because in addition to training and camp chores, they also had to dig a new trench line: "Most Marines would rather be ordered on a dangerous patrol than spend the day digging trench line. It was extremely difficult work. Progress was slow and the work was backbreaking."[50]

No work detail was more demoralizing than recovering and burying the dead. Soldiers grew accustomed, in varying degrees, to the carnage of the battlefield, but some men never got used to burying their own comrades. Bob Hoffman certainly did not: "In the beginning we had a fear of the dead. We hated to touch them. Some of the hardest experiences of my life were taking identification tags from my dead friends."[51] Doughboys, especially if veterans, found burying enemy dead, or the many horse carcasses common to World War I, far less traumatic but still distinctly unpleasant and arduous. A dead, bloated horse, Hoffman explains, required a hole ten feet square and six feet deep—somewhat smaller if the animal's rigid legs were chopped off first.[52]

In part because of the detrimental effect on the doughboys' morale of having to bury their own comrades, the army moved more quickly in later wars to establish a graves-registration organization. Sometimes, however, graves-registration personnel were unavailable or were swamped with work, and soldiers again had to recover or bury the bodies of their comrades. Rifleman Robert Kennington volunteered, along with several others, to recover the bodies of five men from their company hastily buried earlier during combat on Guadalcanal. The bodies, wrapped in ponchos, were badly decomposed: "We were puking. It was terrible. After a while we got everyone out. The flesh did not adhere to the bones. We could really only get the bones out. Having in your mind what the guys looked like alive, and then seeing this was horrid."[53]

Even when the graves-registration system worked efficiently, the task of recovering friendly dead still befell the frontline troops if the bodies were under enemy observation and fire. Martin Russ recounts a "snatch party" during the Korean War, in which he and several others successfully recovered a dead marine killed in front of the friendly trench line.[54] Matthew Brennan and his fellow grunts in the aerorifle platoon of an air cavalry troop in Vietnam frequently drew the mission of recovering bodies from crashed helicopters. This work was not only dangerous, since the enemy who shot down the helicopter was usually still in the area, but also grim. On one mission Brennan found "three smoldering bodies" still strapped into their crashed observation helicopter, "staring straight ahead through hollow sockets. The pilot's jaws were frozen open in a final prayer or a cry for help."[55]

From recovering bodies to digging fortifications, the soldier's workload was burdensome in the best of conditions, but conditions were seldom ideal. The soldier fought and struggled to survive in appalling climates and terrain, amid gruesome carnage, while hungry and thirsty. The soldier in Vietnam and in much of the Pacific area during World War II toiled in punishing heat and humidity. Much of the fighting in the Pacific occurred in jungle terrain.[56] James Salafia described the jungle on New Georgia in the Solomons: "The mud in the jungle had a distinct and powerful smell. A damp, musty, dank smell. The odor was unpleasant, but we got used to it. You did not grow accustomed to the noise. The sounds were constant. . . . And there were the land crabs. Sometimes we thought they were Japs trying to sneak into us."[57]

During the seizure of Cape Gloucester on New Britain Island in the Bismarck Archipelago monsoon rains made life sheer misery. Bob Stiles believed that "they should have given us submarine pay for Cape Gloucester; there was more water there than at Coney Island."[58] Soldiers were soaked to the skin for days on end. Mud brought movement to a virtual standstill in an area of the world where roads, bridges, and rail lines were almost nonexistent.

Conditions were similar on the large island of New Guinea. E. J. Kahn slept on the jungle floor, where the ground "is seldom dry and it harbors a vast menagerie of things that crawl and sting." He and his comrades lost weight in the "continuous heat and humidity." The perspiring troops were constantly thirsty, but safe drinking water was at a premium, despite the saturated climate. And Kahn led the relatively comfortable life of a staff soldier. When he saw the combat troops, he realized that he had nothing to complain about: "The men at the front in New Guinea were perhaps among the most wretched-looking soldiers ever to wear the American uniform. They were gaunt and thin, with deep black circles under their sunken eyes. They were covered with tropical sores and had straggly beards. They were clothed in tattered, stained jackets and pants. Few of them wore socks or underwear. Often the soles had been sucked off their shoes by the tenacious, stinking mud."[59]

Kahn was describing the early days of the New Guinea fighting, when such basic items as uniforms and boots were in short supply. But even in Vietnam, where supplies were generally adequate and more easily delivered, if only because of the helicopter, conditions remained taxing, to say the least. Lieutenant Caputo describes how the combination of heat and humidity could literally kill: "The mercury level might be 98 degrees one day, 110 the next, 105 the day after that; but these numbers can no more express the intensity of that heat than the reading on a barometer can express the destructive power of a typhoon. The only valid measurement was what the heat could do to a man, and what it could do to him was simple enough: it could kill him, bake his brains, or wring the sweat out of him until he dropped from exhaustion."[60]

Vietnam, like much of the Pacific area, was visited by monsoons. Charles Strong, a machine gunner in the Americal Division, reported that "it rained for 15 days and 15 nights continuously. We started catching cramps and charley horses. And guys' feet got messed up."[61] Contrary to the popular image of sweltering jungle heat, the arrival of the monsoons, combined with cooler temperatures and brisk winds in the highlands of Vietnam, left soldiers shivering in water-filled foxholes. Marine captain Richard D. Camp was "surprised by how cold it got. My blood had been thinned out by the long months of heat, and then it got cold and windy and wet. I was usually chilled to the marrow and, right off, the docs were treating Marines who had come down with all kinds of colds and winter diseases."[62]

Even colder and wetter were the GIs fighting in the rugged mountains of Italy during World War II. The Germans, skillfully defending from prepared positions, made life dangerous, but for Lieutenant Harold L. Bond, a mortar platoon leader, the weather was an even greater enemy: "I knew for certain the worst part of the war was not the shooting or the shelling—although that had been bad enough—but the weather, snow, sleet, and rain, and the prolonged physical misery which accompanied them."[63] Klaus H. Huebner, a surgeon marching with his infantry battalion, could not have agreed more: "Along the higher ridges wind whips up the steady rain and chills you to the bone. The rain has soaked through my coat and all my clothing. I feel miserable. As the column momentarily comes to a halt, I sit down on the trail in a puddle of water six inches deep. I no longer care what happens or what I do. I have never felt lower in my life."[64]

While GIs shivered in the cold, wet Apennine Mountains of Italy, other GIs were doing the same in the frontier area between France and Germany. The race across France stalled out in fall 1944 in the rugged terrain of places like the Vosges Mountains, the Ardennes, and the Huertgen Forest. Lieutenant Paul Boesch remembers a miserable night march to conduct a relief in place in the Huertgen Forest. The men in his machine-gun platoon had to carry their guns and ammunition on their backs because the jeeps had mired in the mud. As they stumbled along a forest trail, "the night seemed to get even blacker . . . and the rain came in great wind-driven sheets, drenching every thread of our clothes." Visibility was so bad that the relief was postponed until morning. Boesch and two of his sergeants lay down in the mud to rest, with only their raincoats for protection: "Puddles of rain quickly formed in the folds and dents of the raincoats, so that any move brought water pouring into our faces and down our necks. . . . The coldness of the ground soon added to the other chill so that our teeth began to chatter."[65]

The miserable fall weather gave way to the record-cold winter of 1944–1945. Men with frostbite and pneumonia joined those suffering from immersion foot in the sick-call lines. The GIs did some of their fiercest fighting that winter, notably during the Battle of the Bulge in the Ardennes region. In the bitter-cold nights, falling asleep for too long, without moving about or stamping feet to keep the circulation going, meant serious frostbite. One man in Lieutenant Harold P. Leinbaugh's company fell asleep in his hole. When he was discovered in the morning, "both his hands and feet were frozen. His boots had split, there was ice between his toes, and the skin on his hands was burst open."[66]

The only soldiers of the draft era to fight under worse winter conditions were the marines and GIs of the Korean War. The first winter (1950–1951) was especially miserable because soldiers lacked proper cold-weather clothing, the fighting took place in the desolate mountains in North Korea, and the Chinese intervention in late November 1950 drove the United Nations forces into headlong retreat in appalling weather. Soldiers learned through bitter experience how to fight in the cold. Lubricating oil congealed, causing weapons to malfunction, so soldiers kept them dry and oil free. Drinking water had to be cut with alcohol or it froze inside canteens. Canned rations had to be kept next to the body or they would freeze. Medics learned to thaw morphine syrettes in their mouths and to keep blood plasma next to their skin, but in a major fight, wounded men died who would otherwise have lived because the supply of unfrozen plasma ran out.[67]

Even the spring thaw in Korea did not bring relief, only a new variation on the misery. Private Jerry Emer describes the conditions in late February 1951: "We began to get a lot of cold rain and sleet, and the hills became slippery and soggy. We started taking weather casualties, guys with terrible coughs, maybe some with pneumonia and pleurisy."[68] Spring meant monsoons, as did early fall. Lieutenant Lyle Rishell remembers the fall monsoons that "blew in from the south and hit us with torrents of rain," turning everything into a "mushy mess": "Our hands and fingers shriveled and cracked . . . our boots and socks felt leaden. . . . With the rains came chilling winds, and there was little warmth from the wet clothing. We shivered and shook and remained cold."[69]

Korean summer brought a new climatic enemy—heat and humidity. Though perhaps not as extreme as the heat of Southeast Asia, Korean summers were still tough on the soldiers trudging up and down the hilly countryside. Private Leonard Korgie recalls that "the heat was unbearable. It just steamed in on us. No wind, humid, exposed to the sun, very little water, no salt pills, guys began collapsing."[70] To add to the misery, the irrigated rice paddies were a breeding ground for mosquitoes, and the human excrement used to fertilize them added a nauseous stench.[71] Bill Mauldin, stopping over in Tokyo while en route to cover the Korean War in early 1952, learned that "Korea is not the garden spot of the Orient like the editor said it was when he offered me this job."[72] Most Korean War veterans could only marvel at the understatement.

Few theaters of war were as inhospitable as Korea. The doughboys campaigning in France, for example, did not have to endure such climatic extremes. In fact, life in a quiet sector of the western front could be relatively comfortable. A static front was the norm until spring 1918, and segments of the front remained stable almost until war's end. Many doughboys, especially those in early-arriving units, experienced "breaking-in" stretches in these sectors, where they lived in dugouts, ate hot rations brought forward on a regular schedule, and even slept on wood-and-wire-mesh bunks.[73]

During the campaigns of spring through fall 1918, however, the doughboys fought a different kind of war. They moved frequently, plugging holes torn in the Allied lines by the German spring and summer offensives, and then went on the attack during the Aisne-Marne, St. Mihiel, and Meuse-Argonne offensives. Gone were the cozy bunkers and hot meals. As the weather grew increasingly vile in fall 1918, the doughboys fought in the cold, rain, and mud and slept in a soggy hole scraped in the ground, that is, if they were not marching all night.

As early as August 1918, the doughboys noticed the weather turning for the worse. Sergeant Hoffman could only ponder, in dread, what France would be like when the "real" winter arrived: "Mud everywhere! Not a dry spot on us, we were cold, and most uncomfortable. I had the thought . . . that if we were so desperately cold and uncomfortable in August, how must it be in the actual winter months?"[74]

The Armistice of November 11, 1918, spared Hoffman from having to find out just how miserable fighting in the dead of winter could be, but he and his fellow doughboys did have to endure as the weather grew progressively worse from August to November. Private Elton Mackin describes rising on a cold November morning from the damp ground where he had slept: "The most painful part of such a situation is the necessity of getting up to face another day. Even the balmy breeze of a June morning can feel cold then, whereas the steady knife-edge wind of November is pure agony. It drives inside to meet the chills deep in your bones and makes you shake. Your lower jaw trembles like a loose-hinged gate until you can lash it fast with your helmet strap, pulling your face together to stop the chatter of your teeth."[75]

Fighting, or simply living, in extremes of weather added to the soldier's fatigue and even dulled his mental processes. Harry Brown's novel about an infantry platoon moving to contact in the scorching Italian heat in World War II bears this out: "When a man is uncomfortable, through either heat or cold, he finds it hard to think consecutively. His thoughts come in flashes. He is too conscious of his ever-present discomforts. The body, as always, thwarts the mind."[76] Korean War veteran Sherman Pratt put it even more succinctly—the cold "dulled our senses. It made us move slow. It made us *think* slow."[77]

In addition to suffering mind-numbing, strength-draining extremes of weather, the soldier was harassed by a diverse collection of vermin. No doughboy account is complete without the mentioning of lice, or "cooties," as they were called. In spare moments, doughboys removed their shirts and picked lice from the seams, a practice resembling reading in appearance; hence, they "read" their shirts. Most soldiers passed off the itchy, biting cooties as an unavoidable nuisance, but some were driven to distraction by the bugs. Corporal Minder found them "perfectly disgusting": "They bite and annoy you something awful."[78] To eliminate the lice, artillery scout Horatio Rogers tried a "kerosene cure," rubbing his body and clothes down with kerosene: "By the time I had my clothes on again I was in agony. The stuff burned like fire, and for the rest of the day I roamed around like a dog with a can tied to its tail. It didn't kill the cooties either."[79]

Lice were common in later wars as well, although they were not singled out for damnation to the extent that they were by the doughboys. Soldiers instead condemned an array of pests. Klaus Huebner, enjoying the shelter of a sheepherder's hut in Italy in World War II, fell asleep "sitting on the floor in the corner of the room, completely ignoring the fleas and roaches as well as the mice that scurry between the snoring bodies."[80] Yet nowhere did the variety and viciousness of the vermin equal that of the tropics. Peter Bowman, in his novel about an amphibious landing in the Pacific in World War II, cataloged a list of pests that only a biologist could love: mosquitoes (three types), ticks, flies (multiple varieties), fleas, gnats, mites, leeches, sweatbees, spiders, scorpions, land crabs, chiggers, biting and stinging ants, and yes, the "universally uninvited parasite, the louse."[81]

If Vietnam is typical, then Bowman's list is not exaggerated. Lieutenant Caputo and his battalion, fresh in-country, quickly learned that the Viet Cong were not their only enemy: "Our toughest battle that night was waged against Vietnam's insect life. Mosquito netting and repellents proved ineffective against the horde of flying, creeping, crawling, buzzing, biting things that descended on us. . . . By midnight, my face and hands were masses of welts."[82]

Just as doughboys were disgusted by cooties, some grunts abhorred the leeches common in Vietnam. Walking in the wet jungle or wading through a stream or rice paddy virtually ensured picking up some unwanted passengers. Most soldiers nonchalantly removed them by burning them with a cigarette, which persuaded them to let go, but some grunts, like Dwight Reiland, truly hated the "insidious, evil, dirty kind of trespass" perpetrated by the leeches.[83]

Leeches and other vermin were more than just annoying pests. They spread diseases, some of them deadly. Disease historically had caused more casualties than enemy fire, but during the wars of the draft era, the percentage of men lost to illness dropped significantly because of advances in preventive medicine, vaccines, and treatment techniques.[84] Disease and illness remained a major problem, however. Mosquitoes brought malaria, and flies carried typhus and other diseases.[85] Poor sanitation and contaminated drinking water caused hepatitis, hemorrhagic fever, and that most prevalent of soldier ailments, dysentery—a malady so common as to be nicknamed "the GIs." Some of these diseases, such as typhus, hepatitis, and hemorrhagic fever, almost guaranteed the soldier's evacuation to a hospital.[86] Cases of malaria and dysentery, however, were not always serious enough to warrant hospitalization. Some soldiers thus fought on while suffering the fevers and chills of malaria or the stomach pains and loose bowels of "the GIs."

The problem with dysentery, or even a severe bout of diarrhea, besides the suffering caused by weakness, weight loss, dehydration, and intestinal-tract pain, was that the war did not stop for a soldier's bowels. Captain Camp, while on convoy escort duty with his marine rifle company in Vietnam, suffered an attack of diarrhea, but the trucks could not make an unscheduled stop, so he had to hang his backside out of his jeep as it moved down the road: "That was great fun for the troops at my expense, a little comic relief provided by the skipper for the benefit of company morale." [87]

Though a soldier with the GIs might provide amusing anecdotes, there was a serious side to the problem. Relieving oneself in combat meant leaving the shelter of foxholes, bunkers, or basements to drop trousers and squat down in the open. Soldiers were sometimes killed by enemy fire while relieving themselves, or even shot by their own side, usually at night, because they were mistaken for enemy infiltrators.[88] Soldiers often elected not to leave cover in dangerous situations, choosing instead to defecate in a cardboard ration box or even in their steel helmet.[89]

Diarrhea and dysentery were usually caused by contaminated water, but unsanitary cooking conditions, dirty mess kits, and spoiled food also caused intestinal-tract woes. The soldiers frequently commented about their rations, often in the negative. In theory, unit cooks (usually at the company level, but in some cases at battalion level) prepared hot rations at least once a day with cooking equipment designed for use in the field. These rations were prepared close enough to the front for soldiers to rotate back to the field kitchen to eat or for carrying parties, or perhaps helicopters, to take them forward.

On occasion theory and practice coincided, and some soldier-authors praise their unit cooks for putting out a good meal under adverse conditions, sometimes risking their lives by setting up their kitchen close to the fighting. Kurt Gabel, for example, had nothing but praise for his battalion's field kitchen in World War II, a "culinary Camelot" that closely followed the hungry troops and fed them round the clock.[90] Not all unit mess teams, unfortunately, were so talented, conscientious, and brave. Private Albert M. Ettinger declared his "inept" company mess team the worst in the regiment. Everything the team was given to cook was transformed into an unpalatable stew.[91] Lieutenant Leinbaugh's infantry company in World War II shed not a tear when the mess sergeant was wounded by an artillery shell: "We figured his departure could only improve the quality of our daily meals, and [Sergeant] Lance's reaction, 'Now there's a German gunner who's really on our side,' was typical."[92]

Even mediocre hot chow prepared by a less-than-accomplished mess team was better than no hot chow, and commanders went to some lengths to get fresh-cooked rations to the men. Depending on the weather and the tactical situation, however, the arrival of meals was not always the morale booster it should have been. Soldiers had to stand in line, have the food ladled into their mess kits, and then eat in the open air. Lieutenant Lawrence discovered, during World War I, that dining in a heavy rain meant a mess kit filled with "ten percent food and ninety percent rainwater."[93] Lieutenant Boesch's description of some questionable fare served up in the rainy, pitch-black Huertgen Forest illustrates just how badly a hot meal can misfire as a morale booster: "None of us had any idea what we were being served, and by the time we had groped our way to some spot where we could squat on the ground, the food was cold and soggy from rain. In seeking some place to settle, each of us stumbled over other men who had gone ahead of us. In the end we had to give up and take the food in our filthy hands and cram it in chunks into our mouths. Few of us would argue with the theory that before an attack a man should have a hot meal, but neither would we endorse a hot meal under *any* circumstances, least of all these under which we found ourselves."[94]

Boesch correctly notes that at times hot food could not or should not be served at the front. For days or even weeks at a time, the soldier had to subsist on combat rations. Their quality and diversity improved over the period covered in this book, but they remained monotonous and unappetizing, and sometimes in short supply.

Combat rations in World War I included hardtack, an unleavened cracker of Civil War fame and, doughboys believed, Civil War age. Canned rations consisted of a limited choice of corned beef ("corned willie"), salmon ("goldfish"), and an especially despised French beef ration known as "monkey meat."[95] The most common combat ration in World War II was the "K-ration," which came in a cardboard box offering choices of "breakfast," "dinner," and "supper," with breakfast, according to Captain Charles B. MacDonald, being the "least evil."[96] World War II troops, especially in the Pacific, also ate "C-rations," containing cans of hash, meat, or beans, which appeared to Captain W. Standford Smith "to have been canned years earlier" and were "edible only when warmed," which of course was usually impossible to do.[97]

The ostensibly improved C-ration reemerged during the Korean and Vietnam Wars, offering twelve meal choices, which underwent many changes over the years. The canned fruit contained in some C-ration meals was a prized commodity; but a few meal choices, notably the ham and lima beans, a greasy mix that earned the sobriquet of "ham and motherfuckers" because of the hard, unpalatable, lima beans, were universally hated.[98]

As if monotonous rations, vermin, sickness, and miserable weather were not enough, man and his machines of destruction completed the transformation of the soldier's environment into a nightmare. Artillery was the greatest destroyer. During World War I, sections of placid French countryside were pulverized by artillery shells. Charles MacArthur recalls his first view of the Argonne battlefield, where nature and man alike had been blasted: "The woods were splintered into small bits, green with mustard gas. There wasn't a live leaf in twenty miles. Thousands of dead men sprawled in the ulcerated fields. Horses, their legs awkwardly pointing up, and a general litter of junk. Wagons, rifles, socks, rations, love letters."[99]

The doughboys were especially amazed at how completely a once-quaint French village, with its stoutly built homes, could be demolished. Artillery scout Horatio Rogers often navigated using manmade landmarks; sometimes there was little left of the landmark: "I looked for the town of Samogneux. It was an area of masonry rubble, nowhere more than six feet high—the most complete ruin of a town imaginable."[100]

Battlefield carnage was certainly not unique to World War I. When the American advance on Okinawa in World War II stalled in front of the heavily fortified Shuri Line, torrential rains generated knee-deep mud, and corpses could not be removed because of the constant fighting. Private Sledge describes the nightmarish vista: "For several feet around every corpse, maggots crawled about in the muck. . . . There wasn't a tree or bush left. . . . Shells had torn up the turf so completely that ground cover was nonexistent. . . .The scene was nothing but mud; shell fire; flooded craters with their silent, pathetic, rotting occupants; knocked-out tanks and amtracs; and discarded equipment—utter desolation."[101]

Such macabre scenes occurred less frequently during the Vietnam War because the fighting was usually more sporadic and on a smaller scale. But when major engagements did occur, American firepower could devastate the battlefield. Ogden and his marine battalion participated in a pitched battle against a North Vietnamese regiment. Before it was over, they had pounded the enemy with artillery, naval gunfire, and air attacks: "A chunk of jungle the size of two football fields was missing. It looked like a logging company had moved in, taken the choice lumber, then burned and plowed up the rest. . . . There were bodies and pieces of bodies strewn everywhere, some hanging from surviving trees. . . . Every square inch of the territory I scanned was a new revelation in horror."[102]

The common presence in these descriptions is the dead—often horribly mutilated dead. If soldiers believed in heroic death in battle followed by a dignified trip home on their shield, then the sight of comrades literally blown to pieces or left to rot in the sun because enemy fire prevented recovery of the body soon disabused them of their romantic notions. Sergeant Frankel saw his fellow tank crewmen die such deaths in World War II: "You'd think a man has a right to some dignity in death. What is it that makes a grizzly death grizzly? It is not the blood and guts, the untimeliness, the pain. It is, rather, the complete loss of human dignity, of even looking human. That's what grizzly means."[103]

The ultimate negation of death with dignity occurred when a soldier's obliterated body splattered on his comrades, at times with enough force to cause injury or death. A sergeant in Captain Camp's marine rifle company in Vietnam was struck in the head by a rocket-propelled grenade, blowing gore into the face of the man next to him. The man at first thought he had been blinded, but everything he "had been sprayed with could be washed off."[104] Sergeant William Manchester was seriously wounded by a large-caliber Japanese rocket on Okinawa in World War II. His injuries included a piece of one of his men's shinbones imbedded in his back—the man had been vaporized by the rocket's impact.[105]

Existing amid carnage and filth for weeks at a time, soldiers became disgusted with "living like animals." Private William Hicks, the protagonist in Boyd's novel *Through the Wheat,* was a typically grubby marine doughboy: "He had worn his drab shirt for two weeks, and there were black rings around the collar and wrists. . . . The knees of his breeches were as soiled and uncomfortable as his shirt, and his puttees and shoes were crusted thickly with dried mud. His stock-taking was interrupted by the knowledge that a persistent vermin was exploring the vicinity of his breast."[106]

Private Sledge's description of the World War II rifleman after several weeks in combat is worth citing at length:

During the latter phase of the [Peleliu] campaign the typical infantryman wore a worried, haggard expression on his filthy, unshaven face. . . . His camouflaged helmet cover . . . was gray with coral dust and had a tear or two in it. His cotton dungaree jacket . . . was discolored with coral dust, filthy, greasy with rifle oil, and as stiff as canvas from being soaked alternately with rain and sweat and then drying. His elbows might be out, and his knees frequently were, from much "hitting the deck" on the coral rock. His boon-dockers [shoes] were coated with gray coral dust, and his heels were worn off completely by the sharp coral. The infantryman's callused hands were nearly blackened by weeks of accumulation of rifle oil, mosquito repellant . . . , dirt, dust, and general filth. Overall he was stooped by general fatigue and excessive physical exertion. If approached closely enough for conversation, he smelled bad.[107]

The World War II rifleman's successors in later wars were equally dirty and smelly. Lieutenant Owen and his men had no time, or unfrozen water, for clean-ing up during the retreat from the Chosin Reservoir in December 1950: "Our parkas were all stained with blood, food, gun oil, and dirt. Our filthy faces were matted with bristly beards that bore icicles of mucus and spittle."[108] The grunt living in the boonies in Vietnam was no cleaner. Machine gunner Robert Sanders "stayed dirty and muddy. The mud dried, then I was right back in the rice pad-dies. I was funky. I mean, I stunk, man, I really stunk. It was something to aggra-vate us all the time."[109]

Sanders's aggravation over his filthy condition is an important point. Though leaders sometimes had to order men to clean up, especially in very cold weather when cleaning up meant removing warm clothing or shaving with ice-cold water, on the whole soldiers did not like being filthy, smelly, and vermin-ridden; and they did not feel good about themselves when they were. Frank Hurry, an infantry squad leader in New Guinea during World War II, notes: "You were very unclean, which made you unhappy with yourself. It was degrading. I saw much combat, but the personal filth is one of my most unpleasant memories of the war."[110]

In extreme cases, the dirty, exhausted soldier became "too tired to care," fail-ing to take even elementary precautions, sometimes with predictably unfortunate results. S. L. A. Marshall explains what could happen: "The soldier fails to dig a foxhole, even though he knows that he is in danger. The officer fails to properly inspect his position. Troops fail to reconnoiter the immediate area. . . . In this state of slackness, the attitude of men becomes one of general indifference to the possible consequences of inaction."[111] Correspondent Michael Herr observed this phenomenon in Vietnam: "Every day people were dying there because of some small detail that they couldn't be bothered to observe. Imagine being too tired to snap a flak jacket closed, too tired to clean your rifle, too tired to guard a light, too tired to deal with the half-inch margins of safety that moving through the war often demanded, just too tired to give a fuck and then dying behind that exhaustion."[112]

Perhaps even more psychologically devastating than being too tired to care, the soldier sometimes came to believe that his very surroundings were hostile, or "enemy," a condition especially evident in jungle fighting.[113] Soldiers in the Pacific in World War II loathed and feared the jungle. Private Leckie described Guadalcanal as evil: "The terrain of Guadalcanal seemed composed of steel, over which the demons of the jungle had spread a thin treacherous slime."[114] He later found the jungles of New Britain to be even more malevolent: "New Britain was evil, darkly and secretly evil, a malefactor and enemy of humankind, an adversary really, dissolving, corroding, poisoning, chilling, sucking, drenching."[115]

The grunts found the jungles of Vietnam to be as hostile as their predecessors had the jungles of the southwest Pacific. Gustav Hasford, in his novel *The Short-timers,* in describing a typically grueling march in the boonies, portrays the jungle as a sort of monstrous greenhouse: "Humping in the rain forest is like climbing a stairway of shit in an enormous green room constructed by ogres for the confinement of monster plants. . . . Beneath mountains like the black teeth of dragons we hump. We hump up a woodcutter's trail, up slopes of peanut butter, over moss-blemished boulders, into God's green furnace, into the hostile terrain of Indian country."[116]

Though lacking the vivid similes and metaphors, Lieutenant Caputo also saw the Vietnam jungle as evil as he flew over it in a helicopter: "The manuals we had used in guerrilla-warfare courses cheerfully stated that the modern, civilized soldier should not be afraid of the jungle: 'The jungle can be your friend as well as your enemy.' Looking at the green immensity below, I could only conclude that those manuals had been written by men whose idea of a jungle was the Everglades National Park. There was nothing friendly about the Vietnamese bush; it was one of the last of the dark regions on earth."[117]

## THE EMOTIONAL ENVIRONMENT OF WAR

Even as the soldier contended with a harsh, seemingly evil, physical environment, he also found that war stressed him emotionally. He was never completely safe from harm, except when far to the rear, perhaps attending a military school or in a hospital, and even then he was hounded by the thought of having to return to the fighting. Thus the combat soldier was never completely free from fear and anxiety.

Captain, later congressman, Hamilton Fish recalls being always on edge during World War I: "Another thing that sticks in my mind is the constant feeling of anxiety. The threat of death was always with you, particularly from the shelling. . . . The shells, you see, could come at any time."[118] The intensity of that anxiety could vary, but as World War II veteran Charles Crary noted, it never disappeared completely: "There was the constant fear that a bullet with my name on it or a stray piece of shrapnel would kill me. . . . I guess there were times that the fear of death was not in the forefront of my mind; but certainly that oppressive shadow was constantly with me."[119]

During the Vietnam War, combat was more sporadic and the danger from enemy firepower was less than in the earlier wars of the draft era, but the levels of anxiety, tension, and fear remained high because of the nature of the fighting. The grunt never knew when enemy sappers or booby traps might take their toll, not to mention a more conventional bullet or mortar round. James Martin Davis, a long-range reconnaissance specialist, remembers that the ever-present fear, with its physical manifestations, was unshakable: "It was an uncomfortable, chronic, nausea-inducing condition that was there every day and never completely left. It was fear—pure and simple. It was the body's physical reaction to danger nearby."[120]

Although for Davis, as for most soldiers, the fear "never completely left," its intensity could vary significantly. Certain types of combat operations, for example, were especially nerve-racking, notably patrolling and night watch.[121] Patrols were conducted to gather intelligence on the enemy's position, capture a prisoner, ambush an enemy patrol, or simply keep the men sharp and aggressive. Often these patrols were carried out at night, and regardless of their importance to the prosecution of the war, the soldiers who mounted them hated them.

Patrols were a nightly occurrence during the period of static, trench warfare in the last two years of the Korean conflict, and few soldiers looked forward to them with anything but dread. Lieutenant Matthias, a marine rifle platoon leader, relates how the tension would mount: "It is difficult to describe the feelings and anxieties involved in leaving the security of the lines to go out in pitch darkness to the unknown. No matter how simple or difficult the patrol, certain apprehensions began to develop in the late afternoon. . . . As we got closer to darkness, the tension began to build so much that we actually began to look forward to loading up and getting on with it."[122]

Matthias hit on the key issue—patrols left the safety of friendly lines and therefore even a short patrol carried the danger of enemy contact at any moment. As Martin Russ noted, there were no "routine" patrols in Korea: "Although it may sound as though these patrols are becoming routine—emotionally—each one has been a hair-raiser so far, whether we see anything or not."[123] There were no routine patrols in the Vietnam War, either. Tim O'Brien points out yet another possibility that soldiers on night patrol worried about: "One of the most persistent and appalling thoughts that lumbers through your mind as you walk through Vietnam at night is the fear . . . of becoming detached from the others, of spending the night alone in that frightening and haunted countryside."[124]

While the men departing on patrol were understandably apprehensive, those remaining behind were often only slightly less so, because to them fell the task of standing night watch against enemy infiltrators, patrols, or even a full-scale attack. Boyd describes the tension of standing guard in *Through the Wheat:* "Through the long night that stretched interminably before them they peered into the darkness, fancying . . . that each tree trunk was an enemy. The least noise was sufficient for overworked nerves to press the trigger of a rifle and send a volley of bullets through the leaves of the trees."[125]

Private Leckie, in his foxhole beside a huge tree, guarding Henderson Field on Guadalcanal during World War II, describes how his fear and imagination almost got the better of him: "It was a darkness without time. It was an impenetrable darkness. To the right and the left of me rose up those terrible formless things of my imagination. . . . I could hear the darkness gathering against me. . . . I could hear the enemy everywhere about me, whispering to each other and calling my name. I lay open-mouthed and half-mad beneath the giant tree. I had not looked into its foliage before darkness and now I fancied it infested with Japanese. Everything and all the world became my enemy." Daylight finally arrived without incident, but Leckie now understood "why men light fires."[126] Standing guard at night during the Korean War was equally stressful. The marine manning a listening post or standing watch, writes Lieutenant Matthias, was "alone with his sector and all the possible dangers his senses and imagination can conjure. . . . Unless you have experienced the loneliness and horror of 'knowing there is something out there' it is impossible to imagine the feeling."[127]

For the nervous soldier on guard duty or patrol, the ultimate source of his fear was, of course, the enemy. Ironically, one of the best ways for a soldier to overcome this fear was to confront his foe. Lord Charles McM. Moran, in his insightful study of courage, observed that "in the presence of danger men often found salvation in action."[128] By taking action when under fire, the soldier could focus on the job at hand, the adrenaline kicked in, and fear was temporarily forgotten, or at least overcome. For Lieutenant Owen, performing his duties as a platoon leader helped him to get through it all: "I learned how to deflect the fear. After the first jolt of it, which came with the initial shock of coming under fire, I would force myself upright and attempt to read the situation before the skipper's [company commander's] voice came crackling out of the walkie-talkie. Once I had rammed myself into action, the fear subsided. It never completely went away, though."[129]

During an attack or when soldiers were defending against an enemy assault, the excitement could reach fever pitch, despite the danger and fear. Charles Brooks, a squad leader in the Korean War, was surrounded with six of his men in a bunker on Pork Chop Hill. They were too busy fighting the Chinese to be afraid: "Your adrenaline's going like mad, and as long as you can move around and fire back at the enemy you're generally all right." But Brooks added, when a soldier cannot take action, he has time to dwell on his fears: "It's when you have to lie in a hole under an artillery or mortar barrage, helpless, that's when you're really scared."[130]

Yet all too often, the soldier could not retaliate and sometimes could not even move, and then a sense of helplessness greatly added to his fear and stress.[131] Hoffman observed that men could be brave when closing with the enemy, but enduring a pounding from artillery was another matter: "We could be brave in the broad daylight, rushing forward on an attack like the one on Hill 204. But shelling at night saps the courage from the bravest. Everyone lies there and shakes. Only the strongest can keep in their right minds."[132]

Private George Barrette's first barrage in World War II was especially fierce because the Germans had spotted the command post he was working in as a radio operator and shelled it heavily: "Me and this buddy of mine were in the same hole with only a little brush on top, and I remember I was actually bawling. We were both praying to the Lord over and over again to please stop the barrage. We were both shaking and shivering and crying and praying all at the same time."[133]

The Japanese made less use of artillery than the Germans, but in the later island campaigns they resorted increasingly to fortifications and artillery to counter American firepower. One of the first campaigns in which the Japanese tried out their new firepower-intensive tactics occurred when the marines assaulted Peleliu Island. Private Sledge was an early initiate: "Under my first barrage since the fast-moving events of hitting the beach, I learned a new sensation: utter and absolute helplessness. The shelling lifted in about half an hour, although it seemed to me to have crashed on for hours."[134]

The Vietnam War is rarely associated with heavy shelling by the enemy. The North Vietnamese sometimes launched sharp, deadly mortar or rocket barrages—certainly fear inspiring, but not long lasting. For soldiers (or more often marines) stationed in bases near the Demilitarized Zone or the Laotian border, however, shelling from artillery pieces hidden in sanctuaries was frequent and occasionally heavy. Captain Camp describes what he and his company went through when well over 1,000 artillery rounds and rockets pummeled the Khe Sanh Firebase within the span of six hours: "It was a devastating day—not in terms of casualties, which were blessedly few, but in terms of having to take an hours-long shelling we couldn't do anything about. We just sat in our bunkers and took it. . . . By sunset, I was physically and emotionally drained. All I wanted to do was go to sleep. The adrenaline had been going through me for hours and I was about to fall over."[135]

Although the grunt had to endure mortar, rocket, and even artillery fire, at least he was spared from enemy air attack. Except for occasional bombs from Bed Check Charlie, the Korean War soldier was likewise spared. Doughboys' memoirs, on the other hand, are filled with incidents of being observed, strafed, and bombed by German planes. Air attacks generated feelings of helplessness and fear similar to an artillery barrage. Corporal William L. Langer definitely thought so: "Bombing, like shellfire, has always seemed a bit unfair to me. Somehow it makes one feel so helpless, there is no chance of reprisal for the individual man. The advantage is all with the shell, and you have no comeback."[136]

Father Duffy, who had seen more than his share of the front lines as chaplain of an infantry regiment, surpassed Langer, rating bombing as even worse than shelling: "Even shells can be dodged if not too numerous. . . . But when one lies at night and hears the deep buzz of a plane overhead . . . the one feeling that comes is that if that fellow overhead pulls the lever at the right spot . . . it means sudden and absolute destruction. There is no way of getting away from it. One simply lies and cowers."[137]

The doughboys were not only frightened but also frustrated and demoralized by bombing and strafing attacks. Bitter comments like "the Germans seem to have the air to themselves" crop up in the memoirs.[138] Such comments are largely absent from GI accounts of World War II, however, given Allied success in gaining air superiority. But American soldiers were attacked from the air on occasion and fairly frequently during the early fighting in North Africa and the Pacific.

German air attacks in North Africa, especially by the feared Junkers Ju 87 Stuka dive-bomber, were demoralizing. Lieutenant Franklyn A. Johnson, an anti-tank platoon leader in the First Infantry Division, describes the sudden ferocity of a dive-bombing attack: "Suddenly . . . heard a terrific roar and a shadow blotted out the sun. Bombs from 12 Stukas screamed down on us. Never more terrified in my life. Just lay in my hole and beat the dirt with my fists."[139]

At that same time in the Pacific, other soldiers were also lying in holes as Japanese fighters strafed during daytime and bombers visited at night. Allied airpower eventually gained the upper hand, but Japanese air attacks were common in the early fighting in the Solomon Islands and New Guinea. The first things to greet Lieutenant Gerald P. Averill upon his arrival on Vella Lavella Island in the Solomons were strafing Japanese fighters. Averill and his outfit "were pinned in place, humiliated beyond description as we grovelled in the slime; the whirring, snapping slugs tearing up the palms . . . forcing us deeper into the mire, causing us to cling to the bases of the trees in an effort to escape that wicked, demoralizing fire."[140]

Lieutenant Orville Freeman had a similar experience when he landed on Bougainville Island, also in the Solomons: "The Zeros [Mitsubishi A6M Zero-Sen Japanese fighters] were shocking. It was the first time I'd ever been strafed and that's one helpless feeling. You are running as fast as you can, trying to find some cover because you know there is really nothing else you can do."[141]

Helplessness in the face of air attack or artillery bombardment not only heightened fear but also fed a growing resentment. Soldiers wanted to believe that their contributions and sacrifices made a difference. Some even nurtured romantic notions of besting the enemy in individual combat. Instead, they found themselves in the midst of a machine war in which their personal efforts seemed to count for little, and military prowess could not save them from obliteration by shell or bomb. They felt like cannon fodder, and they naturally resented it.

This revelation was most unexpected, and hence most shocking, for the World War I doughboy, who was the first to experience modern machine warfare. Not surprisingly, the postwar disillusionment literature, as the genre has come to be called, denounced the inhumanity and impersonality of modern war. No novelist played more on this theme than did John Dos Passos in his two war novels, *First Encounter* and the more widely read *Three Soldiers*.[142] *First Encounter* features a protagonist, Martin Howe, an American volunteer ambulance driver, as was Dos Passos. At one point, Howe is lying on a bunk inside a dugout near the front in France, watching his comrades playing cards. He muses on the possibility that a shell could kill them all at any moment, and how meaningless such a death would be: "It would be so silly to be killed in the middle of one of those grand gestures one makes in slamming the card down that takes the trick. Suddenly he thinks of all the lives that must, in these last three years [of war], have ended in that grand gesture. It is too silly. He seems to see their poor lacerated souls, clutching their greasy dogeared cards, climb to a squalid Valhalla."[143]

Dos Passos expanded on this idea of senseless death in a machine war in his next novel, *Three Soldiers*. Taking specific aim at the "machine" itself—the army—Private Dan Fuselli, one of the featured three soldiers, was "seized by despair" because in the army, "he was so far from anyone who cared about him, so lost in the vast machine."[144] Dos Passos is the most vehement but by no means the only soldier-author from World War I to resent the impersonal, uncaring army and the senselessness of death in modern warfare. Private Mackin, listening to the enemy's heavy artillery shells rumbling past overhead, reckoned that he and his comrades did not even count for enough to rate being bombarded by the big guns: "[The shells] were the big ones, not meant for little men. Smaller, screaming shells would do for us. The big ones homed on distant, vital things, on targets of importance, just casually on men. Men don't count."[145]

To some degree, all soldiers in the wars of the draft era had to come to grips with the realization that their individual sacrifices and deaths meant little to the big picture, as did Jesse Glenn Gray and his fellow GIs during World War II: "Even the simplest minds among us could sense that it mattered relatively little to the collective body whether he survived or not."[146] Paul Fussell points out that if the doughboy was "anonymous," then the GI was even less: "If in the First World War you're one of over four million uniformed Americans, you're actually pretty anonymous. But if in the Second World War you're one of sixteen million, you're really nothing."[147]

Some GIs first gained a sense of their own insignificance when confronted with visual proof of the massiveness of the war effort, such as witnessing a huge invasion convoy. For the correspondent Richard Tregaskis, the sights and sounds of a furious naval battle off Guadalcanal brought it home: "In that moment I think most of us who were there watching the gunfire suddenly knew . . . that we were only tiny particles caught up in the gigantic whirlpool of war. The terror and power and magnificence of man-made thunder and lightning made that point real. One had the feeling of being at the mercy of great accumulated forces far more powerful than anything human. We were only pawns in a battle of the gods, then, and we knew it."[148]

Private Sledge, in a gun pit in a miserable mangrove swamp on Peleliu

Island, came to the same realization. He had not witnessed any awesome naval battle, nor could he describe his feelings with the grandeur of Tregaskis, but the jolt to his sense of self-worth was just as great: "Slowly the reality of it all formed in my mind: we were expendable! It was difficult to accept. We came from a nation and a culture that values life and the individual. To find oneself in a situation where your life seems of little value is the ultimate in loneliness. It is a humbling experience."[149]

Even the nickname GI, which stood for Government Issue, added to the soldier's sense of insignificance. Private Atwell did not like it: "I even resent being called a GI, and particularly by someone who isn't one. It's always demeaning."[150] The term GI carried over into the Korean War, and so too did the soldier's sense of being an expendable cipher. Lieutenant Matthias, newly arrived at his regiment's command post in Korea, learned that the platoon he was to lead was but one of many symbols on an operations map: "I was now experiencing the placement of one Lieutenant Matthias in the big picture. I was losing my identity. I was about to be reclassified as a number. . . . This number would be recognized on the maps, charts and strategic overlays. . . . At the time it was difficult to accept that I was to lose my identity. . . . It is easy to see why the frontline Marine often felt unimportant and manipulated."[151]

For the soldier in Vietnam, expendability took on ominous new proportions. The grunt came to believe, at least at times, that the "green machine" was deliberately dangling him as bait to attract the attention of an otherwise elusive foe. Once the enemy took the bait, he would be clobbered with artillery, air strikes, and attack helicopters. And some of the bait was killed in the process.

Several scholars of the Vietnam War have commented on the use of the infantryman as bait, and they are understandably critical of the practice.[152] Two qualifiers are often overlooked, however. First, the use of infantry as bait was not unique to the Vietnam War. The doughboy or GI rifleman was frequently sent to find the enemy, and given a stationary foe prepared to ambush or defend, the enemy usually drew first blood. Rifleman Curtis James Morrow, for example, assesses infantry operations in the Korean War in 1951: "My company got a lot of patrol duties which usually ended up with us walking into an ambush. I was later told that that was the idea behind patrols, to locate enemy positions and pinpoint targets for our artillery and [Lockheed] F-86 [Sabre] fighter jets."[153]

The second qualifier concerns intent. John Helmer condemns the Vietnam-era military for deliberately using soldiers as bait, without concern for losses: "Military performance is primarily a function of damage done to the other side; the price we pay for that is of little or no consequence. The men who are lost are expendable."[154] This argument is absurd. Even assuming a military hierarchy without a shred of human compassion, no army can afford to write off losses as of "little or no consequence." The American military has always been concerned over losses, and that is why the army has historically expended bullets instead of lives.[155]

Nevertheless, the grunt did feel, on occasion, that he and his unit were being used to attract the enemy. And "bait" is the term that appears in the memoirs. Machine gunner Stanley Goff observes: "Night movement, that was a suicidal patrol. That was one of the worst patrols you could ever go out on. The purpose of it was for you to walk up on Charlie and for him to hit you, and then for our hardware to wipe them out. We were used as scapegoats to find out where they were. That was all we were—bait."[156]

The Vietnam War veteran James Webb uses the bait theme in his novel *Fields of Fire:* "Back in the villes again. Somebody said it was an operation with a name, but it had its own name: Dangling the Bait. . . . Inviting an enemy attack much as a worm seeks to attract a fish."[157]

The soldier resented being used as bait, or cannon fodder, because it violated his sense of individual worth. The army sometimes fueled that resentment through policies and practices that further damaged his self-esteem. When the citizen-soldier volunteered to serve, or at least acquiesced, he expected to be treated with the respect befitting a warrior. Instead, he often encountered what Lee Kennett calls "institutionalized inequality."[158] The lower ranking enlisted man had to perform menial services, sometimes for the personal benefit of his noncommissioned or commissioned officers, and he resented the perquisites enjoyed by officers simply because of their rank and station. Kennett was specifically referring to World War II, but this resentment was not limited to the GI.[159]

The soldier got his first taste of the army's caste system during his initial training. Most recruits assumed that once they completed training and were bona fide soldiers, they would be accorded more respect and fewer "shit details." They discovered, however, that a wide gap still remained between their rights and privileges and those of the officer corps. For the soldier en route to war, this gap was painfully evident on the troopship. The officers, while not living in luxury, usually berthed on the more comfortable upper decks and ate in a separate ship's officers' mess. The more sensitive officers realized that such arrangements were bound to cause resentment among the soldiers. Lieutenant Munschauer, en route to the Philippines in World War II, noted that "necessarily, the military is autocratic, not democratic, yet even when that is understood, civilians in uniform who have been reared to believe that all men are created equal cannot easily put aside the notion of equality, especially on a Navy ship, where inequality is flaunted."[160]

To the enlisted soldiers crammed below decks, the officers did indeed seem to be flaunting their shipboard privileges. Corporal Rogers, en route to France on a British troopship in World War I, gazed jealously at the "officers lying in steamer chairs on the upper deck, with Red Cross girls in chairs each side of them. Young fellows, my age, who probably knew no more than I did, but they had stayed in some R.O.T.C. and now they were officers."[161]

The shipboard officers sometimes did things that exacerbated the soldier's resentment. While passing through the Panama Canal en route to the Pacific in

World War II, Captain William Hawkins and his fellow officers chipped in some cash and sent a few of their number ashore to purchase liquor to set up an officers' bar. The men did not fail to notice the booze being loaded aboard. Hawkins recalls, "God, if looks could kill! Naturally, the men are thinking that all the officers will be drinking themselves silly, while the troops are doing all the work. It was a mistake for us to get the liquor all right, but live and learn, I guess."[162]

Arrival overseas did not end the institutionalized inequalities. As Kennett has noted, institutionalized inequality was common in World War II, but it was even more evident in World War I.[163] Officers of all ranks in the AEF were allowed, at least unofficially, enlisted orderlies (dubbed "dog robbers" by their fellow soldiers). Also, the best rations were frequently diverted to the officers' mess table, which was usually set up in the choicest available billets. As Will Judy describes it, "The juiciest cuts of meat in some mysterious way always ended up in the officers' mess. The two or three bedrooms in a village were never soiled by corporal's boots. The supply sergeant could always find a new overcoat for the lieutenant. The major ever cautioned the cook that the eggs must be fresh, and the colonel never wanted for good cigars."[164]

Judy was not merely one of the grousers common to every army, although he complained more vehemently than most. Other soldiers support his claims. Private Mackin was detailed to carry rations to his marine unit's officers' mess while the men went hungry. When word of this inequity spread, complaints were loud and bitter: "What a hell of a war this is. Them damn officers get to go out with the nurses behind the lines, have a dog robber to make their lousy beds and spread their blankets, draw a hell of a lot more pay than we poor bastards—and now beans, for them only."[165]

World War II memoirs make fewer references to preferential rations for officers, at least in units near the front. Nor did junior officers have "dog robbers." GIs nevertheless resented officer privileges. Corporal Carl M. Becker remembers little about the officers in his antiaircraft battalion, except that they enjoyed their perquisites. They were "shadowy figures who had virtually nothing to do directly with our everyday lives. They . . . had their whiskey, women, and steaks and dreamed of higher command and the preference that shoulder straps might give them in civilian life. Theirs was a different Army, a different war, from ours."[166]

Becker's comment about "shadowy figures" reflects the egalitarian GIs' resentment of officers who were standoffish or who assumed an air of superiority. Soldiers understood that their officers had important duties and responsibilities and thus deserved cooperation and respect. But if an officer lorded over his men simply because of his rank, he was immediately resented, as Bill Mauldin notes: "Many old line officers are no doubt shocked at a spirit of passive rebellion which occasionally shows itself in this citizen army. That's the whole answer. It is a citizen army, and it has in its enlisted ranks many men who in civil life were not accustomed to being directed to the back door and the servant quarters. To taking orders, yes; but to taking indignities, no."[167]

The "indignities" caused by institutionalized inequality largely evaporated at the front, as Mauldin himself pointed out: "But most combat outfits scrap tradition . . . when they go into battle. No man who depends upon those below him—not only for his success, but for his very life—is going to abuse his men unnecessarily. Not if he has good sense."[168] Not only did it make "good sense," but also conditions at the front left little room for officer privileges at any rate—the junior officer lived in a hole, ate combat rations, and got shot at like everyone else. Yet the institutionalized inequalities, and the concurrent resentment, could quickly reappear when the bullets stopped flying. Private Leckie observed that victory was close at hand when the officers' mess reappeared: "An officers' mess is one of the surest barometers of military success. So long as the officers continue to pig it with the men, there is danger of defeat. But once the officers' mess appears—raised almost on the bodies of the foe, contrived of sticks and pieces of canvas or perhaps only an imaginary line like a taboo—once this appears, and caste is restored, we know that victory is ours."[169]

Institutionalized inequality is less evident in memoirs from the Korean and Vietnam Wars. When a combat unit came out of the line in Korea or returned from the boonies in Vietnam, the officers did not enjoy a substantially better standard of living than their men. Thus a break from combat did not always result in the reestablishment of institutionalized inequality, but it did allow for a reemergence of what soldiers called "chickenshit," or "Mickey Mouse" in the Vietnam era. Fussell's classic definition remains the best:

Chickenshit refers . . . to behavior that makes military life worse than it need be: petty harassment of the weak by the strong; open scrimmage for power and authority and prestige; sadism thinly disguised as necessary discipline; a constant "paying off of old scores"; and insistence on the letter rather than the spirit of ordinances. Chickenshit is so called—instead of horse- or bull- or elephant shit—because it is small-minded and ignoble and takes the trivial seriously. Chickenshit can be recognized instantly because it never has anything to do with winning the war.[170]

The soldier was first exposed to chickenshit, and in a major way, during initial training. He assumed, as he had in the case of institutionalized inequality, that his graduation as a full-fledged soldier and assignment to a regular unit would put an end to chickenshit. Although abating somewhat, chickenshit did not go away. To the soldier's consternation, it thrived even in the overseas theaters of war. As Fussell explains, "Ultimately the only way to escape most of the chickenshit was to be in combat and so far forward as to be virtually unreachable and surely uninspectable."[171]

To some extent chickenshit was in the eye of the beholder. What was chickenshit to a soldier was the enforcement of standards and discipline to his sergeant or company commander. But sometimes chickenshit was just that, and when a soldier gained a reprieve from combat, he did not want to be bothered or taxed by Mickey Mouse inspections, work details, or regulations. Captain Camp was thus annoyed when he was tasked to provide an honor guard from his marine company for a formal regimental change of command in the midst of the Vietnam War. After several days of preparation for the ceremony, Camp noted that he and his men were eager to return to the dangers of combat: "The Marine Corps being the Marine Corps, we were called upon to shine our boots and clean everything spic and span. The troops were just overjoyed. Then we had to run inspections, do more cleaning and polishing, more inspections, and so forth. By about the third day, the troops were *begging* me to take them back into the field."[172]

Chickenshit had also plagued the grunts' predecessors in the Korean War. Corporal Russ found that "the discipline approaches that of boot camp" when his marine battalion was out of the line—calisthenics at 5:00 A.M. followed by a police of the area, rifle inspection, drill and ceremonies, tent inspection, classes, hikes, and training exercises: "This is what is called 'harassing the troops.' It is suggested that we take out our resentment on the Chinese later. One thousand men with persecution complexes."[173]

Russ was no lone malcontent, nor was chickenshit the sole property of the Marine Corps in Korea. Private Victor Fox found that rotation from the line signaled a return of the "fabled chickenshit of the 1st Cavalry Division," starting with the issuance of yellow paint (the color of the division's emblem) so that everything that did not move, to use an old army expression, could be painted. Inspections and even formal guard mount followed. In short, "everything a garrison soldier endured in the States became routine again."[174]

The veteran combatant resented chickenshit because it deprived him of free time on those occasions when he got a break from the fighting. Furthermore, it was demeaning—appropriate fare for a trainee, perhaps, but not for a warrior. Add in resentment of officer privileges perpetuated by institutionalized inequality and resentment over being treated as an expendable cog in an impersonal green machine, and Corporal Russ's comment about "men with persecution complexes" begins to take on real meaning. Thus resentment, like fear and anxiety, was a part of the emotional environment of war.

## THE VICISSITUDES OF WAR

Although the emotional and physical environment of war proved to be far more taxing than anticipated, most soldiers had entered combat with at least a vague understanding, thanks to their training, that war was dangerous and physically demanding. Training had not prepared the soldier, however, for one aspect of war that proved to be especially damaging to his psyche: he might die a senseless death simply because he was in the wrong place at the wrong time. The soldier learned that death in combat could occur in amazingly arbitrary ways. This discovery was traumatic because it meant that the skills he had worked so hard to master—weapons expertise, tactical savvy, and physical fitness—might all be for nought. In World War II Private Standifer and his fellow platoon scout gained an appreciation for war's potential randomness, even before experiencing combat. They had performed well on a training exercise but were nevertheless assessed as casualties. Standifer's friend said to him, "'Leon, we soldiered today, did everything right, and both got killed.' I agreed with him and was just as worried."[175]

It took a battlefield incident, however, before most soldiers grasped the random nature of death in war. In the midst of a fight in a French village, Bob Hoffman and his comrade simultaneously raised themselves up from behind a wall and began firing their rifles. A German sniper, thus presented with identical targets, killed Hoffman's comrade. More than twenty years later, Hoffman still pondered the sniper's choice, but he realized it was just part of a larger issue: "Many things were hard to understand, especially why one man would die, hundreds, thousands, even millions . . . and some were to live."[176]

Soldiers had difficulty accepting how arbitrary death could be. In James Webb's *Fields of Fire,* several marines were killed or wounded by booby traps set off by other men, a distressingly common occurrence. Will Goodrich, a newly arrived replacement, was thoroughly alarmed by the implications of this tragic incident: "The two booby traps had shaken him. The victims were selected so randomly. You could be 100 percent right and still be 100 percent dead. . . . There's not a goddamn thing you can do about it, either."[177]

Soldiers were further shocked to discover that not only did men die in arbitrary ways in combat, but they also died with alarming frequency in senseless accidents often unrelated to fighting the enemy. Accidents of every imaginable type occurred in the combat zone. Some were distinctly military in nature, involving weapons or equipment. Other accidents, such as falls or vehicular mishaps, could just as easily have occurred in civilian life, although conditions in the war zone often contributed to their frequency or seriousness.

Training accidents were common. Training was dangerous, sometimes involving the use of live ammunition and small explosive charges to simulate the noise, smoke, and confusion of real combat. Occasionally someone was wounded or even killed. Weapons training was also dangerous—soldiers were injured learning to use small arms, grenades, or explosives.[178]

Equally prevalent were traffic accidents. These often occurred for the same reasons that they do on the freeway. Tired drivers fell asleep at the wheel or drove too fast. Rain, ice, and snow added the usual hazards. In other cases, combat conditions contributed to the accident. For example, using headlights in areas under enemy observation was suicidal, so drivers had to negotiate narrow, twisting, dangerous roads using dim black-out lights at most, and accidents resulted.[179]

Perhaps most frequent were accidents involving weapons and explosives. Soldiers were amazingly careless at times, and when everyone was armed to the teeth, accidents were inevitable. Men blew themselves up with grenades, shot each other or themselves while cleaning their supposedly empty weapons, or injured themselves fiddling with captured weapons about which they knew nothing—the story related by Captain Richard M. Hardison of how his driver set off a German *panzerfaust* (bazooka) inside a jeep being a classic example. He accidentally triggered the weapon, launching the rocket warhead through the canvas top of his jeep, over a building, and into an empty field beyond. The driver was treated for burns, but fortunately no one else was injured.[180] And then there is the soldier's puzzling fascination with duds—unexploded ordnance that commonly litters the battlefield. Despite being well aware that these were extremely dangerous and best left for the explosive ordnance disposal experts, soldiers regularly detonated duds by picking them up, thinking they would make a nice souvenir.[181]

Certain units were more prone to accidents because of the nature of their work. Engineers' memoirs are filled with examples of injuries and deaths involving heavy equipment and demolition work.[182] Artillerymen describe faulty shells that exploded prematurely or gun tubes that burst, with devastating results, from wear or overheating.[183] And if the lone pilot's memoir included in this book is any indication, helicopters often fell from the sky in Vietnam without the assistance of the enemy.[184]

Soldiers swam and bathed in streams, lakes, and oceans and sometimes drowned.[185] On cold winter nights in Korea, men were fortunate enough, during the static-warfare stage of the fighting, to have a stove in their bunker to warm themselves but sometimes blew themselves up.[186] Some accidents were simply bizarre. One soldier was seriously injured standing in the chow line when a huge icicle broke off the roof and fell on him.[187] On New Britain Island in the Solomons during World War II, nineteen soldiers were killed by falling trees.[188]

Soldiers did not go off to war expecting to die in a senseless accident. Nor did they expect to die at the hands of their own comrades, but soldiers soon discovered that such deaths occurred with distressing regularity. After nearly being killed by fire from an American tank, Private Sledge spoke for all combat soldiers when he said, "to be killed by the enemy was bad enough; that was a real possibility I had prepared myself for. But to be killed by mistake by my own comrades was something I found hard to accept. It was just too much."[189]

The not entirely accurate term "fratricide" is used to refer to the accidental killing of a soldier by his own side, although the equally unsatisfactory oxymoron "friendly fire" is also frequently used. Curiously, the fratricide phenomenon has received little systematic analysis. Probably the best known study on the subject, prepared by historian and army officer Charles R. Shrader, claims that "the casualties attributable to friendly fire in modern war constitute a statistically insignificant portion of total casualties (perhaps less than 2 percent)."[190] However, more recent studies analyzing battles and campaigns in World War II and the Vietnam War find that conservatively 10 to 15 percent of the casualties were caused by friendly fire.[191] The difference between a 2 percent rate (one in fifty) and a 15 percent rate (one in about seven) is obviously significant. Given the hard realities of war, a 2 percent rate might seem not only acceptable but also unavoidable, as long as battles are fought by scared, tired, error-prone humans. But one in every seven casualties is another matter. Which figure is more accurate?

One way to find out is to ask the soldiers themselves, something few researchers have bothered to do. One exception is the sociologist Arnold M. Rose, who surveyed 1,754 enlisted combat soldiers in Italy in World War II about friendly-fire incidents, among other things. He found that "about 60 per cent . . . reported that they had been fired on in some way by our own troops several times, and 20 per cent more said it happened once."[192] One survey in one campaign is not conclusive, nor do Rose's statistics reveal how many were hit by friendly fire, but the fact that 80 percent of the soldiers surveyed had been fired upon by their own side strongly suggests that Shrader's 2 percent is conservative, and if the testimony from soldiers' memoirs is representative, considerably so.[193]

Soldiers managed to kill one another accidentally in almost every conceivable way, but certain types of fratricide are most frequently mentioned. Being hit by one's own artillery occurred in all the wars of the draft era. Sometimes the artillery was at fault for inaccurately calculating the firing data, improperly setting the data on the guns, or using the wrong amount of propellant charge. At other times, the target location was inaccurately sent to the artillery by the person requesting the fire. On rare occasions, faulty ammunition caused inaccurate fire. A classic example occurred in Lieutenant Lawrence's company during World War I. The Germans began shelling the company's position. The American artillery responded, but their shells fell short, also landing on Lawrence's position. To add insult to injury, the company first sergeant had deserted with the signal rockets, so Lawrence could not signal for the fire to be lifted: "We were caught in both barrages, and it was terrible—shells coming from front and rear at the same time."[194]

An even more traumatic casualty producer, although not as frequent as artillery fratricide, was strafing or bombing by friendly aircraft. At times, pilots mistook friendly troops for the enemy. At other times, planes were directed to attack locations that were supposedly enemy held but in reality were in friendly hands. In fairness to American air and artillery support, more often than not the attacks worked as they were supposed to. The memoirs note, besides the incidents of fratricide, the many times when strafing or bombing saved American lives and inflicted devastating losses on the enemy. Lieutenant Munschauer, fighting in the Philippine Islands in World War II, believed the benefits outweighed the risks: "The risk of being hit by friendly fire was worth it. Getting through that terrain would have been far bloodier without planes to rake fire into the brush."[195]

Munschauer's rational assessment of American fire support is no doubt valid, but for men who had just been strafed by a plane from their own side, anger, not rationality, predominated. Occasionally they even returned fire. Private MacArthur's artillery battery did so in World War I:

> A squadron of American planes appeared and circled overhead in Ferris-wheel formation. Like saps we waved at them. Immediately they dived into the field, spraying us with machine-gun bullets. There was a howl of rage and surprise. . . . The half-wit aviators kept it up, horses and men dropping right and left. Every rifle in the field rattled back. Ray Quisno and Sam Wallace jumped for the battery machine guns, and tracer bullets began to smoke into our bright war birds' back. They sailed away followed by brimstone curses and more shots in the back. If we could have brought one of them down we would have torn his heart out.[196]

This incident serves as lead-in to another variety of fratricide—the shooting down of friendly aircraft by ground forces. One of the most spectacular, and costly, cases of fratricide occurred when American cargo planes, loaded with paratroopers about to make a night jump into Sicily in World War II, were fired upon by American troops and ships.[197] Lieutenant Johnson and his antitank platoon were some of the thousands of soldiers and sailors who blazed away at the aircraft, believing them to be German. The next day, as he recorded in his diary, he learned the truth: "Found out this A.M. that parachutes last night were our own 82nd Airborne. Something all screwed up: army and navy shore outfits not informed of paratroop drop—fired on chutes. A terrible mess. Understand about 400 paratroopers killed."[198] For paratrooper Ross S. Carter, on the receiving end of all that fire, it was indeed a "terrible mess." Gazing from the open door of his cargo plane, Carter saw tracers crisscross the night sky and heard the antiaircraft shells exploding: "Some of our planes tumbled out of the air like burning crosses; others stopped like a bird shot in flight, crumpled and plummeted. Still others exploded and disintegrated."[199] Luckily for Carter, his plane flew through the gauntlet unscathed.

Infantry soldiers alone, improperly armed for engaging aircraft, rarely brought one down, friendly or enemy. When the combat soldier accidentally killed someone from his own side, it was almost always a fellow ground combatant. Armored-vehicle crews, with the hatches closed in the midst of a smoke-filled battle, could not see well and sometimes fired on friendly troops or accidentally ran over them.[200] Sometimes troops at a distance were mistaken for the enemy and fired upon at long range by machine guns or mortars. But most frequently soldiers shot one another at close range at night, mistaking friend for enemy.

Soldiers made mistakes and were killed by their own side, but fear was usually the catalyst that led to triggers being pulled. One of the reasons why soldiers hated night patrols was because their chances of being shot by their own comrades were good, unless everything went according to plan. If a patrol did not follow the prescribed route and return to friendly lines at the anticipated time and location, or if other units in the area were not told that a patrol was going out, then a burst of friendly fire might well be the consequence. Sentries and machine gunners who did not know that a friendly patrol was in the area tended to respond to a noise in front of their position with a thrown grenade or a burst of fire.[201] Challenges and passwords were a normal backup device, but a soldier might forget or not know the password, or be so frightened that he shot first and challenged later.[202]

When the enemy was known to be a skillful and frequent night infiltrator, tensions could reach extremes. While fighting in the Pacific in World War II, and at times in other wars and theaters, American troops were so jittery at night that virtually any movement would draw fire. In the fading light of dusk during the Korean War, a nervous replacement shot an approaching GI, without first challenging him, because the GI was wearing his soft cap, common headgear of the Chinese; Americans usually wore their helmets.[203] A marine in Sledge's unit, fleeing from Japanese infiltrators on Peleliu, was himself mistaken for a Japanese and clubbed and shot.[204]

The soldiers especially feared Japanese infiltrators, who were known to kill with a knife or bayonet. Infantryman Sam LaMagna described how, at night on New Georgia Island, the men hunkered down in one- or two-man foxholes, and it was every man for himself. One of LaMagna's comrades bayoneted his own foxhole mate because he thought he was a Japanese. Another man cracked up and, imagining everyone to be Japanese, began firing indiscriminately, wounding his own comrades, until someone shot him in turn to prevent further casualties and because the commotion was attracting Japanese mortar fire.[205]

This type of close-in fratricide was most demoralizing because the soldier pulling the trigger invariably discovered, after the fact, that he had killed someone from his own side, often from his own unit. Sergeant Frankel nearly opened fire with his tank on a group of approaching infantry. For some reason, perhaps a sixth sense, he held his fire. The approaching infantry he had spared were Americans. By an oversight, he was the only one not informed that friendly soldiers would be approaching. Frankel contemplated the "catastrophic guilt" and the "monumental" consequences to his own "peace of mind" that would have resulted if he had opened fire.[206]

Although the experts may not agree on the statistics, the memoirs provide vivid proof that fratricide was common, and experts and soldiers alike concur with Frankel about the devastating guilt that could result from killing a fellow soldier.

## EXPERIENCING THE "RADICAL DISCONTINUITY"

The environment of war, though undeniably malign, was not unremittingly so. The soldier, who of necessity lived close to nature, recounted moments when bullets were not flying, the weather pleasant, and the view remarkable, even spectacular. Indeed the pleasure derived from these moments of tranquillity was enhanced because they stood in such stark contrast to war's horrors. Corporal Wilder recalled a summer day in France in 1918: "It was a beautiful scene. The valley of one of the great rivers; one could see miles and there was color in the clouds. First time I have forgotten the war for a long time."[207]

The GIs in World War II found moments of beauty and serenity in the same region. Sergeant Giles and one of his comrades enjoyed a walk in the country on one of the first pleasant days of spring in 1945: "The day was beautiful & warm, the sun was shining, everything beginning to turn green & it just felt good to get into the country & be peaceful. We found a pretty little creek & sat on the bank & talked."[208]

Soldiers fighting in the extreme climates and terrain of the Pacific, Korea, and Vietnam did not comment positively on their surroundings as often as soldiers in Europe did, but the Pacific warriors occasionally found pleasure in nature. Even that least appreciated of countries, Korea, had its moments. Lieutenant James Hamilton Dill, for example, enjoyed the "Arcadian" beauty of the isolated little village of Mungol-li, unique for its trees complete with nesting cranes: "Farmers out cultivating fields. Houses intact. Everything green. So beautiful after the desolation I am used to."[209]

Positive comments about Vietnam could also be heard on occasion. Lieutenant Downs appreciated the "terrific view" from his mountaintop defensive position near the South China Sea: "That night we were treated to the spectacle of hundreds of fishing boats up and down the shore as far as we could see. Each boat was allowed to fish if it hung a lantern from the mast at night. From our vantage point, they looked like a line of slowly undulating, illuminated pearls."[210]

Yet even as the soldier appreciated moments of natural beauty, he was struck by how out of place they seemed. He was experiencing, first hand, the "radical discontinuity" between the environments of war and peace described by Eric Leed. Peaceful activities and natural beauty did not belong in the soldier's world. Robert Merrick, after a short truck ride, found it almost disconcerting to have been transported from the one environment to the other: "It certainly seemed strange, after having been at the front, in constant sound of the cannon, to get back of the lines into a flourishing, prosperous town with stores, hotels, cafes, and all the appurtenances of civilization."[211]

Ernie Pyle, in the midst of the fighting near Kasserine Pass in North Africa in World War II, similarly sensed that the environments of war and peace somehow should not coexist: "The battlefield was an incongruous thing. Always there was some ridiculous impingement of normalcy on a field of battle. There on that day it was the Arabs. They were herding their camels, just as usual. . . . Children walked along, driving their little sack-laden burros, as tanks and guns clanked past them. The sky was filled with planes and smoke burst from screaming shells."[212]

Sergeant Frankel experienced the same sense of discontinuity in western Europe in World War II: "Of course, there's often an incongruity between war and the pastoral environment that either bears it or witnesses it; by 1945 we would be totally familiar with this awful paradox."[213] Private Sledge, during a respite from the fighting on Okinawa, also experienced Frankel's "awful paradox" as he rested by a peaceful, fern-lined stream, "a beautiful place . . . so out of context with the screaming hell close above it."[214]

What these soldiers found "out of context" or "incongruous" was not the sound of the guns or the battlefield devastation, but natural beauty and peaceful human activity. These were men so immersed in the physical and emotional environment of war that peacetime sights and sounds seemed strange and out of place. How did the soldier become so totally immersed in that environment, and what effect did it have on him?

# 3
# Immersion in the Environment

The confident, physically fit recruit who went off to battle ended up a dirty, exhausted, fear-ridden combatant so immersed in war that the sight of normal peacetime activities struck him as out of place, even surreal. Lord Charles McM. Moran, a British battalion surgeon in World War I, described this immersion process: "[The soldier] had seen men go till none were left of those who had fought with him. He had gazed upon the face of death too long until exhaustion had dried him up making him so much tinder, which a chance spark of fear might set alight. He was forced at last to see the odds, by a wound perhaps, by a bad part of the line, by gas, by an unhealthy atmosphere in the mess, by some narrow escape that led him to ask can such luck last."[1]

Over time the soldier became aware of the constant danger around him and the distinct possibility of his own demise; at the same time, fear and exhaustion made standing the strain increasingly difficult. Ernie Pyle, covering the fighting in North Africa in World War II, identified another significant aspect of the immersion process: "War coarsens most people. Men live rough and talk rough, and if they didn't toughen up inside they simply wouldn't be able to take it."[2] But just how coarse could a soldier become? For Private Eugene B. Sledge and his fellow marines during the grim fighting on Peleliu Island in World War II, the "fierce struggle for survival . . . eroded the veneer of civilization and made savages of us all."[3]

The brutal environment of war thus presented two closely related problems for the soldier: how to survive while not losing his last shred of humanity in the process. Private Richard E. Ogden struggled to do both in Vietnam: "I was aware of the subtle changes in my mental state. . . . Complex issues and problems were becoming too simplified. There was a gleam of hope in the fact that I was aware of these changes. The fight to remain alive was one problem; the fight to remain human was quite another."[4]

Immersion in war was thus a process of discovering combat's dangers and hardships while struggling to survive and maintain a moral compass. This process, James R. Ebert points out, was inescapably "regressive."[5] The average soldier emerged from the initial shock of combat a confident and effective veteran, but in time he became increasingly aware of the odds against him while suffering the physically debilitating effects of continuous combat, often in a harsh climate. He began to lose his nerve, eventually breaking down or becoming dangerously fatalistic. Only by understanding this regressive process can one begin to comprehend how a soldier could fervently wish for a wound or even inflict one on himself, kill an enemy attempting to surrender in the heat of battle, take genuine delight in seeing rear-echelon soldiers of his own side blown away, or calmly munch on combat rations while sitting amid mangled corpses.

## FROM GANGPLANK FEVER TO FIRST COMBAT

Most soldiers emerged from the training process physically fit and confident. Some were even impatient to get overseas, fearing they might miss the war. These eager warriors, often young and single, did not think about their own mortality. Lieutenant Robert G. Merrick, arriving with his artillery battalion in France in 1918, claimed that he and "every American soldier . . . had been hoping and longing for the day when he would get to the front."[6] Lieutenant Paul Fussell, off to World War II with his infantry division, if not exactly "hoping and longing" for combat, was nevertheless optimistic: "As the 103rd Division sailed away on the troop transport *General Brooks,* I simply radiated college-boy optimism. Later, I would tell encouraging lies to Mother and Dad in my letters, but now I was honest when I wrote home, 'I feel very confident and safe.'"[7]

Private Matthew Brennan and his fellow replacements, about to fly to Vietnam in 1965, were equally confident, even eager: "The replacements at Oakland felt and acted like part of a conquering army. Most of us didn't understand what was really happening in Vietnam. We believed that the war had reached its final stages and that we might arrive after the last big battles were won. . . . We were too naive to be afraid."[8]

Not all soldiers, however, shipped out with the same enthusiasm as Brennan. Anxiety over leaving loved ones and uncertainty about what lay ahead made many soldiers "nervous in the service," to use an army adage. Corporal Carl M. Becker, en route to the Pacific with his antiaircraft battalion in World War II, noticed an atmosphere of bravado, but he knew that it was a façade: "Our apparent courage notwithstanding, we were apprehensive, fearful men and boys. Had we voiced our real feelings, we would have diminished ourselves in one another's eyes. . . . We remembered and longed for our families, girls in our arms. We wished for an immediate ending to the war that would send our ship in a peaceful direction to the United States."[9]

A forlorn Private Randolph Stephens, en route to Korea, watched the American coastline recede as his ship left Puget Sound: "I stayed by the rail a long time, doing some soul searching and wondering if someday I would be seeing those same lights again."[10] As Private David Parks and his comrades in the First Infantry Division prepared for deployment to Vietnam, their morale was not improved by the nightly news: "We listen to the war broadcasts as we pack each day. One minute you're packing; the next minute you're hearing about the number of men killed. And you wonder if someday you'll be in that count. Fear is creeping in now. Nobody talks or jokes as much as they used to."[11]

For those soldiers least motivated and emotionally stable, orders for overseas movement triggered real or feigned physical and mental ailments, a condition the World War II GI nicknamed "gangplank fever."[12] Battalion surgeon Klaus H. Huebner believed that some of these men were "probably excellent actors with more endurance than their medical officer or company commander. Since one rotten apple, however, can spoil a barrel, we got rid of all problem cases."[13] Other soldiers attempted, with varying degrees of success, to go AWOL or to get themselves incarcerated to miss overseas movement.[14]

After the rotten apples were culled out, often by a discharge for medical or disciplinary reasons, the remaining soldiers departed for the combat zone. As early as World War II, individual replacements sometimes flew overseas, but units and their equipment, of necessity, traveled by ship. The voyage was long, boring, and uncomfortable, although not all the journeys were equally wretched. Some ships, notably the luxury liners converted to carry troops, were fast and relatively comfortable, although invariably overcrowded. At the other extreme were the small, old rust buckets that provided few comforts, rode the waves miserably, and took forever to complete a passage.[15]

The memoirs tell a common tale of being packed like sardines in tiers of bunks or hammocks. Seasickness reached epidemic proportions in rough seas, with the overpowering smell of vomit pervading the poorly ventilated sleeping quarters. The troops stood for hours in galley lines for food of dubious origin. The men did calisthenics on deck to keep in shape, but generally their fitness suffered. Training was mostly limited to classroom briefings for lack of space, although a few innovative units practiced firing machine guns and even mortars off their ships' fantails. The bored men read and played cards—gambling pots reached extraordinary sums on occasion, since most players figured that they would not need much money where they were going.[16]

The soldier disembarked in the theater of war either as a member of a unit or as an individual replacement, and his first experience of combat varied accordingly. A soldier who was part of a green unit was buoyed by the presence of comrades he trusted and by the confidence typical of green units. A common theme in World War I memoirs is green-unit eagerness to come to grips with the Hun. Private Albert M. Ettinger's 165th Infantry Regiment (which would not forsake its original National Guard designation, the Sixty-ninth New York), after being gassed and sporadically shelled during its initial stint in the trenches, was more eager than ever for a serious scrap: "The 69th had never flinched from a battle and never would. We were tired of all that mustard gas shit, and now we could get our hands on those Goddamned Germans. Many of the boys just relished that prospect."[17]

Ettinger's regiment was not alone in its eagerness. Doughboys frequently report on the displeasure of war-weary French allies over the arrival of a fresh American unit in their heretofore quiet corner of the front. The impromptu live-and-let-live system in place between the French and the Germans in such quiet sectors was soon disrupted by doughboys scrambling to be the first to pull a lanyard or trigger and draw German blood.[18] Corporal Amos N. Wilder's artillery battery, for example, took up position next to a French battery that had not fired a shell in two months. The French were not happy to see the doughboy cannoneers arrive: "Some in the French billets eye us askance. They have been living on indulgent terms with the Boche for some time. Their artillery had been well enough trained not to irritate the enemy. Now comes the American with his aggressive tactics and stirs up the hornets' nest so that they have to live within two steps of shelters, gas masks and helmets."[19]

Green-unit eagerness was evident in World War II as well. Ernie Pyle, after spending months with veteran troops in North Africa and Italy, visited unblooded units training in England for the invasion of France: "Not for ages had I been with a combat unit which had not yet been in battle. . . . The really noticeable difference was their eagerness to 'get a crack at the Jerries.' After they had a chance to crack at them for a few months, I knew they would be just as eager to let someone else have a turn at it." Combat would undoubtedly be a rude awakening for this unit, but the men's enthusiasm would help sustain them in their first battle. So too, Pyle understood, would their confidence in one another: "They had trained so long that they functioned almost automatically. They all knew every man on the team; they knew his temperament and how he would react. They have faith in each other. Only those who have fought realize what confidence that produces."[20]

American units first on the scene during the Korean and Vietnam Wars were also confident, as Lieutenant Lyle Rishell, an infantry platoon leader in the first division to arrive in Korea in 1950, noted: "There was tremendous optimism shared by the soldiers. Many believed us to be invincible, and most had little awareness of what lay ahead."[21] Lieutenant Philip Caputo and his marine battalion, one of the first units to arrive in Vietnam, were equally confident: "We believed in all the myths created by that most articulate and elegant mythmaker, John Kennedy. . . . There was nothing we could not do because we were Americans, and for the same reason, whatever we did was right."[22]

Caputo soon discovered, as did Rishell, that being American did not automatically guarantee victory. They were not the first to be so deluded, as Pyle pointed out after the embarrassing defeat at Kasserine Pass in America's combat debut against the Germans in World War II: "It was all right to have a good opinion of ourselves, but we Americans were so smug with our cockiness. We somehow felt that just because we were Americans we could whip our weight in wildcats."[23]

Herein lies the downside of going to war as part of a green outfit. Chauvinistic American units invariably believed that they could whip their weight in wildcats, but the reality was that green troops with inexperienced leaders made costly mistakes. They unnecessarily exposed themselves to enemy observation and fire until learning to use cover and concealment. Green soldiers bunched up under fire, resulting in heavy casualties. At night they were careless about noise and light, and trigger-happy lookouts gave away their position and drew enemy fire. Units learned the hard way that running out from under an artillery barrage when caught in the open was less costly than laying down and taking it.[24]

The list could go on. The grunts in John M. Del Vecchio's Vietnam War novel *The 13th Valley* debated the pros and cons of going to war as a green unit versus joining a veteran outfit as a green replacement. The green-unit option came in second as far as Sergeant Daniel Egan was concerned: "I remember, just after I got here, talkin to guys who'd come in around Da Nang. They arrived, some of em, in '67. They'd say that they'd come from the World as a cherry unit and the entire unit would be moved to a ville or someplace to defend and they'd be there the day they arrived. . . . Just right to the boonies. They didn't even have time to get acclimated. That's why so many of em had their shit scattered. They weren't comin in as one cherry among one hundred dudes with time in-country. They were virgin units who'd never been shot at. Didn't take long before they knew the score but by then only half of em were still around."[25]

Egan implies that a green replacement assigned to a veteran unit had a better chance of survival—a valid implication, assuming that the replacements were given an opportunity to train and assimilate. All too often, however, replacements were rushed straight into combat. Whatever the military necessity for doing so, it was a disastrous way of introducing them to the environment of war. The new replacement had no chance to be integrated properly into his unit. Thus he felt alone, even abandoned. Correspondent Pyle questioned the wisdom of sending replacements straight into the line at night in the Anzio beachhead during World War II: "All of us who have had any association at all with the imminence of death know that the main thing a man wants is not to be alone. He wants company, and preferably someone he knows. To go up to the brink of possible death in the nighttime in a faraway land, puzzled and afraid, knowing no one, and facing the worst moment of your life totally alone—that takes strength."[26]

The memoirs verify that replacements were indeed often hustled straight into combat and that Pyle's reservations about the practice are justified. Marine private Elton E. Mackin was part of a group of replacements whisked into the lines to reinforce a decimated rifle company in Belleau Wood in 1918. In the midst of combat, it was every man for himself: "Any men who carried the notion that someone was responsible for guarding them from harm soon knew they were mistaken. Such officers and noncoms as were left when we arrived had other things to do. We who were to live awhile soon knew our way about, without a shepherd. There wasn't time for a proper initiation."[27]

Being thrown into combat without a "proper initiation" was even more traumatic for replacement leaders. Such was the case for Lieutenant John L. Munschauer when he took charge of his infantry platoon in the Philippines during World War II: "When I arrived at Company K, no one told me what was going on, where we were located, where the Japs were, nothing of the immediate tactical situation."[28] Within minutes of his arrival, he and his platoon were shelled and assaulted. Luckily they held against the attack.

On the other hand, when replacements were given additional training and a chance to integrate into their squad and platoon when out of combat, their chances of survival went up. Far more than commonly perceived, soldiers trained when not in combat. Sometimes they were learning new tactics for an upcoming operation, such as an amphibious assault or an attack on a fortified position. At other times they were familiarizing themselves with new weapons or equipment. But frequently they trained, not because the veterans needed it but to integrate replacements.

There was rarely enough time to completely integrate and train replacements, but units did what they could. Father Francis P. Duffy described a four-week training program laid out by his regiment when in a rest camp after the Aisne-Marne offensive: "The training was necessary not so much for the old-timers as for the replacements." Duffy noted that the regiment was trying to avoid what had happened during the previous offensive, "where our replacements had to go into [the] line without anything like proper training."[29]

Lieutenant Wilson, who had to commit fresh replacements straight into combat during the bitter fighting in the Huertgen Forest during World War II, was determined to give the new men he received following the battle a better break: "Even though we were in reserve and were supposed to be recuperating, we had no time for rest. It would be suicidal to take those men into battle. We had to give them some intensive training while we had the chance." A five-day training period ensued, with weapons firing and classes "on the absolutely essential basics," and the men "responded well, being keen to learn and eager to try out all the weapons."[30]

During the Korean War, replacements were again thrown into the meat grinder with little or no preparation. During the desperate fighting around the Chosin Reservoir in winter 1950–1951, marine replacements were flown from Japan to forward airstrips in Korea and sent into combat, all in the same day.[31] The army likewise threw replacements directly into battle, according to Corporal Malcolm H. Dow: "We received replacements the afternoon we were scheduled to move up. The new people didn't even have time to undo their packs. They just rested a few minutes and then moved into action. I felt sorry for these new men; no one knew them and no one was really looking out for them."[32]

By the end of 1951, however, the fighting in Korea had settled into positional warfare, and replacements were more systematically integrated into their units. Divisions established orientation programs for new leaders, and replacement troops joined their units and trained when out of the lines.[33] Similar programs were adopted during the Vietnam War. Virtually every Vietnam War soldier-author who arrived as a replacement mentions receiving some in-country training.[34] This three-to-seven-day training period included classes on Viet Cong tactics, equipment, and booby traps; instructions on patrolling techniques; and the firing of various weapons.[35]

Following in-country training, the Vietnam War replacement joined his platoon or company. The replacement, or "cherry" or "FNG" (fucking new guy), then faced the challenge of fitting into a unit of veteran grunts. Recalling Sergeant Egan's implied theory, a cherry in a unit full of veterans was better off than a cherry in a unit full of cherries because the veterans could protect him and teach him the ropes. This theory further assumes, of course, that the veterans were willing and able to do so. Some historians and veterans point out, however, that the old-timers were more inclined to look out for themselves first. Historian Roger J. Spiller notes that "units long in combat are made up of small cliques of veterans who do not easily admit replacements into their ranks."[36] James Jones believes that veterans even went so far as to sacrifice replacements: "Smart replacements soon learned that they got the dirtiest most-exposed jobs. . . . The lucky, the tough, and the smart survived, and the rest were forgotten, shipped home, or buried."[37]

The notion of self-serving veterans sacrificing replacements should not be carried too far. Spiller is correct in his observation that veterans were reluctant to admit replacements into their ranks, but they did not ignore them or sacrifice them. As Appy points out in his study of Vietnam War soldiers, the FNG got a cool reception from veterans until he had proven himself, but "underneath this surface coolness . . . the more experienced men kept careful eyes on the replacements who joined their units, and the care they did take, however minimal, had an enormous impact on the new men."[38]

Veterans were slow to accept replacements, and even pitied or despised them for their lack of combat prowess, but they did try to teach them how to fight and survive, if only because everyone had to depend on one another. Audie Murphy, then a sergeant in the Anzio beachhead in World War II, displayed a typical mix of contempt yet need for fresh replacements: "The need for reinforcements is desperate. But we are suspicious and resentful of the new men that join us. As the days pass, if they prove their worth, they gradually grow into our clique and share the privilege of riding other replacements."[39]

Veterans did ride replacements, often scaring them with tales of combat, and as Murphy points out, acceptance was not automatic. The veterans first wanted to know, as one Vietnam grunt put it, if a replacement was a "shooter or a shaker."[40] Shooters were accepted. Marine lieutenant Howard Matthias noticed the same attitude during the Korean War: "For the most part the veteran operated under a 'wait and see' philosophy. Any new troops, especially officers, were expected to demonstrate their worth before full acceptance was made."[41] The more perceptive replacements understood this wait-and-see philosophy. Private Stanley Goff, newly arrived at the 196th Light Infantry Brigade in Vietnam, accepted the veterans' standoffishness: "There were cliques. The guys that fought together and had been in the boonies together were all around each other, and I could understand it. So they were sort of looking at us like, 'You got to go out there and prove yourself like we did.' I felt respect for that, and I really tried not to take it personally."[42]

While waiting to see how a replacement would perform, the veterans did what they could to teach him combat skills. During a replacement's breaking-in period, Jones's earlier comment aside, he did not draw the "most-exposed jobs," if only because the most dangerous jobs were also usually the most important, and new replacements could not be trusted with them. Walking point, for example, was a very dangerous job, but as FNG Robert Sanders explains, cherries only walked point after they had gained some experience: "Once we got used to the company and started to learn a little, then the old-timers started to put the cherries . . . out on point to cut through the brush. The only reason they didn't put us up there in the beginning was because they didn't want us to walk into an ambush."[43] Another dangerous job in Vietnam was machine gunner, but again, cherries were not usually entrusted with the M-60 machine gun because it was a vital piece of the squad's firepower. The gun was unpopular because it drew return fire and was heavy and bulky, but only proven "shooters" carried the "pig," as the M-60 was called.[44]

Although replacements avoided many dangerous jobs, they did not miss out on the "shit details." The cherry might not carry the machine gun, but he carried the extra ammunition for it. Replacements found themselves on carrying parties, hauling supplies forward. And new guys usually got last pick of the combat rations, meaning that they drew what the others did not want.

Whether he was an individual replacement or a member of a green unit, the soldier's anxiety level rose with the prospect of actual combat. Despite his awareness that war was a deadly business, the green soldier worried less about being killed than about performing bravely under fire, a condition Lord Moran calls "the stage fright of the novice who does not know if he is going to act badly or well."[45]

Sergeant Henry Giles, waiting in England for his engineer company to be sent to the Normandy beachhead during World War II, could not "help thinking what it's going to be like & will I be able to stand up to it & what kind of guts have I really got. I *hope* I've got enough but won't know till I get there."[46] Private Sledge, nearing the end of his Stateside training and knowing that he and his comrades would soon ship out, had the same concerns: "The fact that our lives might end violently or that we might be crippled while we were still boys didn't seem to register. The only thing that we seemed to be truly concerned about was that we might be too afraid to do our jobs under fire. An apprehension nagged at each of us that he might appear to be 'yellow' if he were afraid."[47]

Apprehension, or prebattle jitters, grew stronger as the time for combat drew near, especially if the green soldier had to pass through the physical evidence of war's destructiveness while en route to the front. Marine Private Mackin and his fellow replacements, heading into the fighting at Belleau Wood in World War I, "heard the war scream and writhe and crash among the distant trees. The guns around us added to the din. . . . Dark of night would have been welcome then, so that a man might hide the terror in his eyes."[48]

The set-piece battles of World War I, even during the relatively fluid fighting late in the war, made passage through battlefield carnage on the way to the front almost unavoidable. The torn countryside, the noise of the artillery, the spectacle of refugees and wounded streaming rearward, and the sight of the dead had a sobering impact.[49] During World War II, troops being trucked forward, or perhaps crossing a recently seized beach, shared that experience. Sergeant Dan Levin and his comrades, fresh out of marine combat correspondents' school, arrived on Saipan shortly after the assault forces had cleared the beaches. It might have been another planet:

> Next came real, sinking-in fright, as we unloaded from the transport and then loaded onto trucks that rumbled past debris of battle: dead oxen, their legs sticking up over bloated bellies, and then in the fields an overlooked human body. The truck was jolting in time to the uneven thump of artillery rounds—like physical shocks hitting us. They were from our guns, but we did not know that. I only knew, all at once, that I was surrounded by violent danger, random death. The ten combat correspondents in the truck sat as if catatonic. There was, we all suddenly understood, another and terrifying dimension.[50]

Once the war in Korea entered its static phase, green replacements experienced a similar, sobering physical transition into the environment of war. Lieutenant Matthias and three other replacements were being trucked to their marine regiment at the front in June 1952. The sudden, deafening roar of a nearby eight-inch artillery battery firing a volley literally knocked Matthias out of his seat: "The four of us checked each other out. Even though there was smiling and small talk, there was no fooling each other; we were scared. The remainder of the trip to regiment was filled not only with anticipation, but also, for the first time, real fear."[51]

The most shocking aspect of this physical transition to war was the sight of the dead. With time, corpses would not occasion a glance or comment, but almost every soldier-author vividly recalls seeing his first dead man. Lieutenant Hervey Allen, on his first trip into the lines with his platoon in World War I, saw mangled corpses: "Here I was ghastly sick of heart and body for a while."[52]

Private Roscoe C. Blunt Jr., moving into combat for the first time in a German town in World War II, encountered a dead GI, a soldier from his own division: "The war was now very close. The corpse was not that of a stranger; this was one of our own. Without looking back, I continued on, but having now actually touched death, I was even less confident of my own abilities. Nearly a half century of time has failed to erase the memory of that first dead G.I."[53]

The often-mangled or bloated dead revolted the green soldier and inspired fear by reminding him of his own mortality. Yet many soldiers were also morbidly curious, even fascinated, by the first dead they saw—for most, it was their first encounter with violent death. "Joker," the protagonist in Gustav Hasford's Vietnam War novel *The Short-timers,* warned against being too curious because it was a sure sign of the FNG: "In Vietnam you see corpses almost every day. At first you try to ignore them. You don't want people to think you're curious. Nobody wants to admit that corpses are not old hat to them; nobody wants to be a New Guy."[54]

Despite such shocking evidence of war's destructiveness and the understanding, at least on an intellectual plane, that combat was a dangerous business, a soldier in his first firefight was in some cases not so much scared as incredulous—the other guy was really trying to kill him! The marine private James Doyle recalled that during his first combat on Guam in World War II, he was slow to take cover when the Japanese opened fire because "it really hadn't sunk in to me that those other people were shooting at us." Only after his failure to take cover drew more fire and a shout from his buddy to "get down, yuh fool," did "the thing become personal. For the first time I realized that the people over on the ridge wanted to kill me. Hell, I didn't even know them. It was a weird feeling."[55]

Doyle's hesitation to act might be written off as a rare case of near-terminal stupidity except that his reaction was not unique. A grunt interviewed by oral historian Mark Baker described how, in his first firefight, he just stood there until his lieutenant literally kicked him in the ass and told him to get down and return fire. The grunt explained, "I wasn't so much scared as I was in awe. 'Those motherfuckers are really shooting at us. They're really trying to kill us.'"[56]

In their initial firefight, some soldiers did not even realize at first that they were being shot at. Marine Corporal Charles S. Crawford, a fresh marine replacement in Korea, just after entering the front-line trenches "heard what sounded like bees buzzing past me."[57] He found out later that the bees were machine-gun bullets. His fellow marines believed his failure to duck for cover had been an act of bravado. Lieutenant Robert Santos, in his first firefight in Vietnam, acted with the same seeming bravado. He moved about constantly, exposing himself recklessly, all the while hearing "these noises. Kind of like *ping, ping*—no idea what that noise was." His radioman, puzzled and alarmed at his new lieutenant's actions, set him straight on what the pings were: "'That's the bullets going over your head.' I never knew it."[58]

It may have taken the soldier in his first battle a few seconds to realize that the strange sounds he heard were incoming bullets and that the enemy really did mean him harm, but once that realization dawned on him, fear verging on terror was a normal reaction. Any prebattle cockiness evaporated. Captain Charles R. Cawthon describes how the soldier in his first fight felt: "On the first day of battle, the foot soldier probes new emotional depths, and the findings, I believe, are fairly universal. One is a conviction that he is abandoned, alone, and uncared-for in the world."[59]

The soldier struggled to overcome his fear and sense of abandonment. For some, fear of appearing cowardly motivated them to act. Machine gunner Philip Dosier, the protagonist in Larry Heinemann's Vietnam War novel *Close Quarters,* was panic-stricken in his first firefight during a night ambush patrol, but he fumbled to bring his gun into action, thinking, "I would lock and load that gun if it was the last natural act of my life. They are going to kill me, but what is it going to look like, the new guy so fucked up he couldn't get off more than a couple rounds?"[60]

Some soldiers could not overcome their fear—they froze. Sergeant Nat Frankel describes a soldier whose hands "have to be pried loose from a pole to which he has grabbed on" during his first combat. "He is too scared to even whimper." He would do better in future encounters, however: "Within a week that soldier is fighting bravely, killing with as much nobility as one can kill."[61]

First combat was a time of fear, shock, and confusion. Many were slow to react, some froze, but most began to perform like soldiers, taking cover and returning fire as they had been taught to do. No baptism of fire was more physically and emotionally abrupt, however, than an amphibious assault. The smoke, noise, carnage, and chaos on the beach were so great that sometimes soldiers had no coherent recollection of what had happened. Sergeant Dan Levin has never been able to piece together what he went through during the landing on Iwo Jima in World War II: "Often I have struggled trying to establish a true chronology for those next hours, to wrench them out of their surreality so I could explain them coherently to others and to myself."[62]

Captain Cawthon's combat initiation was on Omaha Beach on D-Day during the invasion of France in World War II. His otherwise sharp memory is a blur concerning the events of that day: "Perhaps . . . my capacity for registering separate sights and sounds had become saturated. Whatever the reason, the afternoon and night of D-day are a tapestry in which scenes emerge from a generally gray background and then fade or run together."[63]

Whether the sustained horror of a major amphibious assault or the gut-wrenching but brief shock of a firefight, first combat came to an end, and with it came the green soldier's sense of relief over having survived and done his job, or at least not run away. Private Blunt survived his first combat in World War II, fighting for the German town of Geilenkirchen, and even captured some Germans in the process: "When everything finally quieted down and I collected my thoughts, I realized my baptism of fire was behind me. I felt proud."[64] Lieutenant Matthias, after an eventful first twenty-four hours in the line at a forward outpost in Korea, found that combat was neither glamorous nor fun, but "there was some satisfaction: I had passed my baptism of fire. Evidently my work on the outpost met the approval of the troops on the outpost, for word spread fast among the troops that the new Lieutenant was willing to get his hands dirty and make some quick decisions."[65]

## "IT CAN'T HAPPEN TO ME"

Following his successful debut in combat, the soldier lost his anxiety over whether he could perform under fire and regained some of his precombat confidence.[66] Psychiatrists Roy L. Swank and Walter E. Marchand, who observed a combat unit in its first campaign in Normandy in World War II, noted that soldiers became "battle wise" after about a week of combat. They had learned to avoid the mistakes typical of green soldiers and to differentiate the sights and sounds of the battlefield. The battlewise soldier then enjoyed a period of "maximum efficiency," during which he remained confident and in control of his fear.[67]

Despite the death and destruction about them, many battlewise soldiers refused to consider the possibility of injury. In short, they believed that "it can't happen to me." Doughboy Private Ettinger, for example, transferred from the dangerous job of motorcycle dispatch rider to the more dangerous job of Stokes mortarman without giving it a second thought: "During combat, the mortar men and machine gunners were always the first target of the enemy . . . but while I often thought of my dear friend, Jack Perry, who had a premonition of death, I never really thought I'd be killed. I saw it as a matter of luck. . . . I had been lucky and I felt lucky."[68] Three wars later, Lieutenant Frederick Downs felt every bit as lucky as Ettinger, even after a month in Vietnam: "A small part of our mind tried to retain its sanity by reminding itself over and over that it would never happen to us. It can happen to anyone else, but it would not happen to me."[69]

That soldiers like Downs and Ettinger could feel charmed despite the ever-present danger is a matter of some mystery. The cockiness of youth may have contributed to their sense of invulnerability. Lieutenant Fussell observes that "war must rely on the young, for only they have the two things fighting requires: physical stamina and innocence about their own mortality."[70] Scott Wilson, who lived to be an older, wiser sergeant by late in World War II, marveled at his earlier foolhardiness: "At age twenty you're invincible. It's never going to be you, it's going to be the other guy. It's not bravery, it's idiotic adolescence."[71] Corporal Charles S. Crawford, a twenty-one-year-old marine who fought in Korea, remembers that "the thought never occurred to me that I might get killed. I had too much to live for; I was young and I was filled with the optimism of youth."[72]

In addition to youthful optimism (or ignorance), the battlewise soldier's confidence in his own prowess contributed to his belief that "it can't happen to me." The now-experienced soldier came to believe that if he could just avoid mistakes, then he would stay alive. Bob Hoffman attributed his survival to skill and caution: "I never got careless; I always had my gas mask. I always carried a shovel and a pick with me throughout the war. . . . I was the champion digger of the American army."[73] Psychiatrist Peter G. Bourne, who studied a Special Forces team in Vietnam, discovered that they firmly believed in their own expertise. Furthermore, the "occasional calculated exposure to the dangers of combat" bolstered each man's confidence because he attributed his survival, at least in part, "to his own mastery of the situation."[74]

The soldier who believed that his military prowess would keep him alive could at the same time blame the deaths of others on their lack of skill or carelessness. Bourne observed this attitude among several air ambulance medics in Vietnam: "Their awareness of death was predicated on the belief that it was something that happened to someone else, and from which certain superior capabilities which they possessed kept them immune."[75] In a similar vein, when Sergeant Bill Morgan, in Jack Fuller's novel *Fragments,* reported in to his new unit, his platoon leader told him, "'I been with this unit six months now,' he said, pulling out a piece of paper. 'Got written down here the name of every KIA [killed in action] we've had. I take it out from time to time to remind me how they died. They fucked up, that's what happened. . . . That's how people get greased.'"[76]

During this period of peak efficiency, the battlewise soldier was able to master his fears. Some soldier-authors even describe their fear as "useful" because it heightened their senses and reflexes.[77] Veteran scout Martinez, in Norman Mailer's novel *The Naked and the Dead,* conducting a one-man night reconnaissance, "was frightened, but effectively so; he had no panic, and it left him intensely aware of everything he could see or feel."[78] Audie Murphy hated waiting for an attack to begin but knew that he would feel better once his unit moved forward: "The nerves will relax; the heart, stop its thumping. The brain will turn to animal cunning."[79] Lieutenant Downs's senses were most acute during an air assault. As the helicopters headed into the landing zone, "my blood was pounding through my body. Every sense was alert to the action around me."[80]

The battlewise soldier was now immersed in the environment of war. Indeed, as Lieutenant James R. McDonough came to realize in Vietnam, he had become an integral part of that environment: "I had passed during the battle from being in the war to being a part of the war. I was no longer an alien in a strange environment. I could no longer draw a distinction between the war and my presence in it. . . . And though my recognition of that fact was unnerving, I knew that probably within my transition lay the seeds of my ultimate survival."[81]

Although immersed in war, the soldier was not yet overpowered by it. Some newly minted veterans even retained the sense of adventure that had impelled them to join up in the first place. Private Mackin and his three fellow battalion runners, having survived the fierce fighting in Belleau Wood in World War I, "were no longer . . . cowering, scared recruits. . . . We had pride. We were the four aces in the runner group. Strut a bit? Sure! We were leathernecks!"[82] Lieutenant Caputo, in the section of his memoir "The Splendid Little War," explains that his enthusiasm, if anything, was enhanced by his initial experiences in Vietnam. On this particular day, he was annoyed that one of his fellow platoon leaders had garnered more glory than he had: "I *wanted* to get into a fight, I wanted to prove myself the equal of the other officers in C Company. Lemmon had seen the lion's share of action that day, and I envied the tough little Texan. He would probably win a letter of commendation or maybe a medal. I wanted to win one myself."[83]

## "IT *CAN* HAPPEN TO ME"

Caputo's enthusiastic quest for glory did not last, however, nor did Mackin's "four aces" still strut with pride after two of them were evacuated with serious wounds. Like so many other soldiers, they discovered that neither military skill nor good fortune could preserve them from harm forever. Some event, such as the death of a close comrade, exposure to battlefield carnage, or the receipt of a wound, usually prompted this realization, a process Lord Moran calls the soldier's "discovery of danger": "At first he has a strange feeling of invulnerability—a form of egotism—then it is suddenly brought home to him that he is not a spectator but a bit of the target, that if there are casualties he may be one of them."[84] The discovery of danger comes for Ernest Hemingway's Colonel Richard Cantwell, the main character in *Across the River and into the Trees,* when, as a junior officer in World War I, he is seriously wounded:

> He was hit three times that winter, but they were all gift wounds; small wounds in the flesh of the body without breaking bone, and he had become quite confident of his personal immortality since he knew he should have been killed in the heavy artillery bombardment that always preceded the attacks. Finally he did get hit properly and for good. No one of his other wounds had ever done to him what the first big one did. I suppose it is just the loss of the immortality, he thought. Well, in a way, that is quite a lot to lose.[85]

Private Robert Leckie, a veteran marine by the time of the fight for Peleliu in the Pacific in World War II, had lost most of his old comrades and all his sense of adventure: "Gone the pagan naiveté of the first battle. How much easier to be a pagan again and to refuse to take the thing seriously."[86] For Private Stephens, eight days on the line in Korea and a Chinese attack were enough to convince him: "I was beginning to see that this wasn't some kind of sport, that people did get killed doing this."[87] The realization of danger came to Private Parks when his buddy, standing next to him in their armored personnel carrier in Vietnam, was killed in a firefight: "Poor Greenfield. Just a few more inches to the left and it would have been me. Maybe tomorrow will be my day. Who knows?"[88] Vietnam War platoon leader Michael Lee Lanning put it succinctly: "Close brushes with death brought not a feeling that I was invulnerable but rather that my number might be due to turn up at any time."[89]

With the realization of vulnerability came heightened fear and anxiety. The soldier found that his fear was no longer useful but debilitating and increasingly difficult to suppress.[90] The physical symptoms of fear became more pronounced. Surveys of veterans catalog these symptoms, ranging from a pounding heart and weak stomach to a small minority who admit to involuntary urination or defecation.[91] If the frequency with which soldiers wet or soiled themselves in the memoirs is any indication, then more men had difficulty holding to the old military salutation to "keep a tight asshole" than admitted to it in the surveys. Sergeant William Manchester, recounting his experiences on Okinawa in World War II, is probably closer to the mark: "Had I not been fasting I'm sure I would have shit my pants. Many did. . . . We were animals, . . . torn between fear . . . and a murderous rage at events."[92]

Many soldiers described their symptoms of fear and the near-impossibility of controlling them. The ever-candid Private Sledge describes his physical fear as he waited in his amphibious tractor for the signal to hit the beach at Peleliu: "I broke out in a cold sweat as the tension mounted with the intensity of the [preparatory] bombardment. My stomach was tied in knots. I had a lump in my throat and swallowed only with great difficulty. My knees nearly buckled, so I clung weakly to the side of the tractor. I felt nauseated and feared that my bladder would surely empty itself and reveal me to be the coward that I was."[93]

Even Audie Murphy, the country's most-decorated soldier in World War II, was no stranger to fear. Recalling a movement to contact against German defenders in Italy, Murphy explained that he was "well acquainted with fear. It strikes first in the stomach, coming like the disemboweling hand that is thrust into the carcass of a chicken. I feel now as though icy fingers have reached into my midparts and twisted the intestines into knots."[94]

While the symptoms were many, the cause of the soldier's fear was simple enough—the realization that it *could* happen to him—he might be killed or wounded. Soldiers came to fear particular types of wounds.[95] Lieutenant Lanning pointed out that, for grunts, "a wound to the genitals was the most feared injury in this war, as in any other conflict. A man's first question to the medics was not 'Am I going to make it?' but rather 'Do I still have my balls?'"[96] Lanning further explained that the "loss of limbs, genitals, or senses was never far from our minds. Fear of such wounds seemed at times to rival that of death itself."[97]

For armored vehicle crewmen, the constant fear was fire. Until diesel-fueled tanks and armored personnel carriers (APCs) were introduced during the Vietnam War, armored vehicles were powered by volatile gasoline, or "mogas" as the army called it, and as APC crewman Dosier in Heinemann's novel *Close Quarters* pointed out, mogasers "burn like paper soaked with tar."[98] Sergeant Frankel, commanding a gasoline-powered Sherman tank in World War II, observed that if the hatches of a burning Sherman were jammed or broken, a real possibility in a badly damaged tank, what transpired would not be pleasant: "It takes twenty minutes for a medium tank to incinerate; and the flames burn slowly, so figure it takes ten minutes for a hearty man within to perish. You wouldn't even be able to struggle, for chances are, both exits would be sheeted with flame and smoke. You would sit, read *Good Housekeeping,* and die like a dog. Steel coffins indeed!"[99]

Not only did the soldier fear certain types of wounds, or dying in especially gruesome ways, but he also dreaded, for a variety of physical and psychological reasons, certain enemy weapons. As the sociologist John Dollard discovered in his survey of Spanish Civil War veterans, "A weapon may be high on the list [of feared weapons] either because it is especially common and dangerous, perhaps the case with artillery shells, or because something about it arouses irrational fear, perhaps the case with air-bombing. The machine gun should probably be high on the list because it is actually dangerous, but the men feel that, though dangerous, it is in the realm of the familiar and that they know how to cope with it."[100]

The soldiers could "cope" with a machine gun by attacking it, even if, as was often the case, they paid a heavy price. They could not cope with artillery or air attack in a similar fashion, however, so they feared those weapons more. For the same reason, soldiers hated land mines and booby traps. These hidden killers were often difficult to detect or counter. Mines are only rarely mentioned in World War I memoirs because they were just coming into common usage by war's end.[101] From World War II on, however, soldiers mention them frequently, and with loathing.[102]

Soldiers hated mines for several reasons. First, they caused the maiming injuries to limbs and genitals that soldiers most dreaded. The Germans made liberal use of mines in their defense of the Huertgen Forest in World War II, and their effects were quickly and painfully evident, as Lieutenant Boesch recalls: "The parade of men wounded by mines was so constant and depressing that the thought of getting a foot or a leg blown off was with us at every turn. This specter haunted us day and night."[103]

Soldiers also hated mines because they called for constant vigilance. Mines were normally buried and booby traps hidden, hence spotting them required time and a sharp eye. But as Ernie Pyle pointed out during the fighting in Italy, time was often at a premium, and thus mines were found the hard way: "The Germans had mined the country behind them beyond anything ever known before. Our troops simply couldn't take time to go over every inch of ground with mine detectors, so they had to discover the mine fields by stumbling into them or driving over them. Naturally there were casualties, but . . . the greatest damage was psychological—the intense watchfulness our troops had to maintain."[104]

Moreover, as with artillery and air attacks, mines generated a sense of help-lessness and frustration because the soldier could not fight back. Lieutenant Caputo describes this frustration, common to the Vietnam War soldier: "It was not warfare. It was murder. We could not fight back against the Viet Cong mines or take cover from them or anticipate when they would go off. Walking down the trails, waiting for those things to explode, we had begun to feel more like victims than soldiers."[105] Lieutenant Matthias and his men felt the same way during the Korean War, where mines were ubiquitous once the static phase of the fighting set in: "We were mentally able to cope with physical, enemy troops but had trou-ble accepting the nasty, unexpected blast of a mine."[106]

Another dreaded weapon was the German 88-mm high-velocity, dual-pur-pose antiaircraft and antitank gun of World War II. That weapon, as Bill Mauldin wrote, took on mythical proportions: "Their 88 mm. is the terror of every dog-face. It can do everything but throw shells around corners, and sometimes we think it has even done that."[107] In reality, far more damage was done by standard German artillery pieces of the 105-mm and 150-mm varieties, but the mystique of the 88 remained powerful, and some memoirs refer to all incoming artillery rounds as 88s.[108]

Far less flashy than the infamous 88 was the run-of-the-mill infantry mortar, but experienced soldiers learned to fear it. Mortars were common. Compared to artillery pieces, they were less expensive, easier to maintain, lighter to transport, and easier to keep resupplied with ammunition. They lacked the range and punch of artillery but were accurate. The Chinese enemy in the Korean War got high marks from the GIs for his skill with mortars. Lieutenant Matthias explains why mortar rounds were so deadly: "Contrary to larger artillery, there was little warn-ing when the shell came in. There was a sudden WHOOSH and an immediate explosion, so we did not have time to take cover as we might with other artillery rounds."[109] Only if a GI heard the "cough" of the enemy mortar round as it left the tube, a fairly frequent occurrence given the short range of most mortars, did he have time to take cover.

If mortars were feared partly for their silence, then other weapons were feared, in part, because of their noise. The Germans, and to a much lesser extent the Japanese, employed rocket artillery during World War II. Rockets were inex-pensive, simple, and could be of considerable size. Although not known for their accuracy, they made such a horrific noise that they were called "Screaming Meemies" or "Moaning Minnies." Lieutenant Boesch, like most GIs, vividly recalls his first Screaming Meemie attack: "We were hustling along the side of a paved road when we first heard it, a weird, agonizing sound—a sound which grew louder and more terrifying as the projectiles approached. It sounded for all the world like a ghost tearing a board from the wall of a haunted house on Hal-lowe'en."[110]

The soldier's fear of particular weapons or certain types of wounds stemmed from his realization that "it *could* happen to him." At the same time that the soldier came to realize and fear his vulnerability, the harsh physical environment of war began to take its toll. James Jones praised Mauldin and his World War II GI cartoon characters Willie and Joe for portraying the debilitating effects of life in the combat zone: "The great thing Mauldin did was to show people over and over again that it was not only the danger of war that slowly did men in. It was perhaps even more that long haul of day after day of monotony and discomfort and living in perpetual dirt in the field, on and on with no prospect of release and no amenities."[111]

The GIs would have agreed with Jones and Mauldin. Private Lester Atwell, a World War II infantryman in Europe, realized earlier than most what his future held: "What a rotten life this was going to be! Always outdoors, always dirty, devitalized, tired from the broken sleep of guard duty. . . . There was just a general feeling of depression, that flat carelessness that comes from knowing one has hit bottom and will stay there."[112] Atwell's fellow World War II infantryman, Blunt, also serving in Europe, came to the same realization, if not as quickly: "The cold, penetrating March dampness, the constantly wet uniforms and the lack of proper rest and food were gradually wearing me down. One exhausting truck convoy after another, one rubble pile bed after another on top of weeks of cold food were too much for my system."[113] Indeed, Blunt's system soon short-circuited entirely, and he came down with pneumonia.

More than one GI, shivering during the European winter of 1944–1945, no doubt envied his counterparts in the Pacific—at least they were warm. But the Pacific was no tropical paradise. Private Sledge describes how he and his comrades were pushed to the limit during the fighting on Peleliu: "The grinding stress of prolonged heavy combat, the loss of sleep because of nightly infiltration and raids, the vigorous physical demands forced on us by the rugged terrain, and the unrelenting, suffocating heat were enough to make us drop in our tracks. How we kept going and continued fighting I'll never know."[114]

Homer Wright, an officer in the Thirty-second Infantry Division fighting in New Guinea, recalled that "climate and disease wore out good men so fast. We were tired beyond imagination. The first impact was weight loss."[115] Weight losses of twenty pounds or more were not unusual for combat soldiers. The monotonous diet of combat rations and the constant exertion of soldiering caused weight loss well beyond what was healthy for young men who were already lean.[116]

At times the combination of physical and emotional stress generated a feeling of accelerated aging. Soldiers like Lieutenant Robert Santos in Vietnam felt old before their time: "We got old fast. We were exposed to so much shit and you find out so much about yourself—your good, your bad, your strengths and your weaknesses—if you're honest with yourself—so quickly that you might as well have aged."[117]

The once battlewise soldier, realizing that his combat prowess was no guarantee of invulnerability, and with his confidence and physical stamina fading, no longer performed at peak efficiency. He entered what Swank and Marchand

called the "hyper-reactive stage," with symptoms that included abnormal fatiga-
bility, increasing fear reactions, overcautiousness, irritability, and eventually
tremulousness.[118]

One of the first things a soldier did after realizing his vulnerability was to try
to lessen his chances of getting killed. He could do little to reduce the dangers of
his environment, but he could avoid taking unnecessary risks. Sergeant Hoffman
remembered how the men had eagerly volunteered for his company's first combat mission and how those who could not go were genuinely disappointed, but
attitudes changed quickly: "Men who did not get to go on this trip cried real
tears—a direct contrast to the lack of volunteering for dangerous missions a few
months later when they had become war-weary. Then they would go if assigned
to any task, no matter how dangerous, but they did not rush in. . . . They'd die if
it were their turn, but they weren't going to overwork fate."[119]

A young, enthusiastic Lieutenant George William Sefton conducted patrols
on his own initiative after jumping into France on D-Day with the 101st Airborne
Division. While on one of these patrols he came under heavy machine-gun fire
and, deciding that discretion was the better part of valor, returned to friendly
lines: "In retrospect, it was the first time since landing in Normandy that I asked
myself, 'Is this trip really necessary?' Up to now, my mind had simply blocked
out the horrors of combat in the interest of accomplishing the jobs for which we
had trained so intensively. In this particular instance, the instinct for self-preservation had prevailed."[120]

Prudence in the face of heavy enemy fire might keep a soldier alive to fight
another day, as might his battle skills. With the "discovery of danger," however,
came the additional realization that chance and fate, not military prowess, were
the greater arbiters, as Lieutenant McDonough learned in Vietnam: "Rational
decision making or technical and physical skills may save you once or twice. But
a man in combat is exposed a thousand times. A gust of wind blows at the right
moment to take the mortar round ten yards farther to explode harmlessly behind
you. . . . A blade of grass, a bent branch, or an article of equipment deflects a
speeding bullet enough to send it harmlessly through your flopping shirt or bone-
less flesh—or savagely through your brain or liver."[121]

The soldier thus had to deal with the realization that he could only do so
much, and not much at that, to improve his chances of survival. Small wonder
that he became increasingly "hyper-reactive." To make matters worse, the soldier
was well aware that he was becoming hyper-reactive—that he was "shaky" or
"shook up," and he began to wonder how much more he could take. Private
Sledge, after weeks of mud, filth, and combat on Okinawa, knew he was reaching the end of his rope: "I felt a sense of desperation that my mind was being
affected by what we were experiencing. Men cracked up frequently in places
such as that. . . . I vividly recall grimly making a pledge to myself. The Japanese
might kill or wound me, but they wouldn't make me crack up. . . . My secret
resolve helped me through the long days and nights we remained in the worst of

the abyss. But there were times at night during that period when I felt I was slipping. More than once my imagination ran wild during the brief period of darkness when the flares and star shells burned out."[122]

Private Blunt, after months of combat in Europe in World War II, noticed how jumpy and nervous he had become. He hoped that he could hold on until war's end, which he knew, by February 1945, could not be far off. Like Sledge, his fears were worse at night, in this case a murky, foggy one while he was on guard duty:

> The mind becomes dulled by the physical and emotional stresses of war and regresses to the primal instinct of survival at all cost. This, I was afraid, was happening to me. The proof of this was apparent when I recoiled upon abruptly encountering German bodies, by my growing revulsion for mines, my increasing preoccupation with death and now by the gnawing apprehension about what was possibly lurking in the fog that embraced me.
>
> I began to worry, for the one thing I didn't need at this time was a breakdown of my nerves. I had controlled my emotions so far and I didn't want to unravel this close to the end of hostilities.[123]

The rotation system established in the Korean and Vietnam Wars at least gave soldiers a departure date to cling to. Unlike Blunt, they did not have to hold on until the "end of hostilities." But twelve months or more of combat was still a great deal to endure, and stressed-out soldiers wondered, like their predecessors in earlier wars, how much more they could take.[124] Lieutenant James Brady, a marine platoon leader in Korea, noted that men eventually became "shook.": "We were beginning to learn a new word for someone who'd had a bad scare or was losing his nerve. We said he was 'shook.' . . . It was 76's [Chinese artillery rounds] coming in flat and fast or mortars dropping on you or fear of mines or maybe too many duck blinds and night ambushes or a wind that never stopped blowing. Those were what made you 'shook,' everyone agreed, and no fooling."[125]

The once-confident helicopter pilot Mason provides an example from the Vietnam War of being shook. After six months or so of too many hot landing zones, Mason "was jumpy, worried. My nights were getting harder to bear." Things only got worse. By the end of his tour, he suffered from epileptic-like seizures, nightmares, and hallucinations.[126]

Paradoxically, at the same time that the soldier became hyper-reactive to danger, he grew increasingly accustomed to the horrible sights and suffering around him. He had to, if he were to continue functioning. Tobey C. Herzog calls this defense mechanism "psychic numbing": "The process involves becoming oblivious to the horrors of combat, to the death of friends, or to the guilt of killing other human beings."[127] Combat soldiers mention it frequently, occasionally adding that they were alarmed to discover such seeming callousness in themselves. Captain Arthur W. Little, commanding a battalion of doughboys, was grief stricken over the first of his officers killed in battle, but "the day was to come when the abnormality of my mind and heart was to become normal in its new plane. The death of an officer came to affect me, emotionally, not at all."[128]

Private Blunt, detailed to help a graves-registration team find and collect the frozen bodies of soldiers killed during the Battle of the Bulge in World War II, "began considering American and German dead with the same lack of emotion. A corpse was a corpse regardless of what color the uniform was, and war was war. When I returned to my platoon two days later, I wondered what was happening to me that I could become so blasé, so indifferent to death."[129]

Many GIs continued to be shocked by the sight of American bodies, if only because they were stark reminders of the observer's own mortality. But some soldiers, as in the case of Blunt, even grew accustomed to the dead of their own side. Private Matthews and his comrades shared a shell hole with several dead marines on Iwo Jima. They did not give the corpses a second thought: "Our attitude toward the bodies was almost perfunctory. . . . For these were not men we knew; they were the result of man's ferocity and we were used to ferocity now."[130]

American soldiers in later wars saw their share of ferocity as well and likewise grew accustomed to it. In Vietnam, platoon leader Downs noticed that "we were all becoming pretty callous to life," and as if to prove the point, added, "The thought was a small one and soon left me."[131] Not only did the soldier become callous, but the sight of enemy dead also could produce, not horror, but a sense of triumph. Private Ogden, while counting enemy bodies after a major engagement in Vietnam, noted: "Viewing death was a curious and intriguing thing at first, but no more. As a kid I had felt terrible during slaughtering season, and ran and hid; but now I felt almost smug and arrogant: better these little pathetic bastards than me."[132]

Fatigue, fear, and stress figured prominently in generating this "psychic numbing." In its extreme form, it is best summed up by Ernie Pyle's description of what World War II soldiers called the "thousand-yard stare" and marines called the "bulkhead stare": "It's a look of dullness, eyes that look without seeing, eyes that see without conveying any image to the mind. It's a look that is the display room for what lies behind it—exhaustion, lack of sleep, tension for too long, weariness that is too great, fear beyond fear, misery to the point of numbness, a look of surpassing indifference to anything anybody can do. It's a look I dread to see on men."[133]

Sergeant Frankel realized that he was approaching such a state: "There is a condition common to all wars, which in World War II we called the two-thousand-[yard] stare. This was the anesthetized look, the wide, hollow eyes of a man who no longer cares. I wasn't to that state yet, but the numbness was total."[134] Private Sledge and his fellow marines, waiting to be relieved by an army unit on Peleliu, were as close to the edge as Frankel: "During mid-afternoon as we waited for the army infantry, we sat numbly looking at nothing with the 'bulkhead stare.' The shock, horror, fear, and fatigue of fifteen days of combat were wearing us down physically and emotionally. I could see it in the dirty, bearded faces of my remaining comrades: they had a hollow-eyed vacant look peculiar to men under extreme stress for days and nights on end."[135]

## "IT *WILL* HAPPEN TO ME"

At this point the soldier was on the verge of being overwhelmed by the brutal environment of war. He had gone from apprehensive but optimistic novice to battlewise, confident veteran to hyper-reactive yet emotionally numbed survivor. A soldier who reached this physical and emotional nadir could become fatalistic—"it *will* happen to me."

Such deep, despairing fatalism should not be confused, however, with the phenomenon of soldiers' premonitions about their impending doom, generally expressed by the comment "my number is up." Once the soldier realized that it *could* happen to him, he naturally began to wonder how long his luck would hold out. As others died or cracked up around him, the soldier came to believe that it would soon be his turn. Lieutenant Gerald P. Averill, prior to what he knew would be a costly amphibious assault on Iwo Jima in World War II, was "convinced more than ever that I never would leave the island alive."[136] Averill made it, but some premonitions of death came true. A veteran in Lieutenant Harold P. Leinbaugh's Company K decided that it was not going to be his lucky day—it was not. He was killed by a burst of German machine-gun fire.[137]

Men who had premonitions often hurriedly wrote "last letters." The World War II mortarman Howard S. Hoffman, growing increasingly edgy after many close calls, "became convinced . . . that I was not going to survive."[138] He left a letter with the supply sergeant concerning the disposition of his personal gear.

Premonitions of death, as in Hoffman's case, reflected a soldier's growing edginess or, as in Averill's case, a realization that the odds of surviving an upcoming operation were not good. A premonition, however, did not equate to acceptance of death and certainly not to a desire for it. Thus, soldiers with premonitions were more akin to realists than to fatalists. But for some soldiers serving "for the duration," a feeling that the war would never end contributed to a true sense of impending doom.[139] Private Carl Andrew Brannen, for example, after experiencing the costly battles of Belleau Wood and Soissons in the Great War, not surprisingly "reasoned that the war would continue a year or two longer, but that I would not see the finish."[140] By October 1918, in Private Mackin's marine company, only a "battered and bitter handful" of old-timers remained, and they "had long since lost all hope of ever going home."[141]

During the Italian campaign in World War II, Lieutenant Bond, while in the hospital recovering from a severe bout of dysentery, was suddenly depressed: "The war would never end, and we would have to go on until we were all killed, fighting in the rocky mountains, and being shelled, sleeping in the slush. Or we would break."[142] For soldiers in the Pacific, the war seemed even more interminable, especially given the common perception, as expressed by Lieutenant Munschauer, that the Japanese would fight to the bitter end: "They would never give up. They would all die, one by one. We had seen that in the Philippines. By 1949 it would be over. Four more years. Millions would be dead. Odds for survival were nil. Only a severe wound taking me out of action would help to beat the odds."[143]

Soldiers in the Korean and Vietnam Wars occasionally spoke as despairingly as troops in the world wars about their chances of surviving, despite the existence of a rotation system. James R. Ebert points out that for the grunt, "the prospect of a year in combat seemed like a lifetime . . . and they were unable to contemplate completing their tours unscathed."[144] Lieutenant Lanning was one soldier who felt that way. He noticed that grunts with more than six months in the company were considered "old-timers," and there were not many of them: "Few completed a full tour without joining one of the casualty lists."[145]

Soldiers in the Korean War were sometimes equally pessimistic, especially given the enemy's seemingly inexhaustible supply of soldiers. During the heavy fighting around the Pusan Perimeter, Lieutenant Frank Muetzel came to that conclusion: "No one even considered the possibility of getting whipped by the NKs [North Koreans]. But there were a lot of them and few of us. We, me, all of us were eventually going to get it; it was just a matter of when and how bad."[146]

Yet even soldiers like Lieutenant Muetzel, who anticipated death or serious injury, were not truly fatalistic. The fatalistic soldier not only anticipated his death but also accepted it and in some cases even welcomed it. The memoirs provide examples of truly fatalistic soldiers, but they are relatively scarce because few men actually reached that state of mind. Those who did failed to take even elementary precautions in the face of the enemy. Lieutenant Munschauer, whose platoon began receiving sniper fire, noticed that one of his men continued to sit outside his foxhole. He yelled at the man to take cover: "'Aw, Lieutenant,' he said, 'don't worry, when your number is up your number . . .' He never finished. A small round hole in the middle of his forehead oozed blood as he slumped over."[147]

"Scar-Chin," a marine in Leckie's company in World War II, refused to take cover during Japanese air attacks. He told Leckie, "If you're gonna get it, you're gonna get it, and there isn't anything you can do about it." Leckie presented his argument against fatalism, but it had no apparent impact on Scar-Chin: "Argue until you are weary, but men like Scar-Chin still lounge among the falling bombs. Tell them they don't believe it, when they say, 'You go when your time comes.' Suggest that it is they, through their own foolhardiness, who choose the time. Impress upon them that they are their own executioner, that they pull their own name out of the hat. Remind them even if it is fatalism that they want—as opposed to common sense—they still must choose it: they must even choose no-choice."[148]

Leckie is assuming that fatalists have the mental and emotional balance left to make a rational choice. But usually the fatalistic soldier was no longer functioning soundly. Ron Kovic was certainly not thinking rationally when he deliberately set out to trip a booby trap in Vietnam: "I remember walking along, knowing goddamn well exactly what I was doing, just waiting for those metal splinters to go bursting up into my testicles, sending me home a wounded hero. That was the only way I was getting out of this place."[149]

Such an action equaled suicide by enemy bullet, and the truly fatalistic, burned-out soldier sometimes opted for it. Private Mackin's friend "Baldy" had reached that point by early November 1918. During a halt in the advance, Baldy no longer took the elementary precaution of keeping his head down. He stood up while everyone else lay prone: "He . . . stood, straightening up his clothes, peering all the while up the slope ahead, full standing in a line of sprawling men. He was a target then, and it seemed to me he didn't care too much. He long had known he wasn't going home."[150] A sniper obligingly killed him.

Sometimes the suicide-by-enemy-fire was dramatic. Corporal Russ tells of a marine who, during the Korean War, "went berserk . . . and grabbed a BAR one night, leapt out of the . . . trench and headed for goonyland [the Chinese lines] before anyone could stop him."[151] More commonly, however, fatalistic soldiers died because of inaction. They simply no longer cared what happened, so they failed to duck for cover, or put on a helmet or flak jacket, or hide a light or a cigarette at night.

Few soldiers actually sank to the depths of fatalistic despair. Relatively more claimed that they were fatalists, but their own attitudes and actions betrayed them. Ernie Pyle knew the truth: "A dozen times I overheard this same remark: 'Well. I don't worry about it because I look at it this way. If your number's up then it's up, and if it isn't you'll come through no matter what.' Every single person who expressed himself that way was a liar and knew it, but, hell, a guy has to say something."[152]

A few who said it were not lying, as the preceding examples illustrate, but Pyle's observation is generally accurate, as verified by cases where soldier-authors profess no longer to care but then prove by their actions or emotions that they still want to live. Corporal Charles F. Minder, in the midst of the fighting in the Argonne, began volunteering for dangerous carrying parties, claiming that he no longer cared and hence was no longer scared: "I don't seem to be scared any more, and volunteered to go. What if I do get hit; it might get me out of this mess! I don't want to kill any more." Yet a few days later, in recording his reaction to a near-miss from a large artillery shell, Minder revealed just how scared of dying he still was: "The trees crashed, and rocks and dirt tumbled down the side of the hill like an avalanche. It scared the life out of me. . . . I sat there for the rest of my guard trembling."[153] So much for Minder's fatalism.

After months of combat in Vietnam, Lieutenant Caputo was suddenly his old, enthusiastic self again. Like Minder, he chalked up his new attitude to freedom from fear, once he no longer cared what happened: "A sudden and mysterious recovery from the virus of fear had caused the change in mood. I didn't know why. I only knew I had ceased to be afraid of dying. It was not a feeling of invincibility; indifference, rather." Yet when caught in the open in his next firefight, Caputo "made love to the earth" as the bullets zipped by overhead. He then organized a hasty assault, because if he and his platoon stayed where they were, they would be slaughtered. He gathered himself for the rush forward: "My body was tensing itself to spring. Quite separate from my thoughts or will, it was concentrating itself to make a rush for the tree line. And that intense concentration of physical energy was born of fear. . . . I understood then why a cornered animal is so dangerous."[154] So much for Caputo's indifference.

Soldiers like Minder and Caputo genuinely wanted to feel indifferent and may even have temporarily tricked themselves into believing it, because it brought an end to fear and anxiety. The problem, however, was that the will to live was too strong. As long as there was any hope, most soldiers could not succumb to fatalism. One powerful source of hope was the Date of Expected Return from Overseas (DEROS), or rotation date. Many Korean and Vietnam War soldiers despaired of completing a full tour of duty in one piece, and for good reason. But for those who survived to the point where their rotation date loomed as a real possibility, the chances of life after combat began looking better.

Yet the approaching rotation date brought a new problem. The soldier stopped believing, if he ever really did, that it *would* happen to him, but he began to worry that it *might* happen. Thus was born "short-timer's syndrome." The short-timer grew reluctant to risk his life in any way. He feared, almost to the point of obsession, that he would be killed by one of those freak occurrences so common in war, perhaps even on his last day in-country.

Short-timer syndrome is generally associated with the Vietnam War, but it was much in evidence during the Korean War as well. The rundown of short-timer characteristics by Lieutenant Matthias would be familiar to any Vietnam War grunt:

> The amount of time in their bunker began to increase. More C rations were eaten in the bunker rather than walking the trench lines back to chow. There was no more volunteering for any assignments that might have risk. . . . When possible, the shorttimer arranged some swaps of guard duty and patrol duty (I imagine some interesting inducements were provided for some changes). . . . The shorttimer often became more irritable, short tempered and nervous. His conversation often indicated fears of getting hit during the last week or last patrol, especially by a stray shell. Every marine could enumerate instances when some poor bastard got it at that time.[155]

Soldiers serving in the world wars had no rotation date to look forward to, but in some cases, especially in the European theater during World War II, they suffered the equivalent of short-timer syndrome: last-casualty syndrome.[156] The imminent collapse of Germany was obvious by early 1945. The GI was amazed that the Germans, at least the more fanatical ones, could fight on in such a hopeless cause, and he did not want the dubious distinction of being the last American killed by one of those Germans.[157]

The GIs, in other words, could sense the war would end, and the prospect awakened fresh hopes and fears not unlike those felt by the Korean and Vietnam War short-timer. Captain Huebner, as the war drew to a close in Italy, took all the precautions typical of the short-timer: "I am now determined to come out alive. I'll gamble on anything but my life. I'll keep my head down, keep my damn helmet on, probe carefully for mines along my path, keep digging my holes deep, and look for cover as I run. I'll think about each situation first, then face it as planned. No show-off stuff for me. I'll obey all orders to the letter and do nothing more. My instinct for self-preservation is deep seated."[158]

Many soldiers, like Huebner, survived "for the duration," but their last weeks of combat were increasingly nerve-racking as the end of the war drew near. Other soldiers had broken down emotionally long before war's end or even before becoming fully immersed in the environment. Conversely, a few soldiers actually thrived in this malignant climate. Most fell somewhere in between, struggling as best they could, using a variety of coping mechanisms to preserve their physical and mental health, and a measure of humanity, in the dangerous, hostile world of war.

# 4
# Coping with the Environment of War

The soldier lived and fought in a harsh environment, filled with dangers and physical deprivation. "This accumulation of noxious factors,"[1] writes the psychiatrist Leo H. Bartemeier, "add[s] up to an enormous burden." Yet soldiers bore this burden for a remarkably long time, maintaining their sanity—and humanity—through a variety of coping mechanisms, such as the belief that "it can't happen to me," or emotional numbing. The soldier coped with the noxious factors of war in other ways as well. Some of these coping mechanisms were sensible enough. Others, such as the "it can't happen to me" rationale, flew in the face of logic, yet they worked as long as the soldier believed in them. The soldier's first priority was dealing with the stresses of combat, but he also had to devise ways of enduring the privations of army life while far from home and the support of loved ones.

## A BREAK IN THE ACTION

The easiest way to cope with the environment of war was to escape from it. The expedient of rotating soldiers, or more usually entire units, out of combat provided a needed reprieve, but the tactical situation and the availability of troops dictated the frequency with which commanders could do so. The shortage of divisions during World War II and Korea meant that soldiers logged considerable stretches of time in combat. During Vietnam, divisions and separate brigades usually received responsibility for geographical areas of operation and hence were never "out of the line."

Thus, the perception is that the soldier rarely got a break from the action. Soldiers' memoirs reinforce this perception by dwelling on the interesting, unusual, or dramatic events of combat while passing quickly over less memorable periods of boredom or relative quiet. According to historian and World War II combat veteran Bradford Perkins, however, "When units were committed to battle, even for the riflemen intermissions were more common than is generally recognized," and hence, "the picture of battle as an uninterrupted scene of carnage and danger is a distortion of reality."[2]

These "intermissions" were rarely total holidays from hardship and danger, as Perkins acknowledges by adding that even a "quiet sector" of the front could still be "very traumatic," and the overall shortage of units meant that soldiers never got as many real breaks in the action as they needed.[3] Commanders did rotate units out of combat when the situation permitted, but the amount of rest that such a rotation provided varied considerably. A platoon placed in company reserve, for example, was usually out of direct enemy fire and observation, but little more. At the other extreme, on rare occasions an entire brigade or division might be sent rearward to a rest camp or for retraining, freeing it from danger and hardship.

Individual soldiers also got a break from the action in the form of passes or leave. Many lucky doughboys earned a week's rest in the Leave Areas in France, administered by the Young Men's Christian Association (YMCA).[4] Rest camps were established during World War II as well, and soldiers enjoyed short passes to such cities as Vielsalm (in Belgium), Paris, or Rome.[5] During the Korean War, a system of R and R allowed five days' leave in Japan. An R and R system was established during the Vietnam War as well; in addition, many soldiers received short passes, often presented as a reward for good performance, to in-country rest areas such as the famous China Beach.

Whether it was a rotation into company reserve a few hundred yards behind the front or a week's leave in Paris, the soldier was grateful for any reprieve. Even a brief withdrawal from combat allowed for hot rations, mail call, sleep, a bath or shower, and a measure of shelter provided by a two-man tent or a cellar roof. During these respites the soldiers describe, with almost childish delight, enjoying amenities that civilians take for granted. A bath or shower, for example, was a major event for troops who had not removed their clothes for weeks at a time. Doughboy William L. Langer recalls his company's being pulled out of the line for a nine-day rest after more than a month of combat. A bath and clean clothes followed: "We shan't so soon forget what a relief it was to be really clean once more. It actually seemed too good to be true."[6]

A bath might involve a nearby stream or lake. On a warm day, soldiers frolicked in the water, no doubt reminded of happier times at the swimming hole back home. Private Robert Leckie describes the pleasure of swimming in the Ilu River on a scorching hot day on Guadalcanal in World War II: "With incautious shouts we fell upon her. She dissolved us, this river. We became a yelling, splashing, swilling, milling mass."[7]

A break from combat also meant sorely needed sleep. Doughboy Private Albert M. Ettinger slept for thirty-six hours after two weeks in the line under miserable conditions.[8] Corporal Amos N. Wilder slept for forty-eight hours after the exhausting Soissons counteroffensive, stirring himself only for chow call.[9] Ettinger and Wilder were extreme cases, but soldiers exhausted from their stint in combat were typically lethargic for a day or two until fully rested. Private Lester Atwell describes the overly tired soldiers in his battalion on going into bivouac: "No one seemed to care about anything. Sentences went unfinished; listening faces were loose and vacant; everyone yawned, sprawled, wrote letters in a desultory way, waiting for one tiresome, not quite sufficient meal to follow the other."[10]

The more exhausted the soldiers were, the more rest they needed, but those observing the recovery process, in this case Ernie Pyle, were amazed at how the men bounced back: "The startling thing to me about those rest periods was how quickly the human body could recuperate from critical exhaustion, how rapidly the human mind snapped back to the normal state of laughing, grousing, yarn-spinning, and yearning for home."[11]

Leaders also marveled at the recuperative powers of their soldiers and thus came to appreciate the importance of even short breaks in the action. Lieutenant Lyle Rishell saw the value of a two-day rest after a month of combat in Korea: "My platoon moved into a bivouac area. Here we would receive our first beer of the war (we were issued only one can per man), our first shower and clean clothing, and some hot food. The men lazed around, refreshed and happy to have a respite from the fighting."[12]

Once the troops had attended to the basics of cleaning up, eating, and resting, they began looking for diversions. Any entertainment was greatly appreciated. The soldiers mention with gratitude shows put on by American entertainers, amenities provided by mobile canteens, and radio broadcasts, especially of music.[13] From World War II on, movies were a major form of entertainment, often shown close to the front. Movies, Private Roscoe C. Blunt observed, "took our minds off the war and transferred us into a fantasy world for a couple of hours."[14]

Another popular diversion was music. The rock-and-roll generation fought in Vietnam. Private John Ketwig writes, "One day we were dancing or listening to the car radio; the next we were in Southeast Asia. Somebody always had a transistor radio, able to pick up Armed Forces Radio. . . . The music took us away."[15] The Korean War GI listened to Armed Forces Radio based in Japan.[16] GIs in Europe in World War II made purchasing or looting a radio a high priority so that they could listen to the BBC or to the music played by Axis Sally on the German propaganda station.[17] Even in the desolate Pacific, some units picked up music over shortwave radio.[18] In the precommercial-radio days of World War I, doughboys enjoyed singing.[19] World War II GIs also sang to entertain themselves, but group singing is rarely mentioned in Korean and Vietnam War memoirs.[20]

If the break in the action continued, then the soldier's time-honored prerogative of eat, drink, and be merry took precedence. The American soldier was adept at finding or manufacturing alcoholic beverages and scouring for something to eat more palatable than army rations. He also sought female companionship, the availability of which varied considerably by war and by theater of operations. Memoirs from the more recent wars are candid about the search for sexual gratification, but the doughboys of the Great War were no saints either. Sergeant Alvin C. York, a mountaineer who had little respect for the woodsmanship of his city-slicker comrades, did compliment them on their hunting skills in one area of endeavor: "Being soldiers, they was right smart when it come to finding them-there pretty French girls. Some of them shore knowed more about hunting and finding them, too, than I did about trailing coon and fox back there on the mountains at home."[21]

Sergeant Nat Frankel, who mentions several sexual encounters in his World War II memoir, explains that for the combat soldier, sex involved a sense of desperation along with the gratification: "The sexuality of the dogface in Europe was neither flamboyant nor sentimental, nor was it callous. There was great desperation in it and considerable satisfaction . . . every woman might be his last. This is a cliché, but a truthful and powerful one—particularly if you can imagine what it's like to make love while assuming that tomorrow you'll be dead."[22]

In mentioning a sense of desperation in the soldier's sexual couplings, Frankel takes a step toward acknowledging the vital role of women as more than just sexual objects. The soldier, living under great stress in an all-male society, missed the support and attention of his wife, mother, or girlfriend. The soldiers' macho environment precluded an open discussion of any essential need for mothering, but the more honest and reflective soldier-authors admit to it.[23] As James Jones acknowledged, "Men thought about women. In fact, women were probably always in their thoughts when they weren't actually in combat or immersed in work, getting ready for combat. When the presence of death and extinction are always just around the corner. . . , the comfort of women takes on a great importance. Woman is the antithesis of war."[24]

The one situation in which soldiers admitted to a need for mothering was when they were sick or wounded and in a military hospital. The caring, compassionate ward nurse was as important to the soldier's recovery as the medical treatment he received. Sergeant Bob Hoffman, hospitalized with wounds in June 1918, was thrilled to find that the nurses were "young and attractive American girls": "Anyone who has not been far away from women and children for a long period does not know what a necessary part of our lives they are."[25] The nurse's genuine affection touched the soldiers deeply. Private Leon C. Standifer, after recovering from his wounds during World War II, fondly remembers Georgia Yeager, his ward nurse: "Looking back, I appreciate Nurse Yeager's love and support, but I realize that she was more nearly typical than unique. Georgia was an army nurse who loved her country and the skinny little boys who were fighting for it. I was never able to thank her for the love."[26]

Though female companionship was a major element in the soldier's pursuit of eat, drink, and be merry, alcohol (supplemented by drugs during the Vietnam

War) played an even more central role.[27] Alcohol was a more available commodity than women, and it lent itself to group participation, or what historian Richard Holmes calls "communal drinking."[28]

A few soldiers did not drink at all, out of religious conviction, as in the case of Sergeant York, or because they were health and fitness devotees, as was Sergeant Hoffman. Most soldiers did drink, however, and as Bill Mauldin notes, they usually did so as part of a group and as part of their effort to cope: "I'm not trying to say the American army is a drunken army. Most of the men have the same attitude as I have about liquor. I drink very little, and I don't like strong liquor at all. Yet there have been times over here when I have tied one on because I was homesick, or bored, or because I was sitting around with a bunch of guys who had a bottle, and when it came around to me I just naturally took a belt at it."[29]

James Jones and his buddies, serving in the Pacific in World War II, were apparently less circumspect in their drinking: "In my outfit we got blind asshole drunk every chance we got."[30] Chances were limited, however, because alcohol was scarce in the sparsely populated Pacific. GIs fermented their own homebrew, traded war souvenirs with the navy or air force for liquor, and even strained the alcohol out of shaving lotion or hair tonic.[31] On rare occasions, Japanese beer or sake was "liberated."[32]

Finding alcohol was much less of a problem for soldiers in Europe during the world wars. Doughboys' memoirs recount boisterous drinking parties at the local French *estaminet,* which made a good profit on sales to soldiers.[33] The French and Italians were just as eager to sell alcohol to Americans during World War II, and any liquor found abandoned in a cellar or house was fair game, especially once the GIs entered Germany.[34]

Procuring alcohol during the Korean War proved more challenging but not impossible. Some units were adept at fermenting their own brew, often a responsibility of the mess section. Captain Charles M. Bussey had the highest praise for his company's mess sergeant, who not only managed to continue feeding the troops during the precipitous retreat following the Chinese intervention but also rescued the company's batch of raisin jack.[35] The Korean War also saw the first issue, on a regular basis, of alcohol (usually beer) to the troops.[36]

During the Vietnam War, beer was again issued on a regular basis, and hard liquor was also available. But it was the increasing use of drugs, especially marijuana, that became a hallmark of that war. Memoirs from the Korean War make occasional mention of marijuana and heroin but not nearly to the extent that drug use pervades the memoirs of the Vietnam War.[37] Individual exposure to drugs in Vietnam varied considerably, however. Some grunts, especially in early-deploying units, report little or no drug use.[38] Other soldiers mention trying drugs, usually marijuana, for the first time in Vietnam, and some admitted to becoming regular users.[39] By late in the war, hard-drug use was on the rise, notably heroin or opium, and a distinct drug subculture, the "heads," had become well established (as opposed to the "juicers," who stuck primarily to alcohol).[40]

Communal drinking or dope smoking occurred regularly during breaks in the action. Drinking or taking drugs while in combat, however, was a different matter. A drunk or stoned soldier was not reliable or effective. The story that Elliott Johnson, a World War II artillery observer, tells of a drunken soldier who began singing "Row, Row, Row Your Boat" at the top of his lungs during a night river crossing, would be amusing except for the fact that the defending Germans immediately opened up with a deadly mortar barrage.[41] Leaders and soldiers alike considered drinking or drug taking unacceptable when in combat. Stories about incapacitated soldiers at the front are thus the exception.

While sparing in the use of alcohol or drugs in combat, the soldier took no precautions with tobacco, except to guard the lighted tip at night, because smoking did not impair the senses. Many men first took up smoking in the army, which went to some lengths to keep them supplied with tobacco. Corporal Charles F. Minder observed that combat is "a terrible strain on your nerves and, unconsciously, you are continually rolling cigarettes. I smoke two or three packs of Bull Durham a day."[42] Nothing changed with World War II, except that cigarettes were more commonly prerolled. Ernie Pyle noted that "a guy in war has to have some outlet for his nerves, and I guess smoking is as good as anything."[43]

Smoking remained a universally prescribed stress reducer during the Korean and Vietnam Wars. As the only nonsmoker in an entire company in Korea, Lieutenant Dill was the odd man out: "It was not easy to be a non-smoker in the army in 1951; it caused unfavorable comment."[44] Lieutenant Howard Matthias, like Dill a nonsmoker, discovered how critical cigarettes were to his men's morale in Korea when monsoon flooding cut them off from resupply: "The smokers began to move from being irritable to downright antagonistic. . . . While watching the desperate withdrawal of my smoking men I began to realize that it was easier for them to give up food than it was their smokes."[45] Resupply by helicopter finally allowed the smokers to resume their habit.

The environment of war was the catalyst for the eat, drink, and be merry phenomenon. It generated a need to blow off steam, revel in the moment, and forget about what the next day might bring. Even Sergeant York, who as a born-again Christian had sworn off drinking and brawling long before entering the army, nevertheless accepted his comrades' excesses: "I had forgiven it if they drank and tore things up before going to the front. Anyway, that was their own business. If they got happiness that way, it was all right with me. I guess they sorter figured they were going to be mussed up and maybe killed when they got into the trenches, so they figured they might jes as well enjoy things while they had the chance."[46]

Doughboys' memoirs contain numerous accounts of drinking, singing, eating, and fighting. In a letter to his mother, Corporal Minder asked for her understanding and tolerance of his frequent trips to the local bistro: "When we are tired out, a glass of wine or ale braces us up, and makes us feel better right away. For a little while, we forget all about the darn army and the war and the unreasonable officers."[47]

And forgetting, or more accurately, not thinking about the army and the war and what lay ahead was the central goal. John Hersey, awaiting transport to the Pacific in World War II, understood: "I was in uniform and on my way, borne on a tide of servicemen going out to action. San Francisco was the jumping-off place. It did not take much acuity to understand that although fear of death was never mentioned, it was universally shared, and that the way of dealing with it was to eat, drink, have sex if possible, and be very merry."[48] Sergeant Giles and his fellow combat engineers in World War II also adhered to that philosophy: "Drinking & sex & war—they all go together. Doesn't matter if you should or shouldn't, you do. It's got nothing to do with the kind of guy you were back home or want to be when you go back. And that's the jinx—you may not go back. Your life expectancy is durned short. What's here & right now is living & all you may have of it."[49]

The eat, drink, and be merry process was an integral part of the Korean and Vietnam Wars as well. Rotation out of the line in Korea or a return to the firebase after humping the boonies in Vietnam was cause to celebrate. Helicopter pilot Robert Mason describes the process: "What do you do on your first day off after weeks of action when you're feeling tired, depressed, and doomed on a hot, wet day at Camp Holloway, Vietnam? You get in a deuce-and-a-half [truck] and go into Pleiku and drink your brains out. That's what you do."[50]

Soldier revelry was usually a group process, but the goals of immediate gratification and the drowning out of past memories and future fears were ultimately personal. Thus, the individual soldier on pass or leave from the combat zone often pursued an eat, drink, and be merry philosophy as fervently as he did when part of the group. The Rest and Recuperation program established in the Korean War was perfectly suited to this pursuit, as evidenced by how quickly the five-day R and R to Japan was dubbed "I and I" by the GIs: "Intercourse and Intoxication."[51]

The R and R program (now standing for "Rest and Recreation") established during the Vietnam War allowed a seven-day trip to several approved locations in the Pacific area, with Hong Kong, Taiwan, and Japan being popular.[52] Philip Dosier, the main character in the novel *Close Quarters,* described the goals of the grunt heading off to R and R: "I want to get drunk, good and drunk. I want to get laid, laid right, laid into a stupor. I want to go somewhere chilly and sunny, even snow-covered some, somewhere cushy and quiet and calm."[53]

R and R passed all too quickly, however, and the soldier faced the prospect of returning from his new-found paradise to finish the remainder of his tour of duty. More than one soldier, knowing what lay ahead, considered not going back.[54] But the vast majority did return, despite sharing Robert Mason's apprehension over being reimmersed in the environment of war: "A nearly hysterical feeling of fear hit me as I stepped off the plane at An Khe [Vietnam]. The fear welled up within me, changing to a prickly, cold terror in the moist heat."[55]

Mason's rekindled fear raises anew the issue of coping. Although breaks in the action, from a short stint in reserve to seven days of R and R, were invaluable in rebuilding a soldier's physical and emotional well being, they do not explain how he coped while actually in the midst of the fighting. The soldier dealt with the stresses of combat in various ways, not the least of which was to take his job seriously and to feel a sense of accomplishment, even pride, in doing so.

## THE CANNON FODDER FIGHTS BACK

The soldier's realization that he was only a minor, expendable cog in a huge war machine was demoralizing. This realization, however, came from a macroview of his situation, and a soldier rarely dwelled on the big picture. His attention focused instead on the immediate family of his platoon and company. "Combat provincialism," as Peter G. Bourne calls it, was the norm: "[The soldiers] are not only unconcerned about the political and strategic aspects of the war; they are also disinterested in the outcome of any battle that is not in their own immediate vicinity. In this way their emotional energy can be reserved for their primary objective, their own personal physical and emotional survival."[56]

Bourne based his conclusion on his observations of the Vietnam War grunt, but combat provincialism was also evident in earlier wars. The soldiers themselves came to recognize, and marvel at, their lack of concern for anything beyond their immediate horizon. Lieutenant Paul Boesch, whose infantry regiment had stalled in its effort to seize the fortified town of Dinard, part of the German-held defenses of the seaport of St. Malo in France in World War II, discovered that he now cared little about the big picture:

> Lying there in my hole in the hill, I mused from time to time about how my war had suddenly diminished in size. Heretofore I had always tried to keep abreast of the broad strategy, to read about developments in all theaters of operations. . . . But now I found I didn't give a damn about these things. It wasn't a question of how far Patton's tanks had gone that day or how the Russians were faring; I wanted to know how our 3d Battalion was getting along, how many casualties Company F was taking from the shelling, what was being done to blast the stalemate which had developed in our own, particular, private little war.[57]

This attitude was understandable—Boesch had enough to worry about without dwelling on the fate of unknown soldiers elsewhere in the war zone. During the Vietnam War, Lieutenant Lanning observed, "Our interest in the war beyond the company was minimal. . . . Personal survival and taking care of my men overshadowed any curiosity about the general situation."[58]

This provincialism, while a natural condition of combat, also served as a valuable coping mechanism. Within his microcosm, the individual soldier discovered that he still mattered. His actions affected his own and his comrades' survival and their success in combat. The psychiatrists Herbert Hendin and Ann Pollinger Haas, in studying why some Vietnam War soldiers handled stress better than others, discovered that those who fared best had concentrated on the job at hand: "All of these veterans evidenced an ability to deal with the limited objectives of each day's mission. Those who developed stress disorders following combat, on the other hand, tended to see war in less manageable, less rational terms which often permitted the sense of chaos generated by the war to dominate them."[59]

Soldiers who focused on their immediate responsibilities retained a sense of control over their situation, found that their actions made a difference, and took pride in their accomplishments. And contrary to the notion that the combat soldier's job is simple, in reality soldiers often shouldered considerable responsibility and had to act on their own initiative.[60] The doughboy corporal Horatio Rogers, for example, scouted out firing positions, often at night and in bad weather, for his artillery battery. He then led the battery to the new location, a difficult job requiring skill in orienteering. Rogers describes the tremendous weight of responsibility, as well as the skills, called for in reconnoitering a new position: "How carefully I would study the map and plan my route . . . , and how earnestly I would pray, as I rode along through the darkness, to be allowed to find it. I learned to turn every condition to my purpose: the stars, if any showed, the direction of the wind, the slope of the land, the color of the sky around its edges, the shapes of trees that might be recognized on the way back, and how they looked from both directions. My pocket compass was almost worn out from use."[61]

Soldiers like Rogers took their jobs seriously because lives depended on it. In a now-famous tale of heroism in World War II, Private John Ahrens held off Japanese attackers on Tulagi Island in the Solomons all night with his Browning Automatic Rifle. When his commanding officer found Ahrens in the morning, he was mortally wounded, with thirteen dead Japanese in front of his foxhole. The dying marine's only question to his captain was, "They tried to run over me last night, but I don't think they made it. Did they?"[62] Ahrens knew he carried a critical weapon—the automatic rifle. Fighting from a one-man foxhole, he also knew that he alone could stop the Japanese from breaking into his unit's perimeter at the point he was assigned to defend. It is not too much to assume that Private Ahrens died a little easier, once his captain told him that the enemy had not made it through.

Soldiers knew which jobs were especially dangerous or difficult, such as scouting, walking point, or carrying the unit's automatic rifle or machine gun. A man who did one of these jobs well could take special pride in his work. Stanley Goff was reluctant at first to assume responsibility for the M-60 machine gun; it was heavy, and using it attracted enemy fire. Goff soon discovered, however, that he was a good machine gunner, and he thus won the admiration of his comrades: "I was like a new man to the guys. I mean, they had respect for me as an individual that could really handle the pig."[63]

Goff's desire for respect was typical. Soldiers not only believed that they could contribute within the microcosm of their squad or platoon, but they also wanted recognition for doing so. The memoirs contain cynical comments about awards and promotions going to the undeserving, which certainly occurred, but those same memoirs reflect their authors' pride on receiving a decoration. A line from Jones's novel *The Thin Red Line* sums up the soldier's attitude toward awards: "Everyone pretended medals didn't mean anything, but everyone who got one was secretly proud."[64]

World War I chaplain Father Duffy understood the importance of recognition, which he called "a soldier's meed."[65] He was proud of his own Distinguished Service Cross: "There is no man living who can truthfully say that it means nothing to him to receive the bronze cross and red, white and blue bar of our army."[66] Most infantrymen were intensely proud of their Combat Infantry Badge (CIB), an award established in World War II. The badge marked them as a breed apart—men who had been at the cutting edge. Private Blunt was certainly proud of his: "It was the most coveted medal by fighting troops and I felt an inner pride and satisfaction of achievement."[67]

Promotions served a similar function. Higher rank meant recognition for good performance and faith in the soldier's potential. Ernie Pyle noted the importance of promotions and service stripes: "A little thing like a stripe can do wonders for morale."[68] A soldier with a few stripes and campaign ribbons was proud because of what those awards signified: here stands a seasoned and successful combat soldier.[69] Corporal Albert French, convalescing in a Stateside military hospital from a wound received in Vietnam, prepared for his first trip home. He donned his dark-green marine uniform "with red stripes on the shoulders. Somebody stripes, corporal stripes, what-I-was stripes. Had ribbons on my chest too. The ribbons said, *He saw some shit,* if you knew what they said at all."[70]

The soldier's need for recognition was even more elementary than the desire for an award or promotion. He just wanted to be told that he was doing his share and that someone appreciated it. A few simple words of praise for a job well done from a respected leader, for example, meant the world to a young soldier. Private Sledge remembered how his first sergeant called the survivors of the fighting on Peleliu together to tell them, without fanfare, that they had proven themselves good marines in a tough battle: "Words of praise were rare from the heart of such a stern old salt who expected every man to do his best and tolerated nothing less. His straightforward, sincere praise and statement of respect and admiration for what our outfit had done made me feel like I had won a medal. His talk was not the loud harangue of a politician or the cliché-studded speech of some rear-echelon officer or journalist. It was a quiet statement of praise from one who had endured the trials of Peleliu with us. . . . His words meant a lot to me, and they apparently did to my comrades, too."[71]

A few simple words of encouragement and recognition in the midst of combat could mean a great deal. For Private Goff, who had just fought to the point of exhaustion, firing his M-60 machine gun until it literally fell apart, a simple compliment from his commander that "This guy did a hell of a job"—was his soldier's meed: "It made me feel good, like any compliment to somebody for working hard. . . . That the company commander would notice you, out of a hundred men, that would make you feel good."[72] For Private Richard E. Ogden, finding out that his platoon leader had put him in for a Bronze Star for bravery meant more than the medal itself: "Pride, and the idea of a medal, did enlighten my spirits. It is gratifying to know that someone has confidence in you; it fortifies your own."[73]

Thus the combat soldier, while understanding his insignificance in the wider scheme of things, retained his sense of self-worth within his unit. Except in moments of despair, he refused to write himself off as cannon fodder. He also refused to give in to the army "green machine's" perceived effort to treat him as an insignificant cipher.[74] The egalitarian citizen-soldier resisted the chickenshit, the institutional inequalities, and the impersonal treatment in a variety of ways.[75] Primarily, enlisted soldiers could look out for one another. Arnold Rose, a member of the Research Branch in World War II and himself an enlisted man, describes how the enlisted "underground" took care of its own: "The best and surest way for an enlisted man to get the army to do something for him is to talk personally to the enlisted men who 'run' the staff sections at headquarters. These 'underground' channels can more than make up for official callousness and unconcern."[76]

Being on good terms with the unit clerk, supply specialist, or cook might allow the soldier to circumvent the system or use it to his advantage. Even soldiers without special connections could help one another; they regularly covered for each other when going on unauthorized forays. Sergeant Hoffman, who was a model soldier on the whole, nevertheless repeatedly went AWOL while in France, apparently just to prove he could do it. On at least two occasions, he and his buddies returned to the bivouac site to find their unit gone but managed to catch up with it without anyone turning them in. Hoffman was a staunch advocate of doughboy individualism: "The American soldier is a good soldier. He has not had the centuries of drilling to make his own individual self subservient to the will of the commanding officer; he does not like to salute the brass bar of Lieutenant John Brown unless that lieutenant has won his respect through his deeds; he does not like to be regimented, turned into a mere robot; he can think and act for himself."[77]

The soldier could indeed think and act for himself—sometimes in the form of acts of rebellion, which succeeded more often than is commonly perceived in a supposedly rigid, authoritarian, military hierarchy. In one classic act of rebellion, the doughboy cannoneers in Charles MacArthur's battery, after being ordered to discard most of their personal belongings and carry what little remained on their backs because of the shortage of transport and horses, discovered that the battery officers had stashed their substantial bedrolls in the supply wagon. At the first halt, the men tied the officers' blanket rolls to nearby trees with long ropes, so that when the march resumed, "the fat rolls flopped out of the wagon and with them all the German binoculars, French cognac, devilled ham, hair tonic, silk underwear, and other curiosities peculiar to officers. What was sauce for the goose was tabasco for the gander."[78]

Some soldiers gained a reputation for being troublemakers, which elevated them in the eyes of their fellow enlisted men because they had the audacity to buck the system. Private Leckie explained that this sort of troublemaker, in the Marine Corps in World War II, was called a "brig-rat," and Leckie was proud to be one: "A man who lands in the brig is apt to be a man of bold spirit and independent mind, who must occasionally rebel against the harsh and unrelenting discipline of the camp."[79]

At times a soldier even got away with a serious act of rebellion because right was on his side. In Private Ogden's marine battalion, a unit that had just arrived in Vietnam, his platoon sergeant had not yet lost his fondness for peacetime, garrison-style Mickey Mouse. The sergeant ordered Ogden, who had just failed a ludicrously strict weapons inspection, to dig a four-by-four-foot hole for punishment. Ogden tore up his hands digging, but his platoon sergeant would not allow him to go to the medics to have his blisters treated. An argument ensued, insults were traded, and fists flew. Almost as a reflex, Ogden pulled out his .45-caliber pistol and leveled it at the sergeant, who then backed off. To his amazement, Ogden got off with a verbal reprimand from the company commander because the sergeant had so completely overstepped the bounds of normal discipline. Furthermore, because the platoon sergeant was universally despised, Ogden found himself a hero: "I was the toast of the town. The first anti-hero of the war for First Platoon, Hotel Company."[80]

Soldiers rebelled against perceived inequities in the distribution of desirable commodities, such as food or alcohol, by obtaining what they wanted by "midnight requisition." Beyond the immediate enjoyment of whatever loot was procured, successful raids provided a sense of victory over the system. The accomplished scrounger, and every unit had at least one, was valued for his talents, as World War II private Clyde Blue explains: "It's not talked about generally, but in every unit there is a whiskey man and a woman man, meaning wherever they land they can locate these little incidentals in a short period of time, even on a desert island."[81] L Company in Father Duffy's regiment had Fortgang, the "champion moocher."[82] Lieutenant Joseph R. Owen's company had Sergeant Richard, their "acquisition specialist."[83] MacArthur's artillery battery had the amazing "Porch Climber." Scrounging was sometimes an act of pure rebellion. Porch Climber, for example, once stole four cases of canned peaches from the battery officers' mess. MacArthur and crew ate the peaches with gusto, "tossing the empty cans back into the officers' supply wagon for luck."[84] More often, however, scrounging was a way to circumvent a system that seemed nonresponsive or unfair. Soldiers sought to acquire material needed to survive or to improve their living conditions.

The art and science of scrounging, or "salvaging," was so pervasive in World War I that Lieutenant Robert G. Merrick considered it an integral part of the "ethics of the front": "Such was the way of the front. The only sure way to keep anything there was to place a man with a gun on guard over it. According to the ethics of the front, it was all right to take anything you could, provided it helped you in the execution of the war. This was not known as stealing; it was called salvaging. I know of one man who salvaged a Ford, and there were many instances of the salvaging of motorcycles and sidecars, while the salvaging of such things as horses, food, supplies, and ammunition was of hourly occurrence."[85]

Doughboys "salvaged," and World War II GIs "requisitioned," but the process was the same, as Pyle explains: "In war areas where things are scarce and red tape still rears its delaying head, a man learns to get what he needs simply by 'requisitioning.' It isn't stealing, it's the only way to acquire certain things. The stress of war puts old virtues in a changed light."[86] The sort of requisitioning that Pyle and Merrick are describing often received at least the tacit approval of leaders because it benefited the unit. Captain Richard D. Camp's marine supply sergeant in Vietnam, for example, "was a thief of the first order, but I never gave him trouble because he was also one of the most good-hearted souls I ever met. His thieving was dedicated to supporting the company."[87]

The appropriation of vehicles, weapons, or equipment deemed necessary for prosecuting the war was a common occurrence. For example, as Captain Richard M. Hardison's artillery battalion transited England en route to the fighting in France during World War II, its truck fleet mysteriously increased by about a dozen vehicles, complete with freshly painted unit markings; meanwhile, ordnance depot stocks turned up short the same amount.[88] And when Lieutenant Sullivan took over his infantry platoon during the Korean War, it had just returned from guarding enemy prisoners of war on Koje Island. He was pleased to find that the platoon's firepower was considerably enhanced by three light machine guns and three Browning Automatic Rifles, albeit at the expense of a U.S. Navy weapons locker on board the ship that had just returned them from the island.[89]

In the case of Sergeant Ralph Zumbro's tank company in Vietnam, the need was not for entire vehicles or weapons but for parts to keep what they had functioning. A supply depot of the unit they were supporting, however, refused to provide the necessary parts. In a midnight raid that even a Viet Cong sapper would admire, Zumbro and a select team set off charges at the depot that simulated incoming mortar rounds. As the supply clerks dove for cover into their bunkers, the raiders, mounted in an armored personnel carrier, filled their requisitions and sped away.[90]

Sometimes the scrounging was of a more desperate sort. Soldiers learned, of necessity, to ransack the pockets and packs of the dead on the battlefield. Doughboys were chronically short of canned combat rations, and they frequently mention taking food from dead comrades and foes. The cannoneer MacArthur went so far as to praise the Germans for their discipline in not eating their emergency rations, thus ensuring that a doughboy could find a meal in a German pack.[91] Soldiers also took clothing or equipment from the dead. Lieutenant Paul Boesch, whose feet were cold and wet in the miserable autumn weather of the Huertgen Forest during World War II, found a dead GI with rubber overshoes in his size: "As I removed the overshoes from the dead man I felt no emotion other than selfish satisfaction that at last my feet would be protected." Soldiers, especially veteran combatants, rarely felt squeamish about stripping the dead of equipment that they obviously no longer needed. As Boesch added, the dead man "was beyond caring whether his feet were wet or not."[92]

Not only were the belongings of the dead fair game but also anything else found lying about the battlefield, from discarded supplies to abandoned civilian property. Captured enemy food occasionally provided a welcome supplement to combat rations. One of Lieutenant Boesch's men, after they had all enjoyed a meal of German salami and pumpernickel, reckoned that "gastronomically . . . this has been an excellent day."[93] American soldiers were not the only accomplished scroungers, of course. Private Standifer, while scouting an abandoned village in France in World War II, put his rifle aside to chase a rooster: "As I rounded a corner in hot pursuit, the rooster squawked and ran back between my legs. Then I saw why. A German soldier wanted the bird too, and he hadn't been dumb enough to leave his rifle lying on the ground. I turned and ran."[94]

Sometimes the appropriated livestock or garden vegetables had not yet been abandoned by fleeing civilians. Putting it more bluntly, soldiers stole it. Once the GIs entered enemy territory, as occurred in Europe in World War II, looting was especially common. "This is turning into a lootin', tootin' war these days," noted Sergeant Giles after his outfit's entry into Germany.[95] Soldiers did not always steal, electing instead to pay or barter for food and drink, but outright thievery did occur, usually in the form of raids on vegetable gardens and chicken coops, or by the butchering of some unfortunate animal killed by "enemy" fire.[96]

Stealing a chicken, requisitioning supplies at midnight, or going over the hill to party in a nearby town were clear violations of the regulations and, despite the occasional collusion of a junior leader, did not go unpunished by the military authorities. These acts of rebellion against a system that often seemed indifferent or unfair did not signify indiscipline, however. The individualistic American soldier, ever disdainful of chickenshit and spit and polish, was not necessarily an undisciplined fighter, as Private Standifer observes: "The hero of Mauldin's cartoons in *Up Front* was the sloppy, undisciplined, pragmatic American soldier. It was an open secret that when necessary, that slouching, unshaven GI could be strongly disciplined and dedicated to the needs of his unit."[97]

This discipline was not a natural phenomenon but had to be instilled. The bedrock for discipline was "coercive institutional authority," to use a phrase from the World War II Stouffer Study: "The sheer coercive power of Army authority was a factor in combat motivation which must not be forgotten simply because it is easy to take for granted. It was omnipresent, and its existence had been impressed on the soldier from his first days in the army when he was read the many punitive articles from the Articles of War."[98]

This "formal," or "imposed," discipline was only the starting point, however, albeit a necessary one.[99] Beginning with his initial training, and continuing with his integration into a unit, the soldier internalized these formal military rules, procedures, and values. Yet with time he began to think less about the punishment he would receive for disobeying regulations and more about the guilt or shame he would feel if he failed in his duties. This self-discipline became a stronger motivator than formal discipline. Furthermore, self-discipline, reinforced by effective training, helped the soldier cope with the environment of war, a quality the soldiers themselves came to appreciate.[100] As the World War II marine Frank Chadwick observed, "During the chaos, you're so damn busy you don't really think. The training takes over. You're conditioned to act in a certain way. It's the thing to do to save yourself too."[101]

Captain Charles L. Thomas, commanding a tank-destroyer company in World War II, was seriously injured but fought on because of his training and discipline: "I was badly hurt but I didn't have time to think about it. Thinking is your worst enemy in war. . . . My training had been to *do,* particularly in an emergency. I, and many others like me, are proof of the proper automatic behavior that continual training and discipline brings about."[102] The Vietnam War platoon leader James R. McDonough also believed in the importance of discipline: "In the heat of battle there is no time for second-guessing the commander, and it is necessary for a soldier to develop an automatic response to an order. Such instantaneous obedience will overcome all fears, all confusion, all inclinations toward self-preservation. It is the result of unmitigated daily discipline in all things: from taking the daily malaria pill, to shaving each day, to attacking into the face of an automatic weapon."[103]

The Korean War platoon leader and company commander Theodore R. Fehrenbach agrees with McDonough that discipline helps overcome fear in battle and adds an important corollary: well-disciplined soldiers are proud soldiers and this pride, in turn, strengthens self-discipline in a reciprocal process: "On line, most normal men are afraid, have been afraid, or will be afraid. Only when disciplined to obey orders quickly and willingly, can such fear be controlled. Only when superbly trained and conditioned against the shattering experience of war, only knowing almost from rote what to do, can men carry out their tasks come what may. And knowing they are disciplined, trained, and conditioned brings pride to men—pride in their own toughness, their own ability; and this pride will hold them true when all else fails."[104]

## "THE DISPLACEMENT, RESTRICTION, AND DETACHMENT OF ATTENTION"

When soldiers could not physically escape the environment of war through a break in the action, they resorted to a variety of mind games that provided mental escape. The psychiatrist Jonathan Shay summed up these games: "Displacement, restriction and detachment of attention are fundamental survival skills under all conditions of inescapable terror."[105] Although displacing, restricting, or detaching attention suggests the proverbial ostrich putting its head in the sand, these techniques nevertheless helped the soldier cope with the horrors of war by allowing him not to think about them.

Tim O'Brien has pointed out that "soldiers are dreamers."[106] A soldier, or anyone under stress or in danger, "displaces" his attention to a more-pleasant place and time: "We live in our heads a lot, but especially during situations of stress and great peril. It's a means of escape in part, but it's also a means of dealing with the real world—not just escaping it, but dealing with it."[107] Soldiers regularly daydreamed about their seemingly distant, prewar past, or what they would do in the even more distant, postwar future. The military correspondent Harry Brown, in his novel about an infantry platoon in Italy in World War II, describes the process: "The war was incidental to a man's thoughts. It entered into them, of course, but it did not take them over bodily. There had been too many years of life, too many memories, before the war had come along. A man could exist on these memories, he could withdraw into them, he could construct them into an unpierceable shell. They were his defence against the violence of the world."[108]

Soldiers daydreamed and talked among themselves about loved ones at home, former good times, and what they would do when the war was over, or in the case of rotating soldiers, when their tour of duty was up. Corporal Victor Fox explains that such thoughts of the future, no matter how fanciful, were critical for coping with the harsh realities of the present: "Talk of future plans might not always ring true; nevertheless, we believed in them. Being right there on the front lines made most talk of the future seem like wistful fantasy, but the men had to believe they were going to leave Korea, and that some day they would have a future somewhere else."[109] Marine corporal William D. Ehrhart would have agreed: "Facts were easy to ignore in Vietnam; it was a way of life. When facts got in the way, you could conjure a dream by force of will, and make the future bright again . . . an infinite number of dreams can dance on the head of a pin."[110]

Of course, at times daydreaming was a dangerous distraction from the business at hand. A daydreaming soldier on guard duty might fail to see an approaching enemy or, if on patrol, fail to spot an ambush or a booby trap. Corporal French warned of the dangers of daydreaming while on point in Vietnam: "Up front you had to stay with your mind, couldn't daydream, sneak home, think about what you had done or wanted to do when you go there."[111]

Home was undoubtedly what the soldier daydreamed about most. Almost all soldiers had ties to the home front, but the nature and strength of those ties varied. Some soldiers overidealized their home life as a counter to the horrors of combat, which could lead to postwar disappointment when home failed to live up to expectations.[112] Conversely, some soldiers, rather than obsessing about home, found that memories of their previous life grew dimmer the longer they were away and the deeper they became immersed in the environment of war. Ernie Pyle noticed this transition among the GIs in North Africa in World War II: "At first homesickness can almost kill a man. But time takes care of that. It isn't normal to moon in the past forever. Home gradually grows less vivid; the separation from it less agonizing. There finally comes a day—not suddenly but gradually, as a sunset-touched cloud changes its color—when a man is living almost wholly wherever he is. His life has caught up with his body, and his days become full war days, instead of American days simply transported to Africa."[113]

For Lieutenant Lanning, the "full war days" caught up with him after only a week or so in Vietnam: "It already seemed as if my previous life no longer existed."[114] But Lanning, like most soldiers, never entirely forgot about home. Private Ketwig observed that no matter how distant the home front, or "the World" as the grunts called it, seemed to be, and no matter how faded the memories became, the soldier clung to it: "The World existed. All too often the fantasy became clouded over by the day's events. It seemed far away, intangible, even alien; but you couldn't let go of the fact that it existed, or you might never make it back."[115]

Mail provided the major link to that distant world, and Private Blunt speaks for all soldiers when he says that the precious memories of home that mail fostered were well worth any accompanying pangs of homesickness: "Mail call was a very special event for a GI. It allowed him a few minutes to withdraw in his private shell and close out the sordidness of the war around him. These few moments were a precious link to the sanity and stability of our civilian lives."[116] Mail and packages helped the soldier displace his attention, to return to Jonathan Shay's term, to a more pleasant time and place. Packages also helped the soldier cope in a straightforward way—food, clothing, and other useful items from home made life at the front a little easier. Soldiers shared their packages with comrades, as did the men in Lieutenant Owen's platoon in Korea: "The packages had cakes and cookies and an occasional bottle of booze, and these were passed around the squads."[117]

Mail and packages from home were not universally positive morale boosters, however. Sometimes letters brought news of death or illness. Private Sledge was devastated to learn that his beloved pet spaniel had been hit by a car and killed.[118] The news for Captain Hyman Samuelson was worse—his young wife was terminally ill.[119] He at least made it home before she died. More commonly, friends and relatives wrote to complain about how hard times were on the home front, what with rationing and all. These complainers unwittingly upset the soldiers, as Bill Mauldin wrote: "A lot of people aren't very smart when they write to a soldier. They complain about the gasoline shortage, or worry him or anger him in a hundred different ways which directly affect his efficiency and morale. Your feelings get touchy and explosive at the front."[120] For soldiers facing death and living in miserable conditions, complaints and problems broached in letters from home seemed irritatingly petty. Lieutenant Lanning's comment during the Vietnam War is typical: "When we received letters or read articles about problems back at home because of weather, money, or living conditions, we smiled and shook our heads. Correspondence about car accidents, lost jobs, or broken love affairs seemed ludicrous. If anyone wanted to find out about a hard life, let them join us."[121]

Short of the death or serious illness of a loved one, no bad news from home was more demoralizing than the Dear John letter. Thoughts of a special girl back home, and the belief that she would wait for her soldier to return, were all that kept some men going. With appalling frequency, the memoirs relate tales of soldiers who broke down, deserted, committed suicide, or became fatally careless in battle after receiving a Dear John letter. The World War II paratrooper Ross Carter, whose buddy Willie was taken away in a straitjacket after receiving a Dear John letter, described the devastating effects: "I saw more than one Willie leave in a strait jacket [sic]. As long as the boys fought in the belief that their sacrifices and hardships meant at least enough to the woman they loved to hold her loyalty, they could usually endure the hell of mechanized battle. When cruel letters jackknifed their faith, their moral fibers crumpled and some of them fell apart."[122]

Private Ehrhart, after months of regular correspondence with his fiancée while he was in Vietnam, received no mail from her for a month. When he finally got a letter, it was a Dear John. He was devastated: "Death I could have understood. Anything. But this. 'This isn't possible,' I thought. 'This isn't *possible!* Eight fucking months!' Long letters. Passionate letters. Filled with every imaginable endearment. A perfect chain, like a rosary, a lifeline, a beacon. Gone just like that?"[123] Ehrhart did not break down or attempt suicide, but he never got over losing his "lifeline."

No news from home was almost as devastating as bad news because it was invariably taken as an ominous sign. As in Ehrhart's case, this rationale all too often proved correct. Sometimes, however, no mail simply reflected the erratic postal system.[124] For a few soldiers, scarcity of mail had nothing to do with the failings of the postal system; they had no one at home who cared enough to write. Private David Parks, who regularly received letters and packages while in Vietnam, felt sorry for his sergeant, who had not received a letter in three months: "I hope he gets a letter soon. . . . It's tough when you don't have any letters on the pony express. Some guys walk away with a handful. Some walk away with a sad face. If only the people back there knew how a few lines cheer you up, change your whole outlook. I hated to face [Sergeant] Emory today. Here he was with nothing and I got letters from Marie Ann, Ziggy, Mother and a package of brownies and another great letter from Deedee."[125]

Homefront civilians did not always understand the importance of mail, but veterans did. While in Vietnam, Sergeant Zumbro received a Christmas package from his cousin, a Korean War veteran, only the box was not for him. The cousin sent a note accompanying the package: "In every outfit, there's one poor troop who doesn't get anything for Christmas, so here is his box." Sure enough, one man in the company had nothing on Christmas day—Zumbro's package brought grateful tears to his eyes.[126]

Thus, the mail usually provided a few cherished minutes of escape for the soldier, allowing him to displace his attention from the grim realities of combat. Soldiers also learned to "restrict" their attention, to use Shay's second term, to the routine tasks at hand. By absorbing themselves in the details of preparing for battle, and by concentrating on their job once in combat, such as keeping a crew-served weapon or armored fighting vehicle in action, soldiers were too busy to be aware of their fears.[127] Corporal Wilder found that the demands of bringing an artillery battery into firing position absorbed his attention: "There is a great anesthesia to danger in the common risk. Dashing into position with a battery, the intricate moves and absorption in tasks for which one has been trained, all this dull[s] one's individual anxiety."[128]

Peter Bourne, in his study of stress in Vietnam, discovered that when soldiers kept themselves busy preparing for an anticipated action, they had no time to work up anxieties. Some Special Forces soldiers he was observing threw themselves into preparations to meet an expected attack by laying mines, stringing barbed wire, and stocking ammunition and medical supplies. These men were "action oriented individuals who characteristically spent little time in introspection. Their response to any environmental threat was to engage in a furor of activity which rapidly dissipated the developing tension."[129] Bourne also observed helicopter medics in action. Evacuating wounded soldiers by helicopter, often under fire, was hazardous work. One of the medics, Bourne learned, used "well-ingrained ritualistic compulsive behavior" to alleviate stress when en route to pick up the wounded: "He would mentally review in minute detail every single action he would perform from the moment the helicopter touched the ground. In some ways it was as though he had taken the old Army adage that if you do your job right you will stay out of trouble, and extended it to cover even the intransigencies of combat."[130]

Restricting attention to routine matters assumes that there are established routines to focus on in the first place. To the extent possible, a soldier clung to routine in the form of standard operating procedures (SOPs), battle drills, minor military rituals, and daily mundane duties, not only because they diverted his attention from more unpleasant thoughts but also because they provided a sense of normalcy and predictability in an inherently unstable environment. Tim O'Brien describes this process: "The routinization of the war, which helped make it tolerable, included even trivial things—what to talk about and when, the times to rest and the times to march and the times to keep the guard, when to tell jokes and when not to, the order of march, when to send out ambushes and when to fake them. These issues were not debatable. They were governed by the informal SOPs, and these SOPs were more important than the Code of Conduct."[131]

Informal SOPs provided a small measure of stability in an uncertain world. Lieutenant Raleigh Couzens, a platoon leader in Pat Frank's Korean War novel *Hold Back the Night,* made C-ration coffee for himself and his company commander every morning, conditions permitting: "This was a bond between them, their first morning coffee. . . . It gave some continuity to a life that at best was nomadic and insecure."[132] For Lieutenant Lanning, in Vietnam, using the same grubby, plastic spoon every day, despite the inclusion of a clean one in each C-ration meal, provided a similar measure of continuity: "In a war where everything was in a constant state of change, including the men who fought it, my spoon was my one bit of permanency."[133]

Soldiers also learned to "detach" their attention, to use Shay's third term, from the immediate past and future. Dwelling on past combat meant recalling dead comrades and terrifying moments. Thinking about future combat was even more counterproductive, invariably leading to thoughts about how much more the soldier could take, or when his number would be up.[134] Better to live for the moment, but as Ernest Hemingway noted, that requires the suspension of imagination—something not easily accomplished: "To live properly in war, the individual eliminates all such things as potential danger. Then a thing is only bad when it is bad. It is neither bad before nor after. Cowardice, as distinguished from panic, is almost always simply a lack of ability to suspend the functioning of the imagination. Learning to suspend your imagination and live completely in the very second of the present minute with no before and no after is the greatest gift a soldier can acquire."[135]

Lieutenant Philip Caputo would agree with Hemingway about the dangers of an active imagination: "A man needs many things in war, but a strong imagination is not one of them." He also agrees that suppressing imagination is easier said than done. Some "unimaginative" grunts in Vietnam did "not feel afraid until there was obvious reason," but Caputo and most of his comrades "suffered from a constant expectancy, feeling that something was about to happen, waiting for it to happen, wishing it would happen just so the tension would be relieved."[136] Private Leckie also found it difficult to avoid thinking about the future, especially in quiet periods, and such thinking was not healthy: "Each fresh trial leaves a man more shaken than the last, and each period of tedium—with its time for speculative dread—leaves his foundations worn lower, his roots less firm for the next trial."[137]

Detaching attention from the immediate past and future was thus difficult for most soldiers, but some succeeded in doing so, at least some of the time. Lieutenant Hervey Allen claimed that he and his doughboys could do it: "There is no man who is so totally absorbed by the present as the soldier. It claims all his attention and he lives from moment to moment in times of danger with an animal keenness that absorbs him utterly. This is a happy and saving thing. With time to brood, conditions would often seem intolerable. To the soldier, *now* is everything."[138]

The marine correspondent Sergeant Dan Levin succeeded in suspending his imagination long enough to get him through the traumatic experience of the amphibious assault on Iwo Jima in World War II: "When I clamored to go ashore . . . on D-day, I had no concept of the experiences ahead. There was a refusal to think, to recognize facts. . . . Refusal to think and failure of imagination—that saving grace."[139]

## "OTHERWORLDLY FAITH"

By displacing, restricting, and detaching his attention, the soldier replaced anxious thoughts with pleasant dreams or simply refused to think at all about anything except the present and the mundane. Yet soldiers relied on more than just these mind games to cope. For some individuals, faith in a higher being and salvation was a major sustaining force. The overall role of religion as a coping mechanism, however, is complex and not in all cases positive. To begin to understand the impact of religion on the soldier, organized religion must be addressed as distinct from personal faith.

Organized religion supported in varying degree all the wars of the draft era. America's fight against the barbaric Hun or godless Communist was a righteous one. Most of this preaching was undertaken in the sincere belief that America was on the side of justice, but as one critical commentator points out, to place God exclusively on "our" side is to legitimize war: "God sanctifies *our* social order, *our* way of life, *our* values, *our* territory. Thus, warfare is applied theology."[140]

At times, and the Crusades come to mind, warfare was indeed applied theology. The secular-minded soldiers of the draft era, however, were as leery of religious proselytizing about "crusading" as they were of saber-rattling political pronouncements. One basic reason why soldiers took such pronouncements with a grain of salt was that the preachers and politicians who called them to arms would not usually be joining them on the crusade. For those men of the cloth who did go along—the uniformed chaplains—credibility could be lost if they failed to share in the dangers that they called upon the troops to endure in the name of God. During the Korean War, for example, Private Curtis James Morrow had no use for his unit's chaplains, who were always quick to disappear after pronouncing God's blessings on forthcoming attacks: "They usually came around just before a major assault. I could see the fear in their faces. Man, they could barely wait to get the hell out of there. . . . After a short prayer from their Bible, usually the 27th Psalm, they would proceed to do just that, get the hell out of there. And we, the poor unfortunate combat infantrymen, with the blessings of their version of God, would be sent on our way to kill, maim, suffer, and die."[141]

Conversely, chaplains like Father Duffy who avoided proclamations about God fighting on America's side and administered instead to the personal needs of their flock, sharing the hardships and dangers in the process, earned the men's respect and admiration.[142] These were "good," as opposed to "bad," chaplains. Lieutenant Lanning describes the difference: "The good ones sought out grunts in the field regardless of denomination. They were good for morale and were great at leaving a sense of calm and well-being behind. Other chaplains were rarely, if ever, seen in the field. Never leaving their BMB [Brigade Main Base] chapels, they administered to their assistants and to those in the rear. Whether they feared for their own personal safety or felt that we grunts were godless individuals, I do not know."[143]

The memoirs provide examples of both types, but good chaplains outnumbered the bad, and their ministration was often sought out by the soldiers who, though skeptical about organized religion's support of war, still retained their personal religious beliefs—at least many of them did. Actually, two distinctly contradictory attitudes toward personal faith are evident in the memoirs. Some soldiers lost their faith—what sort of God would allow this horrible carnage to occur? Other soldiers claimed that their religious beliefs grew stronger and that faith in God sustained them in combat. Jesse Glenn Gray addresses this dichotomy: "For soldiers who have entered military service with a firm otherworldly faith, there is frequently little difficulty in continuing to regard death as they did before, and the violence all about may well strengthen, rather than weaken, their convictions. On the other hand, soldiers whose religious faith is chiefly this-worldly, that is, social and ethical in content, often find war's destruction wreaking havoc with their belief."[144]

The soldiers themselves tended to generalize based on which side of this dichotomy their own beliefs put them. Some claimed that there were "no atheists in foxholes" and that faith sustained all soldiers. They noted the high attendance at religious services, often before or after a major battle, and took it as a sign of religious faith. Lieutenant Leslie W. Bailey noticed that his infantry battalion's attendance at church services was nearly 100 percent following the Battle of Fondouk Pass in North Africa in World War II. He concluded, "Evidently there were not many atheists among us."[145] Lieutenant Boesch was another World War II soldier who believed that foxholes and atheists were incompatible: "Many [soldiers] were devout with deep religious roots—others could trace their religious conviction to the same time they heard their first German artillery. But no matter what their religion, almost all were closer to God than they had been for years. . . . The religion of the foxholes was a serious matter to all of us, and no man hid his piety."[146] And Private Morrow observed a similar religious conversion on the battlefield in Korea: "All atheists become believers after their first serious engagement with the enemy, after the first time they experience a barrage of enemy artillery or mortar fire."[147]

That some soldiers found religion in the foxhole is indisputable. Add to these the men who came into the service with "deep religious roots," as Boesch noted, and clearly a substantial number of soldiers did rely on faith to help them cope. Just what they expected from God, however, was not always evident. A soldier often claimed, as the Korean War veteran Uzal Ent did, that "for me personally, my faith" was what kept him "going," but no elaboration followed.[148]

Certainly some soldiers possessed "otherworldly faith" as Gray defines it. They did not expect divine intervention on their behalf, but they did believe in God and salvation. That comforting thought helped the paratrooper George William Sefton make it through World War II: "There is just one effective shield against the mental and emotional stresses of combat. It is the firm conviction that there is a Supreme Being who decides the extent of your survival. So you do your job to the best of your ability and let Him call the shots."[149] World War II rifleman Leon Standifer also believed in God and placed his fate in his hands: "I wasn't looking for assurance that my life would be spared. People get killed in combat. I didn't expect God to favor me above other Christians."[150]

Many soldiers, however, expected, or at least prayed for, exactly that—they wanted God to spare them. They were not so much comforted by a belief in salvation as they were by a conviction, or hope, that God would protect them. Klaus H. Huebner wished for such protection: "The chaplain and I walk together. It is definitely comforting to have him at my side. I know he is a better Christian than I am. God will surely spare him, and if He does I, walking with him, will probably be spared also. I have suddenly become a superstitious foxhole Christian."[151]

During the Vietnam War, Specialist Dominick Yezzo "found" religion for the same reason. After a near-miss on his hootch by an enemy rocket, he noted in his diary, "I know there is a God. I'm sure of it. I started to give some thought to the popular G.I. theory of fate: when it's your time to go, you'll go. Maybe it's not my time to go. I never put much stock in that thought before, but I do now."[152] Yezzo even realized that this reliance on heavenly protection was "somewhat of a crutch," but he held on to it, nevertheless.[153]

In some cases this belief in divine protection was a soldier's primary coping mechanism, as Bourne discovered in his study of Vietnam War helicopter medics, one of whom was "a sincerely religious Catholic who believed that God would protect him no matter how great the danger."[154] Sergeant York, a devout man, was convinced that God had blessed his participation in the fighting and had also guaranteed his safety: "I done settled it all with my God long ago before I went overseas. I done prayed and prayed to Him; He done given me my assurance that so long as I believed in Him He would protect me, and He did."[155]

Although some soldiers clung to a belief in salvation, or more often divine protection, others found no solace in religion. Turning to the other half of the dichotomy, there were atheists in the foxholes. They put no stock in divine protection and, in the case of the more embittered nonbelievers, had no patience for those who did. Corporal Minder's platoon atheist openly scoffed at his comrades who prayed for God's protection: "What the hell good is all that praying going to do you? If your name is on one of those shells, you are going to get it no matter how much you pray. Don't you think that the men who have been killed already in this war for the past four years prayed?"[156]

Some soldiers, of course, had arrived on the battlefield as atheists. Religion obviously did not help them cope, but neither were they stressed by the burden of questioning or losing completely a previous faith that no longer seemed relevant or true. Soldiers who arrived on the battlefield with "this-world" faith, on the other hand, went through a painful process of questioning, and sometimes rejecting, their beliefs. Private Sledge and his fellow World War II marines wanted to believe, but they grew increasingly skeptical and "couldn't help but have doubts about . . . God in the presence of constant shock and suffering."[157]

Specialist Harold Bryant was a religious man before he went to Vietnam, but what he saw and suffered there, especially the death of his closest friend, put an end to his faith: "I guess deep down in my head now I can't really believe in God like I did because I can't really see why God would let something like this happen. . . . Why He would take such a good individual away from here. . . . I have read the Bible from cover to cover. I keep looking for the explanation. I can't find it. I can't find it."[158]

For soldiers like Bryant and Sledge, the death and horrors of combat could only mean that God did not exist or did not care. Yet other soldiers trusted in that same God for protection or salvation. Faith as a means of coping with the environment of war thus gets mixed reviews, as it did from Lieutenant Frederick Downs as he and his platoon participated in a memorial service for slain comrades during the Vietnam War: "Some of the men drank in [the chaplain's] words like the desert sand drinks in moisture. To some of us the moisture fell on bare rock to be carried away by the empty winds. To others the water was held in a pool of unknowing."[159]

Interestingly, soldiers who would not put their faith in God would sometimes blindly trust in talismans or superstitions. Even soldiers who kept the faith resorted to talismans—better to be safe than sorry. And often there was a connection between the faith and the charm, as with a crucifix or religious medal. Just as often the treasured talisman had no religious significance but might have a connection to home, something given to the soldier by a loved one as he departed.[160] A talisman bolstered a soldier's belief that "it can't happen to me." Given the random nature of death on the battlefield, why not trust to good luck charms or superstitions?

For doughboys of the Forty-second Division, whose emblem was a rainbow, the sight of one was a good omen. Charles MacArthur and thousands of his comrades saw a rainbow just before going into an attack: "The division for which it was named let out a yell that rang high above the roaring barrage. Obviously it meant *Gott Mit Uns*."[161] Private Sledge noticed that despite the wear and tear of the fighting on Peleliu in World War II, his dungaree jacket, like him, had survived without a scratch. He therefore wore it in the next campaign as well and has it still: "I later wore this same lucky jacket through the long, muddy Okinawa campaign. Faded now, it hangs peacefully in my closet, one of my prized possessions."[162]

In Matthew Brennan's aerorifle platoon in Vietnam, the talisman was rosary beads. The Catholic chaplain was amazed to find that the entire platoon had turned out for services one Sunday, and each man received a black plastic rosary: "The word was out about the rosaries, and everyone had agreed that they would bring us good luck. By the next morning, most of the soldiers were wearing the rosaries around their necks for ornament. The platoon had finally got religion."[163]

Sometimes the talisman was not a keepsake but a person. Often a soldier, or a unit, would get a reputation for being lucky or, conversely, for being jinxed. In William March's World War I novel about a marine rifle company, Private John McGill had survived many close calls unscathed: "The men in my company marveled at my luck. Before going over the top many of them would put their hands on my forehead, hoping thereby to become lucky themselves."[164] During the Korean War, Lieutenant Matthias learned that "troops in combat were superstitious" and that they put stock in individual luck. He discovered that his men considered him one of the lucky ones and preferred that he lead them on patrols: "My men requested that I take them out, during special hazardous assignments. I am sure it was not because I was the better leader but because they felt I brought them luck."[165]

At the opposite extreme were leaders or units that the soldier believed were unlucky. The supply convoys in Lieutenant Alfred S. Bradford's infantry battalion in Vietnam had been ambushed so often that the transportation lieutenant who led them had earned three Purple Hearts in three months and the nickname "Magnet." Bradford recalls the reaction of a "relatively composed" soldier on hearing that Magnet would be leading his convoy: "Magnet? Jeez! Where'd I put my flak jacket?"[166]


## HUMOR AND RUMOR

No matter how questionable the rationale for carrying talismans, in doing so soldiers at least felt that they were taking some small step to improve their odds of survival. Often they could do little else to affect their situation, and at times, when the going got tough, their only other recourse was to laugh at their own predicament. "It is not the least of his fighting assets," points out Samuel L. A. Marshall, "that the American soldier has a sense of humor which can survive the shock and strain of engagement."[167] It was this humor that Bill Mauldin most wanted to capture in his cartoons of GIs, "who are able to fight a ruthless war against ruthless enemies, and still grin at themselves."[168] Humor helped soldiers make light of miserable physical conditions. One marine, plodding forward in the cold, muddy Argonne in November 1918, fell into a water-filled shell hole hidden beneath the slime. Private Mackin and his buddies waited for the blistering curses sure to follow, but it was not to be: "He came up, standing thigh deep in the hole and glanced around to note his audience, threw back his head and roared with laughter. Men who hadn't laughed for days laughed with him. . . . What a strange spectacle, a little band of men. . . . They knew the fellowship of laughter, miles from home."[169]

As with this mud-covered marine, the source of the humor was often some hapless soldier. Private Blunt, climbing off a truck after a cold winter convoy, found that his legs were numb from lack of circulation. He promptly fell on his backside, strewing gear in all directions, which "brought roaring laughter" from his squad. Rather than become angry or embarrassed, he knew it was all part of the game: "In the military, especially during combat or other trying periods, tension and frustration were kept in check by laughing at others and their misfortunes. It was accepted behavior. You either laughed or were laughed at, and to take offense wasn't allowed."[170]

Lieutenant Audie Murphy, who went to some lengths in his memoir to capture the bantering and jokes typical of the World War II GI, recalled a classic quip from one of his jokesters as his company moved into the front lines on a bitterly cold day near Colmar, France: "Bergman, with his peculiar sense of humor, is a great help when the going is rough. Sensing the mood, he now shouts, 'Nobody can say we're not moving into action as cool as cucumbers.'"[171] Bergman was no doubt one of those cutups who had provided recruits with comic relief during initial training. The unit comedian was an invaluable morale booster in combat units as well.[172]

Soldiers sometimes found humor even in the most dangerous situations. Lieutenant Boesch and several of his men were carrying a wounded man down a steep, slippery hill in the Huertgen Forest when they had to put the litter down and take cover because of incoming enemy artillery. The wounded man, with an arm in a sling and a bandage wrapped around his head, had appeared to be in bad shape, but when the shells began coming in, he "leaped to his unsteady feet, bandages trailing, and with the unerring instinct of the infantryman, dived into the nearest empty hole." The exhausted Boesch could not help but laugh: "While the enemy barrage poured out a venomous and far from humorous message, I roared with laughter."[173]

Sometimes soldiers' humor was decidedly black and could be appreciated only by men caught up in the brutal environment of war. Black humor included using enemy corpses or body parts in various macabre displays or even having a laugh at the expense of a dead or wounded friendly soldier. This black humor, as Peter Aichinger explains, served as "a means of coping with the horror of war" because "it momentarily relieves the trauma."[174]

Fear of death was one of the traumas that black humor helped relieve. "Corpse humor," for lack of a better term, trivialized death by poking fun at it. During World War I, Private Mackin encountered a dead German at a fork in the trail with one upflung arm caught in the branches of a bush: "Some humorous soul had laced a cardboard sign between the dead man's fingers. Rough lettering spelled out the words 'Battalion P.C.' [post of command] above an arrow pointing west."[175]

Gags involving corpses also demeaned the enemy by adding insult to injury. Lieutenant Downs and his platoon surprised several Viet Cong in the process of placing a large booby trap in the road. The startled enemy accidentally blew themselves to pieces. One of Downs's men picked up a severed hand, placed a cigarette between the fingers, and stuck the hand upright in the dirt: "Everyone took pictures of this bizarre construction. We never thought it was ghoulish. The hand with the cigarette was just our way of releasing emotion against an elusive enemy finally caught."[176]

Corpse humor was not restricted to enemy dead. Sometimes American bodies provided comic relief, although soldiers retained enough respect for their own dead not to demean them by staging gags. Lieutenant Boesch awoke from a sound sleep during World War II to find a dead American soldier next to his foxhole. He learned that the body had been rolled off a stretcher and left by medics after the man had died, given that their priority was to evacuate the living. One of Boesch's men, knowing his lieutenant had been a wrestler before the war, could not resist saying, "I can just imagine the wrestling match you would have had . . . if they had rolled him in on top of you in the dark."[177] Boesch responded that at least it was one match he could have won. He then commented on the GIs propensity for black humor: "Were we irreverent to the dead? Perhaps. But who had a better right to be irreverent, even callous, than the men who might join the dead before another sun set? And who could live with death and horror as constant companions unless he found something to balance the score?"[178]

Thus, by developing a black sense of humor, the soldier salvaged a little levity from the otherwise grim realities of death on the battlefield. A similar process of seeking out the positive occurred with rumors, which abounded in the combat zone. The ones that turned out to be true were more often than not unpleasant, such as the World War II rumor that soldiers would be shipped to the Pacific after Germany's defeat to join in the certain-to-be-bloody invasion of the Japanese home islands. Soldiers, however, focused on those rumors that they wanted to believe in, and as Sergeant Hoffman explains, these were the positive ones: "We practically lived on rumors—usually of a favorable nature. Wishful thinking and hoping apparently gave birth to them."[179]

Popular doughboy rumors included returning to the United States to serve as recruiters and instructors, being sent on furlough to Paris or to rest camps in southern France, or (in the case of the marines) being sent on sea duty.[180] The most outrageous rumor, but one that undoubtedly generated interesting debate around the mess wagon, was that selected volunteers would help repopulate France because so many French males had been killed or crippled in the fighting.[181] Father Duffy, who understood that rumors, along "with eating and growling, . . . constitute our chief forms of recreation," discovered that they were often attributed to him.[182] What more reputable source than the chaplain!

As Duffy indicates, swapping rumors, or "scuttlebutt" as the marines called them, was a pleasant form of social interaction when soldiers had a chance to congregate. Like daydreaming, rumors allowed the men to displace their attention, hence the emphasis on positive rumors. Ernie Pyle points out that rumor-mongering was a useful diversion for the World War II GI: "When the Army doesn't have women, furloughs, ice cream, beer, or clean clothes, it certainly has to have something to look forward to, even if only a faint hope for some kind of change that lies buried in an illogical rumor."[183]

Rumors during the Korean War remained steadfastly positive, although not exclusively so. Lieutenant Owen summarizes the scuttlebutt circulating in his unit following the Inchon landing and the subsequent routing of the North Korean People's Army: "We heard that Navy transports were in the [Inchon] harbor, waiting to take us to the States. Or, that all reservists were going to be immediately released from active duty. Or, that the 1st Marine Division was getting permanent occupation duty. The least desirable of all the rumors was that we would make an amphibious landing somewhere in North Korea and finish off the enemy soldiers who had escaped above the thirty-eighth parallel."[184]

The "least desirable" rumor, of course, was the correct one. There were transports in the harbor—to take the marines to the east coast of Korea, as part of the Tenth (U.S.) Corps, to help complete the destruction of North Korean forces. Yet such realities never dampened the soldiers' enthusiasm for outrageously optimistic rumors.

## SCHEDULED AND UNSCHEDULED DEPARTURES

Grandiose rumors are curiously absent from Vietnam War memoirs. The rotation policy and the reality of a long war no doubt explain the lack of rumormongering. Prior to the commencement of troop withdrawals, the grunts knew that neither they nor their unit were going anywhere outside the confines of Vietnam. Transfers to jobs as recruiters, trainers, or sea marines would come only after the tour of duty was completed. Grunts resorted less to spreading wildly optimistic rumors than their counterparts in earlier wars because they had something more reliable than rumors to believe in—their DEROS. When a soldier stepped off the plane in Vietnam, he knew exactly what day, twelve months hence for army personnel and thirteen for marines, he would leave.

Rotation may have caused problems for unit cohesion and effectiveness, but as a coping mechanism for the individual soldier, it was a winner. The promise of a DEROS, explains Peter Bourne, greatly reduced the hopelessness previously felt by soldiers who had to serve "for the duration": "The G.I. in Viet Nam knows that if he can merely survive for 12 months his removal from combat is assured. There is not the sense of hopelessness that prevailed in previous conflicts where death, injury, or peace became the only possible ways in which the soldier could find himself extricated from combat."[185]

Time became an obsession for the grunt, who counted down the remaining days of his tour of duty using a short-timer's calendar or stick. Sergeant Bill Morgan, in the novel *Fragments,* notes the importance of time: "Three hundred sixty-five days or life, whichever came first. Time was the enemy. Time was the objective. And so we had calendars in our pockets, calendars scratched into our steel-pots, elaborate calendars in our heads. We divided up the year a hundred different ways, triangulating on the seasons, on holidays, on the phases of the moon."[186] This obsession with time provided yet another avenue for displacing attention. The grunt could daydream about his DEROS. Tim O'Brien passed the time while waiting in ambush "counting up the number of days I had left in Vietnam. I figured it out by months, weeks, and hours."[187]

Though less well known than the DEROS, a rotation system was also established during the Korean War. The system was based on points, with more points going to men serving in combat zones than in rear areas. Changes in the point-awarding process and in the total number of points required for departure made for an end-of-tour date that was less firmly fixed than in Vietnam. Nevertheless, as marine lieutenant James Brady observes, the Korean War GI, unlike his World War II predecessor, at least had hope: "The Marine Corps was eminently sensible about some matters. No man was to be left in Korea a day beyond what was necessary; there was no testing yardstick of machismo or brute endurance. . . . There were to be no marathons as during the last war, when a man might spend thirty-six or forty months in the Pacific with no hope of home until war's end or a bad wound."[188]

Doughboys and World War II GIs, however, had no DEROS to count down to or rotation points to calculate. Their departure from overseas was strictly unscheduled and, as they came to realize, would most likely involve a coffin or a hospital ship. With no other end in sight, soldiers began to hope for a "million dollar wound"—one that would provide an exit from combat without permanently maiming them. Corporal Fife, in *The Thin Red Line,* ponders the sort of wound that would keep him out of the rest of the war: "At any rate, clearly the best way to be wounded, if one must be wounded at all, was to have a wound so bad that you would almost die, one that would leave you sick long enough for the war to get over, but which when you recovered from it would not leave you crippled or an invalid. Either that, or receive a minor wound which would incapacitate or cripple you slightly without crippling fully."[189]

Doughboys also yearned for a million dollar wound, referring to it in terms borrowed from the British (a "blighty," or a wound just serious enough to get the soldier sent to "blighty," meaning England) or from the French (a "bon-bless-ey," typically Americanized, meaning a "good wound"). Captain John W. Thomason Jr., after months of fighting, hoped for his million dollar wound in the upcoming attack on Blanc Mont: "I want to get wounded in this fight. A bon blighty, in the arm or the leg, I think. Something that will keep me in a nice dry hospital until spring."[190]

Some doughboys were even content with a serious wound if it meant that they would not have to return to the fighting. Father Duffy, visiting the hospital, found a soldier about to be operated on to have his damaged eye removed. Duffy tried to console him, telling him that "Uncle Sam will look after you," to which the doughboy replied, "I'm not thinking about Uncle Sam at all. There's a girl back in New York who doesn't care whether I have one eye or two."[191]

A million dollar wound provided an honorable escape from combat. The wounded soldier had done his duty, and his comrades were glad for his good fortune. A popular young runner in Private Mackin's marine battalion in World War I was told by his friends to milk his leg wound for all it was worth: "Now you keep limping, see? You keep limpin' 'til you get back of that old Statue of Liberty and get a discharge."[192] Sometimes the million dollar wound was so fortuitous that the wounded man's comrades could not hide their envy. One of Boesch's fellow lieutenants got a flesh wound in the arm just as his company was moving into the line in World War II: "Crowding around to have a look, the men made no effort to conceal the envy in their glances or their remarks. A million-dollar wound was one that did no permanent damage to bone or structure yet still was serious enough to put a man in the hospital for a while. Hospital was a magic word which meant rest, attention, beds, hot food, and—what was most important—nobody shooting at you."[193]

Lieutenant Gerald P. Averill witnessed the perfect wound during the amphibious assault on Iwo Jima. A marine was hit by a piece of mortar shrapnel in the calf of his leg just as he was stepping off the landing craft. He fell back into the boat, the ramp came up, and the landing craft departed. Averill could not conceal his jealousy: "A Purple Heart, a battle star on the Asiatic-Pacific ribbon, and a free ride to the hospital ship without even setting foot on Iwo."[194]

Vietnam and Korean War soldiers wished less often for a million dollar wound than their world war counterparts—better to hope instead to reach that magical rotation date in one piece.[195] They still appreciated a million-dollar wound when they saw one, however. The Korean War GI talked of a "Pusan wound," referring to the large hospital established at Pusan in South Korea.[196] Better still a trip to a hospital in Japan, as was granted to Lieutenant Sullivan, whose wounded thumb required some delicate orthopedic surgery: "I had my million-dollar wound! That evening I went to sleep with the knowledge that I was leaving Korea, probably for good. I had never felt better in my life."[197]

The grunt could also appreciate a million dollar wound. Private Ogden, while helping a wounded man limp off the battlefield, asked him why he was grinning. The marine pulled up his trouser leg to reveal a clean flesh wound through the calf. Ogden rendered his own layman's opinion: "You know, this looks like a million-dollar wound to me."[198] The correspondent Michael Herr, while visiting a medical aid station, listened to a doctor tell a marine with a wounded knee that he would undoubtedly be evacuated to the States: "At first the boy was sure that the doctor was kidding him, then he started to believe it, and then he knew it was true, he was actually getting out, he couldn't stop smiling, and enormous tears ran down into his ears."[199]

Hoping for a million dollar wound was but one of a variety of coping mechanisms that soldiers relied on. Religion might sustain one man while another held on desperately to thoughts of loved ones at home. One important coping mechanism, however, has yet to be addressed—comradeship. Soldiers counted on their buddies to help them through the tough spots. Comradeship was not only a coping mechanism but also a motivator—soldiers fought for their comrades. As a motivating factor, comradeship cannot be separated from unit esprit and the soldier's belief in his cause. Thus, the complicated and important issue of comradeship warrants a separate, closer examination.

# 5

# For Comrades and Country

The coping mechanisms that soldiers used most were "props," as opposed to "motivators," to borrow terms from historian Richard H. Kohn.[1] They supported the soldier emotionally and physically, but they did not necessarily motivate him to take the fight to the enemy. Wishing for a wound to escape further combat, daydreaming about home while on patrol, or boozing it up in a rest camp might help a soldier cope, but they did not contribute to the achievement of victory. The bonds formed within the small circle of comrades in a crew, squad, or platoon were yet another prop, in that the soldier relied on his buddies for physical and moral support.

The soldier's need for his comrades' acceptance, however, took him beyond props and into the realm of motivators. To gain the group's respect and support, the soldier strove to succeed in combat within the standards of performance set by the group. "The fighter is often sustained solely by the determination not to let down his comrades," observes Jesse Glenn Gray, and no motivator was more powerful: "Such loyalty to the group is the essence of fighting morale. The commander who can preserve and strengthen it knows that all other psychological or physical factors are little in comparison."[2] Group loyalty, or "primary-group cohesion," was thus both a significant prop and motivator.[3]

Soldiers have always understood the importance of group bonds, but only during World War II did military psychologists and sociologists begin to examine systematically the workings of the primary group.[4] After much study and debate, these students of soldier behavior came to realize that primary-group cohesion could not be considered in isolation. The soldier was certainly motivated by group norms, but the group did not formulate these norms in a vacuum, as Morris Janowitz and Roger W. Little explain: "The goals and standards or norms that primary groups enforce are hardly self-generated; they arise from the larger military environment and from the surrounding civilian society. Conse-

124

quently, the empirical study of primary groups must extend beyond the factors that contribute to social cohesion in the smallest tactical units."[5]

Thus, the primary group must be examined in the context of its larger military organization and the values of the society that sent it to war. The political scientist and army officer Stephen D. Wesbrook asserts that motivating men in combat "first depends on the soldiers' moral involvement with their primary groups and either their unit or their national sociopolitical system, but ideally both."[6] Therefore, primary-group bonds, unit esprit, and belief in cause and country must be considered in determining why American soldiers fought.

## THE COMPLEXITIES OF COMRADESHIP

Since World War II, the trend in the growing body of literature on primary groups is toward an appreciation of the complexity and diversity of relationships among group members. Each soldier formed unique friendships, for differing reasons. As a general rule, soldiers strove to maintain a good working relationship with all the members of their primary group, since teamwork was critical to survival and success. The group was also bound by shared adversity, as Sergeant Alvin C. York declares: "They were my buddies. That's a word that's only understood by soldiers who have lived under the same blankets, gathered around the same chow can, and looked at death together. I never knowed I loved my brother-man so much until I was a doughboy."[7]

As in any closely knit family, the death of a member was a loss that all felt. Captain Richard D. Camp watched the bodies of his men, killed in a desperate fight the previous day, being loaded into a helicopter: "I felt the sting in my eyes. Though I lowered my head to try to hide the tears, I noticed that many of the marines in the [landing] zone were crying too."[8] Yet soldiers learned to accept the death of comrades as an inevitable part of war. They were saddened by the loss, but they did not dwell on it. Chaplain Francis P. Duffy, a compassionate man who presided over many burials and memorial services for the doughboys, understood that neither he nor the men could handle the emotional strain of lingering too long over departed comrades: "We can pay tribute to our dead but we must not lament for them overmuch."[9] James Jones writes that a soldier could do nothing to bring back a dead comrade, and that life must go on: "When a man was hit and killed outright, there was nothing anyone could do. The man had ceased to exist. The living went right on living, without him. On the other hand, the wounded were evacuated. They would live or die someplace else. So they too ceased to exist to the men they left behind, and could be forgotten also. Without a strong belief in a Valhalla, it was as good a way to handle the problem as any, and made everybody feel better."[10]

Death was such a common occurrence on the battlefield that soldiers grew accustomed to it, or at least less shocked by it. Lieutenant Lyle Rishell was saddened and angered by the death of several of his men by artillery fratricide during the Korean War but found that he quickly put the incident behind him. He wondered at his own seeming indifference: "Was it because I had gotten calloused with the death and dying that was ground combat, or was it because I recognized my own mortality and could do nothing about it? I believe that we lose our sensitivity after a while. It is not that we harden our minds to the suffering or death of others, but rather that we have to move on."[11]

Soldiers thus lamented the loss of comrades, but they moved on. Sometimes a soldier found it especially difficult, however, because the lost comrade had been a dear friend. For some soldiers, according to Jules W. Coleman, a division psychiatrist in World War II, a general commitment to the primary group was enough to provide them needed physical and emotional support. But other men needed a close friend to get by, or a "direct dependency relationship."[12] Roger W. Little, who studied infantrymen during the Korean War, found direct-dependency relationships, or "buddy relations" as he called them, to be common. The GIs considered themselves part of the squad and platoon but beyond that had one or two buddies with whom they were especially close. These buddies shared a foxhole, as well as letters, hopes, fears, and interests: "Buddies became therapists to one another."[13]

Buddy relationships are evident in the memoirs. The World War I marine Carl Andrew Brannen had a special friend in Horace Cooper. Brannen noted that they became friends for the usual mix of practical and emotional reasons: "The buddy system worked well because of the companionship, and at night behind the lines one could lay his blanket on the ground for both and cover with the other, as each man carried only one blanket." Brannen, on returning to his unit after recovering from a minor wound, was glad to find his buddy still there and "gave Cooper an extra pair of clean underwear which I had brought along. Was he glad to get them and discard those cootie nests he was wearing."[14] Typical of friends, it was the little considerations that counted.

Private Roscoe C. Blunt Jr. writes that he would not have made it through World War II without his buddy Joe Everett, to whom he dedicates his memoir. They shared foxholes, swapped stories, and went scrounging together. Everett nursed Blunt through pneumonia and frostbite and literally saved his life on at least one occasion. Near war's end, he consoled a depressed Blunt, who was close to a breakdown: "I withdrew into an emotional shell. Everett, sensing my grief, put his arm around me and we rode in silence."[15] Having a friend who cared was the only way for some soldiers to endure the hardships and dangers.[16]

The terrible downside of friendship in combat was the death of a good buddy. Losses from among the soldier's primary-group family were disconcerting enough, but the loss of a special friend was cause for agonizing grief, rage, and guilt.[17] Sergeant York received permission to return the next day to the site of his famous shootout with a German machine-gun unit, for which he later received the Congressional Medal of Honor (CMH), to look for missing comrades. All he found were fresh graves, including that of his best friend: "Corporal Murray Savage, my best pal, dead. Oh, my, it seemed so unbelievable. . . . I would never share the same blanket with Corporal Savage. We'd never read the Bible together again. We would never talk about our faith and pray to our God. I was mussed up inside worser than I had ever been. I'm a-telling you when you lose your best buddie and you know you ain't never going to see him again, you sorter know how terrible cruel war is."[18]

Sergeant Henry Giles, evacuated to a hospital with a serious ear infection, languished in a replacement depot after his recovery while his battalion fought to stem the German advance during the Battle of the Bulge in World War II. By the time he made his way back to his old platoon, one of his best friends had been killed while manning Giles's machine gun in his absence. For Giles, guilt mingled with grief over his friend's death. He blamed himself for not being there: "He's still much on my mind & it depresses me to think he's gone."[19]

Lieutenant Howard Matthias, a marine platoon leader during the Korean War, had grown especially close to his radioman: "We had experienced some real hairy experiences together and had developed a mutual respect." Matthias was thus devastated to learn from his platoon sergeant that the radioman had been killed by a random shell as he stood in the chow line. The considerate sergeant then left Matthias alone in his bunker: "I must admit that I cried for the first time in Korea."[20] Matthias at least had an opportunity to grieve in peace. Soldiers sometimes had to press on even though a buddy had just been killed before their eyes. Boris R. Spiroff, a platoon sergeant in the Korean War, watched his best friend get hit in the midst of an attack: "Reaching him, I notice a neat hole in his forehead and bleeding from the back of his head. He is dead. I feel awful, sick to my stomach and so helpless, but have to keep moving on."[21]

For some soldiers, the sense of loss was too much. After losing a buddy, they avoided getting close to anyone else because they never again wanted to suffer such shock and pain.[22] Walter Johnson's best friend was killed on New Georgia Island in World War II: "After that I didn't get very close to people. There were so many replacements over time. After you're in and have been through combat, it's harder to make new friends for some reason. Guess you don't want them to die and hurt you."[23] During the Korean War Private Doug Michaud also stopped making friends: "I had changed. I no longer wanted any buddies. Afraid I'd lose them. If I liked someone, I believed he'd get killed. Who needed the additional trauma?"[24]

The nature and strength of the bonds that soldiers formed thus varied, depending on the personalities involved. Most soldiers maintained good relations with their primary group, even if they chose not to make any close friends. Primary-group ties shifted and re-formed as casualties or rotation thinned the ranks and replacements arrived. However, while the faces changed, the group retained a "core identity," and part of that identity was a set of group norms.[25]

The combat soldier was no stranger to the workings of group norms. He had experienced them during his initial training, when his platoon ostracized or physically punished nonconforming recruits who were generating disfavor with the drill sergeant. The military group continued to regulate his life after he completed training, exercising what the Stouffer Study calls "social control." The group berated those who were "too GI," "bucking for promotion," or "brownnosing" on the one hand, and those who, on the other hand, created trouble for the group by excessive goldbricking or incurring the wrath of superiors.[26]

Social control took on new meaning and importance, however, when the soldier and his primary group entered the environment of war. Group norms, notes Frederick J. Kviz, became "survival-oriented": "By killing one of the enemy, an individual reduces the threat not only to his own survival but to that of all other members of his combat group as well. Similarly, if he commits an error, he endangers the survival of all the other members of the group in addition to his own. Thus, any action taken by any individual which may affect his or any of the other group members' survival is of great significance for the entire group."[27] The group did not condone individuals whose actions jeopardized its survival or forced other members to have to take up the slack. Soldiers who avoided combat or did not perform their assigned duties when under fire, variously known as slackers, malingerers, stragglers, goldbricks, shirkers, or ghosts, were treated with contempt. For example, during a fierce struggle for control of the town of Fismette, Sergeant Bob Hoffman had to roust shirkers from their cellar hideouts: "Some insisted that they were sick. . . . I got them out just the same. I used strong arm methods if necessary, even kicked them in the pants."[28]

Doughboys' enthusiasm, especially among units composed largely of volunteers, was real enough, but many soon lost their eagerness for combat; others were reluctant draftees short on enthusiasm from the outset. Straggling, or slacking, became a serious problem, especially late in the war.[29] One of the most common straggler techniques was to get lost. Lieutenant Joseph D. Lawrence made the mistake of letting two of his men go to the rear to retrieve some grenades they claimed to have seen lying by the roadside. They said they would be back in a few minutes but "did not appear again until the fight was over; they were 'lost' in the woods."[30]

As long as some soldiers held a greater regard for their personal safety than for the group's welfare, shirking occurred, despite the group's condemnation and the possibility of punishment for cowardice or desertion. Shirking occurred in World War II as well. Rifleman Lester Atwell describes a malingerer, Braaf, who became "suddenly unpopular" with his comrades because "in attacks he stayed low in his foxhole and wouldn't advance with the rest of the men. Later, he'd rejoin the company, claiming he never heard the order to go ahead, or he'd get conveniently lost."[31]

Some goldbricking was tolerated by the group, with the usual caveat that other soldiers not be endangered or excessively burdened as a consequence. However, in Robert G. Thobaben's infantry battalion, conducting mopping-up operations on Peleliu in World War II, he and his fellow aidmen did not shirk when it was their turn to accompany the daily patrols sent to find Japanese hold-outs: "Everybody—I repeat, everybody—took his turn, and you just didn't show up for sick call on the day you were supposed to act as the aidman for the patrol. There is a lot of 'goofing off' (we called it goldbricking) in the military, but there are times when you take your turn. . . . There was an unsaid rule that you went when it was your turn to go and you were selected."[32] Thobaben is describing, in essence, the enforcement process—his group would not condone a goof off who skipped out on a difficult, dangerous patrol. The group could make life for a per-sistent malingerer miserable and even hazardous, as it did for Private Johnson in Lieutenant Lanning's platoon in Vietnam. Johnson "complained constantly and avoided doing anything more than the minimum" and had once tried to get out of the field by faking heat exhaustion. Johnson had "become a loner, as few would have much to do with him." He finally went too far when, in an attempt to get himself sent for a psychological evaluation, he lied to the battalion com-mander, denigrating the accomplishments of his platoon in the process. The com-mander did not buy his story. Later that night Johnson was found in the shower hootch with a broken nose and jaw. Lanning "accepted the report about John-son's fall in the shower but, of course, knew better."[33]

Unlike Johnson, few soldiers were willing to malinger to the point of being ostracized. Most soldiers lived up to the group's norms, not so much out of fear of group punishment but because they positively identified with their group and wanted to do their share. Private Sanders took a punji stake in the foot in Viet-nam, but he hobbled on with his platoon, refusing medical evacuation until his foot hurt too badly for him to continue. His rationale for staying as long as he did speaks volumes about the bonds of comradeship: "I wouldn't mind going to the rear anytime, I tell you that, but I had partners here. That was the key to the whole deal. You never wanted to be lagging, what we called half-stepping or ghosting. Ghosting was kicking back in the rear. We didn't want to be back there ghosting and have somebody say, 'Hey man, your partner got killed.' You felt that you could have been there and helped him, you know? That was the kind of understanding we had, man."[34]

Not only did the group have little use for soldiers who ghosted, but it also did not appreciate needless heroics. An overly zealous warrior might draw the group into an unnecessary fight or at least get himself wounded or killed, thereby leaving the group a man short.[35] Blunt was one such impulsive GI who volun-teered for dangerous jobs and considered combat a personal challenge. He and his buddy Everett, returning from a reconnaissance patrol that they had volun-teered for, discovered that their comrades were not impressed with their martial enthusiasm: "The others chided us for glory hunting instead of sleeping when we had had the chance."[36] Private Victor Fox, in describing the awards system dur-ing the Korean War, explained that grandstand heroics did not impress the rank and file: "Everyone was honestly glad for men who earned a medal, as long as that individual did not intentionally kill himself or endanger the lives of others.

Teamwork is so vital in combat that an act of individual heroism usually comes more as a surprise than as a contrived action. This left out the John Wayne types."[37] John Wayne was not welcome in the boonies either, as Sergeant Bill Morgan, in *Fragments,* discovers when he attends his initial in-country training: "Strange lessons the lifers [instructors] taught us at Phouc Vinh. They were definitely not interested in heroes. John Wayne was a term of derision. They were indoctrinating us in survival, and we were not hard to sell."[38]

Along with shirkers and John Wayne types, the group had a low tolerance for those who made mistakes in performing routine combat duties. During the fighting on Peleliu Island in World War II, a marine in Private Eugene B. Sledge's company fell asleep on night watch, and two Japanese infiltrators were able to sneak into the company's position; a marine died as a consequence. The sleeping marine had "committed an unforgivable breach of faith": "The men were extremely hard on him for what had happened. He was visibly remorseful, but it made no difference to the others who openly blamed him. He whined and said he was too tired to stay awake on watch, but he only got sworn at by men who were equally tired yet reliable."[39]

GIs were just as tired during the Korean War, but again the group would not tolerate a soldier asleep on duty. In Matthias's company, if marines fell asleep while on ambush, then the others took their weapons and left them in no-man's land: "When they awoke and found themselves alone without a weapon, they hurried in and we never had to worry about their sleeping again. I can imagine the stark fear they must have faced waking up alone and weaponless."[40]

Since group norms promoted survival, a soldier was usually more than willing to abide by them. Equally important, compliance meant group acceptance and support. In turn, except for the dedicated malingerers who cared only about themselves, a soldier felt a responsibility to return that support, generally expressed as a desire not to let his buddies down. If his comrades "stuck it out," then he would too. The normally trite phrase "death before dishonor" took on real meaning at such times.[41] The doughboy Merritt D. Cutler felt that way: while advancing in the midst of artillery fire, "the only thing I could concentrate on was to keep moving—don't let your buddies think you're yellow; I think I was more concerned with this than with the Germans."[42]

Concerned about his standing in the group, a soldier might not even mind a little hype if it enhanced his reputation. Private Brannen's bayonet tip was clipped off by a bullet during the heavy fighting at Blanc Mont in World War I. One of his marine comrades, seeing the bayonet stub, exclaimed that Brannen must have broken it off inside a German. Brannen did not bother to set the record straight.[43]

GIs were as concerned as the doughboys about group acceptance. Bradford Perkins, a World War II artillery forward observer, believes his fear of disgracing himself in front of his comrades was what kept him going: "Because those near you were not strangers, you especially did not want to disgrace yourself. I frequently felt this pressure, and I am sure that it was common."[44] Soldiers in the Korean and Vietnam Wars likewise cared about the group and their standing in it. Private Arnold Winter charged up a hill in Korea, not because he was brave and fearless but because his fellow marines were doing it: "When they gave you an order to go, you went, in spite of everything. And there was also the fear of letting your buddies down. There's an almost unbelievable loyalty among men in a rifle company, and you don't want to be the guy to break that bond. You didn't want to die, but you also didn't want to embarrass yourself by failing your buddies."[45]

During the Vietnam War, the grunts' belief in the cause wore thin, but comradeship remained strong, at least until late in the war. Lieutenant Alfred S. Bradford understood that no one, "unless they were very, very, stupid," believed that they were succeeding in stopping the spread of Communism: "So what did keep the GIs going?" He quotes a typical grunt response: "I don't know. I ain't a lifer. I ain't gung-ho. I just can't let the others down." Like soldiers in earlier wars, grunts cared about their reputations. Bradford provides an example of a medic nicknamed "Shanker" who, by treating a casualty while under fire and getting wounded in the process, redeemed himself in his comrades' eyes: "Shanker wrapped his knee and hopped toward the dust-off [helicopter]. A big grin kept breaking out on his face—the wound was simple, no loss of limb, but a broken kneecap meant a medevac to Japan; he had risked his life and saved his man, despite the other medics, who had said he cared too much about himself to ever be much good."[46]

When soldiers like Shanker set out to prove themselves in the eyes of their comrades, vowing to "stick it out" and "not let their buddies down," acts of heroism ensued. Not surprisingly, these heroic actions often involved a soldier's attempt to protect his comrades. A study of Congressional Medal of Honor recipients during the Vietnam War reveals that a majority of these medals awarded to enlisted soldiers were for "soldier-saving" acts—rescuing wounded comrades, falling on grenades, or performing rear-guard actions.

The study also notes, however, that a sizable minority of CMHs awarded to enlisted men and a significant majority of those awarded to officers were for "war-winning" acts involving aggression against the enemy, leadership initiative, or refusing medical attention to carry on the fight.[47] The accomplished warrior, or "center-pillar guy" as he was sometimes called, was a valued asset as long as his bravery was directed toward the accomplishment of the group's mission and not for personal aggrandizement of the John Wayne variety. By accomplishing the mission and killing the enemy, the courageous soldier helped bring the fighting to an end, at least for the moment. Hence, courage of the war-winning variety was appreciated for its inherent soldier-saving aspects—a dead, captured, or repulsed enemy was no longer a threat to the group.

Understandably, once a soldier had made trusted friends and gained his comrades' respect, he did not want to be reassigned, as became clear to the leaders in Captain Charles R. Cawthon's 116th Infantry Regiment when they attempted to consolidate units depleted in four days of heavy fighting in Normandy in World War II: "This effort ran into immediate opposition as squads, reduced to three and four men, still insisted on keeping their identity and opposed consolidation with others; men also declined promotions that meant going to another platoon or company. The past four days had developed powerful bonds between those who had supported each other through them. I believe that things were finally left very much as they were."[48]

The group's veterans trusted one another, had endured many hardships together, and drew a measure of security and comfort from one another. Despite the seemingly obvious value of keeping such veteran combatants together, the army followed a destructive policy in the world wars of putting soldiers who had recovered from a wound or illness in the general replacement pool instead of returning them to their old outfit.[49] The bankruptcy of this personnel policy was evidenced by the frequency with which soldiers went "AWOL to the front," leaving hospitals or replacement depots without permission because they did not want to be sent to fight with strangers in some new outfit.[50]

Father Duffy received letters on a daily basis from doughboys pleading for help in returning to the regiment. Some did not wait for help: "Many of the men took the matter in their own hands and worked their way across France, dodging M.P.'s, stealing rides on trucks and trains, begging meals . . . , and finally, if their luck held out, getting back amongst their own."[51] Father Duffy, still trying to retrieve his men at war's end, vented his spleen on the system: "There is nothing that stirs my blood like the petty arrogance of some officials in hospitals and casual camps who rebuke the requests of men . . . to rejoin their former outfits. My malison on their tribe."[52]

GIs evacuated for wounds or illness in World War II were as unpleasantly surprised as the doughboys to discover that they would not be returned to their old outfit after their recovery. Bill Mauldin, a rifleman in the Forty-fifth Infantry Division before becoming a *Stars and Stripes* correspondent, found himself in a replacement depot in Sicily after recovering from a wound. He and two other men from his division made their break one night and returned to their unit: "Later I learned that soldiers often languish in repple depples [replacement depots] for months, only to be snapped up eventually by some outfit with which they are not familiar. A soldier's own outfit is the closest thing to home he has over here, and it is too bad when he has to change unnecessarily."[53]

Some soldiers went AWOL to the front even before learning that they would be sent to a different outfit, indeed even before their wounds were fully healed, drawn back to their old outfit by their sense of responsibility. Their buddies needed help, and they could not let them down. Private Leon C. Standifer, comfortably ensconced in the hospital with a wound received during the siege of Lorient, learned that his division was en route to the front in Germany. He could not, in good conscience, remain behind. After being transferred to a replacement depot from the hospital, he went AWOL to the front: "I was homesick for my platoon. They were out there fighting, and that's where I belonged."[54] Like Standifer, Sergeant William Manchester could not lie about in a hospital while his comrades fought. He went AWOL to the front in time to join in a dangerous amphibious assault: "It was an act of love. Those men on the line were my family, my home. They were closer to me than I can say, closer than any friends had been or ever would be. They had never let me down, and I couldn't do it to them. I had to be with them, rather than let them die and me live with the knowledge that I might have saved them."[55]

Personnel managers belatedly took comradeship into account, and during the Korean and Vietnam Wars soldiers were returned to their original units after recovering from a wound or an illness. Although men were routinely returned to their own units, enough exceptions still occurred to make them nervous. Corporal Donald Chase feared, unnecessarily as it turned out, that he would not be sent back to his old infantry company during the Korean War: "I was . . . anxious to get back to the company. It had been about six weeks since I'd been hit in the thigh, and if I didn't return soon, I was afraid I'd be sent to a different outfit—something everyone tried to avoid. Sometimes, though, it happened. So even though I wasn't 100 percent recovered, with the shortage of frontline manpower it was not difficult to show that I could be returned to active duty."[56]

Some soldiers simply did not feel comfortable being away from their unit; they belonged there and were lonely without their friends. Lieutenant Philip Caputo, after attending a staff officers' course in Japan, was glad to be back with his marine outfit in Vietnam: "I had been lonely the whole ten days in Japan, and now, sloshing in the mud of the camp, I knew why. My friends and my outfit were in Vietnam. I belonged there."[57]

## UNIT ESPRIT AS SUPPLEMENTARY MOTIVATOR

Comradeship was thus a powerful motivator. Soldiers fought and died for their comrades and for their own honor. But they also fought and died to take a hill or defend a position. The assumption thus far has been that the group accepted the need to accomplish its assigned missions. In reality, this acceptance was not automatic. In sociological terminology, "vertical bonding" or "hierarchical cohesion" had to be achieved first, meaning that the primary group had to have faith in the larger organization assigning those missions and at least a tacit belief in the war's objectives.[58]

Hence, the motivating factors of unit esprit and belief in the cause also came into play. Recalling Stephen Wesbrook's theory, motivated soldiers are committed to their primary group, but they must also have a "moral involvement" with "either their unit or their national sociopolitical system, but ideally both."[59] In applying this theory to American military history, there may have been times when primary-group cohesion combined with unit esprit sufficed to motivate soldiers without their concern about the justness of the cause, as when army or marine regulars conducted interventions in support of American gunboat diplomacy.[60] For the American citizen-soldier of the draft era, however, an implicit belief in the "national sociopolitical system" was essential. If the nation's cause came into question, as it did in the late stages of the Korean and Vietnam Wars, then serious motivation problems emerged. Primary-group cohesion and belief in cause and country were thus an essential combination, with unit esprit a supplementary motivator.

Unit esprit was no less powerful a motivator, however, for being supplementary. The American soldier displayed an extra measure of determination if he was proud of his unit's accomplishments and confident in its abilities. The value of this esprit is evident in John Dollard's survey of veterans of the Abraham Lincoln Brigade, a group of American volunteers who fought in the Spanish Civil War: "Practically every informant emphasized that being a member of a distinguished outfit had made him a better soldier. Even when that outfit faced the grimmest tasks, the answer is still the same."[61]

Unit esprit refers to the soldier's identification with organizational levels above his primary group. Most American soldiers of the draft era were proud of, and identified with, their higher organization. Corporal Amos N. Wilder describes the esprit in his artillery regiment: "Discipline and morale were strongly affected by such human factors as pride in one's squad or battery and its officers with the associated emulation vis-à-vis other competing units. It may seem paradoxical, but artillerymen . . . risked their lives for the reputation of their outfits as well as for the objectives in the field of battle."[62]

Wilder touches on the two related reasons why unit esprit was such a valuable motivator. First, soldiers who were proud of their outfit fought not only for their comrades and their own self-respect but also because they had a standard of fighting excellence to uphold. Second, the soldier drew a significant measure of self-esteem in return—he belonged to a crack outfit, thus by association, he too was an accomplished fighter.

The level of command with which a soldier identified varied. He might take pride in his outfit at several levels. Wilder, for example, was proud not only of his regiment but also of his division: "I guess now no one will deny that ours (Second) is the best division in the army. Our doughboys and Marines [one of the division's two brigades were marines] have made child's play of what has stopped all the other divisions and even Frenchmen."[63] Doughboys often identified with their division.[64] The divisional shoulder patch was first introduced during World War I, and soldiers were proud to wear them. Divisional loyalty was common during World War II as well. Bill Mauldin was proud of his division, and after becoming a *Stars and Stripes* reporter, discovered that other GIs were equally proud of theirs: "During the three years I spent in the 45th Division, I was certain that it was not only the best division in the army, but that it *was* the army. Since then I have kicked around in more than fifteen other divisions, and

I have found that the men in each of them are convinced that their division is the best and the only division. That's good. Esprit is the thing that holds armies together."[65]

During the Korean War Roger W. Little, who studied an infantry company in combat, concluded that divisional pride, or indeed esprit at any level above the company, was not evident at the front: "For these men . . . the Army began with their buddies and extended little farther than the platoon and company. Beyond these levels the organization was as meaningless as it was complex."[66] What Little is really describing, however, is combat parochialism—the soldier's tendency in battle to care little about what happened outside the microcosm of his primary group. Combat parochialism, however, did not preclude a soldier's sense of pride in his unit, as Little himself acknowledged: "Even the men of this company, who expressed or displayed no identification with the regiment while with the company, would be heard boasting of their membership, wearing the regimentals [insignia], and using distinctive calls, while in the rear or in Japan at rest centers."[67]

More important, Little notes that the company still held "meaning" for the soldier. Samuel L. A. Marshall saw company-level esprit as the critical element in the Eighth Army's revitalization after its demoralizing retreat in winter 1950–1951 following the Chinese intervention: "The key to recovery of the Eighth Army was the revival of the spirit of the good company—an intense pride in unit, the feeling of Able that it was better than Baker and could prove it when the chips were down."[68] Soldiers probably identified more often, and more closely, with their company than with any other level of command beyond their primary group. The World War II rifleman Leon Standifer was proud of his company and recognized, in retrospect, the importance of his commander's efforts to build esprit: "Looking back, I can see that Captain Simmers was carefully building K Company into a proud, close-knit unit. . . . Our phonetic designation was King Company, and he considered us as just that: the best rifle company in the regiment."[69]

At whatever level the soldier identified with his higher organization, Private Sanders, a grunt in the 173d Airborne Brigade in Vietnam and proud of it, makes it clear that unit esprit served to motivate: "We felt that nobody could kick our ass. We felt tough and strong, because we had a unity and harmony that I don't think was matched in Vietnam by any other unit. In fact, we not only felt that the Vietnamese couldn't beat us, we felt sure there was no other American unit that could beat us if it came down to that."[70] Although any number of grunts from equally proud units would be quick to take issue with Sanders's claim, no outfit would jump to the challenge more quickly than the U.S. Marines.[71] Individual regiments and divisions within the Marine Corps developed a sense of esprit, and competition, not unlike that in army units. Marine Raiders and paratroopers in World War II, for example, considered themselves superior to run-of-the-mill gyrenes.[72] The Sixth Marines proudly wore a French *fourragère* awarded in World War I, and other marines were quick to call the cord, worn around the shoulder, a "pogey bait" whistle ("pogey bait" being marine slang for candy).[73] Moreover, for marines like Sledge, the company could be a powerful source of pride and esprit, just as it was for soldiers: "I realized that Company K had become my home. . . . It was not just a lettered company in a numbered battalion in a numbered regiment in a numbered division. It meant far more than that. It was home; it was 'my' company. I belonged in it and nowhere else. Most Marines I knew felt the same way about 'their' companies in whatever battalion, regiment, or Marine division they happened to be. This was the result of, or maybe a cause for, our strong esprit de corps."[74]

Yet beyond allegiance to company, regiment, or division, marines felt a unique commitment to "the Corps," something instilled in them beginning in boot camp. Corporal Martin Russ notes that although the men in his squad in Korea bitched about the Marine Corps, they were also proud of it: "Although its members change, the squad retains an inherent spirit, a combination of intense, but unspoken, pride, and intense, but definitely voiced, discontent. . . . It's the same old cornball story: they claim to loathe the Corps and all it represents, and yet . . . when they get home none of them would hesitate to take a poke at anyone who speaks disparagingly of the outfit."[75] Pride in their unit thus provided soldiers and marines a measure of self-esteem and an extra incentive to perform honorably in combat: they were the best damned soldiers in the force because they belonged to the best damned outfit in the world.

## BELIEF IN CAUSE AND COUNTRY AS AN ESSENTIAL MOTIVATOR

Unit esprit contributed toward aligning the primary group's norms with the goals of the higher organization. If the group had confidence in its leaders and pride in its parent unit, then it was more willing to accomplish the mission, without questions or qualms. But willingness to obey orders ultimately hinged on the group's believing, at least implicitly, in the legitimacy of the cause and the country that sent it to war. Some men believed explicitly in the cause, rallying to the flag for idealistic reasons. The conventional wisdom, however, is that few American soldiers even understood their country's war aims, let alone were motivated by them. During World War I, concern over the conscripted soldiers' lack of motivation led to the establishment of a Morale Branch in the War Department, tasked, among other things, to explain to the troops what they were fighting for. The Morale Branch established Camp Morale Officers, but the system came too late in the war to have much impact.[76]

Concern over the troops' lack of understanding of war aims was even greater in World War II. Ongoing surveys during the war by the Research Branch consistently revealed, as summed up by the sociologist Hans Speier, that "the American soldier had neither any strong beliefs about national war aims nor a highly developed sense of personal commitment to the war effort."[77] The Research

Branch discovered that the average GI's "war aim" was simply to get the war over with and get home in one piece.[78] This attitude was prevalent in both world wars, and as the soldiers themselves acknowledge, it did not exactly inspire commitment or heroics. The marines in Captain John W. Thomason's company, on the verge of what would be a bloody fight at Blanc Mont in World War I, would gladly have let some other outfit garner the glory:

> "Wish to God we could go up an' get this fight over with!"
> "Yes, an' then go back for the winter. Let some of these here noble National Army outfits we've been hearin' about do some of the fightin'! There's us, and there's the 1st Division, and the 32d—Hell! we ain't hogs! Let some of them other fellows have the glory—"[79]

Lieutenant O'Brien believed that this "let's get it over with and go home" attitude was at least a backhanded motivator—the sooner the doughboys finished off the Germans, the sooner they could leave: "One of these days Jerry Hun is going to learn something to his disadvantage. Yanks hate war. Crab incessantly. Anxious to go home, so all for hurry-up in Kultur-extermination."[80] The GI in World War II was just as eager to get home.[81] As with the doughboys, this essentially negative goal provided motivation of a sort, although Captain Ralph Ingersoll probably overstates its value: "Like everyone else in the American army in the [North African] theater of war, they lived only to get home. To get home— 'to get back to tell my lies'—that was their war aim. . . . To get on with winning—so as to get home—can become a desire so strong that men will and do risk their lives to satisfy it."[82]

The World War II marine Robert Leckie was probably more on target, however, when he pointed out that winning the war is a "conclusion," not a cause to believe in: "If a man must live in mud and go hungry and risk his flesh you must give him a reason for it, you must give him a cause. A conclusion is not a cause. Without a cause, we became sardonic."[83] Calls such as Leckie's for instilling more positive war aims did not go unheeded, as evidenced by the establishment of the Morale Branch in World War I and the various troop indoctrination programs conducted by the Research Branch's parent organization, the Information and Education Division of the War Department, in World War II.[84] However, despite the apparent need for ideological war aims to motivate soldiers, indoctrination programs met with little success. The reality was that the American soldier was skeptical of what he considered "propagandizing" and had little use for ideologues in his ranks.

Lieutenant O'Brien described the doughboys' disdain for the American idealists who had joined the French army prior to America's entry into the war and who now wanted to transfer to the American Expeditionary Forces: "Pathetic Bohemians, from U.S. Enlisted in fine fervor of idealism, and find themselves in French army. Want to get in ours. Red tape in way. Nothing army hates so much as idealist."[85] The divisional clerk Will Judy noted that "almost nine-tenths" of the doughboys' conversation concerned wine, women, and food—no one was interested in ideology: "In truth I have not heard more than a half dozen times during my year in the army a discussion among the men or even the officers, of the principles for which we fight. We read of them here, there and everywhere but the men of their own accord and in an informal way seldom or never talk of them."[86]

The GI proved to be no more interested in war aims than the doughboy. The Research Branch discovered that although the indoctrination effort of the Information and Education Division did serve to improve the soldier's knowledge of war-related events, and hence was a valuable information program, it did little to increase the GIs' personal commitment to the country's war aims.[87] Herbert X. Spiegel, a psychiatrist who served as an infantry battalion surgeon in North Africa, found that combat troops were decidedly skeptical of indoctrination programs: "While on the battle field it was difficult to gather men together for pep talks because dispersion was so essential, and during the lull between battles, tired soldiers did not seem to care for speeches about how wicked the enemy was, or why Fascism is an evil force. Combat soldiering became too personal, realistic and concrete to attract an audience with remarks resembling ethical or political platitudes."[88]

Soldiers in general, and soldiers in combat in particular, had little interest in or time for matters beyond their immediate needs and concerns. Little had changed by the time of the Vietnam War. Charles Moskos, who interviewed grunts in Vietnam, found that "quite consistently, the American combat soldier displays a profound skepticism of political and ideological appeals. . . . They dismiss patriotic slogans or exhortations to defend democracy with 'What a crock,' 'Be serious, man,' or 'Who's kidding who?'"[89]

Except for an ideologically motivated minority, an often scoffed-at minority at that, American soldiers were ignorant or skeptical of ideological and political aims. Yet they recognized the authority of their superiors and the legitimacy of their orders and carried them out to the best of their abilities. "Hierarchical cohesion" had thus somehow been achieved, despite the soldiers' seeming lack of interest in war aims. The experts puzzled over how this cohesion could form in the absence of ideological beliefs. The Research Branch hit upon the answer when it discovered that the same GIs who could not explain Allied war aims nevertheless held a "tacit and fairly deep conviction that we were on the right side of the war and that the war, once we were in it, was necessary."[90] Edward A. Shils similarly concluded that the GIs, while they just wanted to finish the "job" of winning the war and go home, "must, in some way, have accepted the legitimacy of the 'job' and felt some degree of obligation to carry it out."[91]

The primary group thus accepted the legitimacy of its leaders and their orders because it tacitly believed in the legitimacy of the cause and country those leaders represented. Moskos believes that a similar tacit patriotism, or "latent ideology," motivated soldiers during the Vietnam War:

Primary groups maintain the soldier in his combat role only when he has an underlying commitment to the worth of the larger social system for which he is fighting. This commitment need not be formally articulated, nor even perhaps consciously recognized. But he must at some level accept, if not the specific purposes of the war, then at least the broader rectitude of the social system of which he is a member. Although American combat soldiers do not espouse overtly ideological sentiments and are extremely reluctant to voice patriotic rhetoric, this should not obscure the existence of more latent beliefs in the legitimacy, and even superiority, of the American way of life.[92]

The sum of these theories is that the American soldier believed, at least implicitly, that he was fighting on the side of the good guys and that American society was materially and morally superior and hence worth fighting for. Soldiers and war correspondents confirm the importance of "latent ideology" as a motivator. A well-known passage from Ernie Pyle's *Here Is Your War* is sometimes quoted out of context as evidence of the GI's lack of commitment in World War II: "I believe our soldiers over here would have voted—if the question had been put—to go home immediately, even if it meant peace on terms of something less than unconditional surrender by the enemy." However, the follow-on point Pyle makes is often overlooked—that this homesickness was being tempered by the GI's growing realization that the war must first be won: "Sure, they all still want to go home. . . . But there is something deeper than that. . . . I can't quite put it into words—it isn't any theatrical proclamation that the enemy must be destroyed in the name of freedom; it's just a vague but growing individual acceptance of the bitter fact that we must win the war or else."[93]

After continuing to watch American soldiers risk their lives in battle, Pyle became even more convinced that "something bigger" must be motivating these men: "I think it was just the application of plain, unspoken, even unrecognized, patriotism."[94] The correspondent Ira Wolfert, covering the fighting on Guadalcanal in the Solomon Islands in World War II, also pondered over what motivated American soldiers. He concluded, much as Pyle had, that national pride and a subconscious patriotism must be at work: "It's just guessing to say what it is that lives in our fellows all the time and gives them the strength to be as tough as the Japs. But I think it's pride in being an American. Nobody I knew ever thought much about being an American, or would fail to be embarrassed by mention of it. . . . But it seems to me now, after all those red-letter days in the Solomons, that it's the truth that Americans subconsciously, and without really knowing it themselves, are very arrogant about being Americans."[95] The GIs themselves, in moments of reflection, realized that their pride in being Americans motivated them. Lieutenant Paul Boesch believed that although his men "waved no flags and made no speeches, underneath they felt a surge of patriotism, a sense of duty that made it impossible to quit."[96]

Belief in cause and country is rarely mentioned in the memoirs of the

Korean and Vietnam Wars, and the cause increasingly came into question, but Moskos's latent ideology was nevertheless at work. Captain William Patrick, commanding a marine rifle company in Ernest Frankel's Korean War novel *Band of Brothers,* had reservations about the war, but for reasons he could not entirely fathom, still believed that what America was doing must somehow be right: "Even if you don't actually put it in words, or even consciously think about it, you still know we stand for something. I mean, it's like . . . you don't sit around talking about patriotism or honor or courage or duty . . . but that doesn't mean those things don't exist."[97]

The Vietnam War grunt, even more likely than his Korean War counterpart to have reservations about what he was fighting for, nevertheless shared Captain Patrick's belief that America still stood for something. Peter G. Bourne captured the essence of the grunt's diffuse but real belief in his country: "Although the American soldier in Vietnam may be unclear as to the exact nature of the evil against which he is fighting, he is very conscious of an amorphous positive entity that may be labeled 'Americanism,' for which he is fighting. . . . While professing profound skepticism for the officially stated United States policy of defending democracy in South Vietnam, the average American soldier is unerringly dedicated to the protection of his own national identity and the privileges to which he feels it entitles him."[98]

Private Dominick Yezzo's "Americanism" was typical. He was "very young" when he went to Vietnam and thus "had not yet been able to form firm convictions about anything." Nevertheless, "I had faith because I was taught by my parents and teachers that America was as solid as a rock. I was also taught to believe in America and its policies."[99]

Like his predecessors in the world wars, the grunt believed in America, and because he did, he also cared about what his fellow Americans thought of him. He did not want to return home disgraced. Roger W. Little, in his study of soldier motivation in the Korean War, found that the attitudes and judgment of hometown family and friends mattered a great deal: "It was not enough that [the soldier] heard about patriotism, the flag, and our way of life in the abstract and general way of indoctrination. He had to hear about them from persons who represented those values to him intimately, persons whose evaluations of his behavior as good or bad were of great significance to him."[100]

General George S. Patton Jr. understood the soldier's concern for his hometown reputation. His famous speech to units joining his Third Army in World War II regularly included words to this effect: "When it's all over and you're home once more, you can thank God that twenty years from now, when you're sitting around the fireside with your grandson on your knee and he asks you what you did in the war, you won't have to shift him to the other knee, cough, and say, 'I shovelled shit in Louisiana.'"[101] Lieutenant O'Brien worried about having to answer exactly that question. An older soldier with a wife and children, he was relieved to have a relatively safe job as a staff officer, but he also worried about what his young son would think of him in the years to come: "Half the soul-sickness of these days is out of fear of what he will think of me, when he grows up and learns how I fought the war from behind a typewriter."[102]

The paratrooper George William Sefton was not behind a typewriter but no doubt wished that he were, instead of in a transport plane on D-Day during the invasion of France in World War II—a plane he believed was off course and over the ocean. Yet Sefton jumped out of that plane, largely because he did not want to disgrace his father, who had donned his uniform for a second war: "They had made it perfectly clear in England that to return to base with the plane would constitute desertion in the face of the enemy. A capital offense by military justice standards. Then there was the prospect of disgracing the family name, what with my father back in the service and all. Obviously, I had to jump, then and there, regardless of consequences."[103] Fortunately, Sefton's ocean turned out to be a shallow flooded area, and instead of certain death by drowning, he landed safely on solid ground.

Lieutenant James Brady, off to war in Korea, knew he would soon be leading a marine rifle platoon. Like most green soldiers, he worried about how he would perform in combat. He did not want to embarrass himself in front of his men, but just as important, he wanted to make the folks back home proud: "I hoped only that I would not run away or get men killed out of cowardice or weakness, hoped I might accomplish things in which people who knew me might take a modest pride."[104] In a similar vein, Paul Berlin, in Tim O'Brien's Vietnam War novel *Going After Cacciato,* was concerned about doing anything that would blemish his hometown reputation: "More than any positive sense of obligation, I confess that what dominates is the dread of abandoning all that I hold dear. I am afraid of running away. I am afraid of exile. I fear what might be thought of me by those I love. I fear the loss of their respect. I fear the loss of my own reputation. Reputation, as read in the eyes of my father and mother, the people in my hometown, my friends."[105]

## SACRIFICES IN VAIN

As long as soldiers like Paul Berlin maintained an abiding faith in America, they would care about what friends and relatives at home thought of them and would implicitly believe that the cause was just, even if complex or unclear, simply because it was an American cause. The soldier's belief in country, and hence in cause, was a critical motivating factor, and perhaps the best way to illustrate that is to examine what happened in Vietnam when that belief began to sour. The legitimacy of the cause in Vietnam and the methods used to pursue it became so questionable in the mind of the grunt that he began to believe his sacrifices were in vain or, in the words of Christian G. Appy, that it was "a war for nothing."[106]

The first thing that most grunts noticed was that, whatever the legitimacy of the cause, there was no valid measurement of progress toward victory. In previous conflicts, including the Korean War before the fighting stalemated by the end of 1951, possession of terrain was tangible evidence of progress. Pat Frank put it simply but accurately in his novel about a marine rifle company in Korea in late 1950: "Geography is the scorecard of war."[107] Specific geographic objectives provided reasonable, attainable goals for soldiers who might otherwise be overwhelmed by war's seeming magnitude.[108]

No war was larger or seemingly more endless than World War II, but the parochial soldier, living within the microcosm of his squad or platoon, nevertheless gained a sense of contributing to victory with each objective captured. The "let's get it over with and go home" attitude translated, at the small-unit level, into rivers crossed, towns taken, and hills seized.[109] Ernie Pyle, visiting an artillery battery in Italy in World War II, concluded that the artillerymen "would have been willing to fire all day and move all night every day and every night if only they could keep going forward swiftly. Because everywhere in our army 'forward,' no matter in what direction, is toward home."[110]

Conversely, the loss of territory could devastate morale. Captain Francis Fenton's company of marines, after a costly advance during the fighting in the Pusan Perimeter in Korea, was ordered to abandon the ground it had just seized because their battalion was being shifted to stem a North Korean breakthrough elsewhere in the perimeter. The marines were incredulous: "The men couldn't believe it. I couldn't believe it. It didn't seem possible, with all the lives we'd lost taking this ground, that we'd now just walk off and leave it."[111]

Yet soldiers in Vietnam walked off and left ground every day. Geographic objectives meant little beyond the killing of the enemy that might be found there. Men died attacking a village or enemy base camp only to have the surviving grunts walk away, often to find themselves fighting at the same location again later. The correspondent David Halberstam, in his 1967 Vietnam War novel *One Very Hot Day,* warned of the demoralizing effects of what seemed to the grunt like erratic wandering around the countryside. Captain Beaupre, the main character and a World War II veteran, explains to his young assistant adviser, Lieutenant Anderson, that in World War II, "we walked, but in a straight line. Boom, Normandy beaches, and then you set off for Paris and Berlin. Just like that. No retracing, no goddamn circles, just straight ahead." But here in Vietnam, "you walk in a goddamn circle, and then you go home, and then you go out the next day and wade through a circle, and then you go home and the next day you go out and reverse the circle you did the day before, erasing it. Every day the circles get bigger and emptier."[112] The circles likewise got bigger and emptier for Private Sanders and his fellow grunts, and some of them died in the process of making them: "We'd take one hill, we'd lose a lot of dead, there'd be a lot of bloodshed. And then, the next thing I'd know, we were gone from this hill. A couple of months later, we had to go back and take the same hill again. We were just out there walking and looking. And it seemed like we were going in circles. . . . All the guys felt the same way. We just weren't accomplishing anything."[113]

Sanders and his comrades were accomplishing one objective. In tracing their circles and retaking their hills, they killed Viet Cong and North Vietnamese soldiers, and that was what they were supposed to do. Attrition warfare, or the body count, substituted for geography as a measurement of victory in Vietnam. Unfortunately, the body count was not only overinflated but also kept to bearable levels by an enemy who in most cases decided when and where he would fight.[114] Thus, from the grunt's perspective, no matter how favorable a particular battle's kill ratio, the enemy did not seem to run out of bodies for the body count. Lieutenant Frederick Downs and his men were frustrated because they never knew for sure how badly they were hurting the enemy, while their own losses were all too apparent: "The attrition on our side was terrible on our morale. Although we killed and wounded many of the NVA we never knew how much it hurt them. It seemed there was an unlimited number to take their places. But on our side, when we lost a man we knew it and it wore heavily on our minds."[115]

Adding to the grunt's frustration was the growing realization that the enemy controlled the tempo of operations, and hence his losses, thus making the concept of the body count as a yardstick for victory a "patent absurdity," to use Tim O'Brien's words.[116] The helicopter pilot Robert Mason, arriving with the First Cavalry Division early in the war, soon learned that the Viet Cong "seemed to control the situation. We wanted them to stand and fight and they wouldn't—very frustrating."[117] This frustration largely accounts for the frequently heard call to "go north" or to "go to Hanoi."[118] While an invasion of North Vietnam would have been a costly and probably disastrous escalation of the war, the idea of going north appealed to the grunt because, like Rome, Paris, and Berlin in World War II, Hanoi was a concrete, geographical goal—something they could understand.

Not only did the frustrated grunt question the way the war was being fought, but ultimately he also came to question why it was being fought. The actions and attitudes of the supposed beneficiaries of his effort, the South Vietnamese, provided the most visible reason for questioning the cause. The American soldier, though rarely an ideologue, nevertheless understood that America's goal in Vietnam was to save the democratic south from being overrun by godless Communists.[119] He arrived in Vietnam, therefore, with two expectations—that the people would be glad to see him and that they would be willing, with his assistance, to fight for their own freedom.[120] The grunt was disabused of his first expectation, that the people would be glad to see him, almost as soon as he stepped off the airplane, as was the case for the newly arrived Private John Ketwig and his fellow replacements as they rode the bus to the replacement center:

We crept out of the air base, through a main gate . . . into the mainstream of Vietnamese peasant life. We marveled at the ragged hovels and piles of garbage. The stink was almost overpowering, as if trapped to rot by the weight of the humidity. The people were tiny, like caricatures. As they saw us approaching they hurried to the edge of the street. A chorus of "Go home,

GI" and "Fuck you, GI" was accompanied by a barrage of assorted garbage and trash bouncing off the wire mesh that covered the windows. Somebody in the back of the bus hollered, "Hey, you fuckin' gooks. We're supposed to be here to save your fuckin' puny asses!"[121]

The people were not happy to see their arriving liberators. Apparently their "puny asses" were not in need of saving. American culture shock at the poverty of the Vietnamese added to the fading of expectations. Were these poor, dirty "gooks" worth saving? Corporal William D. Ehrhart expressed his dawning realization that not all Vietnamese welcomed him with open arms with a bit of understatement: "I don't even think these people like us."[122]

Even worse, some of the people not only disliked Americans, but they also wanted to kill them. The wire mesh on the bus windows, arriving soldiers learned, was not just to keep out the garbage but also the occasional grenade. David Parks summed up the problem: "I'm not sure the native people are with us. They smile at us in the daytime and their sons shoot at us at night. It's hard to spot the real enemy."[123] When the people whom the grunts were there to save reacted by killing them, fading expectations were completely dashed.

The grunt also discovered that when the South Vietnamese were not actually trying to kill him, they were trying to steal from or con him. Outright theft of American property was common, as was the selling of everything from soda to sex at marked-up prices, which got higher as the war progressed and the influx of American dollars drove up inflation. Demirgian, the semifictional grunt in the journalist John Sacks's *M,* expressed his hatred of the Vietnamese for their less-than-scrupulous entrepreneurial practices: "Come to help their miserable country and what? Anyone get any thanks? No, dead or alive—crippled, I could be blind, a basket case and they wouldn't care, not if they had my damn piasters [Vietnamese currency] first! Money is all they care, the crooked bastards! Give me—give me—that's the extent of it, give 'em a stick of soap, though, do you supposed they'd use it, the filthy people? No—they'd sell it, the filthy bastards!"[124]

Demirgian's tirade is extreme but not unique. Private Sanders felt the same way: "We were in Vietnam helping them and they would try to beat us out of the little money we had. I felt they exploited the GIs." He added, "Plus they wouldn't help us fight. . . . We were fighting for them and they [the South Vietnamese army] were scared to fight for themselves. They used to pick up and run. . . . They wouldn't even fight for their own country; we didn't see any reason why we should."[125]

Thus the grunt's second expectation, that the South Vietnamese would be willing to fight for their own country, faded almost as quickly as his expectation that he would be welcomed as a liberator and protector. The grunt expected the uniformed, regular forces of South Vietnam, specifically the Army of the Republic of Vietnam (ARVN), to do their fair share of the fighting. The almost universal perception in the memoirs is that they did not. Much of the grunt's animosity toward the ARVN was undeserved but nevertheless real. Private Sanders hated the ARVN, for example, because they never seemed to do anything: "We never did see the regular South Vietnamese army in the field. They would be guarding the bridges or be hidden away in some compound."[126] No one told Sanders that the South Vietnamese soldiers were doing what American strategy at that time called for them to do—provide area security while American forces conducted field operations against the Viet Cong and North Vietnamese regular forces.[127]

When the ARVN, often ill-equipped, inadequately trained, and poorly led, did conduct field operations, they did not always perform well. Although some ARVN units were effective, it took only one instance of ARVN cowardice or incompetence to turn the grunts against them. Robert Mason transported South Vietnamese soldiers to a landing zone in his UH-1 helicopter, but they would not get out until his crew chief waved a pistol in their faces. Disgusted, Mason's reaction was typical: "I've never seen anything like that. How the fuck are they going to win this stupid war if they fight like that!"[128] The rifleman Robert Rawls sums up the grunts' lack of faith in the ARVN: "They weren't worth a cent. In a fire fight those ARVNs would drop everything and run to the rear. That's why I hate them, those Vietnamese. I wish I'd never see one of them as long as I live 'cause we was over there fighting for them and they were constantly ripping us off. Stealin' stuff."[129]

Yet nothing was more demoralizing and nonsensical to the grunts than seeing ARVN troops killing one another, as they did during the internal struggles for power in South Vietnam. Lieutenant Caputo, with a "ringside seat" on a hilltop, watched two simultaneous battles—marines fighting the Viet Cong and ARVN fighting one another, including a South Vietnamese plane strafing an ARVN truck convoy: "It was incredible, a tableaux of the madness of the war." This incident was the final straw for Caputo: "I knew then that we could never win. With a government and an army like that in South Vietnam, we could never hope to win the war."[130]

The discovery that the South Vietnamese people did not seem to want him there and that their army was lukewarm, at best, in fighting for its own cause demoralized the grunt.[131] But these factors alone did not destroy his belief in the cause his country had sent him to fight. What did destroy it was his growing awareness that his fellow Americans had lost faith in the war and did not want him in Vietnam any more than the Vietnamese did.

A majority of citizens initially supported American involvement in Vietnam. The units and replacements that went to the war early on believed in the cause, or at least in America, as evidenced by Moskos's "latent ideology" and Bourne's "Americanism," concepts that significantly were based on the former's 1965 and 1967 visits to Vietnam and the latter's 1964–1965 tour of duty there.[132] Many of the early-deploying soldiers were regulars and volunteers. The vocal, but small, antiwar movement centered on the college campuses did not have much influence on them, according to Bourne: "Both in the subjective view of combat performance and in the crudely objective measures of psychiatric casualties and disciplinary actions, antiwar sentiment in the United States appears to have had little effect upon the motivational level of the troops in the field."[133]

Following the enemy's 1968 Tet Offensive, however, a majority of Americans, from all walks of life, turned against the war. The heavy casualties and the unexpected strength and fury of the enemy's attacks convinced many Americans that the war was unwinnable unless America upped the ante and invaded North Vietnam. If the country's leadership was not willing to do that, then America should cut its losses and get out.[134] This turn against the war affected the grunts' attitudes. The replacements arriving in Vietnam after the Tet Offensive were increasingly skeptical about the war because they came from a society that was itself increasingly skeptical, and as the supply of eager volunteers dried up, more and more of those replacements were reluctant draftees.[135]

Skeptical, reluctant draftees made skeptical, reluctant grunts. Appy notes that before the Tet Offensive, discontent focused primarily on the way the war was being fought, but after it the grunt increasingly questioned the legitimacy of the cause itself: "In the earlier years the central thrust of disenchantment concerned the strategic aims of the war and the lack of convincing signs of progress. Among those who fought in the latter years, there was a more widespread sense that the war was not worth fighting on any terms; there was a more profound sense of the war's pointlessness."[136]

Moskos also noticed that the grunts' belief in the war deteriorated after Tet. "Latent ideology" was no longer the motivating force it had been earlier in the war: "It was patently evident that soldiers assigned to Vietnam after 1969 differed noticeably from their predecessors in that they were coming from an antiwar milieu that contrasted markedly with that of the early years of the Vietnam War."[137]

Veteran soldiers, returning for second tours in Vietnam, also detected this shift for the worse in grunts' attitudes and motivation. Captain Joseph B. Anderson Jr., returning for a second tour in Vietnam in 1970, noticed a decline in aggressiveness and morale, and he blamed it on faltering homefront support: "What was very clear to me was an awareness among our men that the support for the war was declining in the United States. The gung ho attitude that made our soldiers so effective in 1966, '67, was replaced by the will to survive. They became more security conscious. They would take more defensive measures so they wouldn't get hurt. They were more scared. They wanted to get back home."[138]

Declining homefront support also affected the answer to the question that had so concerned soldiers in earlier wars: "What did you do in the war?" People at home no longer seemed to care about the answer or even believed that the best answer was "nothing." This loss of homefront support damaged one of the grunt's important coping mechanisms, as Dave Grossman observes: "Psychiatric casualties increase greatly when the soldier feels isolated, and psychological and social isolation from home and society was one of the results of the growing antiwar sentiment in the United States."[139] Even worse, the antiwar movement, at least the vocal segment of it centered on the college campus, actively denounced the soldier, adding to his sense of isolation, even alienation. Paradoxically, he was condemned by his countrymen for his role in supporting a cause that his country had sent him to fight for, as Moskos notes: "Not only was the war in Vietnam opposed, but for many militants the basic legitimacy of military service was brought into question. For some, moreover, to be against the war in Vietnam entailed denigrating the moral qualities of the American fighting man. Much of the radical antiwar rhetoric portrayed American soldiers as proto-Fascist automatons and wanton perpetrators of atrocities against Vietnamese civilians."[140]

The grunt naturally resented these attacks and hated the middle-class college crowd that perpetrated them while dodging military service with various student and occupational draft deferments. The growing antiwar sentiment nevertheless caused him to question why he was in Vietnam, and it certainly damaged his motivation to fight.[141] Even early in the war, Bourne's comment to the contrary, the grunts began to be aware that antiwar protest was growing, even if still a minority opinion. Mason and his fellow pilots, bored during a lull in the action, sat around their tents in late 1965 "wondering why they were here." These emerging doubts were aggravated by the statements of the antiwar movement: "It didn't help that the anti-Vietnam-war demonstrators were becoming prominent in the news. With the company in such a black mood, the protestors' remarks were so much salt in our wounds. No one likes being the fool. Especially if he finds himself risking his life to be one."[142]

The antiwar news from the States increased in volume and vehemence, often denouncing the grunts and what they were doing. Even letters from friends and family reflected little pride in the soldier and his accomplishments, simply urging instead that he avoid the vices and dangers of Vietnam. Sergeant Egan, in John M. Del Vecchio's *The 13th Valley,* set in Vietnam in 1970, launches a diatribe against the demoralizing impact of this increasingly negative news from home: "All the papers from the World, they all the time tellin how this place is fucked up. . . . Everybody gets letters askin why we so fucked up. Mothers cryin, askin if their little Joey-boy is smokin dope or rottin with the sif [syphilis]. Tellin em ta cover his ass, take care and come home in one piece cause nobody there wants to take care of a two-piece man. Man, they just don't know."[143]

Grossman believes that faltering homefront support even led to an increase in Dear John letters: "As the war became more and more unpopular back home, it became increasingly common for girlfriends, fiancées, and even wives to dump the soldiers who depended upon them. Their letters were an umbilical cord to the sanity and decency that they believed they were fighting for."[144]

Especially painful to the grunt were the actions of radical, sometimes well-known protestors like Jane Fonda and Dr. Benjamin Spock, who actively aided the enemy cause by visiting North Vietnam or by raising medical supplies for the enemy or at least by rooting for a North Vietnamese victory. A vehement comment by Corporal Ehrhart concerning the traumatic amputation and relocation of the sexual genitalia of these two activists need not be quoted, but suffice it to say that soldiers felt betrayed and confused by such actions taken by their own countrymen.[145] John Sack, who followed a group of individual replacements to Vietnam after leaving their Stateside training company (Company M), summed up the difference in soldiers' expectations of homefront support versus the realities: "M believed that America should believe in M, and M felt betrayed by all acts of Vietnikism: literally betrayed . . . *if we're going to die over there, at least people at home should support us.*"[146]

Ultimately, in a complete reversal of attitudes from the world wars, peer and social pressure discouraged rather than promoted wartime service. A young man, especially from a middle-class or well-to-do background, who volunteered or submitted willingly to the draft, without taking advantage of the numerous educational, occupational, or medical deferments, was considered a fool or worse. Appy notes that draft avoidance was encouraged: "In middle-class circles, especially on many college campuses, the effort to avoid the draft was commonly accepted as legitimate. . . . Techniques of avoidance were openly discussed, shared, and supported."[147] Samuel Hynes, teaching literature on campus during the Vietnam War, reached the same conclusion: "Anyone who taught in an American college during those years . . . remembers the reigning spirit of evasion. Among the students it was not considered dishonorable to avoid the draft; the dishonorable (and stupid) thing was to go."[148]

This overtly negative attitude toward service was generally restricted to the college campus and to middle- and upper-class communities, but it was loudly extolled by the antiwar movement, hence Mason's comment about "being the fool" for serving in Vietnam while others did not. John Ketwig, vehemently antiwar and antiarmy after his service in Vietnam and Thailand, nevertheless dreaded returning home because he would have to face his old friends, who would consider him, and his wartime comrades, fools for fighting and dying in Vietnam: "Smug and confident, they would pity me because I had not been smart enough to beat the draft. . . . It wouldn't be so bad that they laughed at me; I should have taken my scholarship and stayed out of the draft too. . . . But their laughter would be directed at everyone who had gone to The Nam. . . . Fine people, good people, whose only crime had been poverty or a different set of values. Some of them had died, and if anybody laughed at that . . . well, I would have to be awful damn careful."[149]

Many grunts shared Ketwig's fear that their sacrifices were in vain. They had been sent by an increasingly unsympathetic, even hostile, America to fight a war that they did not seem to be winning for people who did not want them there. As the army officer and personnel specialist William L. Hauser writes, motivation and efficiency suffered accordingly: "The people of the United States had decided . . . that the game was not worth the candle, that our forces were fighting a losing (some said *wrongful*) war and ought therefore to get out. The officers and noncoms who were charged with making the troops continue fighting had a near-hopeless task, for their authority to compel risk of life and limb had lost the legitimacy which national purpose bestows."[150]

A soldier who questions the legitimacy and achievability of his cause loses the will to fight. In a marvelous debate between the grunt medic "Doc" and an Iranian *Savak* officer in *Going After Cacciato,* the *Savak* officer points out that although soldiers may fight for their comrades and for their self-respect, they must also ultimately fight for a just cause: "Does not the absence of good purpose jeopardize the soldier's own ego, thus making him less likely to fight well and bravely? If a war is without justice, the soldier knows that the sacrifice of life, his own valued life, is demeaned, and therefore his self-respect must likewise be demeaned."[151]

More simply put by the "Old Fox," a brigade commander in *The 13th Valley,* "If you do not believe in what you are fighting for, you fight badly."[152] In Vietnam, as belief in the cause ebbed, grunts began to fight badly. Primary-group cohesion did not disintegrate, but hierarchical cohesion did. Group norms became "disarticulated," to use John H. Faris's term, from the goals of the higher military organization.[153] Stephen Wesbrook writes that this disarticulated group no longer cared about the mission, only about survival: "If the soldier does not feel a moral involvement with either the military organization or the nation, he will feel no obligation to comply with their demands and will stop fighting except as a matter of personal or group survival."[154] Add to group disarticulation the reality, late in the war, of troop withdrawals and peace negotiations, and the grunt's obsession with surviving to his DEROS in a no-win war becomes completely understandable.

Given that survival became the group's only goal, grunts found ways to avoid taking risks. As Stanley Goff writes, "The smartest people didn't try to find anything. You didn't go anyplace. You just went as far as where you thought the CO [commanding officer] wouldn't be able to hear you. And who the fuck in the squad was going to say any God damn thing?"[155] In their effort "not to find anything," grunts faked patrols. They went out from base camp or the unit's defensive perimeter only far enough to be out of sight and sound. If required to send in periodic reports on the radio, then phoney reports went in on schedule. To cut short an ambush patrol, a squad might fake enemy contact by firing off a few rounds and then beating a retreat. On other occasions, the enemy was allowed to pass by unharmed, because initiating a firefight could mean friendly casualties, even if the grunts had the advantage in numbers and surprise.[156]

Even for those junior leaders who did their best to carry out their assigned missions, and the majority undoubtedly fell into this category, the yardstick for measuring success increasingly became a low number of friendly casualties, not damage done to the enemy. Thus, for the platoon leader Anderson, what was important was that he "lost only one man" during his first tour.[157] Lieutenant Archie Biggers "only lost two kids" in his platoon.[158] Lieutenant Robert Santos, also a platoon leader, felt "responsible for bringing these guys home. Eight of my men died over there and two got wounded."[159] And the squad leader "Paul," a case study of the psychiatrists Hendin and Haas, "was proud of the fact that none of the men in his squad was killed during his tour."[160]

Frugality with men's lives has always been a trait of good leadership, but in Vietnam, by late in the war, it became the only criterion that mattered. Junior leaders who refused to overlook combat avoidance, or who the grunts believed were too enthusiastic in carrying out orders that placed them in harm's way, were persona non grata. These leaders were warned in various subtle and not-so-subtle ways that group survival, not some futile mission in a senseless war, came first. If a leader did not back off, then his men might kill him outright, or "frag" him, a term referring to a fragmentary grenade, the weapon often used in such murders. The psychotherapist Sarah Haley, in working with Vietnam veterans, encountered cases of fraggings. "Bob," one of her patients, a former marine squad leader, explained how his new, inexperienced platoon leader had insisted on assaulting a hill strongly defended by Viet Cong: "Bob reported, 'It was me and my men or him.' He was ambiguous about who killed the officer but stated coolly, 'We didn't go up no shit hill and next week we had a new lieutenant.'"[161]

Bob's ambiguity was in a sense natural because a fragging was often group-sanctioned, even if only one man carried it out. How many fraggings occurred is a matter for debate, but their frequency increased dramatically later in the war. Nor were the motives for fraggings always clear. Not all were about survival. Some involved issues of race or drug use or were simply personal vendettas.[162]

Primary groups in Vietnam, disarticulated from their leaders and higher headquarters, sanctioned combat avoidance and fraggings for the sake of group survival. Survival, however, had always been the main concern, even in primary groups that had not become disarticulated. Hence, combat avoidance and the elimination of dangerously enthusiastic or incompetent leaders happened in other wars as well. Combat avoidance occurred when the men believed that accomplishing the mission was not worth the risk involved. During World War II, Lieutenant Wilson, to his amazement, was ordered to lead a twenty-man patrol into a German-held town at night, engage in hand-to-hand combat using only knives, bayonets, and grenades, take a prisoner, and then return. Needless to say, no one volunteered for this mission. Wilson finally ordered the loudly protesting men from two of his squads to accompany him on the patrol. They went, but each time Wilson moved forward, the men deliberately ruined any chances of surprise, and hence success, by breaking into fits of coughing. Wilson finally "realized my orders were impossible," so he left the "rebellious coughers" behind and took a few trusted men to scout out the town, abandoning the gung-ho scheme for hand-to-hand combat.[163]

Combat avoidance could also occur if soldiers did not like the odds. Captain Cawthon writes that there was "an unwritten soldiers' maxim" at work in his infantry battalion in World War II: "If you shoot at the enemy, he is likely to shoot back, and, therefore, it is an action that requires a fine calculation of the odds."[164] Fear of retaliation largely explains how a live and let live attitude can develop. The British sociologist A. E. Ashworth notes that the live and let live system that evolved in the trenches in World War I was based on "the soldier's realization that if he refrained from offensive activity, the enemy would in all likelihood reciprocate. The soldiers on both sides had a vested interest of a biological sort in the perpetuation of such a situation."[165]

The eager, newly arrived doughboys often upset the "live and let live" system, at least until they learned to appreciate its benefits, and the same thing occurred on occasion during World War II. An enthusiastic Lieutenant Fussell, during his first stint in the lines, while manning an observation post in a farmhouse, spotted some German soldiers in the open and called mortar fire in on them. He was rewarded with a German shell that blew out the window he had just walked away from after completing the call for fire. The lesson to be learned was not lost on Fussell: "As we became more experienced, we learned not to do such showy things anymore. They inevitably brought retribution, and both we and the Germans found that in the absence of orders to the contrary, the best policy was to leave well enough alone."[166]

Incompetent, uncaring, or excessively enthusiastic leaders were occasionally killed by their own men, or left to fend for themselves in a dangerous situation, with sometimes fatal consequences. Bob Hoffman believed that an especially despised sergeant suffered such a fate: "I have always strongly suspected that he received what was often called a 'blue bean'—a shot from his own men. There were men in action that day who had occasion to actually hate him. He had been a martinet."[167]

During World War II, an enthusiastic new lieutenant named Galicki arrived to take over the machine-gun platoon in Kurt Gabel's battalion. The lieutenant immediately began talking about sending out combat patrols to "harass the Krauts," which made the men "a little restless."[168] Several troopers then lured the inexperienced lieutenant to the chow line and deliberately formed a cluster around him, knowing that such a tempting target would draw artillery fire. The men then scattered for their foxholes, leaving the lieutenant "alone and utterly bewildered," just moments before the expected artillery rounds hit. Gabel reports, "I saw Galicki's mess kit and canteen cup fly high in the air, eggs, pancakes, and coffee clear against a gray sky, and Galicki himself sliding along the ground, presumably toward a crater. It was the last time I ever saw that lieutenant."[169]

Combat avoidance and fraggings were thus not unique to the Vietnam War, but group disarticulation ensured that such incidents occurred with much greater frequency. The potential difficulties involved in sustaining the grunts' belief in the cause might have been better appreciated if the lessons of an earlier, unpopular war had been learned.[170] A few historians and journalists writing about the Korean War warned of future problems, but these warnings went unheeded. Theodore R. Fehrenbach, in his 1963 history, foretold what would happen if America again drafted large numbers of citizen-soldiers to fight in a limited war, far from home, for less than compelling reasons: "Reservists and citizen-soldiers stand ready, in every free nation, to stand to the colors and die in holocaust, the big war. Reservists and citizen-soldiers remain utterly reluctant to stand and die in anything less. None want to serve on the far frontiers, or to maintain lonely, dangerous vigils on the periphery of Asia. There has been every indication that mass call-ups for cold war moves may result in mass disaffection."[171] "Mass disaffection," of course, is exactly what America got when it again sent reluctant citizen-soldier draftees to the "periphery of Asia."

Like the grunts, the GIs who went to Korea understood the basic war aims, which were not radically different from those pursued in Vietnam: to contain Communism and save an ostensibly democratic country from being overrun. This theme is evident in Pat Frank's Korean War novel, in which Sergeant Ekland says it is better to fight Communism in Korea than to wait until it spreads: "[The American people] want us to stay out here and fight. They'd rather have us fight on the Yalu than on the Mississippi."[172] The Korean War GI also understood that he was saving South Korea from being overrun by force, and after witnessing the brutality of the North Koreans, many felt, as did Lieutenant James Hamilton Dill, that this cause was worthwhile: "Having had much opportunity to observe what the Communists did to people, the alternative to war and destruction was far worse. Liberty or death was not an idle phrase in a history book in Korea."[173]

The Chinese intervention in late 1950 drove the United Nations forces into headlong retreat, and for a time disaster loomed. But after a series of offensives and counteroffensives, the war stalemated near the Thirty-eighth Parallel, the original border between the two Koreas. The goals of containing Communism and saving South Korea had thus been achieved; but total victory, meaning the defeat of North Korea and reunification of the country, was out of the question. Further fighting, therefore, struck the GI as senseless. Geographical measures of victory no longer mattered—the mission was simply to hold in place. Body count also seemed meaningless, as Lieutenant Dill's comment indicates: "We had inflicted hideous losses [on the enemy], but so far as anyone could tell, we could have spent the rest of our lives eliminating Chinese without making a dent in their army."[174]

Thus the GI, much like the grunt in post-Tet Vietnam, came to see personal survival until his rotation date as the only goal of any importance, as Lieutenant John A. Sullivan, who served in Korea in 1952 and 1953, quickly learned: "For the GI's the general idea was to stay alive. The army wasn't going anywhere, and everyone knew it. There would be no big push to end the war. The name of the game was to hang in there and survive until something happens at the peace talks in Panmunjom. To get killed was to be wasted, and no one wants to be wasted."[175]

The GIs grew increasingly bitter over being "wasted." As in Vietnam, their sacrifices seemed to be in vain. Corporal Martin Russ certainly thought so. He describes a regimental memorial service in May 1953 and relates his bitterness over the chaplain's words that his fellow marines had not died in vain, because in fact they had: "None of those men died gloriously. And most of them died in vain.

Only the ones that died while saving the lives of others did not die in vain. The most disturbing thing of all is that not one of them knew why they were dying."[176] Whatever understanding of and support for the war's aims that the GIs had during the early fighting largely dissipated in the senseless stalemate of the last two years of the war. Surviving until rotation became an obsession for the Korean War GI, just as it became for the grunt. As Lieutenant Marvin Muskat pointed out, "Thirty-six points was the score needed for rotation. Everyone knew this, and the result was that there was a real tendency to just keep one's head down, take no unnecessary risks, and collect points. It wasn't like World War II; you knew there was no big push coming, no fighting until the enemy surrendered. This was a war that was going nowhere."[177] In a war going nowhere, combat avoidance was inevitable. The memoirs do not mention fraggings, but Korean War soldiers faked patrols and ambushes with increasing regularity as the war dragged on. Lieutenant Sullivan's case was typical: he was to lead an ambush patrol to a dangerous and exposed location. After talking it over with his sergeants, he decided they would go out only part way because, after all, "since the army was not going anywhere, there didn't seem to be any reason to risk our lives."[178]

The Korean War GI did not want to be killed in a war that was going nowhere, and he also did not want to die for people who seemed unwilling to fight for themselves. The South Koreans and the GIs did not dislike each other as intensely as the grunts and the South Vietnamese did, but GIs frequently complained about the lack of fighting spirit in the Republic of Korea (ROK) Army. Much of its bad reputation was undeserved, but that does not lessen the reality that the GI perceived he was dying for people who were not doing their share of the fighting.[179] The attitude of Floyd Baker, whose marine unit was rushed into the line to plug a gap left by fleeing ROK troops, was typical: "I was amazed . . . to see the South Korean soldiers bugging out. Here we were, in their country, fighting for their freedom, and they're hightailing it like scared rabbits. We knew some of us were going to get killed, and for what? These clowns?"[180] Lieutenant Matthias displayed the usual marine distaste for army dogfaces, but he reserved his serious disdain for the ROK Army: "U.S. Army troops felt the Marines were prima donnas and we felt the soldiers were overrated as fighting men. Even then our respect for the U.S. Army was five hundred percent greater than for ROK . . . troops."[181]

The Korean War GI not only resented what he believed was an insufficient effort by the ROK Army, but he also came to resent the lack of support from the home front. Americans never displayed the antiwar sentiment that they did during the Vietnam War, but neither did they exhibit much enthusiasm for the "forgotten" war nor appreciation for the sacrifices of the GIs. Lieutenant Frank Meutzel, a marine medically discharged after losing a leg in Korea, encountered public indifference when he left the grounds of the naval hospital: "Off the base, it was as if there was no war taking place. While very few civilians were consciously rude or offensive, it became quickly evident the man on the street just didn't care. The war wasn't popular and no one wanted to hear anything about it."[182]

The soldiers in Korea were well aware of homefront indifference. Lieutenant Anderson in Frankel's novel *Band of Brothers* expressed his anguish over sacrificing for an uncaring America: "I just want them to know and to give a damn. But they don't know and they don't care. Because it doesn't touch them."[183] Marine Lieutenant Matthias likewise resented the home front's lack of interest in the war: "The letters from home confirmed the fact that we were a forgotten bunch of men. Few people back home faced up to the full realization that this was a war. They were too removed from the situation and there was no full mobilization or war effort. . . . As a result, most of us felt we were victims of a forgotten war."[184]

Just as during the Vietnam War, the foxholes had to be filled with growing numbers of draftees once the volunteers, regulars, and recalled reservists had become casualties or had been rotated home. These draftees understood that Americans were indifferent to the war, that the fighting no longer made sense once the war was stalemated, and that life in Korea was not pleasant. Private Morrow, en route to Japan in spring 1952, shared a troop transport with replacements, mostly draftees, bound for Korea. He noticed their distinct lack of enthusiasm: "Some of them made it clear that if it were left up to them there would be no fuckin' war, and they also made it clear that they could find a hell of a lot of other things to do rather than killing people or possibly being killed or maimed for life. Living in muddy holes for the next six months or so wasn't their idea of heroism, and many of them prayed every free minute for God to end the war before they arrived."[185]

Thus the Korean War was a precursor to Vietnam in several important ways. It was fought by increasingly reluctant warriors who viewed survival as their only goal in a conflict that had become unwinnable and that lacked homefront support. The oral historian Rudy Tomedi sums up the similarities: "Both [were] unpopular, both largely misunderstood in their time, and both, in their aftermath, [left] thousands of combat veterans and at least an equal number of civilians wondering if it had all been worth it."[186]

# 6

# Failing to Cope with the Environment of War

The combat environment, according to Jonathan Shay, generates "psychologically catastrophic conditions" that can break a soldier.[1] Eric Bergerud agrees: "The interaction between fear, stress, exhaustion, and illness created a dreadful dynamic that threatened to break the spirit of fighting men."[2] Despite their best efforts to cope with war's catastrophic conditions, some soldiers "couldn't take it any more" and broke down, ran away, or inflicted wounds on themselves to escape combat.

That soldiers could break down psychologically from the stresses of combat first became widely recognized during World War I, when such breakdowns were called "shell shock." By the end of World War I, shell shock had been replaced by "war neurosis" and "psychoneurosis," which gave way during World War II to "combat exhaustion" and then "combat fatigue." Combat fatigue remained in use through the Vietnam War but was supplemented by terms such as "combat reaction."

These shifts in terminology were more than just a semantics drill. The chosen term reflected the catalyst that psychiatrists considered to be the primary cause for breakdown, and this cause, in turn, conferred or denied legitimacy. Shell shock, for example, reflected the belief early in World War I that soldiers broke down because of the physiological effects of concussion from shelling. Because the soldier had no control over the enemy's artillery, breakdown from shell shock was legitimate, according to Albert J. Glass: "Members of the combat . . . group, including commanders and medical officers, could readily understand and accept 'shell shock' as a direct consequence of unavoidable events of battle which might happen to anyone."[3]

Terminology was important for another reason as well. Soldiers who broke down tended to display the symptoms appropriate to the recognized cause, because subconsciously they wanted their exit from combat to be accepted.[4]

Shell-shocked soldiers therefore displayed symptoms of concussion. By the time America entered World War I, doctors had largely discounted concussion as a cause of breakdown, but the term "shell shock" nevertheless remained common to the vernacular. Descriptions in the memoirs of doughboys who broke down thus refer to enemy shelling as the cause and concussion as the effect. Sergeant Merritt D. Cutler, in describing shell shock to oral historian Henry Berry decades after the war, still attributed its occurrence to shelling: "Most of the shell-shock victims of World War I weren't what we'd call today battle fatigue. Real shell shock was the actual scrambling of a man's brain by concussion. If you've ever seen a man actually lose his wits through shelling, you'd never forget it. The poor guys became jibbering idiots."[5]

In reality, concussion cases were rare. Many doughboys came to realize, as did the doctors, that psychological problems were the real cause of breakdown. Sergeant Earl Goldsmith learned that after months of hard fighting, some men just could not take any more: "Some of our lads . . . just snapped. I can think of one man in particular. He went through all those fights we had in July and August [1918]. Then he finally collapsed. . . . Why, the poor guy just sat down and started to bawl like a baby."[6]

By war's end, the term "war neurosis" had replaced shell shock because it reflected psychological rather than physiological causes for breakdown. "War neurosis" and "psychoneurosis" were the terms in use when American soldiers next engaged in serious ground combat in North Africa in World War II. Unfortunately, psychoneurosis implied a personality defect as the primary cause for breakdown, hence psycho cases, as they were inevitably nicknamed, were not always viewed as legitimate casualties. As Glass explains it, "With such labeling and connotation of psychopathology, psychiatric casualties were not accepted by the combat group as being the result of battle conditions. Rather, they were considered to be weaker or predisposed individuals."[7]

Not surprisingly, commanders and even medical personnel sometimes considered these casualties cowards, or at least morally deficient individuals, as evidenced by the notorious incidents in which General George S. Patton Jr. slapped "cowardly" psychiatric patients.[8] Furthermore, psycho casualties unconsciously adopted the symptoms proper for the cause, which reinforced the appearance of character deficiencies: "Many psychiatric casualties from the Tunisia fighting were described as manifesting dramatic and bizarre reactions . . . which seemed to portray the fearful plight of the individual unable to cope with battle conditions."[9] These casualties exhibited terror states, gross tremors, severe startle reactions, mutism, and catatonic-like syndromes.[10]

The belief in character disorders as the main cause of breakdown came into question as the fighting progressed. Much like the case described by Sergeant Goldsmith, GIs who had performed bravely under fire for weeks or even months began to snap. Roy R. Grinker and John P. Spiegel, serving in North Africa, began to notice that soldiers with no prior indication of character disorders were breaking down. They concluded that external factors must be as important as character flaws, or perhaps more important: "As in the etiology of any neurosis, constitutional factors and the individual's life history, including the genetic background of his personality, are very important. Yet many observers have given these factors undue weight. The realities of war, including the nature of army 'society,' and traumatic stimuli, cooperate to produce a potential war neurosis in every soldier."[11]

In May 1943 the terminology changed from "psychoneurosis" to "exhaustion," and eventually to "combat exhaustion" or "combat fatigue," to emphasize these external factors.[12] Glass notes that this new term reestablished the legitimacy of breakdowns: "'Exhaustion' was readily accepted by both psychiatric casualties and the combat reference group. . . . Almost all combat personnel could appreciate that anyone could become exhausted by the stress and strain of continued battle."[13]

This shift in terminology again stimulated a shift in symptoms. The often hysterical psycho casualty was joined by the shaky, "burned-out," battle-fatigued soldier. The correspondent Richard Tregaskis describes a lieutenant he knew who ended up in a hospital in Italy suffering from exhaustion: "He looked lost. His eyes were sunken; his chin and neck jerked nervously in spasms, like a turtle's head poking out of its shell. But he recognized me, and confided, 'It's the Goddamnedest feeling. I can't sleep, and I can't rest. I can't stop the jitters.'"[14]

"Combat fatigue" continued as the accepted term in the Korean and Vietnam Wars. It was common in the Korean War, especially in the first year or so, but the sporadic nature of the fighting in Vietnam, though intense on occasion, did not generate many cases of classic combat fatigue of the type brought on by long-term exposure to constant fighting. Military psychiatrists in Vietnam did see cases, however, of psychiatric casualties in response to short but intense combat, often coupled with a traumatic event such as the loss of a comrade or trusted leader. One psychiatrist dubbed this phenomenon "combat reaction."[15] Some psychiatrists returned to the issue of personality, attributing most Vietnam War psychiatric breakdowns to "character and behavior disorders." One psychiatrist called it "pseudo-combat fatigue" because these casualties exhibited symptoms of classic combat fatigue, but in reality they suffered from various "personality disorders."[16]

The sum of experience in four wars was that external factors generated internal stresses and anxieties—Bergerud's "dreadful dynamic"—that led to a soldier's breakdown. In some cases, character or behavior flaws hastened the process. How many soldiers broke down as a result of this dreadful dynamic? No one can be certain. Men with physical ailments were sometimes misdiagnosed as combat-fatigue cases, or vice versa. Commanders occasionally abused the combat-fatigue category to get rid of malcontents or soldiers with drug or alcohol problems. Conversely, some commanders tried to minimize the number of reported cases of psychiatric casualties because a high rate might be construed as an indicator of morale and leadership problems. Further, combat-fatigue cases treated at the lowest levels often did not make it into any statistical count. Some soldiers broke down more than once and hence were double counted. Moreover, there is the issue of "deferred" casualties—soldiers or veterans who broke down only after leaving combat.[17] Whatever the actual number of psychiatric casualties, it is safe to say, as Richard A. Gabriel does, that it was significant: "In every war in which American soldiers have fought in this century the chances of becoming a psychiatric casualty—of being debilitated for some period of time as a consequence of the stresses of military life—were greater than the chances of being killed by enemy fire. The only exception was the Vietnam War, where the chances were almost equal."[18]

The extent of the problem becomes even more significant if Gabriel's criterion of debilitation "for some period of time" is liberally interpreted. Many soldiers suffered what Bergerud calls "transient breakdown": "A death of a friend, an ugly firefight, or a host of other things could trigger momentary loss of will. Sometimes friends helped men through dark hours, sometimes they worked it through themselves."[19] These cases varied from a panic of short duration to an emotionally and physically exhausted soldier who just needed a few days' rest.[20]

For a panicking soldier, a few sharp words or a slap in the face might suffice to bring him around. In the midst of an attack in World War II, Lieutenant George William Sefton discovered the artillery forward observer "cowering face down in the ditch."[21] Knowing his company needed fire support, Sefton proceeded to motivate him: "My heated verbal suggestions that he get on with his job proved ineffective, but an unrestrained kick in the butt restored his devotion to duty."[22]

Sometimes the transient breakdown took more than a few sharp words or a kick in the pants to overcome. Private Roscoe C. Blunt Jr. lost his nerve during an intense barrage in World War II. He jumped out of his foxhole and began running around in the midst of the shelling, cursing the Germans. His ever-faithful companion Everett forcibly dragged him back to cover. After the barrage ended, Blunt remembered nothing about his actions. His commander had him evacuated for several days' rest, after which Blunt felt fine and returned to his unit.[23]

During a botched night ambush in Vietnam, Lieutenant James R. McDonough was almost killed by a burst of machine-gun fire from his own men, who had mistakenly turned their gun to point inside their ambush position. McDonough lay in the dirt where he had dropped for cover: "A few moments earlier I had been an effective platoon leader doing his job. Now I could actually feel my chest throbbing against the dirt where I lay. . . . I could not think. My body began to tremble, then shiver, then shake uncontrollably."[24] He continued to lie in the same spot, too scared to move, even though he was attacked by an ant colony and then drenched in a monsoon downpour. Only at dawn did he regain control of his shattered nerves.

## EVERYONE HAS HIS BREAKING POINT

At what point does temporary panic or short-term breakdown qualify as combat fatigue? The difficulty in answering this question illustrates why statistics on the occurrence of combat fatigue are suspect. A more useful way of thinking about combat fatigue is to accept what the soldiers themselves came to understand— everyone has his breaking point. A man may have personality traits that make him susceptible to anxiety and breakdown, but no soldier is immune, as the World War II military correspondent Ralph G. Martin notes, "Every man has his breaking point. You can hear just so many shells, see just so many torn bodies, fear just so much fear, soak just so much rain, spend just so many sleepless nights."[25]

Doughboys and their psychiatrists were the first soldiers of the draft era to appreciate that every man had his breaking point. John H. W. Rhein, in examining 320 cases of breakdown among doughboys, found that less than half had any previous history of nervous disorders or phobias. The combat environment was the main culprit: "The experiences at the front in combat were so intense, so strenuous and so exhausting that one acquired in a short time a state of nervous instability which in civil life would require months or years to bring about."[26]

Sergeant Bob Hoffman describes what just five days of heavy fighting for the French town of Fismette did to his company: "Men began to go out of their heads—shell shocked if you could call it that, or just crazy from weakness, strain, suffering and hunger, with death all around them."[27] Lieutenant Joseph D. Lawrence and his company were in equally bad shape after four days of continuous combat in the Meuse-Argonne: "Many of our men were showing signs of cracking under the strain. We had been under continuous shellfire, rifle and machine-gun fire, gassing, attacks by planes, no food, and only what muddy rainwater we could get from holes in the ground. It was drizzling rain and cold, the men were wet to the skin, cold, hungry, thirsty, some of them frightened, many sick from the gas, all in dread of the never-ceasing, screaming, crashing shells. The strain was terrible."[28] After nine days of combat, Lawrence's company was finally relieved by another outfit. Such breaks in the action allowed for sorely needed rest, but they provided only temporary reprieves. Over time, a soldier's bank account of courage, to use Lieutenant Paul Fussell's analogy, was spent: "We came to understand what more have known than spoken of, that normally each man begins with a certain full reservoir, or bank account, of bravery, but that each time it's called upon, some is expended, never to be regained. After several months it has all been expended, and it's time for your breakdown."[29]

The deeper and longer the soldier was immersed in the environment of war, the more it wore him down. Finally, often after some sort of last straw, or "precipitating shock" as the World War I psychiatrist Frederick W. Parsons called it, the soldier broke down: "His chum is killed by his side; his officer is wounded in a particularly distressing manner; or, being detailed to escort walking wounded to the dressing-station, he is shocked by what he sees."[30] The World War II psychiatrists Roy L. Swank and Walter E. Marchand also observed how a final traumatic event often pushed a soldier over the edge: "A soldier with combat exhaustion usually continued in battle until he was exposed to an acute and severe 'incident,' such as a 'near miss' from artillery or mortar fire or a heavy artillery barrage. In many instances a close friend was . . . killed before 'his very eyes.' This usually provoked a violent emotional explosion."[31]

Raymond Sobel, a division psychiatrist in World War II, called this process of deterioration "Old Sergeant Syndrome," because it happened to seasoned veterans who broke down after months of satisfactory, even distinguished, combat service. These soldiers had lost confidence in their martial and leadership skills, had long since abandoned any illusions that "it couldn't happen to them," were nervous and physically run down, and no longer felt close to a primary group that by then contained few of their old comrades: "Being unable or disinclined to form permanent attachments to new men, the 'Old Sergeants' found themselves running on depleted reserves."[32] Despite the group's overall ability to form new bonds as its composition changed, some veteran soldiers did not want the pain of new ties that would again be broken by death or injury.

The memoirs provide examples of veteran soldiers who just couldn't take it any more. Lieutenant Paul Boesch describes how his predecessor in command of G Company, Captain Black, broke down in the midst of the fighting in the Huertgen Forest after two of his sergeants were killed and his executive officer lost his leg to a mine: "'Why did it happen to them?' he cried. He dropped his head in his hands and began to sob. 'Why didn't it happen to me? McCarthy gets both his legs blown off. Men get killed and wounded all around me. Those two sergeants were with me ever since I got here. I made them sergeants. Now they're dead. Joe loses his leg. Why doesn't it happen to me?'"[33]

Often when a veteran like Captain Black finally broke, he lost all ability to function. After weeks of heavy fighting on Okinawa, a seasoned marine in Eugene B. Sledge's outfit snapped. While under heavy enemy fire, "suddenly he began babbling incoherently, grabbed his rifle, and shouted, 'Those slant-eyed yellow bastards, they've killed enougha my buddies. I'm goin' after em.' He jumped up and started for the crest of the ridge." Sledge and a nearby sergeant managed to drag the marine back to cover, undoubtedly saving his life, and turned the sobbing, trembling man over to the corpsmen. The broken marine had fought bravely in two previous campaigns. The sergeant summed it up: "He's a damn good Marine. . . . I'll lower the boom on anybody says he ain't. But he's just had all he can take. That's it. He's just had all he can take."[34]

During the heavy fighting in the first year of the Korean War, before the rotation system was established, veteran combatants broke down much like Sobel's "old sergeants." A forward observer, Sergeant Thomas Randell, sent to support a rifle company, encountered an old acquaintance named Blackburn, who by March 1951 had been in Korea for about seven months and was one of the few survivors of the original complement: "We talked for a while, and he told me about his friends, now all dead or wounded." During the ensuing battle, a rifle grenade landed next to him but failed to explode: "This was one close call too many for poor Blackburn, who took one look at the unexploded grenade lying next to us and completely cracked up. The man had reached his breaking point, then gone beyond it." Until that moment, Blackburn had been a "fine and dependable soldier," according to his company commander, but the "burden had become just too heavy to bear."[35]

Psychiatric casualties of the Old Sergeant Syndrome type declined sharply in the late stages of the Korean War and during the Vietnam War, in part because of the reduced intensity of the fighting, but also because of the hope for escape from combat provided by rotation.[36] Nonetheless, some soldiers still broke down after too much combat. Lieutenant Philip Caputo, who served for a while as his regiment's casualty reporting officer during his tour in Vietnam, noticed the rise in psychiatric casualties in his old battalion after months of combat: "The war was beginning to take a psychological toll. . . . The phrases *acute anxiety reaction* and *acute depressive reaction* started to appear on the sick-and-injured reports. . . . I noticed, in myself and in other men, a tendency to fall into black, gloomy moods and then to explode out of them in fits of bitterness and rage. It was partly caused by grief, grief over the deaths of friends."[37]

Soldiers and psychiatrists thus came to understand that everyone had his breaking point. The only debatable issue was how long this breakdown process took for the average soldier. Swank and Marchand, in their study of infantry soldiers in the Normandy campaign in World War II, noticed that symptoms of "emotional exhaustion" began to appear after forty to forty-five days of combat. GIs became mentally slow, listless, and tremulous. If not soon treated, then they would break down completely after a final triggering event or would sink into a "vegetative existence."[38] The psychiatrist John W. Appel and the medical statistician Gilbert W. Beebe estimated that infantrymen in North Africa in World War II broke down after 200 to 240 aggregate days of combat.[39] The Research Branch surveyed infantry divisions in Italy in World War II and found that the breakdown rate increased after nine months in the combat zone.[40]

There are differences in these time estimates because Swank and Marchand are considering continuous days of combat; Appel and Beebe look at aggregate days, and the Research Branch simply considers time in the combat zone. Exposure to continuous combat without breaks in the action precipitated breakdowns. Furthermore, the more intense that combat, the sooner soldiers broke down. The violent Pacific island campaigns in World War II, for example, although of short duration, produced cases of Old Sergeant Syndrome long before the soldier made it to the rank of sergeant.[41] As Lieutenant Gerald P. Averill put it, Iwo Jima was "a hell of a place to get snapped in," referring to a novice marine's first exposure to combat.[42] Private Allen R. Matthews was one of those marines who got "snapped in" on Iwo Jima. After twelve days of continuous fighting, he was the only one left from his original squad. He could no longer function physically or mentally and was evacuated to a hospital ship. Matthews describes his condition: "I was tired. My muscles ached and my joints hurt and I could not co-ordinate my mind and my actions. . . . My mind and my body seemed disconnected, as if they were standing apart one from the other, each glaring at the other in impotent confusion."[43]

In extreme conditions of danger and hardship, soldiers could wear out in a matter of weeks rather than months. But what about the men who broke down after a few hours in combat, or even before reaching the front? Some soldiers cracked long before the brutal environment of war had a chance to do its worst. Indeed, the occurrence of psychiatric casualties even before doughboys were in harm's way was a reason for ruling out shell shock as the cause of all breakdowns. John F. W. Meagher saw numerous "cases suffering from neuroses who never reached a position nearer the firing line than Liverpool [England]."[44]

Soldiers broke early in World War II as well. While some soldiers looked forward to their first combat with naive eagerness, Ernie Pyle noticed that others were overwhelmed by anxiety: "I suppose the anticipation during the few days before a man's first battle is one of the worst ordeals in a lifetime. Now and then a soldier would crack up before he ever went into action."[45] Private Lester Atwell, who worked in his battalion's aid station, saw men who cracked up almost immediately: "Different men had different breaking points. . . . Some with the best of intentions . . . would go to pieces in the first big attack, perhaps in its first five minutes."[46]

Ironically, and tragically, some green soldiers were so overwhelmed by their fear of combat that they committed suicide. General Mark W. Clark, as a young captain and infantry company commander in World War I, discovered a man missing on the morning the company was to move to the front: "The poor devil, he just didn't want to go. He'd deserted just before we left New York, but I'd had him sent over on the next boat. . . . Of course, we all felt he'd gone AWOL again, but we were wrong—he'd walked over to the woods and blown his brains out."[47]

The rotation system established in the Korean and Vietnam Wars was a significant factor in reducing long-term, or classic, combat fatigue, but some soldiers still broke down early in their tours of duty.[48] Matthew Brennan described his new platoon sergeant as a tall, nervous man in his forties who "had spent the last four years [serving] in Italy, doing everything in his power to stay out of Vietnam."[49] The sergeant fell apart in his first firefight. Brennan found him hiding under a helicopter tail boom, "shaking and talking to himself."[50]

Seeing a man go to pieces even before the first incoming shell or curl up in a ball and shiver during his first firefight sharply impressed on the soldier that he had more to fear than just death or injury.[51] Lieutenant McDonough, newly arrived in Vietnam, began talking to a veteran lieutenant from the same outfit he had just been assigned to, typically seeking information about "what it's like." McDonough soon realized, to his horror, that the lieutenant was no longer sane: "Earlier, I had been afraid only of being physically maimed or killed. But now I saw that there was another threat, that of a madness born of terror and dehumanizing ferocity. The veteran lieutenant was mad. Perhaps once he had been like me. He was alive, but he had not really survived. Physically he was unmarked; spiritually he was dead; mentally he was. . . mutilated and twisted. . . . If this could happen to him, could it happen to me? I was shaken to my bones."[52]

Lieutenant George Wilson, who pointedly notes that his training in Officer Candidate School in World War II did not include even a mention of soldier breakdown, was taken by surprise when a man in his platoon cracked up after only three days of fighting in Normandy. The man began to shake violently and broke into loud sobs. Wilson finally told the medics to take the man away, but "it was too late . . . to keep the fear from spreading. My men looked sick, and they wouldn't look me in the eye."[53]

Psychiatrists discovered that soldiers who broke down early often suffered from character flaws that made it especially difficult for them to cope with combat. They were "predisposed" to breaking down under stress.[54] Surveys of men who broke down early during World War II revealed that they were less intelligent, less able to adjust socially, and more anxiety-ridden than the average soldier.[55] Thus, while every man had his breaking point, the threshold was lower for some than for others. The importance of intelligence in coping with combat stress came as a surprise to some, but military sociologists and psychiatrists have verified that intelligent, well-educated soldiers are better soldiers, in combat and peacetime. Slow-witted soldiers had difficulty learning basic skills and thus could not function successfully within the group.[56] Intelligent soldiers were not only less likely to break down in combat but were also more likely to be superior soldiers, or "fighters," as one study of Korean War GIs called them: "Perhaps the most striking difference between the fighter and the non-fighter is the fighter's relatively greater intelligence." A soldier lacking intelligence, the study added, was "simply not adept enough to perfect easily the many techniques and skills which are necessary for efficient performance."[57]

The educational screening conducted during induction and the demands of initial training weeded out most of the dullards, but a few slipped through the system; they did not fare well on the battlefield. Private Atwell describes the case of Dick Gann, a fellow GI in his medical detachment who was a "mental defective of sorts." He was "morose and slow," stuttered, and mumbled to himself.[58] He tried his best, but he was not soldier material. The battalion surgeon evacuated Gann, who was on the verge of cracking up, as a medical casualty. The men were glad to see him go: "We never expected or wanted to see him again. . . . Hell, he never belonged up here [at the front] in the first place."[59]

Soldiers who broke down early also tended to have difficulty forming ties with the group. Jesse Glenn Gray labeled these soldiers "constitutional cowards": "The coward may have comrades, but they are not able to sustain him emotionally. His relation to them is not one of depth or inner community." The constitutional coward was not motivated by the group because he felt no attachment to it. He faced the prospect of combat emotionally alone, and thus, Gray noted, his fears were overpowering: "Death is a personal enemy of his, a relentless, absolute, all-encompassing enemy. But the coward's inner poverty of life and love makes him no fit antagonist."[60] And as Sergeant William Manchester puts it, "Any man in combat who lacks comrades who will die for him, or for whom he is willing to die, is not a man at all. He is truly damned."[61]

Constitutional cowards crop up as loners, braggarts, or shirkers who did not fit in, and most of them broke down sooner rather than later. Lieutenants Harold P. Leinbaugh and John D. Campbell describe one of the replacements who arrived in their company in World War II as "a real braggart, tough-acting, who kept saying, 'Boy, let me at 'em!'" The braggart lasted less than a day. After being shelled and shot at by a machine gun, "the guy broke down completely. He couldn't cope. He was worse than useless and we had to send him back."[62]

Just prior to shipping out for Europe, Standifer's platoon received a replacement named Lehrer. He wanted to take over Standifer's job as scout, but no one trusted him, according to Standifer's friend George: "'Hell, no, I don't want Lehrer up there [in front] or on my flank. He won't carry his part of the load when things get rough. Lehrer is a loner. He has the guts to do a job if it benefits him, but he will never be a team man.' George had hit the key point that worried me. The squad was my family, and I was ready to risk my life for them. I wasn't sure that Lehrer would." George's assessment proved correct. Lehrer was useless in combat because he did not fit in: "Patrols terrified him, probably because he knew that if he got into trouble no one would want to help him out."[63]

The psychological screening of recruits, which occurred during all the wars of the draft era, was supposed to identify those men who could not perform effectively. The high incidence of breakdowns, however, despite the rejection of thousands of men deemed psychologically unfit for service, indicates that screening was marginally effective at best.[64] The most obvious misfits and psychopaths could be identified, but the quick, assembly-line interviews conducted at the induction stations could not begin to reveal deep-seated flaws and phobias. Aggravating the problem were the recruits who attempted to appear unstable in hopes of getting rejected and, conversely, the men with real disturbances who tried to hide them because they wanted to serve or did not want to be labeled a psycho.[65] Many unstable soldiers were weeded out during training or deployment, but it often took the stress of combat to reveal who was emotionally ill-equipped to cope with war.

## THE DEBATE OVER CAUSES

Psychiatrists and sociologists agree that a mix of behavioral and situational factors affected a soldier's ability to function in combat.[66] But what were the situational factors that drove a soldier to the breaking point? Physical exhaustion caused by the hardships of combat was common and so seemingly overwhelming that observers like Ernie Pyle attributed breakdown to physical wear and tear alone: "A large proportion of those [neurosis] cases were brought about by complete fatigue, by fighting day and night on end with little sleep and little to eat."[67]

Yet this plausible theory did not hold up. During periods of rapid advance, for example, troops were pushed beyond the point of exhaustion, but the incidence of breakdowns dropped off dramatically. Albert Glass and Calvin S. Drayer cited the victorious American advance into the Po River Valley in Italy late in the war as "a final demonstration that physical fatigue alone . . . was not productive of psychiatric casualties."[68]

Psychiatrists did believe, however, that exhaustion contributed to psychological breakdown. Meagher found that fatigue slowed the recovery of neurosis cases: "The lack of sleep, whether from the arduous work in the trenches accentuated by a state of anxiety, or from other causes, was an important factor in delaying recovery."[69] World War II psychiatrists agreed, and the adoption of the terms "combat exhaustion" and "combat fatigue" reflected their acceptance of the role of physical as well as psychological factors in causing breakdown. According to Grinker and Spiegel, "When fatigue, hunger, and thirst are combined with continuous exposure to danger and the constant pounding of heavy artillery and aerial bombs, the resistance of even the strongest to the development of anxiety may become impaired."[70] If physical exhaustion was at most a contributing factor, then only psychological trauma remained to explain why, beyond personal characteristics, a soldier broke down. But students of soldier behavior are not in accord over what fears and anxieties most contributed to that trauma. A few argue that anxiety over having to kill and the guilt that resulted from doing so made a major contribution to soldier stress and hence breakdown.[71] Samuel L. A. Marshall argued, for example, that the World War II GI, who as a civilian had been taught that aggression was wrong, was stressed over having to kill. He cited unnamed military psychiatrists in the European theater who had found that "fear of killing, rather than fear of being killed, was the most common cause of battle failure in the individual."[72]

Although psychiatrists did encounter cases in which anxiety or guilt over killing appeared to be the primary precipitator of combat fatigue, a majority of psychiatrists, Marshall's unnamed sources aside, considered stress produced by the fear of death or mutilation to be the main cause of breakdown.[73] The U.S. Army Medical Department's history of neuropsychiatry in World War II notes that a unit's ratio of psychiatric breakdowns directly reflected the casualty rate and adds: "Clearly, the immediate and continued threat of battle danger was the essential element in . . . psychiatric breakdown."[74] Appel and Beebe agree: "The key to an understanding of the psychiatric problem is the simple fact that the danger of being killed or maimed imposes a strain so great that it causes men to break down."[75]

The soldiers themselves, in their candid admissions of fear over dying, add convincing evidence to this argument. Ernie Pyle noticed that casualties were psychologically bearable to the GI only when there were not too many, too often: "It's when casualties become so great that those who remain feel they have no chance to live if they have to go on and on taking it—that's when morale in an army gets low."[76] For Private Rudolph W. Stephens, that feeling set in after about three weeks of combat in Korea: "As I saw other men wounded and killed, I began to wonder when my time would be up. Every day I would hear of someone getting hit one way or another, and the dread of death was always on my mind. The feeling was as if something was picking at your very soul. No matter what you did, you couldn't get rid of the feeling."[77]

It is more succinctly put by one of Mark Baker's Vietnam veterans: "The hardest thing to accept is that it's for real and forever. [Death] was permanent." The veteran added that he had tried not to dwell on his mortality, "but you're so tired, your mind is weak. When death comes into your head, you don't have the strength to push it aside."[78]

Fear of a serious wound was a natural extension of the fear of death. Lieutenant Lyle Rishell explained that this fear grew stronger when the rugged Korean terrain made evacuating the wounded difficult: "The fear of being wounded was always on our minds, especially when we were exposed in some inaccessible area, because we figured our chances of getting out were slim. I know that bringing a seriously wounded man off the mountain required several hours."[79] Rishell and Stephens were not atypical and certainly not cowardly in admitting their fears. Surveys confirm the axiom that anyone who says he is not scared in combat is a liar, and what soldiers feared most was death or crippling injury.[80]

While psychiatrists and soldiers alike considered fear of death the primary stress producer, they acknowledged that a host of other malevolent factors were also at work. Some soldiers did feel anxiety and guilt over killing. Most were physically worn down by the hardships of the combat zone. The green soldier feared that he might not hold up in his first combat, revealing himself to be a coward. Many men suffered from loneliness and longed for the affection of their loved ones. Some soldiers were torn by grief or rage over the loss of close comrades. Others dreaded the uncertainty and feelings of helplessness generated by the random nature of combat. And the almost total lack of privacy demoralized some soldiers.[81]

Nor is this list of deleterious factors complete. Soldiers were stressed by yet other aspects of their combat environment. They not only grieved for lost comrades but also suffered guilt over surviving.[82] Sergeant Dan Levin felt he had no right to live while so many good men had died: "The sense that I was taking up earth-space that belonged to better, braver, less lucky men, that I had given only a frightened, reluctant minimum and had been unaccountably and undeservedly spared, would grow like a subterranean echo."[83] More typically, anguished soldiers believed, sometimes irrationally so, that they could have done more to save a buddy. Corporal Albert French lost his best friend, Vernon, in a firefight in Vietnam. French had already been seriously wounded by the time his friend was killed, but he still faulted himself for not continuing with his squad—perhaps he could have made a difference: "I'm sorry I didn't keep going, keep moving.

Maybe I might have said, 'Let's go this way, keep down, spread out.' Maybe I would have seen something, seen it coming, got us out of the way. I don't know, man, but I think just maybe I was too scared to move on. Just wanted to lie behind the [rice paddy] dike, not wanting to know who was dying, not wanting to die."[84]

Stress was also caused by a rapid transition from relative comfort and safety to danger and carnage. This phenomenon came to psychiatrists' attention during World War II, when air crews experienced just such an abrupt transition, called "discontinuity," on almost a daily basis.[85] The helicopter brought discontinuity into the realm of ground combat in Vietnam. Psychiatrist Peter G. Bourne, who accompanied helicopter medics on several missions, discovered how stressful it could be: "The pilots are busy with the multiple demands of flying the helicopter and have little time to think of anything else, but there is no anxiety-relieving task on which those in the back can concentrate. Minutes ago they were drinking coffee in the comfort and security of the office; now they are flying into a jungle battle about which they know little except that two men have already lost their lives, and all they can do is sit and wait and think about the impending danger."[86]

Those in the back nervously waiting were often grunts conducting an air assault. Tim O'Brien describes the shock of departing the safety of a base camp on a "hopelessly short ride" to the landing zone. In a matter of seconds, the post exchange and servicemen's club were left behind, replaced by rice paddies and jungle. "You begin to sweat," despite the cool air. All too soon comes the descent: "We started to go down. The worst part of the Combat Assault, the thing you think about on the way down, is how perfectly exposed you are. Nowhere to hide. A fragile machine. . . . You sit in your helicopter, watching the earth come spinning up at you. . . . The helicopter nestled into its landing area, hovering and trembling over the [rice] paddy, and we piled out like frantic rats. We scrambled for paddy dikes and depressions and rocks."[87]

The stress created by a rapid transition into the environment of war was not limited to air assaults but could occur to any soldier reentering combat after a break in the action. Private Blunt recalled how "jumpy" soldiers could be, including himself, when going back to the front line during World War II: "To be totally immersed in the horror of war for months and then to be suddenly trans-planted temporarily to the relative tranquility of a rear area, only to be abruptly returned without any mental preparation to combat again, strained the nervous system's ability to compensate for the upheaval, and the man could easily become paralyzed with fear. The bravery born of necessity often deserted him."[88]

As if the trauma of discontinuity, survivor's guilt, and the other perilous factors were not enough, in some theaters of war the soldier was stressed to the point of breakdown by his very surroundings. A harsh environment could generate what Eli Ginzberg and his team, examining soldier effectiveness in World War II, called "location stress": "Military service can prove to be a particularly severe burden for the soldier who is assigned to a locale that he despises—a rugged mountain area or the tropics."[89] Location stress coupled with loneliness and boredom could cause a man to break, even without the pressures of combat. David Rothschild, a psychiatrist in the Pacific in World War II, noted that the troops called such a breakdown "going tropical" or "jungle wacky": "Many soldiers feel they are entering a remote corner of the earth in which vaguely defined mysteries and dangers are lurking. They find the climate unpleasant and taxing."[90]

Private Robert G. Thobaben's infantry battalion saw only sporadic combat while performing security duty on various Pacific islands in World War II, but it did see a great deal of boredom and privation, and he explains how alien this existence was to the typical young GI: "We were at an age when female companionship was the rule, but there were no women. We lived a life of celibacy, an armed monastic order. The normal freedom to move, particularly the freedom to jump in your car and just go, is practically eliminated for soldiers on an island. The normal involvements in school, listening to pop music and just hearing the news, are a rare luxury overseas in these island paradises. Even the normal craving for some solitude is denied the soldier; one is constantly immersed in a sea of humanity where there is no escape, no privacy."[91]

Isolated Pacific islands were not the only "armpit," to use an old army saying, that soldiers had to serve in. The cold, desolate mountains of Korea were perhaps even worse. Private Dean Westberg described the stress and discomfort caused by the biting Korean wind: "A howling wind blew the snow and cold into the foxhole . . . the noise of the wind makes it seem danger is lurking everywhere."[92] The wind's howl, day in and day out, could drive a man over the edge, as occurred in Lieutenant James Brady's marine company: "Kelso, the machine-gun sergeant, lost a man. . . . It wasn't the gooks that did it but the wind. We'd been on line three weeks and the wind never stopped. One night Kelso's corporal went berserk, firing off a heavy machine gun inside the bunker, trying to kill rats that no one else saw. They carried him off in the morning, cursing the wind and the rats, drooling and trying to tear off his clothes."[93]

## THE TREATMENT OF COMBAT FATIGUE

From howling wind to island tedium, the soldier faced myriad situational stresses. Although each man wrestled with his own personal mix of noxious factors, the fear of death or mutilation, accompanied by some degree of physical exhaustion, remained the main stress producers. The techniques found most useful in treating psychiatric casualties, therefore, were remarkably similar in all the wars of the draft era.

The principles for treating battle fatigue, as the army currently calls it, are captured by the acronym PIES (proximity, immediacy, expectancy, and simplicity). Proximity refers to the treatment of battle-fatigue casualties as far forward as possible. Immediacy means treating them expeditiously. Expectancy calls for casualties to be reassured that they will quickly recover and return to duty. Simplicity refers to the need for keeping the treatment process simple and straightforward. These principles are found in current army literature, but their origins can be traced directly to the experiences of treating psychological casualties in World War I.[94]

World War I psychiatrists did not use the terms "proximity, immediacy, expectancy, and simplicity," but they learned through experience to apply these principles. Official treatment policy in the AEF called for the use of "persuasion" and "rest" to bring about the "speedy restoration and return to their organizations of those in whom exhaustion is the chief or only factor." Doughboys were to understand that "the disorders grouped under the term 'shell shock' are relatively simple and recoverable rather than complex and dangerous." Further, evacuation of patients was to be controlled to ensure forward treatment.[95]

Unfortunately, these treatment principles and the need for specialists and facilities to apply them were forgotten during the interwar years or, more accurately, were set aside as no longer needed. Given postwar advances in the diagnosis and treatment of the mentally ill, the army's Medical Department concluded that a modernized version of the psychological screening of recruits as conducted during World War I could identify those men unfit for service and hence cases of psychoneuroses would be few. With the advent of a high rate of combat neuroses during the North African campaign in World War II, however, it became apparent that screening had not eliminated those men predisposed to breakdown, if only because all soldiers were susceptible to breaking down over time.[96]

The army spent the rest of World War II catching up in the treatment of combat fatigue. Division psychiatrists and psychiatric hospitals were established, much as they had been during World War I, and the treatment principles from that earlier war again proved effective. William C. Menninger, director of the army's Neuropsychiatric Consultants Division, Office of the Surgeon General, summarized treatment practices in terms similar to those used by his World War I counterparts: "If intensive treatment was provided early, in an environment in which the expectation of recovery prevailed, remarkable results were obtained."[97]

Other World War II psychiatrists likewise describe the success of proximity, immediacy, expectancy, and simplicity, although still not using exactly those terms.[98] Fortunately, these treatment principles were not forgotten or ignored again. Albert J. Glass, who had been a division psychiatrist in World War II and was the psychiatric consultant to the Far East Command during much of the Korean War, wrote in 1955 that enough "evidence has accumulated" after three wars to "permit crystallization of certain operational principles of field psychiatry."[99] He advocated "decentralization" (a combination of proximity and immediacy, which go hand in hand), "expectancy," and "simplicity," principles that remain in effect.[100]

In application, these principles meant treating the combat-fatigue casualty at or near a forward aid station, allowing for rapid treatment. The casualty was placed out of immediate danger and allowed to rest, have a hot meal, and clean up. In some cases he was given medicine to help him sleep. The battalion or regimental surgeon and his aidmen (who ideally had been trained by the division psychiatrist to identify and treat combat fatigue) assured him that he would soon feel fit and rested and rejoin his outfit. Not all battle-fatigue cases recovered quickly and some never did, but a significant number responded well to this simple treatment and within a few days were able to return to their unit.[101] An examination of why this process worked reveals a few facts about soldiers' fears and motivations.

Austere treatment close to the front worked precisely because it was close to the front—the casualty was not completely removed from the environment of war. He was safe enough, perhaps in the cellar or dugout of a battalion aid station, to have a much needed physical respite and, even more important, to get relief from the stress caused by fear of imminent death. But he was not far from his unit and was still treated like a soldier, not a patient. Frederick Parsons explains that for the milder cases of war neuroses, this simple treatment returned many soldiers to combat in short order: "Men go for days without sleep, have insufficient food, suffer from lack of water, reach a stage of absolute physical exhaustion, and perhaps are nervous, dazed, and jumpy. After twenty-four or thirty-six hours rest, they are well and . . . they want to get back to the company."[102]

The soldier, despite his breakdown, still considered himself part of his unit and did not want to let his buddies down. He also did not want to embarrass himself by seeming to be shirking or cowardly; thus he wished to rejoin his outfit. Glass, reflecting on his experiences in two wars, noted that the soldier's bond to his group was key: "At a forward level of therapy, where the psychiatric casualty is still emotionally tied to his unit, efforts to improve lowered physical capacity and foster the sustaining power of group identification are appropriate and remarkably successful in restoring previous ability to maintain combat effectiveness."[103]

Once a battle-fatigue casualty had been bedded down in a safe, clean hospital, however, his chances of recovering sufficiently to return to combat dropped off dramatically. Some psychiatric casualties had such severe symptoms that hospitalization was the only option, but too often battle-fatigue cases were "overevacuated," especially if forward treatment was not possible because of the lack of psychiatric specialists and medical facilities, or if the existing treatment organizations were swamped by casualties. Once removed from the environment of war, the battle-fatigue casualty resisted, albeit subconsciously, returning to it. His symptoms, which could include depression, amnesia, psychosomatic illnesses, extreme startle reaction, irritability, insomnia, grief, apathy, and extreme physical weakness, tended to harden and his recovery proceeded slowly, if at all.[104]

Thomas W. Salmon, head of neuropsychiatry for the American Expeditionary Forces, admitted that overevacuation had been a problem until adequate facilities for forward treatment were established in September 1918: "In consequence, many hundreds of men suffering from exhaustion, concussion neurosis, fear, and other emotional states found themselves, within a few days after leaving their organizations, in hospitals a hundred miles or more away from the front. Very few of these men ever returned to active duty."[105]

Overevacuation occurred again early in World War II because of the lack of psychiatric care specialists and facilities, as Glass notes concerning the North African campaign: "The winter and spring battles of the Tunisian campaign in late 1942 and early 1943 . . . brought forth large numbers of psychiatric casualties. As in the early phase of World War I, these patients were evacuated hundreds of miles to rear hospitals whose psychiatric facilities were insufficient. . . . There resulted a fixation of symptoms and the formation of chronic disabling syndromes. Relatively few psychiatric casualties were recovered for combat duty."[106]

Men subconsciously lost their will to recover once they had been evacuated to a hospital because recovery meant a return to the war. Even soldiers initially hospitalized for wounds or ailments sometimes developed psychiatric disorders as they began to recover physically, in a subconscious attempt to remain hospitalized. Of the 3,921 World War II combat soldiers in Eli Ginzberg's study who had been hospitalized and eventually discharged from the army as psychologically unfit, 1,707 had been admitted as psychiatric casualties, but the remaining 2,214 had been admitted for wounds or illness. Only when in the hospital did they develop serious symptoms of psychiatric disability. Ginzberg attributes this phenomenon to the "hold of the hospital": "These figures suggest the 'holding power' of the hospital. It was not easy for men to return to combat or to remain effective once they had been exposed to the security and comfort of the hospital."[107]

World War I psychiatrists also witnessed the hold of the hospital. Rhein, who commanded a neurological hospital in the American Expeditionary Forces, noticed that patients healed of wounds and about to be returned to the front "began to complain of physical ailments," which proved to be "in the nature of hypochondrical [sic] manifestations," no doubt resulting "from the opportunity to think over the dangers of the front in comparison with the safe and comfortable conditions under which the soldiers found themselves" in the hospital.[108]

The veteran soldier who did return to combat after recovering from a physical or psychiatric ailment was burdened by his knowledge of what lay ahead. Some hospital returnees did not last long before they broke down.[109] Late in World War II, a lieutenant rejoined Audie Murphy's company after recovering from a serious wound caused by enemy artillery fire. This lieutenant was liked and respected, and he tried his best, but whenever he came under artillery fire, he went to pieces: "His nerves collapse again. His mouth sags; his speech becomes jerky; and his hands shake so that he can hardly insert an ammunition clip into his carbine. Whether he knows or wants it, he is through. Finished."[110] Murphy sent the lieutenant to the rear and asked his battalion commander not to send him forward again.

Sometimes a hospital returnee did not even make it back. Amos N. Wilder, returning to his artillery battery after several days in the hospital for minor surgery, broke down during the ambulance ride: "En route back alone in flying ambulance had a mental crisis. It seemed I never would get any strength—and they were rushing me back into that hell of life in the Battery with enthusiasm gone to the last and alone." The ambulance returned Wilder to the hospital for "further attention." He spent time in a convalescent camp and eventually rejoined his outfit, where he was assigned to "more congenial tasks" as a clerk at regimental headquarters.[111]

Lieutenant Fussell spent most of February 1945 in the hospital recovering from pneumonia. He overcame the pneumonia, but overcoming his fear of future battles was another matter: "That month away from the line helped me survive for four weeks more but it broke the rhythm and, never badly scared before, when I returned to the line early in March I found for the first time that I was terrified, unwilling to take the chances that before had seemed rather sporting. My month of safety had renewed my interest in survival, and I was psychologically and morally ill prepared to lead my platoon in the great Seventh Army attack of March 15, 1945."[112]

## SELF-INFLICTED WOUNDS AND DESERTION

A soldier worn out from too much combat often sensed that he was nearing the end of his emotional rope, but his breakdown was ultimately a subconscious act. Some soldiers, however, made conscious decisions to escape the fighting. Typically they tried to shirk their combat duties, but some took more drastic measures, inflicting wounds upon themselves or fleeing from the battlefield.

The frequency of occurrence of self-inflicted wounds is impossible to determine. Soldiers who wounded themselves invariably claimed it was an accident or that they had been hit by enemy fire. Although the incidence of self-inflicted wounds may be difficult to ascertain, the rationale for them is clear enough. If a million-dollar wound provided an escape from combat without causing permanent injury, then why wait for the enemy to do it? Besides, who could count on the enemy's aim?

More soldiers contemplated a self-inflicted wound than actually attempted it. John Saddic, a marine in the Korean War, considered falling into a hole in such a way that he would "accidentally" break his hand but decided against it: "I'm not the slightest bit ashamed of thinking about it. Ask any guy who's been in combat. You're bound to think that way at one time or another. But in the long run, most guys don't do it. After all, you have to live with yourself."[113] Soldiers had such thoughts when they were demoralized and exhausted. Private Standifer, sick and miserable on a bitterly cold day in Germany in 1945, had almost reached his breaking point: "I've got to get out of here. . . . To hell with courage. I've got to leave this God-forsaken place. If I don't get sick enough to leave by the time of the next attack, I'm going to find a way to get wounded."[114] Before he did anything drastic, he was evacuated with pneumonia and frostbite.

Some soldiers did resort to self-inflicted wounds, however, despite the shame associated with it, not to mention possible disciplinary action if the medics or a witness turned them in. A self-inflicted wound was a court-martial offense. In Private Carl Andrew Brannen's company in World War I, a marine replacement lying just behind him shot off his own trigger finger. Yet only the most distraught soldiers so blatantly inflicted wounds on themselves. Most shot themselves while "cleaning" their weapon.[115] Klaus H. Huebner was sometimes asked to rule on supposedly accidental shootings. It was not easy to do so: "A self-inflicted wound always poses somewhat of a problem. Is it intentional or accidental? Carbine wounds through the web of toes, through the heel, and through hands do occur now and them. I hate to accuse a man of shooting himself in order to be evacuated. I suppose most are accidental, although I can never be too sure."[116]

Even more difficult to judge were cases of self-inflicted illnesses. Some GIs in the Pacific in World War II deliberately avoided taking their antimalaria medicine, hoping to catch a case of malaria serious enough to get them evacuated.[117] Soldiers fighting in wet, cold climates exposed their extremities in order to come down with immersion foot or frostbite. Private Atwell saw several cases of self-inflicted frostbite come through his battalion aid station. The men talked among themselves about it: "They envied those who had been wounded and sent home, and in an uncritical way they talked of men deliberately freezing their feet, leaving them outside the covers at night or even holding them in a helmet filled with ice and snow."[118]

With the advent of rotation in the Korean and Vietnam Wars, soldiers were less likely to consider wounding themselves, just as they were less likely to wish for a million-dollar wound. Self-inflicted wounds did occur, however, and the pattern was similar to that of the world wars. Like the replacement marine in Brannen's company who shot off his trigger finger, some Korean and Vietnam War soldiers inflicted a wound on themselves early on. Like men who broke down early or committed suicide, these soldiers could not face what lay ahead. Private Floyd Atkins tells of a new lieutenant who arrived in his outfit in Korea: "He spent one day with us on the line. Then he took his .45 automatic and shot himself in the foot. I think he did it on purpose. That first day he said he wouldn't be in Korea long."[119]

At the other extreme were men like Standifer, who contemplated or inflicted a wound on themselves only after they were physically and emotionally worn out. After nine months in Vietnam, corpsman Douglas Anderson "couldn't take it anymore. I told this friend of mine . . . that I was going to throw a grenade around the corner of this hootch and stick my leg out. I wanted to go home, I wasn't going to do this anymore."[120] His friend talked him out of it, and shortly thereafter Anderson was transferred to duty at a hospital.

Rather than shooting themselves, some soldiers elected to desert. Studies of deserters from combat are scarce, but two that exist for the Italian campaign in

World War II indicate that soldiers deserted for the same reason that they broke down or inflicted a wound upon themselves—they were overcome by fear.[121] According to one of the studies, "three out of four subjects frankly stated that fear of combat was the cause of their AWOL." The deserter thus "consciously elects to avoid combat as a result of chronic anticipatory anxiety deriving from accumulated battle experiences."[122] These deserters had often endured several months of combat, some had been hospitalized for wounds, many were physically worn out, and some exhibited the excessive anxiety and group adjustment problems common to soldiers who broke down early on. They were so stressed out by the time they elected to desert that even the probability of apprehension did not deter them. Ties to the group no longer sufficed to hold them. In some cases they felt little connection to the group because their original comrades were gone.[123]

## GROUP NORMS AND THE FAILURE TO COPE

As with self-inflicted wounds, more soldiers contemplated desertion than actually did so. Loyalty to the group and concerns over personal reputation kept most men from deserting. Richard Newman thought about "bugging out," as desertion from combat was called during the Korean War, but he never seriously considered doing it: "You did not want to let your buddies down. How could you face them if you bugged out? Oh, there were plenty of times when I wondered what the hell I was doing there, but I never considered taking off."[124] Given the primary group's disdain for malingerers, the logical conclusion is that it would consider a deserter or a soldier who inflicts a wound on himself the lowest of the low, according to S. Kirson Weinberg: "The unit increases the individual's endurance and courage by challenging him to uphold his self-esteem. When a group realizes that a member is looking for an 'out' and is about to depart, the attitudes of the others may be expressed as follows: 'The yellow so-and-so is going. He's a quitter, leaving us to take it—get hurt and maybe killed.'"[125]

Weinberg, who was describing a typical group of World War II soldiers, is generally correct in his assessment, but the reality was not so simple, as Weinberg himself noted by adding this qualifier: "These attitudes vary with the conditions under which the soldier departs."[126] Specifically, if a soldier had endured at least some combat and had pulled his own weight before deserting or wounding himself, then his comrades tended to excuse his actions. During World War II, Arnold M. Rose found that veteran soldiers "do not condemn the typical AWOL from combat; rather they tend to sympathize with him. . . . One reason why non–AWOL's sympathize with most AWOL's is that they know about the strains of combat and they realize that some men 'can't take it' as well as others."[127] This attitude is apparent in the memoirs. Marine Private Richard Suarez noticed that during the gruelling retreat from the Chosin Reservoir during the

Korean War, "not everyone was John Wayne. . . . Our battalion had three self-inflicted wounds. . . . A lot of [the men] were at the limit of what they could take. I saw one officer sitting by the side of the road crying. I guess he just cracked under the strain. Everybody has a breaking point, and everybody's breaking point is different."[128]

Sergeant Glenn Hubenette, wounded and evacuated to a Mobile Army Surgical Hospital during the Korean War, heard a surgeon berate a young GI who had shot himself in the foot. The doctor "told the kid if he had his way, he'd let him bleed to death, and that the guy didn't belong in the same army with men who'd been legitimately wounded." Hubenette, however, was inclined to give the GI the benefit of the doubt: "Who knew what the kid had gone through before he shot his foot? When the GI and I were alone in the hallway, I told him, 'Take it easy, kid.'"[129]

During World War II, Private Atwell pondered the varying attitudes of his comrades toward self-inflicted wounds. He noted that an unpopular sergeant who had wounded himself in the unit's first battle was condemned but that a man who deliberately induced frostbite after enduring weeks of combat was forgiven: "No one . . . criticized Nugent for deliberately freezing his feet, yet from what I heard, feeling was mounting steadily against Sergeant Weems for taking a similar way out of combat. Wherein did the difference lie? In the fact that Jack Nugent . . . was likable and popular and Sergeant Weems was not? Or was it that Sergeant Weems had shot himself through the foot on the first day of combat, whereas Jack Nugent had gone through attack after attack, patrol after patrol, and had come at last to feel, as most of them felt, that his chances for survival were fast running out?"[130]

As in the case of Sergeant Weems, soldiers did not condone desertion or self-wounding by a man who had not first made a reasonable effort to cope and to do his share. Frank Chadwick knew a sergeant on Guadalcanal who was ostracized for deliberately allowing his jungle rot to fester: "He wouldn't take care of it because he wanted to get the hell out of there. And he did. But before he left everyone understood what he was doing, and they blackballed him. No one had anything to do with him."[131]

To further complicate matters, the attitudes of the soldiers passing judgment on deserters or men who wounded themselves shifted over time. Men not yet deeply immersed in the environment of war were less tolerant because they did not yet appreciate the possibility that they, too, might reach a point where they could not take it anymore. Lieutenant Louis Brockway and his fellow doughboys, yet to experience combat, were appalled to hear veteran British troops talking about million-dollar wounds: "How naive we all were at this point. I remember hearing those Tommies talking about how nice it would be to get a little 'blighty' so they could get the hell out of there. We all felt this was awful; how were they going to win the war that way? What we didn't think about was how long the British had been bleeding. It didn't take us very long to understand their feeling."[132]

Shortly after Boesch took over his platoon in World War II, his platoon sergeant deserted from combat. Boesch was furious, not only because the sergeant deserted but also because the company commander declined to court-martial the man, who had been through a "tough time" before Boesch's arrival. The commander elected instead to reduce the sergeant's rank and transfer him. With more combat experience, however, Boesch's anger changed to ambiguity: "Perhaps if I had been more experienced at the time, I might have insisted on court martial. Then again, after all I saw later, would I have been more mellowed perhaps, more understanding?"[133]

The group's attitude toward deserters and self-inflicted wounds thus varied from condemnation to sympathy, depending on how much combat the group itself had seen and its perception of how long and hard a compatriot had tried to cope before seeking an out. The reaction to psychological breakdowns was similar. The Research Branch discovered during World War II that the group did not blame men for "being afraid or for being emotionally upset by the threat of danger, but they were expected to try to put up a struggle to carry on despite their fear." A soldier could be "visibly shaken," even "trembling violently," but he "was not regarded as a coward unless he made no apparent effort to stick out his job."[134] Lieutenants Leinbaugh and Campbell differentiated between a combat-fatigue case who had tried to stick it out and one who had not: "One of the men who went to the exhaustion center was a first-rate NCO who'd tried his damnedest, but couldn't stay up [on the front line]; he'd be back to try again. Another who went back for a rest wasn't held in such high esteem. The difference between the two was a matter of will: One wanted to be with the company, and the other didn't."[135]

Soldiers who broke down early in combat, or even before reaching the battlefield, were thus often denigrated for cowardly behavior. A sergeant in Howard Matthias's marine company in Korea broke down on his first night patrol. He was transferred to a different platoon within the company and again failed to perform. No one sympathized with his plight: "His fellow NCO's criticized him and none of the enlisted men would have anything to do with him."[136] The man was soon transferred out of the company.

On the other hand, soldiers who had obviously tried their best before breaking down were usually viewed with sympathy by their fellow combatants. Dan Levin's first dispatch about the fighting on Iwo Jima concerned a marine who broke down and had to be carried off. This man had endured three previous island campaigns. Levin quoted one of the marine's buddies, who said that his broken comrade was "a good man": "How much can one man take? Too much is too much."[137]

Even men who broke down relatively early in their combat careers might be accorded a measure of sympathy if the group believed they had good reason to crack up. Two men in Private Blunt's squad in World War II broke down after only five days of combat. Their best friend had been killed in the unit's first fight, and they were "unable to cope with their loss. When both eventually became too terrified to venture out onto the street, some of us brought them their meals. Whenever a shell exploded in the city, they cowered in a corner trembling." The two men were transferred to a rear-area job, but Blunt did not resent it: "Battle fatigue hit men of all ages and in many different ways. No one ridiculed them. We all knew it could happen to anyone at any time, and we realized that understanding was called for."[138] The primary group thus accepted or condemned psychological breakdown, desertion, and self-inflicted wounds based on individual circumstances and the mind-set of the group at the time.

Thus far combat has been portrayed as unremitting physical and emotional travail, with death, injury, or psychological breakdown the inevitable consequence. How then could so many Americans set out, more or less willingly, to fight four major wars in fifty years? Certainly each new generation's ignorance of the nature of war explains much, but another factor was also at work—one not often candidly discussed. Some aspects of combat and army life were stimulating, even enjoyable, or at least were nostalgically viewed as such. Furthermore, some men did more than endure war. They were good at it and even thrived on it.

# 7

# The Joys of War

Near the end of *Men Against Fire,* Samuel L. A. Marshall's famous study of the American combat soldier in World War II, he issued a caveat: "Yet if all I have said thus far conveys an idea that all soldiers should be trained to believe that combat is a life of incessant strain and hardship, it is an impression which requires full correction."[1] Although fear, carnage, and deprivation were integral to the malevolent environment of war, soldiers' memoirs verify that there was indeed more to life in the combat zone than incessant strain and hardship. Soldiers discovered that war had redeeming qualities and appeals. They cherished the camaraderie, enjoyed seeing new sights, were awed by the spectacle of war, took pride in their martial accomplishments, and even admitted to a sense of exhilaration while plying their deadly trade.[2] Furthermore, a significant minority proved to be especially avid warriors who excelled at and even thrived on the business of fighting a war.

## THE JOYS OF WAR AND THE AVERAGE SOLDIER

The typical American soldier was not an avid warrior. He did not like the army, certainly did not like fighting a war, and yearned for the day when he would again be a civilian. Yet often to his surprise, he found that the experience of soldiering was not universally negative. He might fondly remember, for example, comrades who saved his life, shared meager possessions, raised spirits, or lent a sympathetic ear. "The enduring emotion of war, when everything else has faded, is comradeship," says the Vietnam veteran William Broyles Jr.[3] It certainly was for Chaplain Francis P. Duffy: "The sense of congenial companionship more than makes up for the hardships incidental to a campaign. What I am going to miss most is the friendships I have formed."[4]

For Private Eugene B. Sledge, as for many veterans, comradeship was the one saving grace of an otherwise nasty experience: "War is brutish, inglorious, and a terrible waste. Combat leaves an indelible mark on those who are forced to endure it. The only redeeming factors were my comrades' incredible bravery and their devotion to each other."[5] Given an often brutal, seemingly senseless, and ultimately unsuccessful war in Vietnam, grunts were even more likely than their predecessors to claim, as Lieutenant Philip Caputo did, that "devotion, simple and selfless, the sentiment of belonging to each other, was the one decent thing we found in a conflict otherwise notable for its monstrosities."[6]

Shared danger was one of the reasons why the camaraderie was so intense. Danger could also generate excitement, as it did for the World War II scout Leon C. Standifer: "Combat is a many-faceted experience. The excitement comes from facing fear, looking it directly in the face, and surviving."[7] Conversely, Lieutenant Paul Boesch found the fighting in the Huertgen Forest to be anything but exciting. He was cold, wet, miserable, and lived with the constant fear of land mines and artillery fire. All that changed abruptly, however, when he led his infantry company through the town of Huertgen, driving the German defenders before him: "It was a wild, terrible, awe-inspiring thing, this sweep through Huertgen. Never in my wildest imagination had I conceived that battle could be so incredibly impressive—awful, horrible, deadly, yet somehow thrilling, exhilarating."[8]

Soldiers might dread the prospect of combat or be reduced to a shaky bundle of nerves afterward, but during the actual fight they were often too busy, and the adrenalin was flowing too freely, to be scared. Captain Charles M. Bussey, after describing a vicious nighttime fight between his engineers and attacking North Korean soldiers, admitted to being thrilled by such deadly melees: "Although I participated in ground combat because duty demanded it, I actually enjoyed the heightened thrills, the gross apprehension of uncertainty, and the adrenalin-induced drunkenness that mortal combat produced."[9]

James Martin Davis, a Vietnam War grunt, also found combat exciting: "Like it or not, combat is the most intense moment in a man's life. It is hard to explain, but once in a fire fight, our fears are usually erased by the actions of that instant and, for a short period of time, our entire bodies become alive."[10] Dominick Yezzo experienced the same sensation when the jeep he was driving was ambushed and he had to spring for cover, returning fire with his M-16 rifle: "I felt my heart racing and I could hardly get my breath. It's funny but the whole thing was so exciting; it made me feel so terribly alive and vibrant. I was aware of my young strength and body, my whole being. I can never explain the sensations of war, they are strange, numerous, and various."[11]

For some men, combat would be the most exciting, even defining, event of their lives. Nothing in their peacetime experience would equal its intensity, as Samuel Hynes explains: "War expands and extends what is possible in life for an ordinary man, that for once he need not be simply a man mending shoes . . . or an insurance salesman. War offers experiences that men value and remember: shoes and insurance don't do that."[12]

Even before the fighting had ended in 1945, Captain Richard M. Hardison intuitively sensed that he was winding up the greatest experience of his life: "I knew my life would never be the same again. I was sad in a way. Without quite being able to put it into words, I sensed that future relationships and experiences could never equal in intensity what I had seen and experienced these past few months."[13]

War could not only be exciting at times, but it also provided, as Broyles explains, "an escape from the everyday into a special world where the bonds that hold us to our duties in daily life—the bonds of family, community, work—disappear. In war, all bets are off. It's the frontier beyond the last settlement, it's Las Vegas."[14] The soldiers' wartime behavior was considerably more lax than what was considered acceptable in polite society, and some men reveled in it. The eat, drink and be merry philosophy not only helped the soldier forget about the horrors of past and future combat, but it was also fun. Lieutenant John L. Munschauer and his men, ostensibly mopping up Japanese snipers in the Philippine capital of Manila in World War II, were pleased to find that despite the destruction, the local gin joints were open for business. They enjoyed themselves in one of these "sleazy places" and were soon embroiled in a fight with the Army Air Corps: "It was wonderful, just like a fight scene in a Wild West saloon." As Munschauer added, "There were fun times in the army, and this was one of them."[15] Those times—the hell-raising, partying, and midnight requisitioning—are relived with obvious relish in veterans' memoirs.

War's spectacles are almost as common a recollection as the hell-raising. Much like spectators fascinated by fireworks displays, parades, and sports spectaculars, awestruck soldiers watched aerial dogfights, offshore naval engagements, massive artillery preparations, and the life-and-death drama of distant battles. Jesse Glenn Gray refers to this phenomenon as "the lust of the eye": "While it is undeniable that the disorder and distortion and the violation of nature that conflict brings are ugly beyond compare, there are also color and movement, variety, panoramic sweep, and sometimes even momentary proportion and harmony. If we think of beauty and ugliness without the usual moral overtones, there is often a weird but genuine beauty in the sight of massed men and weapons in combat."[16] As the World War I marine Elton E. Mackin put it, "When watching and not under direct fire, a fellow is inclined to inch upward for a better view of things. It is always a show, no matter how terrifying."[17]

As Mackin implies, soldiers even took calculated risks to get a better seat at the big show. Howard V. O'Brien describes how doughboys new to the war would go outside to watch the German air raids on Paris, but the French civilians, veterans of such raids, "shrug shoulders, mention 'imbeciles' and skip for cellar."[18] The doughboys in Captain Arthur Little's battalion perched themselves on the parapet of their trench to watch the fighting going on across the river from their position—that is, until they attracted enemy artillery fire.[19]

Lieutenant Howard Matthias was similarly intrigued by the sights of combat during the Korean War, as long as he was not the target: "A firefight or exchange of artillery can be an amazing spectacle. At night it can become dazzling. A bombardment of an opposing ridge line was often beautiful. . . . When it was landing on us, that was another story."[20]

James Jones, watching his first air raid in World War II "as if watching a football game," wondered how he could be so detached: "It seemed strange and curiously callous, then, to be watching and cheering this game in which men were dying." After experiencing combat in the jungles of Guadalcanal, however, he stopped worrying about callousness and just enjoyed the show, in this case one of the naval battles not far offshore: "We would sit in our bivouac on the hills above Henderson Field and watch the pyrotechnic display of a naval night battle off Savo Island with . . . insouciance, and not feel callous at all. They took their chances and we took our chances."[21]

The sheer magnitude of war could leave men feeling insignificant and expendable, but it also provided some powerful imagery. Ernie Pyle was awed by the sight of the massive invasion convoy he was part of in World War II: "Hour after hour I stood at the rail looking out over that armada of marching ships—they did really seem to march across the ocean—and an almost choking sense of its beauty and power enveloped me."[22] In Vietnam, Lieutenant Frederick Downs found that "the ballet of helicopters over an LZ is beautiful."[23] Or, as Michael Herr put it while watching the sleek little observation helicopters going about their lethal business of flushing out the enemy, "you had to stop once in a while and admire the machinery."[24]

The modern war machine provided awesome spectacles, but even the relatively mundane sights of the countryside could prove pleasant and memorable. Most soldiers were young and had never been far from home; seeing new countries and cultures was a novel experience. Doughboys, for example, were fascinated by the antiquities of France. Father Duffy noticed the men's curiosity over a Roman amphitheater near their bivouac site: "I shan't say the men are not interested in these antiquities. They are an intelligent lot, and unsated by sight-seeing, and they give more attention to what they see than most tourists."[25] Indeed, doughboy tourism was encouraged, with the YMCA providing the tour guides, as a preferred alternative to the eat, drink, and be merry activities that the soldiers might otherwise pursue if left to their own devices.[26] For Robert Rasmus, a young World War II GI, the new sights, at home and abroad, were intriguing: "I'd never been outside the states of Wisconsin, Indiana, and Michigan. So when I woke up the first morning on the troop train in Fulton, Kentucky, I thought I was in Timbuktu. Of course, I was absolutely bowled over by Europe, the castles, the cathedrals, the Alps. It was wonderment. I was preoccupied with staying alive and doing my job, but it seemed, out of the corner of my eye, I was constantly fascinated with the beauty of the German forests and medieval bell towers. At nineteen, you're seeing life with fresh eyes."[27]

Even by the time of the Vietnam War, many young soldiers, especially those from modest backgrounds, had never ventured far from their hometowns or neighborhoods. For them, the recruiting poster's call to "join the Army and see the world" held a certain attraction. Private David Parks, heading west by train from Kansas with the First Infantry Division, en route to Vietnam, noticed that his companion was fascinated by the trip: "My train buddy is a guy named Tubbs, and he is really enjoying the ride. I don't think he has ever been on a train before. He looks out of the window and smiles at 'most everything he sees."[28]

Once in the war zone, there was little time for sightseeing. The soldier had more pressing priorities, notably staying alive. He was there to do more than just survive, however. The citizen-soldier may have had little taste for army life, but he realized that he was now a combat soldier trained to kill the enemy and seize his territory. One of the most elemental joys of soldiering, therefore, was pride in self and unit over victory in battle. "The G.I.," observed Lee Kennett, "could sometimes see himself as a warrior and like what he saw. . . . There were times when the unheroic and unenthusiastic soldier saw himself in quite a different light; it could happen on maneuvers, for example, when a gun crew was working furiously during firing exercises, and the realization spread among them that they were really good—it made them all proud and they worked all the harder."[29]

Even the Vietnam veterans in Robert Jay Lifton's rap group, most of whom were having difficulty reconciling their war experiences and America's involvement in Vietnam, nevertheless retained a measure of pride in their martial accomplishments, a feeling that Lifton refers to as "the John Wayne thing":

> We have seen the John Wayne thing to be many things . . . its combat version, as far as the men in the rap group were concerned, meant military pride, lust for battle, fearless exposure to danger, and prowess in killing. I was impressed by the extent to which the men had been initially involved in this constellation, and by the persistence of elements of it even in the face of the chaos and absurdity of the Vietnam environment. For the John Wayne thing is related to honor; and it would seem that men at war hunger for honor no less than they do for an enemy—that indeed the two feed the same hunger.[30]

Honor comes with success in battle, and soldiers relate instances of that success with satisfaction and pride, as did Leo Cuthbertson, advancing during the successful Soissons counteroffensive: "As we walked along the roads yesterday we could look on either side and see dead Huns—boys who had died with their boots on in the defense of their country. Strange as it may seem, my heart is hardened to a point where such a sight, while pitiful, is a pleasure. For surely that is one way of defeating our enemy—put him in his grave."[31]

Soldiers like Cuthbertson did not enjoy killing per se, but a slain enemy was tangible proof of victory. James Jones witnessed the same process at work in the

World War II GI: "He had his professionalism, first of all. The craft he had mastered from a raw apprentice and had come to love. That could give him pleasure now. The doing of a job—from its projection and inception on through to its completion—even if it meant shooting and killing a lot of other people who perhaps felt about the whole thing the same as he."[32]

The job did not necessarily even have to involve killing. As a combat engineer, Sergeant Henry Giles and his battalion built the first military bridge across the Rhine River at Remagen in World War II. Some of his comrades died or were wounded doing it, but when the sign went up declaring it the longest tactical bridge yet built, compliments of the 291st Engineer Battalion, Giles declared, "Our tails are high! *The 291st built the first bridge across the Rhine.* By george, we have a right to feel good. Our morale is high."[33]

During the Vietnam War, the lack of meaningful geographical objectives and the futile goal of pursuing the body count deprived the grunt of a sense of progress toward victory. In the realm of tactical operations, however, success still provided the same feelings of satisfaction, even elation, that it did for soldiers in earlier wars. After being ambushed, Lieutenant Caputo and his platoon recovered quickly, maneuvered skillfully, and defeated the enemy. When the fight was over, Caputo admitted to a "thrill" the likes of which "he had never experienced . . . before. . . . When the line [of marines] wheeled and charged across the clearing, the enemy bullets whining past them, wheeled and charged almost with drill-field precision, an ache as profound as the ache of orgasm passed through me."[34]

Some soldiers confessed to experiencing more than mere pride in their soldierly skills or excitement in the midst of a firefight. They discovered that they took a certain pleasure in their deadly work—what Jesse Glenn Gray calls the "delight in destruction." Gray found this delight "sinister" and disturbing but one that could not be explained away.[35] Christian G. Appy, in his study of Vietnam War soldiers, concluded that a similar phenomenon was at work, which he calls the "hedonism of destruction." He agrees with Gray that this sinister hedonism cannot be ignored: "There is a tendency to portray soldiers as reluctant and regretful killers, as men who kill only on behalf of noble ideals or merely to survive or because they were ordered to do so or because they are driven to it by the most extreme physical and psychological pressures. The more troubling and complicated reality, however, is that war can engender not only the capacity to kill but the desire to kill."[36]

It is impossible to generalize about the extent to which soldiers actually did delight in killing. In many cases they did in fact kill without enthusiasm, accepting it as a distasteful, if necessary, part of their job, and they considered those in their ranks who enjoyed it as not entirely normal. A GI in Captain Charles R. Cawthon's battalion in World War II, while manning a forward outpost with other soldiers, shot several retreating Germans "very much as in a shooting gallery. . . . The rifleman who had done the shooting had a wolfish grin; the rest looked on without speaking. There were few avid killers in our ranks."[37]

Yet Gray and Appy are also correct. Too many soldiers took delight in destruction to write off the phenomenon as an aberration. Some soldiers enjoyed the sense of power that a weapon gave them.[38] The World War II GI Joe Hanley loved his Browning Automatic Rifle: "I never had hand-to-hand combat with any of the enemy, but I know I was responsible for many deaths. It's so easy when you're swinging a BAR, a Browning automatic, firing away. It's a machine gun. I liked the weapon and every time I got the opportunity, I used it."[39]

If a Browning Automatic Rifle provided a sense of power, then perhaps bigger guns were even better. During the 1968 Tet Offensive in Vietnam, Sergeant Ralph Zumbro and his tank company were defending Pleiku Air Base. Several air force men volunteered to fill out shortages in the tank crews. After beating off a battalion-sized Viet Cong attack with tank-mounted machine guns and canister rounds fired from the tank cannons, one awestruck airman quipped, "You know, you can really express yourself with one of these things."[40]

A few soldiers candidly admit that they enjoyed the power trip they were on. One of Mark Baker's interviewees, a door gunner on a helicopter in Vietnam, recalled an especially bloody engagement: "Blood lust. I can't think of a better way to describe it. Caught up in the moment. I remember thinking this insane thought, that I'm God and retribution is here. . . . It was a slaughter. . . . I was doing it enthusiastically."[41]

Some soldiers thus drew a measure of satisfaction, even exhilaration, from plying their deadly trade. Relatively more soldiers, if not delighted by destruction, took pride in their military prowess, were sometimes caught up in the adrenalin rush of a firefight, cherished the bonds of comradeship, enjoyed seeing the world, or were fascinated by war's panoramic displays. In sum, they discovered that war was not all hell; consequently, veterans are often ambiguous when assessing their combat experiences.[42] Some, like Lieutenant Caputo, frankly admit that war both repelled and attracted them: "I could not deny the grip the war had on me, nor the fact that it had been an experience as fascinating as it was repulsive, as exhilarating as it was sad, as tender as it was cruel. . . . Anyone who fought in Vietnam, if he is honest about himself, will have to admit he enjoyed the compelling attractiveness of combat. It was a peculiar enjoyment because it was mixed with a commensurate pain."[43]

Lieutenant James Brady, in the midst of the Korean War, came to a similar conclusion. He was simultaneously exhilarated and terrorized by combat, even if he could not understand exactly why: "I knew too much now to be frightened by everything and too much ever to turn smug. Yet combat was still a great mystery, mingled fear and exhaustion, a sense of accomplishment offset by neurotic guilt, sheer joy at coming through a firefight, and nauseating terror. Wanting to flee the battle, you were drawn to its furious center. No one who had not fought could possibly imagine the contradictions or the nuances."[44]

Veterans typically denounced combat's horrors and hardships, yet they could not deny that their wartime experience had somehow been exciting, adventuresome, a source of pride, or an emotional high point. These mixed emotions generated contradictory statements such as Richard M. Prendergast's: "Looking back on the war, in spite of the really bad times, it was certainly the most exciting experience of my life. . . . As I see it, at that young age, we hit the climax. Everything after that is anticlimactic."[45]

Will Judy was even more ambiguous: "The twenty-two months in the army has taught many things to me. My experiences I would not trade for any ten years of my life. I have learned to like and to hate the army."[46] Robert G. Thobaben was equally contradictory: "I wouldn't want to do it again. I wouldn't give up the experience for anything."[47] And Lieutenant Matthias, speaking in the third person, had few positive memories of his experience as a marine in the Korean War, but he was typically proud of his service: "He hated war and swore that no son of his would fight like he had fought or endure the conditions that he had endured. He was proud of his accomplishments but would never want to prove himself under combat conditions again."[48]

## "SOLDIER-ADVENTURERS"

Most soldiers, even those proud of their skills and accomplishments, were at best only "moderately capable," writes Gray. "Few men ever reach superlatives in the realm of destruction; most of us remain, as in the domain of creation, moderately capable." He adds, however, that a certain type of warrior, the "soldier-adventurer," excelled at combat. The soldier-adventurer was not without fear, but he nevertheless loved the game of war: "Without wishing it, his nature is too intoxicated by war's promise of intense, forbidden experience."[49]

Other observers of soldier behavior have similarly identified a type of soldier uncommonly adept at fighting in war. Thomas C. Leonard calls them "connoisseurs of violence," and Christian G. Appy discusses "aesthetes of war" who are "connoisseurs of its skills, sensations, and spectacles."[50] Gwynne Dyer asserts that "There is such a thing as a 'natural soldier': the kind of man who derives his greatest satisfaction from male companionship, from excitement, and from the conquering of physical and psychological obstacles. He doesn't necessarily want to kill people as such, but he will have no objections if it occurs within a moral framework that gives him a justification—like war—and if it is the price of gaining admission to the kind of environment he craves."[51]

The soldiers themselves distinguished between the typical, scared GI just trying to get by and the exceptional soldier who excelled at war. Most soldiers, like Fred Olson, a GI in Lieutenants Harold P. Leinbaugh's and John D. Campbell's Company K in Europe in World War II, considered themselves and most of their companions to be average GIs just trying to do their duty: "None of us were heroes. We were just there and trying to do the best we knew how under the circumstances. Maybe some days not doing a very good job of it. But as miserable an existence as it was, I felt very strong about it—goddamnit, do the best I could."[52]

James Jones, another self-avowed average GI, put it more bluntly: "I went where I was told to go, and did what I was told to do, but no more. I was scared shitless just about all of the time."[53] Corporal Fife, a GI in *The Thin Red Line,* was undoubtedly modeled after the author if only because Fife was also "scared shitless" most of the time. He was comforted by the fact that most of his comrades were also scared, but he was also envious of the men who acted coolly and efficiently when under fire: "Fife realized that by far the great majority of the company were reacting like himself. But there were still those others who, for one reason or another of their own, got up and walked about and offered to do things without being told first. Fife knew it, because he had seen them—otherwise he wouldn't have believed it. His reaction to these was one of intense, awed hero worship composed of about two-thirds grinding hate, and shame. But when he tried to force *his* body to stand up and walk around, he simply could not make it do it."[54]

Many soldiers mention, often with a mix of awe and envy, that their outfits contained such exceptional soldiers. Fife reckoned that there were four of these men in his infantry company.[55] Lieutenant Uzal Ent believed they constituted only a small minority: "Some people are exhilarated by combat. They love it. They seem to thrive on it. I knew people like that. Most people, though, ninety-nine percent of them, are scared to death. Including myself."[56] However many soldier-adventurers there were, Captain Cawthon writes that they had an impact on the battlefield far beyond their numbers: "That war turns upon a man, and not upon men, is hardly an original observation, but it is generally applied to the head of state, or the commander at the stratospheric level. I found it equally applicable at the platoon and company level. There was no successful action of the 2nd Battalion that was not made possible by one or two souls who burned for the moment at a white-hot flame."[57]

What motivated the soldier-adventurer to perform so bravely and effectively in battle? Why was he thrilled by war instead of being simply "scared shitless"? Even the seasoned war correspondent Ernie Pyle would not hazard an opinion: "I don't know what it is that impels some men, either in peace or in wartime, to extend themselves beyond all expectation, or what holds other men back to do just as little as possible. In any group of soldiers you'll find both kinds."[58] One seemingly plausible explanation was that these soldier-adventurers were crazy. Who but a psychopath would act that way? Some soldiers with hidden psychotic tendencies did make it to the battlefield, where the stresses of combat caused those traits to emerge. The psychiatric-casualty statistics show a small but fairly constant number of soldiers hospitalized for various psychoses, as opposed to battle fatigue.[59]

Yet the psychopathic soldier acted differently from the soldier-adventurer. He was fearless; the soldier-adventurer was merely adept at overcoming his fears. The psychopath enjoyed killing, but the soldier-adventurer, though a capable killer, did not. Fearlessness and blood lust were useful traits in combat, however; hence, the psychiatrists Roy R. Grinker and John P. Spiegel discovered that the psychotic soldier could perform effectively, at least for a while: "Schizoid individuals . . . frequently perform feats of valor and heroism on the battlefield. Because they are able to express hostility for a time without fear or anxiety, they are able to carry on for a long period, apparently unaware of the danger."[60]

Nevertheless, the psychotic soldier's paranoia and extreme hostility eventually led to his demise. He became totally self-absorbed, and as Grinker and Spiegel observe, he "begins to view his comrades with suspicion" and often became "convinced that certain of the officers or men are in league with the enemy." Furthermore, psychotics "prove somewhat troublesome to their leaders because of their bad judgment, their intolerance of long periods of waiting without action, and their unwillingness to retreat."[61] In sum, the psychopath became a liability. For the soldiers, a psychotic in their midst was like harboring a John-Wayne type on the verge of losing control. James Jones knew only two totally fearless men during World War II, "but they were both crazy, almost certifiably so."[62] Stanley Goff describes a fellow soldier nicknamed "Hardcore," an efficient killer and pointman but also dangerous and scary: "They called him Hardcore. . . . He'd wipe out a rabbit. Just a real cold-blooded dude. Steely eyes, he could shoot a twig off a branch a hundred meters away; he could hit anything. He was our point man, a mean guy. . . . I didn't want to deal with him. With a guy like that, you'd have to go for broke. Nobody had an argument with him. . . . He was always friendly, but I could tell he was sort of 'crazy friendly.' You've seen guys like that. They're friendly but you know they'll just go for broke on you in a minute."[63]

If not a psychopath, then what was the soldier-adventurer? The army, aware that some unknown but significant percentage of soldiers somehow excelled at war, conducted a study of combat infantrymen during the Korean War to determine why some were "fighters" and others "nonfighters." The fighters had shown bravery, technical skill, and initiative on the battlefield. They had been selected for the study by their own peers and leaders, indicating that they were accepted, even admired, unlike the dangerous, loner psychopaths. The study determined that fighters were more intelligent, more masculine, more aggressive, more emotionally stable, more confident in their soldier skills, and in better health and physical condition than the average soldier.[64]

The study optimistically claimed that "the qualities of fighters are potentially measurable and [it] gives promise of the possibility of identifying fighters by appropriately developed tests." The researchers added an important caveat, however: some of these fighter qualities might well be "transient characteristics which accrue from Army experience, including combat itself" and thus not reflective of a soldier's precombat makeup.[65] As the World War II paratrooper Ross S. Carter put it, "It is hard to predict the fighting cock in the chick and the true soldier before he has been in battle. A man who is a man doesn't say so. A man who isn't often does."[66]

Sergeant Lee Childress made the same discovery. One of his men in Vietnam was nicknamed "Boo" because he was "scared shitless—made the plane rattle on the way over [to Vietnam], that kind of a dude." But Boo proved to be a "center-pillar sort of guy" in a firefight, and Childress learned a lesson about machismo: "You know, all the macho motherfuckers kind of bellied up, and I was one of those belly-ups, right? And the guys that seemed to be just the opposite were the ones in those situations that seemed to have the strength."[67]

Who would prove to be a soldier-adventurer could not be accurately predicted. Some men were abysmal peacetime soldiers but indomitable fighters. Lieutenant Ent recalls a soldier who, just before the outbreak of the Korean War, was being considered for discharge from the army as a disciplinary problem. But he proved to be an outstanding BAR man in a firefight. Ent decided that "you just can't tell ahead of time who's going to perform well in combat. Very often it's the guy who gives you the most trouble in peacetime."[68]

The Korean War study identified the characteristics of the soldier-adventurer, but determining what motivated him was not so easy. Even self-avowed soldier-adventurers, and these are relatively scarce, could not always fathom why they took to war so readily. Some realized that perhaps for the first time in their lives, they were good at something—fighting. Soldiering was a challenge requiring the mastery of numerous skills, at least it was for Broyles, a marine platoon leader in Vietnam: "War is a brutal, deadly game, but a game, the best there is. . . . Nothing I had ever studied was as complex or as creative as the small-unit tactics of Vietnam. No sport I had ever played brought me to such deep awareness of my physical and emotional limits."[69]

Like Broyles, Sergeant Fitzgerald, one of Lieutenant Brady's squad leaders during the Korean War, was enamored of the technical details and tactical challenges. For example, he threw himself into planning a deception intended to catch attacking Chinese by surprise: "Fitzgerald liked the whole thing; he was full of ideas on how we could profit if the gooks really did come up the hill, how close he wanted them to get, whether he would hit them first with grenades or automatic weapon fire. This was Fitz's kind of war, laying traps and killing people."[70]

Soldier-adventurers were known for their combat skills, and while they were not foolhardy, they often took on the difficult, dangerous jobs. Sergeant Van Horn, in Corporal Martin Russ's marine platoon in Korea, was admired for his night patrolling skills: "I was immediately impressed by Van Horn's stealth. . . . He has a reputation for this, and for being a good man to have around in a fire fight. He made no sound whatever as he moved. That takes talent."[71] In Lieutenant Lanning's platoon in Vietnam, a replacement named Private Morford, a professional dancer in civilian life, seemed an unlikely candidate for soldier-adventurer, but he proved to be an excellent point man: "Some were better than others at one job or the other, and men like Morford, who possessed a keen sense of direction, lightning-swift reactions, and a personal pride in his reputation, did the same duty much more often than others."[72]

Morford's concern for his reputation gets to the heart of the motivation issue. Soldier-adventurers were recognized and admired for their skill and bravery, and they liked it. Matthew Brennan volunteered to extend his tour of duty and also transferred to the air cavalry to serve in an aerorifle platoon. He "wanted to experience war, not just read about it in books and have other people tell me about it."[73] He discovered that he was good at his job, and when the extension on his tour of duty was up, he was reluctant to leave Vietnam and the army to return to "the obscurity of life in a small Indiana town," where "the people remembered me as a bookworm and an unpromising athlete."[74] As anticipated, Brennan was bored and unhappy with civilian life and was soon back in the army and with the aerorifles in Vietnam.

The soldier-adventurer thus stayed in the army, at least while there was a war on, because it was where he felt most comfortable, useful, and respected. Another type of soldier also stayed in the service, not because he liked combat but because he had "found a home in the Army." Many of these men came from less-than-ideal family and community backgrounds. They not only found "three hots and a cot" in the army but also friends who treated them as equals and a superior, perhaps a squad leader or platoon sergeant, who cared about their welfare and provided a measure of paternal support. These men may not have exhibited the skills of the soldier-adventurer, but they were eager to do their share and intensely loyal to the group.

Lieutenant James Hamilton Dill tells the poignant story of Private Robbins, a GI in the infantry company that he was serving with as artillery forward observer during the Korean War. The company commander called Robbins to his command post after receiving a letter from the soldier's father claiming that the boy was under the legal age for military service. To the surprise of Dill and the company commander, a tearful Robbins pleaded to stay, despite the miserable conditions he was living and fighting in, claiming he had joined the army to escape his drunken, poverty-stricken, abusive father: "I ain't the same as I was last year. I've done been somebody since I joined the army. If the army won't keep me, I ain't going back there lessen it's to kick Pa's head off. I've done shot gooks that was better than him. I'll find some place to hang out until they let me back in the army again. Sir, the army is my home now. It's the only home I ever had. I want to stay."[75] His platoon sergeant vouched for Robbins's good behavior and dedication to duty, and the company commander decided to let him stay.

Matthew Brennan provides the case of "Combat Bolton," a "small and sad-looking teenager" who proved to be an exceptional machine gunner who kept volunteering to extend his tour of duty in Vietnam. Bolton, after a childhood spent bouncing among foster homes, had found a real home in the First Cavalry Division: "I don't have a family, just foster homes growing up. The state pays some greedy bitch to feed you. Where else can I walk into a club where there's a Ninth Cav [cavalry] guy and have him always buy me a drink? These people here really care."[76]

The soldier-adventurer also found a home in the army, or more precisely, a profession that he was good at and one that accorded him respect and recognition. But as the term "soldier-adventurer" implies, not only was he good at his job, but he also found it exciting. Amazingly enough, as Samuel Hynes observes, some "war lovers" continued to view combat as an exhilarating personal contest, despite its brutal realities: "What is it, exactly, that war lovers love? Not the killing and the violence, I think, but the excitement, the drama, and the danger— life lived at a high level of intensity, like a complicated, fatal game (or a Wagnerian opera)."[77] Private Don Doll in *The Thin Red Line* discovers during his first Japanese bombing attack that he can control his fear and thus "convince everybody he had not been afraid." He performs bravely in combat, becoming a squad leader admired for his courage and leadership ability. He discovers, while in the midst of risking his life, that he is fascinated by the life-and-death sport of combat: "It was like facing God. Or gambling with Luck. It was taking a dare from the Universe. It excited him more than all the hunting, gambling and fucking he had ever done all rolled together."[78]

This fictional portrayal of a soldier-adventurer may seem excessive, but the type was real enough. Roscoe C. Blunt considered combat an arena for proving his personal prowess. He collected the paybooks (*Soldat Buchen*) from the bodies of the German soldiers he killed, sometimes risking his own life to retrieve them. He noted, almost in passing, that "it is apparently a strange quirk in some men's personality that prompts them to collect trophies when an adversary has been vanquished."[79] And besting adversaries in individual combat, like some gladiator of old, was what excited Blunt.

Sergeant Mario Lage, who earned a battlefield commission during World War II, was a self-confessed soldier-adventurer. He had fought on Guadalcanal, where he came down with a serious case of malaria and was evacuated to the United States. Despite recurring bouts with the disease, Lage managed to get assigned to Leinbaugh's and Campbell's Company K, becoming one of the few soldiers to fight in the Pacific and in Europe. He knew that his love for battle "was irrational, ridiculous, completely senseless, but he found himself looking forward to returning to combat." For Lage, as for Blunt and most other soldier-adventurers, combat was a test of soldierly prowess, an exciting game, and an irresistible challenge: "The excitement of war overshadowed everything else— it's the supreme sport. In a bullfight the poor bull doesn't have a chance. But combat is more even, more fair, because at least the other guy's got a shot at you. . . . Being in a roller coaster bothers me, but getting shot at doesn't. It was exhilarating. . . . You can go through a thousand lifetimes running the usual gamut of emotions and never have the opportunity to see something like that."[80]

Lieutenant Andrew Barr was another self-proclaimed soldier-adventurer. He went to Korea confident in his skills and looking for excitement: "I was plenty good, plenty sharp, I knew what it was about. My morale was high. I didn't mind at all going to Korea. It was an adventure." Barr "absolutely loved" being a forward observer: "I was out there all by myself, literally calling all the shots. There was a real sense of power involved, the power of life and death." His unit was decimated during the retreat into the Pusan Perimeter, and the survivors "were pretty demoralized . . . , but in all honesty I wasn't."[81] He earned a Silver Star for his gallantry during the retreat.

Soldier-adventurers were not the product of military training and indoctrination, which at best produced soldiers only "moderately capable" of destruction. Personal predilection rather than conditioned behavior was the key differentiator between the war lover and the average soldier, as perhaps best illustrated by the attitudes of certain war correspondents who, without any significant military training or experience, proved to be as enthralled with combat as any soldier-adventurer. Ernie Pyle cannot be accused of glorifying war, yet he admitted to a certain fascination with combat that undoubtedly kept correspondents like him close to the action: "I've written that war is not romantic when a person is in the midst of it. Nothing happened to change my feeling about that. But I will have to admit there was an exhilaration in it; an inner excitement that built up into a buoyant tenseness seldom achieved in peacetime."[82]

Like Pyle, Richard Tregaskis was always close to the fighting. He received a serious head wound in Italy, and Pyle was killed at the front in the Pacific. After being tied down covering the political news in Naples, the arrival of another correspondent freed Tregaskis to return to his first love—reporting the war from the front. "The lure of the front is like an opiate. After abstinence and the tedium of workaday life, its attraction becomes more and more insistent. Perhaps the hazards of battle, perhaps the danger itself, stir the imagination and give transcendent meaning to things ordinarily taken for granted. The basic drama of men locked in a death struggle, with the stakes their own lives, offers a violent contrast to the routine conflicts in Naples."[83]

The experiences of correspondent-adventurers parallel those of soldier-adventurers. Both were thrilled by the challenges and dangers of combat, and unlike the psychopathic soldier, they were not interested in killing for the sake of killing. Indeed, as noncombatants, correspondents were prohibited from taking up arms and rarely did so.[84] But what was the average soldier's reaction to killing? Attitudes varied by enemy and war, but more important, by individual. Generalizations about soldiers' attitudes toward the enemy must be made with the understanding that killing was ultimately a personal act, especially in ground combat.

# 8

# Closing with the Enemy

The soldier's mission, at its most primal, was to kill the enemy. The recruit was trained to use his weapons and told that destroying America's enemies was necessary and justified. He was then immersed in an environment in which his main source of stress came from someone in a different uniform who was trying to kill him first. Under those circumstances, as one Vietnam veteran observed, and contrary to what a few students of soldier behavior claim, most men do not hesitate to shoot back: "People say, well, I could never kill a man. That's bullshit. They can. Anybody can kill. It takes more to make one man kill than it does the next. The training helps a lot; it gets you there. But combat—you know, once they start shooting at you, if you don't shoot back you're a damned fool."[1]

Though willing and able to accomplish his deadly mission, each soldier reacted differently to killing. Some killed impassively, a few eagerly. Some soldiers were plagued by guilt, but most accepted killing as a distasteful part of the job and did not dwell on the matter. The degree to which a soldier hated and dehumanized his enemy affected how reluctantly, or willingly, he killed. The leaders and the primary group set limits on what was acceptable behavior in accomplishing this deadly mission. But sometimes soldiers went beyond the acceptable bounds, killing prisoners of war or unarmed civilians.

## PREPARING FOR THE KILL: SANCTIFICATION AND JUSTIFICATION

Preparing the soldier to carry out his mission began in earnest during initial training, when he was taught to use the basic tools of his trade, such as the rifle, bayonet, and grenade. Perhaps equally important, the trainee learned that killing America's enemies was not only legally sanctioned but also his duty.[2] For most soldiers, this license to kill did not automatically instill willingness; soldiers also wanted to believe that the enemy deserved to die. The reasons why the enemy had to be fought and defeated varied by foe and by war, but some themes were remarkably constant—what philosopher Sam Keen calls "archetypes of the enemy": "Wars come and go, but—strangely, amid changing circumstances—the hostile imagination has a certain standard repertoire of images it uses to dehumanize the enemy."[3] America thus viewed its enemies as godless, evil, barbaric, greedy for conquest, even bestial.[4]

The effect of this imagery, as Keen notes, was to dehumanize the enemy, and since the ideal human was an American, the ideological, racial, and cultural differences, real or exaggerated, between America and its enemies made them easier to dehumanize.[5] Much of this process occurred as part of an overall propaganda effort, especially during the world wars. Before and after donning their uniforms, men were repeatedly exposed to inflammatory comments in the media, in sermons, and in the speeches of opinion leaders about America's actual or potential enemies. Anti-German propaganda was common in the years before America's entry into World War I, and its impact was evident, writes Mark Meigs, in the doughboys' speech and letters: "Soldiers themselves adopted the language of propaganda, often calling the German enemy 'Huns,' or sometimes, in reference to the often recounted stories of atrocities committed by Germans, 'baby killers.'"[6] Will Judy was aware of this propagandizing and deemed it essential if distasteful: "The leaders must preach patriotism to warm us to war, then must begin to grind hate out of the mills of publicity. . . . Patriotism is a beautiful thing and worthy of worship; but war prostitutes it of necessity."[7]

Propagandizing in the form of lurid accounts of Japanese and Nazi brutalities prior to America's entry into World War II similarly created hostile sentiments. Leon C. Standifer, a devout Baptist, explained that part of this propagandizing came from the pulpit: "'Thou shalt not kill' became less clear. We started learning about justified killing. It came on slowly until Pearl Harbor. After that, 'Kill the dirty Japs' was a popular sentiment."[8]

The propaganda effort before and during the world wars undoubtedly helped to turn opinion against the "Huns," "Krauts," and "Japs." What is less clear is the extent to which military training and indoctrination, beyond sanctioning the soldier's mission of killing, contributed to this process. Formal indoctrination efforts started too late in World War I to have an impact. During World War II, indoctrination failed either to boost the soldiers' commitment to the country's war aims or to enhance their hatred of the enemy.[9] Furthermore, soldiers who comment on their training during the world wars rarely mention a deliberate effort by their trainers to disparage the enemy or to instill blood lust.[10]

The process changed, however, by the Vietnam War era. The dehumanization of the Viet Cong, or the "gooks" as they were called, became integral to the training process. Jonathan Shay writes, "Vietnam-era military training reflexively imparted the image of a demonized adversary. The enemy soldier was pictured as evil and loathsome, deserving to be killed as the enemy of God and as

God-hated vermin, so inhuman as not really to care if he lives or dies."[11] Shay overdramatizes the case, but this dehumanization process was nevertheless blatant enough to elicit comments from historians and soldiers alike.[12] Private Reginald Edwards recalls what he learned about the Vietnamese enemy while in marine boot camp: "The only thing they told us about the Viet Cong was they were gooks. They were to be killed. Nobody sits around and gives you their historical and cultural background. They're the enemy. Kill, kill, kill."[13] The message received by the army trainee was the same, as Specialist Haywood T. Kirkland remembers it: "Then they told us when you go over in Vietnam, you gonna be face to face with Charlie, the Viet Cong. They were animals, or something other than human. They ain't have no regard for life. . . . [The trainers] wouldn't allow you to talk about them [the Viet Cong] as if they were people. They told us they're not to be treated with any type of mercy. . . . That's what they engraved into you. That killer instinct."[14]

Dave Grossman believes that this dehumanization of the enemy and the "deification of killing" was intentionally added to the Vietnam-era training process to heighten trainee aggressiveness.[15] He may be correct, but there was a more basic reason for stirring up hatred of the "gooks." The average Vietnam-era trainee entered service with little animosity toward and hence no particular urge to kill an enemy about whom he knew next to nothing. During the world wars, on the other hand, as a result of the steady stream of widely publicized German and Japanese aggressions and atrocities, those joining the military were already convinced that the enemy was evil, or at least fought for sinister causes, and had to be stopped. The Vietnam War draftee, however, was likely to ask, "Where is Vietnam and why should I care?"

After completing training, the soldier understood that he possessed the skills to kill and that doing so was sanctioned and even expected of him. Yet many soldiers echoed the sentiments of the World War II sergeant Charles Brown: "I think the biggest thing in war is to untrain you from the influences that say you don't kill. . . . I feel the men I was with did not become untrained from the civilization in which they grew up. It takes time to make a killer out of a man."[16] For Standifer, even after completing his infantry training, being told that "killing the dirty Japs" was permissible did not mean that he was eager to get started: "What bothered me most was knowing that I now had the skill to kill quickly and easily, but still feeling deep revulsion at the possibility of having to do so."[17]

Even the grunt heading off to Vietnam did not necessarily feel ready or eager to kill, despite the dehumanized image of his enemy that his training cadre had attempted to instill in him. Private David Parks recorded in his diary a question that his drill sergeant had asked him and his fellow trainees. Though intended to be rhetorical, it was not so for Parks: "The sergeant asked a tough question today. He wanted to know if we were ready to kill. I've thought about this for a long time now. I don't know. I don't think so."[18]

## THE CATALYST OF THE BATTLEFIELD

As Sergeant Brown observed, it took time to make a killer, and many green soldiers, like Parks and Standifer, were not at all sure that they were ready to become one. The environment of war, however, quickly turned most soldiers into capable if not enthusiastic killers, although the conversion process could be painful—a first killing was a traumatic experience for many. The first enemy soldier that William Manchester shot was at close range. Manchester, who had always had a "deep-seated" horror of violence, emptied his .45-caliber pistol into a Japanese sniper and watched him die, after which "a feeling of disgust and self-hatred clotted darkly in my throat, gagging me." He vomited, wet himself, and began shaking uncontrollably.[19]

For Manchester, reluctance to kill was overcome by the need to shoot an armed enemy who, if not quickly dispatched, would have shot him instead. Jon Neely's first encounter with the enemy in Vietnam was under similar circumstances. A Viet Cong soldier stepped from behind a tree and leveled his weapon at Neely's squad leader. Instinctively, Neely pulled up his M-79 grenade launcher and fired: "I hit the guy dead center and there wasn't much left of him." Neely vomited from the shock: "To physically kill someone—it really got to me and it took me a few days to get over that."[20]

In some cases, soldiers not in imminent danger hesitated to make their first kill. Whayland Greene, a fresh replacement in the Philippines in World War II, had a clear shot at an unsuspecting Japanese soldier but held his fire, hoping that one of his comrades would do the killing instead. A nearby sergeant obliged him.[21]

Some soldiers did not hesitate, however, even when making their first kill. Their understanding that killing the enemy was sanctioned and expected sufficed to allay any qualms. One of Mark Baker's interviewees arrived in Vietnam at the height of the enemy's Tet Offensive. During his first night in-country, he found himself defending a perimeter: "The VC were coming in the wire and I was shooting them. . . . I killed a couple myself. I thought in the back of my mind that I was going to break down and cry because I killed one, but to me it was nothing. . . . It didn't bother me."[22]

Audie Murphy's first kill came during the invasion of Sicily, when he calmly dropped to one knee, sighted in on two Italian officers escaping on horseback, and shot them out of the saddle with a bullet apiece. Murphy's green lieutenant hollered, "Now why did you do that?" A nonplussed Murphy responded, "That's our job isn't it? They would have killed us if they'd had the chance. That's their job. Or have I been wrongly informed?'" Murphy learned with experience that some soldiers, like his lieutenant, adapted more slowly to battlefield realities than others: "In the training areas we talked toughly, thought toughly; and finally we believed we really were tough. But it is not easy to shed the idea that human life is sacred. The lieutenant has not yet accepted the fact that we have been put into the field to deal out death. I have."[23]

Sooner or later, most soldiers accepted, as Murphy did, that they were indeed there to deal out death, and if they did not deal it out first, then the enemy would.[24] In the environment of combat, most soldiers quickly overcame any reluctance, or queasiness, about killing. Several weeks after killing his first enemy—weeks of nearly continuous combat on Okinawa—Sergeant Manchester won a shootout with another Japanese sniper. As he approached his dead enemy, there was none of the shaking, vomiting, or remorse that had accompanied his first kill. Indeed, his only reaction was anger because this Japanese soldier had obviously been living in a warm, dry cave or bunker: "To my astonishment, and then to my rage, I saw that his uniform was dry. All these weeks I have been suffering in the rain, night and day, this bastard had been holed up in some waterproof cave. It was the only instant in the war when I felt hatred for a Jap. I swung back my right leg and kicked the bloody head."[25]

The night before landing with his marine battalion in Vietnam, Private Richard E. Ogden had a "chilling thought": "The thought of killing someone terrified the hell out of me." Several months later, however, after killing a Viet Cong sapper with his bare hands, Ogden's sense of self-preservation had clearly asserted itself: "I told myself that never again would I feel remorse or sadness for killing, because I was alive and it felt wonderful."[26]

Most soldiers took little pleasure in killing, but once immersed in the environment of war, few remained overly troubled by it, either. Ernie Pyle observed how the GIs in World War II adjusted to their new profession: "The most vivid change was the casual and workshop manner in which they talked about killing. They had made the psychological transition from their normal belief that taking human life was sinful, over to a new professional outlook where killing was a craft. No longer was there anything morally wrong about killing. In fact, it was an admirable thing."[27]

Lieutenant Paul Boesch had made that transition by the time he killed his first German face-to-face in World War II. He had fired at the enemy many times before, but this time "there could be no doubt" that he had personally shot the man now dying at his feet. Yet he felt no remorse: "I could stand there and watch him die and feel absolutely no qualms of any kind. . . . It was as if I were a carpenter and had driven home a nail which secured one beam to another, the job I was assigned to do."[28]

David Parks, who was not sure if he could answer in the affirmative his drill sergeant's question about his readiness to kill, discovered in Vietnam that he was: "Charlie [the Viet Cong] isn't easy to find, but when you do catch up with him he'll fight like a cornered rat. They blast away and we blast away. Everyone has killing on their mind. I don't have the fear about it that I thought I would. All I want to do is get it over with."[29] The soldier might not like killing, but as Lieutenant Philip Caputo notes, he did not hesitate if his life was at stake: "Self-preservation, that most basic and tyrannical of all instincts, can turn a man into a coward or, as was more often the case in Vietnam, into a creature who destroys without hesitation or remorse whatever poses even a potential threat to his life. A sergeant in my platoon, ordinarily a pleasant young man, told me once, 'Lieutenant, I've got a wife and two kids at home and I'm going to see 'em again and don't care who I've got to kill or how many of 'em to do it.'"[30]

Though the killing was often necessary, it was not always done dispassionately. Soldiers sometimes killed in anger, especially if a close buddy had been killed or comrades lost to "cowardly" or "unfair" practices, such as sniping or booby trapping.[31] Private Robert Stiles's buddy was killed by a Japanese sniper hiding in a treetop. They had been close friends for two years. "I was stunned," said Stiles, "but only for a minute." He grabbed a Browning Automatic Rifle and went after the sniper: "I sprayed that fuckin' tree with a whole clip and down came the Nip. As I look back on it, what the hell, he was only doing his job, same as me, but I'm still glad I was the one who got him."[32]

Lieutenant Caputo's platoon, while on a typical sweep operation in Vietnam, was caught in the blast of a command-detonated mine. Nine men were wounded, five seriously. As Caputo carried one of his wounded men to the medevac helicopter, "I felt my own anger, a very cold, very deep anger that had no specific object." He soon found an object to hate, however—the wires used to detonate the mine were discovered and traced back to a nearby village. The Viet Cong who set off the explosion were by then undoubtedly mixed in with and indistinguishable from the villagers. Without hesitation, Caputo ordered the village set ablaze with white-phosphorous bazooka shells: "All right, I thought, tit for tat."[33]

Such fits of rage were usually short-lived, as Elmar Dinter notes: "Feelings of hatred and revenge are the results of fleeting frustrations. If for instance a good friend has just been killed, these emotions increase, but as time passes, they diminish rapidly again. The average soldier does not maintain constant feelings of hatred and revenge."[34] Some soldiers did, however. For them, killing was no longer business; it was personal, as it was for Lieutenant Franklyn A. Johnson, beginning with the day his best friend was killed in Sicily in World War II: "For me, like others who lose a buddy, the day Dick is killed is when the war gets personal, and my hatred of our enemy becomes a continual, gnawing thing."[35]

The anger, frustration, and inability to retaliate in kind generated by the enemy's use of booby traps and mines in Vietnam produced a similar hatred in many grunts, as one of Mark Baker's interviewees recalled: "We changed a lot. The change was individual. It was silence. It was reserve. The anger came from within, for seeing the guys blown up. The unspoken words behind the anger were, 'You fucking bastards, you're going to get it now. Let me find one of you and you're going to die just like they died. I'm going to blow your fucking brains out.' We went into the jungle angry and silent and very determined to do what we were trained to do—which was to kill."[36]

Some soldiers thus burned with a steady hatred while for others anger and a desire for vengeance were passing emotions. Sometimes, when soldiers were engaged in heavy, close combat, the adrenalin flowed, noise and chaos abounded, and rational thought almost ceased. The terms "blood lust" and "in the heat of battle" appear in the memoirs to describe such moments.[37] Soldiers often retained only disjointed recollections of what had happened during this sort of fighting. Bob Hoffman attempted to describe the bloody assault in which he won a Distinguished Service Cross and ended up in the hospital with multiple wounds, but his account is sketchy: "I don't remember all the battle—didn't when it was over."[38]

In close combat, the killing became automatic, and no quarter was given. Lieutenant Joseph D. Lawrence and his men, during an assault in the Meuse-Argonne campaign, showed no mercy to a fleeing enemy who, just moments earlier, had been firing on them. His men opened up with aimed rifle fire, and "the execution was heavy." Lawrence leveled his pistol at a German and fired, "the bullet striking just above the ear and tearing off the top of his head. . . . As I look back on the scene it is horrible, but then, while the heat of battle was upon us, it was thrilling."[39] Attacking doughboys who watched their comrades falling all around them were not in a charitable mood if they lived long enough to close with their tormentors. As Captain John W. Thomason recalled, "A man can stand just so much of that. Life presently ceases to be desirable; the only desirable thing is to kill that [machine] gunner, kill him with your hands!"[40]

After an intense fight, the adrenalin subsided and the survivors were physically exhausted. The loss of comrades began to register, and soldiers grieved, but they also realized, with a rush of relief and elation, that they were still alive. Lieutenant James Brady, returning unharmed from a failed attack during the Korean War in which thirty-two of sixty-four marines were killed or wounded, knew he would grieve for the dead, but that would come later: "I don't know how anyone who hasn't been shot at up close in a real firefight can possibly understand how good you feel afterward. Men have been killed and hurt, the fight has been won or lost, but there is only the one truly significant fact: that you are still alive, you have not been killed."[41]

It was better still, according to the platoon leader James R. McDonough, if survival was accompanied by victory. The enemy dead were tangible evidence of that victory; hence their death was cause for neither remorse nor guilt but triumph:

> Could it be—repugnant thought that it was—pleasure that one feels at the sight of an opponent's body? How could a civilized man feel such a thing?
>     Perhaps the emotion was born of relief. Ground combat is personal. . . . It is a primordial struggle. . . . Emotions flow with an intensity unimaginable to the nonparticipant: fear, hate, passion, desperation. And then—triumph! The enemy falls, lies there lifeless, his gaping corpse a mockery of the valiant fight he made. Your own emotions withdraw, replaced by a flow of relief and exhilaration, because he is dead and not you.[42]

## GERMAN FOES

The implication thus far has been that it did not matter who the enemy was, and up to a point that was true. The soldier went to war knowing that his job was to kill America's evil, barbaric, grasping, or at least woefully misguided foes. Once on the battlefield, the realities of kill-or-be-killed sank in, and he fought to survive, to avenge his dead comrades, to save his buddies, and to accomplish the mission, regardless of who the enemy might be.

On the other hand, who the enemy was and how he fought mattered a great deal. The physical environment and the enemy's combat methods ensured that the fighting in the Pacific and Asia, for example, was especially brutal. Racial hatred played a lesser role in generating this brutality than is commonly perceived, but the influence of race cannot be ruled out. Unlike the Asian foe, the German enemy was ethnically and culturally akin to white America, as an incident related by Lieutenant George William Sefton illustrates. One night during the fighting in World War II, a lost German soldier stumbled into American lines and was killed. Sefton remembers that "the dead German was very young. His pale face had a two-day stubble of wispy growth. His combat uniform pockets contained several apples and a harmonica. He reminded me of my brother who had turned 18 in January."[43] American soldiers rifling through the pockets of dead Asian foes did not feel the emotional tug of seeing a dead "Jap" or "gook" who reminded them of their kid brothers back home.

Not that the American soldier harbored any special love for Germans. He believed that the Prussian militarists of the first war and the Nazis of the second war were evil people intent on conquest and domination. The soldier tended to differentiate, however, between the average German soldier and his political masters. Hence, there were "good" Germans, who were deluded and perhaps coerced into supporting an evil system, and "bad" Germans, who were the Prussian nobility or the Nazis and their *Schutzstaffel* (SS) functionaries.[44]

Differentiating between average Germans and their racist, autocratic, greedy-for-conquest leaders allowed American soldiers to approach their German counterparts with an open mind or even with a measure of compassion. The doughboys and GIs had absorbed some of the dehumanizing propaganda about barbaric Huns and cruel, self-proclaimed Nazi supermen, but the realities of contact with the German *Frontkämpfer* belied these images.[45] Lieutenant Robert G. Merrick's first "view of the despised Boche" in World War I was a prisoner-of-war work party: "They paused slightly in their work and watched us file by. With their small round caps and pea-green uniforms inscribed with an enormous white 'P.G.' *(Prisonier de Guerre),* they did not appear like such ferocious characters to us."[46]

The World War II GI also discovered that his German foe appeared human enough and certainly did not look the part of supermen. Private Roscoe C. Blunt recalled seeing his first Germans, a bedraggled group of freshly captured *Volks-grenadiers:* "These frightened, half-starved Kriegs Gefangener (war prisoners) didn't look at all like the images of vicious German soldiers with cruel, distorted, snarling faces displayed on posters back in basic training lectures. Facing them close up brought the war into sharper focus for me. I was dealing with men just like ourselves, only in different uniforms, speaking a different language and fighting for a different cause."[47]

For most doughboys and GIs, first encounter with the German enemy dispelled notions of a barbaric foe. German actions on the battlefield, with some notable exceptions, reinforced the impression of a human enemy. The German soldier generally acted "correctly," that is, according to American expectations. He surrendered if his situation was hopeless and in turn accepted the surrender of Americans and usually treated them properly. He cared about his own casualties, honored the Red Cross emblem by not firing on medics or vehicles displaying it, and even agreed to occasional truces to allow recovery of the dead and wounded.[48] Doughboys went to France expecting bestial behavior from the Germans, but to their surprise they witnessed few instances of cruelty. Bob Hoffman recalled the "usual atrocity stories," but he "never saw any examples of such torture, killing and mutilation."[49] Nor could Father Francis P. Duffy, at war's end, condemn German behavior: "We fought the Germans two long tricks in the trenches and in five pitched battles and they never did anything to us that we did not try to do to them. And we played the game as fairly as it can be played. We followed their retreat through three sectors, in two of which they had been for years, and we never witnessed at first hand any of the atrocities we read about."[50]

The Germans, during their occupation and subsequent retreat from portions of Belgium and France, certainly exploited the local populace and often looted or destroyed private property, but Hoffman's and Duffy's assessments are consistent with other doughboy memoirs, which contain few references to German battlefield atrocities.[51] German cruelty was more in evidence during World War II as GIs entered German-occupied territories. Some GIs who had been inclined toward a humane view of their German enemy even began to change their minds.[52]

This change of heart tended to come only late in the war, however, usually after GIs had witnessed the horrors of the concentration and displaced-persons camps. Even then, the "good German–bad German" rationale worked to limit the scope of American hatred. For example, the worst battlefield atrocities on the western front occurred during the Battle of the Bulge in 1944, notably the slaughter of American prisoners of war by SS troops near the town of Malmédy. Word of this massacre spread like wildfire through the American forces, but the resulting hatred and retribution were generally restricted to the SS. Private Blunt's attitude was typical: "There was a vast difference between Wehrmacht Soldaten and SS storm troopers. One took prisoners, the other executed them and perpetrated unspeakable atrocities against defenseless civilians."[53] Lieutenants Harold P. Leinbaugh and John D. Campbell, whose infantry company was one of many committed to stemming the German offensive of December 1944, asserted that fair play was out the window after Malmédy, but only against the SS: "If Company K's reaction to the atrocity was typical, the Germans had committed their worst mistake of the war on the Western Front. We had fought by rules of a sort. In the heat of battle, prisoners were sometimes killed. We knew that. But this was mass murder, and the SS was going to have to pay and pay heavily."[54]

After Malmédy, SS troops attempted surrender only at their own peril, but GIs continued to fight "by rules of a sort" when facing *Wehrmacht* troops. This distinction between *Wehrmacht* and SS troops was not entirely inappropriate. The battlefield atrocities of the SS were the shocking exceptions that validated the general rule that most Germans "fought fair." They also fought well. Father Francis P. Duffy provides the doughboys' opinion of their enemy: "They judge the German soldier by their own experience and by soldier standards. They do not fear him, they do not hate him, they do not despise him either. They respected him when he put up a good fight or made a clean getaway, and that was most of the time."[55] Hoffman was more grudging but also positive: "They were entirely worthy foes. I disliked them, but I was forced to admire them, too, for the way they fought."[56]

The Germans again proved to be worthy foes in World War II. Like his doughboy predecessor, the GI respected his German counterparts as fighters. As Bill Mauldin observed, "Because our men soon learn to be more or less professional fighters at the front, they have a deep respect for the German's ability to wage war. You may hear a doggie call a German a skunk, but he'll never say he's not good."[57] Klaus Huebner, after watching the Germans fight in Italy for over a year, conceded that "even though enemy, we must admit that they have been excellent soldiers."[58] According to Lee Kennett, this view of the German as a worthy adversary who normally conducted himself properly on the battlefield was critical in keeping the fighting, as harsh as it often was, within bounds. He adds that the European environment also helped to ameliorate the brutality. The European culture and countryside were similar to America. A GI might find a bottle of wine, a chicken to stew, and even a roof over his head. The soldier in the Pacific, however, "found himself in a strange and forbidding region inhabited by primitive people with a culture that had little or no attraction for him" and that provided few amenities.[59]

## ASIAN FOES

Ground combat against the Germans, though invariably bloody, thus retained a measure of restraint, and most American soldiers did not deny the enemy his humanity. America's Asian foes, on the other hand, were hated and dehumanized, and none more than the Japanese.[60] Jesse Glenn Gray points out that restraint fell by the wayside once the Japanese were dehumanized to the point of being perceived by GIs as some sort of animal or vermin: "The enemy is sought out to be exterminated, not subdued. There is no satisfaction in capturing him. . . . There is also, of course, no safety in it [either], since he is held to be incapable of grasping civilized rules of warfare."[61] American racism undoubtedly played a role in this dehumanization process. John Hersey, in a reissue of *Into the Valley*, his 1943 story about marines on Guadalcanal, apologized for the racism evident in his book but elected to keep it in because it was an integral part of the war environment:

> I have resisted the strong temptation to revise *Into the Valley* for this edition. The first passages to be cut would have been those that refer to the Japanese as animals. It was all very well—and "truthful" enough, for such things were indeed being said—for me to quote a Marine as wishing he were fighting against (white, blond?) Germans, who "react like men," instead of against these Japanese animals, who "take to the jungle as if they were bred there." But to my shame I am not quoting someone else when, after a mortar barrage begins, I write that I envisage "a swarm of intelligent little animals" fussing around the mortar tubes on the other side of the river.[62]

This demeaning racism was evident well before Pearl Harbor. Racial stereotyping had led Americans to believe that the Japanese could not possibly be their match, and thus Japan's early successes in the war generated shock, alarm, and fear.[63] The reaction of Gerald P. Averill and his fellow marines to the attack on Pearl Harbor was typically incredulous: "It was inconceivable. We stared at each other blankly, stunned. Like all other Americans growing up in the late thirties and early forties, we had been fed the national theme—the Japanese were stumpy, bowlegged, half-blind. They could not shoot; their ships were made from melted-down American beer cans; their aircraft, made of wood and cloth, without armor or armament, had no striking power. Yet in the span of those few hours . . . these same inferior people, with their substandard war machinery, had devastated major United States naval and air bases."[64]

As the string of Japanese victories continued in the months after Pearl Harbor, American soldiers shifted from underestimating their opponent to endowing him with almost superhuman fighting capabilities, and dehumanizing racism again played a role in the process. The Japanese soldier was possessed, it seemed, of animal-like cunning, stealth, endurance, and night vision, making him a superior jungle and night fighter.[65]

With the Japanese defeat on Guadalcanal by the end of 1942, yet another shift in perception occurred. Japanese soldiers were inflexible and often committed tactical blunders and hence were not superhuman. After repulsing the disastrous Japanese charge across the Tenaru (Ilu) River on Guadalcanal, Captain William Hawkins commented, "Seeing all those [Japanese] corpses, and realizing how stupid the attack really was, knocked the aura of the Japanese superman into a cocked hat."[66] Racism again influenced the perception process, however. The enemy was still an animal, just no longer an exceptionally cunning and skillful one. He was now seen as some sort of especially nasty beast or vermin to be exterminated.[67] Han Rants, fighting in the Philippines, expressed the GI's common view that the Japanese were savage animals to be dispatched forthwith: "The great majority of enemy soldiers we faced were worse than uncivilized savages or wild beasts seeking to kill. . . . Each of us had to cope with their butchery in our own way but for me vengeance was the answer."[68]

In Peter Bowman's novel about an amphibious assault in the Pacific, published before war's end, the protagonist reminds himself to be on the alert for the animalistic enemy, "stocky of build, with almost no perceptible waistline, that moves . . . with a shuffle rather than a stride . . . with yellow skin inclined toward hairiness, and buck teeth and a pair of squinting eyes slanted toward the nose and a characteristic odor like the smell of wild animals."[69]

This racism, and the Japanese were equally guilty of it, helped ensure that the war in the Pacific would be fought with unparalleled brutality, as Eugene B. Sledge writes: "Official histories and memoirs of Marine infantrymen written after the war rarely reflect that hatred. But at the time of battle, Marines felt it deeply, bitterly, and as certainly as danger. . . . My experiences on Peleliu and Okinawa made me believe that the Japanese held mutual feelings for us. . . . This collective attitude . . . resulted in savage, ferocious fighting with no holds barred. This was not the dispassionate killing seen on other fronts or in other wars. This was a brutish, primitive hatred, as characteristic of the horror of war in the Pacific as the palm trees and the islands."[70]

American soldiers also held racist opinions of their North Korean, Chinese, and Vietnamese foes. As had occurred with the Japanese, racist attitudes sometimes caused the soldier initially to underestimate his opponents' worthiness. Green units typically exhibited overconfidence prior to combat, but in the case of the first American units on the scene during the Korean War, that confidence was further boosted by the belief that no Asian foe could stand up to American troops. Captain Charles M. Bussey and his engineer company, part of the first American division to arrive in Korea, did not expect to be there long: "The word was that we would put up a show of force in the field in Korea, and when the enemy quaked and returned across the 38th Parallel—which was inevitable—we would return to home stations."[71]

By the time that Lieutenant Uzal Ent arrived in Korea with the Twenty-fifth Infantry Division, which followed on the heels of Bussey's Twenty-fourth Division, the North Korean People's Army had not only failed to scurry back across the Thirty-eighth Parallel but had also severely handled the first American troops to arrive. Ent noticed that racist assumptions about the enemy were not holding true: "What really bothered us was that the North Koreans hadn't shown any awe, any respect if you will, for the American units that had been put in their way. There had been a definite feeling, not articulated maybe but very much in people's minds, that the North Koreans would quit when they found out they were facing American troops. Of course they hadn't quit."[72]

A steady influx of American ground and air forces finally stopped the North Koreans and then drove them back across the Thirty-eighth Parallel. United Nations forces then continued attacking northward, intending to occupy North Korea and reunite the country, which triggered a massive intervention by the Chinese Communist Forces (CCF). The American leadership had discounted such an intervention, and the overextended UN forces were driven into headlong retreat in winter 1950–1951. Beyond numbers, this Chinese military success was attributed to the enemy's animal-like cunning, stamina, and stealth, as Pat Frank described it in his novel: "This new enemy was not orthodox. This new enemy did not expose itself except on ground, and at a time, of its own choosing. Then it rose, as if birthed on the spot by the mud of Asia, in full strength and ferocity. . . . This new enemy slithered around your flanks, and stabbed your rear, and ate at your guts. You could not put your hands on him. It was like trying to strangle a jellyfish."[73]

Endowing the enemy with superhuman, or, more accurately, nonhuman, attributes allowed Americans to explain away Chinese success without conceding that the enemy might possess such human qualities as military skill, bravery, or dedication. This dehumanized portrait, however, also inspired fear. How can such a fanatical, animalistic enemy be stopped? Samuel L. A. Marshall chastised the press for demoralizing UN forces in winter 1950–1951 by depicting the Chinese as unstoppable hordes: "Correspondents worked overtime portraying the new enemy in the most terrible aspect permitted by their imaginations; he was described as a fanatic horde breaking over our lines in irresistible waves, charging into the cannon's mouth with maniacal fury, as if under the spell of some drug."[74]

As with the Japanese and the North Koreans before them, the Chinese Communist Forces eventually proved to be beatable. Even their numerical superiority could not overcome American firepower. The discovery that the Chinese enemy was mortal, however, did not necessarily make him more human, just more killable. Lieutenant Ent did not feel any "personal animosity" toward his North Korean and Chinese enemies, but he believed that most GIs did, and he added that dehumanizing the enemy made it easier to kill them: "Many men fought with a visceral hatred of the enemy. Maybe the fact that they were Orientals had something to do with it. 'Gooks' was the standard term for them, and it was easier to think of them as not quite human, as something beneath us."[75]

Underestimation of the enemy born of racism was not as evident in the first American units to deploy to Vietnam, perhaps because the Viet Minh had already proven themselves capable foes against the French. Grunts nevertheless expected the Viet Cong (VC) and North Vietnamese Army (NVA) to be appropriately awed by American superiority; at least Robert Mason and his fellow helicopter pilots did: "The Cav [First Cavalry Division] is here now, and those gooks are going to shit when they see us in action."[76] Lieutenant Caputo and his marine battalion were equally optimistic about a quick victory over an inferior Asian foe: "We believed in our own publicity—Asian guerrillas did not stand a chance against U.S. Marines."[77]

The VC and NVA were, in fact, disconcerted by the Americans and their helicopters and firepower, but they adjusted quickly and soon proved alarmingly adept at night fighting, concealment, and ambushes. As they had with earlier Asian foes, Americans attributed VC and NVA skills to animal-like qualities of endurance and stealth, as Lieutenant Alfred S. Bradford's brigade staff did: "Staff adrenalin was flowing and so were staff jitters. For the first time I realized what a monster their imaginations had made out of the NVA. He could do anything. He could sneak up on an American and snip the buttons off his jungle fatigues. He could break through any barrier. He could mass any number of men. He never ran short of supplies. He could live on a handful of rice and a scoop of muddy water. He never got sick."[78] Headquarters staffs were not the only Americans to have jitters over the enemy's animal-like instincts. The grunt on the perimeter at night also marveled at the VC's seemingly supernatural stealth and cunning. The marines in Private Ogden's company were amazed that the enemy could steal emplaced Claymore mines from under their noses and call out the names of unit members, threatening to come and get them: "The enemy was no longer warm flesh and blood; they were now an intangible, evil, macabre force."[79]

Although Americans never did get the upper hand at night in Vietnam, they did discover that the enemy was not invincible. Grunts more often than not came out ahead in a firefight. As in earlier Asian wars, however, the enemy's mortality did not equate to humanity. The enemy, and the Vietnamese people in general, were considered something less than human. The dehumanization process may have started back in training, but it continued and accelerated once the soldier arrived in-country.[80] Americans did not understand Vietnamese culture and considered the natives poor and ignorant. Lieutenant Frederick Downs, newly arrived in Vietnam, learned from the soldier driving him to his unit that all Vietnamese, not just the enemy, were called "gooks." The soldier explained why: "Friendly or not, they're all called the same. Look at them. They don't even know what good living is. They're ignorant as owl shit, you know?"[81] One of Mark Baker's interviewees noted that this view was common: "Too many of us forgot that Vietnamese were people. We didn't treat them like people after a while. . . . I really didn't like to mistreat people over there. I tried as hard as I could . . . not that I didn't from time to time."[82]

As insidious as racism was in dehumanizing the enemy, thus making him easier to kill, the way America's Asian foes fought was perhaps even more significant in generating hatred. Their methods and standards violated American concepts of fair play.[83] In the South Pacific in World War II, Japanese battlefield brutality goes a long way toward explaining why the fighting became so vicious. American soldiers may have been initially reluctant to retaliate in kind, but as Ore Marion pointed out, they learned fast: "We learned about savagery from the Japanese. Those bastards had years of on-the-job training on how to be a savage on the Asian mainland. But those sixteen-to-nineteen-year-old kids we had on the Canal [Guadalcanal] were fast learners."[84]

One of the first things GIs learned was that the Japanese did not seem to hold life dear. Enemy soldiers committed suicide or made hopeless banzai charges rather than surrendering. This "fanaticism," more than American racism, the correspondent Dan Levin argues, explains why GIs came to loathe the Japanese: "I heard no crap about the 'yellow peril' among our young Marines. The mass suicides on Saipan—both the suicide banzais and the leaps off the cliffs at Marpi Point—had made many of our fellows believe they were facing a mysterious nation of fanatics; that's something else."[85] American soldiers could never understand why the Japanese would commit suicide rather than surrender. The GI rationale simply became, if the Japanese do not care if they live or die, then why should we?

The next Asian foes to seem especially heedless of life were the Chinese during the Korean War. Although lurid accounts of human-wave attacks by screaming, fanatical Chinese have been overdone, the Chinese did often press their assaults with seemingly suicidal determination, according to the war correspondent Marguerite Higgins: "They frequently seemed to care very little for life and were willing to die unquestioningly. They would keep right on surging toward a target even though wave after wave of them were blown up in the process."[86] The machine gunner Ted White, fighting to hold off Chinese assaults during the enemy's April 1951 offensive, agreed: "They kept coming in waves, and I kept firing. I fired my machine gun all night long. Everybody else was firing. And the artillery was dropping all around us. The artillery did a good job of keeping them off us. And all night long I'm thinking, These people are crazy. They're dying in droves, and they just keep coming on."[87]

This seemingly suicidal fanaticism mystified the GIs as much as Japanese banzai charges had in the previous war. Some GIs believed the rumor that the Chinese were "hopped up" on opium—how else to explain such behavior?[88] The Viet Cong and North Vietnamese enemy did not usually expend lives as prodigiously as the Chinese and Japanese, nor did they normally commit suicide. Yet the grunts questioned the value that yet another Asian enemy placed on life because of the Viet Cong's willingness to use women and children as combatants. The American belief that women and children should be spared the horrors of combat was thus violated, as Dave Grossman observes: "The standard methods of on-the-scene rationalization fail when the enemy's child comes out to mourn over her father's body or when the enemy is a child throwing a hand grenade. And the North Vietnamese and Vietcong understood this."[89]

The low value that the Asian foe seemed to place on his own life was incomprehensible to Americans, but what really stirred up hatred was the enemy's disregard for American lives. The American soldier expected his enemy to accept his surrender and treat him humanely, to respect the Red Cross emblem, to care for the wounded of both sides, and to spare noncombatants undue suffering and deprivations. The Asian foe often refused to play by these rules. In the case of the Japanese, asserts Dixon Wecter, this refusal incurred considerable American wrath: "Still greater hatred boils against the Japanese, with their studied Oriental sadism and refusal to pay even lip-service to the rules of the game. The death-march on Bataan, execution of flyers in Tokyo, beheading of prisoners, killing of medics trying to help the wounded, and machine-gunning of life rafts, add up to a rancor that generations are not likely to forget. 'Kill the bastards' is the war-cry of the Pacific."[90]

Wecter writes with a vehemence typical of the war years, but postwar historians acknowledge that Japanese actions of the sort he describes started a downward slide into hatred and brutality early in the war.[91] E. J. Kahn, in his brief memoir about his experiences in New Guinea, reveals the hatred generated by Japanese fighting methods: "Although Japanese exploits with knives have been well publicized, the New Guinea campaign . . . did not disclose any great proficiency on their part in this line, beyond bayoneting bound victims, raiding hospitals and stabbing the patients, and committing hara-kiri, at all of which they had already been known to be adept."[92] Japanese cruelties, actual and rumored, to prisoners, civilians, and wounded prompted GI hatred and responses in kind. As Peter Bowman put it in his novel, "Do unto Japs as Japs do unto you—but first."[93]

The next Asian enemy, the North Koreans, seemed almost as brutal as the Japanese. Soldiers captured by the North Koreans were often tortured, killed, and their bodies mutilated. Mass executions of American prisoners occurred, and many more died from starvation and maltreatment.[94] The Chinese exhibited less outright brutality and committed fewer atrocities than the North Koreans, but their treatment of prisoners was also far from humane, especially during the first winter of the war.[95] Bill Mauldin, visiting the front in 1952, talked to a rifleman who said that the enemy in his sector were North Koreans, who "kill medics just for the fun of it" and were the ones, as opposed to the Chinese, who "have done most of the prisoner killing you hear about."[96] Lieutenant Beverly Scott summed up the GI's opinion of North Korean fanaticism and brutality in terms reminiscent of those used to describe the Japanese, to whom the North Koreans were frequently compared: "They'd come right into your hole, try and shoot you or stab you or bite you if they didn't have a weapon. Just fanatical as hell. Maybe thirty or forty of them would come straight at us in a kind of banzai attack, where they'd all get killed, but it was just to distract us while more of them were trying to sneak around us somewhere else. And they were vicious people. They mutilated bodies. They shot prisoners. Just, nasty, nasty people."[97]

The GI learned that he could expect no quarter from such "nasty people" and was therefore disinclined to grant any. The American soldier in Vietnam similarly concluded that the Viet Cong were also nasty. Grunts were appalled at the Viet Cong terror campaign deliberately waged against their own people. Dominick Yezzo initially sympathized with the enemy, and the first enemy prisoners he met seemed like decent fellows. But after witnessing several Viet Cong atrocities, he changed his mind: "The Communist forces are continuing their wave of terrorism on the cities and civilian populated areas. . . . It's awfully disgusting and churns my stomach. I can't sympathize with North Vietnam any longer."[98]

It was the Vietnamese enemy's disregard for American life, however, that really provoked hatred. The discovery of slain Americans whose bodies showed signs of torture and execution, often followed by mutilation, generated a visceral urge for vengeance.[99] Grunts quickly learned that the enemy, who had no logistical infrastructure for moving or caring for prisoners, often did not bother to take them, especially if wounded, nor did he leave them behind alive.[100] Robert Sanders, after describing various mutilations of American corpses, explained the standard grunt reaction: "Here's what guys felt: 'If Charlie can do it, then we're going to do the same thing to him if we kill him.' All the mutilation did was just piss you off. Charlie turned you into an animal."[101] The marines in Caputo's brigade absorbed the same lesson: "They learned rather quickly that Vietnam was not a place where a man could expect much mercy if, say, he was taken prisoner. And men who do not expect to receive mercy eventually lose their inclination to grant it."[102]

The Asian foe's disregard for life violated American concepts of proper behavior in combat, and so too did his refusal to "fight fair." Up to a point, ruses and deceptions were an acceptable part of the deadly game. If the enemy tricked or scared a unit into opening fire at night, for example, thus giving away its position and perhaps bringing down an artillery barrage as a consequence, then that was "score one" for the enemy. Some tricks, however, went too far. Even the German enemy occasionally attempted ruses that Americans considered foul play, such as using Red Cross vehicles or stretchers for moving weapons and ammunition, or the "*Kamerad* trap" of feigning surrender to draw doughboys into the open, then opening fire.[103]

It is indicative of the American soldiers' desire to maintain a degree of restraint on the battlefield that these unsavory German tricks did not suffice to destroy the rules of fair play. The Asian foe, however, played relatively more, and more egregious, dirty tricks, providing one more reason for Americans to adopt a harsh, no-mercy policy. That the Japanese would commit suicide rather than surrender was unfathomable to the GI, but worse, some played dead or feigned surrender in an attempt to take a few Americans with them. Richard Tregaskis noted that even before the fighting on Guadalcanal was over, GIs had learned to be wary of Japanese playing dead: "Jap dead are dangerous, for there are usually some among them alive enough to wait until you pass, then stab or shoot you. Our marines had by this time learned to take no chances. The dead were shot again . . . to make sure."[104]

Dan Levin described in one of his dispatches from Saipan how the Japanese used civilians as a ruse: "A group of Japanese civilians approached a group of Marines, as if to surrender. Suddenly they part and run aside, revealing the rifles of Japanese troops behind them. One Marine is slain, others wounded. The rest leave no enemy alive."[105] It did not take many instances of Japanese deviousness for GIs to adopt a no-prisoners policy. If a Japanese soldier, even a wounded one, could not be trusted to surrender in accordance with the rules, then he would not be given the opportunity.

The North Korean enemy also proved to be devious. Higgins reported that "an amazing number of Chinese and Koreans spoke a little English. These men would strip overcoats and parkas from our dead soldiers and try to make us believe they were friends. Others learned to yell 'medic, medic' and trick us into revealing our positions."[106] North Korean soldiers frequently slipped on civilian clothes and attempted to infiltrate in the guise of refugees or local inhabitants. The marine forward observer Charles S. Crawford was convinced that the Korean funeral procession he was observing with his binoculars was actually a disguised cart, full of ammunition. He called in mortar fire on the procession, killing the four people accompanying the ox-drawn cart. There was no secondary explosion, however, and Crawford was never able to verify if he had killed civilians or enemy soldiers.[107]

The dilemma of sorting out innocent civilians from enemy combatants was even more pronounced during the Vietnam War, and William D. Ehrhart pointed out that there was often little time to decide: "There's Vietnamese around here, and there's VC. And most of the time, you don't know which is which until it's too late."[108] Hiding behind civilian clothes was a violation of the American soldier's concept of fighting fair, Jeff Yushta, a marine, asserted: "I could respect the NVA. . . . They put on the uniform and they came at you head on. . . . I never believed that there was honor between warriors on opposite sides of a battle, but I see that there is. But dealing with the Viet Cong was real hard because they didn't stand up and fight like men." The effect of facing an enemy who did not "fight like men," Yushta added, was that "it was real easy for me to dehumanize the Viet Cong."[109] Against an Asian foe who refused to fight fair, Americans tended to shoot first and take prisoners, or ascertain civilian status, later.

Moreover, Asian combat techniques contributed to the brutal nature of the fighting. The Asian foe, unlike the German, was firepower poor compared to his American enemy and therefore resorted to night fighting or unconventional warfare. The cover of darkness, often coupled with rugged terrain or jungle, allowed the enemy to infiltrate American positions, set up ambushes, or launch sharp assaults with little warning. Even in daytime, given the dense jungle terrain of the Pacific and portions of Vietnam, the killing was often at close range.[110] Hersey, covering the fighting on Guadalcanal, noted the enemy's seemingly animal-like jungle senses but also understood that the jungle protected him from American weaponry: "On the ridges, the Americans could dominate the jungle with their firepower, and they could see what was going on. In the jungle, the Japs could hide themselves in ambush, and they could lead the Americans into easy traps."[111]

Small wonder that Americans were loath to go into that jungle or down "into the valley," as Hersey entitled his account. But go they did, and some brutish fighting resulted. Daytime jungle fighting involved brief, small-unit encounters generally limited to small-arms fire. Such firefights were actually less lethal than the firepower-intensive combat of Europe, but they were shockers, as Clifford Fox, fighting on Guadalcanal, recalled: "Sometimes you'd exchange fire with some Japanese along a ridgeline. That might be a little way off. But in the jungle, it was always close, very close. It was face-to-face sometimes. Lord, sometimes men fought with bayonets."[112]

But the nastiest, most frightening combat occurred when the GIs dug in for the night and the Japanese infiltrators came calling. The infantryman Sam LaMagna describes the hellish nights on the Munda Trail on New Georgia Island: "At night it was an individual war with everyone fighting for his life. The screams pierced the jungle night and sent chills up my spine. . . . Every morning I'd hear who was killed or wounded. . . . Rumors went around that the Japs were yanking GIs out of their hole[s] by the helmets and to keep helmets unbuckled. At night I could hear teeth chattering."[113]

In Korea, the Asian foe did not have the benefit of jungle concealment, but the North Korean and Chinese enemy learned to move, infiltrate, and attack at night. Captain Averill, a marine fighting his second Asian war, conceded that "all of the Orientals play the night games extremely well."[114] S. L. A. Marshall noted that close-in night fighting, much like jungle fighting, deprived Americans of their long-range firepower: "Recognition of the enemy, as he comes forward, is most likely to occur at some distance between 15 and 150 yards . . . too close and too late for practical and successful artillery intervention."[115] Furthermore, unless barbed wire and mines were thickly laid, the enemy was also too close to stop before reaching American foxholes. Hand-to-hand combat was common fare in the Korean War. Corporal Joe Scheuber's description of a Chinese night assault captures how vicious this type of combat could be: "The fighting was heavy and confused. I turned to look back, hoping that some more of our people might be coming up to reinforce us. As I did, an enemy soldier shot my steel helmet off my head. I hit the ground and lost my rifle. I grabbed a grenade and threw it, never hearing it explode, though it must have. I saw the [South] Korean soldier who had been with me in the foxhole run his bayonet into a Chinese. There was a tremendous amount of noise and confusion, with bullets flying in every direction."[116]

During such close combat, dehumanizing racial stereotypes aside, all soldiers fought like animals, and no quarter was granted. Close-in fighting also occurred during the Vietnam War, given the jungle terrain, the enemy's tendency to move at night, and his preference for initiating ambushes at close range to preclude American use of artillery or air support. The grunt's frustration and anger levels were raised not only by the close-in nature of this fighting but also by the enemy's ability to run away after taking his toll. And when he ran away, he left behind his favorite calling cards, the booby trap and mine. The grunt was under the constant threat of danger from a populace containing enemies in civilian clothes who might snipe, throw a grenade, or plant a mine almost anywhere at any time. Private Ogden describes the demoralizing impact of this type of Viet Cong warfare: "Their spooklike hit-and-run tactics left gaping holes in our morale. The frustration of not being able to react in time creates a condition of tired, angry blood. . . . The Vietcong knew exactly what they were doing, and they were effective. Their continual harassment and evasion kept our anger, frustration, and jagged nerves at an optimum peak."[117]

A common analogy in the memoirs refers to shadow-boxing; John Sack described how it could wear on grunts: "On many, *most* of the veterans in Vietnam, one will discern an uneasy flitting of the eyes or an irresolute twitch at the corner of the mouth, it testifies how they've been a year in the field boxing shadows, taking up arms against a sea of unseen essences."[118] The enemy in Vietnam, in sum, violated just about every American conception of fair and conventional fighting.

The American soldier hated and dehumanized his Asian foes to varying degrees. The Viet Cong, for example, were more despicable for hiding behind civilian clothes and resorting to guerrilla warfare than were the North Vietnamese army regulars who fought conventionally and in uniform. Korean War GIs rated the North Koreans as more brutal, and hence more hated, than the Chinese. The Japanese enemy was probably the most loathed. The more the hatred, the greater the tendency to grant no mercy. Such foes should be hunted down like animals or even exterminated like vermin.

But where is the honor in extermination? Dave Grossman explains that killing a gallant foe confers honor on the victor: "The soldier is able to . . . rationalize his kill by honoring his fallen foes, thereby gaining stature and peace by virtue of the nobility of those he has slain."[119] But what happens to the victor when the enemy has been so dehumanized that he is no longer a noble adversary but a rabid animal to be destroyed? Sam Keen believes the victor is equally demeaned as a consequence: "The use of bestial images seems initially to be one of the better ways of dehumanizing an enemy because it allows soldiers to kill without incurring guilt. But the problem is that it allows the warrior-become-exterminator little sense of dignity or pride in his skill in battle. There is little emotional purgation gained from the slaughter of such an enemy—no heroic sparring with a worthy opponent. . . . Only an escalating brutality and insensitivity to suffering and death."[120]

That the American soldier often thought in terms of exterminating his less-than-human Asian foes is true enough, and occasional comments like the one by a sergeant in Bowman's novel imply that there was indeed little honor in such work: "Hell, . . . killing Japs isn't war. It's K.P.!" Yet in that same novel, which contains numerous virulent and demeaning comments about "Japs," Bowman adds: "He's an expert in counterpatrolling and skilled in preparing ambushes. He's got an instinct for camouflage, and patience and trigger-discipline. . . . He's counting on you to underestimate his toughness and spirit and the quality of his weapons and accuracy of fire, and he wants you to think he's stupid as hell when all the time he's a resourceful, wily little bastard who knows more about you than you know about him."[121]

The enemy may have been subhuman, treacherous, and heedless of human life, but he was also tough, clever, and determined. Mixed statements about the Japanese enemy, simultaneously professing their bravery and their inhumanity, were therefore common. Robert Stiles credited the "Nips" with being "tough, brave guys," but their practice of asking and giving "no quarter" could "become pretty crummy."[122] The army supply officer John Higgins admired "the fighting ability of the Japanese" but lost "respect for them as human beings" after witnessing the results of their massacres of Filipino civilians.[123]

Soldiers in later wars also acknowledged the skill and determination of their Asian foes. Captain Averill, who had fought in the Pacific in World War II, compared the North Koreans to the Japanese: "I was given the chance to do battalion operations against the Chinese and the North Koreans, the latter, in my estimation, coming very close to the Japanese in ferocity and tenacity."[124] Lieutenant Joseph R. Owen made a similar assessment of the North Koreans, who "were tough, skilled fighters, every bit as tenacious in battle as the Japanese had been in the bitter Pacific island fighting of the last war."[125]

The North Vietnamese army and, to a lesser extent, the Viet Cong were similarly accorded a measure of respect, even if the grunt could not understand or condone many of the enemy's methods. "Alice," a grunt in Gustav Hasford's *The Short-timers,* has mixed sentiments reminiscent of his predecessors' in earlier Asian wars: "Alice really understands the shrewd race of men who fight for survival in this garden of darkness—hard soldiers, strange, diminutive phantoms with iron insides, brass balls, incredible courage, and no scruples at all. They look small, but they fight tall, and their bullets are the same size as ours."[126]

Robert Sanders and his comrades "took care of business" when they met the enemy, confident that they could "get some scunnions out there on Charlie's ass," but they did not underestimate him: "He was good. 'Sir Charlie,' that was what we called him. We respected Charlie."[127]

Thus the Asian enemy, who did not fight by American rules and was hated for it, was nevertheless a skilled, tough, and determined opponent. The American soldier, therefore, was more than Keen's "warrior-become-exterminator," devoid of dignity, but instead took pride in overcoming a capable if vicious enemy. Robert Leckie could not decide if his Japanese enemy was brave or just inhumanly fanatical, but then it really did not matter. He was tough to beat in either case: "I can only wonder about this fierce mysterious enemy—so cruel and yet so courageous—a foe who could make me, in his utmost futility, fanaticism, if you will, call upon the best of myself to defend against him."[128] William Manchester revealed the heart of the matter when he pointed out that dehumanizing the Japanese enemy in no way diminished the pride of effort in defeating him: "At the time it was impolitic to pay the slightest tribute to the enemy, and Nip determination, their refusal to say die, was commonly attributed to 'fanaticism.'

In retrospect it is indistinguishable from heroism. To call it anything less cheapens the victory, for American valor was necessary to defeat it."[129]

## KILLING BEYOND THE REALM OF THE SANCTIFIED AND JUSTIFIED

The American soldier expected his enemy to fight by the same rules, or norms, that he did. To some extent these rules were formalized by various Hague and Geneva conventions, but in any case they reflected the American soldiers' sense of what was fair and proper: noncombatants (to include medics and chaplains) should not be harmed, soldiers should be permitted to surrender, prisoners should be treated humanely, and enemy dead should be properly, if unceremoniously, buried. Beyond humanitarian concerns, these norms helped ensure the combat soldier's survival if wounded or forced to surrender. Hence, if the enemy restricted himself to the justifiable killing of armed American combatants, then he would reciprocate.

Once the American soldier perceived that the enemy was regularly violating these norms by killing or torturing prisoners, mutilating corpses, or firing on medical personnel, however, he retaliated out of anger and a desire for revenge. A vicious downward spiral into brutality could then occur, with each side reacting to the other's atrocities. James J. Weingartner points out that conditions in the Pacific were ripe for just such a degeneration: "The mixture of underlying racism exacerbated by wartime propaganda in combination with hatred generated by Japanese aggression and real and imagined atrocities was a potent brew."[130]

On the battlefield, this potent brew could be powerful and fast acting. During his first campaign on Peleliu, Private Sledge saw the bodies of three dead marines that had been grotesquely mutilated by the Japanese. That was enough for him: "My emotions solidified into rage and a hatred for the Japanese beyond anything I had ever experienced. From that moment on I never felt the least pity or compassion for them no matter what the circumstances."[131]

The Vietnam War was nearly as brutal as the Pacific in World War II, and again a potent brew was at work: underlying racism, a harsh physical environment, atrocities, and an enemy whose unconventional fighting methods were alien to American conceptions of proper battlefield conduct. For Lieutenant Caputo, that meant a war without restraints:

Everything rotted and corroded quickly over there: bodies, boot leather, canvas, metal, morals. . . . We were fighting in the cruelest kind of conflict, a people's war. It was no orderly campaign, as in Europe, but a war for survival waged in a wilderness without rules or laws; a war in which each soldier fought for his own life and the lives of the men beside him, not caring who he killed in that personal cause or how many or in what manner and feeling only contempt for those who sought to impose on his savage struggle the mincing distinctions of civilized warfare—that code of battlefield ethics that attempted to humanize an essentially inhuman war.[132]

The fighting in Vietnam was undeniably vicious, but Caputo overstates the case in claiming that there were no rules and that the grunt did not care whom he killed. Even during the Vietnam War, the group set boundaries on which actions were justified. Leaders at all levels also played a key role in setting the standards of acceptable behavior. If senior leaders talked about the enemy in racist, exterminationist terms, then their soldiers felt less constrained. As Gerald Astor points out in his oral history of the fighting in the Pacific, "The denigration of the enemy as 'little yellow bastards' from the top brass down just made the killing easier."[133]

Even more influential in establishing group norms of behavior were the junior leaders. The men expected their leaders to tell them which actions were acceptable. Frederick Downs, in an article written years after his experience as a platoon leader in Vietnam, wrote that the leader made the difference between a disciplined unit and a murderous mob: "An officer's first job is to keep his men under control. . . . If he condones an immoral act, then they will lose respect for him—and he will lose control. . . . His behavior determines whether his men conduct themselves with dignity or become a mob, operating with a mob mentality in which all common sense and decency are washed away."[134]

Downs had learned this lesson the hard way in Vietnam. After a firefight in which several men were killed or wounded, a lightly wounded grunt began beating and kicking the lone NVA soldier whom they had captured. "It was obvious" that the grunt was "going to kill him," but Downs and the rest of his men, enraged over their losses, simply "stood smoking and watching." At that point the company commander intervened, rescuing the prisoner and chewing out Downs for failing in his responsibilities. After cooling off, Downs admitted, "I wanted the dink dead but the captain was right."[135] Downs had allowed his platoon to become a mob. In extreme cases, if the leadership did not restrain the men or, worse, if they condoned such actions, then a massacre on the scale of My Lai could occur.[136]

The killing of prisoners and other unacceptable acts, such as rape, pillaging, and the destruction of civilian property, occurred in varying degrees in all the wars of the draft era, and the junior leader's role in condoning or preventing these acts was often decisive. Lieutenant Lawrence, hearing a commotion on the line, arrived just in time to prevent his doughboys from killing a wounded German soldier. He then escorted the prisoner to the nearest dressing station, where he was told by the harried, overworked doctors to "take him out and shoot him."[137] Lawrence eventually got medical aid for the German and saw him safely to the rear with other prisoners.

During the Korean War, local villagers came to Lieutenant Brady, then serving as the intelligence officer for his battalion, and told him that two marines had raped two women at gunpoint. Brady was sent to investigate by his battalion executive officer, who told him, "I don't mind marines being a little wild. And I don't much like gooks. But we're not going to have rape. This battalion is going to have discipline."[138] Brady investigated diligently, and the guilty marines were identified and sent for court-martial.

The grunts in Matthew Brennan's aerorifle platoon destroyed an NVA kitchen area one day and captured several prisoners, one of whom was an attractive young woman. Several of the grunts were well along in their plans to rape and then kill her when their platoon leader, Lieutenant Rosen, arrived and put a stop to it: "'Forget it. I've already called in the prisoners [on the radio]. . . . The choppers are on their way in for extraction.' That took courage to say, considering our mood."[139]

Some junior leaders failed in their responsibilities to maintain discipline, however, often because they had grown as callous or vengeful as their men. During World War II, Captain Charles B. MacDonald's company was ordered to disengage from a firefight and withdraw. After successfully completing this difficult maneuver, MacDonald discovered that three German prisoners held by his second platoon were no longer present. Bringing the prisoners back in the midst of a fighting withdrawal would have been difficult, and it was unlikely that his men had simply left the prisoners behind alive. But MacDonald asked no questions: "Company G today committed a war crime. They are going to win the war, however, so I don't suppose it really matters."[140]

Junior leaders thus played a central role in setting and enforcing, or failing to enforce, standards of acceptable behavior toward prisoners and the civilian populace. These standards were also strongly influenced, however, by the group's desire to survive. A no-prisoners attitude was adopted in fighting the Japanese, for example, because of the widespread fear that a Japanese soldier, even a wounded one, would try to kill himself along with his would-be captors. Enough Japanese soldiers feigning surrender had grenades or explosives strapped to their bodies to add credence to that fear.[141] Even bringing in the occasional Japanese prisoner for interrogation proved difficult, as Astor notes: "Although U.S. higher-ups in search of intelligence — not for reasons of mercy — constantly urged the taking of prisoners, they were foiled by the unwillingness of the soldiers. The foremost reason given was an inability to trust the surrender as genuine."[142] Lieutenant Emil Matula's instructions to his platoon sums it up: "Shoot them first, and then question them later."[143]

A no-prisoners attitude crops up in other wars as well, although it was usually motivated by vengeance, not survival, as was the case with German SS troops after the Malmédy massacre. The military cameraman Walter Rosenblum filmed GIs shooting SS prisoners in Munich, Germany. He was upset by this brutality, but shortly thereafter he witnessed the handiwork of the SS at the Dachau concentration camp near Munich. Thereafter he accepted the massacre of SS prisoners: "These SS troops were so brazen. They acted as though nothing could hurt them. And they sneered at you. They acted the superrace."[144] Lieutenant Christopher Sturkey's tank-destroyer outfit "had no problem with regular German soldiers" who wanted to surrender, but the SS were another matter: "We had to kill SS men because they wouldn't surrender and wanted to fight to the death; they wanted it the hard way and that's just the way they got it."[145]

A no-prisoners attitude was not as consistently evident toward other enemies, but the discovery of enemy atrocities did generate relatively brief but often intense periods of revenge. The frequent excesses of the North Koreans often triggered such a response. During his first weeks of fighting in the Pusan Perimeter, Private Arnold Winter did not recall "having an opportunity to take prisoners," but after the discovery of mutilated marine bodies, he did not "think it was likely we would have taken any even given the chance." Winter had "no sympathy for the North Koreans. I never saw any of their atrocities myself, but there were quite a few reports of American GI's who were found shot in ditches with their hands tied behind their backs. Apparently they took no prisoners."[146]

Sometimes a no-prisoners attitude applied to specific enemy soldiers in retaliation for not abiding by American concepts of fairness. During World War I, the doughboys' nemesis was the machine gun, which the Germans made increasing use of in lieu of dwindling manpower. Carl Andrew Brannen noted that the operators of these death-dealing weapons received no quarter: "A machine gunner's only chance was to be taken while he was away from the gun and his captors did not know he had any connection with it. The reason is obvious, for when a man sat behind a gun and mowed down a bunch of men, his life was automatically forfeited."[147]

GIs felt the same way about snipers. Ernie Pyle understood why: "Sniping, as far as I know, is recognized as a legitimate means of warfare. And yet there is something sneaking about it that outrages the American sense of fairness."[148] During Private Blunt's first stint in combat, a German sniper killed a GI and then attempted to surrender when Blunt's squad closed in on his location: "A white flag started waving from a window and the sniper surrendered. We surrounded him and then, in a spontaneous outburst of hatred, every man in the squad fired at once. It was an eye for an eye. Many times later I learned that snipers were seldom taken alive."[149]

At times, neither survival instincts nor revenge, but simple convenience, provided the impetus for a no-prisoners attitude. Exhausted, harried captors could not be bothered with escorting a few enemy prisoners rearward. During the successful but exhausting and bloody Allied Soissons counteroffensive in World War I, Elton Mackin's friend Bill was escorting German prisoners, some of them wounded, to the rear. After four days of combat and continuous advancing, Bill "showed the effects of heavy cannon fire and nerve shock. He showed the strain of thirst and hunger; of weariness and—was it stifled fear?" After a brief halt, one of the wounded Germans could not go on: "The man sitting on the stump refused to move, or tried, then shook his head in helplessness."[150] Bill shot him and the rest of the prisoners moved on.

In the dead of winter on a frozen mountaintop in Korea, a lone North Korean soldier appeared before the American trench line. His feet were horribly frostbitten and he wanted to surrender. Taking him prisoner meant escorting him down the steep, ice-covered mountain, and as Corporal Crawford pointed out, "A man would have to go down the hill slow, really slow, and with a gook prisoner in front of him, his downward progress would be more severely curtailed . . . [and] the enemy looked for a target of opportunity."[151] The North Korean soldier shuffled up and down the trench line on his frozen feet, waving a surrender leaflet, but no one would accept his surrender. Finally, a marine killed him with a burst of machine-gun fire.

The considerable trouble and risk involved in escorting this enemy soldier off the mountain explains why he was shot instead. In some cases, however, killing for convenience made no sense at all except that some soldiers seemed to enjoy it, or at least did it without a second thought. During World War II, Sergeant Nat Frankel, perched in the commander's hatch of his tank, chafed at his snail's-pace progress as he herded four German prisoners in front of him. A sergeant from the infantry outfit that he was supporting pulled up in a jeep and asked if he could relieve Frankel of his burden. The tank sergeant readily agreed, and the infantryman loaded the prisoners into his jeep. The jeep then disappeared around an embankment, and Frankel drove off in his tank. Before going very far, Frankel heard gunfire from behind the embankment and a few seconds later the infantry sergeant drove his empty jeep past Frankel's tank: "He smiled as he drove past, smiled and waved."[152]

The group might condone the killing of surrendering enemies if survival or revenge were at stake, but this sort of blatant, cold-blooded killing did not meet with the average GI's approval. Individual standards of behavior usually came into play at these times. Some soldiers, often the psychopathic ones, liked killing and did not especially care if it was within the bounds of what the group considered acceptable. Peter Watson, citing his own and other studies of Vietnam veterans who admitted to mutilating bodies or mistreating prisoners, concluded that "although the conditions of war may make anyone a potential mass murderer, some men *are* more prone to kill indiscriminately than others."[153] Or as William B. Gault put it, the atmosphere of war allows for "the natural dominance of the psychopath."[154]

Lieutenant Caputo loved the marines in his platoon in Vietnam, but he also came to realize that they were not angels: "I had seen them as contemporary versions of Willie and Joe, tough guys who at heart were decent and good. I now realized that some of them were not so decent or good."[155] Matthew Brennan provides an illuminating rundown of the more "interesting fellows" in his aerorifle platoon: a squad leader named James who kept extending his tour "because I like to kill"; a medic named "Hippie Doc" who once bandaged a wounded NVA soldier and "then stabbed him to death as he thanked Doc for saving his life"; and a machine gunner, Hill, who "carried an enormous Bowie knife" for cutting off ears and even heads of enemy dead and who "once stomped an NVA to death" with his size-thirteen boots.[156]

The group did not approve of such excesses, and in some cases soldiers or junior leaders reported these atrocities to higher authorities. The group also did not condone, but understood and usually overlooked, the excesses of soldiers who temporarily "went crazy" out of grief and rage. In Leinbaugh's and Campbell's Company K in World War II, "One man whose best friend had just been killed took revenge on four prisoners. He said they had jumped him and tried to escape—maybe they had, but he got no more escort duty."[157]

During the Vietnam War, Robert Mason's helicopter was dispatched to pick up NVA prisoners. Arriving, he discovered to his horror that a sergeant was systematically executing the trussed-up prisoners with a bullet to the head. Mason began to protest, but a grunt explained to him that the previous night the enemy had tortured and killed six of the sergeant's men. The sergeant could hear their screams all night. In the morning the bodies were discovered with their dismembered genitals shoved in their mouths: "This isn't murder; it's justice. . . . You'll get 'em. They'll just be dead, is all."[158]

At the other extreme from those who loved the killing were the soldiers who, no matter how provoked, retained a measure of restraint. For most soldiers, situational ethics could excuse only so much. Peter Marin observes that although some grunts "participated mindlessly" in the Vietnam War, "countless others, even in the middle of battle, made anguishing moral choices."[159]

Soldiers in all wars were confronted with tough moral choices. The doughboy William H. Houghton was captured during the Argonne fighting. He was escorted to the rear by a young, friendly, and obviously inexperienced German soldier who led, rather than followed, his prisoners and kept his rifle slung on his shoulder. Houghton had a large pocket knife—the Germans had failed to search him thoroughly—and he considered stabbing his lone guard and escaping. Such a move would have been acceptable behavior in almost any soldier's estimation, but Houghton "just didn't have the heart to kill a young boy in cold blood like that. I'd fired my rifle any number of times in combat, but that was different. All in all, I'm glad I didn't do it."[160]

During World War II, Roscoe Blunt witnessed the execution-style shooting of two German prisoners for no apparent reason. Blunt had killed many armed opponents and hated the SS, but he drew the line at murdering unarmed *Wehrmacht* prisoners: "I was torn, on the one hand, between my hatred for the Germans for their atrocities in Belgium and, on the other hand, what I considered the limits of human decency. What I had witnessed went beyond that limit. I was ambiguous about how I should feel about the episode, but I was certain about one thing: I never could have committed such a brutal murder."[161]

During the retreat from the Chosin Reservoir during the Korean War, the marines had difficulty evacuating their own equipment and personnel, let alone enemy prisoners, and a no-prisoners attitude was much in evidence. Private

Ernest Gonzalez discovered the hard way, however, that this policy went beyond what he in good conscience could do: "Word was passed to kill all enemy wounded. I found one Chinese curled up, lying facedown. He had a head wound . . . . I fired into his midriff. He turned slowly and looked at me as if saying, 'Why must you make me suffer more?' Although it remained a common practice on both sides, I never again killed another wounded Chinese soldier."[162]

While some soldiers refused to mistreat or kill enemy prisoners for moral and ethical reasons, others realized that abandoning restraint was foolish for pragmatic reasons. Lieutenant Hervey Allen rejected the recommendation of his unit's British and French trainers in World War I to take no prisoners because, "aside from any other considerations, this was a stupid policy."[163] Surrenders must be accepted, "otherwise the enemy resisted to the last, which cost us many unnecessary casualties," but a lenient policy "encouraged the Germans to surrender more easily."[164]

During a conflict like Vietnam, with its elements of unconventional and civil war, mistreating prisoners or civilians would certainly not contribute to the critical goal of winning the hearts and minds of the people. A grunt in Private Parks's outfit killed a VC suspect in front of his wife and three children, claiming the man had tried to escape. Parks understood that whatever the suspect's guilt, this grunt had just made new enemies: "I can't stop thinking about those kids. They'll hate us the rest of their lives. And who can blame them?"[165]

Most soldiers thus refused, for a variety of practical and ethical reasons, to kill or destroy indiscriminately. Yet the environment of war greatly complicated the process of determining whether killing was justified or not. Were soldiers in the Pacific justified in killing all Japanese attempting to surrender because in some cases it was a ruse? Enough Japanese legitimately attempted to surrender to prove that not all were suicidally inclined. Was an enraged soldier justified, or to be forgiven, for killing a surrendering sniper who had moments before shot his best buddy? Were grunts to be faulted for destroying a village that undoubtedly harbored the Viet Cong who had just triggered a deadly command-detonated mine? The "critical issue," as Tobey C. Herzog sees it, is "who or what is ultimately responsible for . . . [the] descent into this brutish state. . . . Does the burden of responsibility rest with individuals (the evil within), or is the war environment to blame (the evil without)?"[166]

Soldiers had to deal with this issue of responsibility. Some believed their actions were justified because the environment of war left them no choice. Sergeant Frankel freely admits that "there were times that we acted like butchers," but so be it: "The longer you're in a war, the more your moral attentiveness wears down. You become less scrupulous, or at least less assiduous. Well, all soldiers are expected to behave like butchers. Eventually you become one."[167]

If the environment of war is to blame for turning soldiers into butchers, then the Vietnam War produced, according to Caputo, some real "brutes": "It was the dawn of creation in the Indochina bush, an ethical as well as a geographical wilderness. Out there, lacking restraints, sanctioned to kill, confronted by a hostile country and a relentless enemy, we sank into a brutish state."[168] Lieutenant Downs agrees with Caputo, pointing out that "the philosophical arguments in favor of man's ability to resist the slide into barbarism sound noble and rational in a classroom or at a cocktail party," but in the kill-or-be-killed environment of war, "every day we spent in the jungle eroded a little more of our humanity away."[169]

Given the number of veterans suffering some degree of guilt or remorse over what they did during their wars, however, it is clear that if a soldier went beyond what was justifiable and necessary in combat, then he was likely to pay an emotional price. Robert Jay Lifton points out that even though the soldier was immersed in a brutalizing environment that fostered atrocities, he was not absolved of "an irreducible element of individual responsibility."[170] "Joker," the protagonist in *The Short-timers,* after killing an old farmer in a fit of rage, understood too late the implications—he could not leave his personal responsibility behind when he left Vietnam: "I was defining myself with bullets; blood had blemished my Yankee Doodle dream that everything would have a happy ending, and that I, when the war was over, would return to hometown America in a white silk uniform, a rainbow of campaign ribbons across my chest."[171] As a platoon leader, James McDonough considered it his responsibility to prevent grunts like "Joker" from crossing that line, because they would not then be able to erase what they had done: "War gives the appearance of condoning almost everything, but men must live with their actions for a long time afterward. A leader has to help them understand that there are lines they must not cross. He is their link to normalcy, to order, to humanity. If the leader loses his own sense of propriety, or shrinks from his duty anything will be allowed. And anything can happen."[172]

Throughout the Vietnam War novel *Fragments,* Sergeant Bill Morgan grapples with the issue of responsibility in war. Blaming the environment for one's own excesses seemed to have advantages: "There was something seductive about surrendering to forces outside your control, beyond choice or blame." But like McDonough, he realizes that "if you surrendered" to those dark forces, then "how could you be sure you wouldn't go too far? This was the knot: Either there was nothing you could do about it or else there wasn't anything you might not do. . . . That was the personal problem." Morgan eventually concludes that the soldier could not abdicate his responsibility, even, to borrow from Caputo, in the "wilderness" of Indochina: "I understood . . . now, understood it all. . . . The war was to blame, but we were the war. Facts and forces drove us, but we gave them their mortal shape. The final necessity was choice."[173]

## GUILT AND THE RATIO OF FIRE

If only for his own peace of mind, the average soldier would not kill or commit destructive acts beyond what he and the group considered justified or necessary.

Soldiers who crossed the line and committed atrocities in a fit of rage or because they had lost their moral compass in the wilderness of combat often paid a heavy price in guilt. What the group considered justifiable killing varied by war and by foe, but in all cases the uniformed and still-resisting enemy was fair game. Killing him was what the soldier was there to do. Some historians and psychologists believe, however, that despite sanctification, justifications, and the catalyst of the battlefield, the American soldier retained an ingrained reluctance to kill that enemy.

The most famous proponent of this argument is Samuel L. A. Marshall. Based on his findings from four hundred company-level, postcombat interviews in the Pacific and European theaters in World War II, he claimed that at most 25 percent of the American infantry soldiers capable of bringing their weapons to bear during a battle did so. Marshall attributed the GI's reluctance to fire in part to the "paralysis which comes of varying fears. The man afraid wants to do nothing; indeed, he does not care even to think of taking action." But even more important, the "average, normal man who is fitted into the uniform of an American ground soldier" did not shoot because of his socialized aversion to killing:

He is what his home, his religion, his schooling, and the moral code and ideals of his society have made him. The army cannot unmake him. It must reckon with the fact that he comes from a civilization in which aggression, connected with the taking of life, is prohibited and unacceptable. . . . This is his great handicap when he enters combat. It stays his trigger finger even though he is hardly conscious that it is a restraint upon him. Because it is an emotional and not an intellectual handicap, it is not removable by intellectual reasoning, such as: "Kill or be killed."

Furthermore, the soldier's junior leaders "pay little attention to the true nature of this mental block," erroneously assuming that the soldier, based on his training, "loves to fire" and does so in combat.[174]

Students of soldier behavior, having no reason to doubt Marshall's claim that his ratio of fire was based on exhaustive personal observation and research, accepted the fact that three out of four American soldiers did not fire in combat because they were too scared or put off by the thought of killing. Richard Gabriel states that "during World War II, no more than 15 percent of the soldiers in American frontline combat battalions ever fired their weapons at the enemy regardless of whether they were attacking or being attacked. Most soldiers were simply so afraid that they did nothing but stay in their holes."[175] The Canadian historian John A. English, after citing Marshall's fire ratio, added that "it should not be surprising, then, that the most common cause of local defeat in minor tactics is usually attributed to 'the shrinkage of fire,' whereas the Germans had little problem maintaining their volume of fire."[176] The historian Russell F. Weigley cited

Marshall's ratio in his history of the campaign in Europe as evidence that the American infantry was "not particularly aggressive." Weigley agreed with Marshall that this lack of aggressiveness was in part because "almost all American soldiers were conditioned from infancy not to kill."[177]

Harold P. Leinbaugh came across Marshall's ratio of fire while researching for his history of his rifle company, *The Men of Company K*. He arrived at a radically different conclusion from the historians, however. He decided that Marshall's theory was "absurd, ridiculous, and totally nonsensical." Canvassing his fellow K Company veterans, he found that "none of them recalled any experience of failure to fire. One old K Company sergeant asked, 'Did the SOB [Marshall] think that we *clubbed* the Germans to death?'"[178]

Leinbaugh discussed his doubts about Marshall's ratio of fire with the historian Roger J. Spiller, who then sifted through Marshall's notes and journals and interviewed his contemporaries, only to find that Marshall had not surveyed the companies he had interviewed on the issue of refusing to fire. Nor had Marshall and his assistants conducted any number close to 400 company-level interviews. Spiller's convincing findings were published in articles in 1988 and 1989 and concluded that "the systematic collection of data that made Marshall's ratio of fire so authoritative appears to have been an invention."[179]

Spiller's findings should have prompted anyone writing after 1989 to use Marshall's theory only with serious reservations, yet some authors continued to cite his ratio without qualifications.[180] In addition to Spiller's research, which by itself raises serious doubts about Marshall's fire ratio, the findings of other historians and psychiatrists and the further testimony of soldiers like Leinbaugh's sergeant refute the idea that a significant number of infantrymen, let alone 75 percent, consistently failed to fire on the enemy in the midst of battle. Based solely on the evidence of American performance in combat in World War II, Marshall's ratio of fire seems highly improbable. A 1994 study of American tactics in the European theater by the historian Michael D. Doubler provides a needed corrective to the image of the American infantryman as unaggressive and even cowardly by showing how versatile and effective he really was. Not surprisingly, Doubler has serious doubts about the validity of Marshall's ratio: "An exhaustive review of anecdotal evidence, unit after-action reports, and training literature suggests that Marshall's figures on the number of active firers are too conservative and that many more soldiers were pulling the trigger. Furthermore, it is hard to believe that an army attacking prepared defenses for the better part of an entire year could have accomplished much of anything with only one quarter of its soldiers firing their weapons."[181]

The anecdotal evidence Doubler refers to comes from soldiers' memoirs and interviews. Captain MacDonald described a desperate fight during the Battle of the Bulge in which, after a series of German assaults, his company was overrun. Succeeding waves of attacking German infantry were met with "volley after volley" from MacDonald's defending platoons. "All three platoons and the 60mm mortars began to beg for more ammunition," and MacDonald sent runners to find some. "Seven times the enemy infantry assaulted, and seven times they were greeted by a hail of small-arms fire and hand grenades that sent them reeling down the hill, leaving behind a growing pile of dead and wounded." MacDonald's company, possessing only one bazooka and three shells, was overrun only when German Tiger tanks attacked.[182]

Lieutenant Wilson's platoon was caught in a surprise attack by about forty German soldiers just as his men were starting to dig in following an advance in the Huertgen Forest: "We instantly dropped our shovels, lay down in the shallow beginnings of our foxholes, and fired back with all we had." The Germans, armed mostly with bolt-action rifles, "proved no match for the volleys of our Browning Automatic Rifles . . . and semiautomatic M-1 [rifles]. The Krauts were stopped about seventy-five yards in front of us."[183]

As Wilson implies, the GIs discovered that volume of fire often made the difference.[184] On the other hand, marksmanship was not obsolete, especially when defending positions. Sergeant Ross S. Carter and his fellow paratroopers stopped a German counterattack in Italy with aimed fire: "Since only a few of our machine guns and automatic rifles had reached us, it was up to the riflemen and tommy gunners to hold off the assault." The troopers hunkered down in their holes and "calmly squeezed off their shots. . . . American riflemen were always the best in the world, and our . . . riflemen were among the best in the army. In about thirty minutes the attack was broken up."[185]

These examples, provided by junior leaders, indicate not only that a majority of infantrymen engaged the enemy but also that the leaders themselves were well aware of the volume and effect of their units' fires. Marshall's contention that the junior leader in World War II was not even conscious of nonfiring is a dubious theory. Leaders and men alike were aware of, and did not condone, nonfirers—and there were a few, usually men too scared to take action. A nonfirer threatened the group's survival and was not doing his share. Private Standifer was one of those soldiers who had genuine qualms about killing, but he decided that refusing to fire was not fair to the rest: "Some had shot to wound, but not to kill. All of that was considered reasonable; what was contemptible were the eight balls who simply wouldn't fight. This wasn't a matter of integrity, but of simple cowardice: when you fire your rifle, it attracts attention and you get shot at. The men who wouldn't fire were a complete drag, without the courage to fight or to refuse. If you won't fire your rifle, you are useless."[186]

World War II psychiatrist Edwin A. Weinstein noticed that some of his psychiatric casualties were "passive, dependent" types who "developed anxiety rapidly" and often broke down early. One such broken soldier arrived in Weinstein's hospital, complete with a note from his platoon leader: "I personally have never seen him fire his rifle at the enemy—when all the others were out of their holes and in firing position he would seem to be 'froze' in his hole with his head down. . . . All in all . . . he does not come up to par with the average infantryman and is decidedly a bad influence on the other men."[187]

This lieutenant certainly noticed his nonfirer, and it is also evident that this soldier was the exception and that his inaction was unacceptable to the group. Lieutenant Wilson, now a company commander, was again caught by surprise, this time by a German patrol armed with machine pistols, not bolt-action rifles. The heavy enemy fire drove his men, many of whom were new replacements, under cover, and "very few of them even attempted to fire back." The officers immediately returned fire and began "yelling at the men to start shooting." Wilson rousted a dozen soldiers from their holes and led them on a flanking attack, killing several Germans and capturing one.[188] This short, sharp, deadly action is informative. The officers were well aware of nonfiring, brought on by the understandable fact that the enemy had pinned the men down. Wilson and his leaders reacted quickly to correct the problem and to drive off the enemy with handheld infantry weapons.

If historians and veterans of the European theater in World War II put little credence in Marshall's theory, then historians who have studied the vicious, no-mercy fighting in the Pacific are especially dumbfounded that Marshall would claim that American soldiers were reluctant to kill. Craig M. Cameron, in his study of the First Marine Division, found Marshall's theory a "specious argument to assuage moral sensibilities among civilians." In reality, Americans put into uniform and given guns "proved as adept and ruthless in the exercise of violence as their totalitarian enemies."[189]

Gerald Astor, who interviewed dozens of veterans of the Pacific fighting, found the notion ludicrous that three out of four infantrymen failed to engage the enemy: "The interviews with the sources for this book indicate that only a desire to avoid giving away a position kept fingers off the triggers." For those green soldiers who did have reservations about killing, "the experience of enemy fire and the deaths of fellow GIs swiftly snuffed out regard for the Sixth Commandment."[190]

Some students of soldier behavior, like Elmar Dinter, even hold to a theory diametrically opposed to Marshall's: "The average person does not particularly worry about killing. Such 'fear' is an ancient myth and it can be removed from the list of possible anxieties. Deep down in his subconscious, man seems to enjoy killing."[191] Though some soldiers did enjoy killing, Dinter undoubtedly overstates his case. His observation, however, that soldiers do "not particularly worry about killing," as long as that killing falls within the bounds of what is justified, contains much truth. Jules W. Coleman, a division psychiatrist in World War II, found that "there is little guilt associated with killing the enemy." Furthermore, "The destruction of the enemy is an act of vengeance, and serves the purpose of adequately discharging emotions of hatred and impulses of aggression."[192]

The main flaw in Marshall's theory, or in Dinter's for that matter, is the assumption of social homogeneity. Cameron takes Marshall to task for presenting a "monolithic image . . . both as related to how all American soldiers feel and regarding the cultural heritage used as a measure."[193] Soldiers' attitudes toward killing were more diverse than Marshall's theory allowed for. Some soldiers, although nothing close to three out of four, were indeed reluctant, for religious or ethical reasons, to kill even an armed opponent. Yet the consciences of most soldiers were assuaged by society's sanctification and the combat group's justifications for killing the enemy. And indeed a few amoral or pathological types found slaughter to their liking.

The memoirs reflect this range of attitudes toward killing and guilt. Corporal Crawford, after killing his first enemy soldier in Korea (there would be eighty-five confirmed kills—he kept count), found that it "did not make me happy, nor did it make me unhappy." He decided to ask his buddies how they reacted to killing, and he received a variety of answers: "Some of the grunts said they felt guilty but couldn't give me any reason for their guilt; it was, after all, their job to kill gooks. Other grunts said that, because of their religious beliefs, they were afraid after they knew for certain they had killed a gook, but they couldn't explain their fear. Some grunts said they found it exciting, the knowledge they had just killed someone."[194]

Lieutenant Downs provides a similar survey of how the soldiers in his platoon in Vietnam reacted to killing. Like Crawford, he found a wide range of attitudes, although he includes no category of soldiers who abstained totally from firing:[195]

It turned out that most of us liked to kill other men. Some of the guys would shoot at a dink much as they would at a target. Some of the men didn't like to kill a dink up close. The closer the killing, the more personal it became.

Others in the platoon liked to kill close in. A few even liked to torture the dinks if they had a prisoner or cut the dead bodies with knives in a frenzy of aggression.

A few didn't like to kill at all and wouldn't fire their weapons except to protect their buddies.

Mostly, we all saw it as a job and rationalized it in our own way. Over it all ran the streak of anger or fear that for brief moments ruled us all.[196]

Downs raises another issue affecting the willingness to kill. Many soldiers did not like to kill up close, but at long range the killing was impersonal. Dave Grossman provides a good analysis of the effect of distance on attitudes toward killing. As the physical distance increases, the resistance to killing decreases, because, as Grossman notes, "from a distance, you don't look anything like a friend."[197]

Soldiers confirm the relative emotional ease of killing at long range. In World War I Elton Mackin and his fellow marines waited for the order to open fire on attacking Germans with unconcealed eagerness: "Men craned their necks to watch the officers, impatient for the word to open fire. Even our replacements felt the urge of it. Killing at long range is such an impersonal thing: a sporty test of the nerves, like practice on the training range. Here was fair game." The marines, known for their marksmanship, stopped the attack solely with aimed rifle fire. Everyone fired and, Mackin believes, almost all shot to kill: "Do very many *try* to miss? Some fellows tell you things in confidence, but you seldom hear them mention that."[198]

Mackin's hunting and target-practice analogies are common in descriptions of long-range killing. Flushing a covey of quail is a frequently repeated analogy. MacDonald's men opened fire on some Germans fleeing across a field: "The infantrymen sat calmly at the bases of trees and shot at them as if they might have been quail on the rise."[199] Lieutenant Sefton shot a fleeing German, remembering "to lead the angling runner like a rising quail."[200]

Enemies killed up close, however, were not quail, but people. Lieutenant James Hamilton Dill was ambushed at close range by Chinese soldiers during the Korean War. Miraculously, he was not hit, and the GIs with him cut down the ambushers: "It was not my first close call, and I was sure it would not be the last, but I had looked directly into the face of a man trying to kill me. I then watched him die in agony. I had never before had an experience so personal."[201]

Nothing was more personal, or more traumatic for some soldiers, than hand-to-hand combat. During a commando-style raid by Rangers in North Africa in World War II, Sergeant James Altieri found himself face-to-face with an Italian soldier in a narrow slit trench. Altieri reacted first, plunging his knife into the soldier's stomach: "'*Mamma mia,*' he cried. '*Mamma mia.*' I felt the hot blood spurt all over my right arm as I pulled the knife out, then rammed it home again and again. As the body sagged and slid to the ground, I reeled and vomited."[202]

Close-up killing was common during the night fighting in Korea. Sergeant Warren Avery's platoon, rushing forward to help a sister platoon caught in a Chinese ambush, overran some enemy positions almost before they realized it: "I jumped over an enemy foxhole; the Chinese soldier looked up at me and I down at him. I didn't have the guts to blow him away with my carbine, but I did throw a grenade after I got beyond him. At least I didn't have to look at him when he died."[203] Avery was not the only soldier who was squeamish over the thought of having to kill a man face-to-face.

Conversely, some soldiers discovered that they liked killing, at whatever distance, and this realization gave rise to guilt over not feeling guilty. For Private Blunt, "killing had become a challenge, even a need, and I found myself constantly seeking fulfillment."[204] He enjoyed killing, not in cold blood, but as part of the game of besting the enemy. He knew he was not supposed to feel this way and it bothered him:

I worried about the killing lust that I knew had built up inside me. I tried to convince myself that I was only impartially doing the job I had been trained to do, but still, I was experiencing troubled emotions. . . . I was well aware my moral conscience was constantly in conflict with my familial and religious upbringing, but I seemed powerless to resolve the differences. Circumstances had forced me into a life over which I had no control, but still I was concerned that I wasn't even trying to control it, just going along with it—and even, distressingly, sometimes enjoying it.[205]

Lieutenant Caputo became disillusioned with the war in Vietnam by the end of his tour there, but for a long time, like Blunt, he reveled in the challenge of combat: "I knew . . . that something in me was drawn to war. It might have been an unholy attraction, but it was there and it could not be denied."[206] Also like Blunt, he knew that the average, God-fearing American should not feel this "unholy attraction." After a fierce firefight culminating in the destruction of a village, Caputo was "disturbed" over "the dark, destructive emotions I had felt throughout the battle . . . urges to destroy that seemed to rise from the fear of being destroyed myself. I had enjoyed the killing of the Viet Cong who had run out of the tree line."[207]

Dan Levin carried Caputo's and Blunt's thought process a step further: feeling guilty over enjoying killing was just a rationalization. After joining his comrades in gunning down a fleeing Japanese soldier "like furious animals after prey flushed from hiding," Levin "suddenly realized" that this prey was human, but "even as I felt this horror at myself, I knew it was a device for taking the curse off my eager joy at being the hunter."[208] Private Sledge, after killing a Japanese soldier at close range, shared Levin's initial horror: "That I had seen clearly the pain on his face when my bullets hit him came as a jolt. . . . The expression on that man's face filled me with shame and then disgust for the war and all the misery it was causing." Feelings of horror, however, were quickly displaced by feelings of foolishness: "My combat experience thus far made me realize that such sentiments for an enemy soldier were the maudlin meditations of a fool . . . feeling ashamed because I had shot a damned foe before he could throw a grenade at me! I felt like a fool and was thankful that my buddies couldn't read my thoughts."[209]

A few soldiers actually felt the way Marshall said they should. For religious and cultural reasons, they had an aversion to killing. Yet even these reluctant warriors did not fail to shoot to save their own or their comrades' lives. Sergeant York killed twenty or more Germans during the famous fight for which he won a Congressional Medal of Honor because it was "them or me." But the pious sergeant remained troubled by it: "Jes the same I have tried to forget. I have never talked about it much. I have never told the story even to my own mother."[210]

Lieutenant Elliott Johnson, an artillery forward observer in World War II, was equally troubled by killing. He once called a destructive barrage of high-explosive and white-phosphorus shells on a massed target of German vehicles and soldiers. He could not put the resulting carnage out of his mind: "The dev-astation on that little piece of land . . . was incredible. It's one of my bad memo-ries, the suffering." Johnson even killed a "German boy" face-to-face while clearing bunkers: "Again, an unpleasant memory." He was a confirmed pacifist by VE-Day: "I was raised in a house that believed in God. . . . But it took some-thing like this [war] to hammer it home to me: I am totally averse to killing and warfare."[211]

Religious beliefs were often the main cause of a soldier's anxiety over killing. Douglas Anderson encountered marines in his battalion in Vietnam who, having been brought up in religious Baptist families, "were having a lot of trou-ble killing people." Though Anderson did not mention nonfirers, he believed that these reluctant killers sometimes hesitated an extra moment before shooting, and that could prove fatal: "This cost some of them their lives because the minute they would begin to think, they would move just a little less quickly . . . and pause just a little bit more before shooting at somebody."[212]

If a soldier did suffer guilt over killing, his comrades would try to console him as long as they believed his actions were justified. A soldier in Brennan's platoon captured a khaki-clad enemy who appeared to be unarmed, but the man suddenly reached into his pocket. The grunt, assuming he was reaching for a pis-tol or a grenade, killed him. The shot attracted the other grunts, who found their buddy standing over his victim with "big tears rolling down his cheeks." The enemy soldier, it turned out, was a doctor; he had been reaching for bandages to prove his noncombatant status. The distraught grunt was justified in shooting, however, so his comrades tried to make him feel better. His platoon sergeant said, "Don't take it so hard. This is war and people get killed."[213]

People did indeed get killed in war, and the close-range, personal killing done by the infantry was the hardest. Few men enjoyed that sort of killing, but most did it willingly enough when their comrades' and their own lives were on the line. Nor did most soldiers suffer guilt, especially in quantities sufficient to stay trigger fingers, over dispatching an armed enemy whose killing was sancti-fied and justified by country, cause, and comrades. Rather than a guilt-ridden GI frozen with fear, the picture that emerges from the literary evidence is that of an American soldier confident in his ability to defeat his enemies. One of the rea-sons for this confidence was the GI's faith in his leaders. Soldier-memoirists comment frankly on their leaders, good and bad, thus providing valuable insights into the role of the junior combat leader and the qualities he needed to succeed.

# 9
# Leadership in Combat

.

If the skills and attributes desired in an officer in peacetime, when serving on the staff, or on attaining senior grade were added up, the list would be quite lengthy. But for the junior leader in combat, as Lord Charles McM. Moran discovered during World War I, the "simplest virtues" sufficed: "When . . . I search the pages of my diary, which is concerned with the personal leadership of platoons, companies, and the battalion itself, for the particular qualities which give to a few dominion over their fellows I can discern only the simplest virtues."[1] Lee Kennett, in his study of the World War II GI, provides a succinct yet comprehensive summary of those virtues: "G.I.s did not hesitate to point out the qualities they looked for in those who led them: They wanted officers—and noncoms—who led by example, who had confidence in themselves, and who knew their jobs; but they also wanted leaders who knew and cared about the men, shared jokes and hardships with them, and were careful to keep them informed and to explain the purpose of their missions."[2] What men wanted and deserved, then, were tactically and technically proficient leaders who took care of them and shared in their privations and dangers. Simple virtues indeed, though easier listed than realized. Memoirs of American soldiers and junior leaders from World War I through the Vietnam War provide eloquent testimony to the importance of these virtues.

## TACTICAL AND TECHNICAL PROFICIENCY

The expertise required to lead a platoon or company in combat is more complex than most laymen appreciate. The leader must be able to deploy his men tactically and have a working knowledge of his unit's weapons and equipment. Bill Mauldin, in his version of the attributes desirable in a combat leader, placed expertise at the top of the list: "The ideal officer in any army knows his business. . . .

He is saluted and given the respect due a man who knows enough about war to boss soldiers around in it."[3] Such expertise was essential because men's lives hung in the balance, as Frederick Downs, a platoon leader during the Vietnam War, noted: "The chain of command was counting on the officer for the success of the mission and the men were counting on the officer to survive the mission. The men did not give a hoot in hell whether the officer came from West Point, ROTC, or the moon. They wanted the officer to keep them alive and not do anything stupid."[4]

The skills a leader needed obviously varied by type of unit, but they generally included, according to William Darryl Henderson, a "proven ability to carry out a tactical plan, to arrange for and adjust artillery, to demonstrate professional expertise with weapons, to navigate well, and to provide medical care and supplies."[5] Successful leaders understood the importance of this "expert power," as Henderson calls it, in gaining the confidence of the men. The platoon leader Michael Lee Lanning, on the day of his promotion to first lieutenant in Vietnam, understood that green second lieutenants were sometimes the "brunt of jokes" and were "often portrayed as naive bumblers." But if that "bumbling" second lieutenant had paid attention during his training, then he was likely to be "the most knowledgeable soldier in the platoon. . . . His abilities to call in artillery, air, and dust-offs [medevac helicopters] were qualities not to be joked about."[6]

Before a lieutenant could call in artillery, airstrikes, or medevac helicopters, however, he had to know precisely where he was. Lanning realized that "the easiest way to lose the confidence of the men was not to know the unit's location at all times."[7] One of those long-standing lieutenant jokes is that there is nothing more dangerous than a second lieutenant with a map and compass. But for the men whose officer was inept at using these tools, the joke was not funny. For example, the doughboy Joseph D. Lawrence, before departing for officers' candidate school, learned how not to lead a night patrol from his platoon leader, nicknamed "Mr. Hook" because "he was awkward in his movements." Within minutes of leaving friendly lines, "we were lost. Being lost in no-man's-land was no joke." They encountered a barbed-wire entanglement, not knowing if it was on the friendly or enemy side of the lines, and Mr. Hook "got badly entangled." The men freed their intrepid leader without incident and proceeded. Just before dawn they finally found friendly lines, whereupon Mr. Hook boldly marched his patrol straight through a gap in the wire, only to be met by cursing British troops who informed him that his unannounced arrival had almost been greeted with a burst of machine-gun fire. The British soldiers had held their fire only because they had been told that lost doughboys were stumbling around in no-man's-land.[8]

Soldiers had a low tolerance for a leader's incompetence because mistakes cost lives. Yet as Private Eugene B. Sledge pointed out, all jokes aside, the men were sympathetic to the plight of the new lieutenant: "The new officers bore a heavy burden. . . . [Being] faced with heavy responsibilities and placed in a position of leadership amid hardened, seasoned Marine combat veterans . . . was a difficult situation and a terrific challenge. . . . No one I knew in the ranks envied them in the least."[9] The men also understood that no new leader, regardless of how well trained, possessed all the skills and knowledge that he would need in combat. They therefore responded favorably to leaders who admitted that they did not know everything, displayed a willingness to learn, and listened to the advice of their veteran soldiers.

Lieutenant Howard Matthias, on taking command of a veteran marine platoon in Korea, was one of those green, young officers wise enough to listen to his platoon sergeant, who had broken in enough lieutenants to know how to advise without offending or embarrassing: "Sgt. Miller not only quietly carried out his orders but also provided me with common sense guidelines for my behavior. He seldom recommended any specific actions but would drop subtle hints as [to] what might be best."[10]

After operating without a lieutenant for some time, Sergeant Ralph Zumbro's tank platoon in Vietnam got a new leader, Joe Somolik, who immediately impressed the tankers, not with his expertise but with his desire to learn:

This officer, Lieutenant Joe, was not normal by any standards. He insisted on a crash course in crew duties, as well as a Vietnam indoctrination. So for a week, the Assassin [the platoon leader's tank] hardly stopped as he put himself through all of the crew positions, learning the tasks of loader, gunner, and driver, as well as of tank boss. He spent his evenings either with the crews, listening to them recount savage battles, or with the officers in the command bunker, learning the tricks of getting helicopter supplies delivered on time, and how to deal with infantry commanders.[11]

Lieutenant Somolik's apparent ignorance of tank-crew duties might raise questions about what he and his instructors at Fort Knox had been doing during Armor Officers' Basic Course, but Somolik probably knew more about fighting a tank than he let on. The crew drills allowed him to get to know his men and to assess their abilities while also sharpening his own skills.

Captain Richard D. Camp, upon taking command of a rifle company in Vietnam, had never been in combat before, but he did have five years' experience as a marine infantry officer. Like Somolik, however, he prudently took an unobtrusive approach: "I decided to wait and see how good they [his men] were or if their techniques were better than my ideas." Camp was impressed with what he saw but knew from his training that a few of the things they were doing were wrong. His mortarmen, for example, insisted that in the field, the bipods for their 60-mm mortar tubes were "just a lot of extra weight, so we fire them free hand." Rather than put a stop to this "unmitigated bullshit" out of hand, however, Camp asked his self-proclaimed mortar aces to hit a tree outside their company position. The result: "They never landed one anywhere near that tree."[12] Bipods were humped in the boonies forthwith.

At the other extreme from the officer who admitted his inexperience and displayed a willingness to learn was the one who tried to hide his lack of skills behind a mask of bluster and authoritarianism. Private Richard E. Ogden's marine squad leader in Vietnam, "Chicken Foot" Trudeau, was a classic example: "The squad was a mockery in the field and training. He was incapable of taking advice. . . . His egomania and insensitivity got him into hot water. . . . The pressure was on him, and he attempted to conceal his insecurities by yelling and screaming all the time."[13]

An unskilled leader was bad enough, but a martinet who refused to acknowledge his shortcomings or learn from his mistakes was doubly dangerous. Paul Sponaugle, a squad leader in the Pacific in World War II, pointed out that veteran combatants were desperate men playing a deadly game and that they had no time for petty authoritarianism at the front: "Good soldiers, the ones who made it through all the rotten things, were tough and used to killing. If a leader they didn't respect gave them a foolish order just to show them who was in charge, he was taking his life in his hands."[14]

Captain Neal, Lieutenant Philip Caputo's company commander in Vietnam, was a humorless authoritarian who never accompanied his platoons into the field. His marines were exhausted from the grueling routine of nightly patrols and defending the company's base camp, within which Neal slept comfortably in his tent. He suddenly decided one day that an in-ranks, parade-ground-style rifle inspection was in order, thus yielding to the incompetent leader's penchant for doing what he knows how to do, no matter how inappropriate. His men not only considered this inspection blatant harassment but also extremely dangerous because they were a tempting target for enemy mortarmen as they stood in ranks. Fortunately, the enemy did not open fire, but Caputo's fellow platoon leader predicted that Captain Neal was not long for this world: "You know, I think the skipper's nuts. Somebody's going to put a bullet in the back of his head one of these days." Caputo responded, "Whoever does, I hope they give him the Congressional Medal of Honor . . . the war's bad enough without having to put up with that goddamned tyrant."[15]

The men were not opposed to discipline, as long as it was not simply harassment coming from an insecure, incompetent officer trying to assert himself. Lieutenants Harold P. Leinbaugh's and John D. Campbell's company commander, Captain George Gieszl, "never mollycoddled" the men and was a "tough, fair taskmaster," but he "never asked his men to do anything that he could not do—and Gieszl could do almost everything the army asked of a leader."[16] A competent leader did not have to resort to harassment to maintain discipline and control, as exemplified by Arthur Neumann, the sergeant in charge of Robert G. Thobaben's battalion aid station: "He never tried to harass or intimidate anyone. He rarely used profanity and was never rude or cruel. Like any outfit, we had a clown, a goof-off, a neurotic, a psychotic, and a con man, but Neumann seemed able to handle them all."[17]

Doughboys from the Thirty-ninth Infantry Regiment queue up to board French trucks, or *camions*. More often than not, infantry soldiers in the wars of the draft era got from one place to another by marching, but a truck ride, even in World War I, was not uncommon. Though perhaps better than walking, a ride in a truck with solid-rubber tires and a rudimentary suspension system over rough, often damaged, roads was no Sunday outing. The soldier was further unsettled by thoughts of what lay ahead. A truck ride often meant something significant and unpleasant was about to happen, as was the case for these doughboys on their way to the Argonne front. (National Archives)

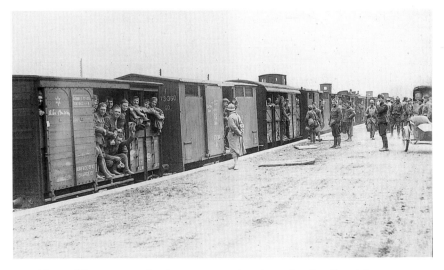

Doughboys of the Twenty-sixth Infantry Regiment jam themselves into French boxcars, known as "forty and eights," in Maron, France, in April 1918. The wooden cars had neither seats nor heat, and soldiers were usually packed in so tightly that they did not have room to stretch out. Additional discomfort was added if the cars had not been cleaned after the previous equine passengers had detrained. The nickname "forty and eight" refers to the boxcar's posted capacity. Stenciled on the side of the first car is "hommes 32-40, chevaux 8," and as one soldier quipped, "I wouldn't treat a horse that way." (National Archives)

During the world wars, African-American soldiers served in segregated units, mostly as service troops because of nagging suspicions on the part of America's white leadership that blacks could not fight. The 369th Infantry Regiment, shown here in France in 1918, with French arms and equipment, was one of a handful of black combat units. Fighting with the French army, the 369th Infantry compiled an admirable record, but other African-American combat units gained reputations as poor performers. Not until blacks were given the opportunity to prove themselves while fighting beside their white comrades in integrated units did the army hierarchy come to understand that any shortcomings in black-unit performance had been the result of the insidious effects of segregation and discrimination and not of any inherent racial flaws in African Americans. (National Archives)

A German machine gunner dead at his post in France in November 1918. Machine-gun crews often fought to the death because they knew that attempting to surrender was futile. Doughboys, otherwise inclined to accept the surrender of German soldiers, often made an exception of machine gunners. As one doughboy put it, when a German "sat behind a gun and mowed down a bunch of men, his life was automatically forfeited." (National Archives)

A grinning young World War I doughboy, with a casualty tag pinned to his jacket, shows off his wounded arm. Whatever pain he is feeling is more than compensated for by the knowledge that his immediate future involves a well-earned period of comfort and rest in a convalescent camp as opposed to the mud and shelling at the front. He might even be contemplating the gold wound stripe that he will sew on his right sleeve and show off proudly. (National Archives)

GIs stacked five deep on canvas cots depart San Francisco on a transport ship in November 1942, bound for the Pacific theater. Depending on the destination of the ship and its speed, usually slow, these soldiers face a three-week trip on an overcrowded transport devoid of amenities. (National Archives)

*(Top)* Marine chaplain Rufus W. Oakley holds services near the front on Peleliu in September 1944. Unit chaplains who shared in the hardships and dangers while administering to the soldiers' religious needs were appreciated and respected. Many soldiers "got religion" in the foxhole, if they did not already have faith, praying for salvation or for God to spare them. For others, war was proof that there was no God or that he did not care. How could God allow such carnage and destruction? (National Archives) *(Bottom)* Pfc. Shellnut (left) holds a piece of silk cut from a parachute flare on Okinawa in 1945. He and his buddy, Pfc. Dobbins, both of the Sixty-ninth Division, will soon have that piece of silk converted into a "genuine" Japanese battle flag like the one Dobbins is holding. Manufacturing war souvenirs was a cottage industry in every war of the draft era. Souvenir-hungry servicemen were always ready to purchase or trade for flags, swords, knives, uniform items, weapons—anything to impress the folks back home. (National Archives)

*(Opposite, top)* GIs from the 347th Infantry Regiment line up for chow near La Roche, Belgium, in January 1945. Hot meals were a real morale booster, and commanders went to some lengths to provide rations in insulated containers to even the most forward-deployed troops. Nevertheless, soldiers often went for days, even weeks, eating only cold, monotonous, canned combat rations. (National Archives)

A GI, Browning automatic rifle in hand, accepts the surrender of a German officer in Illy, France, in September 1944. American soldiers in both world wars usually allowed Germans to surrender, with the hated *Schutzstaffel* (SS) often being an exception in World War II because of the atrocities SS soldiers had committed against civilians and GI prisoners. In the wars in the Pacific and Asia, American soldiers often believed that their foes did not fight fairly or treat prisoners humanely and thus sometimes responded with an unwritten no-prisoners policy. (National Archives)

Sergeant Wyman P. Williams, an assistant squad leader in the Twelfth Infantry Regiment, Fourth Infantry Division, rests near Villedieu, France, August 3, 1944. He is armed with an M-1 Garand rifle and hand grenades. (National Archives)

Soldiers of the Eighty-eighth Infantry Division wind their way across a small valley near Itri, Italy, May 18, 1944, during Operation DIADEM, the Allied offensive that led to the capture of Rome. The Eighty-eighth was one of the first "draftee" divisions, composed primarily of conscripted soldiers as opposed to regulars or called-up National Guardsmen, to see action. The division performed well in its combat debut. (National Archives)

A column of American vehicles crosses a military bridge and moves through the shattered remains of a German village in March 1945. Soldiers struggled to survive amid the natural and human wreckage created by modern firepower, living in a hostile, alien, even surreal environment. Some soldiers became so immersed in this environment that occasional moments of tranquillity or the experience of normal peacetime activities seemed unreal. (National Archives)

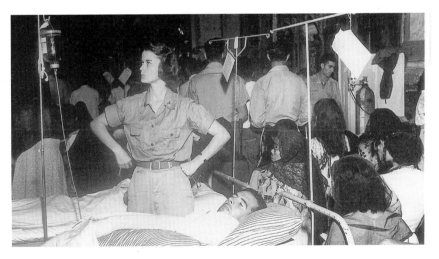

Lieutenant Phyllis Hocking, an army nurse at the Thirty-sixth Evacuation Hospital in the Philippines in December 1944, checks a wounded soldier's glucose intravenous drip. The hospital is set up in a church. The Filipino congregation kneels during Christmas Eve services while doctors and nurses attend to the wounded. The otherwise macho soldier freely admitted to the need for a little mothering while recuperating, and GI memoirs are universal in their praise of the care given by the army's compassionate, dedicated ward nurses. (National Archives)

Marines in Korea dig fighting positions. Note the rolls of concertina barbed wire in the foreground, to be strung in front of the position once it is completed. At the end of a hard day of marching, and perhaps fighting, the exhausted soldier often faced the task of digging in for the night. Remaining stationary the next day or so brought only limited relief, as positions needed to be improved by adding sandbags, overhead cover to protect from artillery airbursts, and more barbed wire and perhaps mines and trip flares. (National Archives)

An integrated machine-gun crew in Korea in November 1950. The U.S. Army entered the war with segregated units and emerged in 1953 with integrated units. The exigencies of war, rather than any enlightened racial policy, led to that integration. More African-American replacements began arriving than were needed by black units, and white units did not have enough, so black replacements were assigned to white outfits. Studies soon showed that not only did such newly integrated units not suffer a drop in morale or effectiveness but also that racial harmony was actually improved as GIs of all races learned to live, work, and fight together. (National Archives)

Pfc. Preston McKnight, Nineteenth Infantry Regiment, huddles under his poncho in Korea in January 1951 to escape the frigid, biting wind. Chinese intervention in winter 1950–1951 and the precipitous retreat by United Nations forces that followed made for conditions as harsh and miserable as any endured by soldiers in the wars of the draft era. (National Archives)

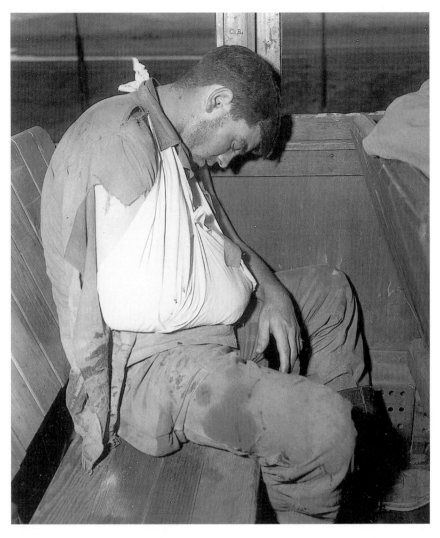

Grimy, blood-stained, and exhausted, Pfc. Orvin L. Morris, Twenty-seventh Infantry Regiment, sleeps on the hospital train evacuating him to Pusan, Korea, in July 1950. Hit in the arm with mortar shell fragments, he has earned his "Pusan wound" and a much-needed period of rest and recuperation. (National Archives)

Thomas S. Robinson, a marine, finds a quiet spot to read a letter from home while serving in Korea in 1952. Mail was the lifeline linking a soldier to home and loved ones, whose support and approval were key to helping him cope with the harsh environment of war. As Tim O'Brien, Vietnam War veteran and novelist, has pointed out, "soldiers are dreamers," and words of endearment and descriptions of hometown events brought by the mail transported the soldier to a happier time and place, if only for a few moments. (National Archives)

Marines fresh from the front in Korea in December 1951 strip off their stained, filthy clothes for the first time in weeks, to be followed by a hot shower and an issue of clean fatigues, or utilities, as the marines called them. Sometimes, such as in the dead of winter, leaders had to enforce standards of hygiene among soldiers who did not want to remove warm clothing or shave with icy cold water. More commonly, however, soldiers could not avoid being filthy, nor could they wash or even take off their dirty fatigues. The chance to bathe in a stream or take a shower brought welcome relief. (National Archives)

One of four dead GIs from the Twenty-first Infantry Regiment found bound and shot through the head by North Koreans in July 1950. Such vicious acts generated hatred and a visceral desire for revenge. North Koreans attempted to surrender at their own peril if their would-be captors had recently witnessed such an atrocity. (National Archives)

The first step in converting the recruit from civilian to soldier occurred at the induction center, or reception station as it was known in the Vietnam War era. All things civilian were literally stripped away. Here recruits have exited the clothing issue point of the reception station at Fort Bliss, Texas, in January 1966. They have turned in their civilian clothes and possessions and have received their uniforms. The third man in line is struggling to get in step with the two recruits in front of him. The first two recruits reflexively feel the stubble on the back of their necks where hair had once grown. The smirk on Drill Sergeant Joe Benolken's face over the predicament of his flock is ill-concealed. (National Archives)

During army basic training at Fort Riley, Kansas, in 1965, Staff Sergeant John Archer, a drill instructor, bellows out orders to trainees during hand-to-hand combat training. Imposing drill sergeants like Archer inspired fear and awe among trainees. Over the course of their training, however, most recruits came to realize that their drill instructors had their best interests at heart. After graduation from basic and advanced training, these recruits faced the stressful environment of war. The drill sergeants were preparing them mentally and physically for what lay ahead. (National Archives)

Marine mortarman R. Jones (standing), muddy, drenched by monsoon rains, and exhausted, takes a break from humping the boonies in Vietnam in December 1967. In addition to the packs and equipment strapped to the men, note the mortar implements on the ground that the crew is carrying—a baseplate, ammunition canisters strapped to a pack frame, and aiming stakes in a canvas bag. Mortar and machine-gun crews habitually carried loads of eighty or more pounds in the wars of the draft era. (National Archives)

George W. Barber, a machine gunner in the Seventh Marine Regiment, opens up on a suspected Viet Cong position in the thick bushes in South Vietnam in November 1968. The marine standing behind Barber is no doubt the assistant gunner, feeding the ammunition belt into the M-60 machine gun and observing the impact of the rounds. The M-60, or "pig" as it was called, was heavy and cumbersome, and it attracted enemy return fire. Yet it was the infantry squad's heavy firepower, and only a trusted marksman carried the pig. Machine gunners carried the M-60 proudly because of the respect and occasional accolades given to a good gunner. (National Archives)

A marine from the Ninth Regiment pries a punji-stake trap from his boot in January 1966. Punji stakes were bamboo or metal barbs, sometimes dipped in feces to ensure infection. Although the stakes have punctured the rubber soles and leather side of his boot, this marine was not hurt, thanks to the metal plate added to the jungle boot to counter the stakes liberally scattered by the Viet Cong. Unfortunately, the Viet Cong and North Vietnamese made increasing use of more sophisticated mines and booby traps provided by the Soviets and the Chinese. The enemy was also adept at improvising booby traps from unexploded or abandoned American munitions. Grunts patrolling the boonies were in a state of near-constant anxiety trying to spot these hidden killers. (National Archives)

A second lieutenant in the Ninth Marine Regiment observes through field glasses the results of an air strike he has called for in Vietnam in March 1967. Jokes about green, bumbling "butter bars" (referring to the gold rank insignia of a second lieutenant) are standard military fare, but the skills possessed by a well-trained lieutenant, such as the ability to call in an accurate air or artillery strike, were indispensable. Being a junior leader in combat, however, was a hazardous profession. Notice that this lieutenant must stand to observe the impact while his men crouch in the tall grass. (National Archives)

Marines carry a dead comrade in a makeshift litter in Vietnam in October 1967 to a point where the body can be further evacuated, often by helicopter, to a graves-registration point. An unwritten marine rule in the wars of the draft era was that no one would be left behind. A marine was thus comforted by the thought that his remains would be properly attended to, but the impact on morale to the survivors who had to evacuate their dead buddies can be imagined. Not to mention, as Tim O'Brien once observed, "Dead human beings are heavy and awkward to carry." (National Archives)

Gilbert J. Davis, a marine corporal, trains South Vietnamese local defense forces, known as the "Ruff Puffs" (Regional and Popular Forces). Grunts often disparaged the performance of their South Vietnamese allies. To the extent that this bad reputation was justified, poor leadership, inadequate training, and equipment deficiencies were to blame. Note in this photograph, for example, that the marine carries a modern M-16 rifle while the Vietnamese soldiers are armed with World War II–vintage M-1 rifles. Some South Vietnamese units fought well, but the overall feeling among grunts was that if these people wouldn't fight for themselves, why should Americans do it for them. A similar, if less extreme, attitude was evident in the GIs' opinion of the fighting qualities of their Republic of Korea Army allies in the Korean War. (National Archives)

A grief-stricken marine bows his head in anguish over the death of his boonie buddy in Vietnam in May 1967. The M-16 rifle stuck bayonet-first into the ground marks the spot where a dead marine lies, awaiting evacuation to a graves-registration point. The unfinished foxhole the marine is standing in indicates that his buddy may have been killed while digging in for the night. The seemingly unconcerned marines in the background are, in reality, respecting the grieving man's space and his need for a moment alone in a world where privacy is virtually nonexistent. (National Archives)

## TAKING CARE OF THE MEN

The competent leader earned respect because his skill directly translated into saved lives. Technical and tactical competence alone, however, was not enough. The leader also had to take care of his men, which in its most basic form meant doing everything reasonable to ensure that they were fed, clothed, sheltered, equipped, and rested. Though soldiers were adept at scrounging or foraging, ultimately they had little control over what they ate, when they rested, and where they went. Thus, they expected the army to provide for their needs, and their leaders had what Jonathan Shay calls a "fiduciary responsibility" to do so: "The vast and distant military and civilian structure that provides a modern soldier with his orders, arms, ammunition, food, water, information, training, and fire support is ultimately a moral structure, a *fiduciary*, a trustee holding the life and safety of that soldier."[18]

The junior leader directly controlled few material assets, but he nevertheless played a vital role in anticipating and requesting what his men would need to survive and to do their jobs. Lieutenant Hervey Allen considered the unglamorous business of taking care of doughboys to be one area in which junior leaders could make a difference: "The men expected to be fed, and they looked to the officers to feed them. To feed, clothe, equip, and pay the men,—that is about all a line officer can do anyway,—pictures of sword flourishers in battle notwithstanding."[19] Taking care of the men paid dividends in improved efficiency. Bill Mauldin offered an apt comparison: "An officer is not supposed to sleep until his men are bedded down. He is not supposed to eat until he has arranged for his men to eat. He's like a prizefighter's manager. If he keeps his fighter in shape, the fighter will make him successful."[20]

Providing for the soldiers' material needs was the most obvious but not the only aspect of taking care of the men. The caring leader also did his best to ensure fairness. Soldiering was hard work, and the trooper did not want to carry more than his fair share of the unit's equipment or fill more than his quota of sandbags. More important, he did not want to take more than his share of the risks. Hence, the wise leader distributed the dangerous jobs as equitably as possible. Patrolling in World War II was one of those dreaded jobs that had to be assigned fairly, as far as Lieutenant Paul Boesch was concerned: "Somehow in the movies men always step forward briskly to ask for dangerous missions, but in the real infantry men looked on volunteering as an easy way to end a military career. While they might be fully willing to take on any task specifically assigned them, they had no desire to ask for trouble." Boesch ensured fairness by "keeping a duty roster for patrols just as we kept duty rosters for other onerous tasks. Each man took his turn."[21]

Another onerous task was being lead unit. In Albert French's marine company in Vietnam, the commander was careful to rotate that dangerous job among his platoons. While on a mission one day, French estimated that it would be his platoon's turn at point after the noon chow break, but for the moment he and his comrades enjoyed the coveted position of center platoon in the column: "You didn't have to worry that much about booby traps or being the first to walk into an ambush."[22]

Sharing the burdens and dangers seems simple enough, but it was complicated because certain individuals or units were better than others. Always putting the most skilled and experienced soldier on point, for example, might save lives when he spotted a booby trap or uncovered an ambush, but how fair was that to the point man? And using the best men helped to ensure the success of the mission, something of more than passing interest to the junior leader's superiors. During World War II, Lieutenant George Wilson noticed that his commanders "used their most experienced men for the tough jobs." He could see how this practice "might appear unfair to the men asked to undertake repeated risks," but using the best men allowed for "a better chance of getting a difficult job done with the least losses." Wilson accepted this method of assigning missions and even "used it myself," even though he had personally been given so many "tough assignments" because of his proven track record that he was beginning to wonder "how many such jobs I could survive."[23]

Unlike their leaders, the men tended to put fairness before mission, and they not only expected their leader to distribute burdens equitably, but they also counted on him to stand up to higher authorities if they perceived that orders from above were unfair, ill-conceived, or inappropriate. Henderson notes that the junior leader who went to bat for his men proved that he cared, even if he failed:

Cohesion occurs when . . . leaders act to protect the soldier from and to regulate relations with higher authorities. An example involves the situation when soldiers perceive orders or allocations from higher headquarters as being unfair or inadequate. The sergeant, platoon leader, or company commander who goes to higher headquarters and wins relief or who merely makes the attempt not only increases his influence among his soldiers but also significantly contributes to their sense of belonging to a group that can deal with an otherwise uncaring environment.[24]

During the fighting in the Philippines in World War II, Captain W. Stanford Smith's regimental commander ordered him to employ his cannon company's lightly armored, self-propelled artillery pieces in an assault, as if they were tanks. Two of the guns were promptly hit and three of Smith's men killed. When the regimental commander again told him to carry out this maneuver, Smith was "incensed" and protested so vehemently that his colonel rescinded the order. Unknown to Smith, one of his sergeants had witnessed him "get really pissed off at the regimental commander and slam his helmet on the ground."[25] It was not long before the entire company knew that Smith had stood up for them.

The junior leader had to pick his battles with his superiors carefully, however. Morris Janowitz and Roger W. Little point out that although the men right-fully expected their leader "to defend them against arbitrary and unwarranted intrusion from above," the junior officer was also "the final representative of coercive higher authority. For him to overidentify with his men would impair the system of authority."[26] The leader thus occupied a difficult middle ground between protecting his men and carrying out his orders. If he became unreason-ably protective, it usually led to his relief from command for disobeying orders or, more commonly, for not carrying them out with sufficient speed and vigor because he feared for his men's lives. The case of Lieutenant Johnson, Rudolph W. Stephens's platoon leader, illustrates how difficult occupying that middle ground could be. As a leader in a war in Korea that by late 1952 was obviously stalemated, Johnson began faking what most of his men had come to consider senseless patrols: "[Johnson] was just as brave as the next man; he just wouldn't waste a man's life on some of those silly patrols, and his men respected him for his actions. No one in the platoon would rat on him for any reason. If there was some action against the enemy that would show some results, then he would give it all he had, but to throw away a life for nothing was out of the question."[27]

From the perspective of his superiors, Johnson was disobeying orders and undermining discipline. Furthermore, it was not his place to decide if the patrols were "silly" or not. From the perspective of his men, he was being sensible with their lives in a war that was going nowhere. Too often, in the late stages of the Korean and Vietnam Wars, leaders found themselves in such unenviable, no-win situations.

The opposite of the overprotective leader was the one who volunteered for dangerous missions or carried out orders in a reckless manner because of his love of fighting or simply from personal ambition. John Dollard's survey of American veterans of the Spanish Civil War revealed, to no one's surprise, that they believed "a commander worthy of respect will take no unnecessary risks with men's lives."[28] Leaders who, in the men's estimation, were heedless of lives gained reputations as "glory hounds." Sergeant Warren Avery's platoon leader in Korea was typical: "He was a real gung-ho second lieutenant who was going to make first lieutenant even if it killed us. The lieutenant was constantly volun-teering us for patrols, or to advance on the point each time the company was in the attack."[29]

In contrast to Sergeant Avery's platoon leader was Lieutenant James Brady, whose sergeant said on Brady's departure to become executive officer of his company in Korea: "You know, Mr. Brady, when you come up to us I was afraid. I thought you was gonna try to win medals with this platoon. That scared me. But you didn't, and that was a good thing. We liked having you as platoon leader."[30]

Sometimes a gung-ho leader was not out to enhance his career or reputation but was simply green and overeager. Most leaders, if they lived long enough, learned the virtues of caution. Captain Camp, in one of his first missions as a company commander, led a platoon-sized patrol deep into "Indian country" in

Vietnam, in search of enemy rocket sites. Only after returning unscathed did he reflect on what a dangerous risk he had just taken. Camp vowed to exhibit more prudence in the future: "I realized that I needed to start getting concerned about my attitude; I might have allowed my enthusiasm to lead us all into a situation in which we would have needed help. The thwarting of my impulsive enthusiasm proved to be a valuable early lesson, for I soon realized that the same sort of emotional response had killed my predecessor and, no doubt, countless others."[31]

The leader who cared for his men was not only frugal with their lives but also went out of his way to keep them informed. Given the soldiers' combat parochialism, they had little interest in the wider war, but they cared a great deal about what was happening within the microcosm of their platoon and company. Junior leaders often knew little themselves about what was going on, but they usually knew more than the men. The wise leader told his soldiers as much as possible, because information about an upcoming move or mission reduced uncertainty, which in turn reduced anxiety. The army officer Joseph J. Ondishko pointed out that the "absence of information" is one of the conditions that fosters panic in troops: "Fears arise from matters they don't understand—keep men informed."[32]

The leader who consistently passed on what he knew also gained his men's trust. They perceived that he was playing it straight with them, even if the news was not all good, as Elmar Dinter observes: "The groups take a burning interest in everything that directly affects their future. This is precisely the kind of information that a clever leader will be able to obtain. . . . If his information proves to be accurate, and if he passes it on without twisting it, then a kind of trust will be created."[33]

The leader who went to the trouble of keeping his men informed helped to dispel their nagging conviction that they were just ciphers or expendable cogs in a large, impersonal machine. Soldiers resented being treated like sheep or kept in the dark. Klaus H. Huebner, although a captain, was consistently left out of the information loop, perhaps because he was a noncombatant. Like all soldiers, he resented not knowing what was to happen next. In North Africa in World War II, he found himself on a train "to where, no one again seems to know. That's what I like about the Army; you never know anything. You are just a serial number, you do what you are told, and it's as simple as that."[34]

Sometimes security precautions or a lack of time precluded passing on information, but the leader who explained what he could showed his men that he cared. The simple act of just talking to a soldier about anything helped establish trust, as long as the conversation was sincere. Captain "Ack Ack" Haldane, who commanded Private Sledge's marine company, was a beloved skipper because his interest in the men was genuine. During a footmarch while training for the upcoming assault on Peleliu in World War II, Haldane asked Sledge, then a fresh replacement, about his background and family and then "moved along the column talking to other men as he had to me. His sincere interest in each of us as human beings helped to dispel the feeling that we were just animals training to fight."[35]

Captain Charles B. MacDonald, as a green replacement commander of a veteran infantry company, typically worried that his men would not accept him. He knew he had made the grade when he inadvertently overheard one of his men talking about him to another soldier: "He doesn't seem scared to come around and see you once in a while, no matter where the hell you are. He seems to care what happens to you."[36]

Leaders like MacDonald and Haldane genuinely cared, and the soldiers sensed it and reciprocated. Lieutenant George William Sefton wisely observed that bonhomie and artificial familiarity, on the other hand, did not win trust: "I learned never to underestimate the intelligence of my men. They will see through bluff and bluster, perceive and resent any cavalier attitude. . . . They will respect you in direct ratio to the consideration you exercise on their behalf."[37]

Although a leader's concern had to be genuine, much of the process of exhibiting it was straightforward enough. He ensured that his men were rested and resupplied, duties were equitably shared, and as much information as possible was passed on. Beyond that, however, taking care of the men was anything but a disinterested, mechanistic process. The junior leader lived with his men and got to know them. He could not be dispassionate about ordering them to do something that might get them killed. Herein lies one of the greatest burdens of junior leadership in combat, one stressful enough to contribute significantly to junior-officer breakdowns, according to Leo H. Bartemeier: "The officer patients . . . manifested attitudes of care and appreciation for their men. . . . It was clear, too, that they had suffered a good deal, emotionally, from the necessity of leading and ordering their men on and on to death, mutilation, and psychiatric disablement."[38]

The leader had to care about his men while somehow steeling himself against the inevitable losses, an emotional dilemma not easily resolved. Perhaps, as Frederick Downs suggests, the most that a junior leader could do was to be aware that sooner or later he would have to face that traumatic dilemma: "Even if the officer does his job perfectly, he will lose men. He will make mistakes that will kill men. He will lead his men out to face the enemy knowing full well some will die. That's his job. Some combat officers will not be able to assume such responsibility for very long. Some will handle it well."[39]

Downs would be the first to admit that this advice is easier given than internalized. His first wounded soldier had a knee shattered by a Viet Cong grenade. As Downs cradled the man's head while the medic bandaged him, "I felt my own tears well up at the impact of seeing one of my men, a man I was responsible for, hurt and bleeding."[40] One of Lieutenant Wilson's men was accidentally run over and killed by an American tank during the fighting in Normandy. This especially senseless death was the second casualty in his platoon since he had taken over, and he realized that he would not last long if he dwelled on each loss: "I knew then I'd never survive if I let myself get tied in with every case. It was vital for me to build some sort of protective shield within myself and concentrate only on what had to be done in the present and how to do it. I forced myself to suppress all thoughts of prior losses and gruesome mental pictures of the tragedy of war."[41]

Only the truly callous leader could be insensitive to the loss of his own men. Most coped by adopting some version of Wilson's sensible recommendation to focus on the job at hand. The leader had a responsibility to those still alive and could do nothing about the dead. If he believed that his mistakes had caused those deaths, however, the weight of guilt could be oppressive. Captain Camp accompanied one of his squads on a routine daytime patrol in Vietnam. On the way back to base camp, the squad proceeded by the easiest and most obvious route, moving down a road. Smitty, the squad leader's radioman, was abruptly mangled before Camp's eyes by a command-detonated mine and mercifully died shortly thereafter. Camp was devastated because he knew they should not have been on that road: "Inside, for all the years since, I have carried the image of Smitty's death deep inside me as a sign of my frailty. I knew it then, clearly, that I never should have let the patrol proceed up that open roadway. I could have said something sooner. I should have. If ever a group of Marines was ambush bait, that patrol on that open road leading out from that village was the best example I ever heard about. . . . I knew better."[42]

## SHARING THE HARDSHIPS AND DANGERS

The leader not only had to order the men he cared for into harm's way, but he also had to be willing to take the same risks himself. The men did not respect a leader who would not share their dangers and hardships. Lieutenant Matthias understood that "respect was given more openly to the officer that would live the life of the 'grunt' on line. This meant eating, sleeping, and struggling the same as the other men."[43] Sergeant Nat Frankel pointed out that only by living like their men could leaders appreciate what they were going through: "What is the difference between an officer for whom we would die and another whom we would just as soon kill? It is, in the long run, the extent to which they share the common lot of their men. Are they distant, protected, scrubbed clean, sterile? If so, they are nothing but computers issuing indifferent orders. Or are they accessible, exposed to the gamut of danger and misfortune, with dirt in their fingernails and an instinctive understanding of and respect for our view of the world? If so, they become one with their units."[44]

In the combat zone, junior leaders had little choice but to live as their men did. Nevertheless, officers still enjoyed some privileges, which the wise leader was careful not to abuse. During World War II and the Korean War, officers were allowed a hard-liquor ration while the men were not. The officers had to pay for the liquor, and it did not always arrive on schedule, but the ration was a potential source of GI resentment. MacDonald and his officers turned potential discontent into a morale booster, however, by sharing the liquor: "The bottles were passed among all the men of the platoons until they were exhausted, which was accomplished rather rapidly, and we wondered at letters to the editor in the *Stars and Stripes* complaining about officers getting whiskey rations when enlisted men did not."[45]

Leaders also had transportation at their disposal, but during a grueling, four-day march in the summer heat of France, Charles F. Minder's company commander dismounted and marched with his men. He even carried the straggling Minder's pack for a while to allow him to catch up: "The Captain did other wonderful things for the fellows. I saw him give a couple of fellows some water from his own canteen. He walked his horse instead of riding him, and that's something that few officers would do."[46] Captain Gieszl, Leinbaugh's and Campbell's company commander, also marched with his men: "He was always fair, and that made all the difference. He didn't take advantage of his jeep on marches. He marched further than the rest of us, moving back and forth along the column."[47]

Captain Gieszl, by actually marching farther than his men, was doing more than just sharing the hardships. He was setting the example. The smart leader not only respected the soldier's view of the world by sharing it, as Sergeant Frankel suggested, but also set the standards to be achieved in that world. He could only do so through personal example. Lieutenant Brady provided a time-honored rule of leadership as he stood last in line behind his platoon at a showerpoint in Korea: "You sent the enlisted men first if it was something pleasant, chow or a shower; you went first yourself if it wasn't. The rules were so simple once you learned them."[48]

Simple to learn, perhaps, but the rules were not always easy to live by. Sometimes the junior leader had to summon his last reserves of strength and resolve to continue to set the example. During the abysmal Korean winter of 1950–1951, Lieutenant Joseph R. Owen and the other leaders in his marine rifle company exerted a maximum effort to keep the exhausted men scrabbling up and down the slippery, frozen hills: "The officers and NCO's earned their pay. When the men faltered we coaxed and cajoled, cursed and threatened. We pulled some men to their feet, and we spelled the machine gunners, mortarmen, and ammo carriers, carrying their heavy loads ourselves."[49]

Sharing dangers and hardships allowed the leader to set the example and to understand what his men were going through, but there was an even more basic reason for risk taking. He had to expose himself to danger in order to do his job. He had to observe the enemy so that he could direct his unit's fire and movement, call for artillery or air support, and report the situation to higher headquarters. He had to position weapons personally to provide covering fire or when organizing a defense. He had to leave the safety of his own foxhole at night to check his unit's position. He was often called upon to lead a patrol or raid.

The men were well aware that the leader had to place himself in danger to do his job under fire. Robert Sanders's company commander was nicknamed "Rabbit," not because he was scared, but because he was a fast mover in a fire-fight:

If you had a sharp company commander, he could take just one glance and tell what was happening. If you had one that got his face buried down in the fucking ground, soon as that shit started coming in, he was trying to hide from the heat, then your whole unit could get killed right there. Rabbit never got down on the ground. Half the time he was the only motherfucker up, checking things out. Where was the automatic weapons fire coming from? Where was the main body of the ambush? Then he would give you orders to move in—in the right direction![50]

Leaders certainly paid the price for taking such risks. A platoon leader in Lieutenant Alfred S. Bradford's battalion died in a firefight when he raised his head to look around. Someone remarked that "he shouldn't have stuck his head up," but a veteran lieutenant responded, "Sometimes, . . . when you're the leader, you've got to."[51] Junior leaders died or were wounded with appalling frequency in the performance of their duties. Lieutenant James Hamilton Dill was not surprised to learn that many of the artillery sergeants in his battery in the Korean War refused battlefield commissions: "New lieutenant of artillery equaled instant forward observer. Too many of those who accepted appointments were promptly killed in action."[52]

The men appreciated the risks that their leaders took, but they also expected it. The junior leader who looked after himself first was despised, not only because he was not sharing the same dangers that he was ordering his men into but also because he was not doing his job effectively. Captain Staley, commanding a company of doughboys in Lieutenant Lawrence's battalion, never left the safety of his dugout: "Captain Staley's confinement to his dugout, a German-built, concrete dugout, became known throughout the battalion." His cowardly behavior left his men in the forward trenches leaderless. Lawrence, leading the platoon next to Staley's company, found himself doing double duty because Staley "did not visit his line. I was the only officer to whom his men could look for instructions."[53]

Bob Stiles, during the fighting on New Britain in the Pacific in World War II, learned that men died when leaders failed to lead. Stiles, a battalion scout and sniper, was advancing with a platoon when they came under friendly artillery fire. He tried to find the platoon leader to have him radio back to lift the fire. A sergeant told Stiles that the lieutenant was in his usual location during an advance: "He's way back —keeping his eye out for stragglers, he tells us." Stiles knew that men had died needlessly as a result: "Well, hell, his job is to be on the lines and relaying the position of the forward men to our artillery so they can lift their elevation on the guns. If someone isn't doing this, the men up forward have their ass out in the cold."[54]

Leaders who abdicated their responsibilities quickly lost the respect of their men and usually did not last long. One of Lieutenant Owen's mortar squad leaders panicked during a Chinese night attack in Korea, abandoning his mortar and telling his men to run for it. The next morning, the squad leader admitted his error and begged for another chance, but Owen knew that the damage was irreversible: "I can't give you another chance. Your men don't respect you. You report to the CP. They'll give you orders from there."[55]

Although some leaders failed out of fear, far more braved the dangers of combat and fulfilled their responsibilities, earning the trust and respect of their men in the process. The soldiers were looking for a particular type of bravery, however. Impulsive, reckless behavior, no matter how courageous, was not what they wanted in a leader. Recklessness might get them killed. The leader who remained cool and unflappable in the midst of chaos, on the other hand, inspired confidence and obedience. In times of danger, men wanted someone to tell them what to do, and only a level-headed leader with his emotions in check could make the correct decisions.

Lord Moran noticed that the successful British leader in World War I possessed "phlegm": "Alone in its influence over the hearts of men I place phlegm—a supreme imperturbability in the face of death which half amused them and half dominated them—the ultimate gift in war."[56] Successful leaders avoided overreacting in the midst of carnage and confusion. The greatest praise a leader could receive from his soldiers was that he was "cool" under fire, as was Colonel William J. Donovan, who commanded Father Francis P. Duffy's infantry regiment in World War I: "'Cool' is the word the men use of him and 'Cool' is their highest epithet of praise for a man of daring, resolution and indifference to danger."[57] Albert M. Ettinger's mortar sergeant was "cool as a cucumber" under fire and "always out front directing the mortar fire."[58] Coolness remained a valuable asset in later wars as well. The machine-gun platoon leader in Allen R. Matthew's marine battalion in World War II was "as cool under fire as he was on the parade ground."[59] Lieutenant Owen admired one of his fellow platoon leaders in the Korean War who was tactically savvy and, more important, "never seemed to get ruffled, and he wasn't a shouter."[60] Tim O'Brien's platoon leader, despite his nickname "Mad Mark," was "not a hysterical, crazy, into-the-brink, to-the-fore" type. "Rather, he was insanely calm. He never showed fear. He was a professional soldier, an ideal leader of men in the field."[61]

Conversely, the leader who could not maintain a calm and confident demeanor spread fear and doubt. Marine Robert Leckie looked at his commander's face after the company's first nerve-racking night in the jungles of Guadalcanal, and he was rattled by what he saw: "I peered at the captain. Anxiety was on his face as though carved there by the night's events. It startled me. Here was no warrior, no veteran of a hundred battles. Here was only a civilian, like myself."[62] Many leaders were as green and anxious as Leckie's company commander, but the smart ones understood that they had to conceal those anxieties from the men. Captain Charles Rigaud was as inexperienced as the marines in his weapons company when they were ambushed by the Japanese on Guadalcanal. His men began falling back without orders, at which point Rigaud stood up in the midst of the firing, and according to John Hersey, "by a combination of blistering sarcasm, orders and cajolery" got the men "in a mood to fight again." Hersey was sure that the young captain was as scared as everyone else, but he never showed it: "I am certain that all along, Captain Rigaud was just as terrified as the rest of us were, for he was eminently human. And yet his rallying those men was as cool a performance as you can imagine. I could feel my own knees tremble; I could see the rifle shake in the hands of the man nearest me. But I kept quite close to Captain Rigaud and I could not see a single tremor."[63]

In Vietnam, Lieutenant Lanning likewise comported himself calmly in his first serious firefight. He was scared, but he instinctively understood that he could not show signs of faltering: "I was frightened—actually, scared as hell is a better description. Still, I remained calm on the radio and delivered my instructions with confidence. Nobody panicked. Everybody did his job."[64]

The successful combat leader had to exhibit coolness under fire and a willingness to take risks in the normal course of his duties, but his men did not expect him to take unnecessary risks simply to prove his bravery. Herbert Spiegel, who served as an infantry battalion surgeon in World War II, noted that replacement officers nevertheless felt a sometimes fatal need to do just that: "It was not surprising that some of these leaders acted in a foolhardy way just to convince themselves and the men that they were not afraid. Nor was it surprising that physical casualties among them was very high."[65]

The leader took enough risks just in doing his job, and as Michael D. Doubler points out, the men much preferred a live leader they trusted to a dead hero: "Men in the ranks thought it was foolhardy when officers needlessly exposed themselves to danger. Soldiers instinctively knew the importance of keeping key leaders alive and often asked them not to lead the way in hazardous situations."[66] Sometimes "follow me" was necessary, but not always. Doubler cites an example from MacDonald's World War II memoir. During a night advance in the Battle of the Bulge, MacDonald decided to take the lead of his company column to expedite matters. His sergeant stopped him: "Goddamit, Captain, . . . you've got to stay farther back. At least get some scouts out front." The chastised MacDonald took up a more appropriate position behind his lead platoon: "His admonition reminded me that it was foolish for me to lead the column. The foolish days of 'leading' one's troops into battle were past, even though correspondents persisted in telling of daring generals who preceded their troops, firing from the hip or brandishing a bayonet."[67]

Leaders did not have to tempt fate. Coolness under fire, not foolhardy bravado, was what the men expected. A dead leader could not issue the orders so critically needed in the midst of battle.

## WHEN THE "SIMPLEST VIRTUES" ARE LACKING

The relative importance of sharing hardships and dangers, taking care of the men, and possessing technical and tactical competence is difficult to assess because these qualities are interrelated. A platoon leader lacking tactical expertise, for example, probably did not possess the confidence to remain cool under fire. A leader without physical courage most likely lacked the moral courage to stand up for his troops' welfare. The leader who did not care about his men felt little compunction to share their hardships or lead by example.[68]

Lest the aspiring junior leader despair over not possessing these virtues in ample abundance, he could take heart from knowing that he did not need to be a budding Napoleon. Elmar Dinter notes that in the stress of combat, "the only things that many group members require of their leaders are clear orders and a will to succeed."[69] In short, men in danger craved a little leadership. They tolerated some flaws and weaknesses as long as their leader took counsel, learned from his mistakes, and had his heart in the right place. Lieutenant Sefton, as he made his way through the fields of Normandy in search of his outfit on D-Day, collected lost paratroopers from a mix of units. His lack of an inspiring plan of action did not seem to bother his wards: "I did not encounter anyone who failed to ask, 'Lieutenant, what's your plan?' Nor did I find one who seemed dissatisfied with my answer, 'Follow me.' At the very least, it kept them from remaining alone in the dark."[70]

Though it is difficult to assess what constituted a minimal level of leadership proficiency, it is not at all hard to determine what happened in a unit whose commander clearly lacked the virtues of leadership. Units with incompetent or uncaring leaders suffered excessive casualties, low morale, and poor cohesion. Roy R. Grinker and John P. Spiegel concluded that poor leadership led to increased psychological strain and breakdown: "Bad leadership and lack of faith in . . . commanding officers have an immensely deteriorating effect upon morale. In the American army, where the relation between the officers and the enlisted men is more personal than traditional, the officer must win the confidence of his men. If this has not been accomplished, the psychological strain on each individual is greatly increased."[71]

An experienced leader like Captain Gerald P. Averill, who was commissioned from the ranks and led combat soldiers in two wars, understood firsthand what poor leadership could do to men's confidence: "Marines are trained to believe in their leaders, both non-commissioned and commissioned officers alike. If those officers show weakness or fear or, worse still, a lack of interest in the safety and welfare of their troops, the individual Marine loses not only confidence in his leaders but also in himself, and that lack of confidence is transmitted to his peers."[72]

Considering how dangerous and stressful it was to lead soldiers in combat, what possessed men to want to do it? As demanding as the job was, leading soldiers was not without its compensations. Junior leaders derived intense pride and satisfaction from their men's accomplishments. Sometimes that satisfaction came from knowing that long hours of training had paid off. Captain Smith's cannon company, in one of its first combat missions, helped to break up a Japanese night attack with well-placed artillery fire: "That kind of precision fire in the middle of the night under adverse conditions could only come from gun crews who were both highly skilled and conscientious. I was proud of them."[73]

Lieutenant Owen found himself in charge of a mortar section that, like the rest of the Seventh Marine Regiment, had been hastily patched together during the Korean War and fleshed out with called-up reservists. As it turned out, he had five weeks to train his men, most of whom knew nothing about mortars, before hitting the beach at Inchon. They proved up to the challenge, and after a few weeks of combat Owen was proud of his salty marines. Following a successful nightlong defense in which his mortars had played a prominent role, Owen asked his sergeant to ring up the company commander on the telephone: "I wanted to tell him that we had just saved battalion's ass, and that Baker-One-Seven [B Company, First Battalion, Seventh Marines] had the best goddamn mortar section in the regiment. Just as I had promised him at Camp Pendelton."[74]

The junior leader could take pride not only in his men but also in himself. He had trained and led them and had proven his abilities under fire. Lieutenant John A. Sullivan was thrust into combat as soon as he arrived at his company in Korea. Like most green replacement leaders, he worried about how he would perform. When his platoon rotated off outpost duty a few days later, his men picked up his gear without being asked and carried it. Sullivan's platoon sergeant explained that they did so because they had accepted him as their leader: "You took care of them, and they're going to take care of you." Sullivan was bursting with pride: "'*Now* I'm a platoon leader,' I said to myself. It felt good. It was worth the shit of the past few days, for whatever I had been trying to prove to myself was proven beyond all doubt."[75]

The combat leader who was competent and caring was rewarded with a loyalty and devotion for which the word "touching" does not begin to do justice. After his platoon had successfully beaten off a Viet Cong attack, Lieutenant James R. McDonough prepared to lead one of his squads on a counterattack. He was deeply moved by the men's willingness, despite the obvious danger, to follow him: "As the squad lined up . . . , I looked at their young faces tightened to stifle the fear building up inside their bodies. . . . No words of complaint from any of them. They were American infantrymen and would do the job they were asked to do. . . . I felt proud to be with them and glad to share their company. Their qualities of moral and physical courage, of unselfish dedication to each other amid the difficult jobs they were called upon to do, marked them in my mind as among the noblest of human beings."[76]

To experience just one such moment of unquestioned loyalty and devotion in the face of danger, as Lieutenant Caputo did when his platoon executed a flawless attack under heavy enemy fire, was reward enough: "And perhaps that is why some officers make careers of the infantry, why they endure the petty regulations, the discomforts and degradations, the dull years of peacetime duty in dreary posts: just to experience a single moment when a group of soldiers under your command and in the extreme stress of combat do exactly what you want them to do, as if they are extensions of yourself."[77]

# 10

# Dwellers Beyond the Environment of War

The combat soldier lived in a cruel world unknown to support troops living a mere mile or so behind the lines.[1] No matter that these troops kept the combatants supplied and backed by supporting arms—the frontline soldier resented them, as Private Eugene B. Sledge noted: "In our myopic view we respected and admired only those who got shot at, and to hell with everyone else. This was unfair to noncombatants who performed essential tasks, but we were so brutalized by war that we were incapable of making fair evaluations."[2]

That many of these noncombatants had successfully sought to avoid combat assignments only fueled this resentment. In World War II, the Research Branch discovered that the Army Ground Forces, which contained the combat arms, were less popular than the Army Service Forces and Army Air Forces. Furthermore, many of the soldiers assigned to the Ground Forces wanted no part of the Infantry Branch: "The Infantry offered a maximum chance of death or injury, and was not only a certain ticket for overseas duty but also was recognized as having hard, dirty, disagreeable work; its opportunities for promotion were less than in some, if not in most, other branches; and it provided little chance to learn skills specifically useful in civilian life."[3]

The ultimate affront to the infantryman occurred when rear-echelon soldiers were punished by being sent to do what he did as a matter of course. In the Philippines in World War II, Han Rants, an infantryman, was surprised to see men from the supply echelons arrive to spend several days at the front as punishment for stealing supplies. The reaction of Rants and his comrades can well be imagined: "We were wild-eyed angry because if this was a punishment, why were we there every day and having to go through years of it?"[4] In a highly publicized incident in Europe in World War II, a railway unit was caught in the act of black-marketing cigarettes, chocolate, and gasoline. Stealing supplies

246

intended for the fighting troops was bad enough, but even worse, those found guilty were allowed to serve in the infantry as their punishment. Lieutenant Paul Boesch's infantrymen were apoplectic on reading about it in *Stars and Stripes:*

> We scarcely could believe what we read!
> "Since when is fighting for your country a punishment?" Sergeant Hobbs demanded in a real fury. "I've been in the infantry four long hard years, not to escape jail either."
> "Who the hell wants to join the infantry," another man asked, "when they make it the dumping ground for all the dirty bastards in the world?"[5]

Combat soldiers, resentful over bearing the burden of fighting while so many others avoided it, developed a bitter pride. They, not the rear echelons, were the real soldiers, because they did the killing and the dying. They considered it their right, indeed one of their few perquisites, to lord it over anyone who was not part of their exclusive club, as Bill Mauldin reports: "While men in combat outfits kid each other around, they have a sort of family complex about it. No outsiders may join. . . . If a stranger comes up to a group of them when they are bulling, they ignore him. . . . Combat people are an exclusive set, and if they want to be that way, it is their privilege. They certainly earn it."[6]

Combat soldiers did more than ignore outsiders, they ridiculed them. Amos N. Wilder, on board a train filled with soldiers returning to their units at the front, discovered that harassing rear-echelon troops encountered en route was the main entertainment: "The funniest thing to me, constantly repeated, was the derision with which the whole trainload would greet M.P.'s or S.O.S. [Services of Supply] men, or other men of the rear. Of course we were old-timers—out of the hospital and seasoned in wars out-of-time. . . . It's surprising how a bunch of fellows who have been at the front are proud of it, and how superior they feel to anyone that hasn't."[7]

The combatants' club even had its own distinctive emblem, at least the infantry did—the Combat Infantryman's Badge. Introduced during World War II as a measure for boosting the prestige of the Infantry Branch, the CIB was an instant success because it clearly marked its wearer as a man who had been in combat, as Mauldin notes: "Everybody these days wears combat boots and combat jackets. A lot of people who never saw more infantry than basic training wear the infantry blue on their caps. The combat badge is about the only thing that sets the front-line man apart, and he has reason to be proud of it."[8]

The CIB remained a coveted award in the Korean and Vietnam Wars. Lieutenant John A. Sullivan remembers his pride upon receiving his CIB in Korea: "I had placed my life at risk for my country, and I had earned the respect of those who had done so before me. I had really joined the club!"[9] Lieutenant Michael Lee Lanning remains proud of his CIB, awarded in Vietnam: "Personally, I felt on that day . . . the same way I feel now: I have received no higher award or honor than the rifle and wreath of the CIB."[10]

## DOG ROBBERS, POGUES, AND REMFs

The infantryman was not the only soldier to risk his life in combat, however, and the infantry was not the only branch of service to seek recognition for doing so. Shortly after the CIB was established, a Combat Medic's Badge was introduced. Other branches, notably Armor, have clamored at times for similar recognition for their combatants. Whatever their branch, the combat soldiers' disdain for those outside their exclusive club was evident by their various names for their rear-echelon compatriots: dog robbers, chair-borne commandos, pogues (a marine term), and REMFs (rear-echelon motherfuckers).

Determining who deserved these disparaging labels was not an exact science but depended on the viewpoint of the soldier slinging the epithet. For the infantryman in a forward foxhole, for example, the company mortarmen were "rear echelon," yet the mortarmen envied the safety and comfort enjoyed by the cannoneers of their supporting artillery battalion. REMF, in short, was a relative term. The perceptive Mauldin was an expert on REMF relativity: "To the dogface out on patrol, his platoon command post, with its machine-gun emplacement, is rear echelon . . . and the safest place in the world."[11] The infantry platoon leader ensconced in that command post might well be surprised to learn that he was in the rear echelon, as Lieutenant Boesch was when he called his forward outpost one night only to be chastised by the soldier on the other end of the telephone for talking too loudly:

> A hoarse whisper came at last from the other end.
> "All right, all right, Jeezus Cuhrist, ya don't have to *shout!*"
> Then still in a low, almost inaudible whisper, the voice continued. "It may be all right for you guys to shout—you're way back there!"
> I sat stunned for a moment. Way back there! *We* were way back there![12]

Thus Boesch learned about rear-echelon relativity. He himself came to consider combatants other than the infantry to be relative REMFs because they enjoyed certain comforts: "Outside of the Infantry, men almost always were able to find blankets at night when it got cold, food when they were hungry, water when they wanted to drink. Their vehicles carried extra rations, small stoves, and other comforts we could only dream about."[13]

A soldier might be praised one day and condemned as a pogue the next, depending on what he was doing. A marine engineer sergeant in Korea explained to Mauldin that "pogue" was "sort of a relative word. When the engineers are picking up mines ahead of the infantry we're great men but when they catch us with picks and shovels back on a supply road we're pogues."[14]

The criteria for determining who was rear echelon thus varied, depending on the perspective of the soldier passing judgment, but in any case the combatant came to believe that there was a vast "they" to his rear who were guilty of various sins, the most basic of which was living in comfort and safety.[15] During World War I, doughboys' resentment of the rear echelon focused on the SOS and on dog robbers—those enlisted soldiers serving as officers' orderlies, staff clerks, and runners. Lieutenant Joseph D. Lawrence, bringing his men out of the line in October 1918, was "tired, and we all were weak, starved, sick, emaciated." While heading rearward, his ragged platoon passed through French villages occupied by service troops: "I envied those men in a house with the comfort of light and perhaps heat. We were like the animals of the forest, without light or heat and sleeping on the ground in the weather."[16]

No rear-echelon troops were more despised by the doughboys than the military police, or "S.O.S. Cowboys," as Private Charles MacArthur called them.[17] The reason was simple enough. Not only did MPs live in safety and comfort, but they also enforced codes of dress and conduct on combat troops visiting the rear areas. Private John O'Brien, an artilleryman intent on enjoying his first break in the action in weeks, was arrested on his way to the local *estaminet* and returned to his unit by the MPs because his dirty, worn-out uniform "looked like something you'd find on the Bowery." His understanding battery duty officer merely advised him not to get caught next time. As it turned out, "It was a good thing I was arrested and sent back. That night one of our men shot an MP, and there was hell to pay. We weren't overly fond of those fellows, you know."[18]

During World War II, combat soldiers resented MPs and supply-and-service troops with the same passion that their doughboy counterparts had. Audie Murphy and his comrades, briefly encamped in Rome following its liberation, noticed with disdain how the rear echelons "pour into town" as "the battle lines crawl northward": "Our attitude toward them is irrational. With the smell of mud and death still in our nostrils, we resent the pressed uniforms and gaiety of men who have spent the war in relatively safe areas."[19]

At least Murphy got to enjoy Rome for a few days. Lieutenant Harold L. Bond and his Thirty-sixth Infantry Division led the triumphal march into Rome, enjoyed the cheering crowds, and then marched out the other side again in pursuit of the retreating Germans: "The pleasures of Rome were not to be for the infantrymen. . . . Unlike the troops of old, taking a great city, the soldiers of this modern army left the comforts and pleasures of Rome to the men in the army headquarters, the service battalions, and the Allied military governors."[20]

Early on in the war in the Pacific, support troops were overworked, lived in spartan conditions, and were harassed by Japanese infiltrators. As the logistics buildup progressed, however, disparities between front line and rear area grew. With increasing efficiency, captured islands could be transformed into substantial, safe, and comfortable bases. Private Sledge and his marine regiment, after clearing the southern end of Peleliu, traveled back through the beach areas that they had assaulted about ten days earlier. They were amazed at the changes: "Heavy construction equipment was everywhere, and we saw hundreds of service troops living in tents and going about their duties as though they were in Hawaii or Australia." The neatly dressed, clean-shaven service troops "eyed us curiously, as though we were wild animals in a circus parade." When Sledge took stock of himself and his comrades, he realized why: "We were armed, helmeted, unshaven, filthy, tired, and haggard. The sight of clean comfortable noncombatants was depressing."[21]

The GI in the Korean War also resented the disparity between frontline and rear-echelon conditions. Once the front stabilized by late 1951, those disparities increased. Static warfare meant some improvements at the front in the form of bunkers with stoves, better rations, and trips to the showerpoint, but the transformation in the rear area was truly remarkable. Lieutenant Sullivan sarcastically describes life at the Seventh Infantry Division Rear Headquarters: "Complete with officers' and NCO clubs, fully stocked with booze, and even having a small theater for the occasional USO show (girls, girls, girls, plus the obligatory comedian), this area provided a safe haven for the rear echelon personnel needed to support one-tenth their number on the front line."[22]

The static nature of the command and logistics system in Vietnam again ensured a wide disparity between combat and rear-area living conditions. Grunts "humped the boonies" and set up defensive perimeters at new locations on almost a daily basis, and small firebases moved with some regularity, but brigade and larger headquarters, major logistics bases, and airfields became semipermanent facilities. This infrastructure did not spring up overnight, but once in place it provided an unprecedented degree of safety and comfort. At some point in his tour in Vietnam, almost every grunt got a chance to visit one of these installations, either as a hospital patient, while on pass as a reward for performance of duty, en route to R and R, or to board the Freedom Bird for the flight home. Like rubes visiting the big city, grunts were agog over the air-conditioned service clubs, electric lights, mess halls serving hot chow, tents or even permanent billets, movie theaters, post exchanges, and indoor plumbing.[23]

Amazement gave way to resentment. Sergeant Philip Dosier, the protagonist in Close Quarters, provides a harsh view of rear-echelon soldiers, or "housecats" as he calls them, while passing through Tan Son Nhut Air Base at the end of his tour: "Where have I been? All these dudes getting hostile fire pay. Fifty-five a month for doing this." And, of course, he resented their comforts: "Hot and cold running water, real toilets, everybody has a jeep, eight kinds of eggs for breakfast, and round-eyed pussy walking the streets just like back in Des Moines." Dosier assessed the gravest danger facing these housecats to be death by boredom: "Can't you just see it? A bunch of housecats strolling down the avenue to the USO. One of them suddenly clutches his throat and stumbles to the ground in gagging convulsions. 'It's boredom! He's got boredom. My God, get a medic, get a chaplain, get a dust-off! This man has boredom. . . .' The plague spreads. . . . Like some disgusting consumptive gunge, some lingering and lethal, virulent plague . . . it sweeps back and forth across the rear echelon. Thousands succumb."[24]

The combat soldier assumed that the rear echelons could live in such comfort because they were raking off the top from the flow of supplies, according to Boesch: "What irritated us about the whole process was that we knew when the PX shipment first started out it contained many choice items like fountain pens, cigarette lighters, lighter fluid, watches, combs, razors, things that the men genuinely needed. But as each succeeding echelon got its hands on the shipment, it dwindled in size and selection."[25]

Soldiers also perceived inequities in the distribution of essential clothing, such as boots and winter uniforms. Private Lester Atwell noticed that the headquarters soldiers in his battalion in World War II were always well attired: "Staff sergeants at Battalion Headquarters, men who worked indoors in clerical positions, pulled strings to secure articles of clothing intended first for combat troops. You saw them, ahead of anyone else, striding about in stiff new yellowish combat boots, brand-new pants, new shirts, new field jackets: Big Time Operators, easily recognizable through minor victories."[26]

The front-line soldier resented this short-stopping, but they were absolutely enraged over reports of rear-area black-marketeering. That their own side could sell or trade supplies needed at the front was a crime that fighting soldiers could not forgive. The combat engineer Henry Giles and his buddies noted with growing anger the stories of black-market activities in France in World War II: "And that burns the hell out of us. As if they didn't have the softest job of anybody, sitting on their fat asses in their big plush headquarters in Paris, they had to go stealing from their own troops."[27]

Grunts believed, not without cause, that rear-echelon black-marketeering was rampant in Vietnam. William D. Ehrhart and his fellow marines puzzled over how street vendors could be selling American goods that their unit was not able to acquire: "How the Vietnamese managed to lay hands on canned Coca Cola and American beer—items we could not beg, borrow or otherwise obtain through regular channels—baffled everyone. Clearly, the supply sergeants at the big bases . . . were making a killing off the war in Vietnam."[28]

Another sin committed by the rear echelons in the eyes of the fighting man was their propensity to grant themselves medals for valor—even the awards were being raked off the top. At war's end in Europe in 1945, Private Atwell was part of a group of men from various combat units temporarily assigned to their division's personnel section to help process soldiers' records. The sight of divisional clerks wearing CIBs did not sit well with the temporary help who had earned theirs the hard way: "On the first day we saw them, all had been wearing the blue-and-silver Combat Infantry Badge, which by right they should not have been issued; and such a howl went up from some of the new arrivals that the clerks were instructed to put their combat badges away until they went home on furlough."[29]

Lieutenant Scott Higgins, a supply officer at Headquarters, II Field Force (roughly a corps-level headquarters) in Vietnam, described how a ranking officer put himself in for a Purple Heart after stubbing his toe ("foot abrasions") while running from his trailer during the Tet Offensive. Higgins added that his fellow REMFs were accomplished at procuring medals: "And there was a lot of that. A lot of Air Medals went out that way, the kind you get for hazardous duty, for acts of valor in the air. A lot of officers would go out and just fly around and put themselves in for Air Medals or a Service Cross."[30]

Moreover, the frontline soldier came to believe that the people in the rear did not have a clue as to what the combatants were going through and, worse, did not seem to care.[31] Impossible orders, nonsensical directives, and demands for seemingly trivial information strengthened this perception. Captain Ralph Ingersoll, about to accompany a combat engineer company on a night attack in North Africa, found that its officers considered their own battalion staff to be out of touch with reality: "To hear the brothers [the tightly knit group of five A Company officers] speak of battalion headquarters and what went on there, you would think it was in Algiers and its officers remote and protected from the realities of war. The officers of A Company respected the officers of the other three line companies of engineers. These were equals. But the officers at battalion were old fogies and could not possibly understand what life was really like."[32]

Peter G. Bourne found the same attitude in a Special Forces A Team in Vietnam. As the Special Forces men were preparing their camp to meet an anticipated Viet Cong assault, Bourne noticed that they placed the blame for their predicament on their higher headquarters: "A . . . target for the hostility of the group is their higher command, the 'B' team forty miles away in Pleiku. There is a feeling that the 'B' team bears much of the responsibility for the military threat to the camp, and complaints are made that they live in comfort, care little about those who are 'really fighting the war,' and fail to support the camp adequately."[33]

Displays of rear-echelon distaste for the frontline soldier added to the perception that REMFs did not understand or care. Lieutenant Lanning and his radioman, straight in from the field to visit wounded men at a hospital in Saigon, went to the post exchange to fill their platoon's shopping list only to find that grubby, smelly grunts were not welcomed with open arms: "The American MP at the PX door explained to us—not any too politely—that we would have to leave our weapons outside. His attitude was that we dirty grunts were not really welcome. . . . We gathered the items on the lists as quickly as possible. Again we felt out of place. Most of the patrons looked at us as they would at whores in church. Just smelling our fatigues was about as close as many of them ever would get to the real war."[34]

Combatants' antagonism toward the rear echelon was to some extent unavoidable. Senior commanders and staff understood that their presence at the front would help reduce this antagonism by showing the men that they really did care and wanted to understand what conditions were like. Such visits could backfire, however, if the soldiers perceived them to be self-serving or insincere. The troops were instantly suspicious, for example, of rear-echelon visitors who showed up only when things were calm. Captain Charles B. MacDonald discovered to his dismay that once his company had moved into a quiet sector, "every officer in the division with the rank of major or above wanted to inspect the company area." These visitors pointedly avoided his First Platoon's exposed position, however, claiming "that it was a bit far to walk, but we laughed inwardly, knowing that it was the threat of enemy shelling that kept most of them away." The visits eventually slacked off, "either from my protest or the fact that all the inspection-minded 'brass' had satisfied their egos with visits to 'the front.' We wondered how many Silver Stars and Distinguished Service Crosses came from the visits."[35]

Combat soldiers were equally put off by senior visitors who, rather than coming by to learn about conditions or the tactical situation, showed up to "inspire" them. Corporal Martin Russ, a marine manning the trenches in Korea, rarely saw anyone above the rank of captain. One day, however, his regimental commander came by to glad-hand: "The colonel, escorted by a fire team, came around to each hole for a minute or two of Good Guy conversation. Standing above our hole, he asked us where we were from, etc. . . . Then he left, to receive his combat pay and Dingleberry Cluster for valour in action."[36]

In contrast to the visit that Russ experienced was a visit by a regimental commander in Korea to the infantry company that the forward observer James Hamilton Dill was supporting. The company was in a dangerous forward position, yet the colonel walked several miles to get there, unescorted except for a single orderly, allowing him to assess the terrain and the precarious nature of the position. He flew out by helicopter, thus indicating that the footmarch was by choice. He talked at some length with the company commander, looked around, and decided to pull the company back from its exposed position. This visit was not his first: "He showed up in the positions of front-line companies regularly and frequently. It took a high degree of dedication to make the physical effort required to climb so many ridges." There was no handshaking or backslapping. The men appreciated that this "brass hat" was here to do his job, not to posture: "Men on line usually have a nagging suspicion that 'higher headquarters,' whatever that mysterious entity is, did not have the foggiest notion what was happening to them. This time 'higher headquarters' had been present in person and obviously knew everything about us. Decisions had been made which gave us a better chance of getting out alive than we had expected. The men sensed this with the perception soldiers have to the moods of their officers."[37]

If the men were uninspired by visits from posturing, self-serving brass, they were completely alienated by rabble-rousing pep talks. Such speeches might inspire trainees, or green units before a battle, but veteran combatants had little use for them. Prior to dispatching Tim O'Brien's infantry company on a dangerous mission in Vietnam, the battalion commander formed the men in a semicircle about him to give them some fatherly advice on fighting the Viet Cong: "You're American soldiers. You're stronger than the dink. You're bigger. You're faster. You're better educated. You're better supplied, better trained, better supported. All you need is brains." After the colonel flew off in his helicopter, one of the company officers summed up the effect of this inspirational speech: "Christ, what a pompous asshole." When the battalion commander was killed a few days later, "a lieutenant led us in song, a catchy, happy, celebrating song: Ding dong, the wicked witch is dead. We sang in good harmony."[38]

O'Brien's apparent glee, or at least lack of regret, over the death of his battalion commander may seem callous, but soldiers did not care much about what happened to those outside their own group. They could sympathize with the plight of their fellow combatants and were even willing to fight to save a sister unit in trouble, if only because they expected others to do the same if they were in need of such help. But on occasions when rear-echelon soldiers got into a tight spot, combatants' reactions varied from indifference to actual delight over their predicament. Private Elton E. Mackin, on night watch during World War I, was relieved to find that the incoming shells he heard were the "big stuff," destined for targets in the rear. His buddy was more than relieved. He wished the shells godspeed: "Go get them slackers, baby, those goddamn politicians in the Service[s] of Supply."[39] During the fighting in the Pusan Perimeter in the Korean War, a North Korean artillery barrage struck the command post of Lieutenant Frank Muetzel's marine infantry battalion: "The troops thought this was pretty funny. They said it was about time the CP got into the war."[40]

Combat troops had even less sympathy for rear-echelon soldiers who unnecessarily put themselves in harm's way, either because they were lost or were poking around where they should not have been. According to William Manchester, combat soldiers had no use for rear-echelon souvenir hunters: "I shall never understand men whose jobs kept them away from the front, who could safely wait out the war . . . yet who deliberately courted death in those Golcondas of mementos, the combat zones. You heard stories about 'Remington Raiders,' 'chairborne' men ready to risk everything for something, *anything,* that would impress families and girls at home. I didn't believe any of them until I saw one."[41] The souvenir hunter he saw, an army quartermaster soldier, ended up mortally wounded. Manchester could not mourn for a rear-echelon soldier on a fool's errand: "Though I could still cry, and did, I saved my tears for the men I knew. This GI was a stranger. His behavior had been suicidal and cheap."[42]

The rear-echelon soldier was selfish and uncaring, from the perspective of the combatant. In reality, most rear-echelon soldiers worked hard, conscientiously, and honestly to support the combat soldier. The more perceptive support troops were well aware of how much better off they were than their compatriots at the front and genuinely sympathized with the combat soldier's plight.[43] Lieutenant Howard V. O'Brien was trained as an artillery officer, but because of his fluency in French, ended up as a liaison officer in the French War Ministry in

World War I. He was alternately bored and homesick but had to admit that he had little to complain about: "What's [the] use of struggling? Take it as it comes. Got a safe job, and comfortable. 'Doing my bit,' etc., etc. I'm lucky, and a damned fool to squawk about it."[44]

During World War II, the headquarters clerk E. J. Kahn was one of those rear-echelon soldiers who, early in the Pacific fighting, did not live appreciably better than the combatants. He realized, nevertheless, that he was relatively better off: "All in all my life in New Guinea was a cinch compared to that of the soldiers in the front lines, who, in order to kill Japs, had to incur endless risks and incredible hardships. Sometimes we soldiers who weren't in a position to destroy any of the enemy thought we were having it tough, but we weren't."[45]

Sergeant Giles, as a combat engineer in World War II, worked hard and was often in danger, usually from artillery fire. He still counted his blessings every time he saw the infantry slogging by: "I never saw a line of them going up [to the front] that I don't think, poor bastards. . . . You feel guilty for thinking, thank God it isn't me, but you feel it just the same, and at the same time you just wish to God there was something you could do."[46]

The fact that many rear-echelon soldiers realized their good fortune, sympathized with the plight of the combat soldier, and performed their duties in an admirable fashion did little to change the frontline soldier's attitude toward them, however. REMFs were not part of the exclusive club and hence deserved no respect.[47] Mauldin, using the especially despised Military Police as an example, explains why the rear echelons will forever be resented by the combat soldier: "It wouldn't do any good to show [the combat GI] that these MPs . . . are a part of the tremendous machine that keeps him fed and clothed and supplied. It wouldn't do any good, because the doggie lives a primitive life and hasn't time for reasoning. He says to himself, 'This is nothing but a bunch of rear echelon bastards. . . .' Soldiers who are in danger feel a natural and human resentment toward soldiers who aren't."[48]

This disdain for the rear echelons, however, did not preclude all but the most ardent soldier-adventurer from quitting his exclusive club to join their ranks, given the chance.[49] Lieutenant James Brady writes that survival came first: "You didn't want to be a rear-echelon pogue, you wanted to be with a line outfit, but once you'd seen combat and lost people and had the usual close calls, for most of us, that was sufficient."[50] Occasionally a combatant landed a safer job because of some special skill or special connections. The commander of the 196th Light Infantry Brigade in Vietnam decided he wanted a brigade bugler. Suddenly, Stanley Goff's skill with the coronet was his ticket out of the boonies. Goff took the job, although he felt guilty about leaving his comrades: "It was very sad; here I was, picked out of all these guys to go. Any one of them was good enough to go. Any of them. I can't ever really give you the feeling of what I felt as I walked by those guys—tears were in my eyes."[51]

Like Goff, soldiers felt guilt over leaving comrades behind to carry on the fight while they took a job in the rear. Beyond the desire to survive, however, an additional factor made departing easier to bear, as illustrated by the example of Captain Bob Fay, a veteran company commander who left Boesch's battalion to join the Ninth Army staff: "We hated to lose Bob, and he disliked going, but all of us realized that men live longer in a rear headquarters, and we were glad to see him get the break. He had already proved his ability and courage in combat so that a rear echelon job was something he could wear with dignity."[52] A soldier like Fay, who had done his share and proven himself in battle, could accept a life-saving, rear-echelon job with his pride intact. Furthermore, his comrades, although understandably jealous of his good fortune, genuinely wished him well because he had earned it.

## SLACKERS, HOME GUARDS, AND WAR PROFITEERS

In the same breath that the combat soldier cursed the rear echelon, he vented his spleen against the home front. During the Korean and Vietnam Wars, soldiers complained, often bitterly, about Stateside indifference and even hostility. The soldier in the world wars could at least draw comfort from knowing, as the historian Dixon Wecter has explained, that the home front supported him: "Bracing to his morale was the knowledge that they, the mass of Americans, stood behind him, working hard, buying Bonds, giving blood, putting up with minor sacrifices without complaint."[53]

This encouraging picture of national unity aside, the combat soldier in the world wars strongly resented homefront saber rattling, complaints about how difficult life was at home, and civilian ignorance of conditions at the front. The soldier hated saber rattlers because they would not be the ones wielding the swords. Lieutenant O'Brien noted that for the doughboy "sitting in [a] muddy shell-hole" with artillery shells whizzing by overhead, it was "no comfort to reflect that four thousand miles away some slob, his fat belly cushioned in arm-chair, is telling neighbors Hun should be punished for crimes."[54] From the doughboy's perspective, the cure for saber rattling was simple enough, as O'Brien pointed out: "Curious how a little personal experience of H.E. [high explosive] tempers passion for triumphal march down Unter den Linden [in Berlin]. If a storm-brigade of editorial writers, officered by politicians, were put on the line, the old war would be over in 45 minutes."[55]

The combat soldier was further annoyed by civilian whining over how, given wartime shortages, they were suffering while exhibiting no appreciation for the privations of life at the front. Private Sledge and his comrades in the Pacific received letters from buddies who had returned to the States that were "disturbingly bitter and filled with disillusionment." Some of those veterans, apparently men discharged for medical or psychological reasons, or perhaps among the handful rotated home, even wished they could rejoin the old battalion.

Their letters were full of "talk of war profiteers and able-bodied men who got easy duty at the expense of others. Some letters said simply that folks back in the States 'just don't understand what the hell it's all about, because they have it so easy.'"[56]

For Audie Murphy and his comrades in Italy, a review of the headlines in the hometown newspapers left them with the impression that the home front knew nothing about what the GIs were going through. One of Murphy's buddies provided a rundown of the news:

> Caskell . . . says, "While waiting at the aid station, I read some old Chicago papers."
> "What's new?" asks Brandon.
> "Charlie Chaplin wants a second front."
> "A second front! Jeezus! Give him this one."
> "The cigarette shortage continues; and people are demanding an explanation for the scarcity of tobacco."
> "My piles bleed for them."
> "The public is warned that meat rationing will be more severe in the coming months."
> "Meat?"
> "Yeah. The kind that doesn't come in cans. Remember?"
> "Lord, yes. Steak."
> "Night clubs may be forced to close at midnight to conserve fuel and the energies of factory workers who like to guzzle too late."
> "I can't stand it."[57]

Although doughboys and GIs excoriated the home front in general for warmongering and failing to appreciate its good fortune, they reserved some of their most vituperative comments for their fellow soldiers who had somehow landed a Stateside billet. Soldiers overseas spoke disparagingly of the homefront military as the "USO boys" or the "home guard" who, as a marine in Thomas Boyd's World War I novel put it, "guard our women while we're over here."[58] Soldiers in the Pacific in World War II expressed their resentment to the Research Branch: "Let them USO boys get some of this chow once in a while, then they will know what it is like to sleep in the mud with mosquitoes buzzing around. . . . Then they will know what life is in this damn Pacific. . . . It is hard to be here and read in every paper . . . from home where Pvt. Joe Dokes is home again on furlough after tough duty as a guard at Radio City."[59] Men overseas clearly resented the soldiers at home who were "guarding" the women and the whiskey, but as Ernie Pyle discovered, to really set a GI off, bring up the subject of war workers striking for more pay: "Just mention a strike at home to either soldier or officer, living on monotonous rations in the mud under frequent bombing, and you had a raving maniac on your hands."[60] That workers were prospering as a result of the war was enough to make GIs see red. Throw in a strike over wages, and they could indeed rave, as Win Stracke's antiaircraft gun crew did after hearing about a United Mine Workers' strike: "I can remember heated discussions when John L. Lewis pulled out the miners. Oh, the terrible bitterness. 'Those sons-o'-bitchin' miners are makin' a hundred and fifty or two hundred bucks a week and we're bustin' our asses for a hundred dollars a month. They oughta string 'em up.'"[61]

The soldier's resentment of war profiteering was not so much directed at the wealthy industrialists, whom he certainly despised but did not know personally, as it was against the guy living down the street back home who had landed a lucrative, war-essential job: "The [World War I] soldier felt aggrieved by the profits certain civilians had garnered from his war. Old classmates in high school who had convinced draft boards of the flatness of their feet were now married, living in comfortable houses, driving snappy cars. Some, in government jobs, had weathered the war in swivel chairs, at salaries dwarfing his dollar-a-day."[62]

The combat soldier further resented that the draft-age men profiting from the war could do so because they had acquired a medical or an occupational draft deferment. The Selective Service System was established to manage the manpower needed not only for the armed forces but also for an expanding wartime industry and agriculture. From the perspective of the draft-eligible male, the central question was how this system decided who carried a rifle versus who served safely in the rear, or never donned a uniform at all. Not surprisingly, many of those chosen to carry rifles questioned the equity of the selection process.

In all the wars of the draft era, soldiers believed, with varying degrees of conviction, that men of education, wealth, and influence landed safe jobs in the rear or wangled a deferment. Amos Wilder, a volunteer, noticed that the draftee replacements arriving to flesh out his artillery battalion not only lacked his enthusiasm but also had chips on their shoulders because of those men who had escaped service: "One . . . heard the usual diatribes against pacifists, slackers, and profiteers on the homefront."[63] Lieutenant O'Brien felt the same way: "But the draft-evader—he's not playing fair. Defaulted on the social contract, and ought to be made to pay up."[64]

Similar diatribes are evident in the World War II memoirs. Lieutenant Paul Fussell, who became an academic after serving in the infantry, was more than a little annoyed over colleagues who had dodged the service, or at least the front: "I was bitterly angry at men of my age who had managed to survive the war in comfort and cleanliness. I was especially furious at those given to bragging about their cleverness in avoiding the combat their social inferiors had to perform."[65] That some people considered combat duty fit only for those without education or technical skills accounts in part for the bitterness and cynicism of the members of the "exclusive club." Private Robert Leckie leveled a blast at American society for its disparaging view of the World War II combat soldier: "Keep it up, America, keep telling your youth that mud and danger are fit only for intellectual pigs. Keep on saying that only the stupid are fit to sacrifice, that America must be defended by the low-brow and enjoyed by the high-brow."[66]

Just how accurate were these charges that men of intellect or influence avoided service, or at least combat, at the expense of the less well-endowed? Some historians claim, as Lee Kennett does in his study of the World War II GI, that the army as a whole was representative: "The Army was the nation itself, an authentic slice of American society with all its many layers. Given the amount of manpower mobilized, it was probably necessary that the Army be that way; given the principles for which the nation fought, it was also somehow appropriate."[67]

Kennett's claim that the World War II army reflected American society is no doubt substantially accurate, and it was certainly more representative than the armies that took to the field in Korea and Vietnam. But the charges leveled by Fussell and Leckie also have merit. Relatively more of the men who did poorly on the Army General Classification Test (AGCT), administered to all recruits to determine basic intelligence and trainability, were allocated to the Army Ground Forces. Conversely, the Army Air Forces received a substantially larger percentage of men who did well on the AGCT. Further, of those with high scores who were assigned to the Ground Forces, many were skimmed off for special schooling, notably the Army Specialized Training Program, although some of these men, along with Air Corps and Service Forces personnel, were involuntarily transferred to the infantry late in the war to meet the growing demand for replacements.[68]

The net result of these programs and policies was to leave the impression that the unlucky and the losers ended up at the front, hence the bitterness evident in Leckie's and Fussell's statements. This perception, and the resentment it generated, grew stronger during the Korean War and culminated in bitter charges of "class war" during the Vietnam era. During these wars, relatively fewer men, compared to the world wars, had to be inducted to meet military requirements; thus draft boards could be more liberal in dispensing deferments. Furthermore, since these wars were less popular than the world wars, more young men sought these deferments or exemptions. And as in World War II, of those men who did serve, few wanted to join the infantry's exclusive club.

The reluctance to serve was evident in a 1952 survey of draft-age college students. Eighty-two percent did not want to be drafted because military service would disrupt their lives. They also considered their educational deferments "fair," because they were only postponing, not avoiding, military service. Moreover, more than half questioned American involvement in Korea.[69] The result, even more than during World War II, was that the relatively undereducated and underprivileged served in combat. Morris Janowitz and Roger W. Little noted that the effect of the selective service process during the Korean War was to "procure a relatively larger number of lower class youth for the Army," simply because they were "less likely to have acquired occupational or educational deferment."[70]

Further, as Little discovered while studying combat infantrymen in Korea, for those youths who were inducted into the army, "personnel assignment policies introduced an additional screening effect," specifically that men with civilian skills or education were assigned to rear-echelon duties but that "men assigned to the rifle company were most likely to lack highly valued social attributes (usually associated with educational experience)."[71] Or in the more colorful words of Lieutenant Anderson in Ernest Frankel's novel: "If they've got a kid in [the] service, drafted of course, then Mamma and Daddy'll be pissed off if the Army doesn't make sonny a cook or a radio repairman or a medical technician— anything but a soldier. That's what's wrong with us. Nobody wants to fight."[72]

A survey of Korean War casualties from the Detroit area, published in 1955, verified Little's theory that those lacking "highly valued social attributes" did indeed end up as combatants. Men killed, captured, or reported missing came disproportionately from nonwhite and low-income neighborhoods, thus substantiating "charges made by a number of observers that Korea was a 'poor man's war.'"[73]

As with just about every other aspect of the "forgotten war," however, these warnings about a "poor man's war" went unheeded. Following the Korean War, men continued to be drafted into the peacetime army, and both draftees and volunteers increasingly came from poor or working-class backgrounds.[74] Thus, the issue of "poor man's war" inevitably resurfaced during the Vietnam War, and the debate still continues over the extent to which the working classes were forced by the system to fight and die in the jungles and rice paddies while the middle and upper classes landed safe jobs in the rear or avoided service altogether.

Complicating this debate is the difficulty inherent in determining what constitutes class in America. Numerous surveys exist on the Vietnam War soldier, but their conclusions vary, depending on what economic, occupational, and residential factors were selected as the basis for comparison.[75] At the risk of oversimplifying, the relatively few surveys concluding that Vietnam was not substantially a class war either factor in officers, which boosts their statistics on soldiers' education levels and economic status, or claim that although the upper echelons of society avoided going to Vietnam, the resulting additional burden placed on the lower classes serving in their stead was minimal.[76]

A larger group of historians and sociologists argues that Vietnam was indeed a class war. They claim that the Selective Service System's philosophy of "channeling" virtually ensured that it would be. The intent of channeling, as explained in an orientation kit given to new draft board members, was to "channel" young men into "activities which were considered essential to the Nation." Occupational deferments would thus encourage men to keep working in defense-related jobs to avoid the draft. Educational deferments would likewise encourage men to stay in school, thereby ensuring a supply of teachers, engineers, and scientists.[77]

This plan for managing young men's lives seems sinister, but it was not without its logic to the leadership of a country embroiled in a Cold War, the winning of which could hinge upon maintaining a technological and industrial edge.

As for individuals who "could not participate" in "essential" activities, they would be eligible for the draft and would thus also benefit the nation by serving in the military. Channeling therefore made sense in the midst of the Cold War or in the case of a full mobilization, when the most efficient use of all manpower would be critical. The problem arose in the gray area of limited war. Fighting the Vietnam War required about only 6 percent of the draft-age male population.[78] As young men scrambled to avoid being part of that 6 percent, they used their money and influence to obtain a deferment or a safe billet in the reserve forces, few of which were called up during the Vietnam War. Lawrence M. Baskir and William A. Strauss, members of President Gerald R. Ford's post–Vietnam Presidential Clemency Board, explained that this scramble did not benefit the nation: "Aside from giving the armed forces the soldiers needed to fight the war, the draft did little to 'channel' a generation of draft-age men in directions that served the national interest. Instead, it created distortion, dislocation, and above all, class discrimination."[79]

Channeling generated class discrimination because the 6 percent who were drafted generally lacked the money and influence necessary to avoid the draft through deferment. If the overwhelmingly middle-class officer corps is not factored into the picture of who served in the foxholes in Vietnam, then survey results clearly indicate, as one survey summarizes, that "men from disadvantaged backgrounds were about twice as likely as their better-off peers to serve in the military, go to Vietnam, and see combat."[80]

Determining exactly how discriminatory channeling and the military's personnel policies were in assigning men of lower educational and economic status to the exclusive club of the combat soldier may never be possible. Nor, as Baskir and Strauss point out, can the "discriminatory social, economic, and racial impact" of these policies "be fairly measured against other wars in American history." Arguably, war at the cutting edge has always been a poor man's affair. Baskir and Strauss contend, however, that the perception of a class war had never been stronger than during the Vietnam War era: "The American people were never before as conscious of how unevenly the obligation to serve was distributed. Few of the nation's elite had sons or close friends who did any fighting."[81]

The grunt felt this inequity keenly. Charles Moskos found a streak of "class hostility" among grunts aimed at their more privileged peers, who not only did not serve but also had the temerity to denounce those who did: "To some extent the soldier's dislike of peace demonstrators is also an outcome of class hostility. To many combat soldiers—themselves largely working class—peace demonstrators are regarded as socially privileged college students."[82] Grunts resented the middle- and upper-class youths who had the educational and occupational deferments or who landed positions in the reserves and National Guard.[83]

Larry Heinemann was one of those working-class grunts, drafted when he ran out of money to continue his college education. He believed that he was chosen to fill the draft quotas so that his more privileged peers could stay in Chicago:

"I got drafted, just like that; got scarfed up, just picked up real quick, because a lot of kids on the North Shore had more money than I did, and ironclad deferments. It's a very affluent part of the country. So they were picking up everybody they could. It was mostly guys like me."[84]

Lieutenant Lanning took an informal survey of the grunts in his platoon in Vietnam in 1969. A few were volunteers, but by this point in the war, most were draftees, and most had been "on the street" before being drafted: "There was, of course, no one in my platoon with a white-collar background or even an inclination in that direction."[85] Only one of his men had a college degree. The college boys, he noted, were at home: "All a man had to do to avoid the draft was to stay in school with a deferment until he was twenty-six years old. At that magic age, he was no longer considered for conscription. Many of today's lawyers and Ph.D.s strived for their academic degrees solely to miss another type of struggle—the one to survive in Vietnam."[86]

If the sons of the wealthy and influential could take advantage of draft deferments that poorer men could not, then they might at least be modestly thankful for their good fortune, but some were not. The editor James Fallows, after describing the various ways that he and his Ivy League compatriots dodged military service, condemned the class arrogance of some of his fellow avoiders in claiming, as one Rhodes scholar and eventual corporate lawyer did, that being spared from the fighting was only their due: "There are certain people who can do more good in a lifetime in politics or academics or medicine than by getting killed in a trench." These self-avowed elites, noted Fallows, had nothing but "disdain for the abilities, hopes, complexities of those who have not scrambled onto the high road."[87] The grunt's opinion of his supposed betters can be imagined, but the Vietnam War veteran James Martin Davis spells it out: "Among some of the college students who successfully avoided the war and among some of the press who reported it, but did not have to fight it, there was an elitism, an arrogance and a snobbishness that flew in the face of our national democratic ideals. Many of my generation considered themselves better than the soldiers who had gone to Vietnam. They considered themselves 'too good' to have to go."[88]

In the wars of the draft era, the men carrying the rifles naturally resented those on the home front who were safe, comfortable, and even prospering. That even a few of those fortunate stay-at-homes during the Vietnam War era could complacently claim that it was only right that "lesser men" fight and die in their stead, however, was a disturbing development in a most disturbing war.

## THE AMBIGUOUS RELATIONSHIP WITH THE HOME FRONT

Despite his resentment of the home guards, draft dodgers, and war profiteers, the combat soldier was not totally alienated from the home front. He clung to his ties with friends and family, and their continued love and support were essential to his coping with war's horrors. Furthermore, because his country had sent him to war, he believed that he deserved its recognition for his sacrifices and accomplishments. Fussell pointed out that "*credit* became a crucial concept" for the World War II GI, who "never forgot" his "all-important home-town audience."[89] Mauldin observed that this desire for hometown recognition and pride in country, balanced against the GI's resentment of homefront selfishness and easy living, produced an ambiguous relationship: "The attitude of the dogface toward America and the home front is a complex thing. Nobody loves his own land more than a soldier overseas, and nobody swears at it more."[90]

Returning from their war, soldiers expected to receive some of that credit Fussell mentions. Father Francis P. Duffy and his regiment, the 165th Infantry, returned after World War I to a tickertape parade in New York City. Duffy was "not a militarist, nor keen for military glory," but this parade "was a deserved tribute to a body of citizen soldiers who had played such a manful part in battle for the service of the Republic."[91]

Not all soldiers returning from the world wars were welcomed with a tickertape parade, but most were recognized for their accomplishments and thanked for their sacrifices, even if the home front could not fully fathom the nature of those sacrifices. Soldiers returning from Korea and Vietnam also wanted recognition, but as a general rule, they were disappointed. Mauldin, visiting Korea as a civilian correspondent in early 1952, accurately identified the problems that limited war, individual rotation, and the lack of a clear-cut victory would cause for soldiers' recognition: "[The GI] fights a battle in which his best friends get killed and if an account of the action gets printed at all in his home town paper, it appears on page 17 under a Lux ad. There won't be a victory parade for his return because he'll come home quietly and alone, on rotation, and there's no victory in the old-fashioned sense, anyway, because this isn't that kind of war."[92]

Vietnam was not that kind of war, either. Vietnam veterans, returning as individuals from a war not yet won, and not likely to be won, knew there would be no parades, bands, or speeches, but they did expect some recognition, and certainly acceptance. Sergeant Bill Morgan, in the novel *Fragments,* describes the returning veteran's need for homefront stability and acceptance: "You wanted to be home again, home where old connections were waiting like strong, open bonds ready to embrace you and hold you firm. You wanted to plug yourself into them again: parents, friends, ideas and images as innocent as youth." Plugging in again, however, was possible only with the help of the people: "You wanted them to understand because they were your jury; they had sent you off to war, and now that you had returned, they alone had the power to honor and excuse."[93]

Too often, however, returning grunts were not honored and excused but denounced and accused, especially by the hostile elements of the antiwar movement. Blaming the war on the men who had fought it was, Jonathan Shay points out, a gross "betrayal of what's right": "Support on the home front for the soldier, *regardless of ethical and political disagreements over the war itself,* is essential."[94]

The soldier not only wanted to be thanked for his service when he returned home, but he also craved recognition while still overseas. The combat soldier scoured the newspapers sent from home for any scrap of information about himself or his unit. Bob Hoffman was comforted by the thought that, whatever happened, his actions in an earlier fight had already been lauded at home: "I thought of my father and mother. I knew that they were very proud of me, for in my pocket was a clipping, columns and columns, from a Pittsburgh newspaper telling of my exploits on Hill 204."[95] Hoffman was later awarded a Distinguished Service Cross for his fight on Hill 204, but recognition for lesser accomplishments also meant a great deal. Jules Coleman's division in the Pacific in World War II sent notices to hometown newspapers about promotions and awards. Coleman attests to their value: "Items to hometown newspapers were sent out in huge volume. The items themselves were not necessarily of great moment, for example, promotion from private to private first class, but they were important to the men, and to their families."[96]

Beyond personal accomplishments, the soldier wanted recognition for his unit, with which he closely identified. Sergeant Giles was happy to see reporters show up to interview the men in his engineer battalion after they had built the first tactical bridge across the Rhine River at Remagen: "This first bridge across by the Americans will be the biggest story since the Bulge. . . . I wrote Janice [his wife] and told her to watch the headlines. . . . When the story about it comes out in S&S [*Stars and Stripes*] I hope I can get a copy to send her."[97]

Giles and his fellow engineers deserved credit for their bridge, but often soldiers did not receive the recognition they deserved, or thought they deserved. Captain Hyman Samuelson complained that his engineer construction battalion in the Pacific in World War II never got any attention from the press. For example, the papers announced the occupation of the Trobriand Islands only when the "marines and infantry move in and 'take' the island without enemy opposition. Hurrah for them." The press failed to mention that the engineers had already been on those islands for a month preparing docks and facilities.[98]

The soldier often blamed his lack of media and hence homefront recognition on the glory-grabbing marines. This precedent was set in World War I when the marines were recognized for their fighting in Belleau Wood while the army got short shrift, in part because censorship prevented naming specific units but allowed for use of the term "marines," which could only refer to the lone marine brigade serving in France. Bob Hoffman complained that "the publicity [the marines] received would make one believe that they had won the entire war single-handed."[99] And Charles MacArthur described army-marine animosity and blamed its vehemence partly on the fact that "The Fighting Few seemed to be grabbing all the credit for the war."[100]

Soldiers resented marine headlining in later wars as well. The Marine Corps's star was again ascendant after Guadalcanal. From the GI's perspective, marines garnered the glory in the Pacific for their amphibious assaults while the soldiers received minimal recognition for their costly "mopping up." As James Jones observed, "Everybody now knows, at least everybody of my generation," about the gallant fight of the First Marine Division on Guadalcanal, but "not many, even of my generation, know that from about mid-November, 1942, on, U.S. infantry was doing much of the fighting on Guadalcanal."[101] Those unheralded army units included Jones's Twenty-fifth Infantry Division.

During the Korean War, as Craig M. Cameron has pointed out, "Public relations remained one of the corps's greatest strengths."[102] The marines were praised for their role in the Inchon landing, and as the army lieutenant Ralph Hockley noted, with ill-concealed bitterness, the sole marine division in Korea managed to stay in the headlines thereafter: "Sometimes to hear marines talk, you would think that the Punchbowl and Heartbreak Ridge—and, for that matter, the whole damned war—was some sort of purely marine operation. That just isn't so."[103]

The depth of soldiers' rancor over what they considered marine grandstanding indicates how important homefront recognition was to them. They just wanted the people at home to appreciate how difficult, dangerous, and traumatic their war was. No one tried harder than Ernie Pyle to convey that message, and he never forgot how important it was to do so, because the soldiers did not let him forget. While following an infantry company fighting in the suburbs of Cherbourg in Normandy, Pyle was nearly accosted by an infantryman who "said, almost belligerently, 'Why don't you tell the folks back home what this is like? All they hear about is victories and a lot of glory stuff. They don't know that for every hundred yards we advance somebody gets killed. Why don't you tell them how tough this life is?'"[104]

Virtually every correspondent who spent time with combat troops heard a similar, often emotional plea. During the bleak, early days of the Korean War, as American and South Korean troops retreated into the Pusan Perimeter, a lieutenant approached Marguerite Higgins "in a fury": "As his lips trembled with exhaustion and anger, he said, 'Are you correspondents telling the people back home the truth? Are you telling them that out of one platoon of twenty men, we have three left? Are you telling them that we have nothing to fight with, and that it is an utterly useless war?'" The combat soldier had no one else to turn to but the correspondents to tell his story, and as Higgins asserts, those correspondents who stayed close to the troops tried to do so, even when the news was not good: "We felt it our responsibility to report the disasters as we saw them. And we knew how passionately the guys who were doing the fighting wanted the 'folks back home' to know what they were up against."[105] Again during the Vietnam War, the soldier wanted his story told, as the correspondent Michael Herr reports: "And always, they would ask you with an emotion whose intensity would shock you to please tell it, because they really did have the feeling that it wasn't being told for them, that they were going through all of this and that somehow no one back in the World knew about it."[106]

The soldier's penchant for war souvenirs further attests to his desire for homefront recognition. Returning home with some campaign ribbons and an award for valor was a good way for a soldier to prove that he had earned a hero's welcome, but proof could also take the form of a Japanese battle flag or a German pistol. Doughboys were inveterate souvenir hunters. Lieutenant O'Brien recalls a standing joke about why Americans fought: "England fighting for Freedom of Sea; France for La Patrie; U.S. for Souvenirs."[107] German helmets, bayonets, pistols, insignia, and belt buckles were popular.[108]

Soldiers in later wars were also avid souvenir hunters. Combat soldiers collected souvenirs for themselves but also used them to trade with rear-echelon troops for food or liquor. The reason the rear echelons wanted souvenirs was obvious enough, as Lieutenant George William Sefton explained while trading war booty acquired in Normandy to some naval officers: "It was evident from the start that the officers' respective craving for something to show the folks back home was exceeded only by the ship's larder of choice edibles with which to dicker the deals."[109]

Soldiers hoped that souvenirs would impress the folks back home. Matthew Brennan, after volunteering to extend his tour of duty in Vietnam, was granted some Stateside leave. He suddenly realized that he had no souvenirs to take with him. During one of his last operations before going home, he found a Viet Cong flag boldly flying over a deserted village: "The platoon formed a line and walked cautiously toward the flagpole, but I was greedy. I wanted to take that flag home with me. I ran to the pole and pulled down the red, yellow, and blue flag." Turning around to show his buddies the flag, he found them scrambling for cover. They had sensibly assumed that such a tempting souvenir was deliberately left behind and booby-trapped. Brennan "felt like a fucking idiot" for taking such a chance. Even worse, when he got home and "showed my family the flag," it "meant nothing to them." Hence his attempt to impress the home front was for nought.[110]

The combat soldier craved homefront recognition while simultaneously resenting those in the States or in the rear areas who were safe, comfortable, and possibly even profiting from the war. He believed that he deserved their appreciation for risking his life and suffering privations. One group of soldiers was especially desirous of recognition for their sacrifices. The African-American soldier believed that fighting for his country would prove his worthiness to be treated as an equal with white citizens. The efforts of black soldiers in the four wars of the draft era would contribute toward that goal, but it was not an easy process.

# 11
# Equal Opportunity in the Foxhole

During both world wars and initially in the Korean War, African Americans served in segregated units. The army integrated during the Korean War era, and thus in Vietnam blacks and whites fought side by side. Integration improved military efficiency and promoted better relations between the races, but it did not resolve all racial problems or eliminate race as a factor in soldiers' attitudes and motivations.

Skin color, for example, affected attitudes toward rallying to the flag. Although young blacks often joined the service for the same reasons as whites, seeking adventure or a career they could be proud of, in the era of segregation in America blacks also enlisted to prove that they could serve their country as effectively and loyally as whites. A GI in World War II told the Research Branch that he and his fellow blacks had volunteered for combat duty "because we all are supposed to be American citizens. . . . Since we are citizens we should be granted the privilege [to fight] that the rest are getting because we are just as good as the next man."[1]

Ironically, considering that any number of reluctant white draftees would have gladly surrendered this privilege to anyone who wanted to take their place, blacks had to clamor for their right to fight. The number of black combat units formed and committed to battle during the era of segregation was relatively low because of the pervasive belief among whites that the black man was not fit to be a combat soldier. Blacks were relegated to service as support troops, often performing menial or disagreeable tasks such as stevedoring, construction, and graves registration. Those black units that did see combat in the world wars did so in no small part because black politicians, the black press, and civil rights advocates demanded a role in the fighting for black Americans. Lieutenant Christopher Sturkey believed that he and his black tank-destroyer outfit saw combat in World War II largely because of this agitation: "The white military opinion was [that] Negro troops were only good for service units to white combat troops . . . the brass said we were too dumb to fight, we'd kill each other. I always will believe the only reason we finally got into the action was because of all the hell the Negro press was raising."[2]

African Americans wanted to fight in part because they believed, or hoped, that by doing so they would prove their worthiness to be treated as first-class citizens. Major Arthur W. Little's battalion of black doughboys endured the "ridicule" of white America "in patience and in fortitude" during training, going on to fight with distinction in France. Little expressed the hope that his doughboys' success would benefit their race: "They had helped not only to win the war, but they had helped, too, in the longdrawn struggle still to be, for the betterment of conditions for their race."[3]

Little was certainly correct in predicting that the African American's struggle for betterment would be long-drawn. In World War II, blacks were still seeking to serve in the hope that they would be rewarded with better treatment at home. General George S. Patton Jr., ever appreciative of what motivated men, told the black GIs of the 761st Tank Battalion that by joining his Third Army they were fighting for their race as well as for the Allied cause. John Long, a black captain commanding a company in that battalion, recalled Patton's words: "He told us, 'Men, you are the first Negro tankers ever to fight in the American army. I would never have asked for you if you were not good. I have nothing but the best in my army. I don't care what color you are as long as you go up there and kill those Kraut sons-of-bitches. Everyone has their eyes on you and are expecting great things from you. Most of all your race is looking forward to your success. Don't let them down, and, damn you, don't let me down!'"[4]

The 761st Tank Battalion did not let Patton down, but their success in combat did little to improve conditions at home. When Private Curtis James Morrow joined the all-black Twenty-fourth Infantry Regimental Combat Team in Korea in 1950, blacks were still hoping that success in combat would aid in their struggle for equality. Morrow and his comrades endured "all the injustice thrown at us," because "given an even chance, we could out-soldier and out-fight any white soldier. And there was no way they could [then] justify their racist attitudes toward their fellow [black] American comrades in war or peace. . . . And all we wanted was the constitutional rights guaranteed all Americans."[5]

While black right-to-fighters repeatedly sought to challenge the perception that they were not fit for combat, other blacks pessimistically believed that nothing they could do would change the attitudes of racist white America or lead to better conditions. These blacks rallied to the flag only with the greatest reluctance.[6] Private Clyde Blue, after hearing about his father's negative experiences as a black doughboy, entered service in World War II as a none-too-enthusiastic draftee: "I went into the army strictly as an interested observer. . . . My father had served with the Buffaloes, 92nd Division, World War I. I expected nothing and the army didn't disappoint me."[7]

Charles Brown, a black sergeant in the Ninety-second Infantry Division in World War II, did not expect his fellow black combatants to effect any changes in white attitudes because, as he perceptively realized, those very attitudes doomed their efforts to failure from the outset: "When you tell the general he must take waiters, busboys and shoeshine boys, he doesn't want them to begin with. The social reflection of the Negro in the United States has some of its greatest effect on the military mind. . . . They start out lacking any confidence in your ability."[8] Private Morrow's buddy, "Red," likewise dismissed the right-to-fight advocates as deluded. He and Morrow discussed writing their memoirs after the Korean War, but Red decided it would be a waste of time—white America would not believe them: "Hell, they think only white soldiers are capable of doing some of the things we've done. . . . They want us to think the only thing we're capable of doing is being a steward, or stevedore, or maybe in some quartermaster corp[s] far behind the front line, playing the part of a happy darkie, like bowing and scraping and kissing White-Folk's asses just to get along."[9]

Even with the end of military segregation, some African-American soldiers expressed a reluctance to serve for the same reason as their predecessors—fighting for their country would not translate into better conditions at home. Robert Sanders and his fellow black soldiers feared that their efforts were in vain: "We used to sit down and have talks over it. We'd say, 'What the fuck are we doing in Vietnam, man? When we get back to the states, we gonna be treated shitty and funky, anyway.' So I could understand where these brothers were coming from. We felt that blacks should not have to fight in Vietnam if, when they got home, they couldn't even get a job."[10]

Though Sanders's buddies had good reason to be skeptical about conditions at home, their efforts were not entirely in vain. The black grunt finally destroyed once and for all the myth that blacks were inferior soldiers and garnered an overdue measure of white recognition for black contributions to the fighting. Thus, in the end, the right-to-fight advocates were at least partially vindicated, but only after the segregated, Jim Crow army was first dismantled, giving black soldiers an even chance to prove themselves while fighting beside their white counterparts.

## SEGREGATION AND DISCRIMINATION

Many young African Americans were less than eager to serve because of what they had heard about army life from family and friends, and a review of the black soldiers' experiences in the segregated army shows that this reluctance was well founded. The army's segregation policies, coupled with the Jim Crow laws vigorously enforced in communities surrounding army posts in the South, ensured separate and unequal treatment for blacks.

Northern black recruits, though no strangers to discrimination, were especially shocked at the pervasiveness of the southern Jim Crow laws.[11] Even after the army was fully integrated in 1954, civilian America was not. Albert French, a black marine returning home to Pennsylvania from Parris Island in South Carolina, was alarmed to find that Jim Crow was alive and well in a North Carolina train station in 1963: "The signs were very clear, WHITE ONLY, COLORED ONLY. . . . Sometime late in '63, on the outskirts of Wilmington, North Carolina, the cross burned in the field and the Halloween sheet motherfuckers stood watching the fire."[12]

Nothing was more demoralizing to black GIs training at segregated camps in World War II than to see their enemy receiving better treatment from white America than they did. Lacey Wilson, a black infantry lieutenant, remembers having to go to the back door of a "whites only" train-station restaurant in Texas while German prisoners of war and their white guards ate inside: "It sickened me so I could not eat a bite after ordering. I was a citizen soldier in the uniform of my country and I had to go through an alley to the back door while some of Hitler's storm troopers lapped up the hospitality of my country."[13]

Shipping overseas at least removed the black soldier from the oppressive segregation of the South. Black doughboys and GIs were pleasantly surprised at the relatively better treatment they received at the hands of foreign peoples. Will Judy, who was white, noticed that the French people showed a lack of prejudice toward black troops that would not have been the case in America: "All American negroes I have seen in France like their stay here. The French have accepted them almost with equality."[14] The Research Branch similarly discovered in World War II that black soldiers "found themselves in new environments where local race prejudice was much less than that which they had experienced in the United States."[15]

Floyd Jones, a black artillery sergeant, appreciated his fair treatment at the hands of the Europeans during World War II, but that does not mean he did not encounter "prejudice and discrimination in Europe, . . . but it was marked, 'made in the United States.' Ole 'Mister Charlie' was there to make sure you never left home, so to speak."[16] Official army segregation policies, reinforced by racist attitudes, ensured that the reality and perception of discrimination did not evaporate overseas. The army, with varying degrees of thoroughness, established racially separate military and even civilian facilities in countries with no Jim Crow laws of their own. Officers' clubs, service clubs, and civilian bars, restaurants, and hotels were segregated, just as they had been in America.[17]

Segregation also meant that white soldiers rarely fought or worked with their black counterparts. If white soldiers physically shared any experience with black troops, it was usually in the performance of manual labor, such as construction and stevedoring. White troops resented having to perform this "niggers' work." Thomas Boyd opens *Through the Wheat* with his disgruntled protagonist, Private William Hicks, "working as a stevedore beside evil-odored blacks, helping to build cantonments. . . . And he was supposed to be a soldier. . . . Soldiering with a shovel. A hell of a way to treat a white man."[18]

With black-white contacts, if they occurred at all, limited to the joint performance of "niggers' work," there was little reason for white soldiers to change their attitudes toward blacks, and as the World War II artilleryman Bradford Perkins admits, these attitudes were not positive: "I was not without prejudice. In the army, like everyone else, I often talked dismissively about 'niggers' and 'jigaboos.' Some of this was simply a function of ignorance. In my entire army service, the only blacks I ever saw, except for a few men on leave in London, were the engineering troops driving trucks in the famous Red Ball Express. . . . I never even glimpsed a contradiction between what we were supposed to be fighting for and the condition of black people in America."[19]

While white soldiers had only limited contacts with black service troops, they saw even less of black combatants.[20] Only a handful of black units saw combat, and unfortunately for the right-to-fight cause, several of these units, notably the Ninety-second Infantry Division during the world wars and the Twenty-fourth Infantry Regiment in Korea, gained reputations as poor performers. Understandably, veterans of these units, like Lieutenant Lyle Rishell, a white platoon leader in the Twenty-fourth Infantry, take issue with charges of poor performance: "The men of the 24th Regiment performed no better and no worse than those of other units, and it is unfair to judge them otherwise because they were black."[21] A recent, careful study of the Twenty-fourth Infantry Regiment, however, verifies that its performance was below that of its white sister regiments. The Twenty-fourth Infantry suffered, at times, from excessive straggling, abandoned equipment, and high leader-casualty rates.[22]

Senior white commanders tended to blame this poor performance on the allegedly inferior qualities of black soldiers, who supposedly panicked easily, were unreliable, careless, and lacked leadership abilities.[23] Captain Charles M. Bussey, a black captain commanding the black engineer unit supporting the Twenty-fourth Infantry, noted that when black units broke and ran, or "bugged out" as it was called, it "implied a racial defect," although "bugging out" by white troops was ascribed to other reasons.[24]

The impact of these beliefs on black soldiers' morale can be imagined. A research team visited Korea in May and June 1951 as part of Project Clear, an army-funded program to examine the feasibility of full integration. At that time, army forces in Korea were a mix of all-white, all-black, and partially integrated units. The team found that all-black units had the lowest morale, because they were repeatedly accused of poor performance.[25]

The myth of the black soldier's inferiority was finally shattered by African-American performance in the Vietnam War, but how then to explain the substandard performance of some segregated units? The answer lies in the system of segregation itself. Not only did whites assume that blacks made poor combat soldiers, but they also assumed that blacks lacked the education and skills to be leaders. Thus, with few exceptions, black units were officered by whites, especially in the senior positions, with some black junior officers serving, usually at company level and below.

This mix of officers in a segregated army was bound to generate friction, distrust, and morale problems. The senior leadership in some black units decided that white officers would not serve under blacks. Along with the generally held belief that blacks lacked leadership ability in the first place, this policy guaranteed that white officers fared better in promotions and assignments than black officers. Robert Millender, a black warrant officer and personnel specialist in the Ninety-second Infantry Division in World War II, was in a position to observe the detrimental effects of this policy: "If this isn't a sweet racket I'd like to see one. . . . The lily-white staff . . . is safe, comfortable, and secure. We had ten white lieutenants come into this outfit and one was sent to a rifle company, but all black lieutenants go to rifle companies. Promotions! Colored lieutenants have remained so for two years and they will promote a white lieutenant who has only been in the ranks five months. Then they wonder why the fighting spirit and morale in this division is so damned low."[26]

The white senior leadership in some black units even enforced segregation within the officer corps, at least to the extent possible. Black officers were billeted separately and could not socialize with their counterparts at the whites-only clubs and messes. Rather than building a sense of cohesion within the officer corps, this policy left black officers feeling ostracized, as Walter Green, a black lieutenant in the Ninety-third Infantry Division in the Pacific in World War II, notes: "In one way we felt we had never left home, for our racial problems still plagued us. The white officers kept to themselves, completely out of touch with the black officers, unless it was in the line of duty. There was no socializing or rapport between us when not on the job."[27]

Black officers and soldiers alike resented serving under whites, who by virtue of their race seemed to get the fast promotions and best assignments. Aggravating this resentment was the nagging suspicion that the army hierarchy would not send the best and brightest of the white officer corps to serve in a black unit. That many white officers did not want to be in a black unit and made no bones about it reinforced the black soldiers' perceptions that the quality of their officers left much to be desired. Roger Walden, a black sergeant in the Ninety-second Division, noticed that many of the white officers arriving at Fort Huachuca, Arizona, to fill out the division before it moved overseas were less than thrilled to be there: "White officers who had goofed elsewhere in white outfits were being sent as senior officers to Fort Huachuca and the 92nd. They had no compunction about letting it be known that they were being punished when sent to Huachuca."[28]

Even worse, some of the white officers were blatantly prejudiced. Many of the army's senior leaders believed that the black soldier preferred being led by white southern officers because they "understood" blacks. In reality, black soldiers preferred to serve under black or at least northern white officers because southern white officers' "understanding" too often turned out to be pure prejudice.[29] Willie Lawton, a black sergeant in the Ninety-third Division in World War

II, observed that his white southern officers did not tolerate "uppity niggers" in uniform any more than they did at home: "If you showed any signs of intelligence, belligerency, or acted like a man, you were immediately put on their 'smart nigger' list. These officers found some pretty nasty ways of trying to break the spirit of those who did not fit into their way of thinking on what kind of behavior and attitude a Negro should exhibit."[30] Even a few prejudiced officers had a detrimental impact on black soldiers' morale because, as Private Morrow pointed out during the Korean War, until a black soldier got to know his officers, he could never be sure if he could trust them, simply because they were white: "And to top it all, any one of the officers calling the shots here could be the very one that put[s] a rope around one of our necks next year some place in the States (America) and just for kicks. Or they may quite possibly be the ones to deny us the very rights that we are here fighting for the South Koreans to enjoy. . . . How can they wonder why we don't trust them?"[31]

Yet not all white officers were prejudiced, nor were they all mediocre. Black troops, while generally preferring to serve under black officers, were willing to follow any junior leader who was competent and caring, as Ivan Harrison, a black lieutenant in the 761st Tank Battalion, noted: "In regards to the Negro soldier preferring to serve under white officers rather than black ones; they prefer serving under officers they have confidence in, black or white, and they will serve such an officer faithfully regardless of his race."[32]

Captain David Williams, a company commander in the 761st Tank Battalion, was one of those white officers who earned the confidence of his men, as Eddie Donald, a black sergeant in the unit, testified: "He is one of us. His men, all black, would follow him to hell and a few steps beyond, so you see its [sic] not the color that Negro soldiers respond to but the leadership exerted and the trust, respect, and confidence the officer can engender."[33]

Thus, although many white officers were competent and relatively free of prejudice, segregation nevertheless ensured that black officers and soldiers reasonably believed that they were being discriminated against in promotions, awards, and assignments. As the Research Branch in World War II discovered, "Many complaints common to soldiers of both races acquired a special significance among Negro soldiers by being invested with the quality of racial discrimination."[34] Even worse, the Research Branch learned that most white soldiers had no idea that blacks felt so discriminated against. A majority of white soldiers surveyed believed that "most Negroes were satisfied with the status of their group in American society."[35]

This ignorance of African-American sensitivity over discrimination sometimes caught otherwise well-intentioned white officers unaware. Major Little, the white commander of a black doughboy battalion, found to his surprise that one of his black company commanders considered his actions prejudiced: "Captain Fillmore did not accept my corrections as being made in good faith. I believe that Captain Fillmore was of the opinion that every correction ever offered him by me was offered on account of his being a colored man, and not on the merits of the good of the service. . . . I believe that Captain Fillmore never did get over his impression that he and all colored officers were victims of racial prejudice, in every development that did not operate to their advancement or personal satisfaction."[36]

Captain Samuelson made the same discovery after taking command of a company of black engineers in World War II. His efforts to instill discipline and improve living conditions were not well received because his soldiers believed he was just playing the part of the typical boss man: "They resent my dictating the whole show. They feel that because I am white and they are colored that I am taking advantage of them. That is one thing that I won't be able to knock out of their heads. Before I die I must help stamp out this crazy idea that the white man has about his superiority over the colored man." A genuinely caring, unprejudiced white officer like Samuelson could eventually win his men over—he noted in his diary about three weeks later that "most of the men are beginning to like me."[37] But overcoming the black soldiers' deeply ingrained suspicions of white motivations made the already daunting task of leading men in combat even more difficult.

Black soldiers perceived discrimination not only in the orders and actions of their white leaders but also in virtually everything unfortunate or unpleasant that befell them. Project Clear researchers found black perceptions of discrimination to be pervasive in Korea, much as the Research Branch had discovered in World War II: "The conviction of most of the soldiers interviewed in all-Negro units [is] that they do not receive treatment equal to that accorded men in white and mixed units. There seems to be almost no aspect of military life in which this belief does not find expression, no familiar GI gripe which is not given a racial twist. The all-Negro unit is alleged to receive discriminatory treatment in equipment, supplies, recreational opportunities, promotions, tough unit assignments, rest rotation, food, clothing, PX rations, medical care, leadership, and publicity."[38]

Many black soldiers did indeed perceive discrimination in everything the army did, even in combat. For example, Harry Duplessis, a black armor officer in World War II, believed that the army scrubbed its plan to combine three black tank battalions into a regiment because the white hierarchy did not want to form such a powerful black unit: "The idea of all of that fire power in an all-black group was just too much for the 'man' to bear so it never came about."[39] In reality, few independent armor regiments of any color were formed during World War II, the intent being instead to employ battalions separately to provide support as needed in each specific situation. In a similar vein, Corporal Horace Evans believed that his separate, black tank battalion was almost never committed together as a complete unit because it would garner too much attention: "One company might be sent to the 87th [Infantry Division], three or four tanks to some other outfit, and so on, so we'd be all over the place. It was definitely a ploy to keep from committing us together as a battalion as much as possible; whole units get credit while a few isolated tanks . . . are overlooked."[40] Yet in reality this sort of dispersion of a supporting tank battalion was common, regardless of the color of the tankers.

Though claims of discrimination in combat were unwarranted in these exam-ples, other cases were not so clear-cut. Many black soldiers believed they were being set up to fail in combat. If black units failed, or were never committed to combat in the first place, then they could not earn the recognition, respect, and appreciation essential for gaining equality on the home front. Given that many whites had no desire to see blacks improve on their second-class citizenship, black soldiers were suspicious of the white hierarchy's motives in employing, or failing to employ, black units. The opinion of Sergeant E. J. Wells, a black infantryman in the Ninety-second Infantry Division in World War II, is typical: "I felt then, and I still do, that the military did not want black combat units, particularly one as large as a division. They most certainly did not want black officers. Everything was done to divide us rather than to unify us into a cohesive . . . unit. During the war only black infantry was made to 'tote that barge, lift that bale,' many times without ever having the chance to win or lose a battle of any size."[41]

Sergeant David Cason believed that his 366th Infantry Regiment, on join-ing the Ninety-second Infantry Division in Italy, was set up for failure, because the white command structure wanted to discredit the regiment's all-black offi-cer corps, one of the few units to have blacks in senior positions: "When the 366th arrived, black from top to bottom, that wreaked havoc with the 92nd hier-archy. There are those who believe that command's answer to this intolerable situation was to throw the 366th into some highly untenable positions and wipe them out."[42]

Thus, given units containing a mix of white officers, some of whom were prejudiced or mediocre, and black officers and troops in an army pursuing seg-regationist policies, it is remarkable that black units functioned at all. Some, like Little's 369th Infantry Regiment in World War I and the 761st Tank Battalion in Patton's army in World War II, compiled admirable records. More typically, however, black combat-unit performance was perceived as below average and the African-American soldier's lack of martial skill as the reason.

In reality, the mistrust and resentment generated by the system of segrega-tion itself made it difficult to build the hierarchical cohesion essential for success in combat. As the historian William T. Bowers and his colleagues note, if some black units like the Twenty-fourth Infantry Regiment did not come up to stan-dard, then segregation was to blame:

> Given the corrosive influence of segregation and the mistrust it instilled, they [the men of the Twenty-fourth Infantry] were sorely handicapped in comparison with their white counterparts. For what matters the most in bat-tle is the loyalty that bonds one man to the next and to his officers and his unit—the instinctive, trusting, mutual dependence that welds the whole into the sort of force that can withstand the worst hardships and tribulations. . . . On that score, even if a few units within the regiment may have measured up, a suspicion lingers that many others did not.[43]

## INTEGRATION: BLACK, WHITE, AND GREEN

In the Jim Crow army, African-American soldiers believed that the white hierarchy discriminated against them in every way imaginable, with the understandable result of low morale and efficiency in many black units. The army belatedly came to realize that segregation, not any inherent racial flaw in blacks, was largely to blame for instances of poor performance by black units. This realization began to dawn on most white soldiers and leaders, however, only after they saw with their own eyes that blacks could soldier if given a fair chance. In the arena of ground combat, two specific events helped to bring about this realization: the insertion of ad-hoc black infantry companies and platoons into white infantry units during World War II and the tentative integration of some white combat units during the Korean War through using black replacements.

The heavy casualties produced by the Battle of the Bulge left the army in Europe critically short of infantry replacements. Despite continued doubts about the black soldier's fitness for combat, black service troops were asked to volunteer to fight as infantry. They were given some training, provided with combat-experienced white officers and sergeants, and sent to the front as infantry platoons and, in some cases, as provisional companies.[44] These hastily formed black units performed well. Shortly after VE-Day, the Research Branch surveyed white officers and soldiers who had served in infantry companies containing black platoons. An overwhelming majority agreed that black soldiers had performed "very well" in combat and were "just the same" or "better" than white infantrymen. Perhaps as important, a majority of white soldiers also said that they had gotten along well with the black soldiers and that their attitudes toward Negroes had improved as a consequence.[45] Granted, these platoons had remained segregated, most of the leaders were still white, and there were too few of them to change the way an entire army thought about black soldiers; but the black infantry-platoon experiment was a successful demonstration of black fighting prowess.

The army, like the rest of the military, remained segregated after World War II. President Harry S Truman is generally credited with ending this segregation by Executive Order 9981 of July 26, 1948, but in reality his order called only for "equality of treatment and opportunity."[46] The order did not specifically direct that units be integrated, and certainly not by a prescribed date. Integration therefore proceeded haltingly. The marines, who had admitted no blacks into their ranks until World War II, and then only as service troops in segregated units, integrated in 1949 and began admitting blacks into all specialties and assignments. The army, however, went to war in Korea in 1950 with still-segregated units.

Nevertheless, the exigencies of war led to a measure of integration. Just prior to the Korean War, the army had eliminated racial quotas in recruiting and induction. The result, in Korea, was an excess of black replacements beyond what the few black units needed. White units, on the other hand, were understrength, an indication of the inherent difficulties in maintaining two separate armies in the middle of a war. This situation led to a decision to place individual black replacements into white combat and support units. The results were favorable. Project Clear researchers found that integrated units did not decline in effectiveness and that the white soldiers in those units acknowledged the abilities of their black comrades.[47] And although this integration by no means put an end to prejudice, relations between the two races improved: "The fear of difficulties or problems is dissipated as contacts between the two groups are placed on an individual personal basis rather than within the framework of preconceptions held by both parties."[48]

Black and white soldiers were apprehensive at first about being thrown together, but as the Project Clear researchers pointed out, these fears dissipated rather quickly. The marines had integrated in 1949, but there were initially few black combat marines, and some units were still all-white when they deployed to Korea. Dave Koegel recalled the arrival of the first black replacements in his marine rifle company, one of whom "was assigned to share a hole with an Alabaman. Knowing looks went around. They were for nothing; the two men became fast friends."[49]

By the time Bill Mauldin visited the Thirty-first Infantry Regiment in Korea in early 1952, the unit had already been integrated, and everyone was getting along: "I kept noticing these guys, about one colored to ten white, all through the company. They seemed to fit in fine, and I never heard any comment about it one way or another. They all seem to be used to it. You will see a colored man and a white man with a southern accent you could cut with a knife, and they will be sharing a two man bunker and kidding each other like they'd been buddies all their lives."[50]

At the risk of detracting from Mauldin's optimistic assessment of army integration, however, the combining of the races did not always take place without friction. Jim Crow laws were still much in evidence in America in the 1950s, and some white soldiers still favored racial separation. Project Clear researchers found that although a majority of white soldiers either supported or "would not object strongly" to integration, a sizable minority "would object . . . strongly" to serving "in a platoon containing both white and colored soldiers, all working and training together, sleeping in the same barracks, and eating in the same messhall."[51]

Some white soldiers, then, were integrated against their will and chose to avoid contact with black soldiers as much as possible.[52] Prejudiced white soldiers were especially chagrined over having to take orders from black sergeants or officers. In Lieutenant Joseph R. Owen's newly formed rifle company, about to embark for Korea, there were about a dozen black marines. Two white marines approached Owen and asked if they could join his still all-white mortar section, because a black sergeant had arrived in their platoon: "We ain't letting them niggers run us. Ain't going to let that happen." Owen stood the men to attention and ordered them back to their platoon, but not until he had explained how things were going to be in the new, integrated Marine Corps: "If I hear you bad-mouthing any NCO in this company, black, white, or polka dot, I'll get you run up for serious brig time."[53]

Lieutenant Howard Matthias's rifle platoon did not contain any black marines until a black replacement showed up after they were already in Korea. Altogether, five black marines arrived while Matthias was platoon leader, and he praised them for meeting the challenges of integration while enduring the stresses of combat. And integrating his platoon was not without its challenges because of the presence of a few "'red necked' boys from the south": "I was naive enough to believe that there was no concern about [the blacks] fitting in under combat conditions. I was wrong. I had to be very concerned who they were assigned under, who they would share a bunker with and any assignment with special hazards. The distrust between the Southerner and the black man was still evident."[54]

The black soldier was thus not welcomed with open arms by all his white comrades, but the majority of soldiers learned to work together, and bonds of camaraderie soon reached across color lines. Integration also went a long way toward erasing the black soldier's perception that all his misfortunes had a discriminatory basis. He discovered that the army's institutional inequality applied, regardless of race. Or as Charles C. Moskos Jr. put it, all privates were treated "like Negroes": "Indeed, it might be argued that relatively little adjustment on the part of the command structure was required when the infusion of blacks into the enlisted ranks occurred as the military establishment was desegregated. In other words, it is suggested that one factor contributing to the generally smooth racial integration of the military was due to the standard treatment—'like Negroes'—accorded to all lower-ranking enlisted personnel."[55]

The Project Clear researchers wholeheartedly recommended that the army proceed with integration, adding that unit morale and efficiency would not suffer as a consequence.[56] By the end of 1954, the army was fully integrated. Black and white soldiers thus fought together by the time of the Vietnam War, respected each other, and perceived the racial climate in the army to be healthier than it was in civilian society.[57] Strong friendships developed between black and white soldiers who perhaps had had little prior contact with people outside their own race. Private Richard E. Ogden, a poor country boy who had known few blacks in civilian life, found himself teamed up with Lance Corporal Johnson, a black from the Watts ghetto, who was suspicious of all whites. Ogden realized that they made an odd couple: "Neither one of us knew what kind of an animal we were up against."[58] After swapping life stories, both men decided that they liked each other. Their common bond grew from Johnson's desire, as an aspiring teacher who had attended college before joining the marines, to educate Ogden, who in turn was eager to learn but had never finished high school. They remained fast friends, until Johnson was killed in combat.

Such unlikely pairings were not uncommon, and even if a soldier did not make a close friend of someone from another race, the demands of combat at least served to forge good relations within the interracial group. Bonds of comradeship grew within the squad and platoon for the sake of mutual support and survival, as Stanley Goff, a black grunt, observed: "The buddy system has to happen. You start realizing that you can't get through not communicating. Guys start opening up. Blacks realize, 'I'm stuck out here in the boonies, and the white guy from the South is stuck out here, and it's life and death, we'd better begin to erase all this coloration immediately.'" Or as Robert Sanders put it, "Charlie had a tendency to make you unify in a hurry."[59] Arthur E. Woodley, a black grunt, explained that soldiers could not afford the luxury of racism or politics: "Once you started to go in the field with an individual, no matter what his ethnic background is or what his ideals, you start to depend on that person to cover your ass."[60]

Unfortunately, equality and comradeship in combat did not automatically lead to racial harmony when soldiers were not in the boonies. Moskos discovered in studying Vietnam-era soldiers that blacks and whites often preferred the company of their "own kind" when not in combat or on the job, a form of behavior he called "racial exclusivism": "The general pattern of day-to-day relationships *off the job* is usually one of mutual racial exclusivism. . . . On the whole, racial integration at informal levels works best on-duty vis-à-vis off-duty, on-base vis-à-vis off-base, basic training and maneuvers vis-à-vis garrison. . . . and—most especially—combat vis-à-vis noncombat. In other words, the behavior of servicemen resembles the racial . . . separatism of the larger American society."[61]

Some soldiers did not mix with those outside their race except when the job required it. To an extent, personal tastes and background accounted for racial exclusivism. Different groups preferred different activities, music, and even conversation. Bigotry, however, was undeniably at work as well. Racial antagonism sometimes bubbled to the surface without the catalyst of danger to keep soldiers working as a team. During his Stateside training, David Parks, a black soldier who hailed originally from Minnesota, recalls his first experience with southern white bigotry: "Never had such bad feelings against white guys before. . . . But then I've never met white guys like these before. They don't let you forget that you're colored and that they're white for one minute." He could not "imagine some of these Southern cats liking me any better than they'll like the Vietcong."[62] Parks's assessment was not far off the mark. Some white racists had no more use for black GIs than they had for the enemy, or in the case of Private Granite in Matthew Brennan's squad, for Yankees: "My main headache was Private Granite. He was a draftee from the hills of Tennessee and recognized no authority from anyone born north of the Mason-Dixon line. . . . His most common profanities were 'nigger' and 'Yankee.' He was in my squad because there weren't any niggers. There was at least one Yankee."[63]

Richard Ogden discovered that Simms, the platoon bigot, did not think much of white men who befriended blacks. Simms told him what they did "back home" to such "nigger lovers": "You know what we do with people who fraternize with niggers? We hang them, that's what we do. We don't mess around back home."[64] Simms then continued with a description of the unnatural sex acts that he supposed Ogden and his black friend Johnson must be performing together, and the fight was on. In a small triumph for racial equality, Ogden thrashed Simms unmercifully.

Simms and Granite are extreme examples, and obviously not all southern whites were bigoted, but white prejudice was prevalent enough to contribute to racial antagonism. The army has a saying that "a soldier isn't black or white, only green," meaning that all soldiers should be treated equally. The integrated army has lived up to that philosophy to an admirable extent, but it took only a few prejudicial actions to fuel black soldiers' perceptions of more pervasive discrimination.

Assignments were one area in which blacks perceived discrimination at work. The choicest noncombat jobs seemed to go to white soldiers, and blacks were overly concentrated in the combat arms. As with most perceptions, this one had a basis in fact. The combat units that deployed to Vietnam early in the war contained a high percentage of volunteers, a disproportionate number of whom, in comparison to the overall military and civilian populations, were black. Black soldiers therefore began dying in greater numbers, relatively speaking, than whites, which generated a storm of protest from black civilian leaders. The army acted to equalize the assignment of blacks to combat and support jobs, and by war's end the overall casualty rate for blacks was only slightly higher than the percentage of blacks serving and slightly less than the percentage of draft-eligible blacks in the general population.[65]

The damage, however, had already been done. Blacks in Vietnam perceived that they were being discriminated against in job assignments, and a few cases of real discrimination kept the perception alive. Arriving in Vietnam in late 1966, Private Parks was transferred to the fire direction center (FDC) of his infantry company's mortar platoon, where he encountered Paulson, a racist white sergeant: "Paulson is a real ass. He's always telling me that Negroes are lazy and won't help themselves, etc. I tell him he's full of shit and end up filling sandbags." Parks, like black soldiers before him, was not a stranger to such abuse, but Paulson's racism had a lethal side. He did not want any blacks in his FDC, a relatively safe place to be in an infantry company. Hence, Parks soon found himself performing the far more dangerous job of forward observer: "Just got kicked out of my beautiful FDC job. The good Sgt. Paulson strikes again. He gave me the news with a smile. I am now Forward Observer Parks, attached to the First Platoon command track [armored personnel carrier]."[66]

Haywood T. Kirkland served as an infantryman in Vietnam in 1967 and 1968, until the last three months of his tour, when his unit was issued 106-mm recoilless rifles. These large weapons were used to defend the battalion base camp, where Kirkland soon became convinced of discrimination in assignments: "The brothers they was calling quote unquote troublemakers, they would send to the field. A lot of brothers who had supply clerk or cook MOS [Military Occupational Specialty] when they came over ended up in the field. And when the brothers who was shot came out of the field, most of them got the jobs burning shit in these 50-gallon drums. Most of the white dudes got jobs as supply clerks or in the mess hall."[67]

Tim O'Brien, a white grunt serving in 1968 and 1969, was one of those white dudes who escaped the exclusive club of the infantry for a safe job as a typist at battalion headquarters. He freely admitted that the best way to acquire such a safe billet was "to burrow your nose gently up an officer's ass."[68] He further admitted that this procedure worked better for whites than for blacks: "For the soul brothers, that route is not easy. To begin with, the officer corps is dominated by white men; the corps of foot soldiers, common grunts, is disproportionately black. On top of that are all the old elements of racial tension—fears, hates, suspicions. . . . With either the hunch or the reality that white officers favor white grunts in handing out the rear jobs, many blacks react as any sane man would. They sulk. . . . They group together and laugh and say shit to the system."[69]

Some African Americans went so far as to claim that this discrimination in assignments was an attempt at genocide. Goff and Sanders, who went through advanced infantry training together in 1968, heard such rumors; and given the racial composition of their training company, they were not so quick to dismiss them: "Nothing but black guys in the whole fucking company. That was particularly alarming to Bob and me. In fact, word was going around, and it wasn't a quiet word, that blacks were being drafted for genocide purposes. Just to get rid of us—to eliminate the black male. And we believed it."[70]

The army was not pursuing a policy of genocide, but black perceptions of discrimination in assignments nevertheless contributed to racial antagonism. Growing militancy among black draftees entering service after 1968 further fueled this discord. Wallace Terry, a black journalist who spent a great deal of time in Vietnam and who interviewed many black grunts for his oral history *Bloods,* describes this growing militancy:

> The war had used up the [black] professionals who found in military service fuller and fairer employment opportunities than blacks could find in civilian society, and who found in uniform a supreme test of their black manhood. Replacing the careerists were black draftees, many just steps removed from marching in the Civil Rights Movement or rioting in the rebellions that swept the urban ghettos from Harlem to Watts. All were filled with a new sense of black pride and purpose. They spoke loudest against the discrimination they encountered . . . in decorations, promotions and duty assignments. They chose not to overlook the racial insults, cross-burnings and Confederate flags of their white comrades.[71]

From the perspective of white soldiers, even those not given to prejudice, this black militancy was a disturbing development. John Ketwig, who volunteered for a tour of duty in Thailand, considered the racial exclusivity he encountered there to be a destructive departure from the interracial camaraderie he had experienced in Vietnam: "Sometimes I was almost homesick for The Nam. Life had been pure there. Simpler. . . . All that mattered was survival, everyone's survival, and that pressure created a society without room for petty bigotry or prejudices. Now, here, the blacks assaulted the whites with loud music, daring some 'honkey mothafucka' to say something. There were black-power closed-fist salutes and complaints that too many 'brothers' were getting wasted in The Nam. What did they know about 'brothers'? Over there we were all 'brothers.' When you're so scared you piss yourself, skin color doesn't matter much. You need the guy next to you, and survival becomes the only real value in all of life."[72]

Even given the imperative to survive, however, black-white relations in Vietnam underwent a similar deterioration. Grunts still cooperated for the sake of survival, but increasingly racial exclusivity reached even into the boonies. O'Brien noticed that while his infantry platoon waited to be picked up by helicopters for an air assault, the blacks had congregated and white soldiers were not welcome: "We lay in private groups on the tarred parking lot of an airfield. The black soldiers joked and were too loud for the early morning. They had their own piece of the helipad, and only officers would interrupt them."[73]

Matthew Brennan's aerorifle platoon had informally segregated itself by spring 1969: "The platoon splintered into an all-black squad and a Southern white squad. I had one of two neutral squads, but most of the men leaned one way or the other."[74] A new platoon sergeant wisely forced a reintegration of the platoon, knowing that teamwork between squads would be impossible otherwise.

Moreover, growing antiwar sentiment among black soldiers added to the racial problems. Since both white and black draftees, especially after 1968, increasingly questioned the reasons for and justness of the war, antiwar attitudes might presumably be a source of common interest and agreement. In reality, the reasons why some blacks opposed the war only served to stir further racial antagonism. Black leaders, notably Martin Luther King Jr., spoke openly against the war, and some militant blacks further condemned it as "whitey's war," sustained by a white-controlled political system using blacks as cannon fodder against a yellow race. Certainly not all black grunts accepted this explanation, but militant blacks espousing this theory often received at least a sympathetic hearing. And militant blacks increasingly advocated racial separatism, thus aggravating the existing trend toward racial exclusivity.

Douglas Anderson, a black corpsman serving in Vietnam in 1967 and 1968, noticed that a "radicalization" process was taking place among black grunts, even in the midst of the war:

> This was during the time that Muhammad Ali refused to go into the service and became a hero. The blacks in the battalion began to question why they were fighting Honky's war against other Third World people. I saw very interesting relationships happening between your quick-talking, sharp-witted

Northern blacks and your kind of easygoing, laid-back Southern blacks. I began to notice certain radicalization processes going on there. Many Southern blacks changed their entire point of view by the end of their tour and went home extremely angry.[75]

Reginald Edwards was one of those black marines who "went home angry" after his tour early in the war (1965–1966). He joined the Black Panthers, many of whom were alienated black veterans like himself: "We had already fought for the white man in Vietnam. It was clearly his war. If it wasn't, you wouldn't have seen as many Confederate flags as you saw. And the Confederate flag was an insult to any person that's of color on this planet."[76]

Even if most black soldiers were not as radicalized as Edwards, they were torn between their duties as soldiers and their identification with a race whose leaders were denouncing the war. Parks wrote in his diary that he was not sure what to think: "Frankly, I'm mixed up. The Stateside news bugs me. On the one hand you have Stokely Carmichael saying Negroes shouldn't be fighting for this country. On the other hand some Negro leaders think just the opposite."[77] Robert Sanders was another black grunt who was "mixed up": "Most of the people were like me; they were naive. We didn't know what the hell was really going on. We knew that Communists were supposed to be bad, and that they were trying to take the South Vietnamese's rice away from them, and that we were out there to stop them. But at the same time, the Black Panther organization, the Muslims, the Kings didn't feel that we should be out there participating in it."[78]

Some African-American soldiers, especially career sergeants and officers, were neither "mixed up" nor antiwar. They continued to perform their duties, and if they had doubts about black participation in the war they kept it to themselves. Their militant black brethren denounced them for their troubles as sell-outs to whitey, calling them "oreos"—black on the outside, white on the inside. Archie Biggers, a black marine lieutenant, was distressed to discover after returning home in 1969 from his tour in Vietnam that he was persona non grata among his own race: "But the thing that really hurt me more than anything in the world was when I came back to the States and black people considered me as a part of the establishment. Because I am an officer. Here I was, a veteran that just came back from a big conflict. And most of the blacks wouldn't associate with me."[79]

Race relations in the military in America's first fully integrated war thus seemed to reach a nadir by the end of the conflict, although interracial camaraderie never completely evaporated in the boonies. Many blacks had clamored for years for their right to fight, only to be told by their brethren that they were now fighting as tools of the white establishment. Blacks had advocated an integrated military to eliminate the discrimination inherent in a segregated army, only to discover that integration did not put an end to prejudice. Indeed, the perception of discrimination in job assignments convinced some blacks that their race was being deliberately sacrificed while whites remained safe in the rear.

Military integration was thus not a cure-all for racial problems. However, despite racial exclusivity and antagonisms—problems that would ease significantly with the end of the Vietnam War and the advent of army initiatives to eliminate any remaining discriminatory policies—the integrated military was an undeniable improvement over the Jim Crow army.[80] Charles Bussey, besides commanding a black engineer company in the Korean War, had been a Tuskegee airman in World War II and remained in the army following the Korean War, retiring as a lieutenant colonel in 1966. He had thus experienced the segregated and the integrated army and recognized the invaluable benefits of military integration, whatever its flaws, for all American soldiers: "I have been haunted by the generalized and not completely objective portrayals and comparisons of how black soldiers performed in the Korean War. If we were so poor then, why did black soldiers get such high marks in the Vietnam War, only fifteen years after Korea? I have some ideas. When the Army began to respect its black soldiers and give them responsibilities, perhaps the Army in return received respect and responsible soldiers."[81] No informed person since the Vietnam War has questioned the African American's right, or ability, to fight for his country, and recognition of his contributions in combat has aided in the continuing fight for equality.

# Conclusion: Don't Expect
# Too Much from War

Seeking answers to James Jones's question—what "makes a man go out into dangerous places and get himself shot at with increasing consistency"—has proved to be a challenging task. In briefest terms, the soldier endured being shot at, along with all the other hazards and hardships of war, by relying on various coping mechanisms while at the same time believing in some combination of comrades, cause, country, and self.

What initially compelled a man to go out into dangerous places, however, has turned out to be a different, though related, issue. A mix of positive and negative incentives motivated men to put themselves in harm's way: belief in cause, submission to peer and social pressure, a sense of obligation, desire for a viable career, and fear of legal prosecution for draft evasion, to name just a few. Perhaps most significant, many men, certainly the eager volunteers but also quite a few draftees, went to dangerous places willingly enough because they had wrongheaded ideas about what they were letting themselves in for. "We all imagine war before we know it," observes Samuel Hynes, but these "wars-in-the-head," as he calls them, "however vivid and violent they may be, are romances: they are war turned into fictions, into shapely untruths. They feed our imaginations with the big abstractions of war—Heroism, Fame, Valor, Glory; they make death sentimental and battle melodramatic."[1]

A soldier going off to war with such romantic notions was in for a ruder shock than one who entertained no illusions of glory.[2] William Manchester discovered the hard way, in the bloodbath of Okinawa in World War II, just how wide of the mark his glorified ideas about battle had been: "I realized that something within me, long ailing, had expired. Although I would continue to do the job, performing as the hired gun, I now knew that banners and swords, ruffles and flourishes, bugles and drums, the whole rigmarole, eventually ended in squalor. . . . My dream of war had been colorful but puerile. It had been so evanescent, so ethereal, so wholly unrealistic that it deserved to be demolished. Later, after time had washed away the bitterness, I came to understand that."[3]

For Audie Murphy, the disillusionment began a few days into his first campaign in Sicily in World War II: "Maybe my notions about war were all cockeyed. How do you pit skill against skill if you cannot even see the enemy? Where is the glamour in blistered feet and a growling stomach? And where is the expected adventure?" After a few more days of fighting and marching, Murphy no longer even entertained such questions: "The Sicilian campaign has taken the vinegar out of my spirit. I have seen war as it actually is, and I do not like it."[4]

Lieutenant James Hamilton Dill, sickened by the slaughter he had caused calling in an artillery barrage on a group of North Korean soldiers and then shocked by the dispatching of South Korean children into enemy territory as spies, came to realize that he had "started out with too many idealized notions about the honor of the profession of arms."[5] Few soldiers went off to war with greater expectations of glory than did Lieutenant Philip Caputo. The circumstances under which the first marine in his unit was killed in Vietnam, however, provided a rude awakening: "Like many inexperienced soldiers, I suffered from the illusion that there were good ways to die in war. I thought grandly in terms of noble sacrifices, of soldiers offering up their bodies for a cause or to save a comrade's life. But there had been nothing sacrificial or ceremonial about Sullivan's death. He had been sniped while filling canteens in a muddy jungle river."[6]

How could so many Americans in three consecutive generations go off to fight with so little appreciation of the inherent hardships, dangers, and grim realities? Hynes, in describing the pre–World War II sources for his own overly optimistic expectations, provides the answer: "I made my war-in-the-head out of *For Whom the Bell Tolls* and *G-8 and His Battle Aces,* and movies like *Hell's Angels* and *The Dawn Patrol,* and all the vestiges of past wars that were around me: the old men marching on Memorial Day, and the bands and the flags; the two-minute silence on Armistice Day; the rows of soldiers' graves at Fort Snelling."[7]

Expectations about the next war derived from the images of the previous ones generated by the mass media, popular literature, and the memorialization process. As Hynes's list of sources indicates, these images were predominantly positive, and Americans would not have it any other way. They did not want to hear about war's hardships and horrors, as the returning Will Judy discovered:

> We have come back hating war, disgusted with the prattle about ideals, disillusioned entirely about the struggles between nations. . . . But the populace refuses to be disillusioned; they force us to feed their own delusions.
>
> Soon we will take on the pose of brave crusaders who swept the battlefields with a shout and a noble charge. . . . An ounce of bravery on the battlefield will become a ton of daring in story as related time and again in the years to come. We as soldiers shall find ourselves made the patriotic guardians of our country, a specially honored class, against our will.[8]

Paul Fussell railed in similar fashion against the sanitizing and glorifying process that turned the vicious struggle that was World War II into a "good war": "Now, fifty years later, there has been so much talk about 'The Good War,' the Justified War, the Necessary War, and the like, that the young and the innocent could get the impression that it was really not such a bad thing after all. It's thus necessary to observe that it was a war and nothing else, and thus stupid and sadistic."[9]

Despite these occasional pleas for a realistic remembrance of war's horrors, Americans wanted to celebrate victories and extol heroes, not dwell on the grim details. Following the Korean War, however, Americans had no victory to immortalize, only a costly stalemate, and the "peace with honor" that ended the Vietnam War had an especially hollow ring. Better to forget that these embarrassing wars had occurred at all. Thus, again, returning veterans found that no one wanted to hear about the realities of their war. Caputo, embittered over his comrades' sacrifices in vain, including the death of his friend Levy, took America to task for ignoring its Vietnam veterans: "You [Levy] were faithful. Your country is not. As I write this, eleven years after your death, the country for which you died wishes to forget the war in which you died. Its very name is a curse. There are no monuments to its heroes, no statues in small-town squares and city parks, no plaques, nor public wreaths, nor memorials. For plaques and wreaths and memorials are reminders, and they would make it harder for your country to sink into the amnesia for which it longs. It wishes to forget and it has forgotten."[10]

Caputo wrote this in 1977, and America has since forsaken much of its collective amnesia. There are now monuments, plaques, and wreaths. But this belated memorialization process, though a fitting tribute to those who fought in Vietnam, did little to advance public understanding about the nature of war. Postwar memorialization tends to simplify and glorify, and again most Americans wanted it that way. Granted, the memorialization of the Vietnam War has been something of an exception. If one word had to be chosen to describe the Vietnam Veterans Memorial in Washington, D.C., it would be "somber." But as the historian G. Kurt Piehler points out, the overall effect of national memorialization, with its emphasis on monuments of classic Greco-Roman design, has been to sanitize and extol: "The widespread use of classicism contributed to the movement to gloss over the brutality of the Civil War and the world wars. It reflected an effort to minimize and rationalize the tremendous suffering these conflicts caused. To a large degree, it encouraged those who wanted to make modern warfare acceptable as it emphasized the heroic nature of battle and of dying for one's country."[11]

In addition to monuments, memorialization following the world wars included the establishment of Stateside and overseas military cemeteries, the Gold Star Mothers, the Tomb of the Unknown Soldier, holidays such as Veterans' Day, military museums, statuary, and battlefield reenactments.[12] The intent of the citizens and veterans promoting these measures was not, as Piehler implies, to "make modern warfare acceptable"; but in their earnest efforts to honor the soldiers who had served and fallen, the overall effect was indeed to rationalize the suffering and to glorify the heroic nature of battle.

The literary critic Malcolm Cowley, a World War I veteran, debating the remembrance and memorialization process with his fellow critic Archibald MacLeish in 1933, proposed that "it is time to inscribe at the entrance to every veterans' graveyard and over the tombs of all the unknown soldiers, *They died bravely, they died in vain.*"[13] Cowley believed that only such a brutally honest approach would stay America from spilling more blood: "For, if we emphasize the useless deaths of the last war, we can be certain of our attitude toward the next. But if, on the other hand, we emphasize the happy illusions of these men who died defending their country—from whom?—and saving democracy—for what?—then we can look forward more or less calmly to the battles in which other generous and loyal men . . . will die in the same courageous fashion."[14]

The problem was that the last thing veterans and the families of men killed in battle wanted to hear, and understandably so, was that those deaths were useless. Dixon Wecter, writing on the verge of the return of millions of servicemen from overseas in World War II, warned that the combat veteran would not want to hear that his sacrifices had been in vain: "On one point and perhaps only one is he unmistakably clear. When the war is over he does not want to be called a fool, or look like one. Whatever the cost to him personally of this war, in time and happiness and wholeness of body or mind, he wants to know that it has all been to some purpose. . . . The returning soldier's fear of any intimation that he has been played for a sucker is linked with his feeling about friends who have paid more than just an installment or two of sweat and pain."[15]

In acknowledging that the human costs had been expended "to some purpose," however, the memorialization process unavoidably emphasized the justness of the cause, the valor of the soldiers, and the necessity of the sacrifices, to the detriment of the realistic portrayal of war's hardships and carnage. The memorialization of the previous generation's war thus contributed to the roseate nature of the next generation's war-in-the-head. The images of battle provided by the popular media further contributed to these optimistic expectations. Some soldiers readily admitted that the war novels, adventure stories, and Wild West tales they had read as adolescents contributed to their misperceptions about battle. Growing up in the interwar years, John L. Munschauer devoured "cheap novels" about World War I: "The stories are long forgotten, but they planted the seed of a notion that there was something fine and heroic in being a soldier. It grew like a virus; it altered something in my personality that would subconsciously start my foot tapping to the beat of war drums."[16]

The bookish Manchester also attributed his "wholly unrealistic" images of battle to the romantic war fiction he read as a teenager prior to World War II. Yet as off base as his expectations about combat were, he believed that he was better off than his fellow marines who had grown up on B movies: "The minority who avoided Hollywood paradigms were, like me, people who had watched fewer B movies than we had read books. That does not mean that we were better soldiers and citizens. We certainly weren't braver. I do think that our optics were clearer, however—that what we saw was closer to the truth because we weren't looking through MGM or RKO prisms."[17]

War movies of the interwar years, with a few exceptions, portrayed the aerial and ground combat of the Great War in glorified terms. Though literary critics debate the relative influence of the antiwar, disillusionist literature of the interwar years compared to the romanticized stories of the sort that Munschauer and Manchester had read, the more important issue may well be the extent to which the rapidly expanding film industry unduly influenced young minds.[18]

The spate of war movies produced during and immediately after World War II had an even greater influence on adolescent minds. Real-world hero Audie Murphy played an imaginary one in westerns and war movies, and John Wayne starred in a series of war, western, and adventure films, most important of which was probably his role as Sergeant Striker in *Sands of Iwo Jima* (1949). John Wayne's influence on the Vietnam War soldiers' war-in-the-head was so significant that Tobey Herzog dubbed it the "John Wayne Syndrome": "By the early 1960's, 'the Duke,' through his movies and political stands, had already approached his present status as a cultural icon representing traditional American values of patriotism, courage, confidence, and leadership."[19] Unfortunately, Wayne's war movies, especially his 1967 film *The Green Berets,* failed to address "the difficult moral issues involved with war; the moments of self-revelation on the battlefield; the confessions of fear, brutal instincts, and frustrations; and the questions of personal responsibility for violent actions."[20] Herzog's assessment can certainly be applied to the post–World War II war-movie genre as a whole—Hollywood continued to refract war through rose-colored prisms.

The impact of these films on Korean and Vietnam War soldiers is evident by their own admissions. Ron Kovic, who enlisted in the marines and went to Vietnam, used to watch movies on Saturday afternoons with his friends. He vividly remembers watching Audie Murphy playing himself in *To Hell and Back:* "It was the greatest movie I ever saw in my life." *Sands of Iwo Jima* was a close second: "John Wayne . . . became one of my heroes." Kovic and his young friends "dreamed of becoming United States Marines and fighting our first war."[21] Caputo was likewise influenced by the silver screen. He joined the marines in 1960 in part because of his movie-inspired visions of martial glory: "The country was at peace then, but the early sixties were years of almost constant tension and crisis; if a conflict did break out, the Marines would be certain to fight in it and I could be there with them. . . . Already I saw myself charging up some distant beachhead, like John Wayne in *Sands of Iwo Jima,* and then coming home a suntanned warrior with medals on my chest."[22]

Movie images thus shaped soldiers' notions of what war would be like, and even entrance into the combat zone did not automatically shatter these notions.

Some Korean War GIs and Vietnam War grunts commented, for example, that war was "just like it was in the movies." When making this claim, however, they were usually referring to some spectacle viewed at a safe distance. Private Fred Davidson, part of the marine force that seized Wolmi-do ("do" meaning island) in Inchon Harbor during the Korean War, sat back and watched the follow-on main forces attack: "From where I sat on top of Radio Hill on Wolmi-do, I could see both landing sites. This was fantastic! It was just like watching a John Wayne movie projected on an enormous 3-D Cinemascope screen."[23]

War at a distance could be spectacular, and observing it required no actions or judgment calls—it was, in short, just like watching a movie. Soldiers soon discovered, however, that being embroiled in combat was another matter. Movie soldiers, Private James Cardinal discovered, did not suffer the way he and his real-life buddies did in Korea: "Believe me, sleeping in foxholes in a drizzling rain, cold and waiting to attack, dodging bullets, and going for three or four days with one small meal is not as romantic as the movies make out."[24]

Soldiers did die in the movies, but heroically, and usually in the midst of a desperate fight. Obliterating a lone North Korean machine-gun nest hidden in a village with a salvo from a battleship, however, was not William Davis's idea of the stuff of movie legends: "We could see the shells coming in. They sounded like freight trains going over. . . . Then there was a gigantic boom. When the smoke cleared, the village no longer existed. In its place was a large, shallow lake with a little straw from the village roofs floating in it. That's when I knew I wasn't in any John Wayne movie."[25]

Add to the misconceptions generated by movies the effect of the memorialization process and the impact of popular notions about America's wars "propagated in such places as textbooks, official histories, popular-culture documents, and public schools," as the literary critic Kali Tal observes, and the result was a glamorized, simplified, "national (collective) myth" about war. Individuals then "borrow from" or "buy into" this national myth when formulating their own "personal myths."[26]

But not all personal myths, or wars-in-the-head, to return to Hynes's phrase, were the same, despite the influence of a collective national myth. Some soldiers went to war with more realistic conceptions than others. Herbert Hendin and Ann Pollinger Haas examined a group of Vietnam veterans who had not broken down in combat and did not have serious postwar adjustment problems. They discovered that one of the reasons why these veterans were not overly stressed by their wartime experience was because they had not expected much good to come from it in the first place: "These veterans experienced combat . . . as a dangerous challenge to be met effectively while trying to stay alive. In contrast to most of those who developed postwar stress disorders, they did not perceive combat as a test of their worth as men."[27]

These soldiers had expected danger and hardship, not adventure or a masculine rite of passage, and although the generalization remains that no green soldier fully anticipates the horrors of war, these men had more realistic expectations than many of their comrades. How to explain this variance in personal myths about war? Some historians posit that less-educated, lower-class youths held less glamorous notions about war. Civilian life meant hard work and a struggle to survive, and combat was more of the same. Conversely, middle- and upper-class youths were not prepared for, nor could they anticipate, war's deprivations, and they discovered too late that lofty ideals about the justness of the cause do not ward off cold, mud, or bullets.[28]

There may well be some validity to this class-based theory, but it is also true that some working-class and poor youths were affected by the national myth. Audie Murphy, a sharecropper's son, and Kovic, the son of a grocery store clerk, volunteered for service expecting to find adventure and heroics. Their wars-in-the-head, in other words, were as off base as anyone else's, although their modest backgrounds may have prepared them better than the typical middle-class youth for enduring the army's institutional inequalities.

At least some soldiers ascribed their more modest expectations about war to what they had learned from realistic, as opposed to overly romanticized, literature. The war-in-the-head of Henry Gole, a young soldier heading for his first combat, was shaped by what he had read, and he was better prepared as a consequence: "My experience as a young infantry soldier in Korea convinced me that having read *The Red Badge of Courage, All Quiet on the Western Front, From Here to Eternity* and *The Naked and the Dead* prepared me better for war than any history I had read to that date. Further, aside from the technical aspects of military training—weapons, tactics, organization and tricks of the trade—the fiction was better psychological preparation than anything I was taught by the Army."[29]

There are valuable insights to be gained about the realities of war by reading memoirs and novels written by combat veterans. Hynes argues that they are important correctives to the national myth: "Personal narratives . . . subvert the expectations of romance. They work at a level below the big words and the brave sentiments, down on the surface of the earth where men fight. They don't glorify war, or aestheticize it, or make it literary or heroic; they speak in their own voices, in their own plain language. They are not antiwar—that is, they are not polemics against war; they simply tell us what it is like."[30]

Tim O'Brien, in telling what his war was like, despaired of providing any profound insights: "Can the foot soldier teach anything important about war, merely for having been there? I think not. He can tell war stories." His self-dismissal aside, however, O'Brien's simple yet eloquent summary of what his war had taught him speaks volumes: "Now, war ended, all I am left with are simple, unprofound scraps of truth. Men die. Fear hurts and humiliates. It is hard to be brave. It is hard to know what bravery *is*. Dead human beings are heavy and awkward to carry, things smell different in Vietnam, soldiers are dreamers, drill sergeants are boors, some men thought the war was proper and others didn't and most didn't care."[31]

Are these "profound" insights? Perhaps not. Are they valuable "scraps of truth" for a young man facing a war? Absolutely. The number of young soldiers who, like Henry Gole, actually availed themselves of such scraps of truth is difficult to determine. Some men do mention, almost as an aside, that war memoirs or novels had helped to bring their war-in-the-head in line with reality. Charles F. Minder had read some of the few accounts published prior to America's joining the fray in 1917 that provided a realistic, meaning grim, portrayal of trench warfare. He was glad that he had: "Today I am going through the same experiences and appreciate all the more the different war books I used to read."[32] Interestingly, accounts of trench warfare in World War I again provided insights several wars later. Marine Lieutenant James Brady, fighting in Korea during the period of stalemated warfare, was thankful for having read a World War I play by R. C. Sherriff: "It was a throwback, this war. I remembered reading *Journey's End* in college. Sherriff *knew!*"[33]

Prior to World War II, Harold L. Bond took the message of the disillusionment literature seriously: "My generation, brought up on *A Farewell to Arms, All Quiet on the Western Front,* and plays such as *Journey's End,* was not easily persuaded that modern war made any sense at all. Most certainly none of us thought any longer of glory and military heroics."[34] Bond was presumptuous, however, in speaking for his entire generation. After all, while he was reading realistic accounts, Manchester was devouring "Kipling, not Hemingway; Rupert Brooke, not Wilfred Owen; *Gone with the Wind,* not Ambrose Bierce and Stephen Crane," and his soon-to-be marine comrades were watching B war movies.[35]

There will probably always be more Manchesters than Bonds, and Hynes further despairs that even the Bonds will not be dissuaded by their reading to forsake war: "In matters of war, cautionary literature and evidence of experience do not change many minds or alter many romantic expectations. Every new generation will respond anew to war's great seduction—not to the uniforms and the parades but to the chance to be where danger is, where men are fighting. War brings to any society its electric, exhilarating atmosphere, and young men rush to join in it, however grim the stories of war they have read and accepted as the truth."[36] Thus even a young man who has absorbed some of the sobering lessons of the "cautionary literature" may still not be able to resist "war's great seduction." Norman Mailer confessed that "despite the First World War and all we knew about it," there "wasn't much pacifism" among his generation, and going off to fight in World War II "seemed romantic to us."[37]

Perhaps the most that realistic accounts of combat can accomplish, therefore, is to warn the novice or potential soldier not to expect too much from war. If this warning tempers a soldier's optimistic war-in-the-head even a little, then the traumatic shattering of expectations he will experience in combat will be less severe. Historians can assist in this warning process. Roger J. Spiller, who teaches officers at the army's Command and General Staff College, believes he has an obligation to ensure that his students have realistic expectations about their dangerous profession: "I teach soldiers the history of war and so contribute to their vision of what war is. Soldiers . . . carry with them into their first combat an expectation of what their war will be like. My responsibility is to see that the distance between what they expect and what they get is as small as possible."[38]

Those teaching history to young people share the same responsibility. The young are the soldiers of the next generation. Someone should tell them what to expect and where to look for insights and answers—the literature of war.

# Notes

## INTRODUCTION

1. William L. Langer, *Gas and Flame in World War I* (New York: Knopf, 1965), pp. xvii–xviii. Langer wrote this book while he was still a doughboy in Europe, and it was distributed to the members of his unit, E Company, First Gas Regiment, in February 1919.

2. Ronald Schaffer, *America in the Great War: The Rise of the War Welfare State* (New York and Oxford: Oxford University Press, 1991), p. 151.

3. James Jones, *WW II: A Chronicle of Soldiering* (New York: Ballantine Books, 1976), p. 6.

4. Alice M. Hoffman and Howard S. Hoffman, *Archives of Memory: A Soldier Recalls World War II* (Lexington: University Press of Kentucky, 1990), pp. 145–146. For a similar assessment, see Paul Fussell, *The Great War and Modern Memory* (London, Oxford, and New York: Oxford University Press, 1975), pp. 326–327.

5. Paul Boesch, *Road to Huertgen: Forest in Hell* (Houston: Paul M. Boesch, 1985), p. 165. The Vietnam veteran Philip Caputo makes the same observation. See *A Rumor of War* (New York: Ballantine Books, 1978), p. 90.

6. Samuel Hynes, *The Soldiers' Tale: Bearing Witness to Modern War* (New York: Allen Lane, 1997), pp. 24–25.

7. Stanley Cooperman, *World War I and the American Novel* (Baltimore: Johns Hopkins University Press, 1967), p. 156.

8. Henry G. Gole, "Literature and History for Soldiers," *Military Review* 68:6 (May 1988): 5.

9. Roger A. Beaumont, "Military Fiction and Role: Some Problems and Perspectives," *Military Affairs* 39:2 (April 1975): 70.

10. Tobey C. Herzog, *Vietnam War Stories: Innocence Lost* (London and New York: Routledge, 1985), p. 96. Herzog's assessment of *The Naked and the Dead* is accurate. I would rank Mailer's novel as the premier American antiwar novel of the twentieth century, which does not mean that it does not contain any number of valuable individual episodes and insights. The full citation for Mailer is *The Naked and the Dead* (New York: Signet, 1948).

11. Hynes, *Soldiers' Tale*, p. 25.

12. Peter Karsten, *Soldiers and Society: The Effects of Military Service and War on American Society*, Grass Roots Perspectives on American History, no. 1 (Westport, Conn., and London: Greenwood Press, 1978), p. 12.

13. Herzog, *War Stories*, p. 3. Joseph Remenyi carries this observation a step further, pointing out that the best literature of war, by dealing with these universal human themes, attracts the most reader empathy and interest. See his "Psychology of War Literature," *Sewanee Review: A Quarterly of Life and Letters* 52:1 (winter 1944): 137–147.

14. Richard H. Kohn, "The Social History of the American Soldier: A Review and Prospectus for Research," *American Historical Review* 86:3 (June 1981): 560.

15. Herbert Hendin and Ann Pollinger Haas, *Wounds of War: The Psychological Aftermath of Combat in Vietnam* (New York: Basic Books, 1984), p. 10.

## CHAPTER 1. RALLYING TO THE FLAG

1. For an excellent discussion of the Selective Draft Act and the rationale behind it, see John Whiteclay Chambers II, *To Raise an Army: The Draft Comes to Modern America* (New York: Free Press, 1987).

2. See ibid., p. 1, for the 72 percent figure. For a discussion of how volunteer enlistments continued to be the main source of manpower for the army from April through December 1917, see Marvin A. Kreidberg and Merton G. Henry, *History of Military Mobilization in the United States Army, 1775–1945,* Department of the Army Pamphlet 20-212 (Washington, D.C.: U.S. Government Printing Office, November 1955), pp. 246–252, especially Table 25, p. 250. In 1918, draft inductions increased significantly, and in August voluntary enlistment in the army was cut out altogether, which explains how, by war's end, 72 percent of the army's personnel were draftees.

3. Michael C. C. Adams, *The Great Adventure: Male Desire and the Coming of World War I* (Bloomington and Indianapolis: Indiana University Press, 1990), p. xiv.

4. Ibid., pp. 51–61. See also David M. Kennedy, *Over Here: The First World War and American Society* (New York: Oxford University Press, 1980), p. 179; Thomas C. Leonard, *Above the Battle: War-Making in America from Appomattox to Versailles* (New York: Oxford University Press, 1978), pp. 152–154; and Charles V. Genthe, *American War Narratives: 1917–1918: A Study and Bibliography* (New York: David Lewis, 1969), pp. 9–13, 32–33, 43–46, and 67–70.

5. Kennedy, *Over Here*, p. 178.

6. These themes are discussed in Adams, *Great Adventure*, pp. 9–44 and 73–84; Genthe, *War Narratives*, pp. 49–52 and 92–98; and Stanley Cooperman, *World War I and the American Novel* (Baltimore: Johns Hopkins University Press, 1967), pp. 44–54.

7. On European society's enthusiasm for war in August 1914, and the values that generated that positive outlook, see Modris Eksteins, *Rites of Spring: The Great War and the Birth of the Modern Age* (New York: Anchor Books, 1989), pp. 115–135; Paul Fussell, *The Great War and Modern Memory* (London, Oxford, and New York: Oxford University Press, 1975), pp.18–29; and Eric J. Leed, *No Man's Land: Combat and Identity in World War I* (Cambridge: Cambridge University Press, 1979), pp. 39–72.

8. For an assessment of the romantic, overwhelmingly pro-Allied war literature pro-

duced by British, American, and Canadian authors from 1914 to 1918, see Genthe, *War Narratives*, pp. 13–17, 37–42, and 76–88; Kennedy, *Over Here*, pp. 180–184; and Cooperman, *American Novel*, pp. 13–44.

9. Henry F. May, *The End of American Innocence: A Study of the First Years of Our Own Time, 1912–1917* (Chicago: Quadrangle Books, 1964), pp. 363–364.

10. Kennedy, *Over Here*, p. 184. For a concurring assessment, see Charles A. Fenton, "A Literary Fracture of World War I," *American Quarterly* 12:1, part 1 (summer 1960): 119–132.

11. May, *American Innocence*, p. 365.

12. Lee Kennett, *G.I.: The American Soldier in World War II* (New York: Charles Scribner's Sons, 1987), p. 89.

13. William E. Matsen, *The Great War and the American Novel: Versions of Reality and the Writer's Craft in Selected Fiction of the First World War* (New York: Peter Lang, 1993), p. 17.

14. For a discussion of the lack of idealism and romantic imagery in American World War II novels, see Peter Aichinger, *The American Soldier in Fiction, 1880–1963: A History of Attitudes Toward Warfare and the Military Establishment* (Ames: Iowa State University Press, 1975), pp. 37–38.

15. Robert Leckie, *Helmet for My Pillow* (Garden City, N.Y.: Nelson Doubleday, 1979), p. 1.

16. Lekachman interview in Studs Terkel, *"The Good War": An Oral History of World War II* (New York: Pantheon Books, 1984), p. 68.

17. Marguerite Higgins, *War in Korea: The Report of a Woman Combat Correspondent* (Garden City, N.Y.: Doubleday, 1951), pp. 17 and 85.

18. Theodore R. Fehrenbach, *This Kind of War: A Study in Unpreparedness* (New York: Macmillan, 1963), pp. 437 and 5.

19. Lawrence M. Baskir and William A. Strauss, *Chance and Circumstance: The Draft, the War, and the Vietnam Generation* (New York: Knopf, 1978), p. 6.

20. Kennedy, *Over Here*, pp. 143, 151–153, and 167.

21. See Ronald Schaffer, *America in the Great War: The Rise of the War Welfare State* (New York and Oxford: Oxford University Press, 1991), p. 182.

22. Amos N. Wilder, *Armageddon Revisited: A World War I Journal* (New Haven and London: Yale University Press, 1994), p. 8.

23. Bulz interview in Henry Berry, *Make the Kaiser Dance: Living Memories of the Doughboy* (New York: Priam Books, 1978), p. 294.

24. Horatio Rogers, *World War I Through My Sights* (San Rafael, Calif.: Presidio Press, 1976), p. 2.

25. Harold P. Leinbaugh and John D. Campbell, *The Men of Company K* (New York: Bantam Books, 1987), p. 2.

26. Stiles interview in Henry Berry, *Semper Fi, Mac: Living Memories of the U.S. Marines in World War II* (New York: Berkley Books, 1983), p. 72.

27. Henry Berry, *Hey, Mac, Where Ya Been? Living Memories of the U.S. Marines in the Korean War* (New York: St. Martin's Press, 1988), p. 220. Berry added, following this quotation, "These pretty much seem to be the feelings of everyone I interviewed" (p. 220).

28. Two historians who do take note of idealistic motivations in the Vietnam War are Christian G. Appy, *Working-Class War: American Combat Soldiers and Vietnam* (Chapel

Hill and London: University of North Carolina Press, 1993), pp. 63–69 and 209–212, and James R. Ebert, *A Life in a Year: The American Infantryman in Vietnam, 1965–1972* (Novato, Calif.: Presidio Press, 1993), pp. 9–12.

29. William D. Ehrhart, "Soldier-Poets of the Vietnam War," *Virginia Quarterly Review* 63:2 (spring 1987): 263.

30. Ron Kovic, *Born on the Fourth of July* (New York: Pocket Books, 1977), p. 74. At a writers' conference in 1985, Kovic reconfirmed his idealistic motivations. He recounted his reaction to John F. Kennedy's famous inaugural address of January 1961: "I sat in my living room . . . and tears streamed down my face because I felt that I had a purpose in my life. I felt that I had an obligation to serve my country." See Timothy J. Lomperis, *"Reading the Wind": The Literature of the Vietnam War* (Durham, N.C.: Duke University Press, 1987), p. 30.

31. William L. Langer, *Gas and Flame in World War I* (New York: Knopf, 1965), pp. xviii–xix.

32. Wilder, *Armageddon,* pp. 4 and 6.

33. Will Judy, *A Soldier's Diary: A Day-to-Day Record in the World War* (Chicago: Judy Publishing, 1931), p. 20.

34. James Jones, *WW II: A Chronicle of Soldiering* (New York: Ballantine Books, 1976), p. 15.

35. Audie Murphy, *To Hell and Back* (New York: Bantam Books, 1983), pp. 6, 7–8.

36. John L. Munschauer, *World War II Cavalcade: An Offer I Couldn't Refuse* (Manhattan, Kans.: Sunflower University Press, 1996), p. 69.

37. John A. Sullivan, *Toy Soldiers: Memoir of a Combat Platoon Leader in Korea* (Jefferson, N.C., and London: McFarland, 1991), p. 2.

38. Ibid., p. 10. For another example, see the John Burns interview in Berry, *Hey, Mac,* p. 181.

39. The Vietnam veteran Tobey C. Herzog, an English professor, has dubbed the influence of popular war movies the "John Wayne Syndrome." See his *Vietnam War Stories: Innocence Lost* (London and New York: Routledge, 1985), pp. 16–24. See also Appy, *Working-Class War,* pp. 60–62.

40. Kovic, *Fourth of July,* p. 73.

41. Alfred S. Bradford, *Some Even Volunteered: The First Wolfhounds Pacify Vietnam* (Westport, Conn., and London: Praeger, 1994), p. 3.

42. Peter Karsten, "Consent and the American Soldier: Theory Versus Reality," *Parameters* 12:1 (March 1982): 42.

43. Ibid., pp. 47–48. See also Richard H. Kohn, "The Social History of the American Soldier: A Review and Prospectus for Research," *American Historical Review* 86:3 (June 1981): 558. Kohn, a historian, makes the same point as Karsten—once the stock of volunteers dries up, as invariably happens, various forms of coercion, notably the draft, must be instituted to spur the more reluctant individuals into fulfilling their obligations.

44. Wilder, *Armageddon,* p. 137.

45. Alvin C. York, *Sergeant York: His Own Life Story and War Diary,* ed. Tom Skeyhill (Garden City, N.Y.: Doubleday, Doran, 1928), p. 150.

46. Herschowitz interview in Berry, *Make the Kaiser Dance,* p. 353.

47. Schaffer, *Great War,* p. 185. The historian Mark Meigs also notes the influence of peer pressure in getting men to join up in World War I and adds, "Peer pressure may

indeed always play a role in sending young men to war" (*Optimism at Armageddon: Voices of American Participants in the First World War* [Washington Square, N.Y.: New York University Press, 1997], p. 24).

48. Carl Andrew Brannen, *Over There: A Marine in the Great War* (College Station: Texas A&M University Press, 1996), p. 5.

49. Charles F. Minder, *This Man's War: The Day-by-Day Record of an American Private on the Western Front* (New York: Pevensey Press, 1931), p. 146.

50. Leon C. Standifer, *Not in Vain: A Rifleman Remembers World War II* (Baton Rouge and London: Louisiana State University Press, 1992), pp. 31–32. For another example, see Carl M. Becker and Robert G. Thobaben, *Common Warfare: Parallel Memoirs by Two World War II GI's in the Pacific* (Jefferson, N.C., and London: McFarland, 1992), pp. 6–7.

51. Jones, *WW II,* p. 17.

52. See a 1969 survey confirming the influence of social and peer pressure in Peter Karsten, *Soldiers and Society: The Effects of Military Service and War on American Society,* Grass Roots Perspectives on American History, no. 1 (Westport, Conn., and London: Greenwood Press, 1978), p. 65.

53. Tim O'Brien, *If I Die in a Combat Zone: Box Me Up and Ship Me Home* (New York: Laurel, Dell, 1987), p. 45.

54. Appy, *Working-Class War,* p. 50.

55. Rudolph W. Stephens, *Old Ugly Hill: A G.I.'s Fourteen Months in the Korean Trenches, 1952–1953* (Jefferson, N.C., and London: McFarland, 1995), p. 25.

56. Baskir and Strauss, *Chance and Circumstance,* pp. 67–90 and 107.

57. Strong interview in Wallace Terry, *Bloods: An Oral History of the Vietnam War by Black Veterans* (New York: Ballantine Books, 1985), p. 55.

58. Samuel A. Stouffer, Edward A. Suchman, Leland C. DeVinney, Shirley A. Star, and Robin M. Williams Jr., *Studies in Social Psychology in World War II,* vol. 1, *The American Soldier: Adjustment During Army Life* (Princeton: Princeton University Press, 1949), pp. 329–337. Only the first two of the four volumes, referred to by their shared title *The American Soldier,* are cited in this book. See bibliography.

59. Baskir and Strauss, *Chance and Circumstance,* p. 55.

60. John Ketwig, *. . . And a Hard Rain Fell* (New York: Pocket Books, 1986), pp. 16–18.

61. Alice M. Hoffman and Howard S. Hoffman, *Archives of Memory: A Soldier Recalls World War II* (Lexington: University Press of Kentucky, 1990), pp. 24–25.

62. Becker and Thobaben, *Common Warfare,* pp. 120–121.

63. James Brady, *The Coldest War: A Memoir of Korea* (New York: Pocket Books, 1991), pp. 9–10.

64. Kennedy, *Over There,* p. 153.

65. Bob Hoffman, *I Remember the Last War* (York, Pa.: Strength and Health Publishing, 1940), p. 31.

66. Jones interview in Mary Penick Motley, *The Invisible Soldier: The Experience of the Black Soldier, World War II* (Detroit: Wayne State University Press, 1975), p. 177.

67. George William Sefton, *It Was My War: I'll Remember It the Way I Want To!* (Manhattan, Kans.: Sunflower University Press, 1994), p. xi. See pp. xi–xiii for Sefton's upbringing.

68. William Manchester, *Goodbye, Darkness: A Memoir of the Pacific War* (Boston and Toronto: Little, Brown, 1979), p. 34. See pp. 15–35 for Manchester's upbringing.

69. Mark Baker, *Nam: The Vietnam War in the Words of the Men and Women Who Fought There* (New York: Berkley Books, 1983), p. 16.

70. Foote interview in Baskir and Strauss, *Chance and Circumstance,* p. 255.

71. Jack Fuller, *Fragments* (New York: Dell, 1985), pp. 28–29.

72. Schaffer, *Great War,* p. 184.

73. Berry, *Make the Kaiser Dance,* pp. 274 and 328. Twelve of Berry's interviewees were National Guardsmen called up to go to the United States–Mexican border in 1916 (p. 341).

74. Janice Holt Giles, ed., *The G.I. Journal of Sergeant Giles* (Boston: Houghton Mifflin, and Cambridge: Riverside Press, 1965), pp. 3–4.

75. Rodriguez interview in Gerald Astor, *Crisis in the Pacific: The Battles for the Philippine Islands by the Men Who Fought Them* (New York: Donald I. Fine Books, 1996), p. 193.

76. Babyak interview in Berry, *Hey, Mac,* p. 112.

77. William C. Menninger, *A Psychiatrist for a Troubled World: Selected Papers of William C. Menninger, M.D.* (New York: Viking, 1967), pp. 557–558.

78. Charles C. Moskos Jr., "Racial Integration in the Armed Forces," *American Journal of Sociology* 72:2 (September 1966): 139. See also Charles C. Moskos Jr., *The American Enlisted Man: The Rank and File in Today's Military* (New York: Russell Sage Foundation, 1970), Table 5.7, p. 220.

79. Moskos, *American Enlisted Man,* p. 117 and Table 5.6, p. 219.

80. See the survey of Vietnam-era enlistees in Patricia M. Shields, "Enlistment During the Vietnam Era and the 'Representative' Issue of the All-Volunteer Force," *Armed Forces and Society* 7:1 (fall 1980): 133–151.

81. Anderson interview in Terry, *Bloods,* p. 221.

82. Albert French, *Patches of Fire: A Story of War and Redemption* (New York: Anchor Books, 1997), pp. 6–7.

83. John Sack, *M* (New York: Avon Books, 1985), p. 28.

84. Woodley interview in Terry, *Bloods,* p. 237.

85. Roy E. Appleman, *South to the Naktong, North to the Yalu* (Washington, D.C.: U.S. Government Printing Office, 1961), p. 180, cited in James H. Toner, "American Society and the American Way of War: Korea and Beyond," *Parameters* 11:1 (spring 1981): 81.

86. Joseph R. Owen, *Colder Than Hell: A Marine Rifle Company at Chosin Reservoir* (Annapolis, Md.: Naval Institute Press, 1996), p. 14.

87. Robert Mason, *Chickenhawk* (New York: Penguin Books, 1986), p. 49.

88. Richard Holmes, *Acts of War: The Behavior of Men in Battle* (New York: Free Press, 1985), pp. 286–287.

89. William H. Mauldin, *Bill Mauldin in Korea* (New York: W. W. Norton, 1952), p. 129.

90. William D. Ehrhart, *Vietnam-Perkasie: A Combat Marine Memoir* (Jefferson, N.C., and London: McFarland, 1983), p. 33.

91. Owen, *Colder Than Hell,* p. 7.

92. Richard D. Camp, with Eric Hammel, *Lima-6: A Marine Company Commander in Vietnam* (New York: Pocket Books, 1989), p. 18.

93. Hoffman, *I Remember,* p. 78.

94. Leinbaugh and Campbell, *Company K,* p. 2.

95. Sullivan, *Toy Soldiers,* p. 31.

96. Murphy, *To Hell and Back,* p. 20.

97. Lester Atwell, *Private* (New York: Popular Library, 1958), p. 16.

98. Matthew Brennan, *Brennan's War: Vietnam, 1965–1969* (New York: Pocket Books, 1986), p. 236.

99. Rosenblum interview in Terkel, *Good War,* p. 384.

100. Michael Lee Lanning, *The Only War We Had: A Platoon Leader's Journal of Vietnam* (New York: Ivy Books, 1987), p. 1.

101. Foote interview in Baskir and Strauss, *Chance and Circumstance,* p. 256.

102. Ibid., p. 25.

103. For a discussion of various peacetime and wartime efforts to turn criminals and social misfits into soldiers, and the general condemnation of the practice as a bad idea, see Roy R. Grinker and John P. Spiegel, *War Neuroses* (Philadelphia and London: Blakiston, 1945), p. 75; Robert H. Ollendorf and Paul L. Adams, "Psychiatry and the Draft," *American Journal of Orthopsychiatry* 14:1 (January 1971): 87; Anne Hoiberg, "Military Staying Power," in *Combat Effectiveness: Cohesion, Stress, and the Volunteer Military,* ed. Sam C. Sarkesian (Beverly Hills and London: Sage, 1980), p. 219; and Peter Watson, *War on the Mind: The Military Uses and Abuses of Psychology* (New York: Basic Books, 1978), pp. 146–148.

104. Becker and Thobaben, *Common Warfare,* p. 112.

105. Rasmus interview in Terkel, *Good War,* p. 39. For another example, in this case a young man who wanted to prove his bravery to his father, see the interview with the Vietnam veteran Richard Deegan in Appy, *Working-Class War,* pp. 74–76.

106. Charles S. Crawford, *The Four Deuces: A Korean War Story* (Novato, Calif.: Presidio Press, 1989), p. 9. For a tale almost identical to Crawford's, see the story of Webster Manuel, who, after being hazed for doing "women's work" as a switchboard operator in the Second Infantry Division in Korea, transferred to a rifle platoon (Donald Knox, with additional text by Alfred Coppel, *The Korean War: Uncertain Victory: The Concluding Volume of an Oral History* [San Diego, New York, and London: Harcourt Brace Jovanovich, 1988], pp. 62 and 73).

107. Philip Caputo, *A Rumor of War* (New York: Ballantine Books, and Toronto: Ballantine Books of Canada, 1978), pp. 6 and 120.

108. Baker, *Nam,* p. 34.

109. Ehrhart, *Vietnam-Perkasie,* p. 89.

110. Morrison interview in Berry, *Make the Kaiser Dance,* p. 323.

111. A study of U.S. Army Basic Training conducted in 1955 by the Walter Reed Army Institute of Research describes this soldierization process as learning carried out simultaneously on two levels. In the "narrower sense," basic training was a straightforward process of teaching the trainee specific combat skills. In the "broader sense," basic training was an "acculturative process" in which the trainee learned "the basic mores, canons and customs of the military subculture, and the arts of living and cooperating with a large group of his fellow men" (David H. Marlowe, "The Basic Training Process," in *The Symptom as Communication in Schizophrenia,* ed. Kenneth L. Artiss [New York and London: Grune and Stratton, 1959], p. 75).

112. Arthur J. Vidich and Maurice R. Stein, "The Dissolved Identity in Military Life," in *Identity and Anxiety: Survival of the Person in Mass Society,* ed. Maurice R. Stein, Arthur J. Vidich, and David Manning White (Glencoe, Ill.: Free Press, 1960), p. 496.

113. Appy, *Working-Class War,* p. 86

114. Gwynne Dyer, *War* (New York: Crown, 1985), p. 111.

115. See Artiss, ed., *Schizophrenia,* p. 76, for a 1955 study that verifies the stressful nature of army basic training.

116. Ebert, *A Life in a Year,* p. 29; see his chapter 2, "Basic Training," pp. 25–42, and chapter 3, "Advanced Individual Training," pp. 43–60, for an excellent overview of the Vietnam-era training process from the trainee's perspective.

117. See Peter G. Bourne, "Some Observations on the Psychosocial Phenomena Seen in Basic Training," *Psychiatry: Journal for the Study of Interpersonal Processes* 30:2 (May 1967): 188, for a discussion of the "environmental shock" experienced by recruits during the reception process.

118. Leckie, *Helmet,* p. 4.

119. Ehrhart, *Vietnam-Perkasie,* p. 12.

120. Hoffman and Hoffman, *Archives,* p. 28.

121. Ehrhart, *Vietnam-Perkasie,* p. 16.

122. Munschauer, *Cavalcade,* pp. 9 and 7.

123. Stack interview in Berry, *Semper Fi,* p. 299.

124. Leckie, *Helmet,* p. 5.

125. Fuller, *Fragments,* p. 40.

126. During World Wars I and II, this platoon was often a tactical unit, and the men continued together into unit training and deployment overseas. For men being trained as individual replacements in the world wars, and for all new recruits in basic training during the Korean and Vietnam Wars, this platoon was strictly a training organization that disbanded on completion of training. In either case, the trainees usually remained together in their platoon, under the tutelage of the same cadre, for the duration of their initial training.

127. Leckie, *Helmet,* p. 10.

128. Hoffman and Hoffman, *Archives,* p. 27.

129. Leon Uris, *Battle Cry* (New York: Bantam Books, 1953), pp. 49–50.

130. The sociologist John H. Faris found group punishments, and the recruits' sense of injustice over them, to be common when he studied basic and advanced individual training in the U.S. Army in the late 1960s and early 1970s (see his "The Impact of Basic Combat Training," *Armed Forces and Society* 2:1 [November 1975]: 117).

131. S. Kirson Weinberg, "Problems of Adjustment in Army Units," *American Journal of Sociology* 50:4 (January 1945): 273.

132. Ebert, *A Life in a Year,* p. 32.

133. Weinberg, "Problems of Adjustment," p. 273. See also Howard Brotz and Everett Wilson, "Characteristics of Military Society," *American Journal of Sociology* 51:5 (March 1946): 375.

134. Stephens, *Old Ugly Hill,* p. 18.

135. Ebert, *A Life in a Year,* p. 32.

136. Sociological studies of basic training note the lack of privacy and the extra measure of discomfort and even stress that resulted. See Faris, "Basic Combat Training," pp. 116–117, and Artiss, ed., *Schizophrenia,* pp. 78–79.

137. Leckie, *Helmet,* pp. 10–11.

138. For a discussion of the trainees' nadir in attitudes three to four weeks into basic training, see Bourne, "Psychosocial Phenomena in Basic Training," pp. 191–192, and Artiss, ed., *Schizophrenia,* p. 89.

139. David Parks, *G.I. Diary* (New York, Evanston, and London: Harper and Row, 1968), pp. 20–21.

140. Appy, *Working-Class War,* p. 104. See also Ebert, *A Life in a Year,* pp. 39–41; Bourne, "Psychosocial Phenomena in Basic Training," pp. 192–193; and Marlowe, in Artiss, ed., *Schizophrenia,* pp. 97–98.

141. Kennett, *G.I.,* p. 56.

142. Leckie, *Helmet,* p. 11.

143. Parks, *G.I. Diary,* p. 25.

144. Klaus H. Heubner, *Long Walk Through War: A Combat Doctor's Diary* (College Station: Texas A&M University Press, 1987), p. 97. For an even more positive testimonial to the value of training marches and a plea to the army never to stop conducting such training, "no matter how many armored personnel carriers it acquires," see Charles R. Cawthon, *Other Clay: A Remembrance of the World War II Infantry* (Niwot: University Press of Colorado, 1990), p. 6.

145. Paul Fussell, *Doing Battle: The Making of a Skeptic* (Boston: Little, Brown, 1996), p. 84.

146. See Marlowe, in Artiss, ed., *Schizophrenia,* p. 97, and Bourne, "Psychosocial Phenomena in Basic Training," p. 193, for the use of recognition and the emerging sense of accomplishment in the buildup phase.

147. Fussell, *Doing Battle,* p. 80.

148. Parks, *G.I. Diary,* pp. 24 and 27.

149. See Faris, "Basic Combat Training," 120; Ebert, *A Life in a Year,* p. 40; and Dyer, *War,* p. 114.

150. Howard Matthias, *The Korean War—Reflections of a Young Combat Platoon Leader,* rev. ed. (Tallahassee, Fla.: Father and Son Publishing, 1995), p. 5.

151. Tuttrup interview in Terkel, *Good War,* p. 175.

152. See Marlowe, in Artiss, ed., *Schizophrenia,* p. 97.

153. For a discussion of griping as a psychological relief valve, see Irving L. Janis, "Psychodynamic Aspects of Adjustment to Army Life," *Psychiatry: Journal of the Biology and the Pathology of Interpersonal Relations* 8:2 (May 1945): 175–176. See also Marlowe, in Artiss, ed., *Schizophrenia,* pp. 86 and 89.

154. Paul Fussell believes that army vulgarity in World War II served, in part, to help the soldiers cope with the frustrations of army life. See *Wartime: Understanding and Behavior in the Second World War* (New York and Oxford: Oxford University Press, 1989), pp. 90–95.

155. Leckie, *Helmet,* p. 14.

156. Kennett, *G.I.,* p. 63.

157. Faris, "Basic Combat Training," pp. 123–124.

158. Uris, *Battle Cry,* pp. 40–41. Uris, incidentally, spared his readers the actual marine term for a World War II era recruit—"shithead" or "shitbird."

159. Becker and Thobaben, *Common Warfare,* p. 120.

160. Janis, "Psychodynamic Aspects," p. 164. See also Stein, Vidich, and White, eds., *Identity and Anxiety,* p. 499.

161. For a discussion of the friendships formed among trainees and the mutual support derived from them, see Artiss, ed., *Schizophrenia,* pp. 89–95, and Paul D. Nelson and Newell H. Berry, "Cohesion in Marine Recruit Platoons," *Journal of Psychology* 68 (January 1968): 63–71.

162. Sefton, *It Was My War,* p. 4.

163. Becker and Thobaben, *Common Warfare,* p. 115. See also Bourne, "Psychosocial Phenomena in Basic Training," p. 193.

164. See Bourne, "Psychosocial Phenomena in Basic Training," p. 193.

165. Fuller, *Fragments,* pp. 52–53.

166. Stanley Goff and Robert Sanders, with Clark Smith, *Brothers: Black Soldiers in the Nam* (Novato, Calif.: Presidio Press, 1982), p. 7.

167. See Dyer, *War,* p. 126.

168. Eugene B. Sledge, *With the Old Breed at Peleliu and Okinawa* (New York: Bantam Books, 1983), p. 13.

169. Stephens, *Old Ugly Hill,* pp. 20–21.

170. Ehrhart, *Vietnam-Perkasie,* p. 19.

171. The soldier-authors are far more positive than negative in their descriptions of their training cadre, but a few accounts portray the drill sergeant as cruel and sadistic, and no doubt this type existed. See the cases of Sergeant Anderson in Ketwig, *Hard Rain,* pp. 19–26, and Sergeant Gerheim in Gustav Hasford, *The Short-timers* (New York: Bantam Books, 1979), pp. 3–33.

172. Dyer, *War,* p. 113. See also Faris, "Basic Combat Training," pp. 118–125; Marlowe, in Artiss, ed., *Schizophrenia,* p. 98; and Holmes, *Acts of War,* pp. 43–47.

173. Leckie, *Helmet,* p. 9.

174. Goff and Sanders, *Brothers,* p. 5. For a similar assessment of his Vietnam-era drill sergeant, see the playwright David Rabe's comments in Eric James Schroeder, *Vietnam, We've All Been There: Interviews with American Writers* (London and Westport, Conn.: Praeger, 1992), p. 204.

175. Dyer, *War,* p. 128. Other observers of the training process, or more typically, observers of combat who thereby came to appreciate the importance of tough, realistic training in preparing men for combat, have echoed Dyer's sentiments. For a World War II example, see Ralph Ingersoll, *The Battle Is the Pay-off* (New York: Harcourt, Brace, 1943), pp. 212–216. For a Korean War example, see the comments of Colonel John Michaelis in Higgins, *War in Korea,* pp. 220–222. Surveys of the soldiers themselves conducted by the Research Branch during World War II and summarized in the Stouffer Study reveal that, if anything, the training should have been even more demanding and realistic. See Samuel A. Stouffer, Arthur A. Lumsdaine, Marion Harper Lumsdaine, Robin M. Williams Jr., M. Brewster Smith, Irving L. Janis, Shirley A. Star, and Leonard S. Cottrell Jr., *Studies in Social Psychology in World War II,* vol. 2, *The American Soldier: Combat and Its Aftermath* (Princeton: Princeton University Press, 1949), pp. 220–231.

176. Jesse Glenn Gray, *The Warriors: Reflections on Men in Battle* (New York: Harper Colophon Books, 1970), pp. 27–28.

177. Robert Jay Lifton, *Home from the War: Vietnam Veterans: Neither Victims nor Executioners* (New York: Simon and Schuster, 1973), pp. 28–29. See also R. Wayne Eisenhart, "You Can't Hack It, Little Girl: A Discussion of the Covert Psychological

Agenda of Modern Combat Training," *Journal of Social Issues* 31:4 (fall 1975): 13–23, for an equally negative assessment of Vietnam-era marine boot camp.

178. Morris Janowitz and Roger W. Little, *Sociology and the Military Establishment,* 3d ed. (Beverly Hills and London: Sage, 1974), p. 67.

179. Kennett, *G.I.,* p. 72.

180. Dyer, *War,* p. 116.

181. Sam Keen, *Faces of the Enemy: Reflections of the Hostile Imagination,* with new preface (San Francisco: Harper San Francisco, 1991), p. 124.

182. The more introspective recruits were themselves aware of the importance of their beliefs and attitudes in shaping their reactions to military service, as evidenced by their tendency to dwell at some length in their memoirs on their civilian upbringing and the importance of values learned prior to joining the military. See, for example, Standifer, *Not in Vain,* pp. 1–40; Manchester, *Goodbye, Darkness,* pp. 15–35; and the character of Robert E. Lee Hodges Jr., in James Webb, *Fields of Fire* (New York: Bantam Books, 1979), pp. 23–36.

183. One of the best warnings about the perils of assuming cultural homogeneity is provided by the historian Craig M. Cameron, who rejects the historian Samuel L. A. Marshall's argument that all recruits brought the same belief, specifically, "Thou shalt not kill," with them into the service: "The argument has serious problems: foremost is the monolithic image Marshall suggests both as related to how all American soldiers feel and regarding the cultural heritage used as a measure" (see *American Samurai: Myth, Imagination, and the Conduct of Battle in the First Marine Division, 1941–1951* [Cambridge: Cambridge University Press, 1994], p. 51 n. 7).

184. Janowitz and Little, *Sociology,* p. 67.

185. John Helmer, *Bringing the War Home: The American Soldier in Vietnam and After* (New York: Free Press, 1974), p. 148.

186. Kurt Gabel, *The Making of a Paratrooper: Airborne Training and Combat in World War II* (Lawrence: University Press of Kansas, 1990), pp. 21–22.

187. Fuller, *Fragments,* p. 40.

188. Eli Ginzberg, James K. Anderson, Sol W. Ginsburg, John L. Herma, and John B. Miner, *The Ineffective Soldier: Lessons for Management and the Nation,* vol. 2, *Breakdown and Recovery* (New York and London: Columbia University Press, 1959), p. 33. For case studies of men discharged for various personal problems, see pp. 13–39; for those with homesickness and family problems, see pp. 40–51.

189. Robert A. Clark, "Aggressiveness and Military Training," *American Journal of Sociology* 51:5 (March 1946): 423–432.

190. Meyer H. Maskin and Leon L. Altman, "Military Psychodynamics: Psychological Factors in the Transition from Civilian to Soldier," *Psychiatry: Journal of the Biology and the Pathology of Interpersonal Relations* 6:3 (August 1943): 263–267.

191. Kennett, *G.I.,* p. 64.

192. Munschauer, *Cavalcade,* p. 10.

193. Marlowe, in Artiss, ed., *Schizophrenia,* p. 84 (note).

194. See the survey results of D. M. Mantell, *True Americanism: Green Berets and War Resisters* (New York: Teachers College Press, 1975), pp. 267–269 and 274–281, cited in Karsten, *Soldiers and Society,* pp. 81–82; Charles W. Brown and Charles C. Moskos Jr., "The American Soldier: Will He Fight? A Provisional Attitudinal Analysis," *Military*

*Review* 56:6 (June 1976): 8–17; William C. Cockerham, "Selective Socialization: Airborne Training as Status Passage," *Journal of Political and Military Sociology* 1:2 (fall 1973): 215–229; and William C. Cockerham, "Attitudes Toward Combat Among U.S. Army Paratroopers," *Journal of Political and Military Sociology* 6:1 (spring 1978): 1–15.

195. Becker and Thobaben, *Common Warfare,* p. 19.

196. Parks, *G.I. Diary,* p. 39.

197. Ketwig, *Hard Rain,* pp. 27 and 28.

## CHAPTER 2. THE ENVIRONMENT OF WAR

1. Eric J. Leed, *No Man's Land: Combat and Identity in World War I* (Cambridge: Cambridge University Press, 1979), p. 3. For a good, though not all-inclusive, synopsis of the various ways in which soldiers' perceptions about combat proved to be erroneous compared to actual experiences in battle, see Anthony Kellett, *Combat Motivation: The Behavior of Soldiers in Battle* (Boston, The Hague, and London: Kluwer, Nijhoff, 1982), pp. 219–225. See also Samuel Hynes's discussion of the "unimaginable otherness of war" in *The Soldiers' Tale: Bearing Witness to Modern War* (New York: Allen Lane, 1997), pp. 52–53. Hynes is a professor of literature and a World War II veteran.

2. John Keegan and Richard Holmes, with John Gau, *Soldiers: A History of Men in Battle* (New York: Viking, 1986), p. 21.

3. Joseph R. Owen, *Colder Than Hell: A Marine Rifle Company at Chosin Reservoir* (Annapolis, Md.: Naval Institute Press, 1996), p. 53.

4. Michael Lee Lanning, *The Only War We Had: A Platoon Leader's Journal of Vietnam* (New York: Ivy Books, 1987), p. 38.

5. Philip Caputo, *A Rumor of War* (New York: Ballantine Books, 1978), p. 57.

6. Elton E. Mackin, *Suddenly We Didn't Want to Die: Memoirs of a World War I Marine* (Novato, Calif.: Presidio Press, 1993), pp. 240–241.

7. George William Sefton, *It Was My War: I'll Remember It the Way I Want To!* (Manhattan, Kans.: Sunflower University Press, 1994), p. 185. Digging in was a staple in all the wars of the draft era. The grunts "humping the boonies" each day in Vietnam, for example, usually stopped several hours before dark, selected a defensive perimeter, and dug in. For an excellent description of how tiring that process could be, see Mark Baker, *Nam: The Vietnam War in the Words of the Men and Women Who Fought There* (New York: Berkley Books, 1983), pp. 86–87.

8. Judd interview in Donald Knox, with additional text by Alfred Coppel, *The Korean War: Uncertain Victory: The Concluding Volume of an Oral History* (San Diego, New York, and London: Harcourt Brace Jovanovich, 1988), p. 310. For a similar comment on the difficulties of bringing water forward during the Korean War, see Howard Matthias, *The Korean War—Reflections of a Young Combat Platoon Leader,* rev. ed. (Tallahassee, Fla.: Father and Son Publishing, 1995), pp. 174–175.

9. Owen, *Colder Than Hell,* p. 75.

10. Eugene B. Sledge, *With the Old Breed at Peleliu and Okinawa* (New York: Bantam Books, 1983), p. 229.

11. John Hersey, *Into the Valley: A Skirmish of the Marines* (New York: Schocken Books, 1989), pp. 85–95. For a similar, though fictional, example, see the saga of the

evacuation of Wilson, a wounded GI, in Norman Mailer, *The Naked and the Dead* (New York: Signet Books, 1948), pp. 482–493, 501–502, and 519–532.

12. Hersey, *Into the Valley*, p. 93. Perhaps the only worse conditions, or at least equally bad, under which casualties had to be evacuated were on the frozen, slippery, rocky slopes of a Korean mountainside. See James Brady's account of a thirteen-hour evacuation in *The Coldest War: A Memoir of Korea* (New York: Pocket Books, 1991), pp. 121–129.

13. Charles MacArthur, *War Bugs* (New York: Grosset and Dunlap, 1929), p. 157.

14. Ibid., p. 286. Other accounts verify how hard the artilleryman worked. See Amos N. Wilder, *Armageddon Revisited: A World War I Journal* (New Haven and London: Yale University Press, 1994), pp. 77 and 107; Horatio Rogers, *World War I Through My Sights* (San Rafael, Calif.: Presidio Press, 1976), pp. 121–123, 137–139, and 227; and Robert G. Merrick, *World War I: A Diary* (Baltimore: privately published, 1982), pp. 68 and 107–108.

15. Frederick Downs, *The Killing Zone: My Life in the Vietnam War* (New York: Berkley Books, 1983), p. 109. For a Korean War example of the work involved in establishing an artillery position, see Knox, *Uncertain Victory*, pp. 271–274. A case can certainly be made that other combat specialties, such as armor and engineers, also worked very hard, but delving into each specialty would be a book in itself. For a personal favorite—the dirty, hot, tired driver working on his armored personnel carrier—see Larry Heinemann, *Close Quarters* (New York: Farrar, Straus and Giroux, 1977), pp. 102–104.

16. William D. Ehrhart, *Vietnam-Perkasie: A Combat Marine Memoir* (Jefferson, N.C., and London: McFarland, 1983), p. 39.

17. Examples of such raids by the Germans and Japanese are common in the memoirs. Cases of raids by North Korean or Chinese aircraft are far fewer, but they did occur. Sergeant Boris R. Spiroff, a First Cavalry Division soldier in Korea, tells of a "Bed Check Charlie": "Though this was only a harassing action, it is eerie hearing the plane overhead. All pray that the bombs do not fall in their area. Everyone is jumpy and precious sleep is disturbed" (*Korea: Frozen Hell on Earth* [New York: Vantage Press, 1995], pp. 59–60). See also Knox, *Uncertain Victory*, pp. 246–250 and 349, and the interview with John Sack, in Eric James Schroeder, *Vietnam, We've All Been There: Interviews with American Writers* (London and Westport, Conn.: Praeger, 1992), p. 13.

18. Robert Leckie, *Helmet for My Pillow* (Garden City, N.Y.: Nelson Doubleday, 1979), p. 81.

19. Accounts of jumpy soldiers on guard duty at night are common. For one of the best, see chapter 3, "The Hole," in Albert French, *Patches of Fire: A Story of War and Redemption* (New York: Anchor Books, 1997), pp. 20–30.

20. A survey of World War II infantrymen revealed that even during a "quiet period," 54 percent got only five to six hours' sleep a day, and 31 percent got four hours or less. See Samuel A. Stouffer, Arthur A. Lumsdaine, Marion Harper Lumsdaine, Robin M. Williams Jr., M. Brewster Smith, Irving L. Janis, Shirley A. Star, and Leonard S. Cottrell Jr., *Studies in Social Psychology in World War II*, vol 2, *The American Soldier: Combat and Its Aftermath* (Princeton: Princeton University Press, 1949), p. 78. Based on his interviews with Vietnam veterans, James R. Ebert estimates that four hours' sleep a day was the norm for grunts in the field. See *A Life in a Year: The American Infantryman in Vietnam, 1965–1972* (Novato, Calif.: Presidio Press, 1993), p. 154.

21. Many students of soldier behavior have commented on the adverse effects of what the army, in recent years, has dubbed "continuous operations." In sum, without adequate rest and relief from combat, soldier efficiency begins to decline, often in a matter of a few days. See Elmar Dinter, *Hero or Coward: Pressures Facing the Soldier in Battle* (London and Totowa, N.J.: Frank Cass, 1985), pp. 27–31; Richard Holmes, *Acts of War: The Behavior of Men in Battle* (New York: Free Press, 1985), pp. 122–125; Kellett, *Combat Motivation,* pp. 231–242; Samuel L. A. Marshall, *Commentary on Infantry Operations and Weapons Usage in Korea, Winter of 1950–51,* Operations Research Office Report 13 (Chevy Chase, Md.: Johns Hopkins University Press, 1953), pp. 29–31; and Arnold M. Rose, "Social Psychological Effects of Physical Deprivation," *Journal of Health and Human Behavior* 1:4 (winter 1960): 285–289.

22. Wilder, *Armageddon,* p. 115.

23. Caputo, *Rumor of War,* p. 237.

24. Charles R. Cawthon, *Other Clay: A Remembrance of the World War II Infantry* (Niwot: University of Colorado Press, 1990), pp. 118–121.

25. Henry Berry, *Make the Kaiser Dance: Living Memories of the Doughboy* (New York: Priam Books, 1978), p. 107.

26. References to the "forty and eights" are ubiquitous. See Carl Andrew Brannen, *Over There: A Marine in the Great War* (College Station: Texas A&M University Press, 1996), pp. 8–9; Albert M. Ettinger and A. Churchill Ettinger, *A Doughboy with the Fighting Sixty-ninth: A Remembrance of World War I* (Shippensburg, Pa.: White Mane Publishing, 1992), pp. 22–23; and Charles F. Minder, *This Man's War: The Day-by-Day Record of an American Private on the Western Front* (New York: Pevensey Press, 1931), p. 219.

27. Again, the references to forty and eights are numerous. See especially Paul Boesch, *Road to Huertgen: Forest in Hell* (Houston: Paul M. Boesch, 1985), pp. 96–103. The GI encountered the forty and eights in French North Africa as well as in metropolitan France. See Klaus H. Huebner, *Long Walk Through War: A Combat Doctor's Diary* (College Station: Texas A&M University Press, 1987), p. 15.

28. George Wilson, *If You Survive* (New York: Ivy Books, 1987), p. 257.

29. John W. Thomason Jr., *Fix Bayonets!* (New York: Blue Ribbon Books, 1926), p. 81. Even artillery pieces were moved by truck on occasion, carried in the truck bed. See Rogers, *Through My Sights,* pp. 128–130.

30. Lester Atwell, *Private* (New York: Popular Library, 1958), pp. 104–109.

31. Boesch, *Road to Huertgen,* p. 70. Or, as one World War I marine put it, "When they took you out of the line, you hiked. But when they wanted to send you up in hurry, it was camions" (Berry, *Make the Kaiser Dance,* pp. 77–78).

32. Joseph D. Lawrence, *Fighting Soldier: The A.E.F. in 1918,* ed. Robert H. Ferrell (Boulder: Colorado Associated University Press, 1985), pp. 74–80. See also William L. Langer, *Gas and Flame in World War I* (New York: Knopf, 1965), pp. 26–27, and Hervey Allen, *Toward the Flame: A War Diary* (New York: Grosset and Dunlap, 1934), chapter 12, "Another Night March," pp. 180–190.

33. Merrick, *A Diary,* p. 89. See pp. 86–91 for his full description of the march. For a similar account, see MacArthur, *War Bugs,* pp. 110–111, 213–214, and 225–232.

34. Ernie Pyle, *Here Is Your War: The Story of G.I. Joe* (Cleveland and New York: World Publishing, 1945), p. 247.

35. Downs, *The Killing Zone*, p. 22.

36. Virtually every Vietnam infantryman's memoir or novel describes the miserable conditions and constant threat under which the grunt humped the boonies. See especially Richard E. Ogden, *Green Knight, Red Mourning* (New York: Zebra Books, 1985), pp. 140–165. See also Ebert, *A Life in a Year,* chapter 8: "Humping the Bush," pp. 151–181.

37. The issue of the soldier's load is the major theme of one of Marshall's books. See Samuel L. A. Marshall, *The Soldier's Load and the Mobility of a Nation* (Quantico, Va.: Marine Corps Association, 1980). He also raised the issue in his study of combat in Korea, *Commentary on Infantry,* chapter 5, "Exhaustible Infantry and 'Inexhaustible' Stores," pp. 42–50.

38. Many soldiers complained about the excessive weight they had to carry, but relatively few itemized their load or estimated the weight. Enough soldiers have done so, however, to give credence to Marshall's claim that soldiers have been consistently overloaded: Private Bailey (World War I Chauchat gunner) carried seventy-two pounds, according to Laurence Stallings, in *The Doughboys: The Story of the AEF, 1917–1918* (New York, Evanston, and London: Harper and Row, 1963), p. 85; Albert M. Ettinger (World War I pioneer), carried a fifty-five pound pack plus eight-pound rifle, bayonet, and 150 rounds of ammunition (see *Fighting Sixty-ninth,* p. 35); William L. Langer (World War I mortarman), carried 105 pounds (see *Gas and Flame,* p. 31); William Manchester (World War II marine rifleman), carried 84.3 pounds during an amphibious landing (see *Goodbye, Darkness: A Memoir of the Pacific War* [Boston and Toronto: Little, Brown, 1979], p. 162). Charles R. Cawthon provides an excellent discussion of the "disastrously overweight" GI on D-Day in Normandy in World War II, without making a specific weight estimate, in *Other Clay,* pp. 42–43; Gerald P. Averill (Marine rifle platoon leader) makes the same point as Cawthon, and itemizes his load, without venturing to make an overall weight estimate, for the World War II landing on Iwo Jima, in *Mustang: A Combat Marine* (Novato, Calif.: Presidio Press, 1987), p. 110; Arnold Winter (Korean War marine BAR man), carried eighty pounds (see Rudy Tomedi, *No Bugles, No Drums: An Oral History of the Korean War* [New York: John Wiley, 1993], p. 24); Martin Russ (Korean War Marine BAR man), carried 110 pounds (see *The Last Parallel: A Marine's War Journal* [New York and Toronto: Rinehart, 1957], p. 18); Robert Sanders (Vietnam War machine gunner), hauled seventy-five to eighty pounds, plus weapon and ammunition (see Stanley Goff and Robert Sanders, with Clark Smith, *Brothers: Black Soldiers in the Nam* [Novato, Calif.: Presidio Press, 1982], p. 53); and Phil Yaeger (Vietnam War marine infantryman), carried seventy to eighty pounds (see Ebert, *A Life in a Year),* p. 171.

39. Lawrence, *Fighting Soldier,* p. 8.

40. Sefton, *It Was My War,* p. 75. See pp. 48–49 for an itemized rundown of all the gear Sefton and his fellow paratroopers carried, although Sefton does not hazard a guess as to the total weight. For other examples of the GI's propensity for ditching his gas mask, see Henry Berry, *Semper Fi, Mac: Living Memories of the U.S. Marines in World War II* (New York: Berkley Books, 1983), p. 96, and Kurt Gabel, *The Making of a Paratrooper: Airborne Training and Combat in World War II* (Lawrence: University Press of Kansas, 1990), p. 195.

41. World War I memoirs frequently refer to a "combat" or "small" pack, as opposed to a "full" pack, when going into combat. See Thomason, *Fix Bayonets!* p. 36, and Minder, *This Man's War,* pp. 230 and 315–316. Harold P. Leinbaugh and John D. Campbell

provide a rundown of the World War II infantryman's combat load and estimate it at "more than thirty pounds," with mortarmen and machine gunners carrying more, in *The Men of Company K* (New York: Bantam Books, 1987), pp. 5–6. Samuel L. A. Marshall estimated the "fighting load" of the Korean War soldier at forty pounds, with radiomen and crew-served weapons crewmen carrying more, in *Commentary on Infantry,* pp. 42–44. Curtis James Morrow mentions carrying about forty-five pounds plus clothing when sent patrolling during the Korean War. See *What's a Commie Ever Done to Black People? A Korean War Memoir of Fighting in the U.S. Army's Last All Negro Unit* (Jefferson, N.C., and London: McFarland, 1997), pp. 13–14. The Vietnam grunt, when not on an extended operation and given helicopter resupply, could likewise pare down his load to about forty pounds. See Al Santoli, *Everything We Had: An Oral History of the Vietnam War by Thirty-three American Soldiers Who Fought It* (New York: Ballantine Books, 1982), p. 37.

42. Marshall, *Soldier's Load,* p. 22.

43. Balsa quoted in Eric Bergerud, *Touched with Fire: The Land War in the South Pacific* (New York: Viking Penguin, 1996), p. 283. For a discussion of soldiers voluntarily overloading themselves during Operation URGENT FURY, see James M. Dubik and Terrence D. Fullerton, "Soldier Overloading in Grenada," *Military Review* 67:1 (January 1987): 38–47.

44. Leon C. Standifer, *Not in Vain: A Rifleman Remembers World War II* (Baton Rouge and London: Louisiana State University Press, 1992), p. 119.

45. Ogden, *Green Knight,* p. 21.

46. Arthur W. Little, *From Harlem to the Rhine: The Story of New York's Colored Volunteers* (New York: Covici-Friede, 1936), p. 99.

47. Lawrence, *Fighting Soldier,* p. 129.

48. Leckie, *Helmet,* p. 82.

49. Franklin interview in Berry, *Semper Fi,* p. 358. Army soldiers were just as likely as marines to find themselves stevedoring. See, for example, Gerald Astor, *Crisis in the Pacific: The Battles for the Philippine Islands by the Men Who Fought Them* (New York: Donald I. Fine Books, 1996), p. 320.

50. Matthias, *Reflections,* p. 152. See also Russ, *Last Parallel,* pp. 106–108. Much of this spadework was done by the Korean Service Corps or hired Korean labor, but the soldiers were put to work as well.

51. Bob Hoffman, *I Remember the Last War* (York, Pa.: Strength and Health Publishing, 1940), p. 164.

52. Ibid., p. 161. See also Mackin, *We Didn't Want to Die,* pp. 43–44, and Thomas Boyd, *Through the Wheat* (Carbondale and Edwardsville: Southern Illinois University Press, 1978), pp. 149–153.

53. Kennington quoted in Bergerud, *Touched with Fire,* p. 468. The novelist James Jones, who also served with the Twenty-fifth Infantry Division on Guadalcanal, describes a similar burial detail in his *WW II: A Chronicle of Soldiering* (New York: Ballantine Books, 1976), p. 116. For another example of combat soldiers having to help recover the bodies of their own comrades, in this case bodies that were frozen solid in the dead of winter during the Battle of the Bulge in World War II, see Gabel, *Paratrooper,* pp. 205–210.

54. Russ, *Last Parallel,* pp. 198–201.

55. Matthew Brennan, *Brennan's War: Vietnam 1965–1969* (New York: Pocket Books, 1986), p. 247.

56. For an excellent description of the jungle terrain of the South Pacific, see Bergerud, *Touched with Fire,* pp. 55–89.

57. Salafia quoted in ibid., pp. 70–71.

58. Stiles interview in Berry, *Semper Fi,* p. 84.

59. E. J. Kahn Jr., *G.I. Jungle: An American Soldier in Australia and New Guinea* (New York: Simon and Schuster, 1943), pp. 108–111 and 121.

60. Caputo, *Rumor of War,* p. 57. For an excellent depiction of heavily laden grunts humping the boonies in such heat, see John M. Del Vecchio, *The 13th Valley* (New York: Bantam Books, 1983), pp. 311–317.

61. Strong interview in Wallace Terry, *Bloods: An Oral History of the Vietnam War by Black Veterans* (New York: Ballantine Books, 1985), p. 55. Vehicular movement became almost impossible except on all-weather roads, and even movement on foot was difficult. Marine corporal Ehrhart got stuck up to his knees in mud and had to be pulled out (*Vietnam-Perkasie,* p. 222).

62. Richard D. Camp, with Eric Hammel, *Lima-6: A Marine Company Commander in Vietnam* (New York: Pocket Books, 1989), p. 210. See also Ehrhart, *Vietnam-Perkasie,* p. 198, and Caputo, *Rumor of War,* pp. 224–225.

63. Harold L. Bond, *Return to Cassino* (New York: Pocket Books, 1965), p. 145. See also pp. 98–104.

64. Huebner, *Long Walk,* p. 126.

65. Boesch, *Road to Huertgen,* pp. 154 and 156.

66. Leinbaugh and Campbell, *Company K,* p. 177. See also Roscoe C. Blunt Jr., *Inside the Battle of the Bulge: A Private Comes of Age* (Westport, Conn., and London: Praeger, 1994), pp. 64–66, and Sefton, *It Was My War,* p. 164.

67. For examples of these conditions, see Henry Berry, *Hey, Mac, Where Ya Been? Living Memories of the U.S. Marines in the Korean War* (New York: St. Martin's Press, 1988), pp. 101 and 128; Henry Knox, *The Korean War: Pusan to Chosin: An Oral History* (San Diego, New York, and London: Harcourt Brace Jovanovich, 1985), pp. 458, 473–474, 512, and 574–575; Charles M. Bussey, *Firefight at Yechon: Courage and Racism in the Korean War* (Washington, D.C., and London: Brassey's, 1991), pp. 244 and 251; and Tomedi, *No Bugles,* pp. 67–68.

68. Emer interview in Knox, *Uncertain Victory,* p. 82.

69. Lyle Rishell, *With a Black Platoon in Combat: A Year in Korea* (College Station: Texas A&M University Press, 1993), p. 77. See also Spiroff, *Frozen Hell,* p. 77, and Rudolph W. Stephens, *Old Ugly Hill: A G.I.'s Fourteen Months in the Korean Trenches, 1952–1953* (Jefferson, N.C., and London: McFarland, 1995), p. 95.

70. Korgie interview in Knox, *Pusan to Chosin,* p. 70. See also pp. 44–45, 102, and 107–110. See also A. Andy Andow, *Letters to Big Jim Regarding Narrul Purigo, Cashinum Iman* (New York: Vantage Press, 1994), p. 54.

71. For comments on mosquitoes and rice-paddy stench, see Tomedi, *No Bugles,* p. 41; Bussey, *Firefight,* p. 137; and Knox, *Uncertain Victory,* p. 196.

72. In his book on the Korean War, Mauldin assumed the guise of "Joe," his famous World War II cartoon figure, who is now a journalist. Joe relates his experiences in Korea to his equally famous cartoon sidekick "Willie," who is now a civilian back in the States (William H. Mauldin, *Bill Mauldin in Korea* [New York: W. W. Norton, 1952], p. 23).

73. For accounts of the doughboy's trench-warfare experiences, see Lawrence, *Fight-*

*ing Soldier,* pp. 13–48; Francis P. Duffy, *Father Duffy's Story: A Tale of Humor and Heroism, of Life and Death with the Fighting Sixty-ninth* (Garden City, N.Y.: Garden City Publishing, 1919), pp. 60–118; Rogers, *Through My Sights,* pp. 132–142; and MacArthur, *War Bugs,* pp. 33–74. Accounts from the positional-warfare period of the Korean War, incidentally, sound remarkably similar, portraying life as relatively comfortable compared to the earlier war of movement. See the memoirs from the static-war period: Russ, *Last Parallel;* Stephens, *Old Ugly Hill;* and John A. Sullivan, *Toy Soldiers: Memoir of a Combat Platoon Leader in Korea* (Jefferson, N.C., and London: McFarland, 1991).

74. Hoffman, *I Remember,* p. 195.

75. Mackin, *We Didn't Want to Die,* p. 241.

76. Harry Brown, *A Walk in the Sun* (New York: Knopf, 1944), p. 147. For an example of an entire company falling asleep at night because of heat-related exhaustion, despite the known enemy threat in the area, see Camp, *Lima-6,* pp. 81–83.

77. Pratt interview in Tomedi, *No Bugles,* p. 68.

78. Minder, *This Man's War,* pp. 126–127; he never got used to the lice either but complained about them throughout his diary (pp. 174, 191, 221, 282, 312, and 342).

79. Rogers, *Through My Sights,* p. 217.

80. Huebner, *Long Walk,* p. 82.

81. Peter Bowman, *Beach Red* (New York: Random House, 1945), pp. 55–56, quotation on p. 56.

82. Caputo, *Rumor of War,* p. 54.

83. Reiland interviewed in Ebert, *A Life in a Year,* p. 169. See also Goff and Sanders, *Brothers,* pp. 127–129, and Lanning, *Only War,* pp. 120–121.

84. See the discussion and statistics in John Ellis, *The Sharp End: The Fighting Man in World War II* (New York: Charles Scribner's Sons, 1980), pp. 177–186.

85. Many of the soldier-authors in this study contracted malaria, and a few ended up in the hospital as a consequence. See Gwendolyn Medlo Hall, ed., *Love, War, and the 96th Engineers (Colored): The World War II New Guinea Diaries of Captain Hyman Samuelson* (Urbana and Chicago: University of Illinois Press, 1995), pp. 192–193 and 231; Leckie, *Helmet,* pp. 230–231; Alice M. Hoffman and Howard S. Hoffman, *Archives of Memory: A Soldier Recalls World War II* (Lexington: University Press of Kentucky, 1990), p. 72; and Audie Murphy, *To Hell and Back* (New York: Bantam Books, 1983), pp. 11–12.

86. Several of the soldier-authors suffered serious bouts of hepatitis, or "yellow jaundice." See Sledge, *Old Breed,* p. 176; John L. Munschauer, *World War II Cavalcade: An Offer I Couldn't Refuse* (Manhattan, Kans.: Sunflower University Press, 1996), p. 143; and Leslie W. Bailey, *Through Hell and High Water: The Wartime Memories of a Junior Combat Infantry Officer* (New York: Vantage Press, 1994), pp. 155–156. For cases of hemorrhagic fever, see Charles S. Crawford, *The Four Deuces: A Korean War Story* (Novato, Calif.: Presidio Press, 1989), pp. 263–268, and Russ, *Last Parallel,* p. 275. To cite all the cases of dysentery or severe diarrhea would be to list most of the memoirs used in this study. For a few of the more serious cases, in which dehydration, weight loss, and weakness forced a soldier-author into the hospital, see Merrick, *A Diary,* pp. 63–64; Bond, *Cassino,* pp. 139–145; and Berry, *Hey, Mac,* pp. 91–92.

87. Camp, *Lima-6,* pp. 72–73. For other examples of the embarrassment and discomfort of trying to soldier when afflicted with diarrhea or dysentery, see Heubner, *Long Walk,* p. 136, and Sefton, *It Was My War,* pp. 143–144.

88. For examples of soldiers shot at while relieving themselves, see Janice Holt Giles, ed., *The G.I. Journal of Sergeant Giles* (Boston: Houghton Mifflin, and Cambridge: Riverside Press, 1965), pp. 245–246; Charles B. MacDonald, *Company Commander* (Toronto, New York, and London: Bantam Books, 1978), p. 53; and Bergerud, *Touched with Fire*, p. 380.

89. See Leinbaugh and Campbell, *Company K*, p. 110; Stephens, *Old Ugly Hill*, p. 142; and Mary Penick Motley, *The Invisible Soldier: The Experience of the Black Soldier, World War II* (Detroit: Wayne State University Press, 1975), p. 164.

90. Gabel, *Paratrooper*, pp. 236–237. See also Nat Frankel and Larry Smith, *Patton's Best: An Informal History of the 4th Armored Division* (New York: Jove Book, 1984), p. 208.

91. Ettinger and Ettinger, *Fighting Sixty-ninth*, p. 28.

92. Leinbaugh and Campbell, *Company K*, p. 272.

93. Lawrence, *Fighting Soldier*, p. 77.

94. Boesch, *Road to Huertgen*, p. 152. Boesch provides another excellent example of the hot-chow theory gone wrong when his battalion commander insisted that they eat a hot turkey dinner on Thanksgiving Day, despite being in a precarious tactical situation. The outcome was three killed and seven wounded when the ration party drew enemy artillery fire (pp. 170–173).

95. For a discussion of World War I combat rations, see Allen, *Toward the Flame*, p. 188; Minder, *This Man's War*, pp. 119–120; Rogers, *Through My Sights*, pp. 24, 160, and 181; and Thomason, *Fix Bayonets!* pp. 198–200.

96. MacDonald, *Company Commander*, p. 29. Other memoirs from the European theater indicate that while C-rations and 10-in-1 rations were also issued on occasion, the K-ration was the most common. See Cawthon, *Other Clay*, pp. 69–70; Wilson, *If You Survive*, pp. 207–208; Richard M. Hardison, *Caissons Across Europe: An Artillery Captain's Personal War* (Austin, Tex.: Eakin Press, 1990), p. 162; and Leinbaugh and Campbell, *Company K*, pp. 107–108. See also Ellis, *Sharp End*, pp. 246–250, for a discussion of World War II combat rations.

97. W. Stanford Smith, with contributions by Leo J. Machan and Stanley E. Earman, *The Cannoneers: GI Life in a World War II Cannon Company* (Manhattan, Kans.: Sunflower University Press, 1993), p. 36.

98. See James Hamilton Dill, *Sixteen Days at Mungol-li* (Fayetteville, Ark.: M&M Press, 1993), pp. 264–266; Tomedi, *No Bugles*, p. 126; Del Vecchio, *13th Valley*, pp. 218–219; Santoli, *Everything We Had*, p. 27; and Ebert, *A Life in a Year*, pp. 116 and 155.

99. MacArthur, *War Bugs*, p. 173. See also Allen, *Toward the Flame*, pp. 128–129.

100. Rogers, *Through My Sights*, p. 227. For a description of the ruined village of Limey, see Langer, *Gas and Flame*, pp. 27–28. For an especially vivid description of a World War I battlefield after the fighting was over, see Ernest Hemingway's short story, "A Way You'll Never Be," in *The Short Stories of Ernest Hemingway: The First Forty-nine Stories and the Play "The Fifth Column"* (New York: Modern Library, 1942), pp. 500–501.

101. Sledge, *Old Breed*, pp. 257–258. See Manchester, *Goodbye, Darkness*, pp. 359–361, for a similar assessment of the fighting on Okinawa.

102. Ogden, *Green Knight*, pp. 272–273.

103. Frankel, *Patton's Best*, p. 74. Students of soldier behavior have noticed the

demoralizing effect that violent and near-total destruction of the human body by modern firepower has on the survivors. The soldier might envision his own death, but not his own obliteration. See Stanley Cooperman, *World War I and the American Novel* (Baltimore: Johns Hopkins University Press, 1967), pp. 72–75; Ellis, *Sharp End,* pp. 107–111; and Lord Charles McM. Moran, *The Anatomy of Courage* (Garden City Park, N.Y.: Avery Publishing, 1987), pp. 62–63.

104. Camp, *Lima-6,* p. 158. Paul Fussell was likewise sprayed with blood and tissue when the man in front of him was hit by a burst of machine-gun fire. See "My War: How I Got Irony in the Infantry," *Harper's,* 264:1580 (January 1982): 45, and *Wartime: Understanding and Behavior in World War II* (New York and Oxford: Oxford University Press, 1989), pp. 270–272.

105. Manchester, *Goodbye, Darkness,* pp. 46 and 384. George Wilson was sprayed by gore, but not injured, when one of his men was hit in the back by a mortar round (*If You Survive,* p. 46).

106. Boyd, *Through the Wheat,* pp. 22–23. See also Allen, *Toward the Flame,* pp. 80 and 123.

107. Sledge, *Old Breed,* pp. 134–135. See also Brown, *A Walk,* pp. 24–25, and Mac-Donald, *Company Commander,* pp. 36 and 84.

108. Owen, *Colder Than Hell,* pp. 211 and 149. See also Brady, *Coldest War,* pp. 131 and 153; Knox, *Uncertain Victory,* p. 405; and Russ, *Last Parallel,* p. 201.

109. Goff and Sanders, *Brothers,* p. 80. For the armored crewman's version of being dirty, in which grease and constant dust figure prominently, see Heinemann, *Close Quarters,* pp. 5–6 and 103–104.

110. Hurry interview in Bergerud, *Touched with Fire,* p. 63. See also Sledge, *Old Breed,* pp. 94–95.

111. Marshall, *Soldier's Load,* p. 48. See also Ernie Pyle, *Brave Men* (New York: Henry Holt, 1944), p. 84.

112. Michael Herr, *Dispatches* (New York: Avon Books, 1978), p. 54.

113. Only a few students of soldier behavior have commented on this phenomenon. See Kellett, *Combat Motivation,* pp. 243–244. For a brief mention of the "hostile" Southeast Asian jungle, see William Barry Gault, "Some Remarks on Slaughter," *American Journal of Psychiatry* 128:4 (October 1971): 84.

114. Leckie, *Helmet,* p. 58.

115. Ibid., p. 220. See also Hersey, *Into the Valley,* pp. 43–45, and especially Manchester, *Goodbye, Darkness,* pp. 93–98 and 159–161.

116. Gustav Hasford, *The Short-timers* (New York: Bantam Books, 1979), pp. 149–150.

117. Caputo, *Rumor of War,* p. 105. See also pp. 79–80. Michael Herr agrees, at least regarding the Central Highlands. See his *Dispatches,* pp. 93–96. While it is jungle terrain that most often appears in memoirs as hostile, other theaters of war could also prove to be inhospitable, if not evil. The historian Michael D. Doubler has noted that fighting in the gloomy Huertgen Forest in Germany in World War II was extremely demoralizing: "Excessive fatigue made troops sluggish and careless, and combat exhaustion became commonplace as the dark, deadly forest blanketed soldiers with a sense of gloom and desperation" (*Closing with the Enemy: How GI's Fought the War in Europe, 1944–1945* [Lawrence: University Press of Kansas, 1994], p. 189). Comments from veterans of the

Huertgen fighting attest to the forbidding gloom. See Boesch, *Road to Huertgen: Forest in Hell* (the subtitle is itself a comment), p. 150, and his description of the fighting on pp. 151–184; and Wilson, *If You Survive,* who also describes the bloody, miserable fighting in chapter 11, "Slaughter in the Huertgen Forest," pp. 131–185.

118. Fish interview in Berry, *Make the Kaiser Dance,* p. 423. For another World War I example, see Minder, *This Man's War,* pp. 246–247.

119. Crary quoted in Bergerud, *Touched with Fire,* p. 445. See also Henry Dearchs, quoted on p. 220. For another World War II example, see Giles, ed., *G.I. Journal,* p. 219. For Korean War examples, see Rishell, *Black Platoon,* p. 36; Berry, *Hey, Mac,* p. 210; Knox, *Pusan to Chosin,* p. 129; and Owen, *Colder Than Hell,* p. 176.

120. James Martin Davis, "Vietnam: What It Was Really Like," *Military Review* 69:1 (January 1989): 36. See also Alfred S. Bradford, *Some Even Volunteered: The First Wolfhounds Pacify Vietnam* (Westport, Conn., and London: Praeger, 1994), p. 109; Ehrhart, *Vietnam-Perkasie,* p. 68; Goff and Sanders, *Brothers,* pp. 84, 130, and 144; Herr, *Dispatches,* pp. 14 and 41; and John Ketwig, *And a Hard Rain Fell* (New York: Pocket Books, 1986), p. 42.

121. The Stouffer Study discusses "combat variables" that affected the World War II soldier's level of stress and exhaustion. The level of danger or uncertainty made some operations more stressful than others. See Stouffer et al., *Combat and Its Aftermath,* pp. 65–67. See Kellett, *Combat Motivation,* p. 250, and Ellis, *Sharp End,* pp. 46–50, for the soldiers' hatred of patrols.

122. Matthias, *Reflections,* pp. 96–97. For discussions of patrolling, see also Wilson, *If You Survive,* pp. 103–105, and Leinbaugh and Campbell, *Company K,* pp. 173–174.

123. Russ, *Last Parallel,* p. 233. See also pp. 237–241.

124. Tim O'Brien, *If I Die in a Combat Zone: Box Me Up and Ship Me Home* (New York: Laurel, Dell, 1987), p. 91. See chapter 9, "Ambush," for a description of a night ambush patrol, pp. 88–99.

125. Boyd, *Through the Wheat,* p. 100. See also Mackin, *We Didn't Want to Die,* pp. 49 and 62.

126. Leckie, *Helmet,* pp. 65 and 66.

127. Matthias, *Reflections,* p. 109. See also Brennan, *Brennan's War,* pp. 34–35.

128. Moran, *Anatomy,* p. 38. See also Holmes, *Acts of War,* pp. 229–231. A survey of American volunteers who fought in the Spanish Civil War revealed that 71 percent experienced fear just before going into combat but that only 15 percent were afraid during combat. Of those exhibiting fear in combat, inability to take action against the enemy (as during a shelling) was a key factor. See John Dollard, with the assistance of Donald Horton, *Fear in Battle* (New York: AMS Press, 1976), pp. 8–9.

129. Owen, *Colder Than Hell,* p. 69. See also Boesch, *Road to Huertgen,* pp. 21 and 27. Boesch found that he could overcome his "foxhole complex" by taking action appropriate for a leader, such as taking charge of a patrol.

130. Brooks interview in Tomedi, *No Bugles,* p. 215. See also the Richter interview in Knox, *Pusan to Chosin,* p. 490; Berry, *Hey, Mac,* p. 211; and Stephens, *Old Ugly Hill,* p. 69.

131. Sociologists, psychiatrists, and historians have noted this phenomenon. See Dinter, *Hero or Coward,* pp. 37–39; John Ellis, *Eye-Deep in Hell: Trench Warfare in World War I* (Baltimore: Johns Hopkins University Press, 1989), pp. 64–65; Ellis, *Sharp*

*End,* pp. 60–65; Roy R. Grinker and John P. Spiegel, *War Neuroses* (Philadelphia and London: Blakiston, 1945), pp. 69–70; Robert H. Scales Jr., "Firepower: The Psychological Dimension," *Army* 39:7 (July 1989): 43–50; and Stouffer et al., *Combat and Its Aftermath,* pp. 82–83.

132. Hoffman, *I Remember,* p. 172. See also Boyd, *Through the Wheat,* pp. 139–140; Lawrence, *Fighting Soldier,* p. 81; Thomason, *Fix Bayonets!* pp. 164–167; and MacArthur, *War Bugs,* pp. 187–189.

133. Barrette quoted in Ralph G. Martin, *G.I. War, 1941–1945* (Boston and Toronto: Little, Brown, 1967), p. 191.

134. Sledge, *Old Breed,* p. 65.

135. Camp, *Lima-6,* pp. 295–296. See also pp. 281–292.

136. Langer, *Gas and Flame,* p. 24.

137. Duffy, *Story,* p. 288.

138. For such remarks, see Minder, *This Man's War,* p. 212; Hoffman, *I Remember,* pp. 304–305; and Allen, *Toward the Flame,* p. 273. For examples of being strafed, see Merrick, *A Diary,* pp. 55 and 81; Thomason, *Fix Bayonets!* pp. 121–122; Rogers, *Through My Sights,* pp. 160 and 187; Hoffman, *I Remember,* pp. 155 and 180; and Ettinger and Ettinger, *Fighting Sixty-ninth,* p. 99.

139. Franklyn A. Johnson, *One More Hill* (New York: Bantam Books, 1983), p. 57. See also pp. 33, 54, 56, and 66. For other examples of air attack during the fighting in North Africa, see Bailey, *Hell and High Water,* p. 78; Ralph Ingersoll, *The Battle Is the Pay-off* (New York: Harcourt, Brace, 1943), pp. 168–169, 174–176, and 179–180; Martin, *G.I. War,* p. 44; and Pyle, *Your War,* pp. 131–133 and 155–156.

140. Averill, *Mustang,* p. 62. See also Captain John L'Estrange interview in Berry, *Semper Fi,* pp. 180–181.

141. Freeman interview in Berry, *Semper Fi,* p. 165. For other examples of Japanese air attacks, see Kahn, *G.I. Jungle,* pp. 99 and 125–133; Hall, ed., *Love, War,* pp. 53, 78, 143–144, and 207–208; and Carl M. Becker and Robert G. Thobaben, *Common Warfare: Parallel Memoirs by Two World War II GIs in the Pacific* (Jefferson, N.C., and London: McFarland, 1992), pp. 138–139, and 143–148.

142. See Stanley Cooperman, "John Dos Passos' *Three Soldiers*: Aesthetics and the Doom of Individualism" in *The First World War in Fiction: A Collection of Critical Essays,* ed. Holger Klein (London: Macmillan, 1976), pp. 23–31.

143. John Dos Passos, *First Encounter* (New York: Philosophical Library, 1945), p. 59.

144. John Dos Passos, *Three Soldiers,* Sentry ed. (Boston: Houghton Mifflin, 1921), p. 63. See also the case of Private John Andrews, p. 228.

145. Mackin, *We Didn't Want to Die,* p. 179. See also Wilder, *Armageddon,* pp. 141 and 146.

146. Jesse Glenn Gray, *The Warriors: Reflections on Men in Battle* (New York: Harper Colophon Books, 1970), p. 99.

147. Fussell, *Wartime,* p. 70. See also Ellis, *Sharp End,* pp. 288–290. The Stouffer Study found that a "fundamental source of strain was the sheer impersonality of combat" (*Combat and Its Aftermath,* p. 84). Students of World War II literature note the pervasiveness of this theme. See Eric Homberger, in Holger Klein, with John Flower and Eric Homberger, eds., *The Second World War in Fiction* (London: Macmillan, 1984), chapter 5: "United States," pp. 192–200.

148. Richard Tregaskis, *Guadalcanal Diary* (New York: Random House, 1943), p. 62.

149. Sledge, *Old Breed,* p. 103. For other examples, some eloquent, and a few equaling the bitterness of Dos Passos, see Bowman, *Beach Red,* pp. 107–108; Leckie, *Helmet,* pp. 86–87; Hall, ed., *Love, War,* p. 15; and Atwell, *Private,* p. 383.

150. Atwell, *Private,* p. 470. Doughboys, though not stuck with the GI label, also found army anonymity demeaning: "The soldier hangs to his name as his last hold on individuality. He likes to be called by his name rather than private" (Will Judy, *Soldier's Diary: A Day-to-Day Record in the World War* [Chicago: Judy Publishing, 1931], p. 19).

151. Matthias, *Reflections,* pp. 27–28.

152. See Christian G. Appy, *Working-Class War: American Combat Soldiers and Vietnam* (Chapel Hill and London: University of North Carolina Press, 1993), pp. 182–190; Ebert, *A Life in a Year,* pp. 209–210; and John Helmer, *Bringing the War Home: The American Soldier in Vietnam and After* (New York: Free Press, 1974), pp. 22–29.

153. Morrow, *Commie,* pp. 9–10. This example was chosen because of its similarity to comments made by the Vietnam grunts about bait. Tales of movement to contact by patrols or larger units are common in the memoirs from all the wars of the draft era. The American soldier was more often than not advancing against a stationary, dug-in, camouflaged enemy who got off the first shots.

154. Helmer, *Bringing the War,* p. 27.

155. For an excellent assessment of the U.S. Army's emphasis on firepower and combined-arms tactics in lieu of expending lives in World War II, see Doubler, *Closing,* especially chapter 10, "The Schoolhouse of War," pp. 265–299.

156. Goff and Sanders, *Brothers,* p. 32.

157. James Webb, *Fields of Fire* (New York: Bantam Books, 1979), p. 155. See also Brennan, *Brennan's War,* chapter 4: "Bait," specifically pp. 53–54.

158. Lee Kennett, *G.I.: The American Soldier in World War II* (New York: Charles Scribner's Sons, 1987), p. 83.

159. The Stouffer Study found enlisted soldiers' resentment of the army's caste system, and the benefits it bestowed on officers, to be pervasive among troops stationed Stateside and overseas. Only when in combat, where junior officers went without perquisites and shared the danger and hardships with their men, did soldiers' resentment largely disappear. See Samuel A. Stouffer, Edward A. Suchman, Leland C. DeVinney, Shirley A. Star, and Robin M. Williams Jr., *Studies in Social Psychology in World War II,* vol. 1, *The American Soldier: Adjustment During Army Life* (Princeton: Princeton University Press, 1949), pp. 71–75, 178–182, 379–382, and 363–381. See also Howard Brotz and Everett Wilson, "Characteristics of Military Society," *American Journal of Sociology* 51:5 (March 1946): 373; G. Dearborn Spindler, "American Character as Revealed by the Military," *Psychiatry: Journal for the Operational Statement of Interpersonal Relations* 11:3 (August 1948): 275–281; and Arthur J. Vidich and Maurice R. Stein, "The Dissolved Identity in Military Life," in *Identity and Anxiety: Survival of the Person in Mass Society,* ed. Maurice R. Stein, Arthur J. Vidich, and David Manning White (Glencoe, Ill.: Free Press, 1960), pp. 494–496 and 502–505.

160. Munschauer, *Cavalcade,* p. 72. See also Smith, *Cannoneers,* pp. 19–22.

161. Rogers, *Through My Sights,* p. 21. See also Becker and Thobaben, *Common Warfare,* p. 133.

162. Hawkins interview in Berry, *Semper Fi,* p. 35.

163. As in the case of the Doolittle Board, convened in 1946 to examine deteriorating officer–enlisted relations during World War II, concern over poor officer–enlisted relations in the American Expeditionary Forces in World War I also prompted an investigation. The resulting Fosdick Report clearly indicated that the doughboys' resentment of institutional inequality was a major part of the problem. Portions of this report are published in Stouffer et al., *Adjustment During Army Life,* pp. 381–382.

164. Judy, *Soldier's Diary,* p. 206. See also Minder, *This Man's War,* p. 313.

165. Mackin, *We Didn't Want to Die,* p. 243.

166. Becker and Thobaben, *Common Warfare,* p. 34.

167. Bill Mauldin, *Up Front* (New York: Award Books, 1976), p. 184. For an example of soldiers' resentment over officers acting "royally," see Atwell, *Private,* p. 127.

168. Mauldin, *Up Front,* pp. 185–186.

169. Leckie, *Helmet,* p. 218. See also the Doyle interview in Berry, *Semper Fi,* p. 286.

170. Fussell, *Wartime,* p. 80. See also Michael C. C. Adams, *The Best War Ever: America and World War II* (Baltimore and London: Johns Hopkins University Press, 1994), pp. 81–82, and Kennett, *G.I.,* pp. 81–83.

171. Fussell, *Wartime,* p. 82.

172. Camp, *Lima-6,* p. 74. See also Ralph Zumbro, *Tank Sergeant* (Novato, Calif.: Presidio Press, 1986), pp. 84–85.

173. Russ, *Last Parallel,* p. 109. See also p. 144.

174. Fox interviewed in Knox, *Pusan to Chosin,* p. 421. See also Corporal James Cardinal's letter, quoted in Knox, *Uncertain Victory,* pp. 148–149, and Sullivan, *Toy Soldiers,* pp. 98–99.

175. Standifer, *Not in Vain,* p. 86.

176. Hoffman, *I Remember,* p. 254.

177. Webb, *Fields of Fire,* p. 252. Attempting, unsuccessfully, to retain a measure of control over one's life in the midst of a war is a major theme in Jack Fuller's Vietnam War novel, *Fragments* (New York: Dell, 1985); follow, in particular, the case of Sergeant James Neumann. Examples of the randomness of death (or survival) in war abound. See Duffy, *Story,* p. 251; Bailey, *Hell and High Water,* pp. 167–168; Berry, *Hey, Mac,* p. 102; Knox, *Uncertain Victory,* p. 387; Spiroff, *Frozen Hell,* pp. 55–56; Bradford, *Volunteered,* pp. 82–83; and Fuller, *Fragments,* p. 65.

178. For training accidents, see Averill, *Mustang,* p. 103; Becker and Thobaben, *Common Warfare,* p. 14; Cawthon, *Other Clay,* pp. 26 and 31; Sefton, *It Was My War,* pp. 191–192; and Dominick Yezzo, *A G.I.'s Vietnam Diary, 1968–1969* (New York: Franklin Watts, 1974), August 27 entry (this book does not contain page numbers, but is organized chronologically by diary entry dates).

179. For traffic and vehicular accidents, see Ettinger and Ettinger, *Fighting Sixty-ninth,* p. 103; Hardison, *Caissons,* p. 69; Merrick, *A Diary,* p. 90; Berry, *Semper Fi,* pp. 99 and 217; Knox, *Pusan to Chosin,* p. 398; Spiroff, *Frozen Hell,* p. 29; and Robert Mason, *Chickenhawk* (New York: Penguin Books, 1986), p. 245.

180. Hardison, *Caissons,* p. 73.

181. For accidents involving weapons, explosives, and duds, see Brannen, *Over There,* p. 41; Huebner, *Long Walk,* p. 194; Jones, *WW II,* p. 41; Sledge, *Old Breed,* p. 99;

Standifer, *Not in Vain,* p. 136; Bradford, *Volunteered,* p. 38; Camp, *Lima-6,* p. 202; David Parks, *G.I. Diary* (New York, Evanston, and London: Harper and Row, 1968), p. 113; Hall, ed., *Love, War,* p. 145; Wilson, *If You Survive,* pp. 128–129 and 217; Hoffman and Hoffman, *Archives,* p. 128; and Russ, *Last Parallel,* p. 146.

182. For engineers' accidents, see Hall, ed., *Love, War,* pp. 80, 151, 247, 276, and 280; Bussey, *Firefight,* pp. 134 and 226; Astor, *Crisis,* p. 203; and Berry, *Semper Fi,* p. 391.

183. For artillery or heavy mortar–related accidents, see Rogers, *Through My Sights,* pp. 160–161; Merrick, *A Diary,* p. 76; Martin, *G.I. War,* p. 285; Hoffman and Hoffman, *Archives,* pp. 107–109 and 134–135; and Smith, *Cannoneers,* p. 52.

184. See the myriad helicopter accidents in Mason, *Chickenhawk,* pp. 127–128, 237–238, 259–260, 262–263, 290, 316, 345–346, 372, and 456–457; he does not exaggerate. Helicopter accidents were the biggest single cause of noncombat deaths in Vietnam (22 percent). See the statistics in Thomas C. Thayer, *War Without Fronts: The American Experience in Vietnam* (Boulder, Colo., and London: Westview Press, 1985), pp. 117–118.

185. For drowning accidents, see Minder, *This Man's War,* p. 193; MacArthur, *War Bugs,* p. 121; and Camp, *Lima-6,* p. 185.

186. For exploding stoves during the Korean War (generally caused by burning too volatile a fuel in them), see Matthias, *Reflections,* pp. 211–212, and Sullivan, *Toy Soldiers,* pp. 55 and 106–107.

187. Blunt, *Inside,* pp. 106–107.

188. Martin, *G.I. War,* p. 279. See also Bergerud, *Touched with Fire,* p. 102.

189. Sledge, *Old Breed,* p. 72.

190. Charles R. Shrader, *Amicicide: The Problem of Friendly Fire in Modern War,* U.S. Army Command and General Staff College Combat Studies Institute Research Study no. 1 (Washington, D.C.: U.S. Government Printing Office, December 1982), p. vii. Despite the 23 percent fratricide ratio in Operation DESERT STORM, Shrader continued to defend his 2-percent figure ("Friendly Fire: The Inevitable Price," *Parameters* 22:3 [Autumn 1992]: 29–44).

191. See Charles F. Hawkins, "Friendly Fire: Facts, Myths and Misperceptions," *U.S. Naval Institute Proceedings* 120:6 (June 1994): 54–59, and Kenneth K. Steinweg, "Dealing Realistically with Fratricide," *Parameters* 25:1 (spring 1995): 4–29. See also Bergerud, *Touched with Fire,* pp. 379–380.

192. Arnold M. Rose, "The Social Psychology of Desertion from Combat," *American Sociological Review* 16:5 (October 1951): 621.

193. I hesitate to mention the following statistic because I am not sure exactly what it tells us, but of the 129 memoirs, oral histories, and novels used as sources for this study, 80 of them mention at least one incident of fratricide or near-fratricide, and many report multiple instances. As with Rose's statistics, one can infer from the sheer frequency with which soldiers report being shot at by their own side that a 2 percent fratricide rate must be conservative.

194. Lawrence, *Fighting Soldier,* p. 111. For other examples of artillery or mortar fratricide, see Ettinger and Ettinger, *Fighting Sixty-ninth,* p. 166; Hoffman, *I Remember,* p. 221; Astor, *Crisis,* pp. 113, 246, and 437; Wilson, *If You Survive,* p. 21; Bailey, *Hell and High Water,* pp. 151–152; Berry, *Semper Fi,* pp. 245, 253–254, and 265; MacDonald, *Company Commander,* p. 99; Manchester, *Goodbye, Darkness,* p. 376; Sefton, *It Was My*

*War,* p. 98; Rishell, *Black Platoon,* pp. 89–91; Knox, *Pusan to Chosin,* pp. 183, 268, and 407; Knox, *Uncertain Victory,* pp. 113–114 and 316; Morrow, *Commie,* pp. 53 and 62; Caputo, *Rumor of War,* p. 184; Camp, *Lima-6,* p. 86; Lanning, *Only War,* p. 92; and Ogden, *Green Knight,* pp. 266–267.

195. Munschauer, *Cavalcade,* p. 139.

196. MacArthur, *War Bugs,* p. 148. For another example of angry soldiers returning fire on friendly aircraft, see Hoffman and Hoffman, *Archives,* p. 104. See also Astor, *Crisis,* p. 437, for a case where the soldiers did not actually shoot at a friendly aircraft that bombed them, but they did cheer when the plane came in too low and crashed. For examples of air-to-ground fratricide, see Bergerud, *Touched with Fire,* pp. 378–379; Wilson, *If You Survive,* p. 197; Boesch, *Road to Huertgen,* pp. 54–55 and 62; Motley, *Invisible Soldier,* p. 290; Murphy, *To Hell and Back,* p. 158; Pyle, *Brave Men,* pp. 430–439; Tomedi, *No Bugles,* pp. 26 and 125; Knox, *Pusan to Chosin,* pp. 113 and 552; and Knox, *Uncertain Victory,* p. 302. The Vietnam War saw the introduction of helicopter gunships and fratricide by same. See Brennan, *Brennan's War,* pp. 219–220; Caputo, *Rumor of War,* p. 207; Mason, *Chickenhawk,* p. 427; and Parks, *G.I. Diary,* p. 124.

197. For an account of this incident and some of the other better known cases of fratricide throughout history, see Geoffrey Regan, *Blue on Blue: A History of Friendly Fire* (New York: Avon Books, 1995); though largely a compilation of friendly-fire accounts from other sources, it is one of the few books specifically to address fratricide.

198. Johnson, *One More Hill,* p. 91.

199. Ross S. Carter, *Those Devils in Baggy Pants* (New York and Toronto: Signet Books, 1951), p. 23. For other examples of ground-to-air fratricide, see Astor, *Crisis,* p. 378; Becker and Thobaben, *Common Warfare,* pp. 59–60; and Johnson, *One More Hill,* p. 56.

200. For examples of fratricide caused by armored vehicles, see Wilson, *If You Survive,* p. 22; Berry, *Semper Fi,* pp. 252–253; MacDonald, *Company Commander,* p. 269; Knox, *Pusan to Chosin,* pp. 178–179; Caputo, *Rumor of War,* p. 208; O'Brien, *If I Die,* pp. 151–152; and Baker, *Nam,* p. 218.

201. For examples of fratricide, or near-fratricide, because of mistakes and fear during patrolling, see Little, *Harlem,* pp. 295–296; Berry, *Make the Kaiser Dance,* pp. 213–214; Wilson, *If You Survive,* p. 219; Crawford, *Four Deuces,* p. 98; Stephens, *Old Ugly Hill,* pp. 152–153; Sullivan, *Toy Soldiers,* pp. 46–48 and 53; Baker, *Nam,* pp. 207–208; Camp, *Lima-6,* p. 207; French, *Patches of Fire,* p. 167; and James R. McDonough, *Platoon Leader* (New York: Bantam Books, 1986), pp. 98–99.

202. For a good discussion and an example of the shortcomings of the challenging procedures, see Paul Fussell, *Doing Battle: The Making of a Skeptic* (New York: Little, Brown, 1996), p. 137, and Allen R. Matthews, *The Assault* (New York: Dodd, Mead, 1980), pp. 106–107.

203. Stephens, *Old Ugly Hill,* pp. 131–132.

204. Sledge, *Old Breed,* pp. 110–111.

205. La Magna interview in Astor, *Crisis,* pp. 190–191.

206. Frankel, *Patton's Best,* p. 71. For an example of a soldier who suffered just such "catastrophic guilt," see Ron Kovic, *Born on the Fourth of July* (New York: Pocket Books, 1977), pp. 194–195.

207. Wilder, *Armageddon,* p. 113. In a similar vein, Hervey Allen drew a measure of

tranquillity from gazing at the stars on a clear night in France. See *Toward the Flame,* p. 26.

208. Giles, ed., *G.I. Journal,* pp. 313–314. See also Bond, *Cassino,* p. 159, and Huebner, *Long Walk,* p. 59.

209. Dill, *Mungol-li,* p. 41. See also pp. 46–47. For other scarce comments on Korea's beauty, see Knox, *Pusan to Chosin,* p. 461, and Knox, *Uncertain Victory,* pp. 221–222.

210. Downs, *Killing Zone,* p. 33. See also Baker, *Nam,* p. 62, for a comment on the jungle's beauty, at least at a distance. Veterans of the Pacific fighting in World War II also occasionally comment on the jungle's beauty, but they almost always limit their admiration to a distant view. See Bergerud, *Touched with Fire,* pp. 87–88.

211. Merrick, *A Diary,* p. 39.

212. Pyle, *Your War,* p. 170.

213. Frankel, *Patton's Best,* p. 8.

214. Sledge, *Old Breed,* p. 302.

## CHAPTER 3. IMMERSION IN THE ENVIRONMENT

1. Lord Charles McM. Moran, *The Anatomy of Courage* (Garden City Park, N.Y.: Avery, 1987), p. 16.

2. Ernie Pyle, *Here Is Your War: The Story of G.I. Joe* (Cleveland and New York: World Publishing, 1945), p. 135.

3. Eugene B. Sledge, *With the Old Breed at Peleliu and Okinawa* (New York: Bantam Books, 1983), p. 123.

4. Richard E. Ogden, *Green Knight, Red Mourning* (New York: Zebra Books, 1985), pp. 274–275.

5. James R. Ebert, *A Life in a Year: The American Infantryman in Vietnam, 1965–1972* (Novato, Calif.: Presidio Press, 1993), p. 236. For an excellent analysis of the moral aspects of this regressive process, see Tobey C. Herzog, *Vietnam War Stories: Innocence Lost* (London and New York: Routledge, 1985), pp. 24–31.

6. Robert G. Merrick, *World War I: A Diary* (Baltimore: privately published, 1982), p. 28.

7. Paul Fussell, *Doing Battle: The Making of a Skeptic* (Boston: Little, Brown, 1996), p. 101.

8. Matthew Brennan, *Brennan's War: Vietnam, 1965–1969* (New York: Pocket Books, 1986), p. 4.

9. Carl M. Becker and Robert G. Thobaben, *Common Warfare: Parallel Memoirs by Two World War II GIs in the Pacific* (Jefferson, N.C., and London: McFarland, 1992), p. 53.

10. Rudolph W. Stephens, *Old Ugly Hill: A G.I.'s Fourteen Months in the Korean Trenches, 1952–1953* (Jefferson, N.C., and London: McFarland, 1995), p. 33.

11. David Parks, *G.I. Diary* (New York, Evanston, and London: Harper and Row, 1968), p. 50.

12. The Stouffer Study found that "anticipatory anxieties about going overseas," especially among infantry replacements, generated "gangplank fever." See Samuel A.

Stouffer, Arthur A. Lumsdaine, Marion Harper Lumsdaine, Robin M. Williams Jr., M. Brewster Smith, Irving L. Janis, Shirley A. Star, and Leonard S. Cottrell Jr., *Studies in Social Psychology in World War II*, vol. 2, *The American Soldier: Combat and Its Aftermath* (Princeton: Princeton University Press, 1949), pp. 439–445.

13. Klaus H. Huebner, *Long Walk Through War: A Combat Doctor's Diary* (College Station: Texas A&M University Press, 1990), p. 5.

14. See the classic case of Private Ciferri in Lieutenant Franklyn A. Johnson's antitank platoon, who, in his effort to miss the Normandy landings in World War II, was caught trying to go AWOL, and then was grossly insubordinate to Johnson, hoping to get left behind in the guardhouse pending court-martial. Ciferri found himself, instead, on the way to Omaha Beach under armed guard by his fellow platoon members; see Johnson's *One More Hill* (New York: Bantam Books, 1983), pp. 134–135.

15. See Lee Kennett, *G.I.: The American Soldier in World War II* (New York: Charles Scribner's Sons, 1987), pp. 114–118, for a good overview of the joys of life on a troopship, to include the GIs' special disdain for the slow, uncomfortable Liberty Ships. If Howard S. Hoffman's twenty-eight-day passage to Italy on a Liberty Ship in World War II is typical, then the GIs' distaste for these otherwise famous, war-winning cargo ships is well founded. See Alice M. Hoffman and Howard S. Hoffman, *Archives of Memory: A Soldier Recalls World War II* (Lexington: The University Press of Kentucky, 1990), pp. 41–47.

16. Almost every soldier-author describes, some in sketchy terms and others in detail, their sea voyages to war. For World War I, see Will Judy, *A Soldier's Diary: A Day-to-Day Record in the World War* (Chicago: Judy Publishing, 1931), pp. 77–84; Charles F. Minder, *This Man's War: The Day-by-Day Record of an American Private on the Western Front* (New York: Pevensey Press, 1931), pp. 5–22; and [Howard V. O'Brien], *Wine, Women, and War: A Diary of Disillusionment* (New York: J. H. Sears, 1926), pp. 7–12. For World War II, see E. J. Kahn Jr., *G.I. Jungle: An American Soldier in Australia and New Guinea* (New York: Simon and Schuster, 1943), pp. 1–13; Johnson, *One More Hill*, pp. 4–7; Gwendolyn Midlo Hall, ed., *Love, War, and the 96th Engineers (Colored): The World War II New Guinea Diaries of Captain Hyman Samuelson* (Urbana and Chicago: University of Illinois Press, 1995), pp. 35–42; W. Stanford Smith, with contributions by Leo J. Machan and Stanley E. Earman, *The Cannoneers: G.I. Life in a World War II Cannon Company* (Manhattan, Kans.: Sunflower University Press, 1993), pp. 19–22; and Becker and Thobaben, *Common Warfare*, pp. 125–127 and 131–134. For the Korean War, see Henry Berry, *Hey, Mac, Where Ya Been? Living Memories of the U.S. Marines in the Korean War* (New York: St. Martin's Press, 1988), pp. 234–235 and 271; Joseph R. Owen, *Colder Than Hell: A Marine Rifle Company at Chosin Reservoir* (Annapolis, Md.: Naval Institute Press, 1996), pp. 41–51; and Martin Russ, *The Last Parallel: A Marine's War Journal* (New York and Toronto: Rinehart, 1957), pp. 33–36. For the Vietnam War, see Ebert, *A Life in a Year,* pp. 70–74, and Parks, *G.I. Diary,* pp. 55–59.

17. Albert M. Ettinger and A. Churchill Ettinger, *A Doughboy with the Fighting Sixty-ninth: A Remembrance of World War I* (Shippensburg, Pa.: White Mane Publishing, 1992), p. 122. Father Francis P. Duffy, the regiment's chaplain, confirms the unit's eagerness to do battle (*Father Duffy's Story: A Tale of Humor and Heroism, of Life and Death with the Fighting Sixty-ninth* [Garden City, N.Y.: Garden City Publishing, 1919], pp. 124–125).

18. For an excellent assessment of the live-and-let-live system on the western front, see A. E. Ashworth, "The Sociology of Trench Warfare, 1914–1918," *British Journal of Sociology* 19:4 (December 1968): 407–423, or his expansion on the subject in his book, *Trench Warfare, 1914–1918: The Live and Let Live System* (New York: Holmes and Meier, 1980).

19. Amos N. Wilder, *Armageddon Revisited: A World War I Journal* (New Haven and London: Yale University Press, 1994), p. 82. See also Alvin C. York, *Sergeant York: His Own Life Story and War Diary* (Garden City, N.Y.: Doubleday, Doran, 1928), pp. 202–203; Bob Hoffman, *I Remember the Last War* (York, Pa.: Strength and Health Publishing, 1940), pp. 271–272; and Minder, *This Man's War,* pp. 205–206.

20. Ernie Pyle, *Brave Men* (New York: Henry Holt, 1944), pp. 343–344.

21. Lyle Rishell, *With a Black Platoon in Combat: A Year in Korea* (College Station: Texas A&M University Press, 1993), p. 25. See also Charles M. Bussey, *Firefight at Yechon: Courage and Racism in the Korean War* (Washington, D.C., and London: Brassey's, 1991), p. 83.

22. Philip Caputo, *A Rumor of War* (New York: Ballantine Books, 1978), p. 66. See also pp. 205–206.

23. Pyle, *Your War,* p. 177.

24. The Stouffer Study includes a survey of World War II veteran soldiers in the European theater who identified three mistakes most frequently made by green troops: bunching up, talking or making noise at night, and shooting before they were able to see their target. See Stouffer et al., *Combat and Its Aftermath,* pp. 283–284. For a sampling of green-unit errors or ignorance, see Hervey Allen, *Toward the Flame: A War Diary* (New York: Grosset and Dunlap, 1934), p. 13; Henry Berry, *Make the Kaiser Dance: Living Memories of the Doughboy* (New York: Priam Books, 1978), p. 298; Gerald Astor, *Crisis in the Pacific: The Battles for the Philippine Islands by the Men Who Fought Them* (New York: Donald I. Fine Books, 1996), pp. 200 and 212–213; Janice Holt Giles, ed., *The G.I. Journal of Sergeant Giles* (Boston: Houghton Mifflin, and Cambridge: Riverside Press, 1965), pp. 36–37; Harold P. Leinbaugh and John D. Campbell, *The Men of Company K* (New York: Bantam Books, 1987), p. 160; Kurt Gabel, *The Making of a Paratrooper: Airborne Training and Combat in World War II* (Lawrence: University Press of Kansas, 1990), pp. 172–173; and Robert Mason, *Chickenhawk* (New York: Penguin Books, 1986), sec. I (appropriately named "Virgins"), pp. 21–229, with specific incidents on pp. 80, 82 and 86, 99–100, and 118–120.

25. John M. Del Vecchio, *The 13th Valley* (New York: Bantam Books, 1983), p. 95.

26. Pyle, *Brave Men,* p. 271. A team of psychiatrists who visited the European theater late in World War II also found this practice psychologically damaging as well as inefficient. See Leo H. Bartemeier, Lawrence S. Kubie, Karl A. Menninger, John Romano, and John C. Whitehorn, "Combat Exhaustion," two-part series, part 2, *Journal of Nervous and Mental Disease* 104:5 (November 1946): 516–517. See also Albert J. Glass, ed., *Neuropsychiatry in World War II,* Medical Department, U.S. Army, Office of the Surgeon General, 2 vols., *Overseas Theaters* (Washington, D.C.: U.S. Government Printing Office, 1973), 2: 122. For a similar assessment from the Korean War, see Samuel L. A. Marshall, *Commentary on Infantry Operations and Weapons Usage in Korea, Winter of 1950–51,* Operations Research Office Report 13 (Chevy Chase, Md.: Johns Hopkins University Press, 1953), p. 56.

27. Elton E. Mackin, *Suddenly We Didn't Want to Die: Memoirs of a World War I Marine* (Novato, Calif.: Presidio Press, 1993), p. 70. See also John W. Thomason Jr., *Fix Bayonets!* (New York: Blue Ribbon Books, 1926), "Replacements," pp. 31–35.

28. John L. Munschauer, *World War II Cavalcade: An Offer I Couldn't Refuse* (Manhattan, Kans.: Sunflower University Press, 1996), p. 103. See also George Wilson, *If You Survive* (New York: Ivy Books, 1987), p. 11.

29. Duffy, *Story,* p. 227. Unfortunately, but typically, this four-week training program was terminated after ten days because the unit was sent back to the fighting (p. 229).

30. Wilson, *If You Survive,* p. 214. For other examples of replacement integration in World War II, see Paul Boesch, *Road to Huertgen: Forest in Hell* (Houston: Paul M. Boesch, 1985), p. 45; William Young Boyd, *The Gentle Infantryman* (New York: St. Martin's Press, 1985), pp. 161–162; Leinbaugh and Campbell, *Company K,* pp. 105–106; and George William Sefton, *It Was My War: I'll Remember It the Way I Want To!* (Manhattan, Kans.: Sunflower University Press, 1994), p. 145.

31. See Doug Michaud interview in Donald Knox, *The Korean War: Pusan to Chosin: An Oral History* (San Diego, New York, and London: Harcourt Brace Jovanovich, 1985), p. 565, and Owen, *Colder Than Hell,* p. 220.

32. Dow interview in Donald Knox, with additional text by Alfred Coppel, *The Korean War: Uncertain Victory: The Concluding Volume of an Oral History* (San Diego, New York, and London: Harcourt Brace Jovanovich, 1988), pp. 392–393.

33. For examples of replacement training and integration during the static period of the Korean War, see ibid., pp. 458–459; Howard Matthias, *The Korean War—Reflections of a Young Combat Platoon Leader* (Tallahassee, Fla.: Father and Son Publishing, 1995), pp. 40 and 69; Stephens, *Old Ugly Hill,* pp. 44–47 and 84–85; and John A. Sullivan, *Toy Soldiers: Memoir of a Combat Platoon Leader in Korea* (Jefferson, N.C., and London: McFarland, 1991), pp. 18–23.

34. The historian Christian G. Appy says that although some replacements received in-country orientation and training, "just as often the need for replacements was so pressing that new men were dispatched [to their units] almost immediately" (*Working-Class War: American Combat Soldiers and Vietnam* [Chapel Hill: University of North Carolina Press, 1993], p. 141). In periods of crisis (Appy provides an example of a marine arriving during the siege of Khe Sanh) replacements may have been sent directly into combat, but this was certainly not the norm. For a good overview of replacement training in Vietnam, see Ebert, *A Life in a Year,* pp. 96–101.

35. While most of the soldier-authors mention in-country training, many do not dwell on the details. Tim O'Brien, for example, mentions his week at the Americal Division's Combat Center but little else (*If I Die in a Combat Zone: Box Me Up and Ship Me Home* [New York: Laurel, Dell, 1987], pp. 74–75). For one of the better descriptions, in this case the Screaming Eagle Replacement Training School, see Del Vecchio, *13th Valley,* pp. 9–19. See also Stanley Goff and Robert Sanders, with Clark Smith, *Brothers: Black Soldiers in the Nam* (Novato, Calif.: Presidio Press, 1982), pp. 18–19 and 52–53.

36. Roger J. Spiller, "Isen's Run: Human Dimensions of Warfare in the Twentieth Century," *Military Review* 68:5 (May 1988): 24. See also John Ellis, *The Sharp End: The Fighting Man in World War II* (New York: Charles Scribner's Sons, 1980), pp. 302–304.

37. James Jones, *WW II: A Chronicle of Soldiering* (New York: Ballantine Books, 1976), p. 68. See p. 249 for an egregious example of the abuse of replacements.

38. Appy, *Working-Class War,* p. 138. Ebert draws the same conclusion in *A Life in a Year,* p. 129.

39. Audie Murphy, *To Hell and Back* (New York: Bantam Books, 1983), p. 108. Two Stouffer Study surveys, incidentally, show that more than 80 percent of the combat soldiers surveyed believed that the veteran soldiers "did as much as they could" to integrate replacements because "it was to the interest of the old-timers . . . to work the replacement into the unit as quickly and completely as possible" (Stouffer et al., *Combat and Its Aftermath,* pp. 278–279).

40. The Vietnam grunt, Tom Schultz, is quoted in Ebert, *A Life in a Year,* p. 111. See Ebert's excellent chapter on FNGs, chapter 6, "Being New," pp. 104–130.

41. Matthias, *Reflections,* pp. 41–42.

42. Goff and Sanders, *Brothers,* pp. 20–21.

43. Ibid., p. 57. See also p. 138.

44. Ibid., p. 64. See also Ebert, *A Life in a Year,* pp. 114–115.

45. Moran, *Anatomy,* p. 26. See also Richard Holmes, *Acts of War: The Behavior of Men in Battle* (New York: Free Press, 1985), "First Blood," pp. 136–148.

46. Giles, ed., *G.I. Journal,* p. 22.

47. Sledge, *Old Breed,* p. 20.

48. Mackin, *We Didn't Want to Die,* p. 19.

49. For several of the better descriptions of green troops marching through carnage while en route to the front, see Allen, *Toward the Flame,* pp. 101–110; John Dos Passos, *Three Soldiers,* Sentry ed. (Boston: Houghton Mifflin, 1921), pp. 177–186; and Thomason, *Fix Bayonets!* pp. 31–45.

50. Dan Levin, *From the Battlefield: Dispatches of a World War II Marine* (Annapolis, Md.: Naval Institute Press, 1995), p. 11. See also Roscoe C. Blunt Jr., *Inside the Battle of the Bulge: A Private Comes of Age* (Westport, Conn., and London: Praeger, 1994), pp. 5–8; Huebner, *Long Walk,* pp. 40–42; and Studs Terkel, *"The Good War": An Oral History of World War II* (New York: Pantheon Books, 1984), pp. 41–42.

51. Matthias, *Reflections,* p. 24. For other Korean War examples, see Charles S. Crawford, *The Four Deuces: A Korean War Story* (Novato, Calif.: Presidio Press, 1989), pp. 45–52, and Stephens, *Old Ugly Hill,* pp. 47–50.

52. Allen, *Toward the Flame,* p. 38.

53. Blunt, *Inside,* p. 13. See also Sledge, *Old Breed,* pp. 254–255; Harold L. Bond, *Return to Cassino* (New York: Pocket Books, 1965), p. 24; Fussell, *Doing Battle,* pp. 104–105; and Charles B. MacDonald, *Company Commander* (Toronto, New York, and London: Bantam Books, 1978), p. 19.

54. Gustav Hasford, *The Short-timers* (New York: Bantam Books, 1979), p. 130. James Ebert also notes that "a macabre fascination with death drew soldiers to their first corpse with more than professional interest" (*A Life in a Year,* p. 146).

55. Doyle interview in Henry Berry, *Semper Fi, Mac: Living Memories of the U.S. Marines in World War II* (New York: Berkley Books, 1983), p. 285.

56. Mark Baker, *Nam: The Vietnam War in the Words of the Men and Women Who Fought There* (New York: Berkley Books, 1983), p. 40. See also Caputo, *Rumor of War,* p. 88, and John Sack, *M* (New York: Avon Books, 1985), pp. 154–155.

57. Crawford, *Four Deuces,* p. 93.

58. Santos interview in Al Santoli, *Everything We Had: An Oral History of the Viet-*

*nam War by Thirty-three American Soldiers Who Fought It* (New York: Ballantine Books, 1982), pp. 112–113. For another example, see Alfred S. Bradford, *Some Even Volunteered: The First Wolfhounds Pacify Vietnam* (Westport, Conn., and London: Praeger, 1994), p. 66.

59. Charles R. Cawthon, *Other Clay: A Remembrance of the World War II Infantry* (Niwot: University Press of Colorado, 1990), p. 54.

60. Larry Heinemann, *Close Quarters* (New York: Farrar, Straus and Giroux, 1977), p. 44.

61. Nat Frankel and Larry Smith, *Patton's Best: An Informal History of the 4th Armored Division* (New York: Jove Book, 1984), p. 14.

62. Levin, *Battlefield,* p. 65; this was Levin's first amphibious assault, although he had experienced some previous combat. See also Allen R. Matthews, *The Assault* (New York: Dodd, Mead, 1980), p. 39; Matthews was also in the assault wave (his first) on Iwo Jima, and he likewise cannot piece together a clear picture of what happened.

63. Cawthon, *Other Clay,* p. 62.

64. Blunt, *Inside,* p. 19.

65. Matthias, *Reflections,* p. 39. See also Mason, *Chickenhawk,* pp. 108–109.

66. This section title and the two that follow are borrowed from Paul Fussell's process of "realization," whereby a combat soldier learns of his mortality: First comes, "it can't happen to me," followed by, "it can happen to me," and finally, "it is going to happen to me." See *Wartime: Understanding and Behavior in the Second World War* (New York and Oxford: Oxford University Press, 1989), p. 282.

67. Roy L. Swank and Walter E. Marchand, "Combat Neuroses: Development of Combat Exhaustion," *Archives of Neurology and Psychiatry* 55:3 (March 1946): 238–239.

68. Ettinger and Ettinger, *Fighting Sixty-ninth,* p. 148.

69. Frederick Downs, *The Killing Zone: My Life in the Vietnam War* (New York: Berkley Books), p. 74.

70. Fussell, *Wartime,* p. 52.

71. Wilson quoted in Eric Bergerud, *Touched with Fire: The Land War in the South Pacific* (New York: Viking Penguin, 1996), p. 444. See also Frank Chadwick quotation on the same page.

72. Crawford, *Four Deuces,* p. 23. See also Rishell, *Black Platoon,* pp. 25 and 29.

73. Hoffman, *I Remember,* pp. 53–54.

74. Peter G. Bourne, *Men, Stress, and Vietnam* (Boston: Little, Brown, 1970), p. 121. John Dollard's survey of American veterans of the Spanish Civil War draws a similar conclusion. Sixty-four percent said they were less fearful in subsequent battles at least in part because they had learned to protect themselves in combat (see *Fear in Battle* [New York: AMS Press, 1976], p. 22).

75. Bourne, *Men, Stress,* p. 97.

76. Jack Fuller, *Fragments* (New York: Dell, 1985), p. 105.

77. Richard A. Gabriel, in his study of military psychiatry, notes that the short-term physical effects of anxiety can serve to key up the body, making it a "more efficient fighting machine by increasing its strength, endurance, and resistance to pain" (*The Painful Field: The Psychiatric Dimension of Modern War* [New York, London, and Westport, Conn.: Greenwood Press, 1988], p. 166).

78. Norman Mailer, *The Naked and the Dead* (New York: Signet Books, 1948), p. 456.

79. Murphy, *To Hell and Back,* p. 98.

80. Downs, *Killing Zone,* p. 105. See also Caputo, *Rumor of War,* pp. 105–106, for the "strange exhilaration" he experienced during his first "hot" landing zone.

81. James R. McDonough, *Platoon Leader* (New York: Bantam, Books, 1986), p. 93. See also Ralph Zumbro, *Tank Sergeant* (Novato, Calif.: Presidio Press, 1986), p. 15.

82. Mackin, *We Didn't Want to Die,* pp. 82–83. See also Horatio Rogers, *World War I Through My Sights* (San Rafael, Calif.: Presidio Press, 1976), p. 58.

83. Caputo, *Rumor of War,* p. 115.

84. Moran, *Anatomy,* pp. 26–27. See also Holmes, *Acts of War,* p. 182.

85. Ernest Hemingway, *Across the River and into the Trees* (New York: Collier Books, 1987), p. 33. See also the case of Lieutenant Kreider in Richard Tregaskis, *Stronger Than Fear* (New York: Random House, 1945), pp. 19 and 65–66.

86. Robert Leckie, *Helmet for My Pillow* (Garden City, N.Y.: Nelson Doubleday, 1979), p. 261.

87. Stephens, *Old Ugly Hill,* p. 57. See also Matthias, *Reflections,* p. xiv.

88. Parks, *G.I. Diary,* p. 112.

89. Michael Lee Lanning, *The Only War We Had: A Platoon Leader's Journal of Vietnam* (New York: Ivy Books, 1987), p. 259.

90. The Stouffer Study includes surveys of combat soldiers in World War II confirming that those who saw friends killed or wounded, or crack up emotionally, exhibited increased symptoms of stress and fear. In sum, they gained a realization of danger and vulnerability (see Stouffer et al., *Combat and Its Aftermath,* pp. 80–82).

91. See the survey results in ibid., p. 201, and Dollard, *Fear in Battle*, pp. 10–11. See also Ronald Schaffer, *America in the Great War: The Rise of the War Welfare State* (New York and Oxford: Oxford University Press, 1991), pp. 159–160; Ellis, *Sharp End,* pp. 97–98; and Fussell, *Wartime,* pp. 277–278.

92. William Manchester, *Goodbye, Darkness: A Memoir of the Pacific War* (Boston and Toronto: Little, Brown, 1979), p. 380. For other examples, see Rogers, *Through My Sights,* p. 63; Astor, *Crisis,* p. 233; Russ, *Last Parallel,* p. 179; and William D. Ehrhart, *Vietnam-Perkasie: A Combat Marine Memoir* (Jefferson, N.C., and London: McFarland, 1983), p. 224.

93. Sledge, *Old Breed,* p. 59. See also Richard Tregaskis, *Guadalcanal Diary* (New York: Random House, 1943), p. 166.

94. Murphy, *To Hell and Back,* p. 95.

95. For example, the Spanish Civil War veterans surveyed by John Dollard most feared abdominal, eye, brain, and genital wounds. See *Fear in Battle,* pp. 12–13.

96. Lanning, *Only War,* p. 71. Lanning provides an example of a sergeant with a shrapnel wound to his penis, from which he recovered. For another example, see James Webb, *Fields of Fire* (New York: Bantam Books, 1979), p. 61.

97. Lanning, *Only War,* p. 210.

98. Heinemann, *Close Quarters,* p. 102. When Sergeant Zumbro's M48 tank was set on fire by a Viet Cong rocket-propelled grenade, the fire extinguisher system put the blaze out: "Thank God for diesel engines. If the old girl had been a gasoline fueled tank, we would be dead" (*Tank Sergeant,* p. 117).

99. Frankel, *Patton's Best,* p. 156. Much like tankers, helicopter crewmen had their fears of crashing and burning. The Vietnam War correspondent Michael Herr called it

"helicopter anxiety": "If you were ever on a helicopter that had been hit by ground fire your deep, perpetual chopper anxiety was guaranteed" (*Dispatches* [New York: Avon Books, 1978], p. 15).

100. Dollard, *Fear in Battle*, p. 14. The Stouffer Study found a similar mix of physical and psychological factors at work in generating fear of certain weaponry and further discovered that the veteran soldier learned to place more weight on the physical factors (the weapon's actual lethality). See Stouffer et al., *Combat and Its Aftermath*, pp. 231–241. See also Holmes, *Acts of War*, pp. 209–213, and Anthony Kellett, *Combat Motivation: The Behavior of Soldiers in Battle* (Boston, The Hague, and London: Kluwer, Nijhoff, 1982), pp. 254–257.

101. Albert Ettinger is one of the few doughboys to mention a land mine casualty. See *Fighting Sixty-ninth*, p. 77. The Germans also left mines behind on withdrawing after the Armistice. See O'Brien, *Wine, Women, and War*, pp. 260–261.

102. The historian John Ellis comments on the psychological impact of mines in *Sharp End*, p. 80. See also Fussell, *Wartime*, p. 279.

103. Boesch, *Road to Huertgen*, p. 164. See also Wilson, *If You Survive*, pp. 111–112.

104. Pyle, *Your War*, p. 153. See also Huebner, *Long Walk*, pp. 51, 73, 111–113, and 139. Huebner, a battalion surgeon, confirms the demoralizing effect of mines because of the maiming wounds they generated.

105. Caputo, *Rumor of War*, p. 273. See also Baker, *Nam*, pp. 71, 83, and 94, and O'Brien, *If I Die*, pp. 125–130.

106. Matthias, *Reflections*, p. 82. See also Crawford, *Four Deuces*, pp. 222–223, and Rishell, *Black Platoon*, pp. 148 and 165.

107. Bill Mauldin, *Up Front* (New York: Award Books, 1976), p. 93.

108. For two memoirs in which all incoming artillery rounds are from 88s, see Lester Atwell, *Private* (New York: Popular Library, 1958), and Giles, ed., *G.I. Journal.* More discerning memoirists, often artillerymen or antitank-gun crewmen, differentiated between high-velocity 88-mm artillery fire versus 105- or 150-mm artillery fire.

109. Matthias, *Reflections*, pp. 51–52. See also A. Andy Andow, *Letters to Big Jim Regarding Narrul Purigo, Cashinum Iman* (New York: Vantage Press, 1994), p. 49, and Berry, *Hey, Mac*, p. 238.

110. Boesch, *Road to Huertgen*, p. 26. For other typical reactions to the rocket artillery, which the Germans had named "*Nebelwerfer*," see Bond, *Cassino*, pp. 37–38; Frankel, *Patton's Best*, p. 95; and MacDonald, *Company Commander*, p. 89.

111. Jones, *WW II*, p. 123.

112. Atwell, *Private*, pp. 35–36.

113. Blunt, *Inside*, p. 143.

114. Sledge, *Old Breed*, p. 149.

115. Wright quoted in Bergerud, *Touched with Fire*, p. 449.

116. Clifford Fox lost thirty pounds on Guadalcanal. See his comment in ibid., p. 442; Boris R. Spiroff lost more than twenty pounds in twelve months (see *Korea: Frozen Hell on Earth* [New York: Vantage Press, 1995], p. 72); Stephens claims to have lost sixty pounds after thirteen months in Korea (see *Toy Soldiers*, p. 160); and Matthias claims a loss of seventy pounds in Korea (see *Reflections*, p. 133).

117. Santos interview in Santoli, *Everything We Had*, pp. 122–123.

118. Swank and Marchand, "Combat Neuroses," pp. 239–240 and diagram on p. 238.

Other psychiatrists have described a condition similar to Swank and Marchand's "hyper-reactive stage." See the discussion of the "incipient stage" of combat exhaustion in Barte-meier et al., "Combat Exhaustion," two-part series, part 1, *Journal of Nervous and Mental Disease* 104:4 (October 1946): 374–375. See also the discussion of "the latency period" prior to combat exhaustion in Gary L. Tischler, "Patterns of Psychiatric Attrition and of Behavior in a Combat Zone," in *The Psychology and Physiology of Stress: With Reference to Special Studies of the Viet Nam War,* ed. Peter G. Bourne (New York and London: Academic Press, 1969), pp. 23–24. Finally, see Lord Moran's discussion of "windiness," which is what the British called the symptoms a soldier displayed on the verge of cracking up, in *Anatomy,* p. 31.

119. Hoffman, *I Remember,* p. 78. See also p. 214.

120. Sefton, *It Was My War,* p. 86.

121. McDonough, *Platoon Leader,* p. 15.

122. Sledge, *Old Breed,* p. 263.

123. Blunt, *Inside,* p. 118.

124. The standard army tour of duty in Vietnam was twelve months, and the marines' tour was thirteen. Rotation in the Korean War was based on a point system that was modified several times, but a twelve-month tour was roughly the norm for a combat soldier.

125. James Brady, *Coldest War: A Memoir of Korea* (New York: Pocket Books, 1991), pp. 137–138. See the case of Sergeant Frank Almy in Knox, *Uncertain Victory,* pp. 217–218.

126. Mason, *Chickenhawk,* pp. 284, 391–392, 394, 415–416, 430, and 468–469.

127. Herzog, *War Stories,* p. 40. See also Jones's discussion of "combat numbness" in *WW II,* p. 185, and Jesse Glenn Gray's discussion of "stupification of consciousness" in *The Warriors: Reflections on Men in Battle* (New York: Harper Colophon Books, 1970), p. 105.

128. Arthur W. Little, *From Harlem to the Rhine: The Story of New York's Colored Volunteers* (New York: Covici-Friede, 1936), p. 248. See also Allen, *Toward the Flame,* p. 121, and Hoffman, *I Remember,* pp. 164–166.

129. Blunt, *Inside,* p. 96. See also Atwell, *Private,* pp. 317–318; Fussell, *Doing Battle,* p. 123; Huebner, *Long Walk,* p. 188; and Hoffman and Hoffman, *Archives,* pp. 153–154.

130. Matthews, *Assault,* p. 227.

131. Downs, *Killing Zone,* p. 84.

132. Ogden, *Green Knight,* p. 272. See also Baker, *Nam,* p. 101; Heinemann, *Close Quarters,* p. 252; Herr, *Dispatches,* pp. 18–19; and Parks, *G.I. Diary,* p. 93.

133. Pyle, *Brave Men,* p. 270.

134. Frankel, *Patton's Best,* p. 102.

135. Sledge, *Old Breed,* p. 128. Incidentally, one of the classic case studies of a soldier's immersion in the environment of war is that of Allen R. Matthews; in his memoir *The Assault,* he describes his transition from fresh replacement to bulkhead stare and combat exhaustion in thirteen days on Iwo Jima.

136. Gerald P. Averill, *Mustang: A Combat Marine* (Novato, Calif.: Presidio Press, 1987), p. 108.

137. Leinbaugh and Campbell, *Company K,* pp. 239 and 243.

138. Hoffman and Hoffman, *Archives,* pp. 102–103. See also Berry, *Semper Fi,* p.

243; Sledge, *Old Breed*, p. 223; Knox, *Uncertain Victory*, p. 59; and Ron Kovic, *Born on the Fourth of July* (New York: Pocket Books, 1977), pp. 216–217.

139. The Stouffer Study includes surveys of combat soldiers in World War II that indicate how demoralizing the war's seeming endlessness was, with death, serious injury, or psychological breakdown as the only ways out. This discovery prompted the formulation of a rotation plan to alleviate the problem although it was not fully implemented before the war ended (see Stouffer et al., *Combat and Its Aftermath*, pp. 88–95).

140. Carl Andrew Brannen, *Over There: A Marine in the Great War* (College Station: Texas A&M University Press, 1996), p. 40.

141. Mackin, *We Didn't Want to Die*, p. 213.

142. Bond, *Cassino*, p. 146.

143. Munschauer, *Cavalcade*, p. 146. See also Becker and Thobaben, *Common Warfare*, p. 172.

144. Ebert, *A Life in a Year*, p. 214.

145. Lanning, *Only War*, p. 45.

146. Muetzel quoted in Knox, *Pusan to Chosin*, p. 184.

147. Munschauer, *Cavalcade*, p. 127. Jones in *WW II*, p. 43, argues that fatalism is a necessary condition that allows soldiers to function under fire; few agree with this thesis: see Stouffer et al., *Combat and Its Aftermath*, p. 189; Ellis, *Sharp End*, p. 206; and Holmes, *Acts of War*, pp. 240–241.

148. Leckie, *Helmet*, pp. 91–92.

149. Kovic, *Fourth of July*, p. 210.

150. Mackin, *We Didn't Want to Die*, p. 233.

151. Russ, *Last Parallel*, p. 236.

152. Pyle, *Brave Men*, p. 6.

153. Minder, *This Man's War*, pp. 329 and 339.

154. Caputo, *Rumor of War*, pp. 247 and 251–252.

155. Matthias, *Reflections*, pp. 163–164. See also pp. 165–166 for his discussion of his personal case of short-timer syndrome. For other examples, see Crawford, *Four Deuces*, pp. 135, 144, and 202; Rishell, *Black Platoon*, pp. 162–164; Stephens, *Old Ugly Hill*, pp. 86–87; Sullivan, *Toy Soldiers*, p. 116; and Knox, *Uncertain Victory*, p. 462. Virtually every Vietnam grunt mentions the impact of growing "short." For a good overview, see Ebert, *A Life in a Year*, pp. 316–338. For personal accounts, see John Ketwig, *And a Hard Rain Fell* (New York: Pocket Books, 1986), pp. 169–170, 177–178, and 187; Parks, *G.I. Diary*, p. 127; and Dominick Yezzo, *A G.I.'s Vietnam Diary, 1968–1969* (New York: Franklin Watts, 1974), diary entries for July 31 to August 16.

156. The term "last-casualty syndrome" is borrowed from Vietnam veteran John G. Fowler Jr., who explains that this syndrome was evident among soldiers in Vietnam late in the war, once troop withdrawals were in full swing. See "Combat Cohesion in Vietnam," *Military Review* 59:12 (December 1979): 27.

157. The Stouffer Study comments on the World War II GIs' renewed hope, toward the end of the fighting in Europe, of surviving the war (see Stouffer et al., *Combat and Its Aftermath*, p. 189). Last-casualty syndrome was much less in evidence in the Pacific in World War II because everyone expected continued hard fighting for the Japanese home islands.

158. Huebner, *Long Walk*, p. 193. See also Giles, ed., *G.I. Journal*, p. 337, and Murphy, *To Hell and Back*, p. 262.

## CHAPTER 4. COPING WITH THE ENVIRONMENT OF WAR

1. Leo H. Bartemeier, Lawrence S. Kubie, Karl A. Menninger, John Romano, and John C. Whitehorn, "Combat Exhaustion," two-part series, part 1, *Journal of Nervous and Mental Disease* 104:4 (October 1946): 368. Bartemeier and his colleagues, for example, classified the soldiers' coping mechanisms as "normal" and "abnormal" defenses, with the abnormal ones possibly being the more important.

2. Bradford Perkins, "Impressions of Wartime," *Journal of American History* 77:2 (September 1990): 565.

3. Ibid. Most commanders appreciated the need for breaks in the action. In World War II, for example, the shortage of American combat divisions meant that, as divisions, they stayed in the line for extended periods, but commanders recognized the need to provide rest and relief for individual soldiers and subordinate units. See Michael D. Doubler, *Closing with the Enemy: How G.I.s Fought the War in Europe, 1944–1945* (Lawrence: University Press of Kansas, 1994), p. 252.

4. For a discussion of the World War I Leave Areas, see Frank Freidel, *Over There: The History of America's First Overseas Crusade,* rev. and abridged ed. (Philadelphia: Temple University Press, 1990), pp. 195–197, and Mark Meigs, *Optimism at Armageddon: Voices of American Participants in the First World War* (Washington Square, N.Y.: New York University Press, 1997), pp. 79–86.

5. For a description by World War II GIs of their activities while on pass to such cities, see Paul Boesch, *Road to Huertgen: Forest in Hell* (Houston: Paul M. Boesch, 1985), pp. 135–142; Leslie W. Bailey, *Through Hell and High Water: The Wartime Memories of a Junior Combat Infantry Officer* (New York: Vantage Press, 1994), pp. 142–143; and Klaus H. Huebner, *Long Walk Through War: A Combat Doctor's Diary* (College Station: Texas A&M University Press, 1987), pp. 99–104, 118–120, 157, and 164–165.

6. William L. Langer, *Gas and Flame in World War I* (New York: Knopf, 1965), p. 69. For similar comments, see Janice Holt Giles, ed., *The G.I. Journal of Sergeant Giles* (Boston: Houghton Mifflin, and Cambridge: Riverside Press, 1965), p. 265; Franklyn A. Johnson, *One More Hill* (New York: Bantam Books, 1983), p. 37; Gerald P. Averill, *Mustang: A Combat Marine* (Novato, Calif.: Presidio Press, 1987), pp. 194–195; James Hamilton Dill, *Sixteen Days at Mungol-li* (Fayetteville, Ark.: M&M Press, 1993), p. 390; and Robert Mason, *Chickenhawk* (New York: Penguin Books, 1986), pp. 129–130.

7. Robert Leckie, *Helmet for My Pillow* (Garden City, N.Y.: Nelson Doubleday, 1979), p. 56. Communal bathing in a stream or river is especially evident in the World War I memoirs; for examples, see Hervey Allen, *Toward the Flame: A World War I Diary* (New York: Grosset and Dunlap, 1934), pp. 84–86; Elton E. Mackin, *Suddenly We Didn't Want to Die: Memoirs of a World War I Marine* (Novato, Calif.: Presidio Press, 1993), pp. 66 and 133–134; and Horatio Rogers, *World War I Through My Sights* (San Rafael, Calif.: Presidio Press, 1976), pp. 145 and 157. In later wars, the army made increasing use of bath and laundry units, and the memoirs speak more often of trips to an army showerpoint than they do of bathing in a stream. Swimming on a hot day remained a popular diversion, however, situation permitting.

8. Albert M. Ettinger and A. Churchill Ettinger, *A Doughboy with the Fighting Sixty-ninth: A Remembrance of World War I* (Shippensburg, Pa.: White Mane Publishing, 1992), p. 167.

9. Amos N. Wilder, *Armageddon Revisited: A World War I Journal* (New Haven and London: Yale University Press, 1994), p. 108.

10. Lester Atwell, *Private* (New York: Popular Library, 1958), p. 286.

11. Ernie Pyle, *Here Is Your War: The Story of G.I. Joe* (Cleveland and New York: World Publishing, 1945), p. 248. Pyle makes a similar observation in his *Brave Men* (New York: Henry Holt, 1944), p. 270. See also Francis P. Duffy, *Father Duffy's Story: A Tale of Humor and Heroism, of Life and Death with the Fighting Sixty-ninth* (Garden City, N.Y.: Garden City Publishing, 1919), p. 260.

12. Lyle Rishell, *With a Black Platoon in Combat: A Year in Korea* (College Station: Texas A&M University Press, 1993), p. 71.

13. For grateful soldiers' comments about entertainment and services provided by organizations like the Red Cross, Salvation Army, and the United Service Organization, see Charles MacArthur, *War Bugs* (New York: Grosset and Dunlap, 1929), p. 133; Will Judy, *A Soldier's Diary: A Day-to-Day Record in the World War* (Chicago: Judy Publishing, 1931), pp. 110–111 and 148–149; Charles R. Cawthon, *Other Clay: A Remembrance of the World War II Infantry* (Niwot: University Press of Colorado, 1990), p. 108; Harold P. Leinbaugh and John D. Campbell, *The Men of Company K* (New York: Bantam Books, 1987), p. 210; Johnson, *One More Hill*, p. 77; John A. Sullivan, *Toy Soldiers: Memoir of a Combat Platoon Leader in Korea* (Jefferson, N.C., and London: McFarland, 1991), p. 46; and John Ketwig, *And a Hard Rain Fell* (New York: Pocket Books, 1986), p. 84.

14. Roscoe C. Blunt Jr., *Inside the Battle of the Bulge: A Private Comes of Age* (Westport, Conn., and London: Praeger, 1994), p. 121. See also Pyle, *Brave Men*, pp. 244–245; Huebner, *Long Walk*, p. 117; and Donald Knox, with additional text by Alfred Coppel, *The Korean War: Uncertain Victory: The Concluding Volume of an Oral History* (San Diego, New York, and London: Harcourt Brace Jovanovich, 1988), p. 295.

15. Ketwig, *Hard Rain*, pp. 236–237. See also Michael Herr, *Dispatches* (New York: Avon Books, 1978), pp. 181–182 and 257–258.

16. For examples, see Boris R. Spiroff, *Korea: Frozen Hell on Earth* (New York: Vantage Press, 1995), p. 39, and Rudolph W. Stephens, *Old Ugly Hill: A G.I.'s Fourteen Months in the Korean Trenches, 1952–1953* (Jefferson, N.C., and London: McFarland, 1995), p. 103.

17. For accounts of European-theater GIs listening to the radio, see Blunt, *Inside*, pp. 80 and 153; Pyle, *Brave Men*, p. 107; and Leon C. Standifer, *Not in Vain: A Rifleman Remembers World War II* (Baton Rouge and London: Louisiana State University Press, 1992), p. 138.

18. For a rare mention of listening to music on a short-wave radio, see E. J. Kahn Jr., *G.I. Jungle: An American Soldier in Australia and New Guinea* (New York: Simon and Schuster, 1943), pp. 134–135.

19. Sing-alongs were common in World War I, generally of popular tunes and ribald drinking songs, often borrowed from the British. See Judy, *Soldier's Diary*, pp. 166 and 215.

20. Group singing was still a popular diversion in World War II. See Giles, ed., *G.I. Journal*, pp. 274–275; Kahn, *G.I. Jungle*, p. 135; Leckie, *Helmet*, pp. 25 and 250; and Richard Tregaskis, *Invasion Diary* (New York: Random House, 1944), p. 191.

21. Alvin C. York, *Sergeant York: His Own Life Story and War Diary* (Garden City, N.Y.: Doubleday, Doran, 1928), p. 198. See also Meigs, *Optimism*, chapter 4: "'Mad'-

moiselle from Armentières, Parlez-vous?' Sexual Attitudes of Americans in World War I," pp. 107–142.

22. Nat Frankel and Larry Smith, *Patton's Best: An Informal History of the 4th Armored Division* (New York: Jove Book, 1984), pp. 85–86.

23. See Richard Holmes, *Acts of War: The Behavior of Men in Battle* (New York: Free Press, 1985), pp. 97–100.

24. James Jones, *WW II: A Chronicle of Soldiering* (New York: Ballantine Books, 1976), p. 174.

25. Bob Hoffman, *I Remember the Last War* (York, Pa.: Strength and Health Publishing, 1940), p. 133.

26. Standifer, *Not in Vain*, p. 195. See also Giles, ed., *G.I. Journal*, pp. 226–233; Pyle, *Your War*, p. 83; Gwendolyn Medlo Hall, ed., *Love, War, and the 96th Engineers (Colored): The World War II New Guinea Diaries of Captain Hyman Samuelson* (Urbana and Chicago: University of Illinois Press, 1995), p. 198; and Paul Fussell, *Doing Battle: The Making of a Skeptic* (Boston: Little, Brown, 1996), p. 151. All the examples cited, incidentally, are army nurses. World War II marines speak harshly of their navy nurses (the navy provides medical care for the marines) because, by training or preference, they took their officers' rank to heart and failed to show the compassion more typical of army nurses. The historian Craig M. Cameron notes this phenomenon in *American Samurai: Myth, Imagination, and the Conduct of Battle in the First Marine Division, 1941–1951* (Cambridge: Cambridge University Press, 1994), pp. 78–79. For examples, see Henry Berry, *Semper Fi, Mac: Living Memories of the U.S. Marines in World War II* (New York: Berkley Books, 1983), p. 172; Leckie, *Helmet*, p. 239; William Manchester, *Goodbye, Darkness: A Memoir of the Pacific War* (Boston and Toronto: Little, Brown, 1979), p. 273; and Leon Uris, *Battle Cry* (New York, London, and Toronto: Bantam Books, 1953), p. 295.

27. The intent, incidentally, is not to portray all soldiers as whoremongers. Most soldiers were young, single, and eager for female companionship, but in defense of the married soldier, some vowed to remain true to their loved ones, despite long separations. Howard V. O'Brien, Henry Giles, and Joseph R. Owen are some of the more conspicuous. They repeatedly mention being wretchedly homesick and make no mention of any sexual liaisons or even point out specific instances when they avoided temptation.

28. Holmes, *Acts of War*, pp. 244–246.

29. Bill Mauldin, *Up Front* (New York: Award Books, 1976), pp. 89–90.

30. Jones, *WW II*, p. 122. In the same passage, Jones praises Bill Mauldin for honestly portraying GI drinking in his famous Willie and Joe cartoons.

31. For examples, see ibid.; Eric Bergerud, *Touched with Fire: The Land War in the South Pacific* (New York: Viking Penguin, 1996), pp. 484–488; Leckie, *Helmet*, p. 250; Ralph G. Martin, *The G.I. War, 1941–1945* (Boston and Toronto: Little, Brown, 1967), p. 299; and Eugene B. Sledge, *With the Old Breed at Peleliu and Okinawa* (New York: Bantam Books, 1983), p. 171.

32. See Martin, *G.I. War*, p. 250, and Manchester, *Goodbye, Darkness*, pp. 288–290.

33. For examples, see Henry Berry, *Make the Kaiser Dance: Living Memories of the Doughboy* (New York: Priam Books, 1978), pp. 38 and 180; Ettinger and Ettinger, *Fighting Sixty-ninth*, pp. 27–28, 52–56, and 118–119; MacArthur, *War Bugs*, pp. 12–13, 15, 30, and 99–101; and Rogers, *Through My Sights*, pp. 93–94, 130, and 252–253.

34. For examples, see Atwell, *Private,* pp. 364, 448, and 473; Huebner, *Long Walk,* p. 167; Leinbaugh and Campbell, *Company K,* p. 231; and Mauldin, *Up Front,* pp. 84–88.

35. Charles M. Bussey, *Firefight at Yechon: Courage and Racism in the Korean War* (Washington, D.C., and London: Brassey's, 1991), p. 246. The head cook in Charles S. Crawford's unit, unlike Bussey's mess sergeant, "couldn't boil water without fucking it up" but was tolerated because he was a skilled moonshiner. See Crawford, *The Four Deuces: A Korean War Story* (Novato, Calif.: Presidio Press, 1989), pp. 156–157.

36. Liquor, often from captured stocks, was issued sporadically during World War II, and the officers received a liquor ration on a fairly consistent basis.

37. See A. Andy Andow, *Letters to Big Jim Regarding Narrul Purigo, Cashinum Iman* (New York: Vantage Press, 1994), p. 58; Bussey, *Firefight,* pp. 111–112; and Martin Russ, *The Last Parallel: A Marine's War Journal* (New York and Toronto: Rinehart, 1957), pp. 294 and 298.

38. For examples, see Richard E. Ogden, *Green Knight, Red Mourning* (New York: Zebra Books, 1985), p. 244, and Mason, *Chickenhawk,* p. 474. (Of course, in Mason's case, he was using prescription tranquilizers with regularity by the time he left Vietnam.)

39. See William D. Ehrhart, *Vietnam-Perkasie: A Combat Marine Memoir* (Jefferson, N.C., and London: McFarland, 1983), pp. 215–217, and Dominick Yezzo, *A G.I.'s Vietnam Diary, 1968–1969* (New York: Franklin Watts, 1974), diary entries for March 13, April 8, May 4, and August 4.

40. For a good overview of the "juicers" versus the "heads" subcultures, see John Helmer, *Bringing the War Home: The American Soldier in Vietnam and After* (New York: Free Press, and London: Collier Macmillan, 1974), pp. 184–208. One of the relatively few novels set late in the war (August 1970), John M. Del Vecchio's *13th Valley* (New York: Bantam Books, 1983), also describes, briefly, the "juicers" versus "heads" subcultures (pp. 124–125).

41. Johnson interview in Studs Terkel, *"The Good War": An Oral History of World War II* (New York: Pantheon Books, 1984), p. 260.

42. Charles F. Minder, *This Man's War: The Day-by-Day Record of an American Private on the Western Front* (New York: Pevensey Press, 1931), p. 284. See also Allen, *Toward the Flame,* p. 61, and Carl Andrew Brannen, *Over There: A Marine in the Great War* (College Station: Texas A&M University Press, 1996), p. 41.

43. Pyle, *Brave Men,* p. 447. See also Leckie, *Helmet,* p. 31, and Allen R. Matthews, *The Assault* (New York: Dodd, Mead, 1980), p. 4.

44. Dill, *Mungol-li,* p. 266.

45. Howard Matthias, *The Korean War—Reflections of a Young Combat Platoon Leader,* rev. ed. (Tallahassee, Fla.: Father and Son Publishing, 1995), p. 148. See also Donald Knox, *The Korean War: Pusan to Chosin: An Oral History* (San Diego, New York, and London: Harcourt Brace Jovanovich, 1985), p. 448.

46. York, *Sergeant York,* p. 213.

47. Minder, *This Man's War,* pp. 103–104. There are innumerable further examples of doughboy eat, drink, and be merry incidents; the exploits of Albert M. Ettinger (*Fighting Sixty-ninth*) and Charles MacArthur (*War Bugs*) and their hell-raising friends are the most illustrative.

48. John Hersey, *Into the Valley: A Skirmish of the Marines* (New York: Schocken Books, 1989), p. xii.

49. Giles, ed., *G.I. Journal,* p. 72. See also Ross S. Carter, *Those Devils in Baggy Pants* (New York and Toronto: Signet Books, 1951), p. 132; Huebner, *Long Walk,* pp. 22 and 169; Carl M. Becker and Robert G. Thobaben, *Common Warfare: Parallel Memoirs by Two World War II GIs in the Pacific* (Jefferson, N.C., and London: McFarland, 1992), pp. 130–131; and John L. Munschauer, *World War II Cavalcade: An Offer I Couldn't Refuse* (Manhattan, Kans.: Sunflower University Press, 1996), pp. 118–119.

50. Mason, *Chickenhawk,* p. 224. For descriptions of unit partying in Korea, see William A. Mauldin, *Bill Mauldin in Korea* (New York: W. W. Norton, 1952), pp. 102–108, and Joseph R. Owen, *Colder Than Hell: A Marine Rifle Company at Chosin Reservoir* (Annapolis, Md.: Naval Institute Press, 1996), pp. 84–85.

51. For a brief description of R and R, see Theodore R. Fehrenbach, *This Kind of War: A Study in Unpreparedness* (New York: Macmillan, 1963), p. 503. For accounts of the R and R experience, see Matthias, *Reflections,* pp. 186–189; Spiroff, *Frozen Hell,* pp. 70–72; Stephens, *Old Ugly Hill,* pp. 156–159; and Dill, *Mungol-li,* pp. 114–115.

52. The psychiatrist Gary L. Tischler describes the "hedonistic pseudocommunity" of the American soldier in Vietnam, for whom R and R was merely the culminating event (see chapter 2, "Patterns of Psychiatric Attrition and of Behavior in a Combat Zone," in *The Psychology and Physiology of Stress: With Reference to Special Studies of the Viet Nam War,* ed. Peter G. Bourne (New York and London: Academic Press, 1969), p. 36. Tischler, who was a psychiatrist at a base hospital in Vietnam, overstates the extent to which the combat soldier was able to partake in the activities of the "hedonistic pseudocommunity" of the rear echelons, but the will was there, if not the opportunities.

53. Larry Heinemann, *Close Quarters* (New York: Farrar, Straus and Giroux, 1977), p. 172. See pp. 172–208 for one of the most hedonistic R and Rs of any Vietnam War novel or memoir. For descriptions of R and R similar to Heinemann's fictional account in theme and plot, if not in degree of excess, see Ehrhart, *Vietnam-Perkasie,* pp. 157–172; Stanley Goff and Robert Sanders, with Clark Smith, *Brothers: Black Soldiers in the Nam* (Novato, Calif.: Presidio Press, 1982), pp. 183–188; Ketwig, *Hard Rain,* pp. 111–124; and Mason, *Chickenhawk,* pp. 323–328.

54. About 5,000 servicemen were discharged for deserting during their tour of duty in Vietnam; about half of those had failed to return from R and R. See Lawrence M. Baskir and William A. Strauss, *Chance and Circumstance: The Draft, the War, and the Vietnam Generation* (New York: Knopf, 1978), p. 113.

55. Mason, *Chickenhawk,* p. 328.

56. Peter G. Bourne, *Men, Stress, and Vietnam* (Boston: Little, Brown, 1970), p. 44. For similar conclusions, see Elmar Dinter, *Hero or Coward: Pressures Facing the Soldier in Battle* (London and Totowa, N.J.: Frank Cass, 1985), p. 71, and John Ellis, *The Sharp End: The Fighting Man in World War II* (New York: Charles Scribner's Sons, 1980), p. 281.

57. Boesch, *Road to Huertgen,* p. 25. See also Munschauer, *Cavalcade,* p. 63; Matthias, *Reflections,* pp. 79–80; and Russ, *Last Parallel,* p. 55.

58. Michael Lee Lanning, *The Only War We Had: A Platoon Leader's Journal of Vietnam* (New York: Ivy Books, 1987), p. 37.

59. Herbert Hendin and Ann Pollinger Haas, *Wounds of War: The Psychological Aftermath of Combat in Vietnam* (New York: Basic Books, 1984), p. 210.

60. The historian Roger J. Spiller argues, contrary to the popular conception that

modern "machine" warfare has made the soldier more insignificant, that the need for individual skill and initiative on today's dispersed battlefield has enhanced the role of the soldier. See "Isen's Run: Human Dimensions of Warfare in the Twentieth Century," *Military Review* 68:5 (May 1988): 18.

61. Rogers, *Through My Sights*, p. 41. See his descriptions of leading the battery into position on pp. 41–43, 54–55, 102–104, 110–114, and 147–149.

62. Marine Brigadier General (ret.) Samuel Griffith related this story to the oral historian Henry Berry in *Semper Fi*, p. 118.

63. Goff and Sanders, *Brothers*, p. 70. See also pp. 66–68.

64. James Jones, *The Thin Red Line* (New York: Charles Scribner's Sons, 1962), p. 429. For a discussion of the importance of awards and recognition as motivators, see Holmes, *Acts of War,* pp. 355–359, and Anthony Kellett, *Combat Motivation: The Behavior of Soldiers in Battle* (Boston, The Hague, and London: Kluwer, Nijhoff, 1982), pp. 201–209.

65. Duffy, *Story*, p. 209.

66. Ibid., p. 230. For other examples, see Boesch, *Road to Huertgen,* pp. 142–143; George Wilson, *If You Survive* (New York: Ivy Books, 1987), pp. 27–28; Goff and Sanders, *Brothers,* pp. 193–194; and Lanning, *Only War,* p. 192.

67. Blunt, *Inside,* p. 38.

68. Pyle, *Brave Men,* p. 136.

69. For soldiers at the bottom of the rank ladder (privates and second lieutenants), even the relatively routine promotion to the next rank was important because it was tangible evidence that they were no longer "rookies." This rationale probably explains why James Brady and his friend Mack were so pleased with their promotion to first lieutenant during the Korean War. See Brady, *The Coldest War: A Memoir of Korea* (New York: Pocket Books, 1991), p. 205.

70. Albert French, *Patches of Fire: A Story of War and Redemption* (New York: Anchor Books, 1997), p. 150.

71. Sledge, *Old Breed,* p. 168. See also Charles B. MacDonald, *Company Commander* (Toronto, New York, and London: Bantam Books, 1978), pp. 137–138.

72. Goff and Sanders, *Brothers,* p. 111.

73. Ogden, *Green Knight,* p. 228.

74. The sociologist G. Dearborn Spindler provides a useful analysis of the World War II citizen-soldier who resisted military discipline, rebelled against the military hierarchy, and retained his self-centered outlook. See "American Character as Revealed by the Military," *Psychiatry: Journal for the Operational Statement of Interpersonal Relations* 11:3 (August 1948): 275–281.

75. The literature professor Peter Aichinger, in his analysis of American war novels, points out that some of the more memorable characters are soldiers who struggle to retain their individualism in a story that "pits the individual against the organization that above all others specializes in reducing men to interchangeable parts of a machine" (*The American Soldier in Fiction, 1880–1963: A History of Attitudes Toward Warfare and the Military Establishment* [Ames: Iowa State University Press, 1975], pp. 109–110).

76. Arnold M. Rose, "The Social Structure of the Army," *American Journal of Sociology* 51:5 (March 1946): 363.

77. Hoffman, *I Remember,* p. 112. See pp. 65–66 and 69–73 for his unauthorized trips and subsequent catching up with his unit.

78. MacArthur, *War Bugs,* p. 217.

79. Leckie, *Helmet,* p. 151. Dominick Yezzo was another soldier who habitually rebelled against the system. See his June 18 diary entry in *Vietnam Diary.*

80. Ogden, *Green Knight,* p. 56.

81. Blue interview in Mary Penick Motley, *The Invisible Soldier: The Experience of the Black Soldier, World War II* (Detroit: Wayne State University Press, 1975), p. 128.

82. Duffy, *Story,* p. 218.

83. Owen, *Colder than Hell,* p. 44.

84. MacArthur, *War Bugs,* pp. 117, 146, 159, 200, and 253–254.

85. Robert G. Merrick, *World War I: A Diary* (Baltimore: privately published, 1982), p. 81.

86. Pyle, *Your War,* p. 299.

87. Richard D. Camp with Eric Hammel, *Lima-6: A Marine Company Commander in Vietnam* (New York: Pocket Books, 1989), p. 212.

88. Richard M. Hardison, *Caissons Across Europe: An Artillery Captain's Personal War* (Austin, Tex.: Eakin Press, 1990), p. 61. See also p. 176 for the addition of a German truck to the battalion's fleet, a fairly common occurrence, especially late in the war as captured stocks increased.

89. Sullivan, *Toy Soldiers,* p. 24.

90. Ralph Zumbro, *Tank Sergeant* (Novato, Calif.: Presidio Press, 1986), p. 65. Stealing equipment and supplies using ruses or even force was common. For other examples, see George William Sefton, *It Was My War: I'll Remember It the Way I Want To!* (Manhattan, Kans.: Sunflower University Press, 1994), pp. 27–28 and 183; Bergerud, *Touched with Fire,* pp. 489–490; Leinbaugh and Campbell, *Company K,* p. 205; and Henry Berry, *Hey, Mac, Where Ya Been? Living Memories of the U.S. Marines in the Korean War* (New York: St. Martin's Press, 1988), p. 89.

91. MacArthur, *War Bugs,* p. 150. See also Brannen, *Over There,* p. 32; Thomas Boyd, *Through the Wheat* (Carbondale and Edwardsville: Southern Illinois University Press, 1978), p. 115; and Rogers, *Through My Sights,* p. 189.

92. Boesch, *Road to Huertgen,* p. 162. See also the Wright interview in Knox, *Pusan to Chosin,* p. 535.

93. Boesch, *Road to Huertgen,* p. 88.

94. Standifer, *Not in Vain,* p. 150.

95. Giles, ed., *G.I. Journal,* pp. 272 and 323. See also Blunt, *Inside,* pp. 135 and 168; Cawthon, *Other Clay,* pp. 169–170; Hardison, *Caissons,* pp. 108 and 175; Terkel, *Good War,* p. 41; and Atwell, *Private,* pp. 363–365 and 416.

96. For examples, see Mackin, *We Didn't Want to Die,* p. 152; John W. Thomason Jr., *Fix Bayonets!* (New York: Blue Ribbon Books, 1926), pp. 1–3; Brannen, *Over There,* p. 9; Atwell, *Private,* pp. 207–208; Mauldin, *Up Front,* pp. 173–174; Motley, *Invisible Soldier,* pp. 285–286; Giles, ed., *G.I. Journal,* pp. 66–67; and Sefton, *It Was My War,* pp. 132 and 134–135.

97. Standifer, *Not in Vain,* p. 240.

98. Samuel A. Stouffer, Arthur A. Lumsdaine, Marion Harper Lumsdaine, Robin M. Williams Jr., M. Brewster Smith, Irving L. Janis, Shirley A. Star, and Leonard S. Cottrell Jr., *Studies in Social Psychology in World War II,* vol 2, *The American Soldier: Combat and Its Aftermath* (Princeton: Princeton University Press, 1949), p.112. See also William

Darryl Henderson, *Cohesion: The Human Element in Combat: Leadership and Societal Influence in the Armies of the Soviet Union, the United States, North Vietnam, and Israel* (Washington, D.C.: National Defense University Press, 1988), p. 16.

99. See the discussion of how "formal" discipline contributes to the soldiers' internalized "sense of duty" in Stouffer et al., *Combat and Its Aftermath,* pp. 117–118. See also Kellett's discussion of "imposed" discipline in *Combat Motivation,* pp. 92–93 and 134–148.

100. See William C. Cockerham's 1976 survey of paratroopers (results published in 1978), in which the Vietnam veterans surveyed recognized more than did the nonveterans that discipline in combat was a "source of stability under stress" ("Attitudes Toward Combat Among U.S. Army Paratroopers," *Journal of Political and Military Sociology* 6:1 [spring 1978]: 1–15, quotation on p. 9).

101. Chadwick quoted in Bergerud, *Touched with Fire,* p. 443.

102. Thomas interview in Motley, *Invisible Soldier,* p. 174.

103. James R. McDonough, *Platoon Leader* (New York: Bantam Books, 1986), p. 73.

104. Fehrenbach, *This Kind of War,* p. 233.

105. Jonathan Shay, *Achilles in Vietnam: Combat Trauma and the Undoing of Character* (New York: Scribner, 1995), p. 175.

106. Tim O'Brien first used this phrase in his memoir, *If I Die in a Combat Zone: Box Me Up and Ship Me Home* (New York: Laurel, Dell, 1987), p. 31. The phrase next appears, attributed to the British World War I soldier-author Siegfried Sassoon, in the frontispiece of O'Brien's Vietnam War novel, *Going After Cacciato* (New York: Dell, 1979).

107. O'Brien interview in Eric James Schroeder, *Vietnam, We've All Been There: Interviews with American Writers* (London and Westport, Conn.: Praeger, 1992), p. 128.

108. Harry Brown, *A Walk in the Sun* (New York: Knopf, 1944), p. 148.

109. Fox interview in Knox, *Uncertain Victory,* p. 263. See also Spiroff, *Frozen Hell,* p. 22.

110. Ehrhart, *Vietnam-Perkasie,* p. 184. See also Gustav Hasford, *The Short-timers* (New York: Bantam Books, 1979), pp. 151–152.

111. French, *Patches of Fire,* p. 77. Daydreaming was often referred to as "World dreaming" by Vietnam War grunts. See Johnnie Clark quoted in James R. Ebert, *A Life in a Year: The American Infantryman in Vietnam, 1965–1972* (Novato, Calif.: Presidio Press, 1993), p. 177.

112. See Eric J. Leed, *No Man's Land: Combat and Identity in World War I* (Cambridge: Cambridge University Press, 1979), p. 188; Lee Kennett, *G.I.: The American Soldier in World War II* (New York: Charles Scribner's Sons, 1987), pp. 74–75; Meyer H. Maskin and Leon L. Altman, "Military Psychodynamics: Psychological Factors in the Transition from Civilian to Soldier," *Psychiatry: Journal of the Biology and the Pathology of Interpersonal Relationships* 6:3 (August 1943): 264–265; Dixon Wecter, *When Johnny Comes Marching Home* (Westport, Conn.: Greenwood Press, 1970), pp. 11–12; and Maria S. Bonn, "A Different World: The Vietnam Veteran Novel Comes Home," in *Fourteen Landing Zones: Approaches to Vietnam War Literature,* ed. Philip K. Jason (Iowa City: University of Iowa Press, 1991), p. 5.

113. Pyle, *Your War,* p. 298.

114. Lanning, *Only War,* p. 38.

115. Ketwig, *Hard Rain,* p. 4. See also p. 8.

116. Blunt, *Inside,* p. 114. See also Minder, *This Man's War,* p. 241; MacArthur, *War*

*Bugs*, p. 9; Merrick, *A Diary*, p. 22; Boesch, *Road to Huertgen*, pp. 44 and 47; Giles, ed., *G.I. Journal*, pp. 42–43, 85, 88, and 103; Johnson, *One More Hill*, pp. 22 and 113; Kahn, *G.I. Jungle*, p. 28; Richard Tregaskis, *Guadalcanal Diary* (New York: Random House, 1943), p. 182; Bussey, *Firefight*, p. 101; Spiroff, *Frozen Hell*, p. 58; Ketwig, *Hard Rain*, pp. 46–48; and McDonough, *Platoon Leader*, p. 23.

117. Owen, *Colder Than Hell*, p. 171.

118. Sledge, *Old Breed*, p. 237.

119. Hall, ed., *Love, War*, pp. 282–284.

120. Mauldin, *Up Front*, p. 24. The results of a post–World War II study of soldier effectiveness reinforce Mauldin's comment. See Eli Ginzberg, James K. Anderson, Sol W. Ginsburg, John L. Herma, and John B. Miner, *The Ineffective Soldier: Lessons for Management and the Nation*, vol. 2, *Breakdown and Recovery* (New York and London: Columbia University Press, 1959), pp. 41 and 46–49.

121. Lanning, *Only War*, p. 95; for similar complaints, see Atwell, *Private*, p. 395, and Manchester, *Goodbye, Darkness*, p. 260.

122. Carter, *Those Devils*, p. 163; for other examples, see Bergerud, *Touched with Fire*, pp. 475–476; Pyle, *Brave Men*, p. 267; Uris, *Battle Cry*, pp. 143–146; Wilson, *If You Survive*, pp. 96–97; Knox, *Uncertain Victory*, p. 264; Spiroff, *Frozen Hell*, p. 63; Berry, *Hey, Mac*, pp. 92–93; and Ehrhart, *Vietnam-Perkasie*, p. 79.

123. Ehrhart, *Vietnam-Perkasie*, p. 132. For his increasing bitterness over losing his fiancée, see pp. 131–132, 135–136, 143, 153–154, and 288–289. The psychologist Dave Grossman believes that Dear John letters became more common as the Vietnam War grew increasingly unpopular. See *On Killing: The Psychological Cost of Learning to Kill in War and Society* (Boston: Little, Brown, 1995), p. 277.

124. For examples of the demoralizing effect of mail delivery problems, see Terkel, *Good War*, p. 281; Wilson, *If You Survive*, p. 14; and Pyle, *Your War*, p. 50.

125. David Parks, *G.I. Diary* (New York, Evanston, and London: Harper and Row, 1968), p. 92.

126. Zumbro, *Tank Sergeant*, p. 88.

127. Eighty-four percent of the Spanish Civil War veterans surveyed by John Dollard said that concentrating on the task at hand made them less afraid. See *Fear in Battle* (New York: AMS Press, 1976), pp. 30–31. See also Kellett, *Combat Motivation*, pp. 287–289, on "distraction."

128. Wilder, *Armageddon*, p. 71. See also the case of Sergeant Ekland in Pat Frank, *Hold Back the Night* (Philadelphia and New York: J. B. Lippincott, 1952), p. 133.

129. Bourne, *Men, Stress*, p. 122.

130. Ibid., p. 97. See also Ebert, *A Life in a Year*, p. 230.

131. O'Brien, *Cacciato*, p. 64.

132. Frank, *Hold Back the Night*, p. 65.

133. Lanning, *Only War*, pp. 261–262.

134. Shay refers to this detachment of attention as the soldiers' shrinking temporal horizon. See *Achilles*, p. 176. See also Stouffer et al., *Combat and Its Aftermath*, p. 190, for a brief discussion of the "shortening of time perspective."

135. Ernest Hemingway, ed., *Men at War: The Best War Stories of All Time* (New York: Bramhill House, 1979), p. xxiv.

136. Philip Caputo, *A Rumor of War* (New York: Ballantine Books, 1978), p. 80.

137. Leckie, *Helmet,* p. 80.

138. Allen, *Toward the Flame,* p. 121. See also [Howard V. O'Brien], *Wine, Women, and War: A Diary of Disillusionment* (New York: J. H. Sears, 1926), p. 80.

139. Dan Levin, *From the Battlefield: Dispatches of a World War II Marine* (Annapolis, Md.: Naval Institute Press, 1995), p. 85. See also Matthews, *Assault,* p. 6, and Ogden, *Green Knight,* pp. 245–246.

140. Sam Keen, *Faces of the Enemy: Reflections of the Hostile Imagination* (San Francisco: Harper San Francisco, 1991), p. 27.

141. Curtis James Morrow, *What's a Commie Ever Done to Black People? A Korean War Memoir of Fighting in the U.S. Army's Last All Negro Unit* (Jefferson, N.C., and London: McFarland, 1997), p. 24. The literature professor Stanley Cooperman discusses the religious cynicism evident in World War I novels and attributes it to the doughboy's disillusionment over organized religion's support for the war. See *World War I and the American Novel* (Baltimore: Johns Hopkins University Press, 1967), pp. 103–113. For examples, see Mackin, *We Didn't Want to Die*, pp. 64–65; William March, *Company K* (New York: Sagamore Press, 1957), p. 91; [O'Brien], *Wine, Women, and War,* p. 95; and John Dos Passos, *Three Soldiers,* Sentry ed. (Boston: Houghton Mifflin, 1921), pp. 156–157 and 209–211. For a discussion of grunts' disillusionment with chaplains' proselytizing, see Robert Jay Lifton, *Home from the War: Vietnam Veterans: Neither Victims nor Executioners* (New York: Simon and Schuster, 1973), p. 163.

142. For praise of Father Duffy as a chaplain, see Berry, *Make the Kaiser Dance,* pp. 310–311.

143. Lanning, *Only War,* p. 101.

144. Jesse Glenn Gray, *The Warriors: Reflections on Men in Battle* (New York: Harper Colophon Books, 1970), p. 119. Students of soldier motivation tend to support one side or the other of this dichotomy. Lee Kennett, for example, claims that "there is . . . evidence that the spiritual factor was an important one in the soldier's life" in World War II, but John Ellis points out in his World War II study that "for many men nothing so utterly and completely dissipated their residual religious beliefs as the randomness and pervasiveness of violent death" (see Kennett, *G.I.,* p. 138, and Ellis, *Sharp End*, p. 99). Both, of course, are correct. See also Holmes, *Acts of War,* pp. 241–242, for a recognition, like Gray's, that a dichotomy does exist, although Holmes rates those soldiers whose beliefs were shattered by war as "a minority."

145. Bailey, *Hell and High Water,* p. 98. See also Joseph D. Lawrence, *Fighting Soldier: The A.E.F. in 1918* (Boulder: Colorado Associated University Press, 1985), p. 130; Berry, *Semper Fi,* p. 288; Pyle, *Your War,* p. 12; Tregaskis, *Guadalcanal,* pp. 21–22; Spiroff, *Frozen Hell,* p. 61; and Knox, *Pusan to Chosin,* pp. 221–222.

146. Boesch, *Road to Huertgen,* p. 22. See also pp. 74–75 and 112. For a similar comment, see marine Bud DeVeer quoted in Bergerud, *Touched with Fire,* p. 470.

147. Morrow, *Commie,* p. 23. See also the Ford interview in Wallace Terry, *Bloods: An Oral History of the Vietnam War by Black Veterans* (New York: Ballantine Books, 1985), p. 35.

148. Ent interview in Rudy Tomedi, *No Bugles, No Drums: An Oral History of the Korean War* (New York: John Wiley and Sons, 1993), p. 28.

149. Sefton, *It Was My War,* p. 216.

150. Standifer, *Not in Vain,* p. 144.

151. Huebner, *Long Walk,* p. 130.

152. Yezzo, *Vietnam Diary,* March 6 entry.

153. Ibid., April 3 entry. See also the case of the World War II soldier Han Rants in Gerald Astor, *Crisis in the Pacific: The Battles for the Philippine Islands by the Men Who Fought Them* (New York: Donald I. Fine Books, 1996), p. 395.

154. Bourne, *Men, Stress,* p. 96.

155. York, *Sergeant York,* p. 276.

156. Minder, *This Man's War,* pp. 331–332.

157. Sledge, *Old Breed,* p. 247.

158. Bryant interview in Terry, *Bloods,* p. 30. See also Caputo, *Rumor of War,* p. 121; Matthew Brennan, *Brennan's War: Vietnam 1965–1969* (New York: Pocket Books, 1986), pp. 57–58; and Ehrhart, *Vietnam-Perkasie,* pp. 82–83.

159. Frederick Downs, *The Killing Zone: My Life in the Vietnam War* (New York: Berkley Books, 1983), p. 201.

160. See Ebert, *A Life in a Year,* pp. 227–228; Ellis, *Sharp End,* p. 100; Paul Fussell, *Wartime: Understanding and Behavior in the Second World War* (New York and Oxford: Oxford University Press, 1989), pp. 48–51; and Holmes, *Acts of War,* pp. 238–240.

161. MacArthur, *War Bugs,* p. 143. Albert M. Ettinger, another Rainbow Division doughboy, also relates the rainbow superstition. See *Fighting Sixty-ninth,* p. 201.

162. Sledge, *Old Breed,* p. 157. See also Blunt, *Inside,* p. 20, for a discussion of a lucky crucifix.

163. Brennan, *Brennan's War,* p. 182. See also Jack Fuller, *Fragments* (New York: Dell, 1985), p. 114.

164. March, *Company K,* p. 71.

165. Matthias, *Reflections,* pp. 69 and 70.

166. Alfred S. Bradford, *Some Even Volunteered: The First Wolfhounds Pacify Vietnam* (Westport, Conn., and London: Praeger, 1994), p. 33.

167. Samuel L. A. Marshall, *Men Against Fire: The Problem of Battle Command in Future War* (Gloucester: Peter Smith, 1978), p. 185. See also Ebert, *A Life in a Year,* pp. 231–232; Holmes, *Acts of War,* pp. 242–244; and Ronald Schaffer, *America in the Great War: The Rise of the War Welfare State* (New York and Oxford: Oxford University Press, 1991), p. 164.

168. Mauldin, *Up Front,* p. 5.

169. Mackin, *We Didn't Want to Die,* p. 248.

170. Blunt, *Inside,* p. 106.

171. Audie Murphy, *To Hell and Back* (New York: Bantam Books, 1983), p. 253.

172. See the case of Wagner, for example, in Cawthon, *Other Clay,* p. 16.

173. Boesch, *Road to Huertgen,* p. 175. For other examples, see French, *Patches of Fire,* p. 90; Ernest Frankel, *Band of Brothers* (New York: Macmillan, 1958), p. 122; Kurt Gabel, *The Making of a Paratrooper: Airborne Training and Combat in World War II* (Lawrence: University Press of Kansas, 1990), p. 204; and Munschauer, *Cavalcade,* pp. 126–127.

174. Aichinger, *Soldier in Fiction,* pp. 96–97. See also Thomas Myers, *Walking Point: American Narratives of Vietnam* (New York and Oxford: Oxford University Press, 1988), pp. 105–139. The Stouffer Study also takes note of "the bitter humor of the front . . . as yet another way in which the soldier could achieve a frame of mind in which it was

possible for him to endure and accept what could not be avoided" (*Combat and Its Aftermath*, p. 190).

175. Mackin, *We Didn't Want to Die*, p. 22.

176. Downs, *Killing Zone*, p. 70. See Hasford, *Short-timers*, pp. 147–148, for a depiction of an enemy skull, complete with Mickey Mouse ears, mounted on a stick. See Brennan, *Brennan's War*, p. 160, and photograph between pp. 140 and 141, for a nonfictional duplicate. See also Lanning, *Only War*, pp. 21–22, and James Webb, *Fields of Fire* (New York: Bantam Books, 1979), p. 269. For corpse humor in the Korean War, see Knox, *Pusan to Chosin*, pp. 569–570, and Knox, *Uncertain Victory*, p. 300.

177. Boesch, *Road to Huertgen*, p. 19.

178. Ibid., p. 20. See also Allen, *Toward the Flame*, p. 52.

179. Hoffman, *I Remember*, p. 60.

180. See Boyd, *Through the Wheat*, pp. 165–166 and 172; MacArthur, *War Bugs*, pp. 45–46 and 116; Mackin, *We Didn't Want to Die*, p. 174; and Minder, *This Man's War*, p. 221.

181. For this rumor, see Hoffman, *I Remember*, pp. 60–61.

182. Duffy, *Story*, p. 104.

183. Pyle, *Brave Men*, p. 90.

184. Owen, *Colder Than Hell*, p. 85. See also Knox, *Uncertain Victory*, p. 141, for another acknowledgment that the "major project of the rumor mills" seemed to be morale boosting by "grinding out continually hopeful views of what lay ahead."

185. Bourne, ed., *Psychology*, pp. 227–228.

186. Fuller, *Fragments*, p. 79. See also Herr, *Dispatches*, p. 118.

187. O'Brien, *If I Die*, p. 95.

188. James Brady, "Leaving For Korea," *American Heritage* 48:1 (February/March 1997): 80; for a similar comment, see Mauldin, *Korea*, p. 41.

189. Jones, *Thin Red Line*, pp. 40–41. See also *WW II*, p. 42.

190. Thomason, *Fix Bayonets!* p. 139. Thomason refers to himself in the third person in his memoir; hence, "the captain" spoke these lines.

191. Duffy, *Story*, p. 73. See also Boyd, *Through the Wheat*, p. 114, and Dos Passos, *Three Soldiers*, p. 199.

192. Mackin, *We Didn't Want to Die*, p. 161.

193. Boesch, *Road to Huertgen*, pp. 159–160.

194. Averill, *Mustang*, p. 110. See also Atwell, *Private*, pp. 55, 60, 75, and 228; Berry, *Semper Fi*, p. 385; Brown, *A Walk*, p. 9; Cawthon, *Other Clay*, pp. 80 and 157; Leinbaugh and Campbell, *Company K* p. 161; Murphy, *To Hell and Back*, p. 191; Pyle, *Your War*, p. 264; Sledge, *Old Breed*, pp. 65–66 and 130; and Standifer, *Not in Vain*, p. 186.

195. Though less frequently than in earlier wars, soldiers still hoped for a million dollar wound during the Korean and Vietnam Wars, particularly at times when they were worn down from a long stretch of combat; for examples, see Knox, *Pusan to Chosin*, pp. 369 and 652; Knox, *Uncertain Victory*, p. 271; Stephens, *Old Ugly Hill*, p. 79; Ogden, *Green Knight*, p. 270; and Mason, *Chickenhawk*, p. 406.

196. See Knox, *Uncertain Victory*, p. 110, for a soldier happy over his "Pusan wound."

197. Sullivan, *Toy Soldiers*, p. 130. See also Berry, *Hey, Mac*, pp. 306–307; Knox, *Pusan to Chosin*, p. 67; Owen, *Colder Than Hell*, p. 68; and Matthias, *Reflections*, p. 206.

198. Ogden, *Green Knight*, p. 207.

199. Herr, *Dispatches*, p. 82. For other Vietnam War examples of million dollar wounds or accidents, see Ketwig, *Hard Rain*, p. 104; Mason, *Chickenhawk*, p. 406; and McDonough, *Platoon Leader*, p. 177.

## CHAPTER 5. FOR COMRADES AND COUNTRY

1. Richard Kohn raises the issue of props versus motivators specifically in the context of primary-group cohesion: "The literature on primary group cohesion has never clearly shown whether solidarity with the group acted as a psychological prop to bolster men to endure the stress or as a motivation to carry out the mission and perform effectively in battle—or both." The answer, as discussed in this chapter, is "both" (see "The Social History of the American Soldier: A Review and Prospectus for Research," *American Historical Review* 86:3 [June 1981]: 561).

2. Jesse Glenn Gray, *The Warriors: Reflections on Men in Battle* (New York: Harper Colophon Books, 1970), p. 40. Samuel L. A. Marshall also believes that group loyalty is the critical motivator in battle: "I hold it to be one of the simplest truths of war that the thing which enables an infantry soldier to keep going with his weapons is the near presence or the presumed presence of a comrade" (*Men Against Fire: The Problem of Battle Command in Future War* [Gloucester: Peter Smith, 1978], p. 42).

3. See Roger Kaplan, "Army Unit Cohesion in Vietnam: A Bum Rap," *Parameters* 17:3 (September 1987): 58. Kaplan responds specifically to Kohn's comment (quoted in note 1 above) that no one had addressed the issue of primary-group cohesion as "prop" or "motivator." In reality, that issue was addressed at least as early as the Stouffer Study (1949), and the answer, again, was "both": The primary group "served two principal functions in combat motivation: it *set and enforced group standards* of behavior, and it *supported and sustained the individual* in stresses he would otherwise not have been able to withstand" (Samuel A. Stouffer, Arthur A. Lumsdaine, Marion Harper Lumsdaine, Robin M. Williams Jr., M. Brewster Smith, Irving L. Janis, Shirley A. Star, and Leonard S. Cottrell Jr., *Studies in Social Psychology in World War II*, vol. 2, *The American Soldier: Combat and Its Aftermath* [Princeton: Princeton University Press, 1949], pp. 130–131). See also the analysis and expanded discussion of the Stouffer Study's findings concerning primary groups in Edward A. Shils, "Primary Groups in the American Army," in *Continuities in Social Research: Studies in the Scope and Method of "The American Soldier,"* ed. Robert K. Merton and Paul F. Lazarsfeld (Glencoe, Ill.: Free Press, 1950), pp. 25–28.

4. See especially the Stouffer Study's discussion of the "informal group" and group interaction in Stouffer et al., *Combat and Its Aftermath*, pp. 130–149. See also the groundbreaking study by Edward A. Shils and Morris Janowitz, "Cohesion and Disintegration in the *Wehrmacht* in World War II," *Public Opinion Quarterly* 12:2 (summer 1948): 280–315. Roy R. Grinker and John P. Spiegel discussed the importance of what they called "group ego" as a coping mechanism as early as 1943 in a report circulated to army medical officers and later published in book form in 1945: "Among the factors which enable the soldier successfully to withstand the onslaught of anxiety in the war situation, is his identification with the group" (*War Neuroses* [Philadelphia and London: Blakiston, 1945], p. 117). For other comments by World War II psychiatrists and psy-

chologists on the importance of group bonds, see Raymond Sobel, "The 'Old Sergeant' Syndrome," *Psychiatry: Journal of the Biology and the Pathology of Interpersonal Relations* 10:3 (August 1947): 320; Edwin A. Weinstein, "The Function of Interpersonal Relations in the Neurosis of Combat," *Psychiatry: Journal of the Biology and the Pathology of Interpersonal Relations* 10:3 (August 1947): 307; and Leo H. Bartemeier, Lawrence S. Kubie, Karl A. Menninger, John Romano, and John C. Whitehorn, "Combat Exhaustion," two-part series, part 1, *Journal of Nervous and Mental Disease* 104:4 (October 1946): 369.

5. Morris Janowitz and Roger W. Little, *Sociology and the Military Establishment,* 3d ed. (Beverly Hills and London: Sage Publications, 1974), p. 94. See also Anthony Kellett, *Combat Motivation: The Behavior of Soldiers in Battle* (Boston, The Hague, and London: Kluwer, Nijhoff, 1982), p. 97.

6. Stephen D. Wesbrook, "The Potential for Military Disintegration," in *Combat Effectiveness: Cohesion, Stress, and the Volunteer Military,* ed. Sam C. Sarkesian (Beverly Hills and London: Sage Publications, 1980), p. 274. See also p. 260.

7. Alvin C. York, *Sergeant York: His Own Life Story and War Diary* (Garden City, N.Y.: Doubleday, Doran, 1928), p. 213. For similar comments, see Janice Holt Giles, ed., *The G.I. Journal of Sergeant Giles* (Boston: Houghton Mifflin, and Cambridge: Riverside Press, 1965), p. 377; Stanley Goff and Robert Sanders, with Clark Smith, *Brothers: Black Soldiers in the Nam* (Novato, Calif.: Presidio Press, 1982, p. 60; and Michael Lee Lanning, *The Only War We Had: A Platoon Leader's Journal of Vietnam* (New York: Ivy Books, 1987), pp. 24 and 95.

8. Richard D. Camp, with Eric Hammel, *Lima-6: A Marine Company Commander in Vietnam* (New York: Pocket Books, 1989), p. 167.

9. Francis P. Duffy, *Father Duffy's Story: A Tale of Humor and Heroism, of Life and Death with the Fighting Sixty-ninth* (Garden City, N.Y.: Garden City Publishing, 1919), p. 69. See also p. 207. Elton E. Mackin echoes Duffy's words: "We learned to close our minds to the memory of men who fell." See *Suddenly We Didn't Want to Die: Memoirs of a World War I Marine* (Novato, Calif.: Presidio Press, 1993), p. 122.

10. James Jones, *The Thin Red Line* (New York: Charles Scribner's Sons, 1962), p. 195.

11. Lyle Rishell, *With a Black Platoon in Combat: A Year in Korea* (College Station: Texas A&M University Press, 1993), p. 91. For another example from the Korean War, see the marines' reaction to the death of their company executive officer in Ernest Frankel, *Band of Brothers* (New York: Macmillan, 1958), pp. 220–221.

12. Jules W. Coleman, "The Group Factor in Military Psychiatry," *American Journal of Orthopsychiatry* 16:2 (April 1946): 224.

13. Roger W. Little, "Buddy Relations and Combat Performance," in *The New Military: Changing Patterns of Organization,* ed. Morris Janowitz (New York: Russell Sage, 1964), p. 200. Note that buddy relationships did not supplant the interpersonal bonds of the primary group, a point made by Little and also by Frederick J. Kviz, "Survival in Combat as a Collective Exchange Process," *Journal of Political and Military Sociology* 6:2 (fall 1978): 228–229.

14. Carl Andrew Brannen, *Over There: A Marine in the Great War* (College Station: Texas A&M University Press, 1996), pp. 46–47 and 51.

15. Roscoe C. Blunt Jr., *Inside the Battle of the Bulge: A Private Comes of Age*

(Westport, Conn., and London: Praeger, 1994), p. 173. For the ongoing Blunt-Everett relationship, see pp. 25, 51, 61, 64, 66, 69, 71, 78, 91, 135, 144, and 180–181.

16. For other examples of close buddy relationships, follow the case of Boesch and Jack Bochner in Paul Boesch, *Road to Huertgen: Forest in Hell* (Houston: Paul M. Boesch, 1985); William Pope and Jim Mahoney in William Young Boyd, *The Gentle Infantryman* (New York: St. Martin's Press, 1985); Kurt Gabel, Jake Dalton, and Joe Cooley in Kurt Gabel, *The Making of a Paratrooper: Airborne Training and Combat in World War II* (Lawrence: University Press of Kansas, 1990); and Lanning and Jerry Woody in Lanning, *Only War,* p. 52.

17. For a discussion of the traumatic impact on the soldier of the death of a close comrade, see Gray, *Warriors,* pp. 93–94, and John Keegan and Richard Holmes, with John Gau, *Soldiers: A History of Men in Battle* (New York: Viking, 1986), pp. 265–266.

18. York, *Sergeant York,* p. 272.

19. Giles, ed., *GI Journal,* p. 239. See also p. 152.

20. Howard Matthias, *The Korean War—Reflections of a Young Combat Platoon Leader,* rev. ed. (Tallahassee, Fla.: Father and Son Publishing, 1995), pp. 178 and 179.

21. Boris R. Spiroff, *Korea: Frozen Hell on Earth* (New York: Vantage Press, 1995), p. 51. The psychiatrist Jonathan Shay, in his work with Vietnam War veterans suffering from Post-traumatic Stress Disorder, found that the obstruction of grief was an important contributing favor in some PTSD cases. Soldiers could not properly grieve for dead comrades because, as in Spiroff's case, the exigencies of combat did not permit it, but also because open grieving was considered "unmanly." The memoirs validate the importance of grieving when a close friend was lost. See Shay's *Achilles in Vietnam: Combat Trauma and the Undoing of Character* (New York: Scribner, 1995), pp. 55–68.

22. For a discussion of some soldiers' reluctance to make new friends in combat, see Shay, *Achilles,* pp. 40–53.

23. Johnson quoted in Eric Bergerud, *Touched with Fire: The Land War in the South Pacific* (New York: Viking Penguin, 1996), p. 441. See also the comments of Adam DiGenaro on the same page.

24. Michaud interview in Donald Knox, *The Korean War: Pusan to Chosin: An Oral History* (San Diego, New York, and London: Harcourt Brace Jovanovich, 1985), p. 670.

25. For a comment about their infantry company's "core identity," see Harold P. Leinbaugh and John D. Campbell, *The Men of Company K* (New York: Bantam Books, 1987), p. xix. See also Charles R. Cawthon, *Other Clay: A Remembrance of the World War II Infantry* (Niwot: University Press of Colorado, 1990), p. 131.

26. For a discussion of "social control," see Samuel A. Stouffer, Edward A. Suchman, Leland C. DeVinney, Shirley A. Star, and Robin M. Williams Jr., *Studies in Social Psychology in World War II,* vol. 1, *The American Soldier: Adjustment During Army Life* (Princeton: Princeton University Press, 1949), pp. 410–423. See also pp. 423–429 on group rewards and punishments. For a discussion of the doughboy "folk identity" and the norms set by the doughboy primary group, see Robert Sandels, "The Doughboy: Formation of a Military Folk," *American Studies* 24:1 (1983): 75–81. For group norms in World War II, see S. Kirson Weinberg, "Problems of Adjustment in Army Units," *American Journal of Sociology* 50:4 (January 1945): 271–278.

27. Kviz, "Survival in Combat," p. 225. For a discussion of group norms in combat in the Korean War, see Little, "Buddy Relations," in Janowitz, ed., *New Military,* pp.

200–219. For group norms in Vietnam, see James R. Ebert, *A Life in a Year: The American Infantryman in Vietnam, 1965–1972* (Novato, Calif.: Presidio Press, 1993), pp. 119–130.

28. Bob Hoffman, *I Remember the Last War* (York, Pa.: Strength and Health Publishing, 1940), p. 227; for other examples, see pp. 180 and 251.

29. Lieutenant General Robert Lee Bullard, a field army commander by war's end, is one of the few senior commanders to attest to a serious straggler problem. See Robert Lee Bullard, with Earl Reeves, *American Soldiers Also Fought* (New York and Toronto: Longmans, Green, 1936), p. 66. See also the discussion of straggling in Mark Meigs, *Optimism at Armageddon: Voices of American Participants in the First World War* (Washington Square, N.Y.: New York University Press, 1997), pp. 60–62.

30. Joseph D. Lawrence, *Fighting Soldier: The A.E.F. in 1918* (Boulder: Colorado Associated University Press, 1985), p. 92. For other examples of doughboy slacking, or straggling, see Mackin, *We Didn't Want to Die,* pp. 207, 144–145, 219, and 230; Hervey Allen, *Toward the Flame: A War Diary* (New York: Grosset and Dunlap, 1934), pp. 62–63, 186, and 235; Brannen, *Over There,* pp. 34–36; Albert M. Ettinger and A. Churchill Ettinger, *A Doughboy with the Fighting Sixty-ninth: A Remembrance of World War I* (Shippensburg, Pa.: White Mane Publishing, 1992), pp. 100–101 and 108–109; Henry Berry, *Make the Kaiser Dance: Living Memories of the Doughboy* (New York: Priam Books, 1978), pp. 214–215; and William March, *Company K* (New York: Sagamore Press, 1957), pp. 141–143.

31. Lester Atwell, *Private* (New York: Popular Library, 1958), p. 166; Braaf continued to shirk, eventually deserted, and was caught and court-martialed (pp. 179, 181, 275, and 528). See also George Wilson, *If You Survive* (New York: Ivy Books, 1987), p. 157.

32. Carl M. Becker and Robert G. Thobaben, *Common Warfare: Parallel Memoirs by Two World War II GIs in the Pacific* (Jefferson, N.C., and London: McFarland, 1992), p. 171.

33. Lanning, *Only War,* p. 198. For another example of a Vietnam War malingerer despised by his platoon and harshly dealt with, see Frederick Downs, *The Killing Zone: My Life in the Vietnam War* (New York: Berkley Books, 1983), pp. 56–58. See also the case of Brennan's radioman in Matthew Brennan, *Brennan's War: Vietnam, 1965–1969* (New York: Pocket Books, 1986), pp. 26 and 37.

34. Goff and Sanders, *Brothers*, p. 87. See also pp. 131 and 145–146.

35. See Herbert Hendin and Ann Pollinger Haas, *Wounds of War: The Psychological Aftermath of Combat in Vietnam* (New York: Basic Books, 1984), p. 208.

36. Blunt, *Inside,* p. 169.

37. Fox interview in Knox, *Pusan to Chosin,* p. 421.

38. Jack Fuller, *Fragments* (New York: Dell, 1985), p. 78.

39. Eugene B. Sledge, *With the Old Breed at Peleliu and Okinawa* (New York: Bantam Books, 1983), pp. 111–112; for another example, see Henry Berry, *Semper Fi, Mac: Living Memories of the U.S. Marines in World War II* (New York: Berkley Books, 1983), p. 78.

40. Matthias, *Reflections,* p. 133. See also p. 134. Rudolph W. Stephens's company in Korea also took harsh measures against men who fell asleep when on patrol. See *Old Ugly Hill: A G.I.'s Fourteen Months in the Korean Trenches, 1952–1953* (Jefferson, N.C., and London: McFarland, 1995), pp. 53–54 and 93.

41. Historians, psychiatrists, and sociologists have noted the critical role of self-esteem, personal honor, pride, "ego-preservation," and so forth, in motivating the soldier within the context of the primary group. See John Ellis, *The Sharp End: The Fighting Man in World War II* (New York: Charles Scribner's Sons, 1980), pp. 312–319; Richard Holmes, *Acts of War: The Behavior of Men in Battle* (New York: Free Press, 1985), pp. 301–307; John Keegan, *The Face of Battle* (New York: Viking Press, 1976), pp. 52–53; Marshall, *Men Against Fire,* pp. 148–149; Herbert X. Spiegel, "Preventive Psychiatry with Combat Troops," *American Journal of Psychiatry* 101:3 (November 1944): 310; Stouffer et al., *Combat and Its Aftermath,* pp. 135–145; and S. Kirson Weinberg, "The Combat Neuroses," *American Journal of Sociology* 51:5 (March 1946): 473–474.

42. Cutler interview in Berry, *Make the Kaiser Dance,* p. 216.

43. Brannen, *Over There,* p. 48.

44. Bradford Perkins, "Impressions of Wartime," *Journal of American History* 77:2 (September 1990): 566. See also Paul Fussell, *Doing Battle: The Making of a Skeptic* (Boston: Little, Brown, 1996), pp. 124–125, and Leon C. Standifer, *Not in Vain: A Rifleman Remembers World War II* (Baton Rouge and London: Louisiana State University Press, 1992), pp. 249–250.

45. Winter interview in Rudy Tomedi, *No Bugles, No Drums: An Oral History of the Korean War* (New York: John Wiley and Sons, 1993), pp. 26–27.

46. Alfred S. Bradford, *Some Even Volunteered: The First Wolfhounds Pacify Vietnam* (Westport, Conn., and London: Praeger, 1994), pp. 150 and 148–149.

47. Joseph A. Blake and Suellen Butler, "The Medal of Honor, Combat Orientations and Latent Role Structure in the United States Military," *Sociological Quarterly* 17:4 (autumn 1976): 561–567. See also a broader survey of Congressional Medals of Honor by Jeffery W. Anderson, "Military Heroism: An Occupational Definition," *Armed Forces and Society* 12:4 (summer 1986): 591–606. Anderson derives a definition of heroism based on the citations for 337 CMHs awarded from 1863 to 1979. This definition contains eight characteristics that involve both "soldier saving" and "war winning" (although Anderson does not use these terms), and this definition held true for all wars from the Civil War through Vietnam.

48. Cawthon, *Other Clay,* p. 74.

49. See Marshall, *Men Against Fire,* pp. 155–156.

50. For a discussion of going "AWOL to the front," see Holmes, *Acts of War,* pp. 299–300, and Lee Kennett, *G.I.: The American Soldier in World War II* (New York: Charles Scribner's Sons, 1987), pp. 139–140.

51. Duffy, *Story,* p. 322.

52. Ibid., p. 209. See also p. 88 and the Krahnert interview in Berry, *Make the Kaiser Dance,* p. 43.

53. Bill Mauldin, *Up Front* (New York: Award Books, 1976), pp. 126–127.

54. Standifer, *Not in Vain,* p. 195.

55. William Manchester, *Goodbye, Darkness: A Memoir of the Pacific War* (Boston and Toronto: Little, Brown, 1979), p. 391. For other World War II examples of going or threatening to go AWOL to the front, see Gerald Astor, *Crisis in the Pacific: The Battles for the Philippine Islands by the Men Who Fought Them* (New York: Donald I. Fine Books, 1996), p. 418; Berry, *Semper Fi,* pp. 100–101; Harold L. Bond, *Return to Cassino* (New York: Pocket Books, 1965), p. 149; Allen R. Matthews, *The Assault* (New York:

Dodd, Mead, 1980), p.167; and Richard Tregaskis, *Invasion Diary* (New York: Random House, 1944), p. 239.

56. Chase interview in Donald Knox, with additional text by Alfred Coppel, *The Korean War: Uncertain Victory: The Concluding Volume of an Oral History* (San Diego, New York, and London: Harcourt Brace Jovanovich, 1988), pp. 152–153.

57. Philip Caputo, *A Rumor of War* (New York: Ballantine Books, 1978), p. 146.

58. For a discussion of "vertical bonding," see Faris R. Kirkland, Paul T. Bartone, and David H. Marlowe, "Commanders' Priorities and Psychological Readiness," *Armed Forces and Society* 19:4 (summer 1993): 579–598. For a discussion of "hierarchical cohesion," see Alexander L. George, "Primary Groups, Organization, and Military Performance," in *Handbook of Military Institutions,* ed. Roger W. Little (Beverly Hills, Calif.: Sage, 1971), pp. 306–311.

59. Wesbrook, "Military Disintegration," in Sarkesian, ed., *Combat Effectiveness,* p. 274 (I also cited Wesbrook in note 6).

60. Morris Janowitz, for example, believes American acceptance of warfare in the late nineteenth century did not require a specific ideological cause: "At the turn of the century the military considered the national purposes of war as self-evident; they did not require explicit ideological justification. . . . It sufficed to operate on the self-evident principle of common defense, and on the implicit moral crusade to enforce American-type law and order" (*The Professional Soldier: A Social and Political Portrait* [New York: Free Press, 1960, prologue added in 1974], p. 262).

61. John Dollard, with Donald Horton, *Fear in Battle* (New York: AMS Press, 1976), p. 46. For other discussions of the value of unit esprit, see Holmes, *Acts of War,* pp. 308–315, and Kellett, *Combat Motivation,* pp. 46–56.

62. Amos N. Wilder, *Armageddon Revisited: A World War I Journal* (New Haven and London: Yale University Press, 1994), p. 145.

63. Ibid., p. 144.

64. See Sandels, "Doughboy," pp. 74–75, for a discussion of the emergence of the division as a focus for unit esprit in World War I.

65. Mauldin, *Up Front,* p. 1.

66. Little, "Buddy Relations," in Janowitz, ed., *New Military,* p. 204.

67. Ibid., p. 205. See also James Hamilton Dill, *Sixteen Days at Mungol-li* (Fayetteville, Ark.: M&M Press, 1993), pp. 402–404, for the importance of regimental esprit.

68. Samuel L. A. Marshall, *Commentary on Infantry Operations and Weapons Usage in Korea, Winter of 1950–51,* Operations Research Office Report 13 (Chevy Chase, Md.: Johns Hopkins University Press, 1953), p. xvi; he also noted that regimental pride was operative during the Korean War, but "there was relatively less interest in loyalty to the division" than there had been in the world wars (p. xvii).

69. Standifer, *Not in Vain,* p. 81.

70. Goff and Sanders, *Brothers,* p. 58. See also pp. 173–174.

71. For an analysis of the Marine Corps' effort to establish and sustain its image as a unique, elite force, see Craig M. Cameron, *American Samurai: Myth, Imagination, and the Conduct of Battle in the First Marine Division, 1941–1951* (Cambridge: Cambridge University Press, 1994).

72. See the comments in Gerald P. Averill, *Mustang: A Combat Marine* (Novato, Calif.: Presidio Press, 1987), p. 98, and Berry, *Semper Fi,* pp. 116 and 125.

73. See Leon Uris, *Battle Cry* (New York, London, and Toronto: Bantam Books, 1953). Uris's novel is based on his World War II service with the Sixth Marines. See especially the classic barroom brawl between Sixth Marines and Eighth Marines in New Zealand, instigated by snide comments about "pogey-bait whistles" (pp. 270–271).

74. Sledge, *Old Breed*, p. 101.

75. Martin Russ, *The Last Parallel: A Marine's War Journal* (New York and Toronto: Rinehart, 1957), p. 133.

76. See Thomas M. Camfield, "'Will to Win'—the U.S. Army Troop Morale Program of World War I," *Military Affairs* 41:3 (October 1977): 125–128.

77. Hans Speier, "'The American Soldier' and the Sociology of Military Organization," in Merton and Lazarsfeld, eds., *Continuities*, p. 116.

78. See Stouffer et al., *Adjustment During Army Life*, chapter 9, "The Orientation of Soldiers Toward the War," pp. 430–485, for the overall findings of the Research Branch concerning the lack of ideological motivation and the War Department's effort to establish troop orientation programs, such as Frank Capra's famous "Why We Fight" films.

79. John W. Thomason Jr., *Fix Bayonets!* (New York: Blue Ribbon Books, 1926), p. 136.

80. [Howard V. O'Brien], *Wine, Women, and War: A Diary of Disillusionment* (New York: J. H. Sears, 1926), p. 37. See also p. 24.

81. Several historians comment on the prevailing attitude among GIs of "let's get the war over with and go home." See Michael C. C. Adams, *The Best War Ever: America and World War II* (Baltimore and London: Johns Hopkins University Press, 1994), pp. 88–89; Ellis, *Sharp End*, pp. 286–288; and Kennett, *G.I.*, p. 140.

82. Ralph Ingersoll, *The Battle Is the Payoff* (New York: Harcourt, Brace, 1943), p. 74.

83. Robert Leckie, *Helmet for My Pillow* (Garden City, N.Y.: Nelson Doubleday, 1978), pp. 25–26; for a similar call for a cause, or "positive aim," see Grinker and Spiegel, *War Neuroses*, p. 119.

84. See Stouffer et al., *Adjustment During Army Life*, pp. 458–485, for a discussion of the Information and Education Division's indoctrination program (see note 76 on the Morale Branch).

85. [O'Brien], *Wine, Women, and War*, pp. 96 and 42. See also Mackin, *We Didn't Want to Die*, p. 55.

86. Will Judy, *A Soldier's Diary: A Day-to-Day Record in the World War* (Chicago: Judy Publishing, 1931), p. 125.

87. Stouffer et al., *Adjustment During Army Life*, pp. 473–484.

88. Spiegel, "Preventive Psychiatry," p. 311. John Ellis also notes the World War II soldiers' lack of interest in ideological issues. See his *Sharp End*, pp. 281–282.

89. Charles C. Moskos Jr., *The American Enlisted Man: The Rank and File in Today's Military* (New York: Russell Sage Foundation, 1970), p. 148.

90. Stouffer et al., *Combat and Its Aftermath*, p. 151.

91. Shils, "Primary Groups," in Merton and Lazarsfeld, eds., *Continuities*, p. 22. See also p. 24.

92. Moskos, *American Enlisted Man*, p. 147. See also William Darryl Henderson, *Cohesion: The Human Element in Combat: Leadership and Societal Influence in the Armies of the Soviet Union, the United States, North Vietnam, and Israel* (Washington,

D.C.: National Defense University Press, 1988), pp. 98–99; Speier, "Sociology of Military Organization," in Merton and Lazarsfeld, eds., *Continuities*, p. 117; Wesbrook, "Military Disintegration," in Sarkesian, ed., *Combat Effectiveness*, pp. 253–256; and Elliot P. Chodoff, "Ideology and Primary Groups," *Armed Forces and Society* 9:4 (summer 1983): 581–582.

93. Ernie Pyle, *Here Is Your War: The Story of G.I. Joe* (Cleveland and New York: World Publishing, 1945), p. 297.

94. Ernie Pyle, *Brave Men* (New York: Henry Holt, 1944), p. 6.

95. Ira Wolfert, *Battle for the Solomons* (Cambridge, Mass.: Riverside Press, 1943), p. 196.

96. Boesch, *Road to Huertgen*, p. 114. For similar statements by GIs about the justness of their cause, see the Norman Mailer interview in Eric James Schroeder, *Vietnam, We've All Been There: Interviews with American Writers* (London and Westport, Conn.: Praeger, 1992), pp. 92–93; Blunt, *Inside*, p. 73; Dan Levin, *From the Battlefield: Dispatches of a World War II Marine* (Annapolis, Md.: Naval Institute Press, 1995), p. 48; Wilson, *If You Survive*, p. 157; and Fussell, *Doing Battle*, p. 99.

97. Frankel, *Band of Brothers*, p. 176.

98. Peter G. Bourne, *Men, Stress, and Vietnam* (Boston: Little, Brown, 1970), pp. 44–45.

99. Dominick Yezzo, *A G.I.'s Vietnam Diary, 1968–1969* (New York: Franklin Watts, 1974), author's note at start of book.

100. Little, "Buddy Relations," in Janowitz, ed., *New Military*, pp. 205–206.

101. Patton's words as recalled by the historian Martin Blumenson, who as a young officer in World War II served on the Third Army staff. See *Patton: The Man Behind the Legend, 1885–1945* (New York: William Morrow, 1985), p. 223.

102. [O'Brien], *Wine, Women, and War*, pp. 168 and 109. See also Judy, *Soldier's Diary*, p. 13.

103. George William Sefton, *It Was My War: I'll Remember It the Way I Want To!* (Manhattan, Kans.: Sunflower University Press, 1994), p. 52. See also the Leacock interview in Studs Terkel, *"The Good War": An Oral History of World War II* (New York: Pantheon Books, 1984), p. 375, and the Johnny DeGrazio interview on p. 162.

104. James Brady, "Leaving for Korea," *American Heritage* 48:1 (February/March 1997): 88. See also Curtis James Morrow, *What's a Commie Ever Done to Black People? A Korean War Memoir of Fighting in the U.S. Army's Last All Negro Unit* (Jefferson, N.C., and London: McFarland, 1997), p. 61.

105. Tim O'Brien, *Going After Cacciato* (New York: Dell, 1979), p. 377. See also p. 68.

106. "A War for Nothing" is the title and theme of chapter 7 in Christian G. Appy's *Working-Class War: American Combat Soldiers and Vietnam* (Chapel Hill and London: University of North Carolina Press, 1993), pp. 206–249. See also Ebert, *A Life in a Year*, p. xii.

107. Pat Frank, *Hold Back the Night* (Philadelphia and New York: J. B. Lippincott, 1952), p. 45.

108. See Gray, *Warriors*, p. 42, and Kellett, *Combat Motivation*, pp. 251–253.

109. The Stouffer Study comments on the value to morale of such "local victories" (*Combat and Its Aftermath*, p. 170).

110. Pyle, *Brave Men*, p. 103. See also Tregaskis, *Invasion*, p. 130, and Blunt, *Inside*, p. 31.

111. Fenton interview in Knox, *Pusan to Chosin*, p. 122. For other examples, see Boesch, *Road to Huertgen*, pp. 105–106; Henry Berry, *Hey, Mac, Where Ya Been? Living Memories of the U.S. Marines in the Korean War* (New York: St. Martin's Press, 1988), p. 208; and Knox, *Uncertain Victory*, p. 13.

112. David Halberstam, *One Very Hot Day* (Boston: Houghton Mifflin, 1967), p. 114. See also Ebert, *A Life in a Year*, p. 188; Appy, *Working-Class War*, pp. 225–226; and Hendin and Haas, *Wounds*, pp. 8–9.

113. Goff and Sanders, *Brothers*, p. 134. For another example, see the Paul Buckman (a pseudonym) case in Hendin and Haas, *Wounds*, p. 206.

114. Virtually every history of the Vietnam War comments on the problems inherent in the body count, both in its accuracy and as a measure of victory. Perhaps most telling is a survey of army generals who had served in Vietnam, which reveals that the senior leaders themselves had serious reservations about the accuracy and usefulness of the body count. See Douglas Kinnard, *The War Managers: American Generals Reflect on Vietnam* (New York: Da Capo Press, 1991), pp. 72–75. See also Thomas C. Thayer, *War Without Fronts: The American Experience in Vietnam* (Boulder and London: Westview Press, 1985), pp. 101–104, and Ebert, *A Life in a Year*, pp. 271–276.

115. Downs, *Killing Zone*, p. 175.

116. Tim O'Brien, *If I Die in a Combat Zone: Box Me Up and Ship Me Home* (New York: Laurel, Dell, 1987), pp. 129–130.

117. Robert Mason, *Chickenhawk* (New York: Penguin Books, 1986), p. 131. Of course, though Mason's observation is generally valid, the enemy did stand and fight the First Cavalry Division when it first arrived in Vietnam and by all accounts suffered heavy losses for their trouble. But the Viet Cong and North Vietnamese Army then backed off to lick their wounds, recover, and learn how to deal with the cavalry's helicopters.

118. For examples of frustrated soldiers clamoring to "go north," see William D. Ehrhart, *Vietnam-Perkasie: A Combat Marine Memoir* (Jefferson, N.C., and London: McFarland, 1983), p. 205; Wallace Terry, *Bloods, an Oral History of the Vietnam War by Black Veterans* (New York: Ballantine Books, 1985), pp. 110–111 and 214; and Ralph Zumbro, *Tank Sergeant* (Novato, Calif.: Presidio Press, 1986), p. 26.

119. Appy and Ebert and the sociologist John Helmer concluded that a majority of Vietnam War soldiers understood that America was in Vietnam to help democratic South Vietnam survive and to contain the spread of Communism, although as Helmer points out, understanding did not equate to personal commitment. See Appy, *Working-Class War*, pp. 209–212; Ebert, *A Life in a Year*, pp. 11–12; and John Helmer, *Bringing the War Home: The American Soldier in Vietnam and After* (New York: Free Press, and London: Collier Macmillan Publishers, 1974), p. 144.

120. See Robert Jay Lifton, *Home from the War: Vietnam Veterans: Neither Victims nor Executioners* (New York: Simon and Schuster, 1973), p. 40. See also Edward Tabor Linenthal, "From Hero to Anti-hero: The Transformation of the Warrior in Modern America," *Soundings: An Interdisciplinary Journal* 63:1 (spring 1980): 79–83. Linenthal describes how the American soldier's view of himself as a heroic figure fighting for a just cause was shaken in Vietnam.

121. John Ketwig, *And a Hard Rain Fell* (New York: Pocket Books, 1986), p. 32.

Ketwig specifically mentions his expectation of being treated as a liberator. He was even more disappointed than the average soldier: "Secretly, I hoped to be greeted like a G.I. liberating France in World War II. The people resented us. . . . Downtown [Pleiku], we were treated like an invading army. Try as I might, I was never able to find the exotic, inscrutable Asian culture. Everywhere I looked, I found a society of murderers, thieves, and carnival hucksters" (pp. 70–71).

122. Ehrhart, *Vietnam-Perkasie*, p. 61. The memoirs provide overwhelming evidence of the American soldiers' dislike, even hatred, for the South Vietnamese, but this dislike has also been verified by surveys. See Byron G. Fiman, Jonathan F. Borus, and M. Duncan Stanton, "Black-White and American-Vietnamese Relations Among Soldiers in Vietnam," *Journal of Social Issues* 31:4 (fall 1975): 39–48. See also Thayer, *War Without Fronts*, pp. 186–188, for surveys of South Vietnamese civilians conducted in 1971 in which a majority admitted to not liking or even hating Americans and believing that the Americans felt the same way toward them.

123. David Parks, *G.I. Diary* (New York, Evanston, and London: Harper and Row, 1968), p. 94. The rate at which a grunt's expectations faded varied, but fade they did. Lieutenant Lanning, for example, used the term "gook" in his diary for the first time only after three months in Vietnam. His decision finally to do so "aptly showed my loss of respect for Vietnamese of both sides" (*Only War*, p. 164). See also the case of Dominick Yezzo, who, as a member of a civil affairs team, tried harder than most to sympathize with the plight of the South Vietnamese but after nine months was "sick of Vietnam and its people." Trace his shifting attitude in his *Vietnam Diary*, entries for September 18 and 29, October 2, and May 11, 14, and 28.

124. John Sack, *M* (New York: Avon Books, 1985), p. 210. See also pp. 188–189.

125. Goff and Sanders, *Brothers*, p. 133.

126. Ibid.

127. These security forces, incidentally, did more fighting than they are generally given credit for, especially the Regional and Provisional Forces, nicknamed the "Ruff Puffs" by the Americans. See Thayer, *War Without Fronts*, pp. 155–167.

128. Mason, *Chickenhawk*, p. 404.

129. Rawls interview in Al Santoli, *Everything We Had: An Oral History of the Vietnam War by Thirty-three American Soldiers Who Fought It* (New York: Ballantine Books, 1982), p. 157. For other examples of grunt disdain for the ARVN, see Bradford, *Volunteered*, pp. 19–20, 115, and 161–162; Ehrhart, *Vietnam-Perkasie*, pp. 61 and 265–266; Ron Kovic, *Born on the Fourth of July* (New York: Pocket Books, 1977), p. 219; and Santoli, *Everything We Had*, pp. 117 and 137. See also Ebert, *A Life in a Year*, pp. 234–235.

130. Caputo, *Rumor of War*, p. 317. See also Mark Baker, *Nam: The Vietnam War in the Words of the Men and Women Who Fought There* (New York: Berkley Books, 1983), p. 93.

131. See comments by Ketwig, *Hard Rain*, pp. 85–86, and Mason, *Chickenhawk*, pp. 440–441.

132. Moskos, *American Enlisted Man*, p. x, and Bourne, *Men, Stress*, p. viii.

133. Bourne, *Men, Stress*, p. 40. See also pp. 43–44.

134. A survey by Howard Schuman shows that antiwar sentiment jumped dramatically after Tet, not for the ideological or moralistic reasons championed by the middle-class, campus-centered antiwar movement but because of growing disillusionment,

especially among the working class, over how the war was being prosecuted and the heavy price being paid in American lives (see "Two Sources of Antiwar Sentiment in America," *American Journal of Sociology* 78:3 [November 1972]: 513–536). Charles Moskos agrees with Schuman's assessment: "American public opinion was moved after 1969 by such pragmatic considerations as the unanticipated strength of enemy forces, the adoption of a 'no-win' military policy, and most important, distress over continued American casualties" (see *S. L. A. Marshall Chair: Soldiers and Sociology*, U.S. Army Research Institute for the Behavioral and Social Sciences [Washington, D.C.: U.S. Government Printing Office, 1988], p. 12).

135. Ebert notes that draftees totaled 21 percent of America's combat force in Vietnam in 1965 but 70 percent in 1970, with a concomitant increase in draftee battle deaths from 16 percent in 1967 to 43 percent in 1970. See *A Life in a Year*, p. 17.

136. Appy, *Working-Class War*, p. 208.

137. Moskos, *S. L. A. Marshall Chair*, p. 12. See also Kurt Lang, "American Performance in Vietnam: Background and Analysis," *Journal of Political and Military Sociology* 8:2 (fall 1980): 279; Thomas Myers, *Walking Point: American Narratives of Vietnam* (New York and Oxford: Oxford University Press, 1988), pp. 140–141; and Samuel Hynes, *The Soldiers' Tale: Bearing Witness to Modern War* (New York: Allen Lane, 1997), pp. 209–211. Grunts' doubts about the cause were also passed from veteran to new guy in-country, "resulting in a slowly maturing pessimism that was inherited and inculcated in the squads and fireteams" (see Ebert, *A Life in a Year*, p. 233).

138. Anderson interview in Terry, *Bloods*, p. 226. See also Brennan, *Brennan's War*, pp. 195–196.

139. Dave Grossman, *On Killing: The Psychological Cost of Learning to Kill in War and Society* (Boston: Little, Brown, 1995), p. 277.

140. Moskos, *American Enlisted Man*, p. 34. See also Thomas J. Begines, "The American Military and the Western Idea," *Military Review* 72:3 (March 1992): 45–46, for a discussion of the growing alienation between the Vietnam War soldier and American society.

141. Incidentally, that a majority of grunts late in the war became disillusioned with either the cause or the way the war was being fought is not in doubt, as evidenced by a survey of returning veterans that was read into the *Congressional Record* in May 1971: 47 percent said the war was a mistake, 40 percent said it was not a mistake but fought incorrectly, and 10 percent said simply that it was not a mistake (survey cited in Helmer, *Bringing the War*, p. 35 and p. 31 n. 75).

142. Mason, *Chickenhawk*, p. 162.

143. John M. Del Vecchio, *The 13th Valley* (New York: Bantam Books, 1983), p. 96.

144. Grossman, *On Killing*, p. 277.

145. Ehrhart, *Vietnam-Perkasie*, p. 204.

146. Sack, *M*, p. 137. See also James Webb, *Fields of Fire* (New York: Bantam Books, 1979), p. 210.

147. Appy, *Working-Class War*, p. 51; he notes, however, that draft avoidance was not as common, or as acceptable, among working-class youth.

148. Hynes, *Soldiers' Tale*, p. 182. See also James Fallows, "What Did You Do in the Class War, Daddy?" *Washington Monthly* 7:8 (October 1975): 5.

149. Ketwig, *Hard Rain*, p. 289. The sometimes hostile reception that returning Viet-

nam veterans received stood in stark contrast to earlier wars; for examples, see Ebert, *A Life in a Year*, pp. 341–343, and the "Homecoming" chapter in Baker, *Nam*, pp. 239–268.

150. William L. Hauser, "The Will to Fight," in Sarkesian, ed., *Combat Effectiveness*, p. 189.

151. O'Brien, *Cacciato*, pp. 240–241.

152. Del Vecchio, *13th Valley*, p. 163.

153. John H. Faris, "An Alternative Perspective to Savage and Gabriel," *Armed Forces and Society* 3:3 (May 1977): 459–460.

154. Wesbrook, "Military Disintegration," in Sarkesian, ed., *Combat Effectiveness*, p. 257. For other discussions about the disintegration of hierarchical cohesion in the Vietnam War, see Chodoff, "Ideology," pp. 588–590; Helmer, *Bringing the War*, pp. 43–48; Kviz, "Survival in Combat," p. 229; Lang, "Performance in Vietnam," pp. 274–276; Moskos, *S. L. A. Marshall Chair*, pp. 12–13; Kellett, *Combat Motivation*, pp. 107–112; and Holmes, *Acts of War*, pp. 316–317.

155. Goff and Sanders, *Brothers*, p. 33; Goff then provides an example on p. 34 of faking contact with the enemy while on a night patrol. The grunts fired a few rounds and scurried back to base camp.

156. For examples of these various forms of combat avoidance, see Baker, *Nam*, pp. 42 and 189; Brennan, *Brennan's War*, pp. 267–269; and O'Brien, *If I Die*, pp. 90 and 108. Even more serious were "combat refusals"—units of company-size and below that openly refused to carry out orders to conduct a specific combat operation. Richard Gabriel and Paul L. Savage believe that as many as 245 such refusals may have occurred in 1970, but they are speculating. See *Crisis in Command: Mismanagement in the Army* (New York: Hill and Wang, 1978), pp. 45–46. Gabriel and Savage's statistics are questionable, but combat refusals did occur; for examples, see Appy, *Working-Class War*, p. 231.

157. Anderson interview in Terry, *Bloods*, p. 223.

158. Biggers interview in ibid., p. 113.

159. Santos interview in Santoli, *Everything We Had*, p. 121.

160. Hendin and Haas, *Wounds*, p. 207.

161. Sarah A. Haley, "When the Patient Reports Atrocities: Specific Treatment Considerations of the Vietnam Veteran," *Archives of General Psychiatry* 30:2 (February 1974): 193. See also Vernon Janick quoted in Ebert, *A Life in a Year*, p. 122.

162. See Appy, *Working-Class War*, pp. 246–247; Gabriel and Savage, *Crisis in Command*, pp. 44–45 and 66–67; Thomas C. Bond, "The Why of Fragging," *American Journal of Psychiatry* 133:11 (November 1976): 1328–1331; and Charles C. Moskos Jr., "The American Combat Soldier in Vietnam," *Journal of Social Issues* 31:4 (fall 1975): 34–35. For fraggings, or threats of fragging, in the Vietnam War literature, see Brennan, *Brennan's War*, p. 286; Ketwig, *Hard Rain*, pp. 88–91; Mason, *Chickenhawk*, p. 384; Terry, *Bloods*, p. 212; Webb, *Fields of Fire*, pp. 140–142; and O'Brien, *Cacciato*, pp. 278–282.

163. Wilson, *If You Survive*, p. 116; for other World War II examples, see Fussell, *Doing Battle*, p. 111, and Mary Penick Motley, *The Invisible Soldier: The Experience of the Black Soldier, World War II* (Detroit: Wayne State University Press, 1975), p. 284.

164. Cawthon, *Other Clay*, p. 121.

165. A. E. Ashworth, "The Sociology of Trench Warfare, 1914–1918," *British Journal of Sociology* 19:4 (December 1968): 420.

166. Fussell, *Doing Battle,* p. 110. For an example of "live and let live" in effect in the Italian campaign during World War II, see Motley, *Invisible Soldier,* pp. 308–309.

167. Hoffman, *I Remember,* pp. 260–261. For a fictional example from World War I, see March, *Company K,* pp. 55–58.

168. Gabel, *Paratrooper,* p. 204.

169. Ibid., p. 205; the lieutenant survived this artillery barrage but was killed later in the war. See also the Eugene Lester interview in Motley, *Invisible Soldier,* p. 307.

170. Comparisons of the Korean and Vietnam Wars are scarce. James Toner, a professor of government, identifies several of the problems in the Korean War that surfaced again in Vietnam: loss of faith in the cause, disdain for the people ostensibly being saved, and the pros and cons of a rotation system. See "American Society and the American Way of War: Korea and Beyond," *Parameters* 11:1 (spring 1981): 79–90.

171. Theodore R. Fehrenbach, *This Kind of War: A Study in Unpreparedness* (New York: Macmillan, 1963), p. 658. See also Toner, "American Society," pp. 88–89, for another call for legions.

172. Frank, *Hold Back the Night,* p. 43. See also pp. 39–40. The issue of American credibility as a Cold War ally also crops up in this novel, foreshadowing similar concerns during the Vietnam War. If America was driven out of Korea by the Chinese and "came back home with its tail between its legs, then the whole world would know that the United States couldn't hold Berlin or Vienna, or the line of the Elbe, or the Dardanelles, or the oil fields of the Middle East" (p. 137).

173. Dill, *Mungol-li,* p. 356.

174. Ibid., p. 170.

175. John A. Sullivan, *Toy Soldiers: Memoir of a Combat Platoon Leader in Korea* (Jefferson, N.C., and London: McFarland, 1991), p. 19. See also p. ix.

176. Russ, *Last Parallel,* p. 293. Comments on and bitterness over the war's senselessness are common in accounts by soldiers who served after the Chinese intervention. For further examples, see Knox, *Uncertain Victory,* pp. 23 and 211; William H. Mauldin, *Bill Mauldin in Korea* (New York: W. W. Norton, 1952), p. 9; Tomedi, *No Bugles,* p. 102; and Matthias, *Reflections*, p. xiii.

177. Muskat interview in Knox, *Uncertain Victory,* p. 406.

178. Sullivan, *Toy Soldiers,* p. 101. For other examples of combat avoidance or complaints about the senseless patrolling in Korea, see Berry, *Hey, Mac,* p. 290; Matthias, *Reflections,* pp. 99–100; and Russ, *Last Parallel,* p. 314.

179. See Fehrenbach, *This Kind of War,* pp. 166 and 218. See also Jim Holton interview in Tomedi, *No Bugles,* pp. 200–201.

180. Baker interview in Berry, *Hey, Mac,* p. 216.

181. Matthias, *Reflections,* p. 78; for other negative comments about ROK Army or KATUSA soldiers, see Charles S. Crawford, *The Four Deuces: A Korean War Story* (Novato, Calif.: Presidio Press, 1989), p. 209; Joseph R. Owen, *Colder Than Hell: A Marine Rifle Company at Chosin Reservoir* (Annapolis, Md.: Naval Institute Press, 1996), pp. 84, 101, and 232; Knox, *Pusan to Chosin,* p. 296; Knox, *Uncertain Victory,* p. 164; and Rishell, *Black Platoon,* p. 33.

182. Muetzel interview in Knox, *Uncertain Victory,* p. 369. See also Berry, *Hey, Mac,* p. 1.

183. Frankel, *Band of Brothers,* p. 177. See also p. 290.

184. Matthias, *Reflections,* p. 170.

185. Morrow, *Commie,* p. 102. Dill also comments on the shift to a force consisting primarily of draftees by late 1951 and implies that this shift was not for the better. See *Mungol-li,* p. 402.

186. Tomedi, *No Bugles,* p. vi.

## CHAPTER 6. FAILING TO COPE WITH THE ENVIRONMENT OF WAR

1. Jonathan Shay, *Achilles in Vietnam: Combat Trauma and the Undoing of Character* (New York: Scribner, 1995), p. 152.

2. Eric Bergerud, *Touched with Fire: The Land War in the South Pacific* (New York: Viking, 1996), p. 445.

3. Albert Glass, introduction, in *The Psychology and Physiology of Stress: With Reference to Special Studies of the Viet Nam War,* ed. Peter G. Bourne (New York and London: Academic Press, 1969), pp. xiv–xv. See also Thomas W. Salmon and Norman Fenton, *The Medical Department of the United States Army in the World War,* 15 vols., *Neuropsychiatry in the American Expeditionary Forces* (Washington, D.C.: U.S. Government Printing Office, 1929), 10: 311. For a shortened version of Salmon and Fenton's volume, see Edward A. Strecker, "Military Psychiatry: World War I, 1917–1918," in *One Hundred Years of American Psychiatry,* American Psychiatric Association (New York: Columbia University Press, 1944), pp. 385–416. Strecker includes verbatim passages from Salmon and Fenton without attribution and might be accused of plagiarism except that Strecker, who served as the psychiatrist for the Twenty-eighth Infantry Division in World War I, was one of the contributing authors to the earlier book, and thus probably extracted his own material.

4. Glass, introduction, in Bourne, ed., *Psychology,* p. xiv. For other discussions of how psychiatric casualties tend to exhibit the accepted or expected symptoms, see Peter G. Bourne, *Men, Stress, and Vietnam* (Boston: Little, Brown, 1970), p. 80; Richard A. Gabriel, *The Painful Field: The Psychiatric Dimension of Modern War* (New York, London, and Westport, Conn.: Greenwood Press, 1988), p. 141; and Larry H. Ingraham and Frederick J. Manning, "Psychiatric Battle Casualties: The Missing Column in a War Without Replacements," *Military Review* 60:8 (August 1980): 20–22.

5. Cutler interview in Henry Berry, *Make the Kaiser Dance: Living Memories of the Doughboy* (New York: Priam Books, 1978), p. 214. For other examples, see Hervey Allen, *Toward the Flame: A War Diary* (New York: Grosset and Dunlap, 1934), pp. 268–269, and Robert G. Merrick, *World War I: A Diary* (Baltimore: privately published, 1982), p. 94.

6. Goldsmith interview in Berry, *Make the Kaiser Dance,* p. 280. See also the case of breakdown on p. 347. Sometimes the doughboys could see that the cause of a man's breakdown was mental, not physiological, but the term "shell shock" was still being used, as in this shell-shock case described by a marine, Carl Andrew Brannen: "I was awakened suddenly by a fellow near me becoming a raving maniac. The strain had been too much and something had slipped in his head. Cases like this were called shell shock" (see *Over There: A Marine in the Great War* [College Station: Texas A&M University Press, 1996], p. 34).

7. Albert J. Glass, ed., *Neuropsychiatry in World War II,* Medical Department, U.S.

Army, Office of the Surgeon General, 2 vols., *Overseas Theaters* (Washington, D.C.: U.S. Government Printing Office, 1973), 2: 991.

8. Ibid., pp. 26–27. See also pp. 130–131.

9. Glass, introduction, in Bourne, ed., *Psychology,* p. xvi.

10. Ibid. See also Roy R. Grinker and John P. Spiegel, *War Neuroses* (Philadelphia and London: Blakiston, 1945), pp. 4–48.

11. Grinker and Spiegel, *War Neuroses,* pp. 66 and 70.

12. Glass, ed., *Neuropsychiatry,* pp. 9–10.

13. Glass, introduction, in Bourne, ed., *Psychology,* p. xviii. The terms "exhaustion" or "combat fatigue" were not entirely satisfactory to World War II psychiatrists, but they generally agree with Glass (who was himself a division psychiatrist) that the terms were an improvement. See Leo H. Bartemeier, Lawrence S. Kubie, Karl A. Menninger, John Romano, and John C. Whitehorn, "Combat Exhaustion," two-part series, part 1, *Journal of Nervous and Mental Disease* 104:4 (October 1946): 386–389, and Francis J. Braceland, "Psychiatric Lessons from World War II," *American Journal of Psychiatry* 103:5 (March 1947): 591–592.

14. Richard Tregaskis, *Invasion Diary* (New York: Random House, 1944), p. 139.

15. For a discussion of combat reaction, see Ted D. Kilpatrick and Harry A. Grater Jr., "Field Report on Marine Psychiatric Casualties in Vietnam," *Military Medicine* 136:10 (October 1971): 801–809.

16. For a discussion of pseudocombat fatigue, see Robert E. Strange, "Combat Fatigue Versus Pseudo-Combat Fatigue in Vietnam," *Military Medicine* 133:10 (October 1968): 823–826. For a discussion of character and behavior disorders in Vietnam War soldiers, see Bourne, ed., *Psychology,* pp. xxiv–xxv and 228–229; Bourne, *Men, Stress,* pp. 63–74; and Franklin Del Jones, "Experiences of a Division Psychiatrist in Vietnam," *Military Medicine* 132:12 (December 1967): 1003–1008.

17. For a discussion of the statistics problem, see Bartemeier et al., "Combat Exhaustion," part 2, *Journal of Nervous and Mental Disease* 104:5 (November 1946): 507–508; Glass, ed., *Neuropsychiatry,* pp. 996–998 and 1013; Glass, introduction, in Bourne, ed., *Psychology,* pp. xx–xxii; and Franklin Del Jones and Arnold W. Johnson Jr., "Medical and Psychiatric Treatment Policy and Practice in Vietnam," *Journal of Social Issues* 31:4 (fall 1975): 60–64.

18. Gabriel, *Painful Field,* p. 30. Nor does this estimate include "deferred" psychiatric casualties suffering from what is now called Post-traumatic Stress Disorder. Psychiatrists cite several reasons, incidentally, for the lower level of psychiatric casualties during the Vietnam War, to include the intermittent nature of the fighting; the relative lack of stress from prolonged bombardment; the psychological boost provided by good training, equipment, medical care, and logistical support; improved psychiatric treatment procedures; and last but not least, the hope of reprieve provided by the rotation system. See Bourne, ed., *Psychology,* pp. xxv–xxvii, 15–16, and 227–228; Bourne, *Men, Stress,* pp. 74–76; and Jones and Johnson, "Treatment Policy," pp. 53–54.

19. Bergerud, *Touched with Fire,* p. 447. See also the discussion of the "occasional coward" in Jesse Glenn Gray, *The Warriors: Reflections on Men in Battle* (New York: Harper Colophon Books, 1970), pp. 111–112.

20. A survey of Spanish Civil War veterans provides statistical evidence of "transient breakdown." Sixty-one percent reported that they "lost their heads for a moment, couldn't

control themselves and were useless as soldiers for a little while." See John Dollard, with Donald Horton, *Fear in Battle* (New York: AMS Press, 1976), p. 4.

21. George William Sefton, *It Was My War: I'll Remember It the Way I Want To!* (Manhattan, Kans.: Sunflower University Press, 1994), p. 123.

22. Ibid. For other examples of panicking soldiers, see Joseph R. Owen, *Colder Than Hell: A Marine Rifle Company at Chosin Reservoir* (Annapolis, Md.: Naval Institute Press, 1996), p. 58; Charles F. Minder, *This Man's War: The Day-by-Day Record of an American Private on the Western Front* (New York: Pevensey Press, 1931), p. 272; and James Hamilton Dill, *Sixteen Days at Mungol-li* (Fayetteville, Ark.: M&M Press, 1993), pp. 321–322.

23. Roscoe C. Blunt Jr., *Inside the Battle of the Bulge: A Private Comes of Age* (Westport, Conn., and London: Praeger, 1994), pp. 26–29.

24. James R. McDonough, *Platoon Leader* (New York: Bantam Books, 1986), p. 122. For other examples of transient breakdown, see Gerald P. Averill, *Mustang: A Combat Marine* (Novato, Calif.: Presidio Press, 1987), pp. 113–114; Henry Berry, *Hey, Mac, Where Ya Been? Living Memories of the U.S. Marines in the Korean War* (New York: St. Martin's Press, 1988), pp. 103–104; Donald Knox, with additional text by Alfred Coppel, *The Korean War: Uncertain Victory: The Concluding Volume of an Oral History* (San Diego, New York, and London: Harcourt Brace Jovanovich, 1988), p. 498; and Richard D. Camp, with Eric Hammel, *Lima-6: A Marine Company Commander in Vietnam* (New York: Pocket Books, 1989), pp. 130–131.

25. Ralph G. Martin, *The G.I. War, 1941–1945* (Boston and Toronto: Little, Brown, 1967), p. 339.

26. John H. W. Rhein, "Neuropsychiatric Problems at the Front During Combat," *Journal of Abnormal Psychology* 14:1–2 (April–June 1919): 11. For similar assessments, see Sidney I. Schwab, "The Mechanism of the War Neuroses," ibid., pp. 3–4, and Lord Charles McM. Moran, *The Anatomy of Courage* (Garden City Park, N.Y.: Avery Publishing, 1987), p. 69.

27. Bob Hoffman, *I Remember the Last War* (York, Pa.: Strength and Health Publishing, 1940), p. 319.

28. Joseph D. Lawrence, *Fighting Soldier: The A.E.F. in 1918* (Boulder: Colorado Associated University Press, 1985), pp. 116–117.

29. Paul Fussell, *Doing Battle: The Making of a Skeptic* (New York: Little, Brown, 1996), p. 138. See also Dave Grossman's discussion of "the well of fortitude" in *On Killing: The Psychological Cost of Learning to Kill in War and Society* (Boston: Little, Brown, 1995), pp. 83–86.

30. Frederick W. Parsons, "War Neuroses," *Atlantic Monthly* 123:4 (March 1919): 337. See also the discussion of "last straws" by the World War I psychiatrist John F. W. Meagher, in "Prominent Features of the Psychoneuroses in the War," *American Journal of the Medical Sciences* 158:3 (September 1919): 347.

31. Roy L. Swank and Walter E. Marchand, "Combat Neuroses: Development of Combat Exhaustion," *Archives of Neurology and Psychiatry* 55:3 (March 1946): 241. See also the case studies in Grinker and Spiegel, *War Neuroses,* pp. 11, 16, 17, 29, 35, and 104, in which a "last straw," usually artillery fire or an air attack, triggered a breakdown.

32. Raymond Sobel, "The 'Old Sergeant' Syndrome," *Psychiatry: Journal of the Biology and the Pathology of Interpersonal Relations* 10:3 (August 1947): 320. See also

Glass, ed., *Neuropsychiatry*, pp. 49–52, and the survey of World War II combat soldiers discharged for psychiatric reasons in Eli Ginzberg, James K. Anderson, Sol W. Ginsburg, John L. Herma, and John B. Miner, *The Ineffective Soldier: Lessons for Management and the Nation*, 3 vols, *Patterns of Performance* (New York and London: Columbia University Press, 1959), 3: 71–88. This survey lends credence to Sobel's "old sergeant syndrome." While some soldiers broke early in combat, others had served satisfactorily for a long time before breaking, had attained corporal's rank or higher, had often been decorated for valor or for wounds in combat, and had served a year or more overseas before breaking down.

33. Paul Boesch, *Road to Huertgen: Forest in Hell* (Houston: Paul M. Boesch, 1985), pp. 167–168.

34. Eugene B. Sledge, *With the Old Breed at Peleliu and Okinawa* (New York: Bantam Books, 1983), p. 308. For an excellent fictional example of a World War II combatant who couldn't take it anymore, see the case of Sergeant Porter in Harry Brown, *A Walk in the Sun* (New York: Knopf, 1944), pp. 10, 16, 78–79, 101, 117–121, 123–124, and 132–133. For other World War II examples, see Audie Murphy, *To Hell and Back* (New York: Bantam Books, 1983), p. 237; Leon C. Standifer, *Not in Vain: A Rifleman Remembers World War II* (Baton Rouge and London: Louisiana State University Press, 1992), pp. 91 and 205; and George Wilson, *If You Survive* (New York: Ivy Books, 1987), p. 91.

35. Randell interview in Knox, *Uncertain Victory*, p. 123. For another Korean War example, see James Brady, *The Coldest War: A Memoir of Korea* (New York: Pocket Books, 1991), p. 112.

36. For a discussion of the reasons for a reduction in the occurrence of classic combat fatigue during the Vietnam War, see the sources cited in note 18. For a discussion of declining psychiatric casualty rates in the latter part of the Korean War, see Donald B. Peterson, "The Psychiatric Operation, Army Forces, Far East, 1950–53," *American Journal of Psychiatry* 112:1 (July 1955): 23–28. Peterson cites improved psychiatric care and facilities as the war progressed as a major factor in reduced casualty rates. See also Glass, introduction, in Bourne, ed., *Psychology,* pp. xxii–xxiii. Glass notes the beneficial effects of reduced combat intensity and the rotation system in lowering the incidence of genuine combat fatigue during the Korean War.

37. Philip Caputo, *A Rumor of War* (New York: Ballantine Books, 1978), pp. 190–191. For other Vietnam War examples, see Stanley Goff and Robert Sanders, with Clark Smith, *Brothers: Black Soldiers in the Nam* (Novato, Calif.: Presidio Press, 1982), pp. 134–135; William D. Ehrhart, *Vietnam-Perkasie: A Combat Marine Memoir* (Jefferson, N.C., and London: McFarland, 1983), p. 235; Michael Lee Lanning, *The Only War We Had: A Platoon Leader's Journal of Vietnam* (New York: Ivy Books, 1987), pp. 269–270; and Wallace Terry, *Bloods: An Oral History of the Vietnam War by Black Veterans* (New York: Ballantine Books, 1985), pp. 96–97.

38. Swank and Marchand, "Combat Neuroses," pp. 240–241.

39. John W. Appel and Gilbert W. Beebe, "Preventive Psychiatry: An Epidemiological Approach," *Journal of the American Medical Association* 131:18 (August 31, 1946): 1470. See also David G. Mandelbaum, "Psychiatry in Military Society," two-part series, part 1, *Human Organization* 13:3 (fall 1954): 8.

40. Samuel A. Stouffer, Arthur A. Lumsdaine, Marion Harper Lumsdaine, Robin M. Williams Jr., M. Brewster Smith, Irving L. Janis, Shirley A. Star, and Leonard S. Cottrell

Jr., *Studies in Social Psychology in World War II*, vol. 2, *The American Soldier: Combat and Its Aftermath* (Princeton: Princeton University Press, 1949), pp. 452–453.

41. These short, violent island campaigns, however, should not be allowed to overshadow the campaigns in New Guinea and the Philippines, which were long and arduous, generating cases of combat fatigue in "old sergeants" not unlike those occurring in Europe. For an example of old-timers in the Sixth Infantry Division cracking up after months of fighting in the Philippines, see Gerald Astor, *Crisis in the Pacific: The Battles for the Philippine Islands by the Men Who Fought Them* (New York: Donald I. Fine Books, 1996), p. 417.

42. Averill, *Mustang*, p. 120. One of Averill's platoon sergeants broke down after several days on Iwo Jima (pp. 120–121); after about a week of combat, the marine rifle company he was in was down to 50 percent strength (p. 124).

43. Allen R. Matthews, *The Assault* (New York: Dodd, Mead, 1980), p. 1.

44. Meagher, "Prominent Features," p. 346. For discussions of the World War II soldier's tendency to break down early on, see Bartemeier et al., "Combat Exhaustion," part 1, 377; Glass, ed., *Neuropsychiatry*, p. 996; and Swank and Marchand, "Combat Neuroses," pp. 241–242.

45. Ernie Pyle, *Brave Men* (New York: Henry Holt, 1944), p. 189. For a case study of a GI who broke down even before reaching combat, see Grinker and Spiegel, *War Neuroses*, pp. 17–18.

46. Lester Atwell, *Private* (New York: Popular Library, 1958), p. 166. For early breakdowns in combat, see the cases of Lieutenant Millbank (p. 73) and litter bearer Cornell (pp. 194–196). For fictional examples of early GI breakdowns, see the cases of Sergeant Stack in James Jones, *The Thin Red Line* (New York: Charles Scribner's Sons, 1962), p. 113, and Hennessey in Norman Mailer, *The Naked and the Dead* (New York: Signet Books, 1948), pp. 32–34.

47. Clark interview in Berry, *Make the Kaiser Dance*, pp. 164–165. For other examples of suicide, or attempted suicide, to avoid combat, see Carl M. Becker and Robert G. Thobaben, *Common Warfare: Parallel Memoirs by Two World War II GIs in the Pacific* (Jefferson, N.C., and London: McFarland, 1992), p. 51; Astor, *Crisis*, p. 347; and Bergerud, *Touched with Fire*, pp. 450–451.

48. Based on a study of 200 soldiers referred for neuropsychiatric evaluation in Vietnam, 23 percent were in the first month of their tour of duty and almost half were within the first four months. See Gary L. Tischler, "Patterns of Psychiatric Attrition and Behavior in the Combat Zone," in Bourne, ed., *Psychology*, p. 25.

49. Matthew Brennan, *Brennan's War: Vietnam, 1965–1969* (New York: Pocket Books, 1986), p. 224.

50. Ibid., p. 227. See also the case of Rayburn, in Albert French, *Patches of Fire: A Story of War and Redemption* (New York: Anchor Books, 1997), pp. 33 and 133.

51. Combat veterans surveyed in the Italian campaign in World War II by the Research Branch verify the adverse effects of seeing fellow soldiers crack up. Seventy percent reported that it made them nervous, depressed, or demoralized (see Stouffer et al., *Combat and Its Aftermath*, pp. 208–209).

52. McDonough, *Platoon Leader*, p. 18.

53. Wilson, *If You Survive*, pp. 41 and 38.

54. Military psychiatrists are virtually unanimous in emphasizing the importance of

external, or "situational," factors in causing breakdown, but most also believe that personal factors affect how well a soldier can cope with these external stresses. For discussions of "predisposition" toward breakdown, see Bartemeier et al., "Combat Exhaustion," part 1, p. 373; Schwab, "Mechanism," p. 4; S. Kirson Weinberg, "The Combat Neuroses," *American Journal of Sociology* 51:5 (March 1946): 468–471; and Edwin A. Weinstein, "The Function of Interpersonal Relations in the Neurosis of Combat," *Psychiatry: Journal of the Biology and Pathology of Interpersonal Relations* 10:3 (August 1947): 310–313.

55. The Research Branch examined the background of maladjusted soldiers (psychiatric cases and AWOLs) and found these characteristics to be in greater evidence than in well-adjusted soldiers. See Samuel A. Stouffer, Edward A. Suchman, Leland C. DeVinney, Shirley A. Star, and Robin M. Williams Jr., *Studies in Social Psychology in World War II*, vol. 1, *The American Soldier: Adjustment During Army Life* (Princeton: Princeton University Press, 1949), pp. 112–147. For similar findings, with an emphasis on intelligence and education levels as being especially important in effective soldiering, see Ginzberg et al., *Lost Divisions*, 1:104–125, and *Patterns of Performance*, 3: 89–116.

56. In addition to the studies cited in note 65, see Robert L. Egbert, Tor Meeland, Victor B. Cline, Edward W. Forgy, Martin W. Spickler, and Charles Brown, *Fighter I: An Analysis of Combat Fighters and Non-Fighters*, Human Resources Research Office Technical Report 44, December 1957, p. 26. See also Mandelbaum, "Military Society," part 1, p. 7; Anthony Kellett, *Combat Motivation: The Behavior of Soldiers in Battle* (Boston, The Hague, and London: Kluwer, Nijhoff, 1982), pp. 62–65 and 310–311; Peter Watson, *War on the Mind: The Military Uses and Abuses of Psychology* (New York: Basic Books, 1978), pp. 138–148; and Anne Hoiberg, "Military Staying Power," in *Combat Effectiveness: Cohesion, Stress, and the Volunteer Military*, ed. Sam C. Sarkesian (Beverly Hills and London: Sage, 1980), pp. 214–218.

57. Egbert et al., *Fighter I*, p. 26.

58. Atwell, *Private*, p. 115.

59. Ibid., p. 324. See also the case of "H. R." in Standifer, *Not in Vain*, pp. 92–93, 137–138, and 178–179.

60. Gray, *Warriors*, pp. 114–115. See also Richard Holmes, *Acts of War: The Behavior of Men in Battle* (New York: Free Press, 1985), p. 81.

61. William Manchester, *Goodbye, Darkness: A Memoir of the Pacific War* (Boston and Toronto: Little, Brown, 1979), p. 391.

62. Harold P. Leinbaugh and John D. Campbell, *The Men of Company K* (New York: Bantam Books, 1987), p. 169; for another early breakdown, see p. 223. For a fictional example of a bully and braggart who broke down and fled in his first fight, see the case of Private Irv Donaldson, in William Young Boyd, *The Gentle Infantryman* (New York: St. Martin's Press, 1985), pp. 170–172, 183, 211, and 216.

63. Standifer, *Not in Vain*, pp. 102 and 164.

64. Fourteen out of every 1,000 inductees, totaling 68,000, were rejected for service during World War I for emotional or mental reasons, which did not preclude another 9 out of every 1,000 doughboys being separated from service for emotional or mental reasons (35,000 men). Screening was even more vigorous during World War II, with 94 out of every 1,000 inductees rejected (1,686,000), yet the separation rate for GIs with emotional or mental instability was 50 out of every 1,000, for a total of 504,000. These numbers lend

credence to claims that screening cannot accurately identify those men who are "predisposed" to breaking down (see Ginzberg et al., *Lost Divisions,* Table 37, 1:145).

65. The chief psychiatrist of the AEF, Thomas W. Salmon, warned that "even after a careful selection, with the elimination of many psychopathic, mentally defective, and unstable men," American divisions "were capable of furnishing a large number of war neurotics under battle conditions" (Salmon and Fenton, *Neuropsychiatry,* p. 306). Despite this warning, psychiatrists put great faith in psychological screening during the early months of World War II, and as the statistics in note 64 indicate, this faith was misplaced. The most comprehensive critique of the screening process (educational and psychological) in World War II can be found in Ginzberg et al., *Lost Divisions*, 1:137–193. See also Braceland, "Psychiatric Lessons," pp. 589–590; William C. Menninger, "Psychiatric Experience in the War, 1941–1946," *American Journal of Psychiatry* 103:5 (March 1947): 582; and Albert N. Mayers, "Dug-out Psychiatry," *Psychiatry: Journal of the Biology and the Pathology of Interpersonal Relations* 8:4 (November 1945): 387–388. Psychiatric screening during the Vietnam War also suffered from various deficiencies: shifting evaluation criteria, inadequate numbers of screeners, and insufficient time for more than a superficial evaluation. See Robert Paul Liberman, Stephen M. Sonnenberg, and Melvin S. Stern, "Psychiatric Evaluations for Young Men Facing the Draft: A Report of 147 Cases," *American Journal of Psychiatry* 128:2 (August 1971): 147–152.

66. One of the best descriptions of these factors, in layman's terms, can be found in Ginzberg et al., *Breakdown and Recovery,* chapter 1, "The Determinants of Performance," 2:1–12. A soldier's effectiveness depends on the interaction of psychological, organizational, and situational "determinants"—in other words, a mix of personal and environmental factors.

67. Ernie Pyle, *Here Is Your War: The Story of G.I. Joe* (Cleveland and New York: World Publishing, 1945), p. 266.

68. Glass, ed., *Neuropsychiatry,* p. 100. See also Weinstein, "Neurosis of Combat," p. 308.

69. Meagher, "Prominent Features," p. 346. See also Salmon and Fenton, *Neuropsychiatry,* p. 310, and Moran, *Anatomy,* pp. 78–87.

70. Grinker and Spiegel, *War Neuroses*, p. 68. For other discussions of the contributing role of physical factors in breakdowns, see John Ellis, *The Sharp End: The Fighting Man in World War II* (New York: Charles Scribner's Sons, 1980), pp. 199–204; Grossman, *On Killing,* pp. 67–73; Shay, *Achilles,* pp. 121–124; and Bartemeier et al., "Combat Exhaustion," part 1, p. 367.

71. See, for example, Morris Janowitz and Roger W. Little, *Sociology and the Military Establishment,* 3d ed. (Beverly Hills and London: Sage, 1974), p. 105.

72. Samuel L. A. Marshall, *Men Against Fire: The Problem of Battle Command in Future War* (Gloucester: Peter Smith, 1978), p. 78. See also Grossman, *On Killing,* pp. 52–54. Grossman, like Marshall, discounts fear of death as a primary cause of breakdown in favor of "resistance to overt aggressive confrontation" (p. 54).

73. For case studies of soldiers who broke down primarily because of anxiety and guilt over killing, see Bartemeier et al., "Combat Exhaustion," part 1, p. 379, and Grinker and Spiegel, *War Neuroses,* pp. 30 and 33–35.

74. Glass, ed., *Neuropsychiatry*, p. 995.

75. Appel and Beebe, "Preventive Psychiatry," p. 1469. For further support for this position, see Tischler, "Psychiatric Attrition," in Bourne, ed., *Psychology,* p. 20; Kurt Lang, *Military Institutions and the Sociology of War: A Review of the Literature, with Annotated Bibliography* (Beverly Hills and London: Sage, 1972), pp. 76–77; Stouffer et al., *Combat and Its Aftermath,* pp. 77–78 and 445–455; Kilpatrick and Grater, "Field Report," p. 809; and Ingraham and Manning, "Battle Casualties," p. 23.

76. Pyle, *Brave Men,* p. 103.

77. Rudolph W. Stephens, *Old Ugly Hill: A G.I.'s Fourteen Months in the Korean Trenches, 1952–1953* (Jefferson, N.C., and London: McFarland, 1995), p. 63. See also pp. 67 and 78.

78. Mark Baker, *Nam: The Vietnam War in the Words of the Men and Women Who Fought There* (New York: Berkley Books, 1983), p. 112.

79. Lyle Rishell, *With a Black Platoon in Combat: A Year in Korea* (College Station: Texas A&M University Press, 1993), p. 80.

80. One of the major findings of John Dollard's survey of Spanish Civil War veterans was that "fear is a normal experience in battle. Experienced men admit it and are not ashamed." Seventy-four percent of those surveyed experienced fear in their initial combat, and 91 percent were "always" or "sometimes" afraid in subsequent actions. And what the veteran soldiers feared was being killed, crippled or disfigured for life, or captured and tortured (see *Fear in Battle,* pp. 4–5 and 18–19). The Research Branch in World War II concluded that "from the standpoint of the individual soldier, it is primarily the danger of death or injury which makes the combat situation so harassing an experience. . . . The threats of being maimed, of undergoing unbearable pain, and of being completely annihilated elicit intense reactions which may severely interfere with successful performances" (Stouffer et al., *Combat and Its Aftermath,* p. 192).

81. For summarizing lists or discussions of the multiple stress-producing factors that could contribute to soldier breakdown, see Brian H. Chermol, "Wounds Without Scars: Treatment of Battle Fatigue in the U.S. Armed Forces in the Second World War," *Military Affairs* 49:1 (January 1985): 27–29; Bartemeier et al., "Combat Exhaustion," part 1, pp. 366–368; Albert J. Glass, "Psychotherapy in the Combat Zone," *American Journal of Psychiatry* 110:10 (April 1954): 727–728; Ellis, *Sharp End,* pp. 212–215; and Stouffer et al., *Combat and Its Aftermath,* pp. 76–95.

82. For a discussion of survivors' guilt, see Robert Jay Lifton, *Home from the War: Vietnam Veterans: Neither Victims nor Executioners* (New York: Simon and Schuster, 1973), pp. 99–133. In his book, Lifton expands the concept of survivors' guilt into "animating guilt," encompassing guilt over killing or committing atrocities, and even guilt over fighting in a "wrong" war. For a more circumscribed discussion of survivors' guilt in combat, see Shay, *Achilles,* pp. 69–75. See also Weinstein, "Neurosis of Combat," p. 311.

83. Dan Levin, *From the Battlefield: Dispatches of a World War II Marine* (Annapolis, Md.: Naval Institute Press, 1995), p. 81.

84. French, *Patches of Fire,* p. 143.

85. For a discussion of discontinuity, see Kellett, *Combat Motivation,* pp. 278–279.

86. Bourne, *Men, Stress,* p. 86.

87. Tim O'Brien, *If I Die in a Combat Zone: Box Me Up and Ship Me Home* (New York: Laurel, Dell, 1987), pp. 112–113. Michael Herr, who flew in and out of combat with

some regularity as a war correspondent in Vietnam, also describes the emotional shock of discontinuity. See *Dispatches* (New York: Avon Books, 1978), pp. 79–80.

88. Blunt, *Inside,* pp. 117–118.

89. Ginzberg et al., *Breakdown and Recovery,* 2:127–132.

90. David Rothschild, "Review of Neuropsychiatric Cases in the Southwest Pacific Area," *American Journal of Psychiatry* 102:4 (January 1946): 458. Indeed, the Southwest Pacific Area in World War II may be the one theater of war in which physical hardship and deprivation proved to be the major, rather than just a contributing, factor in psychological breakdown. See Glass, ed., *Neuropsychiatry,* p. 995.

91. Becker and Thobaben, *Common Warfare,* p. 157. For another example, follow the experiences of Captain Hyman Samuelson and his outfit, the Ninety-sixth Engineers. Samuelson served in New Guinea from April 1942 through September 1944. Except for the early part of this period, the enemy threat was low, but Samuelson records numerous breakdowns and suicides in his regiment because of location stress. See Gwendolyn Midlo Hall, ed., *Love, War, and the 96th Engineers (Colored): The World War II New Guinea Diaries of Captain Hyman Samuelson* (Urbana and Chicago: University of Illinois Press, 1995), pp. 139, 217–218, 234, 241–242, and 252.

92. Westberg interview in Donald Knox, *The Korean War: Pusan to Chosin: An Oral History* (San Diego, New York, and London: Harcourt Brace Jovanovich, 1985), p. 477.

93. Brady, *Coldest War,* p. 114.

94. PIES and battle fatigue are discussed in U.S. Department of the Army Field Manual 8-51, *Combat Stress in a Theater of Operations: Tactics, Techniques, and Procedures* (Washington, D.C.: U.S. Government Printing Office, final approved draft, May 1994), chapter 1, "Control of Combat Stress," pp. 1-1 to 1-16. See also Gabriel's discussion of treatment techniques in *Painful Field,* pp. 145–148.

95. This official policy, promulgated on September 25, 1918, is contained in Salmon and Fenton, *Neuropsychiatry,* pp. 308–309. See also the discussion of treatment at the division-psychiatrist level on pp. 313–318. World War I psychiatrists confirm the validity of this policy. See Parsons, "War Neuroses," pp. 337–338; Rhein, "Neuropsychiatric Problems," pp. 10–13; Schwab, "Mechanism," pp. 6–7; and Tom A. Williams, "The Emotions and Their Mechanism in Warfare," *Journal of Abnormal Psychology* 14:1–2 (April–June 1919): 24–25. For a good overview of the treatment of neuroses in the AEF, see Ronald Schaffer, *America in the Great War: The Rise of the War Welfare State* (New York and Oxford: Oxford University Press, 1991), chapter 12, "The Treatment of 'Shell-shock' Cases in the AEF: A Microcosm of the War Welfare State," pp. 199–212.

96. For the failure to learn, or remember, the lessons of World War I concerning the treatment of combat neuroses, see Lawrence Ingraham and Frederick Manning, "American Military Psychiatry," in *Military Psychiatry: A Comparative Perspective,* ed. Richard A. Gabriel (New York, London, and Westport, Conn.: Greenwood Press, 1986), pp. 33–48; Glass, introduction, in Bourne, ed., *Psychology,* pp. xv–xxii; and Menninger, "Psychiatric Experience," p. 583 (see the World War II references in note 65 for a discussion of the failure of psychological screening).

97. Menninger, "Psychiatric Experience," p. 581.

98. See the discussion of treatment techniques for World War II battle fatigue in Bartemeier et al., "Combat Exhaustion," part 2, pp. 489–506; Braceland, "Psychiatric Lessons," pp. 591–592; and Grinker and Spiegel, *War Neuroses,* pp. 75–77.

99. Albert J. Glass, "Principles of Combat Psychiatry," *Military Medicine* 117:1 (July 1955): 27.

100. Ibid., pp. 31–33. See Jones and Johnson, "Treatment Policy," pp. 58–59, for the application of these treatment principles during the Vietnam War.

101. Recovery rates again raise the sticky issue of statistics. What constitutes recovery? Some soldiers were returned to combat but broke down again. Others "recovered," but were fit only for noncombat duty. Statistics on recovery are thus suspect, but they clearly show that a substantial number of soldiers, perhaps a majority, were returned to some form of useful duty after suffering a breakdown, at least once an adequate treatment infrastructure had been established. See the statistics in Strecker, "Military Psychiatry," pp. 410–411; Menninger, "Psychiatric Experience," pp. 579 and 581; Peterson, "Psychiatric Operation," pp. 25–27; and Jones and Johnson, "Treatment Policy," pp. 61–64.

102. Parsons, "War Neuroses," pp. 337–338.

103. Glass, "Principles," p. 31.

104. The symptoms of battle fatigue varied widely and tended to reflect expected or accepted characteristics of breakdown, depending on the current terminology. For overviews of symptomology, see Holmes, *Acts of War,* pp. 265–269, and Gabriel, *Painful Field,* pp. 37–43.

105. Salmon and Fenton, *Neuropsychiatry,* p. 306.

106. Glass, "Psychotherapy," p. 726. Overevacuation was also a problem in the Pacific early in World War II. See Glass, ed., *Neuropsychiatry,* p. 628. For overevacuation problems in the Third Marine Division during the Vietnam War, see Kilpatrick and Grater, "Field Report." Kilpatrick notes, incidentally, that the army's psychiatric treatment apparatus was more robust, and that overevacuation was apparently not a problem (p. 801).

107. Ginzberg et al., *Patterns of Performance,* 3:138, 152–153. See also Grinker and Spiegel's discussion of "conversion symptoms" in hospitalized soldiers in their *War Neuroses,* pp. 125–126. The evacuation and hospitalization of a psychiatric casualty did not mean that he automatically stopped thinking about the comrades he left behind. Military psychiatrists note the hospitalized patient's continued struggle between his desire for self-preservation and his sense of duty. Some patients condemned themselves as quitters, suffered survivors' guilt, or feared the loss of honor that a "psycho" discharge might bring. In some cases, psychiatric patients claimed, in all sincerity, that they were ready to return to their units but were in no condition to do so. See Meagher, "Prominent Features," pp. 348–349; Bartemeier et al., "Combat Exhaustion," part 1, p. 383; Weinberg, "Combat Neurosis," p. 474; and Grinker and Spiegel, *War Neuroses,* pp. 32–37.

108. Rhein, "Neuropsychiatric Problems," p. 12. See also Parsons, "War Neuroses," p. 337. Hospitalized soldiers during the Vietnam War were also susceptible to the hold of the hospital: "The disabling psychiatric symptoms of wounded soldiers . . . usually developed after hospitalization; or, if present when hospitalized, the symptoms persisted or became more severe, requiring neuropsychiatric consultation" (Jones and Johnson, "Treatment Policy," p. 54).

109. For example, of the 8,057 World War II combat veterans in the Ginzberg study who were discharged from the army as psychologically unfit, 1,140 of them had recovered from physical wounds, had returned to combat, but were then rehospitalized for psychiatric disability. See Ginzberg et al., *Patterns of Performance,* 3:138.

110. Murphy, *To Hell and Back,* p. 259. For another example of a returning officer,

recovered from a wound, who promptly broke down, see Wilson, *If You Survive,* pp. 139–140.

111. Amos N. Wilder, *Armageddon Revisited: A World War I Journal* (New Haven and London: Yale University Press, 1994), pp. 129 and 134.

112. Paul Fussell, "My War: How I Got Irony in the Infantry," *Harper's* 264:1580 (January 1982): 44–45.

113. Saddic interview in Berry, *Hey, Mac,* p. 166.

114. Standifer, *Not in Vain,* p. 210.

115. Brannen, *Over There,* p. 17. See also Minder, *This Man's War,* pp. 189 and 310.

116. Klaus H. Huebner, *Long Walk Through War: A Combat Doctor's Diary* (College Station: Texas A&M University Press, 1987), p. 50. Private Lester Atwell, who worked in a battalion aid station in World War II, also noted the near-impossibility of determining intent, but he knew that most such wounds were deliberate: "In Tillet, a wave of self-inflicted wounds broke out. Time after time, men were carried into the aid station from nearby houses, wincing in pain, shot through the foot. Each swore it was an accident. . . . The circumstances were almost always the same: the man was alone in a room, or a fox-hole, and at most in the presence of his best friend; there would be the one shot, the cry for help, the wound always through the foot" (Atwell, *Private,* pp. 185–186).

117. A 1944 Research Branch survey of GIs in the Southwest Pacific Area revealed that 10 percent believed (incorrectly) that a case of malaria would get them evacuated to the States (see Stouffer et al., *Adjustment During Army Life,* p. 176).

118. Atwell, *Private,* p. 161. See also pp. 186–187. For other examples from the world wars of self-inflicted wounds, see Thomas Boyd, *Through the Wheat* (Carbondale and Edwardsville: Southern Illinois University Press, 1978), pp. 147–149; Lawrence, *Fighting Soldier,* p. 91; Atwell, *Private,* pp. 61–62; Nat Frankel and Larry Smith, *Patton's Best: An Informal History of the 4th Armored Division* (New York: Jove Book, 1984), p. 94; and Studs Terkel, *"The Good War": An Oral History of World War II* (New York: Pantheon Books, 1984), pp. 44 and 67.

119. Atkins interview in Knox, *Pusan to Chosin,* p. 95.

120. Anderson interviewed in Al Santoli, *Everything We Had: An Oral History of the Vietnam War by Thirty-three American Soldiers Who Fought It* (New York: Ballantine Books, 1982), p. 73. For other examples of self-inflicted wounds in the Korean and Vietnam Wars, see p. 156, and also Knox, *Pusan to Chosin,* p. 123, and James Webb, *Fields of Fire* (New York: Bantam Books, 1979), pp. 274–275.

121. The first study was conducted by the Eighty-fifth Infantry Division psychiatrist from September to November 1944 and can be found in Glass, ed., *Neuropsychiatry,* pp. 85–87. The second was a survey conducted by the Research Branch sociologist Arnold M. Rose in March 1945, the results of which are discussed in his article, "The Social Psychology of Desertion from Combat," *American Sociological Review* 16:5 (October 1951): 614–629.

122. Glass, ed., *Neuropsychiatry,* pp. 86–87.

123. These characteristics of deserters are drawn from the two studies cited in note 121.

124. Newman interview in Berry, *Hey, Mac,* p. 237. Eugene B. Sledge voiced a similar opinion in his interview with Studs Terkel in *Good War,* p. 60.

125. Weinberg, "Combat Neurosis," p. 473.

126. Ibid. The variation in soldier responses to fellow grunts who wounded themselves during the Vietnam War, for example, was diverse enough for two students of grunt behavior to come to different conclusions on the subject. Christian G. Appy explains that at least until late in the war, a self-inflicted wound was considered "an understandable but cowardly escape and a betrayal of the group" (*Working-Class War: American Soldiers and Vietnam* [Chapel Hill and London: University of North Carolina Press, 1993], p. 244). Conversely, James R. Ebert has concluded that "soldiers generally treated self-inflicted wounds as none of their business," and he relates examples of grunts who did not turn in comrades for inflicting wounds on themselves (*A Life in a Year: The American Infantryman in Vietnam, 1965–1972* [Novato, Calif.: Presidio Press, 1993], p. 224).

127. Rose, "Psychology of Desertion," p. 627. He adds, "This, of course, would not apply to the few AWOL's who ran away before the strain of combat is intense or long."

128. Suarez interview in Rudy Tomedi, *No Bugles, No Drums: An Oral History of the Korean War* (New York: John Wiley and Sons, 1993), p. 95.

129. Hubenette interview in Knox, *Uncertain Victory,* pp. 60–61.

130. Atwell, *Private,* p. 187.

131. Chadwick interview in Bergerud, *Touched with Fire,* p. 451. For other examples of soldiers who were ridiculed or distrusted for inflicting wounds on themselves, see Boyd, *Gentle Infantryman,* pp. 166–167; Sefton, *It Was My War,* pp. 101–102; and Pat Frank, *Hold Back the Night* (Philadelphia and New York: J. B. Lippincott, 1952), pp. 128–129.

132. Brockway interview in Berry, *Make the Kaiser Dance,* p. 363.

133. Boesch, *Road to Huertgen,* p. 42.

134. Stouffer et al., *Combat and Its Aftermath,* p. 200.

135. Leinbaugh and Campbell, *Company K,* p. 120.

136. Howard Matthias, *The Korean War—Reflections of a Young Combat Platoon Leader,* rev. ed. (Tallahassee, Fla.: Father and Son Publishing, 1995), p. 55; for another example, see Knox, *Pusan to Chosin,* p. 186.

137. Levin, *Battlefield,* p. 70.

138. Blunt, *Inside,* p. 29.


## CHAPTER 7. THE JOYS OF WAR

1. Samuel L. A. Marshall, *Men Against Fire: The Problem of Battle Command in Future War* (Gloucester: Peter Smith, 1978), p. 184. Unfortunately, except for reference to the thrill of danger and a discussion of GI humor, Marshall did not elaborate on his caveat. See also Samuel Hynes, *The Soldiers' Tale: Bearing Witness to Modern War* (New York: Allen Lane, 1997), pp. 28–29, and the discussion of war's "powerful fascination" in Jesse Glenn Gray, *The Warriors: Reflections on Men in Battle* (New York: Harper Colophon Books, 1970), p. 28.

2. Of the students of soldier behavior, Jesse Glenn Gray provides the most complete analysis of war's redeeming qualities and appeals, which he calls war's "three delights" (*Warriors,* pp. 28–58).

3. William Broyles Jr., "Why Men Love War," *Esquire* 102:5 (November 1984):

58. See also Gray, *Warriors,* p. 44; Richard Holmes, *Acts of War: The Behavior of Men in Battle* (New York: Free Press, 1985), p. 398; and John Ellis, *The Sharp End: The Fighting Man in World War II* (New York: Charles Scribner's Sons, 1980), pp. 305–309 and 317–319.

4. Francis P. Duffy, *Father Duffy's Story: A Tale of Humor and Heroism, of Life and Death with the Fighting Sixty-ninth* (Garden City, N.Y.: Garden City Publishing, 1919), p. 325. See also the Win Stracke interview in Studs Terkel, *"The Good War": An Oral History of World War II* (New York: Pantheon Books, 1984), p. 159.

5. Eugene B. Sledge, *With the Old Breed at Peleliu and Okinawa* (New York: Bantam Books, 1983), p. 323.

6. Philip Caputo, *A Rumor of War* (New York: Ballantine Books, 1978), p. xvii. See also Stanley Goff and Robert Sanders, with Clark Smith, *Brothers: Black Soldiers in the Nam* (Novato, Calif.: Presidio Press, 1982), p. 60.

7. Leon C. Standifer, *Not in Vain: A Rifleman Remembers World War II* (Baton Rouge and London: Louisiana State University Press, 1992), p. 246.

8. Paul Boesch, *Road to Huertgen: Forest in Hell* (Houston: Paul M. Boesch, 1985), p. 226.

9. Charles M. Bussey, *Firefight at Yechon: Courage and Racism in the Korean War* (Washington, D.C., and London: Brassey's, 1991), p. 184.

10. James Martin Davis, "Vietnam: What It Was Really Like," *Military Review* 69:1 (January 1989): 39–40.

11. Dominick Yezzo, *A G.I.'s Vietnam Diary, 1968–1969* (New York: Franklin Watts, 1974), December 6 entry. See also Fred Reed, "A Veteran Writes," sidebar in Peter Marin, "Coming to Terms with Vietnam," *Harper's* 261:1567 (December 1980): 44; John Ketwig, *And a Hard Rain Fell* (New York: Pocket Books, 1986), p. 43; and Michael Lee Lanning, *The Only War We Had: A Platoon Leader's Journal of Vietnam* (New York: Ivy Books, 1987), p. 147.

12. Hynes, *Soldiers' Tale,* p. 23. See the case of Arthur W. Little, *From Harlem to the Rhine: The Story of New York's Colored Volunteers* (New York: Covici-Friede, 1936), p. 180.

13. Richard M. Hardison, *Caissons Across Europe: An Artillery Captain's Personal War* (Austin, Tex.: Eakin Press, 1990), p. 167.

14. Broyles, "Men Love War," p. 58. See also Craig M. Cameron, *American Samurai: Myth, Imagination, and the Conduct of Battle in the First Marine Division, 1941–1951* (Cambridge: Cambridge University Press, 1994), pp. 69–70, for a discussion of the marines' sense of "release from societal strictures."

15. John L. Munschauer, *World War II Cavalcade: An Offer I Couldn't Refuse* (Manhattan, Kans.: Sunflower University Press, 1996), p. 111.

16. Gray, *Warriors,* p. 31 ("lust of the eye" appears on p. 30). See also Holmes, *Acts of War,* p. 273, and Broyles, "Men Love War," p. 62.

17. Elton E. Mackin, *Suddenly We Didn't Want to Die: Memoirs of a World War I Marine* (Novato, Calif.: Presidio Press, 1993), p. 41.

18. [Howard V. O'Brien], *Wine, Women, and War: A Diary of Disillusionment* (New York: J. H. Sears, 1926), p. 70.

19. Little, *Harlem,* p. 272.

20. Howard Matthias, *The Korean War—Reflections of a Young Combat Platoon*

*Leader,* rev. ed. (Tallahassee, Fla.: Father and Son Publishing, 1995), p. 79. Matthias, like most soldiers, was also fascinated by the spectacle of aerial warfare. See p. 124.

21. James Jones, *WW II: A Chronicle of Soldiering* (New York: Ballantine Books, 1976), pp. 38–39. Robert Leckie also describes watching, with fascination, the naval battles off Guadalcanal. See *Helmet For My Pillow* (Garden City, N.Y.: Nelson Doubleday, 1979), p. 110.

22. Ernie Pyle, *Here Is Your War: The Story of G.I. Joe* (Cleveland and New York: World Publishing, 1945), p. 14. Pyle reported other instances of lust of the eye in his second wartime book, *Brave Men* (New York: Henry Holt, 1944). See his description of a nighttime naval bombardment (pp. 25–26) and the shelling of an enemy position (p. 81).

23. Frederick Downs, *The Killing Zone: My Life in the Vietnam War* (New York: Berkley Books, 1983), pp. 104–105.

24. Michael Herr, *Dispatches* (New York: Avon Books, 1978), p. 160. For further examples of lust of the eye, see Robert G. Merrick, *World War I: A Diary* (Baltimore: privately published, 1982), p. 100; Bob Hoffman, *I Remember the Last War* (York, Pa.: Strength and Health Publishing, 1940), pp. 97 and 198–199; Charles F. Minder, *This Man's War: The Day-by-Day Record of an American Private on the Western Front* (New York: Pevensey Press, 1931), pp. 64 and 296; Roscoe C. Blunt Jr., *Inside the Battle of the Bulge: A Private Comes of Age* (Westport, Conn., and London: Praeger, 1994), p. 23; Nat Frankel and Larry Smith, *Patton's Best: An Informal History of the 4th Armored Division* (New York: Jove Book, 1984), p. 17; Allen R. Matthews, *The Assault* (New York: Dodd, Mead, 1980), p. 158; Richard Tregaskis, *Guadalcanal Diary* (New York: Random House, 1943), pp. 99–100 and 220–222; Richard Tregaskis, *Invasion Diary* (New York: Random House, 1944), pp. 170–172; George Wilson, *If You Survive* (New York: Ivy Books, 1987), p. 119; Lyle Rishell, *With a Black Platoon in Combat: A Year in Korea* (College Station: Texas A&M University Press, 1993), pp. 53–54; and Ketwig, *Hard Rain,* pp. 157–158.

25. Duffy, *Story,* pp. 43–44.

26. Mark Meigs describes the AEF's effort to sponsor doughboy tourism in *Optimism at Armageddon: Voices of American Participants in the First World War* (Washington Square, N.Y.: New York University Press, 1997), chapter 3, "'From a hayloft to a hotel where kings have spent their summers': Americans' Encounter with French Culture," pp. 69–106. See also David M. Kennedy, *Over Here: The First World War and American Society* (New York: Oxford University Press, 1980), pp. 205–209.

27. Rasmus interview in Terkel, *Good War,* p. 39. For other young soldiers impressed with their first view of the world, see Carl M. Becker and Robert G. Thobaben, *Common Warfare: Parallel Memoirs by Two World War II GIs in the Pacific* (Jefferson, N.C., and London: McFarland, 1992), pp. 122–123, and Leckie, *Helmet,* p. 45.

28. David Parks, *G.I. Diary* (New York, Evanston, and London: Harper and Row, 1968), p. 51.

29. Lee Kennett, *G.I.: The American Soldier in World War II* (New York: Charles Scribner's Sons, 1987), p. 90.

30. Robert Jay Lifton, *Home from the War: Vietnam Veterans: Neither Victims nor Executioners* (New York: Simon and Schuster, 1973), p. 219.

31. Cuthbertson letter quoted in Frank Freidel, *Over There: The Story of America's*

*First Great Overseas Crusade,* rev. and abridged ed. (Philadelphia: Temple University Press, 1990), p. 121.

32. Jones, *WW II*, pp. 184–185.

33. Janice Holt Giles, ed., *The G.I. Journal of Sergeant Giles* (Boston: Houghton Mifflin, and Cambridge: Riverside Press, 1965), p. 296.

34. Caputo, *Rumor of War,* p. 254. See also Richard E. Ogden, *Green Knight, Red Mourning* (New York: Zebra Books, 1985), p. 218.

35. Gray, *Warriors,* p. 51.

36. Christian G. Appy, *Working-Class War: American Combat Soldiers and Vietnam* (Chapel Hill and London: University of North Carolina Press, 1993), pp. 262–263.

37. Charles R. Cawthon, *Other Clay: A Remembrance of the World War II Infantry* (Niwot: University Press of Colorado, 1990), p. 128.

38. For a discussion of the soldiers' love of weaponry and the sense of power thus derived, see Appy, *Working-Class War,* pp. 263–264; Broyles, "Men Love War," p. 62; and Dave Grossman, *On Killing: The Psychological Cost of Learning to Kill in War and Society* (Boston: Little, Brown, 1995), pp. 134–137.

39. Hanley interview in Terkel, *Good War,* p. 273. A similar though fictional example is found in Harry Brown, *A Walk in the Sun* (New York: Knopf, 1944), p. 153.

40. Ralph Zumbro, *Tank Sergeant* (Novato, Calif.: Presidio Press, 1986), p. 98.

41. Mark Baker, *Nam: The Vietnam War in the Words of the Men and Women Who Fought There* (New York: Berkley Books, 1983), p. 135. See also pp. 172–176, 184, and 187, and the example in William D. Ehrhart, *Vietnam-Perkasie: A Combat Marine Memoir* (Jefferson, N.C., and London: McFarland, 1983), pp. 70–71.

42. The historian Ronald Schaffer found this ambiguity in doughboys' memoirs: "As one reads what they wrote about the war, one notices that many of the front-line soldiers developed conflicting feelings about it and about the part in it that they had played. The idea that the experience had been awful appears again and again, but they were glad they had gone through it and would not have missed it for anything" (*America in the Great War: The Rise of the War Welfare State* [New York and Oxford: Oxford University Press, 1991], p. 172).

43. Caputo, *Rumor of War,* p. xvi. See also p. 68.

44. James Brady, *The Coldest War: A Memoir of Korea* (New York: Pocket Books, 1991), p. 260.

45. Prendergast interview in Terkel, *Good War,* p. 58.

46. Will Judy, *A Soldier's Diary: A Day-to-Day Record in the World War* (Chicago: Judy Publishing, 1931), p. 216.

47. Becker and Thobaben, *Common Warfare,* p. 203.

48. Matthias, *Reflections,* p. 225.

49. Gray, *Warriors,* pp. 55 and 125.

50. See Thomas C. Leonard, *Above the Battle: War-Making in America from Appomattox to Versailles* (New York: Oxford University Press, 1978), pp. 169–170, and Appy, *Working-Class War,* pp. 280–282. See also the discussion of combat soldier "drivers" versus "passengers," in Elmar Dinter, *Hero or Coward: Pressures Facing the Soldier in Battle* (London and Totowa, N.J.: Frank Cass, 1985), pp. 19–21; the fighter–nonfighter motivational "continuum" in Anthony Kellett, *Combat Motivation: The Behavior of Soldiers in Battle* (Boston, The Hague, and London: Kluwer, Nijhoff, 1982), p. 334; the dis-

cussion of "killer-angels" in Peter S. Kindsvatter, "Cowards, Comrades and Killer Angels: The Soldier in Literature," *Parameters* 20:2 (June 1990): 43–48; and soldier "sheep" versus "sheep dogs" in Grossman, *On Killing*, pp. 183–185.

51. Gwynne Dyer, *War* (New York: Crown Publishers, 1985), pp. 117–118.

52. Harold P. Leinbaugh and John D. Campbell, *The Men of Company K* (New York: Bantam Books, 1987), pp. 304–305. See also the case of Tim O'Brien, *If I Die in a Combat Zone: Box Me Up and Ship Me Home* (New York: Laurel, Dell, 1987), p. 147.

53. Jones, *WW II*, p. 40.

54. James Jones, *The Thin Red Line* (New York: Charles Scribner's Sons, 1962), p. 205.

55. Fife names the characters of Witt, Doll, Bell, and Dale, who are classic fictional case studies of soldier-adventurers (ibid., p. 315).

56. Ent interview in Rudy Tomedi, *No Bugles, No Drums: An Oral History of the Korean War* (New York: John Wiley and Sons, 1993), p. 22.

57. Cawthon, *Other Clay*, p. 141. Samuel L. A. Marshall came to the same conclusion after studying numerous small-unit actions during World War II: "I came to see . . . that the great victories of the United States have pivoted on the acts of courage and intelligence of a very few individuals" (*Men Under Fire*, p. 208).

58. Pyle, *Brave Men*, p. 71.

59. The accuracy of statistics on psychiatric casualties is questionable, for the reasons discussed in chapter 6, but psychotics exhibited distinct symptoms and usually required medical evacuation and discharge from the service; hence, the statistics on the occurrence of psychoses are probably more accurate than for other types of psychiatric casualties. The rate of U.S. Army overseas hospital admissions for psychoses during World War II was 2.8 cases out of 40.2 cases per 1,000 soldiers for all types of neuropsychiatric disorders. See Table 87 in Albert J. Glass, ed., *Neuropsychiatry in World War II*, Medical Department, U.S. Army, Office of the Surgeon General, 2 vols., *Overseas Theaters* (Washington, D.C.: U.S. Government Printing Office, 1973), 2:1006. Similar low but constant rates of psychosis occurred during the Korean and Vietnam Wars. See Donald B. Peterson, "The Psychiatric Operation, Army Forces, Far East, 1950–1953," *American Journal of Psychiatry* 112:1 (July 1955): 27, and Franklin Del Jones and Arnold W. Johnson Jr., "Medical and Psychiatric Treatment Policy and Practice in Vietnam," *Journal of Social Issues* 31:4 (fall 1975): 62–63.

60. Roy R. Grinker and John P. Spiegel, *War Neuroses* (Philadelphia and London: Blakiston, 1945), pp. 44–45.

61. Ibid. See also Gray's discussion of the "soldier-killer" in *Warriors*, pp. 56–57.

62. Jones, *WW II*, p. 67. Norman Mailer provides an intricate portrayal of a World War II psychotic, Sergeant Samuel Croft. Croft loved killing, considered himself invincible, resented and distrusted his superiors, and did not care about anyone but himself. See *The Naked and the Dead* (New York: Signet Books, 1948), pp. 18, 26, 50, 124–128, 149–155, 342, 346, 411–415, and 466–472.

63. Goff and Sanders, *Brothers*, p. 29. See also Herr's description of the psychotic Long Range Reconnaissance Patrol (LRRP) soldier "Ocean Eyes" in *Dispatches*, pp. 5–7.

64. Robert L. Egbert, Tor Meeland, Victor B. Cline, Edward W. Forgy, Martin W. Spickler, and Charles Brown, *Fighter I: An Analysis of Combat Fighters and Non-fight-*

*ers*, Human Resources Research Office Technical Report 44, December 1957, pp. 4 and 26–31. This study is unique in looking at combat soldiers in the midst of a war, but surveys of GIs in a regiment of the Seventieth Division in World War II, conducted before the unit went to combat and again at war's end, revealed a similar set of characteristics for soldiers rated "above average" in combat performance by their junior leaders: confidence in their skills, lower anxiety levels, willingness to kill as part of the job, and intelligence. See Samuel A. Stouffer, Arthur A. Lumsdaine, Marion Harper Lumsdaine, Robin M. Williams Jr., M. Brewster Smith, Irving L. Janis, Shirley A. Star, and Leonard S. Cottrell Jr., *Studies in Social Psychology in World War II*, vol. 2, *The American Soldier: Combat and Its Aftermath* (Princeton: Princeton University Press, 1949), pp. 30–37.

65. Egbert et al., *Fighter I*, pp. 5 and 7.

66. Ross S. Carter, *Those Devils in Baggy Pants* (New York and Toronto: Signet Books, 1951), p. 31.

67. Childress interview in Al Santoli, *Everything We Had: An Oral History of the Vietnam War by Thirty-three American Soldiers Who Fought It* (New York: Ballantine Books, 1982), p. 63.

68. Ent interview in Tomedi, *No Bugles*, p. 19.

69. Broyles, "Men Love War," p. 58. See also Hynes, *Soldiers' Tale*, p. 28.

70. Brady, *Coldest War*, p. 147.

71. Martin Russ, *The Last Parallel: A Marine's War Journal* (New York and Toronto: Rinehart, 1957), p. 216.

72. Lanning, *Only War*, p. 208. See also pp. 178 and 221–222.

73. Matthew Brennan, *Brennan's War: Vietnam 1965–1969* (New York: Pocket Books, 1986), p. 35.

74. Ibid., p. 182. For fictional examples of soldiers who were good fighters and reveled in it, see the case of "Snake" in James Webb, *Fields of Fire* (New York: Bantam Books, 1979), pp. 20 and 233; Joe Sumeric, in William Young Boyd, *The Gentle Infantryman* (New York: St. Martin's Press, 1985), pp. 82–85, 91, 167–168, 189, and 321; and Charlie Dale, in Jones, *Thin Red Line*, pp. 182, 189–190, and 363–364.

75. James Hamilton Dill, *Sixteen Days at Mungol-li* (Fayetteville, Ark.: M&M Press, 1993), p. 147. For a fictional example of a Korean War marine who had "found a home" in the Marine Corps, see the case of Private Nick Tinker, in Pat Frank, *Hold Back the Night* (Philadelphia and New York: J. B. Lippincott, 1952), pp. 34–35 and 207–209. Tinker came from a background of abuse and poverty, joined the marines as soon as he turned seventeen, and proved to be loyal and brave.

76. Brennan, *Brennan's War*, p. 217. For other examples of Vietnam War soldiers who escaped unhappy home lives and found a new home in the army or marines, see the cases of Billy Cizinski and Bob Foley, in Appy, *Working-Class War*, pp. 66–72.

77. Hynes, *Soldiers' Tale*, p. 28.

78. Jones, *Thin Red Line*, pp. 79, 341, and 174.

79. Blunt, *Inside*, p. 77. For instances of paybook collecting, see pp. 38, 50, 125, 131, and 166.

80. Leinbaugh and Campbell, *Company K*, pp. 18 and 303.

81. Barr interviewed in Tomedi, *No Bugles*, pp. 70, 72, and 77.

82. Pyle, *Your War*, p. 214.

83. Tregaskis, *Invasion Diary*, p. 201. See also John Sack's interview in Eric James

Schroeder, *Vietnam, We've All Been There: Interviews with American Writers* (London and Westport, Conn.: Praeger, 1992), p. 14, and Herr, *Dispatches*, pp. 225 and 245.

84. Herr admits to crossing the line between correspondent and soldier and picking up a rifle on occasion. See *Dispatches*, pp. 67–68. Correspondents were supposed to be unarmed, but some carried unauthorized weapons, especially if they doubted that the enemy would honor their noncombatant status.

## CHAPTER 8. CLOSING WITH THE ENEMY

1. Gwynne Dyer, *War* (New York: Crown, 1985), p. 13.

2. See Elmar Dinter, *Hero or Coward: Pressures Facing the Soldier in Battle* (London and Totowa, N.J.: Frank Cass, 1985), p. 22.

3. Sam Keen, *Faces of the Enemy: Reflections of the Hostile Imagination,* with new preface (San Francisco: Harper San Francisco, 1991), p. 13.

4. Keen provides a catalog of these various "archetypes" (ibid., pp. 16–88).

5. See Richard Holmes, *Acts of War: The Behavior of Men in Battle* (New York: Free Press, 1985), pp. 365–368, and Jesse Glenn Gray, *The Warriors: Reflections on Men in Battle* (New York: Harper Colophon Books, 1970), pp. 131–134.

6. Mark Meigs, *Optimism at Armageddon: Voices of American Participants in the First World War* (Washington Square, N.Y.: New York University Press, 1997), p. 22.

7. Will Judy, *A Soldier's Diary: A Day-to-Day Record in the World War* (Chicago: Judy Publishing, 1931), p. 73. See also p. 37.

8. Leon C. Standifer, *Not in Vain: A Rifleman Remembers World War II* (Baton Rouge and London: Louisiana State University Press, 1992), p. 19. See also p. 34. "Kill the dirty Japs" was a common sentiment, as evidenced by a Research Branch survey of a group of infantry soldiers conducted while they were still Stateside. What is not clear from the survey is the extent to which military training versus social and propaganda influences instilled these attitudes. See Samuel A. Stouffer, Arthur A. Lumsdaine, Marion Harper Lumsdaine, Robin M. Williams Jr., M. Brewster Smith, Irving L. Janis, Shirley A. Star, and Leonard S. Cottrell Jr., *Studies in Social Psychology in World War II,* vol. 2, *The American Soldier: Combat and Its Aftermath* (Princeton: Princeton University Press, 1949), chart 7, p. 34.

9. See the discussion of troop indoctrination in chapter 5. See also John A. Ballard and Aliecia J. McDowell, "Hate and Combat Behavior," *Armed Forces and Society* 17:2 (winter 1991): 229–241, for a review of the literature and research on the role of hatred as a motivator. The authors note that no consensus exists on the value of hatred as a motivating factor in combat.

10. See Dave Grossman, *On Killing: The Psychological Cost of Learning to Kill in War and Society* (Boston: Little, Brown, 1995), p. 252.

11. Jonathan Shay, *Achilles in Vietnam: Combat Trauma and the Undoing of Character* (New York: Scribner, 1995), p. 103.

12. For other discussions of dehumanization as part of the Vietnam-era training process, see Christian G. Appy, *Working-Class War: American Combat Soldiers and Vietnam* (Chapel Hill and London: University of North Carolina Press, 1993), pp. 105–107; James R. Ebert, *A Life in a Year: The American Infantryman in Vietnam, 1965–1972*

(Novato, Calif.: Presidio Press, 1993), pp. 45–52; and R. Wayne Eisenhart, "You Can't Hack It, Little Girl: A Discussion of the Covert Psychological Agenda of Modern Combat Training," *Journal of Social Issues* 31:4 (fall 1975): 18–19.

13. Edwards interview in Wallace Terry, *Bloods: An Oral History of the Vietnam War by Black Veterans* (New York: Ballantine Books, 1985), pp. 5–6.

14. Kirkland interview in ibid., p. 90. See also Ebert, *A Life in A Year,* pp. 49–51.

15. Grossman, *On Killing,* pp. 249–260.

16. Brown interview in Mary Penick Motley, *The Invisible Soldier: The Experience of the Black Soldier, World War II* (Detroit: Wayne State University Press, 1975), p. 271.

17. Standifer, *Not in Vain,* p. 98. See also p. 130.

18. David Parks, *G.I. Diary* (New York, Evanston, and London: Harper and Row, 1968), p. 24. For another example of a Vietnam War soldier who was not sure he was ready to kill, see the case of Sergeant Bill Morgan in Jack Fuller, *Fragments* (New York: Dell, 1985), pp. 57–58.

19. William Manchester, *Goodbye, Darkness: A Memoir of the Pacific War* (Boston and Toronto: Little, Brown, 1979), pp. 3–7.

20. Neeley interview in Ebert, *A Life in a Year,* p. 149.

21. Greene interview in Gerald Astor, *Crisis in the Pacific: The Battles for the Philippine Islands by the Men Who Fought Them* (New York: Donald I. Fine Books, 1996), p. 322. See also the case of paratrooper Rodriguez on pp. 210–211.

22. Mark Baker, *Nam: The Vietnam War in the Words of the Men and Women Who Fought There* (New York: Berkley Books, 1983), p. 63. See also Bob Hoffman, *I Remember the Last War* (York, Pa.: Strength and Health Publishing, 1940), p. 109.

23. Audie Murphy, *To Hell and Back* (Toronto: Bantam Books, 1983), p. 10.

24. For a discussion of self-preservation as a motivator, see Anthony Kellett, *Combat Motivation: The Behavior of Soldiers in Battle* (Boston, The Hague, and London: Kluwer, Nijhoff, 1982), p. 302, and Stouffer et al., *Combat and Its Aftermath,* p. 169.

25. Manchester, *Goodbye, Darkness,* p. 373.

26. Richard E. Ogden, *Green Knight, Red Mourning* (New York: Zebra Books, 1985), pp. 22 and 237.

27. Ernie Pyle, *Here is Your War: The Story of G.I. Joe* (Cleveland and New York: World Publishing, 1945), p. 241.

28. Paul Boesch, *Road to Huertgen: Forest in Hell* (Houston: Paul M. Boesch, 1985), pp. 231–232.

29. Parks, *G.I. Diary,* p. 63.

30. Philip Caputo, *A Rumor of War* (New York: Ballantine Books, 1978), p. xix.

31. See Gray, *Warriors,* p. 140.

32. Stiles interview in Henry Berry, *Semper Fi, Mac: Living Memories of the U.S. Marines in World War II* (New York: Berkley Books, 1983), p. 84.

33. Caputo, *Rumor of War,* pp. 268 and 270.

34. Dinter, *Hero or Coward,* p. 45. See also the survey in Stouffer et al., *Combat and Its Aftermath,* p. 167.

35. Franklyn A. Johnson, *One More Hill* (Toronto: Bantam Books, 1983), p. 98. See also the Renstrom interview in Berry, *Semper Fi,* p. 224.

36. Baker, *Nam,* p. 72.

37. See Gray, *Warriors,* p. 51.

38. Hoffman, *I Remember,* p. 108. Historians have noted that soldier-author accounts of heavy fighting are understandably blurred, sketchy, or surreal. See John Ellis, *Eye-Deep in Hell: Trench Warfare in World War I* (Baltimore: Johns Hopkins University Press, 1989), pp. 98–104; John Ellis, *The Sharp End: The Fighting Man in World War II* (New York: Charles Scribner's Sons, 1980), pp. 102–105; and John Keegan and Richard Holmes, with John Gau, *Soldiers: A History of Men in Battle* (New York: Viking, 1986), p. 263. See also the case of Lewis Millett, who won a Congressional Medal of Honor in Korea but remembers only part of what happened and admits to going "berserk." See his interview in Rudy Tomedi, *No Bugles, No Drums: An Oral History of the Korean War* (New York: John Wiley and Sons, 1993), p. 110.

39. Joseph D. Lawrence, *Fighting Soldier: The A.E.F. in 1918* (Boulder: Colorado Associated University Press, 1985), p. 99.

40. John W. Thomason Jr., *Fix Bayonets!* (New York: Blue Ribbon Books, 1926), p. 17. See also the interview with Sergeant Merritt D. Cutler in Henry Berry, *Make the Kaiser Dance: Living Memories of the Doughboy* (New York: Priam Books, 1978), pp. 216–217.

41. James Brady, *The Coldest War: A Memoir of Korea* (New York: Pocket Books, 1991), p. 256.

42. James R. McDonough, *Platoon Leader* (New York: Bantam Books, 1986), p. 159. For other examples of postcombat elation over surviving, see William Young Boyd, *The Gentle Infantryman* (New York: St. Martin's Press, 1985), p. 37; Curtis James Morrow, *What's a Commie Ever Done to Black People? A Korean War Memoir of Fighting in the U.S. Army's Last All Negro Unit* (Jefferson, N.C., and London: McFarland, 1997), p. 35; Baker, *Nam,* p. 71; and Charles R. Cawthon, *Other Clay: A Remembrance of the World War II Infantry* (Niwot: University Press of Colorado, 1990), p. 67.

43. George William Sefton, *It Was My War: I'll Remember It the Way I Want To!* (Manhattan, Kans.: Sunflower University Press, 1994), p. 129.

44. See John W. Dower, *War Without Mercy: Race and Power in the Pacific War* (New York: Pantheon Books, 1986), p. 34.

45. Observers of soldiers' behavior describe a "*Frontkämpfer* spirit" as common on the western front during the world wars, especially the first war. German and Allied soldiers sympathized with one anothers' condition—they were the ones suffering and dying, not those in the rear areas and on the home front. See Gray, *Warriors,* pp. 135–138; Holmes, *Acts of War,* pp. 367–371; and Thomas C. Leonard, *Above the Battle: War-Making in America from Appomattox to Versailles* (New York: Oxford University Press, 1978), pp. 68–73.

46. Robert G. Merrick, *World War I: A Diary* (Baltimore: privately published, 1982), p. 20. For other examples, see [Howard V. O'Brien], *Wine, Women, and War: A Diary of Disillusionment* (New York: J. H. Sears, 1926), p. 79; Judy, *Soldier's Diary,* p. 116; and Horatio Rogers, *World War I Through My Sights* (San Rafael, Calif.: Presidio Press, 1976), pp. 28–29.

47. Roscoe C. Blunt Jr., *Inside the Battle of the Bulge: A Private Comes of Age* (Westport, Conn., and London: Praeger, 1994), p. 19. See also p. 161. For other examples, see Rasmus interview in Studs Terkel, *"The Good War": An Oral History of World War II* (New York: Pantheon Books, 1984), pp. 44–45; Cawthon, *Other Clay,* p. 130; Kurt Gabel, *The Making of a Paratrooper: Airborne Training and Combat in World War II* (Lawrence: University Press of Kansas, 1990), pp. 156–157; Klaus H. Huebner, *Long Walk Through*

*War: A Combat Doctor's Diary* (College Station: Texas A&M University Press, 1987), p. 75; and Pyle, *Your War,* pp. 274–277.

48. For examples of German "fair play" in honoring the Red Cross emblem or allowing truces for the recovery of casualties, see Carl Andrew Brannen, *Over There: A Marine in the Great War* (College Station: Texas A&M University Press, 1996), pp. 24–25 and 42; Harold L. Bond, *Return to Cassino* (New York: Pocket Books, 1965), p. 57; Blunt, *Inside,* p. 69; Harold P. Leinbaugh and John D. Campbell, *The Men of Company K* (New York: Bantam Books, 1987), pp. 225–226; Charles B. MacDonald, *Company Commander* (Toronto, New York, and London: Bantam Books, 1978), p. 85; and Ralph G. Martin, *The G.I. War, 1941–1945* (Boston and Toronto: Little, Brown, 1967), pp. 77–78.

49. Hoffman, *I Remember,* pp. 185–186.

50. Francis P. Duffy, *Father Duffy's Story: A Tale of Humor and Heroism, of Life and Death with the Fighting Sixty-ninth* (Garden City, N.Y.: Garden City Publishing, 1919), p. 311.

51. For condemnations of the rapaciousness of the German occupation and withdrawal, see Judy, *Soldier's Diary,* pp. 163 and 195; [O'Brien], *Wine, Women, and War,* pp. 222 and 255; and Rogers, *Through My Sights,* pp. 193–194.

52. For examples, see Alice M. Hoffman and Howard S. Hoffman, *Archives of Memory: A Soldier Recalls World War II* (Lexington: University Press of Kentucky, 1990), p. 100, and Janice Holt Giles, ed., *The G.I. Journal of Sergeant Giles* (Boston: Houghton Mifflin, and Cambridge: Riverside Press, 1965), pp. 199–200, 277–278, 322–323, 338, 350, and 352.

53. Blunt, *Inside,* pp. 79–80. For another example of a GI differentiating between "brainwashed" SS troopers and "ordinary" German soldiers, see Terkel, *Good War,* p. 259.

54. Leinbaugh and Campbell, *Company K,* p. 134.

55. Duffy, *Story,* p. 312.

56. Hoffman, *I Remember,* p. 306. See also pp. 120–121. For other positive doughboy assessments of the Germans as soldiers, see William L. Langer, *Gas and Flame in World War I* (New York: Knopf, 1965), pp. xix–xx, and Elton E. Mackin, *Suddenly We Didn't Want to Die: Memoirs of a World War I Marine* (Novato, Calif.: Presidio Press, 1993), pp. 55, 189, and 246.

57. Bill Mauldin, *Up Front* (New York: Award Books, 1976), pp. 51–52.

58. Huebner, *Long Walk,* p. 174. For other positive GI assessments of German fighting ability, see Leslie W. Bailey, *Through Hell and High Water: The Wartime Memories of a Junior Combat Infantry Officer* (New York: Vantage Press, 1994), p. 96; Bond, *Cassino,* pp. 37 and 187; Harry Brown, *A Walk in the Sun* (New York: Knopf, 1944), p. 100; Cawthon, *Other Clay,* p. 76; and Nat Frankel and Larry Smith, *Patton's Best: An Informal History of the 4th Armored Division* (New York: Jove Book, 1984), pp. 110–111.

59. See Lee Kennett, *G.I.: The American Soldier in World War II* (New York: Charles Scribner's Sons, 1987), pp. 155 and 153.

60. Research Branch surveys of combat veterans and soldiers still in training verified that hatred of the Japanese, as revealed by the large affirmative response to the suggestion "wipe out the whole Japanese nation," far outstripped hatred of the German people, who received a much lower affirmative response to the same recommendation (see Stouffer et al., *Combat and Its Aftermath,* chart 9, p. 158).

61. Gray, *Warriors,* p. 149.

62. John Hersey, *Into the Valley: A Skirmish of the Marines,* with new foreword (New York: Schocken Books, 1989), p. xxviii.

63. Prewar racial stereotyping and the resultant underestimation of the Japanese is discussed in Craig M. Cameron, *American Samurai: Myth, Imagination, and the Conduct of Battle in the First Marine Division, 1941–1951* (Cambridge: Cambridge University Press, 1994), pp. 89–95, and Dower, *Without Mercy,* pp. 98–106.

64. Gerald P. Averill, *Mustang: A Combat Marine* (Novato, Calif.: Presidio Press, 1987), p. 18. For similar reactions, see Berry, *Semper Fi,* pp. 294 and 354, and Terkel, *Good War,* p. 87.

65. For a discussion of this shift in perception, see Cameron, *American Samurai,* pp. 104–105; Dower, *Without Mercy,* pp. 111–117; Kennett, *G.I.,* pp. 167–168; and James J. Weingartner, "War Against Subhumans: Comparisons Between the German War Against the Soviet Union and the American War Against Japan, 1941–1945," *Historian* 58:3 (spring 1996): 564.

66. Hawkins interview in Berry, *Semper Fi,* p. 41. For other comments about the loss of Japanese "superman" status, see E. J. Kahn Jr., *G.I. Jungle: An American Soldier in Australia and New Guinea* (New York: Simon and Schuster, 1943), p. 122, and Robert Leckie, *Helmet for My Pillow* (Garden City, N.Y.: Nelson Doubleday, 1979), pp. 197–198.

67. For a discussion of "exterminationist ideology," as Cameron calls it, see *American Samurai,* pp. 114–118 and 166–168. See also Dower, *Without Mercy,* pp. 88–93.

68. Rants interview in Astor, *Crisis,* p. 275.

69. Peter Bowman, *Beach Red* (New York: Random House, 1945), p. 13.

70. Eugene B. Sledge, *With the Old Breed at Peleliu and Okinawa* (New York: Bantam Books, 1983), pp. 37–38. As Sledge notes, the Japanese also contributed to the racism and hatred. For a discussion of Japan's racist view of the West during World War II, see Dower, *Without Mercy,* pp. 240–261.

71. Charles M. Bussey, *Firefight at Yechon: Courage and Racism in the Korean War* (Washington, D.C., and London: Brassey's, 1991), p. 73.

72. Ent interview in Tomedi, *No Bugles,* pp. 16–17.

73. Pat Frank, *Hold Back the Night* (Philadelphia and New York: J. B. Lippincott, 1952), p. 18.

74. Samuel L. A. Marshall, *Commentary on Infantry Operations and Weapons Usage in Korea, Winter of 1950–1951,* Operations Research Office Report 13 (Chevy Chase, Md.: Johns Hopkins University Press, 1953), pp. 118–119.

75. Ent interview in Tomedi, *No Bugles,* p. 18.

76. Robert Mason, *Chickenhawk* (New York: Penguin Books, 1986), p. 63.

77. Caputo, *Rumor of War,* p. 66.

78. Alfred S. Bradford, *Some Even Volunteered: The First Wolfhounds Pacify Vietnam* (Westport, Conn., and London: Praeger, 1994), p. 37.

79. Ogden, *Green Knight,* p. 132.

80. For an analysis of this dehumanizing, racist outlook, see Robert Jay Lifton's discussion of the "gook syndrome" in his *Home from the War: Vietnam Veterans: Neither Victims nor Executioners* (New York: Simon and Schuster, 1973), pp. 191–205.

81. Frederick Downs, *The Killing Zone: My Life in the Vietnam War* (New York: Berkley Books, 1978), p. 7.

82. Baker, *Nam,* p. 173. See also p. 66.

83. See Eric Bergerud, *Touched with Fire: The Land War in the South Pacific* (New York: Viking Penguin, 1996), pp. 404–406. Bergerud does not mention which scholarly accounts he is taking issue with, but the best of the works arguing that racism was the main cause of hatred and brutality in the Pacific in World War II is Dower's *Without Mercy*.

84. Ore Marion interview in Bergerud, *Touched with Fire*, p. 412.

85. Dan Levin, *From the Battlefield: Dispatches of a World War II Marine* (Annapolis, Md.: Naval Institute Press, 1995), p. 58. Ira Wolfert notes that Japanese suicidal tendencies were first encountered on Guadalcanal and were as mystifying to Americans then as they were throughout the war. See *Battle for the Solomons* (Cambridge, Mass.: Riverside Press, 1943), pp. 128–131.

86. Marguerite Higgins, *War in Korea: The Report of a Woman Combat Correspondent* (Garden City, N.Y.: Doubleday, 1951), p. 203.

87. White interview in Tomedi, *No Bugles*, p. 129. See also Freeman interview, pp. 120–121. See also Boris R. Spiroff's comment about a Chinese wave assault during the April 1951 offensive in his *Korea: Frozen Hell on Earth* (New York: Vantage Press, 1995), p. 69.

88. For comments about possible Chinese use of opium, see Henry Berry, *Hey, Mac, Where Ya Been? Living Memories of the U.S. Marines in the Korean War* (New York: St. Martin's Press, 1988), pp. 183–184, and Donald Knox, with additional text by Alfred Coppel, *The Korean War: Uncertain Victory: The Concluding Volume of an Oral History* (San Diego, New York, and London: Harcourt Brace Jovanovich, 1988), p. 434.

89. Grossman, *On Killing*, p. 267.

90. Dixon Wecter, *When Johnny Comes Marching Home* (Westport, Conn.: Greenwood Press, 1970), p. 488.

91. Dower, who stresses that both sides must share the blame for racism and the downward spiral of atrocities, acknowledges that the Japanese had a deserved reputation for brutality even before Pearl Harbor, and their harsh treatment of American prisoners of war captured during their early victories only made matters worse. See *Without Mercy*, pp. 33–52. See also Bergerud, *Touched with Fire*, pp. 403–416.

92. Kahn, *G.I. Jungle*, p. 117. Kahn goes on to describe various Japanese brutalities and dirty tricks. See pp. 117–119. See also the Hoffrichter interview in Astor, *Crisis*, p. 276.

93. Bowman, *Beach Red*, p. 78. This statement concludes a discussion of Japanese cruelty during the Bataan Death March that is superfluous to the plot, except to show the hatred generated by such Japanese actions.

94. Theodore R. Fehrenbach provides a discussion of atrocities and the mistreatment of prisoners by the North Koreans, and to a lesser extent, by the Chinese. See *This Kind of War: A Study in Unpreparedness* (New York: Macmillan, 1963), pp. 199–201, 233, 423–425, 461–469, and 540–549. For eyewitness accounts from the Sunchon Tunnel Massacre in October 1950, and of North Korean brutality in general, see Tomedi, *No Bugles*, pp. 48–59; Donald Knox, *The Korean War: Pusan to Chosin: An Oral History* (San Diego, New York, and London: Harcourt Brace Jovanovich, 1985), pp. 98, 173–175, 330, and 372–373; and Higgins, *War in Korea*, pp. 91–92.

95. Higgins notes that "the Chinese were certainly far more correct in their behavior toward captives than were the North Koreans" (*War in Korea*, p. 208). Hig-

gins is only relatively correct, however. The Chinese were not exactly compassionate jailers, especially during the first winter of the war. See Knox, *Uncertain Victory,* pp. 327–344.

96. William H. Mauldin, *Bill Mauldin in Korea* (New York: W. W. Norton, 1952), p. 94.

97. Scott interview in Tomedi, *No Bugles,* p. 181.

98. Dominick Yezzo, *A G.I.'s Vietnam Diary, 1968–1969* (New York: Franklin Watts, 1974), diary entry for May 14. See February 12 entry for Yezzo's sympathetic view of some North Vietnamese prisoners. See also McDonough, *Platoon Leader,* pp. 192–193; Stanley Goff and Robert Sanders with Clark Smith, *Brothers: Black Soldiers in the Nam* (Novato, Calif.: Presidio Press, 1982), pp. 139–140; Ogden, *Green Knight,* pp. 96–98; Al Santoli, *Everything We Had: An Oral History of the Vietnam War by Thirty-three American Soldiers Who Fought It* (New York: Ballantine Books, 1982), p. 61; and Ebert, *A Life in a Year,* pp. 297–299.

99. For examples, see Mason, *Chickenhawk,* pp. 218–219; Ogden, *Green Knight,* pp. 8–11; and Terry, *Bloods,* pp. 46 and 241–243.

100. Ebert makes this point and provides examples of wounded Americans killed by the North Vietnamese in *A Life in a Year,* p. 282.

101. Goff and Sanders, *Brothers,* p. 142.

102. Caputo, *Rumor of War,* p. xviii.

103. For examples of these tricks and ruses, see Hervey Allen, *Toward the Flame: A War Diary* (New York: Grosset and Dunlap, 1934), p. 46; Berry, *Make the Kaiser Dance,* pp. 39, 165, and 278; Judy, *Soldier's Diary,* pp. 121, 127–129, and 131; Mackin, *We Didn't Want to Die,* pp. 58–65; Thomason, *Fix Bayonets!* pp. 24–27; Amos N. Wilder, *Armageddon Revisited: A World War I Journal* (New Haven and London: Yale University Press, 1994), p. 96; and Laurence Stallings, *The Doughboys: The Story of the AEF, 1917–1918* (New York, Evanston, and London: Harper and Row, 1963), p. 317.

104. Richard Tregaskis, *Guadalcanal Diary* (New York: Random House, 1943), p. 146. For other examples of Japanese soldiers playing dead, see Bergerud, *Touched with Fire,* pp. 410–411; Berry, *Semper Fi,* p. 86; and Astor, *Crisis,* p. 374.

105. Levin, *Battlefield,* p. 22. See also Sledge, *Old Breed,* p. 37.

106. Higgins, *War in Korea,* pp. 202–203.

107. Charles S. Crawford, *The Four Deuces: A Korean War Story* (Novato, Calif.: Presidio Press, 1989), pp. 224–226; for a discussion of the enemy's propensity for infiltration, see pp. 89–90.

108. William D. Ehrhart, *Vietnam-Perkasie: A Combat Marine Memoir* (Jefferson, N.C., and London: McFarland, 1983), p. 56.

109. Yushta interview in Ebert, *A Life in a Year,* p. 296.

110. See Ellis, *Sharp End,* p. 88.

111. Hersey, *Into the Valley,* p. 42.

112. Fox interview in Bergerud, *Touched with Fire,* p. 359.

113. La Magna interview in Astor, *Crisis,* p. 190. The numerous personal accounts in Astor and also in Bergerud, *Touched with Fire,* provide a vivid portrait of the grim, stressful nature of jungle fighting in the Pacific in World War II.

114. Averill, *Mustang,* p. 200.

115. Marshall, *Commentary on Infantry,* p. 6.

116. Scheuber interview in Knox, *Uncertain Victory,* p. 487. See further examples on pp. 48, 286, and 499. See also Howard Matthias, *The Korean War—Reflections of a Young Combat Platoon Leader,* rev. ed. (Tallahassee, Fla.: Father and Son Publishing, 1995), p. xi, for a comment on the Korean and Vietnam Wars being "very personal wars with much close contact with the enemy."

117. Ogden, *Green Knight,* p. 209. See also Tobey C. Herzog, *Vietnam War Stories: Innocence Lost* (London and New York: Routledge, 1985), pp. 51–52.

118. John Sack, *M* (New York: Avon Books, 1985), p. 157; for another shadow-boxing analogy, see Ehrhart, *Vietnam-Perkasie,* p. 194.

119. Grossman, *On Killing,* p. 196.

120. Keen, *Faces,* pp. 61–62. For this point raised specifically in the cases of the Japanese and Vietnamese enemies, see Gray, *Warriors,* pp. 152–153, and Shay, *Achilles,* pp. 115–119.

121. Bowman, *Beach Red,* pp. 20 and 61.

122. Stiles interview in Berry, *Semper Fi,* p. 82.

123. Higgins interview in Astor, *Crisis,* p. 369.

124. Averill, *Mustang,* p. 297.

125. Joseph R. Owen, *Colder Than Hell: A Marine Rifle Company at Chosin Reservoir* (Annapolis, Md.: Naval Institute Press, 1996), p. 45. See also Crawford, *Four Deuces,* pp. 76–77. Positive comments about the Chinese enemy's skill and endurance are also evident in the memoirs. See Lyle Rishell, *With a Black Platoon in Combat: A Year in Korea* (College Station: Texas A & M University Press, 1993), p. 155, and Spiroff, *Frozen Hell,* p. 31.

126. Gustav Hasford, *The Short-timers* (Toronto: Bantam Books, 1979), p. 153.

127. Goff and Sanders, *Brothers,* pp. 130–131. For other sympathetic or respectful comments about the NVA or VC, see Matthew Brennan, *Brennan's War: Vietnam, 1965–1969* (New York: Pocket Books, 1986), pp. 60–61 and 66, and Caputo, *Rumor of War,* p. 262.

128. Leckie, *Helmet,* p. 212.

129. Manchester, *Goodbye, Darkness,* p. 240.

130. James J. Weingartner, "Trophies of War: U.S. Troops and the Mutilation of Japanese War Dead, 1941–1945," *Pacific Historical Review* 61:1 (February 1992): 54. Dower discusses how this mutual racism and hatred spawned reciprocal brutalities, until "no mercy" prevailed. See *Without Mercy,* chapter 3, "War Hates and War Crimes," pp. 33–73.

131. Sledge, *Old Breed,* p. 150.

132. Caputo, *Rumor of War,* pp. 217–218. See Ebert, *A Life in a Year,* pp. 293–315, for a discussion of the problems of fighting an unconventional war and the terrorism, atrocities, and brutalities that occurred on both sides.

133. Astor, *Crisis,* p. 449. See also James J. Weingartner, "Massacre at Biscari: Patton and an American War Crime," *Historian* 52:1 (November 1989): 24–39, for the effect that a "no-prisoners" speech by General George S. Patton may have had in precipitating a massacre of German and Italian prisoners of war by American soldiers during the fighting in Sicily in World War II. For discussions of the role of leaders in either moderating or encouraging brutality, see Robert J. Berens, "Battle Atrocities," *Army* 36:4 (April 1986): 56, and Dower, *Without Mercy,* pp. 66–67.

134. Frederick Downs, "View from the Fourth Estate: Death and the Dark Side of Command," *Parameters* 17:4 (December 1987): 92.

135. Downs, *Killing Zone,* p. 192.

136. See Herbert Hendin and Ann Pollinger Haas, *Wounds of War: The Psychological Aftermath of Combat in Vietnam* (New York: Basic Books, 1984), p. 239.

137. Lawrence, *Fighting Soldier,* p. 104.

138. Brady, *Coldest War,* p. 208. See pp. 206–212 for the entire affair.

139. Brennan, *Brennan's War,* p. 100. See also Goff and Sanders, *Brothers,* p. 140.

140. MacDonald, *Company Commander,* p. 215.

141. For examples of Japanese wounded or soldiers feigning surrender who attempted to take some Americans with them, see Astor, *Crisis,* pp. 373 and 431, and Berry, *Semper Fi,* p. 327.

142. Astor, *Crisis,* pp. 448–449. See also Kennett, *G.I.,* pp. 163–166.

143. Matula interview in Astor, *Crisis,* p. 373; for other GI refusals to take prisoners, despite the intelligence officers' requests to do so, see pp. 278 and 437.

144. Rosenblum interview in Terkel, *Good War,* p. 382.

145. Sturkey interview in Motley, *Invisible Soldier,* p. 171.

146. Winter interview in Tomedi, *No Bugles,* pp. 25 and 28.

147. Brannen, *Over There,* p. 49. For similar doughboy comments about a no-mercy attitude toward machine gunners and snipers, see Hoffman, *I Remember,* p. 306, and Frank Freidel, *Over There: The Story of America's First Great Overseas Crusade,* rev. and abridged ed. (Philadelphia: Temple University Press, 1990), p. 115.

148. Ernie Pyle, *Brave Men* (New York: Henry Holt, 1944), p. 373.

149. Blunt, *Inside,* p. 21. See also Lester Atwell, *Private* (New York: Popular Library, 1958), p. 327, for a captured German sniper forced to dig his own grave and then being shot, on the orders of the division commander, no less. Atwell was one of the few to ponder what was obviously a double standard of GI fairness: "It always struck me as odd: the enemy snipers were unspeakable villains; our own were heroes."

150. Mackin, *We Didn't Want to Die,* pp. 96 and 97.

151. Crawford, *Four Deuces,* p. 195. See also Frank, *Hold Back the Night,* p. 89.

152. Frankel, *Patton's Best,* p. 5.

153. Peter Watson, *War on the Mind: The Military Uses and Abuses of Psychology* (New York: Basic Books, 1978), p. 244.

154. William Barry Gault, "Some Remarks on Slaughter," *American Journal of Psychiatry* 128:4 (October 1971): 84. See also Joel Yager, "Personal Violence in Infantry Combat," *Archives of General Psychiatry* 32:2 (February 1975): 261. Yager sees group dynamics, situational factors, and personality as interrelated in generating atrocities, but "in some instances, the personal factors . . . seem to far outweigh group and situational factors."

155. Caputo, *Rumor of War,* p. 128.

156. Brennan, *Brennan's War,* p. 141. See also pp. 85–86 for the case of Gould, another unrestrained killer.

157. Leinbaugh and Campbell, *Company K,* p. 54. For other World War II examples of prisoners killed in a fit of rage, see Blunt, *Inside,* pp. 84–85, and Manchester, *Goodbye, Darkness,* p. 381.

158. Mason, *Chickenhawk,* p. 435.

159. Peter Marin, "Coming to Terms with Vietnam," *Harper's* 261:1567 (December 1980): 49; Gray also makes this point in *Warriors,* pp. 186–188.

160. Houghton interview in Berry, *Make the Kaiser Dance,* p. 149.

161. Blunt, *Inside,* p. 80. For a fictional example of a World War II soldier who could not kill an enemy prisoner, even though his close friend had just been killed, see the case of Captain Paul Kreider in Richard Tregaskis, *Stronger Than Fear* (New York: Random House, 1945), p. 107. Kreider reasons that "it was not right to kill an unarmed man in cold blood. The fact that the enemy had done that in many cases didn't make it any more right or honorable."

162. Gonzalez interview in Knox, *Pusan to Chosin,* p. 514. See also Ogden, *Green Knight,* pp. 294–295.

163. Allen, *Toward the Flame,* p. 182.

164. Ibid., p. 183. For other examples of soldiers who appreciated how counterproductive killing surrendering prisoners was, see Hoffman, *I Remember,* pp. 308–309; Paul Fussell, *Doing Battle: The Making of a Skeptic* (Boston: Little, Brown, 1996), p. 141; Leinbaugh and Campbell, *Company K,* p. 148; and Berry, *Semper Fi,* p. 67.

165. Parks, *G.I. Diary,* p. 121. For another example, see James Webb, *Fields of Fire* (New York: Bantam Books, 1979), p. 171, for the case of a lieutenant nicknamed "Rock Man" and his platoon, whose cruelties toward the local populace "*made* a lot more VC than they ever end up killing."

166. Herzog, *War Stories,* p. 106, makes the point that wrestling with this "critical issue" is especially prevalent in the Vietnam War literature. See also Cornelius A. Cronin, "Line of Departure: The Atrocity in Vietnam War Literature," in *Fourteen Landing Zones: Approaches to Vietnam War Literature,* ed. Philip K. Jason (Iowa City: University of Iowa Press, 1991), pp. 200–216.

167. Frankel, *Patton's Best,* p. 4.

168. Caputo, *Rumor of War,* p. xx.

169. Downs, *Killing Zone,* p. 162. For a similar statement about the Vietnam War turning the grunt "deep-down mean," see Larry Heinemann, *Close Quarters* (New York: Farrar, Straus and Giroux, 1977), p. 278.

170. Lifton, *Home,* p. 102.

171. Hasford, *Short-timers,* p. 133.

172. McDonough, *Platoon Leader,* p. 62. Tim O'Brien, although not a leader like McDonough, also understood that the grunt could not abdicate personal responsibility. See his interview in Eric James Schroeder, *Vietnam, We've All Been There: Interviews with American Writers* (London and Westport, Conn.: Praeger, 1992), p. 138.

173. Fuller, *Fragments,* pp. 53, 54, and 287.

174. Samuel L. A. Marshall, *Men Against Fire: The Problem of Battle Command in Future War* (Gloucester: Peter Smith, 1978), p. 50, for the 25 percent ratio of fire; p. 53, for Marshall's claim to having conducted approximately 400 postcombat interviews; and p. 54, for his claim that "nearly all hands" could have brought fire on the enemy at some point in each engagement but only 20 to 25 percent did so. See also pp. 71 and 78.

175. Richard A. Gabriel, *The Painful Field: The Psychiatric Dimension of Modern War* (New York, London, and Westport, Conn.: Greenwood Press, 1988), p. 3. Gabriel used a 15 percent figure assumedly because the actual range of Marshall's estimate was

15 to 25 percent firers, with 25 percent being the best that could be expected from "the most spirited and aggressive companies" (see Marshall, *Men Against Fire,* p. 54).

176. John A. English, *On Infantry* (New York: Praeger, 1981), p. 145.

177. Russell F. Weigley, *Eisenhower's Lieutenants: The Campaigns of France and Germany* (Bloomington: Indiana University Press, 1981), p. 38.

178. Fredric Smoler, "The Secret of the Soldiers Who Didn't Shoot," *American Heritage* 40:2 (March 1989): 40.

179. Ibid., p. 43. The two articles referred to are this one and Roger J. Spiller, "S. L. A. Marshall and the Ratio of Fire," *Royal United Services Institute Journal* 133:4 (winter 1988): 63–71.

180. For examples, see Michael C. C. Adams, *The Best War Ever: America and World War II* (Baltimore and London: Johns Hopkins University Press, 1994), pp. 96–97, and especially Grossman, who wholeheartedly embraces Marshall's ratio of fire and guilt rationale in *On Killing,* pp. 4 and 87–93.

181. Michael D. Doubler, *Closing with the Enemy: How GIs Fought the War in Europe, 1944–1945* (Lawrence: University Press of Kansas, 1994), pp. 289–290.

182. MacDonald, *Company Commander,* pp. 124–128.

183. George Wilson, *If You Survive* (New York: Ivy Books, 1987), p. 111.

184. See Fussell, *Doing Battle,* p. 100.

185. Ross S. Carter, *Those Devils in Baggy Pants* (New York and Toronto: Signet Books, 1951), p. 41.

186. Standifer, *Not in Vain,* p. 53.

187. Edwin A. Weinstein, "The Function of Interpersonal Relations in the Neurosis of Combat," *Psychiatry: Journal of the Biology and the Pathology of Interpersonal Relations* 10:3 (August 1947): 312.

188. Wilson, *If You Survive,* pp. 150–151.

189. Cameron, *American Samurai,* p. 51.

190. Astor, *Crisis,* pp. 451–452. A large majority (more than 70 percent) of GIs in a Research Branch survey responded, while still in training, that they would "like" to kill a Japanese soldier or would "feel that it was just part of the job, without either liking or disliking it." Add in the catalyst of the battlefield, as Astor mentions, and the number of GIs too reluctant to shoot at a Japanese soldier must have been small indeed (see Stouffer et al., *Combat and Its Aftermath,* chart 7, p. 34).

191. Dinter, *Hero or Coward,* p. 23.

192. Jules W. Coleman, "The Group Factor in Military Psychiatry," *American Journal of Orthopsychiatry* 16:2 (April 1946): 224. Guilt over killing as a limited factor at most in causing psychological breakdowns is discussed in chapter 6.

193. Cameron, *American Samurai,* p. 51 n. 7.

194. Crawford, *Four Deuces,* pp. 99 and 100.

195. In contrast to Marshall's self-invented ratio of fire from World War II, a bona fide survey of Vietnam veterans from the First Cavalry Division revealed that more than 80 percent engaged the enemy in a firefight. The handful of nonparticipants in a particular battle said they failed to fire because they were performing other duties, had a weapon malfunction, did not want to give away their positions, wanted to avoid fratricide, or froze out of fear. Anxiety or guilt over killing was not mentioned (see Russell W. Glenn, "Men and Fire in Vietnam," two-part series, part 1, *Army* 39:4 [April 1989]: 18–26; part 2, *Army* 39:5 [May 1989]: 38–45).

196. Downs, *Killing Zone,* p. 161.

197. This quotation is from the title of Grossman's section on killing and physical distance. See his *On Killing,* pp. 97–137. For other discussions of the effect of distance on killing, see Gray, *Warriors,* p. 178; Keen, *Faces,* pp. 72–88; and Lifton, *Home,* pp. 346–361.

198. Mackin, *We Didn't Want to Die,* p. 35.

199. MacDonald, *Company Commander,* p. 252.

200. Sefton, *It Was My War,* p. 113. See also the Freeman interview in Tomedi, *No Bugles,* p. 119. For "shooting gallery" analogies, see Leinbaugh and Campbell, *Company K,* p. 188, and Crawford, *Four Deuces,* p. 105.

201. James Hamilton Dill, *Sixteen Days at Mungol-li* (Fayetteville, Ark.: M&M Press, 1993), p. 312. For another example of the traumatic effect of up-close killing, see Morrow, *Commie,* p. 30.

202. Altieri interview in Martin, *G.I. War,* p. 43.

203. Avery interview in Knox, *Uncertain Victory,* p. 48.

204. Blunt, *Inside,* p. 115.

205. Ibid., pp. 115–116. See also Morrow, *Commie,* pp. 63–64.

206. Caputo, *Rumor of War,* p. 68.

207. Ibid., p. 289. Caputo's sense of guilt contradicts his earlier statement (see note 168) that the environment of war was to blame for the grunts' "brutishness." Like most soldiers, Caputo could not absolve himself of some measure of responsibility for his actions, no matter how brutal the environment of war. For an analysis of environmental factors versus personal responsibility in Caputo's *Rumor of War,* see Thomas Myers, *Walking Point: American Narratives in Vietnam* (New York and Oxford: Oxford University Press, 1988), pp. 97–102.

208. Levin, *Battlefield,* p. 26.

209. Sledge, *Old Breed,* pp. 120–121.

210. Alvin C. York, *Sergeant York: His Own Life Story and War Diary* (Garden City, N.Y.: Doubleday, Doran, 1928), p. 236. See also Charles F. Minder, *This Man's War: The Day-by-Day Record of an American Private on the Western Front* (New York: Pevensey Press, 1931), pp. 247–248, 292, and 332.

211. Johnson interview in Terkel, *Good War,* pp. 261, 262, and 263.

212. Anderson interview in Santoli, *Everything We Had,* p. 71. For an example of one such reluctant killer in Vietnam, see the case of Arthur in Brennan, *Brennan's War,* pp. 87–88, 95–96, and 105–106.

213. Brennan, *Brennan's War,* p. 64. For a fictional example of comrades consoling while also congratulating a GI for killing his first Japanese soldier, see the case of Private Bead in James Jones, *The Thin Red Line* (New York: Charles Scribner's Sons, 1962), pp. 150–152.

CHAPTER 9. LEADERSHIP IN COMBAT

1. Lord Charles McM. Moran, *The Anatomy of Courage* (Garden City Park, N.Y.: Avery, 1987), p. 185.

2. Lee Kennett, *G.I.: The American Soldier in World War II* (New York: Charles Scribner's Sons, 1987), p. 142. Research Branch surveys of enlisted men in World War II

verify Kennett's list of desirable junior leader traits. See Samuel A. Stouffer, Arthur A. Lumsdaine, Marion Harper Lumsdaine, Robin M. Williams Jr., M. Brewster Smith, Irving L. Janis, Shirley A. Star, and Leonard S. Cottrell Jr., *Studies in Social Psychology in World War II*, vol. 2, *The American Soldier: Combat and Its Aftermath* (Princeton: Princeton University Press, 1949), pp. 118–130.

3. Bill Mauldin, *Up Front* (New York: Award Books, 1976), p. 178.

4. Frederick Downs, "View from the Fourth Estate: Death and the Dark Side of Command," *Parameters* 17:4 (December 1987): 93.

5. William Darryl Henderson, *Cohesion: The Human Experience in Combat: Leadership and Societal Influences in the Armies of the Soviet Union, the United States, North Vietnam, and Israel* (Washington, D.C.: National Defense University Press, 1988), p. 114.

6. Michael Lee Lanning, *The Only War We Had: A Platoon Leader's Journal of Vietnam* (New York: Ivy Books, 1987), p. 96. For a synopsis of the "esoteric skills and knowledges" required of a platoon leader in Vietnam, see James Webb, *Fields of Fire* (New York: Bantam Books, 1979), pp. 205–206.

7. Lanning, *Only War,* p. 33. After his first two days as a platoon leader in the boonies, Lanning's "abilities to navigate and read a map had gained the respect of the platoon" (p. 36). For an example of the difficulties involved in maneuvering cross-country at night, and the weight of responsibility felt by the leader while doing it, see James R. McDonough, *Platoon Leader* (New York: Bantam Books, 1986), pp. 155–158.

8. Joseph D. Lawrence, *Fighting Soldier: The A.E.F. in 1918* (Boulder: Colorado Associated University Press, 1985), pp. 39–41. For other examples of inept land navigation by World War I leaders, see Henry Berry, *Make the Kaiser Dance: Living Memories of the Doughboy* (New York: Priam Books, 1978), p. 383, and Albert M. Ettinger and A. Churchill Ettinger, *A Doughboy with the Fighting Sixty-ninth: A Remembrance of World War I* (Shippensburg, Pa.: White Mane Publishing, 1992), p. 158. Leaders got men lost while on patrol in other wars as well, sometimes with fatal results; for examples, see James Brady, *The Coldest War: A Memoir of Korea* (New York: Pocket Books, 1991), pp. 216–217, and Larry Heinemann, *Close Quarters* (New York: Farrar, Straus and Giroux, 1977), pp. 37–51.

9. Eugene B. Sledge, *With the Old Breed at Peleliu and Okinawa* (New York: Bantam Books, 1983), p. 222.

10. Howard Matthias, *The Korean War—Reflections of a Young Combat Platoon Leader,* rev. ed. (Tallahassee, Fla.: Father and Son Publishing, 1995), p. 42.

11. Ralph Zumbro, *Tank Sergeant* (Novato, Calif.: Presidio Press, 1986), p. 54.

12. Richard D. Camp, with Eric Hammel, *Lima-6: A Marine Company Commander in Vietnam* (New York: Pocket Books, 1989), pp. 26, 24, and 30–31.

13. Richard E. Ogden, *Green Knight, Red Mourning* (New York: Zebra Books, 1985), p. 33.

14. Sponaugle interview in Eric Bergerud, *Touched with Fire: The Land War in the South Pacific* (New York: Viking Penguin, 1996), p. 438.

15. Philip Caputo, *A Rumor of War* (New York: Ballantine Books, 1978), p. 238.

16. Harold P. Leinbaugh and John D. Campbell, *The Men of Company K* (New York: Bantam Books, 1987), pp. 7–8.

17. Carl M. Becker and Robert G. Thobaben, *Common Warfare: Parallel Memoirs by*

*Two World War II GIs in the Pacific* (Jefferson, N.C., and London: McFarland, 1992), p. 141.

18. Jonathan Shay, *Achilles in Vietnam: Combat Trauma and the Undoing of Character* (New York: Scribner, 1995), p. 15.

19. Hervey Allen, *Toward the Flame: A War Diary* (New York: Grosset and Dunlap, 1934), p. 7.

20. Mauldin, *Up Front,* pp. 179–180.

21. Paul Boesch, *Road to Huertgen: Forest in Hell* (Houston: Paul M. Boesch, 1985), p. 114. See also Shay's discussion of "the fairness assumption" in *Achilles*, pp. 10–14.

22. Albert French, *Patches of Fire: A Story of War and Redemption* (New York: Anchor Books, 1997), p. 77.

23. George Wilson, *If You Survive* (New York: Ivy Books, 1987), p. 159.

24. Henderson, *Cohesion,* p. 15. See also p. 109.

25. W. Stanford Smith, with contributions by Leo J. Machan and Stanley E. Earman, *The Cannoneers: GI Life in a World War II Cannon Company* (Manhattan, Kans.: Sunflower University Press, 1993), pp. 49–50.

26. Morris Janowitz and Roger W. Little, *Sociology and the Military Establishment,* 3d ed. (Beverly Hills and London: Sage, 1974), p. 103.

27. Rudolph W. Stephens, *Old Ugly Hill: A G.I.'s Fourteen Months in the Korean Trenches, 1952–1953* (Jefferson, N.C., and London: McFarland, 1995), p. 128.

28. John Dollard, with Donald Horton, *Fear in Battle* (New York: AMS Press, 1976), p. 44.

29. Avery interview in Donald Knox, with additional text by Alfred Coppel, *The Korean War: Uncertain Victory: The Concluding Volume of an Oral History* (San Diego, New York, and London: Harcourt Brace Jovanovich, 1988), p. 8.

30. Brady, *Coldest War*, p. 151. For a condemnation of officers seeking to enhance their careers at the expense of men's lives, see Matthias, *Reflections,* p. 53.

31. Camp, *Lima-6,* p. 48.

32. Joseph J. Ondishko Jr., "A View of Anxiety, Fear and Panic," *Military Affairs* 36:2 (April 1972): 60.

33. Elmar Dinter, *Hero or Coward: Pressures Facing the Soldier in Battle* (London and Totowa, N.J.: Frank Cass, 1985), p. 54.

34. Klaus H. Huebner, *Long Walk Through War: A Combat Doctor's Diary* (College Station: Texas A&M University Press, 1987), p. 27.

35. Sledge, *Old Breed*, p. 43. See also Sledge's praise for Lieutenant Edward ("Hillbilly") Jones, pp. 92–94.

36. Charles B. MacDonald, *Company Commander* (Toronto, New York, and London: Bantam Books, 1978), p. 96.

37. George William Sefton, *It Was My War: I'll Remember It the Way I Want To!* (Manhattan, Kans.: Sunflower University Press, 1994), p. 215.

38. Leo H. Bartemeier, Lawrence S. Kubie, Karl A. Menninger, John Romano, and John C. Whitehorn, "Combat Exhaustion," two-part series, part 2, *Journal of Nervous and Mental Disease* 104:5 (November 1946): 515. See also Jules W. Coleman, "The Group Factor in Military Psychiatry," *American Journal of Orthopsychiatry* 16:2 (April 1946): 224.

39. Downs, "Death and the Dark Side," p. 95.

40. Frederick Downs, *The Killing Zone: My Life in the Vietnam War* (New York: Berkley Books, 1983), p. 53.

41. Wilson, *If You Survive,* p. 22.

42. Camp, *Lima-6,* pp. 197–198. For other examples of junior leaders struggling with the dilemma of caring for their men while trying to steel themselves against their loss, see Lawrence, *Fighting Soldier,* p. 102; John L. Munschauer, *World War II Cavalcade: An Offer I Couldn't Refuse* (Manhattan, Kans.: Sunflower University Press, 1996), p. 113; William Manchester, *Goodbye, Darkness: A Memoir of the Pacific War* (Boston and Toronto: Little, Brown, 1979), pp. 69–70; and Brady, *Coldest War,* pp. 79–80 and 159.

43. Matthias, *Reflections,* p. 41.

44. Nat Frankel and Larry Smith, *Patton's Best: An Informal History of the 4th Armored Division* (New York: Jove Book, 1984), p. 192.

45. MacDonald, *Company Commander,* p. 101. For other examples of officers sharing their liquor ration, see Wilson, *If You Survive,* pp. 223–224, and Henry Berry, *Hey, Mac, Where Ya Been? Living Memories of the U.S. Marines in the Korean War* (New York: St. Martin's Press, 1988), p. 236.

46. Charles F. Minder, *This Man's War: The Day-by-Day Record of an American Private on the Western Front* (New York: Pevensey Press, 1931), p. 108.

47. Leinbaugh and Campbell, *Company K,* p. 8.

48. Brady, *Coldest War,* p. 154.

49. Joseph R. Owen, *Colder Than Hell: A Marine Rifle Company at Chosin Reservoir* (Annapolis, Md.: Naval Institute Press, 1996), p. 165.

50. Stanley Goff and Robert Sanders, with Clark Smith, *Brothers: Black Soldiers in the Nam* (Novato, Calif.: Presidio Press, 1982), p. 59. "Rabbit" was also a pejorative used by African-American soldiers for whites. Sanders is black, but there is no indication in his memoir that this nickname for his commander was used in this sense.

51. Alfred S. Bradford, *Some Even Volunteered: The First Wolfhounds Pacify Vietnam* (Westport, Conn., and London: Praeger, 1994), p. 40.

52. James Hamilton Dill, *Sixteen Days at Mungol-li* (Fayetteville, Ark.: M&M Press, 1993), p. 255.

53. Lawrence, *Fighting Soldier,* pp. 115 and 114.

54. Stiles interview in Henry Berry, *Semper Fi, Mac: Living Memories of the U.S. Marines in World War II* (New York: Berkley Books, 1983), p. 85.

55. Owen, *Colder Than Hell,* p. 134. See pp. 121–122 for the incident of panic.

56. Moran, *Anatomy,* p. 188. Dollard's survey of Spanish Civil War veterans verifies the importance of coolness under fire: "Coolness is contagious. Ninety-four per cent of the men feel that they fought better after observing other men behaving calmly in a dangerous situation" (*Fear in Battle,* p. 28).

57. Francis P. Duffy, *Father Duffy's Story: A Tale of Humor and Heroism, of Life and Death with the Fighting Sixty-ninth* (Garden City, N.Y.: Garden City Publishing, 1919), p. 270. One of Berry's doughboy veterans agrees with Duffy's assessment of Donovan: "He was the calmest man under fire I ever saw. Oh you'd think he was standing at the corner of Broadway and Forty-second Street, not in the middle of a barrage. And he was always in the middle of everything—Bill was no dugout officer" (see Berry, *Make the Kaiser Dance,* p. 332).

58. Ettinger and Ettinger, *Fighting Sixty-ninth,* p. 147.

59. Allen R. Matthews, *The Assault* (New York: Dodd, Mead, 1980), p. 148.

60. Owen, *Colder Than Hell,* p. 153.

61. Tim O'Brien, *If I Die in a Combat Zone: Box Me Up and Ship Me Home* (New York: Laurel, Dell, 1987), p. 85.

62. Robert Leckie, *Helmet for My Pillow* (Garden City, N.Y.: Nelson Doubleday, 1979), p. 57.

63. John Hersey, *Into the Valley: A Skirmish of the Marines* (New York: Schocken Books, 1989), pp. 78 and 79.

64. Lanning, *Only War,* p. 107.

65. Herbert Spiegel, "Psychiatry with an Infantry Battalion in North Africa," in *Neuropsychiatry in World War II,* ed. Albert J. Glass, Medical Department, U.S. Army, Office of the Surgeon General, 2 vols., *Overseas Theaters* (Washington, D.C.: U.S. Government Printing Office, 1973), 2:122–123.

66. Michael D. Doubler, *Closing with the Enemy: How GI's Fought the War in Europe, 1944–1945* (Lawrence: University Press of Kansas, 1994), p. 238.

67. MacDonald, *Company Commander,* p. 171. See ibid. for Doubler's discussion of this incident.

68. Common sense dictates that these three leadership virtues are interrelated, but two sociological surveys add some empirical evidence. A survey of combat-experienced leaders revealed that the leader who was competent and possessed technical expertise was more willing to expose himself to danger and had closer personal relations with his men than did less competent leaders. See Dean E. Frost, Fred E. Fiedler, and Jeff W. Anderson, "The Role of Personal Risk-Taking in Effective Leadership," *Human Relations* 36:2 (February 1983): 185–202. A survey of leaders and soldiers in peacetime companies in the U.S. Army determined that commanders who were indifferent to their soldiers' welfare had units with poor morale and cohesion, even though these same commanders stressed tactical and technical proficiency. In sum, leaders needed both to care and to be proficient. See Faris R. Kirkland, Paul T. Bartone, and David H. Marlowe, "Commanders' Priorities and Psychological Readiness," *Armed Forces and Society* 19:4 (summer 1993): 579–598.

69. Dinter, *Hero or Coward,* p. 56.

70. Sefton, *It Was My War,* p. 57.

71. Roy R. Grinker and John P. Spiegel, *War Neuroses* (Philadelphia and London: Blakiston, 1945), p. 69. Other psychiatrists came to the same conclusion. See Glass, ed., *Neuropsychiatry,* pp. 634–635; Coleman, "Group Factor," pp. 223–224; John W. Appel and Gilbert W. Beebe, "Preventive Psychiatry: An Epidemiological Approach," *Journal of the American Medical Association* 131:18 (August 31, 1946): 1474; and Bartemeier et al., "Combat Exhaustion," part 2, 518.

72. Gerald P. Averill, *Mustang: A Combat Marine* (Novato, Calif.: Presidio Press, 1987), p. xviii.

73. Smith, *Cannoneers,* p. 50.

74. Owen, *Colder Than Hell,* p. 126.

75. John A. Sullivan, *Toy Soldiers: Memoir of a Combat Platoon Leader in Korea* (Jefferson, N.C., and London: McFarland, 1991), p. 93.

76. McDonough, *Platoon Leader,* pp. 109–110.

77. Caputo, *Rumor of War,* p. 254.

## CHAPTER 10. DWELLERS BEYOND THE ENVIRONMENT OF WAR

1. For example, the Research Branch surveyed soldiers worldwide in July 1945 to determine how many had experienced any combat. Only 27 percent of the soldiers and junior officers claimed to "have been in actual combat," and another 16 to 18 percent said they had been "under enemy fire but not in actual combat," the assumption being that these men endured one or more artillery barrages or air attacks behind the lines. The rest (53 to 57 percent) never came under fire. See Samuel A. Stouffer, Edward A. Suchman, Leland C. DeVinney, Shirley A. Star, and Robin M. Williams Jr., *Studies in Social Psychology in World War II*, vol. 1, *The American Soldier: Adjustment During Army Life* (Princeton: Princeton University Press, 1949), chart 3, p. 165.

2. Eugene B. Sledge, *With the Old Breed at Peleliu and Okinawa* (New York: Bantam Books, 1983), pp. 135 and 138 (quotation is split by a map on pp. 136–137).

3. Stouffer et al., *Adjustment During Army Life*, p. 296. See also "The Making of the Infantryman," *American Journal of Sociology* 51:5 (March 1946): 376.

4. Rants interview in Gerald Astor, *Crisis in the Pacific: The Battles for the Philippine Islands by the Men Who Fought Them* (New York: Donald I. Fine Books, 1996), p. 433.

5. Paul Boesch, *Road to Huertgen: Forest in Hell* (Houston: Paul M. Boesch, 1985), p. 128.

6. Bill Mauldin, *Up Front* (New York: Award Books, 1976), p. 58. See also the discussion of the World War II GI's "status hierarchy," with the combat soldier the self-proclaimed elite, in Samuel A. Stouffer, Arthur A. Lumsdaine, Marion Harper Lumsdaine, Robin M. Williams Jr., M. Brewster Smith, Irving L. Janis, Shirley A. Star, and Leonard S. Cottrell Jr., *Studies in Social Psychology in World War II*, vol. 2, *The American Soldier: Combat and Its Aftermath* (Princeton: Princeton University Press, 1949), pp. 305–312.

7. Amos N. Wilder, *Armageddon Revisited: A World War I Journal* (New Haven and London: Yale University Press, 1994), p. 139.

8. Mauldin, *Up Front*, p. 123. For comments about the importance of the CIB to the World War II infantryman, see Charles R. Cawthon, *Other Clay: A Remembrance of the World War II Infantry* (Niwot: University Press of Colorado, 1990), p. 39, and James Jones, *WW II: A Chronicle of Soldiering* (New York: Ballantine Books, 1976), p. 137.

9. John A. Sullivan, *Toy Soldiers: Memoir of a Combat Platoon Leader in Korea* (Jefferson, N.C., and London: McFarland, 1991), p. 106. For another example of pride in earning the CIB in Korea, see Curtis James Morrow, *What's a Commie Ever Done to Black People? A Korean War Memoir of Fighting in the U.S. Army's Last All Negro Unit* (Jefferson, N.C., and London: McFarland, 1997), p. 86.

10. Michael Lee Lanning, *The Only War We Had: A Platoon Leader's Journal of Vietnam* (New York: Ivy Books, 1987), p. 134.

11. Mauldin, *Up Front,* p. 135. Carrying the relativity concept to its logical extreme, as an infantryman in Harold P. Leinbaugh's and John D. Campbell's company did, the rear echelon was "any son of a bitch behind my foxhole" (*The Men of Company K* [New York: Bantam Books, 1987], p. 74).

12. Boesch, *Road to Huertgen,* p. 125.

13. Ibid., p. 51. For other discussions of rear-echelon relativity, see William Manchester, *Goodbye, Darkness: A Memoir of the Pacific War* (Boston and Toronto: Little,

Brown, 1979), p. 260, and John M. Del Vecchio, *The 13th Valley* (New York: Bantam Books, 1983), pp. 174–175.

14. William H. Mauldin, *Bill Mauldin in Korea* (New York: W. W. Norton, 1952), p. 127.

15. For general discussions of the combat soldier's disdain for the rear echelon, see Richard Holmes, *Acts of War: The Behavior of Men in Battle* (New York: Free Press, 1985), pp. 77–79, and Anthony Kellett, *Combat Motivation: The Behavior of Soldiers in Battle* (Boston, The Hague, and London: Kluwer, Nijhoff, 1982), pp. 119–122.

16. Joseph D. Lawrence, *Fighting Soldier: The A.E.F. in 1918* (Boulder: Colorado Associated University Press, 1985), pp. 131 and 132.

17. Charles MacArthur, *War Bugs* (New York: Grosset and Dunlap, 1929), p. 119.

18. O'Brien interview in Henry Berry, *Make the Kaiser Dance: Living Memories of the Doughboy* (New York: Priam Books, 1978), p. 112.

19. Audie Murphy, *To Hell and Back* (New York: Bantam Books, 1983), p. 160.

20. Harold L. Bond, *Return to Cassino* (New York: Pocket Books, 1965), p. 231. See also Klaus H. Huebner, *Long Walk Through War: A Combat Doctor's Diary* (College Station: Texas A&M University Press, 1987), pp. 90–97.

21. Sledge, *Old Breed*, p. 107.

22. Sullivan, *Toy Soldiers*, p. 17. For another classic, and almost as sarcastic, description of the comfortable life in the rear echelons, in this case a marine ordnance battalion, see Martin Russ, *The Last Parallel: A Marine's War Journal* (New York and Toronto: Rinehart, 1957), pp. 43–44.

23. An excellent account illustrating the yawning gap between the grunt's life in the boonies and the rear-echelon soldier's life of comfort is provided by Al Santoli, who juxtaposes interviews with a marine rifleman and a rear-area supply officer in his *Everything We Had: An Oral History of the Vietnam War by Thirty-three American Soldiers Who Fought It* (New York: Ballantine Books, 1982), pp. 87–99. See also Frederick Downs, *The Killing Zone: My Life in the Vietnam War* (New York: Berkley Books, 1983), pp. 215–221; Lanning, *Only War*, pp. 17–26; Tim O'Brien, *Going After Cacciato* (New York: Dell, 1979), pp. 58–59; William D. Ehrhart, *Vietnam-Perkasie: A Combat Marine Memoir* (Jefferson, N.C., and London: McFarland, 1983), pp. 241–242 and 249; and Stanley Goff and Robert Sanders, with Robert Clark, *Brothers: Black Soldiers in the Nam* (Novato, Calif.: Presidio Press, 1982), pp. 125–126.

24. Larry Heinemann, *Close Quarters* (New York: Farrar, Straus and Giroux, 1977), pp. 285 and 286.

25. Boesch, *Road to Huertgen*, p. 129. See also the Research Branch survey in Stouffer et al., *Combat and Its Aftermath*, p. 297.

26. Lester Atwell, *Private* (New York: Popular Library, 1958), p. 374.

27. Janice Holt Giles, ed., *The G.I. Journal of Sergeant Giles* (Boston: Houghton Mifflin, and Cambridge: Riverside Press, 1965), p. 112.

28. Ehrhart, *Vietnam-Perkasie*, p. 190. See also Santoli, *Everything We Had*, p. 146, and John Ketwig, *And a Hard Rain Fell* (New York: Pocket Books, 1986), pp. 39 and 154–155.

29. Atwell, *Private*, p. 493. See also the case of Captain Sarsfield and his Bronze Star on pp. 491–492, and Leinbaugh and Campbell, *Company K,* pp. 255–256.

30. Higgins interview in Santoli, *Everything We Had,* p. 95. See also the case of Cap-

tain Owen and Warrant Officer White in Robert Mason, *Chickenhawk* (New York: Penguin Books, 1986), pp. 331–332. Richard A. Gabriel and Paul L. Savage are especially critical of the debasement of the awards system in Vietnam. See *Crisis in Command: Mismanagement in the Army* (New York: Hill and Wang, 1978), pp. 14–16.

31. Research Branch surveys confirm the validity of this observation. See Stouffer et al., *Combat and Its Aftermath,* pp. 314–316. See also Hervey Allen, *Toward the Flame: A War Diary* (New York: Grosset and Dunlap, 1934), p. 239.

32. Ralph Ingersoll, *The Battle Is the Pay-off* (New York: Harcourt, Brace, 1943), p. 63.

33. Peter G. Bourne, *Men, Stress, and Vietnam* (Boston: Little, Brown, 1970), p. 115.

34. Lanning, *Only War,* pp. 67–68. See also pp. 110–111 and 242; Gustav Hasford, *The Short-timers* (New York: Bantam Books, 1979), pp. 37–39; and Franklyn A. Johnson, *One More Hill* (New York: Bantam Books, 1983), p. 76.

35. Charles B. MacDonald, *Company Commander* (New York: Bantam Books, 1978), pp. 99–100; for another example, see Leinbaugh and Campbell, *Company K,* p. 231.

36. Russ, *Last Parallel,* p. 95. See also Kurt Gabel, *The Making of a Paratrooper: Airborne Training and Combat in World War II* (Lawrence: University Press of Kansas, 1990), p. 211.

37. James Hamilton Dill, *Sixteen Days at Mungol-li* (Fayetteville, Ark.: M&M Press, 1993), pp. 172 and 188.

38. Tim O'Brien, *If I Die in a Combat Zone: Box Me Up and Ship Me Home* (New York: Laurel, Dell, 1987), pp. 109, 110, and 114.

39. Elton E. Mackin, *Suddenly We Didn't Want to Die: Memoirs of a World War I Marine* (Novato, Calif.: Presidio Press, 1993), p. 179. See also John Dos Passos, *First Encounter* (New York: Philosophical Library, 1945), p. 40.

40. Muetzel interview in Donald Knox, *The Korean War: Pusan to Chosin: An Oral History* (San Diego, New York, and London: Harcourt Brace Jovanovich, 1985), p. 185.

41. Manchester, *Goodbye, Darkness,* p. 313.

42. Ibid., p. 316. See also Cawthon, *Other Clay,* p. 82.

43. The noncombatant in World War II was certainly aware, as the Research Branch discovered, that "relative to the combat men, . . . he had got a fairly good break in the Army" (Stouffer et al., *Adjustment During Army Life,* p. 173).

44. [Howard V. O'Brien], *Wine, Women, and War: A Diary of Disillusionment* (New York: J. H. Sears, 1926), p. 109.

45. E. J. Kahn Jr., *G.I. Jungle: An American Soldier in Australia and New Guinea* (New York: Simon and Schuster, 1943), pp. 113–114. I refer to Kahn as a "headquarters clerk," but he never actually identifies which headquarters he worked in or what his exact duties were, perhaps for security concerns. He served in the Thirty-second Infantry Division, which by all accounts had a rough fight under appalling conditions in New Guinea.

46. Giles, ed., *G.I. Journal,* p. 56. See also Carl M. Becker and Robert G. Thobaben, *Common Warfare: Parallel Memoirs by Two World War II GIs in the Pacific* (Jefferson, N.C., and London: McFarland, 1992), p. 81; David Rabe interview in Eric James Schroeder, *Vietnam, We've All Been There: Interviews with American Writers* (London and Westport, Conn.: Praeger, 1992), p. 199; O'Brien, *If I Die,* pp. 168–169; and Mark Baker, *Nam: The Vietnam War in the Words of the Men and Women Who Fought There* (New York: Berkley Books, 1983), pp. 122–123.

47. The Research Branch discovered that combat troops in both the Pacific and Euro-

pean theaters were generally satisfied with the support they received, but that did nothing to diminish their resentment of the rear echelon. See Stouffer et al., *Combat and Its Aftermath,* pp. 292–295.

48. Mauldin, *Up Front,* pp. 79–80. See also James R. McDonough, *Platoon Leader* (New York: Bantam Books, 1986), p. 3.

49. As the Research Branch learned from its soldier surveys, "However superior the combat man may have felt toward the rear echelon, this feeling of superiority rarely supplanted frank eagerness on his part to change places and fill one of the rear jobs towards which he was so scornful" (Stouffer et al., *Combat and Its Aftermath,* p. 312).

50. James Brady, *The Coldest War: A Memoir of Korea* (New York: Pocket Books, 1991), p. 270.

51. Goff and Sanders, *Brothers,* p. 124.

52. Boesch, *Road to Huertgen,* p. 108. See also the case of Lieutenant Bond, who accepted a job as a general's aide with a mix of joy, reluctance, and guilt (*Cassino,* pp. 171–174 and 178–180).

53. Dixon Wecter, *When Johnny Comes Marching Home* (Westport, Conn.: Greenwood Press, 1970), p. 504. Research Branch surveys confirm Wecter's assessment. A majority of soldiers serving in Europe and the Mediterranean, despite their litany of complaints against the home front, nevertheless believed that the people back home supported them. See Stouffer et al., *Combat and Its Aftermath,* pp. 320–323.

54. [O'Brien], *Wine, Women, and War,* p. 216. See also p. 231.

55. Ibid., p. 183. See also Mackin, *We Didn't Want to Die,* p. 161.

56. Sledge, *Old Breed,* pp. 272–273.

57. Murphy, *To Hell and Back,* p. 134. See also Eric Bergerud, *Touched with Fire: The Land War in the South Pacific* (New York: Viking Penguin, 1986), p. 478; Alice M. Hoffman and Howard S. Hoffman, *Archives of Memory: A Soldier Recalls World War II* (Lexington: University Press of Kentucky, 1990), p. 140; Jones, *WW II,* pp. 141–144; and Ernie Pyle, *Here Is Your War: The Story of G.I. Joe* (Cleveland and New York: World Publishing, 1945), p. 11.

58. Thomas Boyd, *Through the Wheat* (Carbondale and Edwardsville: Southern Illinois University Press, 1978), p. 8.

59. Stouffer et al., *Adjustment During Army Life,* p. 188. Surveys of soldiers in the European and Mediterranean theaters also reveal resentment of the "home guards"; see Stouffer et al., *Combat and Its Aftermath,* pp. 317–319. See also Pyle, *Your War,* pp. 197–198.

60. Pyle, *Your War,* p. 96.

61. Stracke interview in Studs Terkel, *"The Good War": An Oral History of World War II* (New York: Pantheon Books, 1984), p. 160.

62. Wecter, *Johnny,* p. 349; he also discusses the World War II soldier's resentment of war workers (pp. 505–508). See also Huebner, *Long Walk,* p. 59.

63. Wilder, *Armageddon,* p. 70.

64. [O'Brien], *Wine, Women, and War,* p. 42.

65. Paul Fussell, *Doing Battle: The Making of a Skeptic* (Boston: Little, Brown, 1996), p. 213.

66. Robert Leckie, *Helmet for My Pillow* (Garden City, N.Y.: Nelson Doubleday, 1979), p. 241. Paul Fussell levels the same charges in *Doing Battle,* pp. 171–172.

67. Lee Kennett, *G.I.: The American Soldier in World War II* (New York: Charles

Scribner's Sons, 1987), p. 23. See also Bradford Perkins, "Impressions of Wartime," *Journal of American History* 77:2 (September 1990): 564.

68. For an analysis of the Army's AGCT and assignment policies, see Eli Ginzberg, James K. Anderson, Sol W. Ginsburg, John L. Herma, and John B. Miner, *The Ineffective Soldier: Lessons for Management and the Nation,* 3 vols., *The Lost Divisions* (New York and London: Columbia University Press, 1959), 1:41–57.

69. The Selective Service Act of 1948, incidentally, established the student deferment, which figured prominently in Korean and Vietnam War-era draft deferments. The survey findings are from Edward A. Suchman, Robin M. Williams Jr., and Rose K. Goldsen, "Student Reaction to Impending Military Service," *American Sociological Review* 18:3 (June 1953): 293–304.

70. Morris Janowitz and Roger W. Little, *Sociology and the Military Establishment,* 3d ed. (Beverly Hills and London: Sage, 1974), pp. 71–72.

71. Roger W. Little, "Buddy Relations and Combat Performance," in *The New Military: Changing Patterns of Organization,* ed. Morris Janowitz (New York: Russell Sage, 1964), p. 220. See also Theodore R. Fehrenbach, *This Kind of War: A Study in Unpreparedness* (New York: Macmillan, 1963), p. 610.

72. Ernest Frankel, *Band of Brothers* (New York: Macmillan, 1958), p. 177.

73. Albert J. Mayer and Thomas Ford Hoult, "Social Stratification and Combat Survival," *Social Forces* 34:2 (December 1955): 155.

74. See Anne Hoiberg, "Military Staying Power," in *Combat Effectiveness: Cohesion, Stress, and the Volunteer Military,* ed. Sam C. Sarkesian (Beverly Hills and London: Sage, 1980), pp. 219–220.

75. For a discussion of the problems inherent in measuring class in surveys, see Thomas C. Wilson, "Vietnam-Era Military Service: A Test of the Class-Bias Thesis," *Armed Forces and Society* 21:3 (spring 1995): 461–465.

76. For surveys including officers in their statistics, see Allan Mazur, "Was Vietnam a Class War?" *Armed Forces and Society* 21:3 (spring 1995): 455–459, and Arnold Barnett, Timothy Stanley, and Michael Shore, "America's Vietnam Casualties: Victims of a Class War?" *Operations Research* 40:5 (September–October 1992): 856–866. For a survey arguing that Vietnam was only "marginally" a class war, see Wilson, "Vietnam-Era Military Service," pp. 466–471.

77. Extracts from this orientation kit can be found in Peter Karsten, *Soldiers and Society: The Effects of Military Service and War on American Society,* Grass Roots Perspectives on American History, no. 1 (Westport, Conn., and London: Greenwood Press, 1978), pp. 102–106 (quotation on p. 103).

78. For an analysis of channeling and its failure during the Vietnam War era, see Lawrence M. Baskir and William S. Strauss, *Chance and Circumstance: The Draft, the War, and the Vietnam Generation* (New York: Knopf, 1978), pp. 14–17 (see p. 6 for the 6 percent estimate); John Helmer, *Bringing the War Home: The American Soldier in Vietnam and After* (New York: Free Press, and London: Collier Macmillan, 1974), pp. 3–10; and Christian G. Appy, *Working-Class War: American Combat Soldiers and Vietnam* (Chapel Hill and London: University of North Carolina Press, 1993), pp. 28–30.

79. Baskir and Strauss, *Chance and Circumstance,* p. 17.

80. Ibid., p. 9. Baskir and Strauss are here summarizing the results of their own "Notre Dame survey," which the authors briefly describe on p. xviii and refer to, along

with other studies, throughout their book. See also Appy, *Working-Class War,* pp. 11–43; Gilbert Badillo and G. David Curry, "The Social Incidence of Vietnam Casualties: Social Class or Race?" *Armed Forces and Society* 2:3 (May 1976): 397–406; Charles C. Moskos Jr., *The American Enlisted Man: The Rank and File in Today's Military* (New York: Russell Sage Foundation, 1970), pp. 41–54; and Michael Useem, "The Educational and Military Experience of Young Men During the Vietnam Era: Non-linear Effects of Parental Social Class," *Journal of Political and Military Sociology* 8:1 (spring 1980): 15–29.

81. Baskir and Strauss, *Chance and Circumstance,* p. 8.

82. Moskos, *American Enlisted Man,* p. 163. See also Appy, *Working-Class War,* pp. 220–225, for a discussion of grunt "class anger."

83. For an assessment of the dodge of enlisting in the reserves and the fact that those forces, during the Vietnam War era, were manned by middle-class volunteers, see Appy, *Working-Class War,* pp. 36–37; Baskir and Strauss, *Chance and Circumstance,* pp. 48–51; and James R. Ebert, *A Life in a Year: The American Infantryman in Vietnam, 1965–1972* (Novato, Calif.: Presidio Press, 1993), pp. 15–16.

84. Heinemann interview in Schroeder, *We've All Been There,* p. 146. See also Goff and Sanders, *Brothers,* p. xvi.

85. Lanning, *Only War,* p. 86.

86. Ibid., p. 87. See Baskir and Strauss, *Chance and Circumstance,* pp. 28–32, for a discussion of the student deferment as a draft dodge. The deferment for graduate school that Lanning condemns was actually abolished in 1967, but deferments for undergraduate studies continued. See also James Webb, *Fields of Fire* (New York: Bantam Books, 1979), p. 409.

87. James Fallows, "What Did You Do in the Class War, Daddy?" *Washington Monthly* 7:8 (October 1975): 14; see also Baskir and Strauss, *Chance and Circumstance,* p. 7.

88. James Martin Davis, "Vietnam: What It Was Really Like," *Military Review* 69:1 (January 1989): 41.

89. Paul Fussell, *Wartime: Understanding and Behavior in the Second World War* (New York and Oxford: Oxford University Press, 1989), p. 155. For other discussions of the importance of homefront recognition, see Elmar Dinter, *Hero or Coward: Pressures Facing the Soldier in Battle* (London and Totowa, N.J.: Frank Cass, 1985), pp. 49–50; William Darryl Henderson, *Cohesion: The Human Element in Combat: Leadership and Societal Influence in the Armies of the Soviet Union, the United States, North Vietnam, and Israel* (Washington, D.C.: National Defense University Press, 1988), p. 79; and Kellett, *Combat Motivation,* pp. 209–213.

90. Mauldin, *Up Front,* p. 127.

91. Francis P. Duffy, *Father Duffy's Story: A Tale of Humor and Heroism, of Life and Death With the Fighting Sixty-ninth* (Garden City, N.Y.: Garden City Publishing, 1919), p. 329.

92. Mauldin, *Korea,* p. 10.

93. Jack Fuller, *Fragments* (New York: Dell, 1985), pp. 209 and 210.

94. Jonathan Shay, *Achilles in Vietnam: Combat Trauma and the Undoing of Character* (New York: Scribner, 1995), p. 197. For an example, see Ron Kovic, *Born on the Fourth of July* (New York: Pocket Books, 1977), p. 134.

95. Bob Hoffman, *I Remember the Last War* (York, Pa.: Strength and Health Publishing, 1940), p. 310.

96. Jules V. Coleman, "Division Psychiatry in the Southwest Pacific Area," in *Neuropsychiatry in World War II,* ed. Albert J. Glass, Medical Department, U.S. Army, Office of the Surgeon General, 2 vols., *Overseas Theaters* (Washington, D.C.: U.S. Government Printing Office, 1973), 2:626.

97. Giles, ed., *G.I. Journal,* p. 295. See also p. 76.

98. Gwendolyn Midlo Hall, ed., *Love, War, and the 96th Engineers (Colored): The World War II New Guinea Diaries of Captain Hyman Samuelson* (Urbana and Chicago: University of Illinois Press, 1995), p. 211. For a discussion of the combat soldiers' concerns over fair and accurate press coverage, see Mauldin, *Up Front,* pp. 18–23, and Kellett, *Combat Motivation,* pp. 185–188.

99. Hoffman, *I Remember,* p. 80.

100. MacArthur, *War Bugs,* p. 75. See also Berry, *Make the Kaiser Dance,* pp. 114–117.

101. Jones, *WW II,* p. 39. See also Bergerud, *Touched with Fire,* pp. 175–176 and 435.

102. Craig M. Cameron, *American Samurai: Myth, Imagination, and the Conduct of Battle in the First Marine Division, 1941–1951* (Cambridge: Cambridge University Press, 1994), p. 226. There was, of course, more to army-marine antagonism than the issue of publicity. The marines' self-avowed elitism, differences in tactics and doctrine, the marine belief that soldiers were inferior fighters, and the rivalry over missions between two competing ground fighting forces also generated antagonism (see pp. 130–165).

103. Hockley interview in Donald Knox, with additional text by Alfred Coppel, *The Korean War: Uncertain Victory: The Concluding Volume of an Oral History* (San Diego, New York, and London: Harcourt Brace Jovanovich, 1988), p. 383. See also Charles M. Bussey, *Firefight at Yechon: Courage and Racism in the Korean War* (Washington, D.C., and London: Brassey's, 1991), pp. 144–147.

104. Ernie Pyle, *Brave Men* (New York: Henry Holt, 1944), pp. 399–400.

105. Marguerite Higgins, *War in Korea: The Report of a Woman Combat Correspondent* (Garden City, N.Y.: Doubleday, 1951), pp. 84 and 95.

106. Michael Herr, *Dispatches* (New York: Avon Books, 1978), p. 206. See Herr's follow-on example of a marine who asks him to "tell it! You tell it, man" (p. 207). See also John M. Del Vecchio, *The 13th Valley* (Toronto, New York, London, and Sydney: Bantam Books, 1983), acknowledgments page.

107. [O'Brien], *Wine, Women, and War,* p. 157. This joke resurfaces as an apocryphal story in later wars. Correspondent Ira Wolfert reported that a captured Japanese bomber pilot in World War II supposedly quipped, "I understand what we are fighting for—Togo [Tojo Hideki]—and what the Germans are fighting for—Hitler—but your Marines seem to be fighting for souvenirs!" (*Battle for the Solomons* [Cambridge, Mass.: Riverside Press, 1943], p. 50).

108. For other examples of doughboy souvenir hunting, see Robert G. Merrick, *World War I: A Diary* (Baltimore: privately published, 1982), pp. 84 and 97–100; William L. Langer, *Gas and Flame in World War I* (New York: Knopf, 1965), p. 38; Horatio Rogers, *World War I Through My Sights* (San Rafael, Calif.: Presidio Press, 1976), pp. 172, 210, and 212; and Hoffman, *I Remember,* pp. 12 and 124.

109. George William Sefton, *It Was My War: I'll Remember It the Way I Want To!* (Manhattan, Kans.: Sunflower University Press, 1994), p. 94. See also W. Stanford Smith,

with contributions by Leo J. Machan and Stanley E. Earman, *The Cannoneers: GI Life in a World War II Cannon Company* (Manhattan, Kans.: Sunflower University Press, 1992), p. 63; Roscoe C. Blunt Jr., *Inside the Battle of the Bulge: A Private Comes of Age* (Westport, Conn.: Praeger, 1994), pp. 29, 50–51, 89, 117, and 137; and Becker and Thobaben, *Common Warfare,* pp. 179–180.

110. Matthew Brennan, *Brennan's War: Vietnam, 1965–1969* (New York: Pocket Books, 1986), pp. 72 and 75. America's enemies, incidentally, were well aware of the GI's passion for souvenirs and often booby-trapped weapons, equipment, and even corpses.

## CHAPTER 11. EQUAL OPPORTUNITY IN THE FOXHOLE

1. Samuel A. Stouffer, Edward A. Suchman, Leland C. DeVinney, Shirley A. Star, and Robin M. Williams Jr., *Studies in Social Psychology in World War II,* vol. 1, *The American Soldier: Adjustment During Army Life* (Princeton: Princeton University Press, 1949), p. 533.

2. Sturkey interview in Mary Penick Motley, *The Invisible Soldier: The Experience of the Black Soldier, World War II* (Detroit: Wayne State University Press, 1975), p. 170. See also p. 168. For a discussion of the "right-to-fight" issue in World War I, see Mark Meigs, *Optimism at Armageddon: Voices of American Participants in the First World War* (Washington Square, N.Y.: New York University Press, 1997), pp. 19–21 and 54–56, and for World War II, see Stouffer et al., *Adjustment During Army Life,* pp. 526–535.

3. Arthur W. Little, *From Harlem to the Rhine: The Story of New York's Colored Volunteers* (New York: Covici-Friede, 1936), p. 350.

4. Long interview in Motley, *Invisible Soldier*, p. 152. See also the interview with Horace Evans, p. 157, confirming Patton's speech and its positive impact on the black tankers of the 761st Tank Battalion.

5. Curtis James Morrow, *What's a Commie Ever Done to Black People? A Korean War Memoir of Fighting in the U.S. Army's Last All Negro Unit* (Jefferson, N.C., and London: McFarland, 1997), p. 35.

6. Some black soldiers surveyed by the Research Branch "welcome the chance to prove their loyalty and fighting ability in the belief, or at least the hope, that such efforts would be rewarded." A second group of black soldiers, however, expressed "bitterness over the treatment Negroes had received and were receiving at the hands of their country both in and out of the Army, cynicism over expressions of war aims in view of traditional deviations from these professed principles in American racial practice, and skepticism about whether Negroes would in fact receive recognition for the efforts they put forth" (Stouffer et al., *Adjustment During Army Life,* p. 507).

7. Blue interview in Motley, *Invisible Soldier,* p. 122. See also Jones interview, p. 190.

8. Brown interview in ibid., p. 279.

9. Morrow, *Commie,* p. 77.

10. Stanley Goff and Robert Sanders, with Clark Smith, *Brothers: Black Soldiers in the Nam* (Novato, Calif.: Presidio Press, 1982), p. 133.

11. Research Branch surveys verify that blacks from northern states were dissatisfied

with being stationed in southern camps, as were many blacks from southern states, for that matter, and that Jim Crow was the reason. See Stouffer et al., *Adjustment During Army Life,* pp. 550–566. Given the focus on the soldier in combat, the problems of discrimination and segregation in the Stateside army are touched on here only briefly. That Stateside segregation generated black soldiers' resentment and proved detrimental to the training process is without question, however. See the experiences of the black 369th Infantry Regiment training in Spartanburg, South Carolina, in 1917 in Little, *Harlem,* pp. 48–70. See also the Stateside experiences of Motley's interviewees in chapter 1, "The Wrong War in the Wrong Century," of *Invisible Soldier,* pp. 39–72, and Studs Terkel's interviewees in *"The Good War": An Oral History of World War II* (New York: Pantheon Books, 1984), pp. 264–266 and 366–370. And see the Stateside surveys conducted by a team of sociologists in 1951 in Leo Bogart, ed., *Project Clear: Social Research and the Desegregation of the United States Army* (London and New Brunswick, N.J.: Transaction Publishers, 1992), pp. 145–279.

12. Albert French, *Patches of Fire: A Story of War and Redemption* (New York: Anchor Books, 1997), p. 16.

13. Wilson interview in Motley, *Invisible Soldier,* p. 61. See also the interviews on pp. 161, 266, and 326.

14. Will Judy, *A Soldier's Diary: A Day-to-Day Record in the World War* (Chicago: Judy Publishing, 1931), p. 162.

15. Stouffer et al., *Adjustment During Army Life,* pp. 543–544. For other comments by black GIs about good relations with Italian civilians, see Motley, *Invisible Soldier,* pp. 53, 162, 299, 310, and 318.

16. Jones interview in Motley, *Invisible Soldier,* p. 178.

17. For examples of segregated facilities or segregation policies overseas, see ibid., pp. 50–51 and 188, and Terkel, *Good War,* p. 379.

18. Thomas Boyd, *Through the Wheat* (Carbondale and Edwardsville: Southern Illinois University Press, 1978), pp. 1–2. For similar racist comments in World War I novels and memoirs, see John Dos Passos, *Three Soldiers,* Sentry ed. (Boston: Houghton Mifflin, 1921), p. 177; [Howard V. O'Brien], *Wine, Women, and War: A Diary of Disillusionment* (New York: J. H. Sears, 1926), pp. 89 and 298–299; and John W. Thomason Jr., *Fix Bayonets!* (New York: Blue Ribbon Books, 1926), p. 105. For a World War II example, see Gwendolyn Midlo Hall, ed., *Love, War, and the 96th Engineers (Colored): The World War II New Guinea Diaries of Captain Hyman Samuelson* (Urbana and Chicago: University of Illinois Press, 1995), pp. 66–69.

19. Bradford Perkins, "Impressions of Wartime," *Journal of American History* 77:2 (September 1990): 563.

20. The black Ninety-second and Ninety-third Infantry Divisions saw combat in World War I, the latter fighting as separate regiments with the French. The same two divisions were reactivated in World War II. The Ninety-second fought in Italy and the Ninety-third in the Pacific, the latter again never functioning as an entire division. A handful of separate black tank, tank-destroyer, and artillery battalions also fought in World War II. One black infantry regiment, the Twenty-fourth, with its black supporting arms fought in the Korean War, until it was disbanded as part of the integration process.

21. Lyle Rishell, *With a Black Platoon in Combat: A Year in Korea* (College Station: Texas A&M University Press, 1993), p. 47.

22. This study is by William T. Bowers, William M. Hammon, and George L. Mac-

Garrigle, *Black Soldier, White Army: The 24th Infantry Regiment in Korea* (Washington, D.C.: Center of Military History, U.S. Army, 1996).

23. See the comments by white officers in ibid., pp. 114, 120, 123, 167–168, and 268, and in Bogart, *Project Clear,* pp. 11–19.

24. Charles M. Bussey, *Firefight at Yechon: Courage and Racism in the Korean War* (Washington, D.C., and London: Brassey's, 1991), p. 93.

25. Bogart, *Project Clear,* pp. 104–108.

26. Millender interview in Motley, *Invisible Soldier*, p. 316. For other examples, see pp. 96–97, 268, 297, 311, and 322; Bussey, *Firefight,* p. 124; and Rudy Tomedi, *No Bugles, No Drums: An Oral History of the Korean War* (New York: John Wiley, 1993), p. 179. See also Bowers, *Black Soldier,* pp. 55–56 and 72–73.

27. Green interview in Motley, *Invisible Soldier,* p. 90; for similar complaints, see pp. 91, 93, 296–297, and 318.

28. Walden interview in ibid., p. 62; for similar complaints, see pp. 75, 84, 98, 152, 275, 297, and 304. See also Bowers, *Black Soldier,* pp. 168, 257, and 265.

29. See Stouffer et al., *Adjustment During Army Life*, pp. 580–585; Bogart, *Project Clear,* pp. 117–120; Motley, *Invisible Soldier,* p. 334; and Bowers, *Black Soldier,* pp. 57–58.

30. Lawton interview in Motley, *Invisible Soldier,* p. 100.

31. Morrow, *Commie*, p. 34. See also pp. 11–12. For similar comments, see Motley, *Invisible Soldier,* pp. 76, 85, and 99, and Bussey, *Firefight,* pp. 213–214.

32. Harrison interview in Motley, *Invisible Soldier,* p. 157.

33. Donald interview in ibid., p. 166. See also p. 327 for a positive assessment of a white commander.

34. Stouffer et al., *Adjustment During Army Life*, p. 502. Albert J. Glass came to the same conclusion: "Segregation of Negro troops in separate units was a clear communication that they must be considered as inferior beings for separation could have no other purpose" (*Neuropsychiatry in World War II*, Medical Department, U.S. Army, Office of the Surgeon General, 2 vols., *Overseas Theaters* [Washington, D.C.: U.S. Government Printing Office, 1973], 2:89 n. 58).

35. Stouffer et al., *Adjustment During Army Life,* p. 506.

36. Little, *Harlem,* p. 239.

37. Hall, ed., *Love, War,* p. 233.

38. Bogart, *Project Clear,* pp. 53–54. See also pp. 54–55 for several examples provided by interviewees of perceived discrimination in combat support.

39. Duplessis interview in Motley, *Invisible Soldier,* p. 328.

40. Evans interview in ibid., p. 163.

41. Wells interview in ibid., p. 314; for other comments about black combat units being deliberately disbanded, misused, or held out of combat, see pp. 99, 161, 303, and 321–322.

42. Cason interview in ibid., p. 268. See also the interview with the black commander of the 366th Infantry Regiment, who details the misuse of his unit, pp. 334–340.

43. Bowers, *Black Soldier,* p. 65. See also pp. 263–266.

44. See Russell F. Weigley, *Eisenhower's Lieutenants: The Campaigns of France and Germany* (Bloomington: Indiana University Press, 1981), pp. 960–963.

45. Stouffer et al., *Adjustment During Army Life,* pp. 588–589 and 592.

46. Bogart, *Project Clear*, pp. xxix. See pp. xxix–xxxi and 7–10 for an overview of the situation leading to integration in the army in Korea as summarized in the next few paragraphs.

47. Ibid., pp. 22–24 and 93–98.

48. Ibid., p. 98. See also Charles C. Moskos Jr., *The American Enlisted Man: The Rank and File in Today's Military* (New York: Russell Sage Foundation, 1970), pp. 118–121 and Table 5.9, p. 222.

49. Koegel interview in Donald Knox, with additional text by Alfred Coppel, *The Korean War: Uncertain Victory: The Concluding Volume of an Oral History* (San Diego, New York, and London: Harcourt Brace Jovanovich, 1988), p. 268.

50. William H. Mauldin, *Bill Mauldin in Korea* (New York: W. W. Norton, 1952), p. 73.

51. See the questionnaire results in Bogart, *Project Clear,* pp. 88–91.

52. Project Clear researchers in ibid. discovered that the white soldier strongly opposed to integration "does not commit any hostile acts, but rather withdraws as far as he can from [interracial] contact" (p. 101). He might also seek a transfer to an outfit that was not yet integrated (Table A29, p. 102). Conversely, most soldiers of both races responded positively to integration, and 64 percent of whites in integrated units said they had made friends among black soldiers (p. 77).

53. Joseph R. Owen, *Colder Than Hell: A Marine Rifle Company at Chosin Reservoir* (Annapolis, Md.: Naval Institute Press, 1996), pp. 34–35 and p. 21. For a similar example, see James Brady, *The Coldest War: A Memoir of Korea* (New York: Pocket Books, 1991), p. 116. And for an example of this problem from the perspective of a black marine placed in charge of white soldiers for the first time, some of whom were less than eager to serve under a black, see Henry Berry, *Hey, Mac, Where Ya Been? Living Memories of the U.S. Marines in the Korean War* (New York: St. Martin's Press, 1988), pp. 151–152.

54. Howard Matthias, *The Korean War—Reflections of a Young Combat Platoon Leader,* rev. ed. (Tallahassee, Fla.: Father and Son Publishing, 1995), pp. 104–106 (quotation on p. 104).

55. Moskos, *American Enlisted Man,* p. 124.

56. See the recommendations in Bogart, *Project Clear,* pp. 142–143.

57. For surveys supporting these statements, see Byron G. Fiman, Jonathan F. Borus, and M. Duncan Stanton, "Black-White and American-Vietnamese Relations Among Soldiers in Vietnam," *Journal of Social Issues* 31:4 (fall 1975): 39–48, and Moskos, *American Enlisted Man,* pp. 118–131.

58. Richard E. Ogden, *Green Knight, Red Mourning* (New York: Zebra Books, 1985), pp. 189–190. For other examples of interracial "boonie brothers," see Howard and "Rosey" in Wallace Terry, *Bloods: An Oral History of the Vietnam War by Black Veterans* (New York: Ballantine Books, 1985), p. 199, and Charles Strong and Joe, p. 57; "Doc" and "Blond" in John M. Del Vecchio, *The 13th Valley* (New York: Bantam Books, 1983), pp. 129–131; and "Bagger" and "Cannonball" in James Webb, *Fields of Fire* (New York: Bantam Books, 1979), pp. 192–198.

59. Goff and Sanders, *Brothers,* pp. 23 and 131.

60. Woodley interview in Terry, *Bloods,* p. 239; for similar comments, see pp. 23, 38–39, and 59, and Al Santoli, *Everything We Had: An Oral History of the Vietnam War*

*by Thirty-three American Soldiers Who Fought It* (New York: Ballantine Books, 1982), pp. 72 and 157. Historian James E. Westheider provides an overview of the military's growing racial problems in the Vietnam era but acknowledges that interracial cohesion in combat units remained viable. See *Fighting on Two Fronts: African Americans and the Vietnam War* (New York and London: New York University Press, 1997), pp. 6, 86, and 113–115.

61. Moskos, *American Enlisted Man,* p. 122. For other discussions of racial exclusivity, see John Helmer, *Bringing the War Home: The American Soldier in Vietnam and After* (New York: Free Press, and London: Collier Macmillan, 1974), pp. 100–101; James R. Ebert, *A Life in a Year: The American Infantryman in Vietnam, 1965–1972* (Novato, Calif.: Presidio Press, 1993), pp. 327–328; and Westheider, *Two Fronts,* pp. 85–93.

62. David Parks, *G.I. Diary* (New York, Evanston, and London: Harper and Row, 1968), pp. 34 and 41.

63. Matthew Brennan, *Brennan's War: Vietnam, 1965–1969* (New York: Pocket Books, 1986), p. 205.

64. Ogden, *Green Knight,* p. 221.

65. The final proportion of black combat deaths in Vietnam was 12.5 percent, versus a 10 percent level of African-American military presence in Vietnam and a national, black draft-age population of 13.5 percent in 1973. See Thomas C. Thayer, *War Without Fronts: The American Experience in Vietnam* (Boulder and London: Westview Press, 1985), pp. 113–114, and Christian G. Appy, *Working-Class War: American Combat Soldiers and Vietnam* (Chapel Hill and London: University of North Carolina Press, 1993), pp. 18–19. Although the rate of black combat deaths evened out in the long run, the killed-in-action rate for blacks between 1961 and 1966 was 16 percent, yet blacks constituted only 10.6 percent of the military personnel in Southeast Asia during that period. See Moskos, *American Enlisted Man,* p. 116, and Table 5.5, p. 218.

66. Parks, *G.I. Diary,* pp. 86–87.

67. Kirkland interview in Terry, *Bloods,* p. 99. See also pp. 36 and 212–213. Incidentally, as nasty as the "shit-burning" job sounds, it was not simply someone's sick idea of makework. Cutoff fifty-five gallon drums were used to catch human waste in the latrines. These drums could be slid out of the wooden latrines and the waste burned off using diesel fuel. All in all, it was an efficient and sanitary procedure, but understandably no one looked forward to the detail.

68. Tim O'Brien, *If I Die in a Combat Zone: Box Me Up and Ship Me Home* (New York: Laurel, Dell, 1987), p. 171.

69. Ibid. Given this book's focus on the combat experience, real or perceived discrimination in other areas, such as the draft and military justice, is not addressed. See Westheider, *Two Fronts,* pp. 20–65.

70. Goff and Sanders, *Brothers,* p. 11. For other examples of this genocidal theme surfacing, see Herbert Hendin and Ann Pollinger Haas, *Wounds of War: The Psychological Aftermath of Combat in Vietnam* (New York: Basic Books, 1984), p. 225, and Webb, *Fields of Fire,* pp. 270–271.

71. Terry, *Bloods,* p. xiv.

72. John Ketwig, *And a Hard Rain Fell* (New York: Pocket Books, 1986), p. 209.

73. O'Brien, *If I Die,* p. 111.

74. Brennan, *Brennan's War,* p. 235.

75. Anderson interview in Santoli, *Everything We Had,* p. 72.

76. Edwards interview in Terry, *Bloods,* p. 12; for other examples, see the cases of "Franko" in French, *Patches of Fire,* pp. 52 and 59–60; "Jax" in Del Vecchio, *13th Valley,* pp. 88–89, 316–317, and 399; "Panther" in Brennan, *Brennan's War,* p. 254; and "Piper" in Goff and Sanders, *Brothers,* pp. 29–30.

77. Parks, *G.I. Diary,* pp. 115–116.

78. Goff and Sanders, *Brothers,* p. 132.

79. Biggers interview in Terry, *Bloods,* p. 117. See also the case of Sergeant Sadler in Webb, *Fields of Fire,* pp. 344–345, and Sergeant Henry in Brennan, *Brennan's War,* p. 254. See Westheider's discussion of "oreos" in *Two Fronts,* pp. 126–128.

80. Albeit belatedly, the military instituted policy changes and reforms late in the Vietnam War period to improve equality and to eliminate discrimination in such areas as educational testing, military justice, and promotions. See Westheider, *Two Fronts,* pp. 131–139.

81. Bussey, *Firefight,* p. 261.


## CONCLUSION

1. Samuel Hynes, *The Soldiers' Tale: Bearing Witness to Modern War* (New York: Allen Lane, 1997), p. 30. For similar assessments, see Charles V. Genthe, *American War Narratives: 1917–1918: A Study and Bibliography* (New York: David Lewis, 1969), pp. 1–20; John Hellmann, *American Myth and the Legacy of Vietnam* (New York: Columbia University Press, 1986), pp. 103–108; and Edward Tabor Linenthal, "From Hero to Antihero: The Transformation of the Warrior in Modern America," *Soundings: An Interdisciplinary Journal* 63:1 (spring 1980): 79–93.

2. See Richard Holmes's discussion of "dislocation of expectation" in his *Acts of War: The Behavior of Men in Battle* (New York: Free Press, 1985), p. 73.

3. William Manchester, *Goodbye, Darkness: A Memoir of the Pacific War* (Boston and Toronto: Little, Brown, 1979), p. 382.

4. Audie Murphy, *To Hell and Back* (New York: Bantam Books, 1983), pp. 4 and 15.

5. James Hamilton Dill, *Sixteen Days at Mungol-li* (Fayetteville, Ark.: M&M Press, 1993), p. 160. See pp. 158–159 for the artillery incident.

6. Philip Caputo, *A Rumor of War* (New York: Ballantine Books, 1978), p. 153.

7. Hynes, *Soldiers' Tale,* p. 30.

8. Will Judy, *A Soldier's Diary: A Day-to-Day Record in the World War* (Chicago: Judy Publishing, 1931), pp. 211–212. This theme is also evident in Ernest Hemingway's short story "Soldier's Home." See his *The Short Stories of Ernest Hemingway: The First Forty-nine Stories and the Play "The Fifth Column"* (New York: Modern Library, 1942), pp. 243–244. See also Thomas C. Leonard, *Above the Battle: War-Making in America from Appomattox to Versailles* (New York: Oxford University Press, 1978), p. 177.

9. Paul Fussell, *Wartime: Understanding and Behavior in the Second World War* (New York and Oxford: Oxford University Press, 1989), p. 142. The historian Gerald F. Linderman agrees with Fussell. See his *The World Within War: America's Combat Experience in World War II* (New York: Free Press, 1997), p. 362.

10. Caputo, *Rumor of War,* p. 213.

11. G. Kurt Piehler, *Remembering War the American Way* (Washington, D.C., and London: Smithsonian Institution Press, 1995), p. 86.

12. See ibid., pp. 92–153, for a description of the memorialization process following the world wars.

13. Archibald MacLeish, "Lines for an Interment," with a response by Malcolm Cowley, *New Republic* 76:981 (September 20, 1933): 161.

14. Archibald MacLeish and Malcolm Cowley, "A Communication: The Dead of the Next War," *New Republic* 76:983 (October 4, 1933): 216.

15. Dixon Wecter, *When Johnny Comes Marching Home* (Westport, Conn.: Greenwood Press, 1970), pp. 555–556.

16. John L. Munschauer, *World War II Cavalcade: An Offer I Couldn't Refuse* (Manhattan, Kans.: Sunflower University Press, 1996), p. 67.

17. Manchester, *Goodbye, Darkness,* pp. 28 and 67–68.

18. See Holger Klein, with John Flower and Eric Homberger, eds., *The Second World War in Fiction* (London: Macmillan, 1984), p. 181, and Craig M. Cameron, *American Samurai: Myth, Imagination, and the Conduct of Battle in the First Marine Division, 1941–1951* (Cambridge: Cambridge University Press, 1994), pp. 38–48.

19. Tobey C. Herzog, *Vietnam War Stories: Innocence Lost* (London and New York: Routledge, 1985), p. 19. See pp. 16–24 for a full discussion of the "John Wayne Syndrome."

20. Ibid., p. 24. See also Michael C. C. Adams, *The Best War Ever: America and World War II* (Baltimore and London: Johns Hopkins University Press, 1994), p. 15.

21. Ron Kovic, *Born on the Fourth of July* (New York: Pocket Books, 1977), pp. 54, 55, and 56.

22. Caputo, *Rumor of War,* p. 6.

23. Davidson interview in Donald Knox, *The Korean War: Pusan to Chosin: An Oral History* (San Diego, New York, and London: Harcourt Brace Jovanovich, 1985), p. 238. See p. 288 for a similar example.

24. Cardinal interview in ibid., p. 419.

25. Davis interview in ibid., p. 276.

26. Kali Tal, "Speaking the Language of Pain: Vietnam War Literature in the Context of a Literature of Trauma" in *Fourteen Landing Zones: Approaches to Vietnam War Literature,* ed. Philip K. Jason (Iowa City: University of Iowa Press, 1991), p. 224. John Hellmann examines this national myth (or "American myth," as he calls it), the way it influenced soldiers going to the Vietnam War, and the influence of the war in turn on that myth in *American Myth*.

27. Herbert Hendin and Ann Pollinger Haas, *Wounds of War: The Psychological Aftermath of Combat in Vietnam* (New York: Basic Books, 1984), p. 214.

28. One of the most in-depth expositions of this theory is provided by the historian Eric J. Leed, although his examples are based on European soldiers' experiences. See *No Man's Land: Combat and Identity in World War I* (Cambridge: Cambridge University Press, 1979), pp. 75–76 and 80–96. Mark Meigs provides some evidence that education and class may have affected doughboy expectations as well. See *Optimism at Armageddon: Voices of American Participants in the First World War* (Washington Square, N.Y.: New York University Press, 1997), p. 216. And see Christian G. Appy, *Working-Class War: American Combat Soldiers and Vietnam* (Chapel Hill and London: University of

North Carolina Press, 1993), pp. 80–84, for a discussion of the impact of class on Vietnam War soldiers' attitudes and expectations.

29. Henry G. Gole, "Literature and History for Soldiers," *Military Review* 86:6 (May 1988): 3.

30. Hynes, *Soldiers' Tale,* p. 30.

31. Tim O'Brien, *If I Die in a Combat Zone: Box Me Up and Ship Me Home* (New York: Laurel, Dell, 1987), pp. 32 and 31.

32. Charles F. Minder, *This Man's War: The Day-by-Day Record of an American Private on the Western Front* (New York: Pevensey Press, 1931), p. 242.

33. James Brady, *The Coldest War: A Memoir of Korea* (New York: Pocket Books, 1991), p. 237.

34. Harold L. Bond, *Return to Cassino* (New York: Pocket Books, 1965), pp. 38–39.

35. Manchester, *Goodbye, Darkness,* p. 28.

36. Hynes, *Soldiers' Tale,* p. 111.

37. Mailer interview in Eric James Schroeder, *Vietnam, We've All Been There: Interviews with American Writers* (London and Westport, Conn.: Praeger, 1992), p. 92.

38. Roger J. Spiller, "My Guns: A Memoir of the Second World War," *American Heritage* 42:8 (December 1991): 47.

# Bibliography

BOOKS

Adams, Michael C. C. *The Best War Ever: America and World War II*. Baltimore and London: Johns Hopkins University Press, 1994.

———. *The Great Adventure: Male Desire and the Coming of World War I*. Bloomington and Indianapolis: Indiana University Press, 1990.

Aichinger, Peter. *The American Soldier in Fiction, 1880–1963: A History of Attitudes Toward Warfare and the Military Establishment*. Ames: Iowa State University Press, 1975.

Allen, Hervey. *Toward the Flame: A War Diary*. 1926. Reprint, New York: Grosset and Dunlap, 1934.

Andow, A. Andy. *Letters to Big Jim Regarding Narrul Purigo, Cashinum Iman*. New York: Vantage Press, 1994.

Appy, Christian G. *Working-Class War: American Combat Soldiers and Vietnam*. Chapel Hill and London: University of North Carolina Press, 1993.

Artiss, Kenneth L., ed. *The Symptom as Communication in Schizophrenia*. New York and London: Grune and Stratton, 1959.

Ashworth, Tony. *Trench Warfare, 1914–1918: The Live and Let Live System*. New York: Holmes and Meier, 1980.

Astor, Gerald. *Crisis in the Pacific: The Battles for the Philippine Islands by the Men Who Fought Them*. New York: Donald I. Fine Books, 1996.

Atwell, Lester. *Private*. New York: Popular Library, 1958.

Averill, Gerald P. *Mustang: A Combat Marine*. Novato, Calif.: Presidio Press, 1987.

Bailey, Leslie W. *Through Hell and High Water: The Wartime Memories of a Junior Combat Infantry Officer*. New York: Vantage Press, 1994.

Baker, Mark. *Nam: The Vietnam War in the Words of the Men and Women Who Fought There*. 1981. Reprint, New York: Berkley Books, 1983.

Baskir, Lawrence M., and William A. Strauss. *Chance and Circumstance: The Draft, the War, and the Vietnam Generation*. New York: Knopf, 1978.

Becker, Carl M., and Robert G. Thobaben. *Common Warfare: Parallel Memoirs by Two World War II GIs in the Pacific.* Jefferson, N.C., and London: McFarland, 1992.

Bergerud, Eric. *Touched with Fire: The Land War in the South Pacific.* New York: Viking Penguin, 1996.

Berry, Henry. *Hey, Mac, Where Ya Been? Living Memories of the U.S. Marines in the Korean War.* New York: St. Martin's Press, 1988.

———. *Make the Kaiser Dance: Living Memories of the Doughboy.* New York: Priam Books, 1978.

———. *Semper Fi, Mac: Living Memories of the U.S. Marines in World War II.* 1982. Reprint, New York: Berkley Books, 1983.

Blumenson, Martin. *Patton: The Man Behind the Legend, 1885–1945.* New York: William Morrow, 1985.

Blunt, Roscoe C., Jr. *Inside the Battle of the Bulge: A Private Comes of Age.* Westport, Conn., and London: Praeger, 1994.

Boesch, Paul. *Road to Huertgen: Forest in Hell.* 1962. Reprint, Houston: Paul M. Boesch, 1985.

Bogart, Leo, ed. *Project Clear: Social Research and the Desegregation of the United States Army.* 1969. Reprint, London and New Brunswick, N.J.: Transaction Publishers, 1992.

Bond, Harold L. *Return to Cassino.* 1964. Reprint, New York: Pocket Books, 1965.

Bourne, Peter G. *Men, Stress, and Vietnam.* Boston: Little, Brown, 1970.

———, ed. *The Psychology and Physiology of Stress: With Reference to Special Studies of the Viet Nam War.* New York and London: Academic Press, 1969.

Bowers, William T., William M. Hammond, and George L. MacGarrigle. *Black Soldier, White Army: The 24th Infantry Regiment in Korea.* Washington, D.C.: Center of Military History, U.S. Army, 1996.

Bowman, Peter. *Beach Red.* New York: Random House, 1945.

Boyd, Thomas. *Through the Wheat.* 1923. Reprint, with afterword by James Dickey, Carbondale and Edwardsville: Southern Illinois University Press; London and Amsterdam: Feffer and Simons, 1978.

Boyd, William Young. *The Gentle Infantryman.* New York: St. Martin's Press, 1985.

Bradford, Alfred S. *Some Even Volunteered: The First Wolfhounds Pacify Vietnam.* Westport, Conn., and London: Praeger, 1994.

Brady, James. *The Coldest War: A Memoir of Korea.* 1990. Reprint, New York, London, Toronto, Sydney, Tokyo, and Singapore: Pocket Books, 1991.

Brannen, Carl Andrew. *Over There: A Marine in the Great War.* Preface and annotation by Rolfe L. Hillman Jr. and Peter F. Owen; afterword by J. P. Brannen. College Station: Texas A&M University Press, 1996.

Brennan, Matthew. *Brennan's War: Vietnam, 1965–1969.* 1985. Reprint, New York: Pocket Books, 1986.

Brown, Harry. *A Walk in the Sun.* New York: Knopf, 1944.

Bullard, Robert Lee, with Earl Reeves. *American Soldiers Also Fought.* New York and Toronto: Longmans, Green, 1936.

Bussey, Charles M. *Firefight at Yechon: Courage and Racism in the Korean War.* Washington, D.C., and London: Brassey's, 1991.

Cameron, Craig M. *American Samurai: Myth, Imagination, and the Conduct of Battle in the First Marine Division, 1941–1951*. Cambridge: Cambridge University Press, 1994.

Camp, Richard D., with Eric Hammel. *Lima-6: A Marine Company Commander in Vietnam*. New York, London, Toronto, Sydney, Tokyo, and Singapore: Pocket Books, 1989.

Caputo, Philip. *A Rumor of War*. 1977. Reprint, New York: Ballantine Books, 1978.

Carter, Ross S. *Those Devils in Baggy Pants*. New York and Toronto: Signet, 1951.

Cawthon, Charles R. *Other Clay: A Remembrance of the World War II Infantry*. Niwot: University Press of Colorado, 1990.

Chambers, John Whiteclay, II. *To Raise an Army: The Draft Comes to Modern America*. New York: Free Press, 1987.

Cooperman, Stanley. *World War I and the American Novel*. Baltimore: Johns Hopkins University Press, 1967.

Crawford, Charles S. *The Four Deuces: A Korean War Story*. Novato, Calif.: Presidio Press, 1989.

Del Vecchio, John M. *The 13th Valley*. 1982. Reprint, Toronto, New York, London, and Sydney: Bantam Books, 1983.

Dill, James Hamilton. *Sixteen Days at Mungol-li*. Fayetteville, Ark.: M&M Press, 1993.

Dinter, Elmar. *Hero or Coward: Pressures Facing the Soldier in Battle*. London and Totowa, N.J.: Frank Cass, 1985.

Dollard, John, with Donald Horton. *Fear in Battle*. 1944. Reprint, New York: AMS Press, 1976.

Dos Passos, John. *First Encounter*. 1920. Reprint, New York: Philosophical Library, 1945.

———. *Three Soldiers*. Boston: Houghton Mifflin, 1921.

Doubler, Michael D. *Closing with the Enemy: How GIs Fought the War in Europe, 1944–1945*. Lawrence: University Press of Kansas, 1994.

Dower, John W. *War Without Mercy: Race and Power in the Pacific War*. New York: Pantheon, 1986.

Downs, Frederick. *The Killing Zone: My Life in the Vietnam War*. 1978. Reprint, New York: Berkley Books, 1983.

Duffy, Francis P. *Father Duffy's Story: A Tale of Humor and Heroism, of Life and Death with the Fighting Sixty-ninth*. Historical appendix by Joyce Kilmer. Garden City, N.Y.: Garden City Publishing, 1919.

Dyer, Gwynne. *War*. New York: Crown, 1985.

Ebert, James R. *A Life in a Year: The American Infantryman in Vietnam, 1965–1972*. Novato, Calif.: Presidio Press, 1993.

Egbert, Robert L., Tor Meeland, Victor B. Cline, Edward W. Forgy, Martin W. Spickler, and Charles Brown. *Fighter I: An Analysis of Combat Fighters and Non-Fighters*. Human Resources Research Office Technical Report 44, December 1957.

Ehrhart, William D. *Vietnam-Perkasie: A Combat Marine Memoir*. Jefferson, N.C., and London: McFarland, 1983.

Eksteins, Modris. *Rites of Spring: The Great War and the Birth of the Modern Age*. New York, London, Toronto, Sydney, and Auckland: Anchor Books, 1989.

Ellis, John. *Eye-Deep in Hell: Trench Warfare in World War I*. 1976. Reprint, Baltimore: Johns Hopkins University Press, 1989.

——. *The Sharp End: The Fighting Man in World War II*. New York: Charles Scribner's Sons, 1980. Also published as *On the Front Lines: The Experience of War Through the Eyes of the Allied Soldiers in World War II*, New York, Chichester, Brisbane, Toronto, and Singapore: John Wiley and Sons, 1991.

English, John A. *On Infantry*. New York: Praeger, 1981.

Ettinger, Albert M., and A. Churchill Ettinger. *A Doughboy with the Fighting Sixty-ninth: A Remembrance of World War I*. Shippensburg, Pa.: White Mane, 1992.

Fehrenbach, Theodore R. *This Kind of War: A Study in Unpreparedness*. New York: Macmillan, 1963.

Frank, Pat. *Hold Back the Night*. Philadelphia and New York: J. B. Lippincott, 1952.

Frankel, Ernest. *Band of Brothers*. New York: Macmillan, 1958.

Frankel, Nat, and Larry Smith. *Patton's Best: An Informal History of the 4th Armored Division*. 1978. Reprint, New York: Jove, 1984.

Freidel, Frank. *Over There: The Story of America's First Great Overseas Crusade*. 1964. Reprint, revised and abridged, Philadelphia: Temple University Press, 1990.

French, Albert. *Patches of Fire: A Story of War and Redemption*. New York, London, Toronto, Sydney, and Auckland: Anchor Books, 1997.

Fuller, Jack. *Fragments*. 1984. Reprint, New York: Dell, 1985.

Fussell, Paul. *Doing Battle: The Making of a Skeptic*. Boston, New York, Toronto, and London: Little, Brown, 1996.

——. *The Great War and Modern Memory*. London, Oxford, and New York: Oxford University Press, 1975.

——. *Wartime: Understanding and Behavior in the Second World War*. New York and Oxford: Oxford University Press, 1989.

Gabel, Kurt. *The Making of a Paratrooper: Airborne Training and Combat in World War II*. Edited and with an introduction and epilogue by William C. Mitchell, foreword by Theodore A. Wilson. Lawrence: University Press of Kansas, 1990.

Gabriel, Richard A. *The Painful Field: The Psychiatric Dimension of Modern War*. Contributions in Military Studies, number 75. New York, London, and Westport, Conn.: Greenwood Press, 1988.

——, ed. *Military Psychiatry: A Comparative Perspective*. Contributions in Military Studies, number 57. New York, London, and Westport, Conn.: Greenwood Press, 1986.

Gabriel, Richard A., and Paul L. Savage. *Crisis in Command: Mismanagement in the Army*. New York: Hill and Wang, 1978.

Genthe, Charles V. *American War Narratives, 1917–1918: A Study and Bibliography*. New York: David Lewis, 1969.

Giles, Janice Holt, ed. *The G.I. Journal of Sergeant Giles*. Boston: Houghton Mifflin, and Cambridge: Riverside Press, 1965.

Ginzberg, Eli, James K. Anderson, Sol W. Ginsburg, John L. Herma, and John B. Miner. *The Ineffective Soldier: Lessons for Management and the Nation*. 3 vols. Vol. 1, *The Lost Divisions;* Vol. 2, *Breakdown and Recovery;* Vol. 3, *Patterns of Performance*. New York and London: Columbia University Press, 1959.

Glass, Albert J., ed. *Neuropsychiatry in World War II*. 2 vols. Medical Department, U.S. Army, Office of the Surgeon General. Vol. 2, *Overseas Theaters*. Washington, D.C.: U.S. Government Printing Office, 1973.

Goff, Stanley, and Robert Sanders, with Clark Smith. *Brothers: Black Soldiers in the Nam.* Novato, Calif.: Presidio Press, and London: Arms and Armour Press, 1982.

Gray, Jesse Glenn. *The Warriors: Reflections on Men in Battle.* 1959. Reprint, with an introduction by Hannah Arendt, New York, Hagerstown, San Francisco, and London: Harper Colophon Books, 1970.

Grinker, Roy R., and John P. Spiegel. *War Neuroses.* 1945. Reprint, New York: Arno Press, 1979.

Grossman, Dave. *On Killing: The Psychological Cost of Learning to Kill in War and Society.* Boston, New York, Toronto, and London: Little, Brown, 1995.

Halberstam, David. *One Very Hot Day.* Boston: Houghton Mifflin, 1967.

Hall, Gwendolyn Midlo, ed. *Love, War, and the 96th Engineers (Colored): The World War II New Guinea Diaries of Captain Hyman Samuelson.* Urbana and Chicago: University of Illinois Press, 1995.

Hardison, Richard M. *Caissons Across Europe: An Artillery Captain's Personal War.* Austin, Tex.: Eakin Press, 1990.

Hasford, Gustav. *The Short-timers.* Toronto, New York, London, Sydney, and Auckland: Bantam Books, 1979.

Heinemann, Larry. *Close Quarters.* New York: Farrar, Straus and Giroux, 1977.

Hellmann, John. *American Myth and the Legacy of Vietnam.* New York: Columbia University Press, 1986.

Helmer, John. *Bringing the War Home: The American Soldier in Vietnam and After.* New York: Free Press, and London: Collier Macmillan, 1974.

Hemingway, Ernest. *Across the River and into the Trees.* 1950. Reprint, New York: Collier Books, 1987.

———. *The Short Stories of Ernest Hemingway: The First Forty-nine Stories and the Play "The Fifth Column."* New York: Modern Library, 1942.

———, ed. *Men at War: The Best War Stories of All Time.* 1942. Reprint, New York: Bramhill House, 1979.

Henderson, William Darryl. *Cohesion: The Human Element in Combat: Leadership and Societal Influence in the Armies of the Soviet Union, the United States, North Vietnam, and Israel.* With an introduction by Charles C. Moskos. Washington, D.C.: National Defense University Press, 1988.

Hendin, Herbert, and Ann Pollinger Haas. *Wounds of War: The Psychological Aftermath of Combat in Vietnam.* New York: Basic Books, 1984.

Herr, Michael. *Dispatches.* 1968. Reprint, New York: Avon Books, 1978.

Hersey, John. *Into the Valley: A Skirmish of the Marines.* 1943. Reprint, with new foreword by the author. New York: Schocken Books, 1989.

Herzog, Tobey C. *Vietnam War Stories: Innocence Lost.* London and New York: Routledge, 1985.

Higgins, Marguerite. *War in Korea: The Report of a Woman Combat Correspondent.* Garden City, N.Y.: Doubleday, 1951.

Hoffman, Alice M., and Howard S. Hoffman. *Archives of Memory: A Soldier Recalls World War II.* Lexington: University Press of Kentucky, 1990.

Hoffman, Bob. *I Remember the Last War.* York, Pa.: Strength and Health Publishing, 1940.

Holmes, Richard. *Acts of War: The Behavior of Men in Battle.* New York: Free Press, 1985. Also published as *Firing Line,* London: Jonathan Cape, 1985.

Huebner, Klaus H. *Long Walk Through War: A Combat Doctor's Diary*. College Station: Texas A&M University Press, 1987.

Hynes, Samuel. *The Soldiers' Tale: Bearing Witness to Modern War*. New York: Allen Lane, 1997.

Ingersoll, Ralph. *The Battle Is the Pay-off*. New York: Harcourt, Brace, 1943.

Janowitz, Morris. *The Professional Soldier: A Social and Political Portrait*. New York: Free Press, 1960, prologue added in 1974.

———, ed. *The New Military: Changing Patterns of Organization*. New York: Russell Sage, 1964.

Janowitz, Morris, and Roger W. Little. *Sociology and the Military Establishment*. 3d ed. Beverly Hills and London: Sage, 1974.

Jason, Philip K., ed. *Fourteen Landing Zones: Approaches to Vietnam War Literature*. Iowa City: University of Iowa Press, 1991.

Johnson, Franklyn A. *One More Hill*. 1949. Reprint, Toronto, New York, London, and Sydney: Bantam Books, 1983.

Jones, James. *From Here to Eternity*. New York: Signet, 1951.

———. *The Thin Red Line*. New York: Charles Scribner's Sons, 1962.

———. *WW II: A Chronicle of Soldiering*. 1975. Reprint, New York: Ballantine, 1976.

Judy, Will. *A Soldier's Diary: A Day-to-Day Record in the World War*. Chicago: Judy Publishing, 1931.

Kahn, E. J., Jr. *G.I. Jungle: An American Soldier in Australia and New Guinea*. New York: Simon and Schuster, 1943.

Karsten, Peter. *Soldiers and Society: The Effects of Military Service and War on American Society*. Grass Roots Perspectives on American History, number 1. Westport, Conn., and London: Greenwood Press, 1978.

Keegan, John. *The Face of Battle*. New York: Viking, 1976.

Keegan, John, and Richard Holmes, with John Gau. *Soldiers: A History of Men in Battle*. Foreword by Frederick Forsyth. New York: Viking, 1986.

Keen, Sam. *Faces of the Enemy: Reflections of the Hostile Imagination*. 1986. Reprint, new preface, San Francisco: HarperCollins, 1991.

Kellett, Anthony. *Combat Motivation: The Behavior of Soldiers in Battle*. Boston, The Hague, and London: Kluwer, Nijhoff, 1982.

Kennedy, David M. *Over Here: The First World War and American Society*. Oxford, New York, Toronto, and Melbourne: Oxford University Press, 1980.

Kennett, Lee. *G.I.: The American Soldier in World War II*. New York: Charles Scribner's Sons, 1987.

Ketwig, John. . . . *And a Hard Rain Fell: A GI's True Story of the War in Vietnam*. 1985. Reprint, New York: Pocket Books, 1986.

Kinnard, Douglas. *The War Managers: American Generals Reflect on Vietnam*. 1977. Reprint, New York: Da Capo, 1991.

Klein, Holger, ed. *The First World War in Fiction: A Collection of Critical Essays*. London: Macmillan, 1976.

Klein, Holger, with John Flower and Eric Homberger, eds. *The Second World War in Fiction*. London: Macmillan, 1984.

Knox, Donald. *The Korean War: Pusan to Chosin: An Oral History*. San Diego, New York, and London: Harcourt Brace Jovanovich, 1985.

————, with Alfred Coppel. *The Korean War: Uncertain Victory: The Concluding Volume of an Oral History.* San Diego, New York, and London: Harcourt Brace Jovanovich, 1988.

Kovic, Ron. *Born on the Fourth of July.* 1976. Reprint, New York, London, Toronto, Sydney, and Tokyo: Pocket Books, 1977.

Kreidberg, Marvin A., and Merton G. Henry. *History of Military Mobilization in the United States Army, 1775–1945.* Department of the Army Pamphlet 20-212. Washington, D.C.: U.S. Government Printing Office, November 1955.

Lang, Kurt. *Military Institutions and the Sociology of War: A Review of the Literature, with Annotated Bibliography.* Beverly Hills and London: Sage, 1972.

Langer, William L. *Gas and Flame in World War I.* New York: Knopf, 1965.

Lanning, Michael Lee. *The Only War We Had: A Platoon Leader's Journal of Vietnam.* New York: Ivy Books, 1987.

Lawrence, Joseph D. *Fighting Soldier: The A.E.F. in 1918.* Edited by Robert H. Ferrell. Boulder: Colorado Associated University Press, 1985.

Leckie, Robert. *Helmet for My Pillow.* 1957. Reprint, Garden City, N.Y.: Nelson Doubleday, 1979.

Leed, Eric J. *No Man's Land: Combat and Identity in World War I.* Cambridge: Cambridge University Press, 1979.

Leinbaugh, Harold P., and John D. Campbell. *The Men of Company K.* 1985. Reprint, Toronto, New York, London, Sydney, and Auckland: Bantam Books, 1987.

Leonard, Thomas C. *Above the Battle: War-Making in America from Appomattox to Versailles.* New York: Oxford University Press, 1978.

Levin, Dan. *From the Battlefield: Dispatches of a World War II Marine.* Annapolis, Md.: Naval Institute Press, 1995.

Lifton, Robert Jay. *Home from the War: Vietnam Veterans: Neither Victims nor Executioners.* New York: Simon and Schuster, 1973.

Linderman, Gerald F. *The World Within War: America's Combat Experience in World War II.* New York, London, Toronto, Sidney, and Singapore: Free Press, 1997.

Little, Arthur W. *From Harlem to the Rhine: The Story of New York's Colored Volunteers.* New York: Covici-Friede, 1936.

Little, Roger W., ed. *Handbook of Military Institutions.* Sage Series on Armed Forces and Society, Beverly Hills, Calif.: Sage, 1971.

Lomperis, Timothy J. *"Reading the Wind": The Literature of the Vietnam War.* Durham, N.C.: Duke University Press, 1987.

MacArthur, Charles. *War Bugs.* New York: Grosset and Dunlap, 1929.

MacDonald, Charles B. *Company Commander.* 1947. Reprint, Toronto, New York, and London: Bantam Books, 1978.

Mackin, Elton E. *Suddenly We Didn't Want to Die: Memoirs of a World War I Marine.* Foreword by Victor H. Krulak, introduction and annotations by George B. Clark. Novato, Calif.: Presidio Press, 1993.

Mailer, Norman. *The Naked and the Dead.* New York: Signet Books, 1948.

Manchester, William. *Goodbye, Darkness: A Memoir of the Pacific War.* Boston and Toronto: Little, Brown, 1979.

March, William. *Company K.* 1933. Reprint, New York: Sagamore Press, 1957.

Marshall, Samuel L. A. *Commentary on Infantry Operations and Weapons Usage in*

*Korea, Winter of 1950–51.* Operations Research Office Report 13 (ORO-R-13). Chevy Chase, Md.: Johns Hopkins University Press, 1953.

———. *Men Against Fire: The Problem of Battle Command in Future War.* 1947. Reprint, Gloucester: Peter Smith, 1978.

———. *The Soldier's Load and the Mobility of a Nation.* 1950. Reprint, Quantico, Va.: Marine Corps Association, 1980.

Martin, Ralph G. *The G.I. War, 1941–1945.* Boston and Toronto: Little, Brown, 1967.

Mason, Robert. *Chickenhawk.* 1983. Reprint, New York, London, Victoria, Ontario, and Auckland: Penguin Books, 1986.

Matsen, William E. *The Great War and the American Novel: Versions of Reality and the Writer's Craft in Selected Fiction of the First World War.* American University Studies Series 24, American Literature, vol. 48. New York, San Francisco, Bern, Baltimore, Frankfurt am Main, Berlin, Vienna, and Paris: Peter Lang, 1993.

Matthews, Allen R. *The Assault.* 1947. Reprint, New York: Dodd, Mead, 1980.

Matthias, Howard. *The Korean War—Reflections of a Young Combat Platoon Leader.* 1993. Rev. ed., Tallahassee, Fla.: Father and Son Publishing, 1995.

Mauldin, William H. *Bill Mauldin in Korea.* New York: W. W. Norton, 1952.

———. *Up Front.* 1945. Reprint, with a foreword by David Halberstam, New York: Award Books, 1976.

May, Henry F. *The End of American Innocence: A Study of the First Years of Our Own Time, 1912–1917.* 1959. Reprint, Chicago: Quadrangle Books, 1964.

McDonough, James R. *Platoon Leader.* 1985. Reprint, Toronto, New York, London, Sydney, and Auckland: Bantam Books, 1986.

Meigs, Mark. *Optimism at Armageddon: Voices of American Participants in the First World War.* Washington Square: New York University Press, 1997.

Menninger, William C. *A Psychiatrist for a Troubled World: Selected Papers of William C. Menninger, M.D.* Edited, with introductory material, by Bernard H. Hall. New York: Viking Press, 1967.

Merrick, Robert G. *World War I: A Diary.* Baltimore, Md.: privately published, 1982.

Merton, Robert K., and Paul F. Lazarsfeld, eds. *Continuities in Social Research: Studies in the Scope and Method of "The American Soldier."* Glencoe, Ill.: Free Press, 1950.

Minder, Charles F. *This Man's War: The Day-by-Day Record of an American Private on the Western Front.* New York: Pevensey Press, 1931.

Moran, Lord Charles McM. *The Anatomy of Courage.* 1945. Reprint, Garden City Park, N.Y.: Avery, 1987.

Morrow, Curtis James. *What's a Commie Ever Done to Black People? A Korean War Memoir of Fighting in the U.S. Army's Last All Negro Unit.* Jefferson, N.C., and London: McFarland, 1997.

Moskos, Charles C., Jr. *The American Enlisted Man: The Rank and File in Today's Military.* New York: Russell Sage Foundation, 1970.

———. *S. L. A. Marshall Chair: Soldiers and Sociology.* U.S. Army Research Institute for the Behavioral and Social Sciences. Washington, D.C.: U.S. Government Printing Office, 1988.

Motley, Mary Penick. *The Invisible Soldier: The Experience of the Black Soldier, World War II.* Foreword by Howard Donovan Queen. Detroit: Wayne State University Press, 1975.

Munschauer, John L. *World War II Cavalcade: An Offer I Couldn't Refuse*. Manhattan, Kans.: Sunflower University Press, 1996.

Murphy, Audie. *To Hell and Back*. 1949. Reprint, Toronto, New York, London, Sydney, and Auckland: Bantam Books, 1983.

Myers, Thomas. *Walking Point: American Narratives of Vietnam*. New York and Oxford: Oxford University Press, 1988.

[O'Brien, Howard V.]. *Wine, Women, and War: A Diary of Disillusionment*. New York: J. H. Sears, 1926.

O'Brien, Tim. *Going After Cacciato*. 1975. Reprint, New York: Dell, 1979.

———. *If I Die in a Combat Zone: Box Me Up and Ship Me Home*. 1969. Reprint, New York: Laurel, Dell, 1987.

Ogden, Richard E. *Green Knight, Red Mourning*. New York: Zebra Books, 1985.

Owen, Joseph R. *Colder Than Hell: A Marine Rifle Company at Chosin Reservoir*. Foreword by Raymond G. Davis. Annapolis, Md.: Naval Institute Press, 1996.

Parks, David. *G.I. Diary*. New York, Evanston, and London: Harper and Row, 1968.

Piehler, G. Kurt. *Remembering War the American Way*. Washington, D.C., and London: Smithsonian Institution Press, 1995.

Pyle, Ernie. *Brave Men*. New York: Henry Holt, 1944.

———. *Here Is Your War: The Story of G.I. Joe*. 1943. Reprint, Cleveland and New York: World, 1945.

———. *Last Chapter*. New York: Henry Holt, 1946.

Regan, Geoffrey. *Blue on Blue: A History of Friendly Fire*. New York: Avon Books, 1995.

Rishell, Lyle. *With a Black Platoon in Combat: A Year in Korea*. College Station: Texas A&M University Press, 1993.

Rogers, Horatio. *World War I Through My Sights*. 1975. Reprint, with foreword by Walter Muir Whitehill, San Rafael, Calif.: Presidio Press, 1976.

Russ, Martin. *The Last Parallel: A Marine's War Journal*. New York and Toronto: Rinehart, 1957.

Sack, John. *M*. 1966. Reprint, New York: Avon Books, 1985.

Salmon, Thomas W., and Norman Fenton. *The Medical Department of the United States Army in the World War*. 15 vols. Vol. 10, *Neuropsychiatry in the American Expeditionary Forces*. Washington, D.C.: U.S. Government Printing Office, 1929.

Santoli, Al. *Everything We Had: An Oral History of the Vietnam War by Thirty-three American Soldiers Who Fought It*. 1981. Reprint, New York: Ballantine Books, 1982.

Sarkesian, Sam C., ed. *Combat Effectiveness: Cohesion, Stress, and the Volunteer Military*. Vol. 9. Sage Research Progress Series on War, Revolution, and Peacekeeping. Beverly Hills and London: Sage, 1980.

Schaffer, Ronald. *America in the Great War: The Rise of the War Welfare State*. New York and Oxford: Oxford University Press, 1991.

Schroeder, Eric James. *Vietnam, We've All Been There: Interviews with American Writers*. London and Westport, Conn.: Praeger, 1992.

Sefton, George William. *It Was My War: I'll Remember It the Way I Want To!* Manhattan, Kans.: Sunflower University Press, 1994.

Shay, Jonathan. *Achilles in Vietnam: Combat Trauma and the Undoing of Character.* New York, London, Sydney, Tokyo, and Singapore: Scribner, 1995.

Shrader, Charles R. *Amicicide: The Problem of Friendly Fire in Modern War*. U.S. Army

Command and General Staff College Combat Studies Institute Research Study no. 1. Washington, D.C.: U.S. Government Printing Office, December 1982.

Sledge, Eugene B. *With the Old Breed at Peleliu and Okinawa.* 1981. Reprint, New York, Toronto, London, Sydney, and Auckland: Bantam Books, 1983.

Smith, W. Stanford, with contributions by Leo J. Machan and Stanley E. Earman. *The Cannoneers: GI Life in a World War II Cannon Company.* Manhattan, Kans.: Sunflower University Press, 1993.

Spiroff, Boris R. *Korea: Frozen Hell on Earth.* New York: Vantage Press, 1995.

Stallings, Laurence. *The Doughboys: The Story of the AEF, 1917–1918.* New York, Evanston, and London: Harper and Row, 1963.

Standifer, Leon C. *Not in Vain: A Rifleman Remembers World War II.* Baton Rouge and London: Louisiana State University Press, 1992.

Stein, Maurice R., Arthur J. Vidich, and David Manning White, eds. *Identity and Anxiety: Survival of the Person in Mass Society.* Glencoe, Ill.: Free Press, 1960.

Stephens, Rudolph W. *Old Ugly Hill: A G.I.'s Fourteen Months in the Korean Trenches, 1952–1953.* Jefferson, N.C., and London: McFarland, 1995.

Stouffer, Samuel A., Edward A. Suchman, Leland C. DeVinney, Shirley A. Star, Robin M. Williams Jr., Arthur A. Lumsdaine, Marion Harper Lumsdaine, M. Brewster Smith, Irving L. Janis, and Leonard S. Cottrell Jr. *Studies in Social Psychology in World War II.* 4 vols. Vol. 1, *The American Soldier: Adjustment During Army Life;* Vol. 2, *The American Soldier: Combat and Its Aftermath.* Princeton: Princeton University Press, 1949.

Sullivan, John A. *Toy Soldiers: Memoir of a Combat Platoon Leader in Korea.* Jefferson, N.C., and London: McFarland, 1991.

Terkel, Studs. *"The Good War": An Oral History of World War II.* New York: Pantheon Books, 1984.

Terry, Wallace. *Bloods: An Oral History of the Vietnam War by Black Veterans.* 1984. Reprint, New York: Ballantine Books, 1985.

Thayer, Thomas C. *War Without Fronts: The American Experience in Vietnam.* Boulder and London: Westview Press, 1985.

Thomason, John W., Jr. *Fix Bayonets!* 1925. Reprint, New York: Blue Ribbon Books, 1926.

Tomedi, Rudy. *No Bugles, No Drums: An Oral History of the Korean War.* New York, Chichester, Brisbane, Toronto, and Singapore: John Wiley, 1993.

Tregaskis, Richard. *Guadalcanal Diary.* New York: Random House, 1943.

———. *Invasion Diary.* New York: Random House, 1944.

———. *Stronger Than Fear.* New York: Random House, 1945.

Uris, Leon. *Battle Cry.* New York, London, and Toronto: Bantam Books, 1953.

U.S. Department of the Army Field Manual 8-51. *Combat Stress in a Theater of Operations: Tactics, Techniques, and Procedures.* Final approved draft. Washington, D.C.: U.S. Government Printing Office, May 1994.

Watson, Peter. *War on the Mind: The Military Uses and Abuses of Psychology.* New York: Basic Books, 1978.

Webb, James. *Fields of Fire.* 1978. Reprint, New York: Bantam Books, 1979.

Wecter, Dixon. *When Johnny Comes Marching Home.* 1944. Reprint, Westport, Conn.: Greenwood Press, 1970.

Weigley, Russell F. *Eisenhower's Lieutenants: The Campaigns of France and Germany.* Bloomington: Indiana University Press, 1981.

Westheider, James E. *Fighting on Two Fronts: African Americans and the Vietnam War.* New York and London: New York University Press, 1997.

Wilder, Amos N. *Armageddon Revisited: A World War I Journal.* New Haven and London: Yale University Press, 1994.

Wilson, George. *If You Survive.* New York: Ivy Books, 1987.

Wolfert, Ira. *Battle for the Solomons.* Cambridge, Mass.: Riverside Press, 1943.

Yezzo, Dominick. *A G.I.'s Vietnam Diary, 1968–1969.* New York: Franklin Watts, 1974.

York, Alvin C. *Sergeant York: His Own Life Story and War Diary.* Edited by Tom Skeyhill. Garden City, N.Y.: Doubleday, Doran, 1928.

Zumbro, Ralph. *Tank Sergeant.* Novato, Calif.: Presidio Press, 1986.


ARTICLES


Anderson, Jeffery W. "Military Heroism: An Occupational Definition." *Armed Forces and Society* 12:4 (summer 1986): 591–606.

Appel, John W., and Gilbert W. Beebe. "Preventive Psychiatry: An Epidemiological Approach." *Journal of the American Medical Association* 131:18 (August 31, 1946): 1469–1475.

Ashworth, A. E. "The Sociology of Trench Warfare, 1914–1918." *British Journal of Sociology* 19:4 (December 1968): 407–423.

Badillo, Gilbert, and G. David Curry. "The Social Incidence of Vietnam Casualties: Social Class or Race?" *Armed Forces and Society* 2:3 (May 1976): 397–406.

Ballard, John A., and Aliecia J. McDowell. "Hate and Combat Behavior." *Armed Forces and Society* 17:2 (winter 1991): 229–241.

Barnett, Arnold, Timothy Stanley, and Michael Shore. "America's Vietnam Casualties: Victims of a Class War?" *Operations Research* 40:5 (September–October 1992): 856–866.

Bartemeier, Leo H., Lawrence S. Kubie, Karl A. Menninger, John Romano, and John C. Whitehorn. "Combat Exhaustion." Two-part series. Part 1: *Journal of Nervous and Mental Disease* 104:4 (October 1946): 358–389; Part 2: *Journal of Nervous and Mental Disease* 104:5 (November 1946): 489–525.

Beaumont, Roger A. "Military Fiction and Role: Some Problems and Perspectives." *Military Affairs* 39:2 (April 1975): 69–71.

Begines, Thomas J. "The American Military and the Western Idea." *Military Review* 72:3 (March 1992): 39–48.

Berens, Robert J. "Battle Atrocities." *Army* 36:4 (April 1986): 53–56.

Blake, Joseph A., and Suellen Butler. "The Medal of Honor, Combat Orientations and Latent Role Structure in the United States Military." *The Sociological Quarterly* 17:4 (Autumn 1976): 561–567.

Bond, Thomas C. "The Why of Fragging." *American Journal of Psychiatry* 133:11 (November 1976): 1328–1331.

Bourne, Peter G. "Some Observations on the Psychosocial Phenomena Seen in Basic

Training." *Psychiatry: Journal for the Study of Interpersonal Processes* 30:2 (May 1967): 187–196.

Braceland, Francis J. "Psychiatric Lessons from World War II." *American Journal of Psychiatry* 103:5 (March 1947): 587–593.

Brady, James. "Leaving for Korea." *American Heritage* 48:1 (February/March 1997): 69–89.

Brotz, Howard, and Everett Wilson. "Characteristics of Military Society." *American Journal of Sociology* 51:5 (March 1946): 371–375.

Brown, Charles W., and Charles C. Moskos Jr. "The American Soldier: Will He Fight? A Provisional Attitudinal Analysis." *Military Review* 56:6 (June 1976): 8–17.

Broyles, William, Jr. "Why Men Love War." *Esquire* 102:5 (November 1984): 55–65.

Camfield, Thomas M. "'Will to Win'—The U.S. Army Troop Morale Program of World War I." *Military Affairs* 41:3 (October 1977): 125–128.

Chermol, Brian H. "Wounds Without Scars: Treatment of Battle Fatigue in the U.S. Armed Forces in the Second World War." *Military Affairs* 49:1 (January 1985): 9–12.

Chodoff, Elliot P. "Ideology and Primary Groups." *Armed Forces and Society* 9:4 (summer 1983): 569–593.

Clark, Robert A. "Aggressiveness and Military Training." *American Journal of Sociology* 51:5 (March 1946): 423–432.

Cockerham, William C. "Attitudes Toward Combat Among U.S. Army Paratroopers." *Journal of Political and Military Sociology* 6:1 (spring 1978): 1–15.

———. "Selective Socialization: Airborne Training as Status Passage." *Journal of Political and Military Sociology* 1:2 (fall 1973): 215–229.

Coleman, Jules W. "The Group Factor in Military Psychiatry." *American Journal of Orthopsychiatry* 16:2 (April 1946): 222–226.

Davis, James Martin. "Vietnam: What It Was Really Like." *Military Review* 69:1 (January 1989): 34–44.

Downs, Frederick. "View from the Fourth Estate: Death and the Dark Side of Command." *Parameters* 17:4 (December 1987): 91–95. Reprinted from *Washington Post,* August 16, 1987, pp. D1–D2.

Dubik, James M., and Terrence D. Fullerton. "Soldier Overloading in Grenada." *Military Review* 67:1 (January 1987): 38–47.

Ehrhart, William D. "Soldier-Poets of the Vietnam War." *Virginia Quarterly Review* 63:2 (spring 1987): 246–267.

Eisenhart, R. Wayne. "You Can't Hack It, Little Girl: A Discussion of the Covert Psychological Agenda of Modern Combat Training." *Journal of Social Issues* 31:4 (fall 1975): 13–23.

Fallows, James. "What Did You Do in the Class War, Daddy?" *Washington Monthly* 7:8 (October 1975): 5–19.

Faris, John H. "An Alternate Perspective to Savage and Gabriel." *Armed Forces and Society* 3:3 (May 1977): 457–462.

———. "The Impact of Basic Combat Training." *Armed Forces and Society* 2:1 (November 1975): 115–127.

Fenton, Charles A. "A Literary Fracture of World War I." *American Quarterly* 12:1, Part 1 (summer 1960): 119–132.

Fiman, Byron G., Jonathan F. Borus, and M. Duncan Stanton. "Black-White and American-Vietnamese Relations Among Soldiers in Vietnam." *Journal of Social Issues* 31:4 (fall 1975): 39–48.

Fowler, John G. "Combat Cohesion in Vietnam." *Military Review* 59:12 (December 1979): 22–32.

Frost, Dean E., Fred E. Fiedler, and Jeff W. Anderson. "The Role of Personal Risk-Taking in Effective Leadership." *Human Relations* 36:2 (February 1983): 185–202.

Fussell, Paul. "My War: How I Got Irony in the Infantry." *Harper's* 264:1580 (January 1982): 40–48.

Gault, William Barry. "Some Remarks on Slaughter." *American Journal of Psychiatry* 128:4 (October 1971): 82–86.

Glass, Albert J. "Principles of Combat Psychiatry." *Military Medicine* 117:1 (July 1955): 27–33.

———. "Psychotherapy in the Combat Zone." *American Journal of Psychiatry* 110:10 (April 1954): 725–731.

Glenn, Russell W. "Men and Fire in Vietnam." Two-part series. Part 1: *Army* 39:4 (April 1989): 18–26; Part 2, *Army* 39:5 (May 1989): 38–45.

Gole, Henry G. "Literature and History for Soldiers." *Military Review* 68:6 (May 1988): 2–15.

Haley, Sarah A. "When the Patient Reports Atrocities: Specific Treatment Considerations of the Vietnam Veteran." *Archives of General Psychiatry* 30:2 (February 1974): 191–196.

Hawkins, Charles F. "Friendly Fire: Facts, Myths and Misperceptions." *U.S. Naval Institute Proceedings* 120:6 (June 1994): 54–59.

Ingraham, Larry H., and Frederick J. Manning. "Psychiatric Battle Casualties: The Missing Column in a War Without Replacements." *Military Review* 60:8 (August 1980): 19–29.

Janis, Irving L. "Psychodynamic Aspects of Adjustment to Army Life." *Psychiatry: Journal of the Biology and the Pathology of Interpersonal Relations* 8:2 (May 1945): 159–176.

Jones, Franklin Del. "Experiences of a Division Psychiatrist in Vietnam." *Military Medicine* 132:12 (December 1967): 1003–1008.

Jones, Franklin Del, and Arnold W. Johnson Jr. "Medical and Psychiatric Treatment Policy and Practice in Vietnam." *Journal of Social Issues* 31:4 (fall 1975): 49–65.

Kaplan, Roger. "Army Unit Cohesion in Vietnam: A Bum Rap." *Parameters* 17:3 (September 1987): 58–67.

Karsten, Peter. "Consent and the American Soldier: Theory Versus Reality." *Parameters* 12:1 (March 1982): 42–49.

Kilpatrick, Ted D., and Harry A. Grater Jr. "Field Report on Marine Psychiatric Casualties in Vietnam." *Military Medicine* 136:10 (October 1971): 801–809.

Kindsvatter, Peter S. "Cowards, Comrades, and Killer Angels: The Soldier in Literature." *Parameters* 20:2 (June 1990): 31–49.

Kirkland, Faris R., Paul T. Bartone, and David H. Marlowe. "Commanders' Priorities and Psychological Readiness." *Armed Forces and Society* 19:4 (summer 1993): 579–598.

Kohn, Richard H. "The Social History of the American Soldier: A Review and Prospectus for Research." *American Historical Review* 86:3 (June 1981): 553–567.

Kviz, Frederick J. "Survival in Combat as a Collective Exchange Process." *Journal of Political and Military Sociology* 6:2 (fall 1978): 219–232.

Lang, Kurt. "American Military Performance in Vietnam: Background and Analysis." *Journal of Political and Military Sociology* 8:2 (fall 1980): 269–286.

Liberman, Robert Paul, Stephen M. Sonnenberg, and Melvin S. Stern. "Psychiatric Evaluations for Young Men Facing the Draft: A Report of 147 Cases." *American Journal of Psychiatry* 128:2 (August 1971): 147–152.

Linenthal, Edward Tabor. "From Hero to Anti-hero: The Transformation of the Warrior in Modern America." *Soundings: An Interdisciplinary Journal* 63:1 (spring 1980): 79–93.

MacLeish, Archibald. "Lines for an Interment," with a response by Malcolm Cowley. *New Republic* 76:981 (September 20, 1933): 159–161.

MacLeish, Archibald, and Malcolm Cowley. "A Communication: The Dead of the Next War." *New Republic* 76:983 (October 4, 1933): 214–216.

"The Making of the Infantryman." *American Journal of Sociology* 51:5 (March 1946): 376–379.

Mandelbaum, David G. "Psychiatry in Military Society." Two-part series. Part 1, *Human Organization* 13:3 (fall 1954): 5–15; Part 2, *Human Organization* 13:4 (winter 1955): 19–25.

Marin, Peter. "Coming to Terms With Vietnam." *Harper's* 261:1567 (December 1980): 41–56.

Maskin, Meyer H., and Leon L. Altman. "Military Psychodynamics: Psychological Factors in the Transition from Civilian to Soldier." *Psychiatry: Journal of the Biology and the Pathology of Interpersonal Relations* 6:3 (August 1943): 263–269.

Mayer, Albert J., and Thomas Ford Hoult. "Social Stratification and Combat Survival." *Social Forces* 34:2 (December 1955): 155–159.

Mayers, Albert N. "Dug-Out Psychiatry." *Psychiatry: Journal of the Biology and Pathology of Interpersonal Relations* 8:4 (November 1945): 387–388.

Mazur, Allan. "Was Vietnam a Class War?" *Armed Forces and Society* 21:3 (spring 1995): 455–459.

Meagher, John F. W. "Prominent Features of the Psychoneuroses in the War." *American Journal of the Medical Sciences* 158:3 (September 1919): 344–354.

Menninger, William C. "Psychiatric Experience in the War, 1941–1946." *American Journal of Psychiatry* 103:5 (March 1947): 577–586.

Moskos, Charles C., Jr. "The American Combat Soldier in Vietnam." *Journal of Social Issues* 31:4 (fall 1975): 25–37.

———. "Racial Integration in the Armed Forces." *American Journal of Sociology* 72:2 (September 1966): 132–148.

Nelson, Paul D., and Newell H. Berry. "Cohesion in Marine Recruit Platoons." *Journal of Psychology* 68 (January 1968): 63–71.

Ollendorf, Robert H., and Paul L. Adams. "Psychiatry and the Draft." *American Journal of Orthopsychiatry* 41:1 (January 1971): 85–90.

Ondishko, Joseph J., Jr. "A View of Anxiety, Fear and Panic." *Military Affairs* 36:2 (April 1972): 58–60.

Parsons, Frederick W. "War Neuroses." *Atlantic Monthly* 123:4 (March 1919): 335–338.

Perkins, Bradford. "Impressions of Wartime." *Journal of American History* 77:2 (September 1990): 563–568.

Peterson, Donald B. "The Psychiatric Operation, Army Forces, Far East, 1950–53." *American Journal of Psychiatry* 112:1 (July 1955): 23–28.

Remenyi, Joseph. "Psychology of War Literature." *Sewanee Review: A Quarterly of Life and Letters* 52:1 (winter 1944): 137–147.

Rhein, John H. W. "Neuropsychiatric Problems at the Front During Combat." *Journal of Abnormal Psychology* 14:1–2 (April–June 1919): 9–14.

Rose, Arnold M. "Social Psychological Effects of Physical Deprivation." *Journal of Health and Human Behavior* 1:4 (winter 1960): 285–289.

——. "The Social Psychology of Desertion from Combat." *American Sociological Review* 16:5 (October 1951): 614–629.

——. "The Social Structure of the Army." *American Journal of Sociology* 51:5 (March 1946): 361–364.

Rothschild, David. "Review of Neuropsychiatric Cases in the Southwest Pacific Area." *American Journal of Psychiatry* 102:4 (January 1946): 454–459.

Sandels, Robert. "The Doughboy: Formation of a Military Folk." *American Studies* 24:1 (spring 1983): 69–88.

Scales, Robert H., Jr. "Firepower: The Psychological Dimension." *Army* 39:7 (July 1989): 43–50.

Schuman, Howard. "Two Sources of Antiwar Sentiment in America." *American Journal of Sociology* 78:3 (November 1972): 513–536.

Schwab, Sidney I. "The Mechanism of the War Neuroses." *Journal of Abnormal Psychology* 14:1–2 (April–June 1919): 1–8.

Shields, Patricia M. "Enlistment During the Vietnam Era and the 'Representative' Issue of the All-Volunteer Force." *Armed Forces and Society* 7:1 (fall 1980): 133–151.

Shils, Edward A., and Morris Janowitz. "Cohesion and Disintegration in the Wehrmacht in World War II." *Public Opinion Quarterly* 12:2 (summer 1948): 280–315.

Shrader, Charles R. "Friendly Fire: The Inevitable Price." *Parameters* 22:3 (Autumn 1992): 29–44.

Smoler, Fredric. "The Secret of the Soldiers Who Didn't Shoot." *American Heritage* 40:2 (March 1989): 37–45.

Sobel, Raymond. "The 'Old Sergeant' Syndrome." *Psychiatry: Journal of the Biology and the Pathology of Interpersonal Relations* 10:3 (August 1947): 315–321.

Spiegel, Herbert X. "Preventive Psychiatry with Combat Troops." *American Journal of Psychiatry* 101:3 (November 1944): 310–315.

Spiller, Roger J. "My Guns: A Memoir of the Second World War." *American Heritage* 42:8 (December 1991): 45–51.

——. "Isen's Run: Human Dimensions of Warfare in the Twentieth Century." *Military Review* 68:5 (May 1988): 16–31.

——. "S. L. A. Marshall and the Ratio of Fire." *Royal United Services Institute Journal* 133:4 (winter 1988): 63–71.

Spindler, G. Dearborn. "American Character as Revealed by the Military." *Psychiatry: Journal for the Operational Statement of Interpersonal Relations* 11:3 (August 1948): 275–281.

Steinweg, Kenneth K. "Dealing Realistically with Fratricide." *Parameters* 25:1 (spring 1995): 4–29.

Strange, Robert E. "Combat Fatigue Versus Pseudo-Combat Fatigue in Vietnam." *Military Medicine* 133:10 (October 1968): 823–826.

Strecker, Edward A. "Military Psychiatry: World War I, 1917–1918," in *One Hundred*

*Years of American Psychiatry.* American Psychiatric Association, New York: Columbia University Press, 1944.

Suchman, Edward A., Robin M. Williams Jr., and Rose K. Goldsen. "Student Reaction to Impending Military Service." *American Sociological Review* 18:3 (June 1953): 293–304.

Swank, Roy L., and Walter E. Marchand. "Combat Neuroses: Development of Combat Exhaustion." *Archives of Neurology and Psychiatry* 55:3 (March 1946): 237–247.

Toner, James H. "American Society and the American Way of War: Korea and Beyond." *Parameters* 11:1 (spring 1981): 79–90.

Useem, Michael. "The Educational and Military Experience of Young Men During the Vietnam Era: Non-linear Effects of Parental Social Class." *Journal of Political and Military Sociology* 8:1 (spring 1980): 15–29.

Weinberg, S. Kirson. "The Combat Neuroses." *American Journal of Sociology* 51:5 (March 1946): 465–478.

———. "Problems of Adjustment in Army Units." *American Journal of Sociology* 50:4 (January 1945): 271–278.

Weingartner, James J. "Massacre at Biscari: Patton and an American War Crime." *Historian* 52:1 (November 1989): 24–39.

———. "Trophies of War: U.S. Troops and the Mutilation of Japanese War Dead, 1941–1945." *Pacific Historical Review* 61:1 (February 1992): 53–67.

———. "War Against Subhumans: Comparisons Between the German War Against the Soviet Union and the American War Against Japan, 1941–1945." *Historian* 58:3 (spring 1996): 557–573.

Weinstein, Edwin A. "The Function of Interpersonal Relations in the Neurosis of Combat." *Psychiatry: Journal of the Biology and the Pathology of Interpersonal Relations* 10:3 (August 1947): 307–314.

Williams, Tom A. "The Emotions and Their Mechanism in Warfare." *Journal of Abnormal Psychology* 14:1–2 (April–June 1919): 15–26.

Wilson, Thomas C. "Vietnam-Era Military Service: A Test of the Class-Bias Thesis." *Armed Forces and Society* 21:3 (spring 1995): 461–471.

Yager, Joel. "Personal Violence in Infantry Combat." *Archives of General Psychiatry* 32:2 (February 1975): 257–261.

# Index